GOOD
RETIREMENT _{NON}
GUIDE
1996

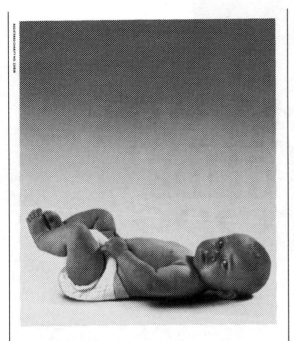

Reduce her chances of being killed by cancer. Can you think of a better legacy?

"I'm afraid you have cancer."

Twenty years ago these words were a death sentence in most cases. As simple and stark as that.

Nowadays, thanks to research, things are very different: 90,000 people survived cancer last year.

160,000 however, did not.

Your clients can reduce that number by leaving us a bequest in their Wills: two thirds of our work is funded by legacies.

Our free booklet explains how to make a Will with the help of a professional adviser.

For copies, and a free display stand write to: Cancer Research Campaign, FREE-POST, 10 Cambridge Terrace, London NW1 0YP.

Or call the legacy office on 0171 224 1333.

With your help Sophie, the girl in the photo, could grow up in a world where more people survive cancer than die of it.

Please remember her when you're drawing up a Will.

GOOD RETIREMENT *NON* GUIDE 1996

Rosemary Brown

ENTERPRISE DYNAMICS

KOGAN PAGE

This edition first published 1996

Copyright © by Enterprise Dynamics Ltd 1996

Kogan Page Ltd, 120 Pentonville Road, London N1 9JN

British Library Cataloguing in Publication Data

A CIP record for this book is available from the British Library.

ISBN 0-7494-1776-5

Typeset by Saxon Graphics Ltd, Derby.
Printed and bound in Great Britain by
Clays Ltd, St. Ives plc.

Contents

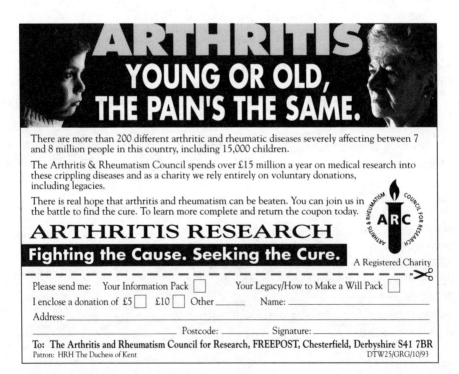

8. Your Home   136

9. Leisure Activities   179

PAYROLL GIVING
TO THE
CHURCH ARMY

Sharing Faith
through
Words and Action

10. Starting Your Own Business   215

11. Looking for Paid Work   265

12. Voluntary Work   296

13. Health   321

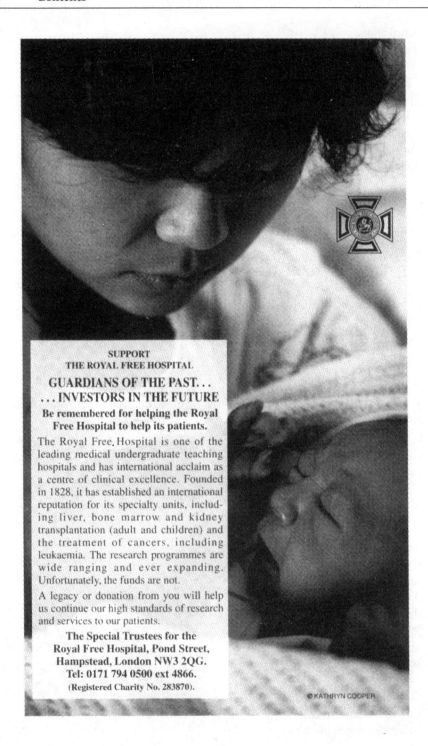

14. Holidays   364

15. Caring for Elderly Parents   404

16. No One is Immortal   445

"It simply isn't cricket not to make a Will!"

*Receive an enamelled lapel badge when you send for this **free** booklet.*

Far too few of us make Wills. In fact, only about one in three has made a record of their wishes. The trouble is that the two who don't may seriously increase the distress of those near and dear to them by adding insecurity to sorrow at the time of their death.

That's why The Royal London Society for the Blind has produced this useful booklet, full of sensible advice about making a Will. It is designed to be easy to read and is available free, by writing to the address below.

If you consider adding a Charity to your Will, I do hope you can support The Royal London Society for the Blind.

GRG

Please complete and return this coupon to:
David Gower, c/o Royal London Society for the Blind,
105 Salusbury Road, London NW6 6RH

Please send me___ copies of the booklet *A Simple Guide to Making a Will.*

Name ....

Address ....

....

....

Post Code ....

Tel: ....

ROYAL LONDON SOCIETY FOR THE BLIND
Registered Charity No: 307892

Without your help, this is the only legacy for Britain's Wildlife

Hunting with dogs is a legacy of cruelty that's been handed down for generations.

Foxes, deer and hares are the defenceless victims, chased by hunters and hounds, then savaged to death.

For fun.

But one thing could eradicate the terrible legacy of bloodsports.

A legacy from you.

By leaving part of your estate to the League Against Cruel Sports, you'll be providing vital funds for our campaigns to abolish these barbaric acts.

Pledging a legacy is easy. Simply write to Sue Rocks, Legacy Officer, at the address below for our free 'Will to Survive' legacy advice leaflet.

Please leave something in your Will for hunted animals or they'll be left to suffer this cruelty for generations to come.

DON'T LET BRITAIN'S WILDLIFE GO TO THE DOGS.

League Against Cruel Sports, Sparling House, 83-87 Union Street, London SE1 1 SG. 0171-403 6155.

Registered in England as a Company No. 2880406.

Introduction

Perhaps it is hardly surprising that the remark people make most often about retirement is: 'I've never been as busy in my life.'

Ask them what they do and you will be regaled with a dizzying account of conservation activity, sporting feats, adventure holidays, art and craft projects, voluntary work initiatives, courses of all descriptions plus a thousand and one other ventures from developing an allotment to starting a business.

Forget any fears you might have of being bored. Once you get going, activities suddenly snowball and, far from wondering how to occupy your time, your biggest problem is likely to be fitting everything in.

With every new edition of the *Guide*, the number of choices gets bigger and better. Whether you plan to take up a new interest, enjoy the outdoor life, become involved in your community, learn a fresh skill or find a worthwhile new outlet for your talents, there are scores of tempting opportunities to explore.

One of the most noteworthy changes over the past year is the number of people seeking – and more to the point, finding – paid work after they retire. Moreover, whereas until recently most openings for mature job-seekers tended to be for unskilled work, today we are increasingly being told of people well into their sixties landing professional and executive jobs.

Some are discovering exciting new challenges in small firms where their experience is really valued. Others are joining the growing number of companies employing interim managers to handle specific assignments, such as a marketing campaign or the installation of a new computer system.

Many of the new jobs coming on to the market are the direct result of the recent downsizing of businesses, which are finding they need skilled people to fill a key gap or which, as is becoming more common, are contracting-out various support services.

This is especially good news for men and women aged 50-plus. Because many vacancies are for high-level temporary work, where experience and reliability are essential, mature candidates are often preferred.

Temporary work has two outstanding advantages today. Not only is it often the quickest route back into permanent employment but, as several current surveys show, 'temping' itself has acquired a high-flying image. Groups most in demand include: accountants, medical staff, computer specialists, fund-raisers, homecare workers and people with training skills.

The campaign to end age discrimination is also gathering pace. In recent months, 90 leading employers have publicly stated that they have added age to their equal opportunity policy and, among other positive changes, no longer specify age limits in their job advertisements. Far from being a token gesture, many are now enthusing that older recruits are proving to be a great asset to the company.

While the decision whether to work or instead enjoy some of the fun leisure pursuits on offer may have little to do with money, your future financial security may well depend on how realistically you budget for the years ahead.

Though prudence is obviously sensible – especially as you may be looking forward to another 25 years or longer after you retire – the evidence suggests that, perhaps through ignorance of their entitlements, some people may have been taking economies to extreme.

The message is: cheer up! Far from being all doom and gloom, in recent months there has been a flurry of good news items. Good news from the Inland Revenue is that some 6 million people, including many retirees, may be better off than they realise as a result of being due a tax refund. Among those most likely to benefit are people on small incomes (i.e. below the taxable limit), whose savings are in banks and building societies but who have not yet signed a form requesting that interest be paid to them in full – without deduction of tax. For further information, call the Taxback line on: 0800 660800; or see IR leaflet, *A guide to people with savings*, obtainable from any tax office.

Though many eligible claimants may not have known about their right to a refund, few readers will have missed the news that – in common with women – men aged 60 are now also entitled to free NHS prescriptions.

Another very helpful measure – specially targeted at more cautious investors – has been the introduction of corporate bond PEPs.

Although almost any investment carries some risk, the new disclosure rules which came into effect during 1995 make it very much easier for individuals to assess what they are being 'sold' and what they will be charged.

Another potentially attractive gain is the annuity deferral option. This allows people with a tax-approved personal pension to delay the purchase of an annuity, with the added advantage that in the mean time they can both take their tax-free lump sum and withdraw a limited income. However, there are risks as well as benefits, so expert advice is essential before taking a decision.

1995 also saw the Sex Discrimination Act extended to include pension schemes, with the result that many part-timers can now join an employer's pension scheme as of right. With most of the reforms of the new Pension Act due to come into effect in 1997, there is a strong argument for the many women who have previously been excluded to take advantage of the opportunity to build up a retirement income of their own.

The November 1995 Budget is also a cause for special cheer. Dubbed by the pundits as 'A Budget for the Over-50s', it promises a number of real benefits for those nearing retirement or already retired.

In particular, the widening of the 20 per cent tax band to £3,900 – together with the enhanced personal and age-related allowances – should take many retirees out of tax altogether.

Another big fillip is the 5 per cent reduction in tax on savings for basic rate taxpayers, which should make a very considerable difference – especially to the many pensioners whose savings are in bank and building society accounts.

However, for many, the best budget news of the lot was the package of new measures to assist with long-term care. These include: the right to keep more of your own money before having to contribute to residential or nursing home costs; the doubling of the £8,000 threshold to £16,000; and tax exemption for long-term care insurance policies.

Another change – due to start in April 1996 – is the switch to a new self-assessment system, which is designed to simplify the process of making tax returns. It will mainly affect the self-employed, higher rate taxpayers and others, including many retired people, who have several different sources of income. Happily, self-assessment is optional, so it is entirely up to you whether to go independent or to leave it to the tax office to work out your liability.

As for me, there is no question of managing on my own when it comes to editing the *Good* non-*Retirement Guide*. This year, as always, I am hugely indebted to the many hundreds of people who generously gave their time in helping to check the information.

While it is impossible to mention everyone by name, I am especially grateful to the several officials at the Inland Revenue, DSS and other government departments for their great good humour, unfailing co-operation and painstaking efforts to notify us of any changes that we need to include.

My assistant, Jean Rosete, is a marvel of efficiency; not only calm in the face of deadlines but also a wonderful friend – and quite simply, I should be lost without her.

A big thank you too to our publishers, Kogan Page, for their enthusiasm and support in producing what is now our tenth annual edition of the *Guide*.

A final word to all our readers, to whom this book is dedicated. To all of you, my very best wishes for lasting happiness and satisfaction in the years ahead.

Rosemary Brown
December 1995

STOP PRESS

November 1995 Budget highlights

Take effect from start of tax year on 6 April 1996:

* Basic rate tax to be cut by 1 per cent to 24 per cent
* Personal allowance to rise from £3,525 to £3,765 – Age-related personal allowance, for ages 65 to 74, increased to £4,910; for ages 75 and over, to £5,090
* Married couple's allowance raised to £1,790 – Age-related married couple's allowance, for ages 65 to 74, increased to £3,115; for ages 75 and over, to £3,155
* Income limit for age-related allowances (personal and married couple's) raised to £15,200
* Blind person's allowance increased to £1,250
* Widow's bereavement allowance and the additional personal allowance for single parents both increased to £1,790
* 20 per cent tax band widened by £700 to £3,900
* Threshold for higher rate tax raised by £1,200 to £25,500
* Tax on income from savings, including bank and building society interest, to be cut from 25 to 20 per cent for basic rate taxpayers
* Capital gains tax exemption increased to £6,300 a year
* Inheritance tax threshold raised to £200,000
* Pension cap raised from £78,600 to £82,200

Other key Budget points

* Burden of long-term care to be eased. Individuals needing to go into a residential or nursing home will be able to keep more of their savings. Those with assets below £10,000 (currently £3,000) will not have to pay anything. The cut-off point for State help to be doubled from £8,000 to £16,000. Details of further measures, including tax exemption for long-term care insurance policies, to be announced later
* Qualifying age for retirement relief from capital gains tax reduced from 55 to 50
* Income from approved PHI and other insurance plans taken out as protection against sickness, disability or unemployment to be exempted from tax
* New measures to assist small businesses include cut in small firms' corporation tax and 5 per cent cap on business rate increases
* Shareholdings in qualifying unquoted companies held for two years exempted from inheritance tax

* New minimum holding period of three years for shares in SAYE and profit sharing schemes
* Executive share options of up to £20,000 treated more generously for tax
* Qualifying age for purchasing Pensioners Guaranteed Income Bonds reduced to 60; maximum holding increased to £50,000.

New benefit up-ratings from April 1996

Highlights include:

* The basic pension for a single person goes up to £61.15 a week; for a married couple, £97.75.
* The basic rate of long-term Incapacity Benefit will be £61.15 a week.
* Attendance allowance is increased to £32.40 at the lower rate and to £48.50 at the higher rate.
* The basic Income Support Allowance goes up to £47.90 for a single adult and to £75.20 for couples.
* Unemployment benefit rises to £48.25 for people under pension age and to £61.15 for those over pension age.
* Disability Working Allowance for single people is increased to £48.25; for married couples and lone parents, to £76.60.
* The new care component figures for Disability Living Allowance will be: highest £48.50; middle £32.40; lowest £12.90. The new mobility components will be: higher £33.90; lower £12.90.

Their circumstances may have changed but why should they?

Helping people face change in later life is never easy.

At DGAA Homelife however, we have been providing the highest levels of care for people of a professional or similar background for nearly a century.

We help as many people as possible to continue living in their own homes. For those who need greater care, we have twelve residential and nursing homes where fees are determined by a realistic combination of ability to pay and charitable contribution.

Please help us in our work by sending a donation, payable to DGAA Homelife, to the address below.

DGAA Homelife, 1 Derry Street, London W8 5HY. Tel: 0171 396 6703
The Distressed Gentlefolk's Aid Association. Registered Charity No: 207812

Home, Residential and Nursing Care for Life.

DG
AA
HOMELIFE

A lasting and living memorial

to your generosity

ALMSWORTH COMMON, EXMOOR. PHOTOGRAPHY BY BRIAN HARRIS FOR CPRE

The English countryside has been the delight of countless generations – yet this very heart of our national heritage is constantly under threat from damaging development.

Working at national and local level since 1926, CPRE has played a major part in the creation and protection of National Parks, the provision of Green Belts around cities and in establishing firm planning controls. Important contributions are also being made to agricultural, forestry, water and transport policies and hedgerow protection. CPRE's success is based on solid research, constructive ideas and reasoned argument.

CPRE is ever-vigilant but its work as a small but cost-effective charity is totally dependent on public support. By making a bequest or a donation to CPRE, you can help to ensure that England's Green and Pleasant Land is enjoyed by future generations. Remember, a legacy to a registered charity like CPRE is exempt from Inheritance Tax.

If you would like further information about remembering CPRE in a will, write to David Conder, Room 14, Council for the Protection of Rural England, Warwick House, 25 Buckingham Palace Road London SW1W 0PP

PATRON HM THE QUEEN

PRESIDENT JONATHAN DIMBLEBY

REGISTERED CHARITY NUMBER 233179

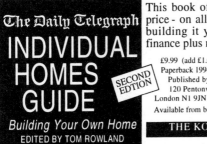

1 Looking Forward to Retirement

Just as there are some people who become engaged within three hours of meeting and live happily ever after, there are others who without any apparent planning enjoy a totally fulfilled retirement, clearly relishing everything it has to offer.

But for most of us life does not work like that. Important events require some preparation if we are to make the most of them and arguably this is more true of retirement than of any other stage.

A majority of people retiring today are fitter, more skilled and better off financially than any previous generation. Also, with early retirement increasingly becoming the norm, a great many of us can realistically look forward to 25 years or more of active life ahead. As a result, planning the future has become even more critically important. The *Good non-Retirement Guide* is not designed to offer you a ready-made philosophy or a few rose-tinted blueprints on the theme 'Life Begins in Middle Age'. Its sole aim is to set you thinking along constructive lines, to indicate what is possible, to advise on the best sources of information and to help you avoid the pitfalls that can trap the unwary.

Key concerns are likely to be the question of money and how you will occupy your time. Others may well include: where you live, how best to keep fit, the effect of your retirement on close personal relationships and perhaps new responsibilities such as the care of elderly parents.

You do not need to be an accountant to know that once you stop earning your income will drop. However, if you complete the Budget Planner (see pages 130-135), you may be pleasantly surprised to find that the difference is far less than you had feared. On the plus side, you will be saving on travel and other work-related expenses as well as enjoying a welcome reduction in tax.

As with all questions affecting retirement, it is sensible if possible to plan ahead. Assess your likely savings including the lump sum from your pension and any insurance policies you may have. Then draw up a plan as to how you can maximise their value. Should you invest your money in a building society, PEP scheme, TESSA, unit trust, stocks and shares or government securities? Does it make sense to buy an annuity?

What are the tax angles for someone in your position? Should you consider consulting a good accountant, stockbroker or other professional adviser? If you are unsure of the answers, then Investment, Chapter 5, may help to clarify your thinking.

Your retirement income may well depend on whether you start a new career, especially if – as has happened to many thousands of people over the past couple of years – you were made redundant with no immediate job prospects on offer. While we are not pretending that starting afresh is easy, a great many men and women do in fact find rewarding work, including some who are well into their sixties. While some individuals turn their talents to something entirely new, others go freelance or become consultants in their existing area of expertise. Chapter 11, Looking for Paid Work, may give you some useful leads.

An increasing number of people are taking the heady step of starting their own business. This is not a decision to be entered into lightly. The risks are legion and most budding entrepreneurs find that they have never worked as hard in their lives. In the early days at least, being your own boss means sacrificing your social life, forgoing a salary and traipsing out in the rain to post your own letters. Moreover, if you are married, unless your partner is solidly behind you there are liable to be domestic tensions – especially if you run the business from home. Against this, many who take the plunge derive enormous satisfaction from building up a family enterprise. If you are seriously flirting with the idea Chapter 10, Starting Your Own Business, provides a lot of the detail you will need to know.

A worthwhile alternative to becoming a business tycoon is to devote your energies to voluntary work. There are literally scores of opportunities for retired people to make a valuable contribution within their own community. You might visit the elderly in their own homes, drive patients to hospital, run a holiday playscheme, help out in your Citizens' Advice Bureau or become a Samaritan. Other ideas which might appeal are conservation work or playing a more active role in politics by joining your local party association. Whether you can only spare the occasional day or are prepared to help on a regular basis Chapter 12, Voluntary Work, lists a fund of suggestions you might like to consider.

A prime requirement, whether you are thinking of paid or unpaid work, or for that matter simply planning to devote more time to your hobbies, is to remain fit and healthy. Good health is the most valuable possession we have. Without it, energy is lacking, activities are restricted and the fun goes out of life. No amount of money can compensate for being bed-ridden or a semi-invalid.

While anyone can be unfortunate enough to be struck down by an unexpected illness, your future good health is largely in your own hands. The reason why the seventies are so often dogged by aches and pains is that sufficient care has not been taken during the fifties and sixties.

As well as all the obvious advice about not smoking, becoming too fat or drinking to excess, there is the important question of exercise. While you could of course do press-ups and go for walks, you will probably have a much better time if you join the new keep-fit brigade.

There are opportunities around the country for almost every kind of sport, with 50-plus beginners especially welcome. Additionally, dancing, yoga, keep-fit-to-music and relaxation classes are readily available through most local authorities as well as being offered by the many specialist bodies listed in both the Health and Leisure Activities chapters.

The only problem is likely to be fitting everything in. The choice of organised leisure pursuits is little short of staggering. If you have ever wanted to learn about computers, take a degree, join a choir, become proficient in a craft, play competitive Scrabble, start coin collecting or become a beekeeper, you will find an organisation that caters for your enthusiasm.

The type of activities you enjoy could be an important consideration in choosing where you will live. Because we are conditioned to thinking of retirement as a time for settling into a new home, many people up sticks without perhaps giving enough thought to such essentials as proximity to family and friends and whether a different area would provide the same scope for pursuing their interests.

A fairly common mistake is for people to retire to a place where they once spent an idyllic holiday, perhaps 15 or 20 years previously with only a minimum of further investigation. Resorts that are glorious in mid-summer can be bleak and damp in winter as well as pretty dull when the tourist season is over. Equally, many people sell their house and move somewhere smaller without taking account of the fact that when they are spending more time at home they may actually want more space, rather than less. This is particularly true of anyone planning to work from home or who has a hobby such as carpentry which requires a separate workroom.

While moving may be the right solution, especially if you want to realise some capital to boost your retirement income, there are plenty of ways of adapting a house to make it more convenient and labour-saving. Likewise, you may be able to cut the running costs, for example with insulation. These and other possibilities, including taking in a lodger and creating a granny flat, are explored in Chapter 8, Your Home.

On the subject of granny flats, if you are caring for elderly parents there may come a time when a little bit of outside help could make all the difference. The range of organisations that can provide you with back-up is far more extensive than is generally realised. For single women especially, who may feel that they have to give up a career, knowing what facilities are available could prove a veritable godsend.

While there may be pressure if a parent, however much loved, requires an undue amount of attention, a more commonplace problem is the effect of retirement on a couple's relationship. Many husbands are puzzled, and sometimes hurt, by their wife's attitude to the event. For years she has been complaining 'I never see anything of you darling' and 'Why can't you spend a little more time with the family?' – so naturally he expects her to be delighted to have him at home. But according to some husbands, the enthusiasm may seem less than whole-hearted. As one recently retired 62-year-old put it: 'I had hardly had a chance to enjoy a couple of days pottering in the garden for the first time in years, when my wife was nagging me to go out and find something to do. She was the one who wanted me to take early retirement. Now she is wishing that I was back at work.'

The reverse situation can also apply, especially if the wife had a high-powered career. Although in general the evidence suggests that it is usually the man's retirement that provokes most friction, this may change as more of today's working wives turn 60 and find themselves facing the same need to make difficult adjustments.

Either way, the point is that after years of seeing relatively little of each other, retirement suddenly creates the possibility of much more togetherness. Put in blunt terms, many wives grumble that having a husband at home during the day means an extra meal to cook and inevitable disruption to their normal routine. And while this may not apply in an 'equal opportunity' marriage, where the domestic jobs are shared equally between husband and wife, in a majority of households women still do the lion's share of the cooking and cleaning. So, if he stays in bed longer in the morning, the chores will be finished later which can be an irritation. But an even greater cause for resentment is that she may feel guilty about meeting her friends or pursuing her usual weekday activities unless her partner is also busy.

If she is still at work, the situation can be even more fraught as, apart from the extra housework, she may find her loyalties uncomfortably divided. Furthermore, quite irrationally, some retired husbands begin to harbour dire suspicions about their wives' working colleagues, imagining romantic entanglements that had never crossed their minds before.

Sometimes too, retired people subconsciously label themselves as 'old' and start denying themselves and their partner the pleasures of a happily fulfilled sex life. It is difficult to know whether this is more ludicrous or tragic. As studies in many parts of the world show, the sexual satisfaction of both partners continues in a high proportion of cases long after the age of 70 and often well into the eighties. A welcome book which discusses the subject frankly is published by Age Concern. Called *Living, Loving and Ageing*, it costs £4.95 and is available from most bookshops or directly from Age Concern.

Usually, problems that coincide with retirement can be fairly simply overcome by willingness to discuss them frankly and to work out a solution that suits both partners. The situation is very much easier today than even ten years ago when male/female roles were far more stereotyped and many couples felt that they had to conform to a set pattern for the sake of convention.

Despite the impression given by some articles, marriage is not the only relationship and many non-marrieds equally find that adjusting to retirement is not always that easy. Relatives may impose new pressures once you are no longer at work. Likewise, close friendships sometimes alter when one friend retires – and not the other. Additionally, many single people admit that they had not realised before how much they relied on their job for companionship and sometimes, even for part of their weekend social life.

Pre-retirement courses

Talking to other people to find out how they plan to tackle the challenges as well as the opportunities of retirement can be immensely helpful. Many companies recognise this need by providing pre-retirement courses. If you are unlucky enough to be in a firm where this is not yet done, or if you are self-employed, there are a number of organisations to which you can turn for advice and help.

Before deciding on a particular course, it is worthwhile giving a little thought to the best time to go and the subjects which the counselling should cover. The traditional view is that the ideal time is somewhere between one and two years before you are due to retire. While this is probably true for most people, it is also important to remember that preparing for retirement really has to be a staged process. Some financial decisions, such as those affecting company or personal pension planning, need to be taken as early as possible. Others, such as whether to move house, can probably only be made much later.

The basic subjects that the best courses address are: finance, health, activity, leisure, housing and the adjustments which will need to be made by both you and your family when you retire.

The crucial test, however, is not the amount of factual information that is contained but the extent to which the course helps to focus and stimulate your own thoughts on the various issues and to lead to discussion with your partner and others in the same situation.

The following is a list of the best known courses available to individuals enrolling independently of company sponsorship.

The Pre-Retirement Association of Great Britain & Northern Ireland, 26 Frederick Sanger Road, Surrey Research Park, Guildford, Surrey GU2 5YD. T:01483 301170. The PRA, the national body for retirement counselling, runs the Retirement Preparation Service which includes both company courses and those for individuals who are not sponsored by their employer. These courses are independent, free from commercial bias and partners are encouraged to attend. PRA also runs *Positive Change Management* courses for mid-life/redundancy in Central London or Guildford; cost is £141 per person, or £235 per couple (including VAT) for a two-day course.

Throughout the UK some of the 37 affiliated local organisations of the PRA arrange their own pre-retirement courses, often in collaboration with other educational authorities. For further details, contact the PRA at the Guildford address above.

Week-long retirement planning holiday courses are run at Barton Hall Chalet Hotel, near Torquay, in the spring and autumn. Price is about £225 which includes full board, accommodation and evening entertainment. Details from Bill Tadd, **Time of Your Life**, 78 Capel Road, East Barnet, Herts EN4 8JF. T:0181 449 4506.

The Retirement Trust, 19 Borough High Street, London Bridge, London SE1 9SE. T:0171 378 9708. Offers individuals the opportunity of a free one- or two-hour discussion on pre-retirement planning. The service is free and is available nationwide. For further information, contact the above address.

Scottish Pre-Retirement Council, Alexandra House, 204 Bath Street, Glasgow G2 4HL. T:0141 332 9427. Runs courses in various regions of Scotland. These are normally held over four days and prices range from about £18 to £40.

Greater London Association for Pre-Retirement, 2 Doughty Street, London WC2N 2PH. T:0171 404 6664. Runs two-day non-residential courses in Central London during February, April, June and October. Subjects covered are leisure, health, money matters and state benefits. Cost for two days, including lunch and book pack, is £105 (£90 for GLAP members).

Jewish Care, Volunteers and Community Development Department, 221 Golders Green Road, London NW11 9DQ. T:0181 458 3282. Offers a course of six workshops (day or evening) in Golders Green, North London, focusing on: attitudes to retirement, financial planning, health, voluntary activity, further education and family relationships. Partners are encouraged to attend and price is approximately £20. For further information, contact Sue Gordon at the above address.

Adult Education Centres
See local telephone directory under your local council listing. As interest in this area increases a growing number of Adult Education Centres are running both day and evening courses. Standards vary but you should be able to get a good idea of the approach from the syllabus.

Workers' Educational Association, Temple House, 17 Victoria Park Square, Bethnal Green, London E2 9PB. T:0181 983 1515. Many of the 900 branches of the WEA run local courses. Check your telephone directory for the nearest branch or contact the London HQ for further information.

Financial organisations

Pensions and people of pension age are a big market as is reflected in the wide range of financial institutions offering pre-retirement courses. The very largest like the Prudential and Standard Life are able to offer these as a genuinely independent extension of their huge pension businesses but many of the smaller firms obviously see them as commercial marketing opportunities. It is, therefore, important to be aware of this if you do go on such a course.

Abbey National Financial Services Ltd., Prestwood House, Corporation Street, High Wycombe, Bucks HP13 6TQ. T:01494 472211. Offer one- and two-day retirement planning seminars in a number of locations around the country. Prices (1995) which are inclusive of lunch are: £110 (£190 for couples) for the one-day seminar and £210 (£370 for couples) for the two-day event; in both cases, VAT should be added. Accommodation, if required, can be arranged. For further information, contact Penny Freshney at the above address.

Godwins Ltd., Briarcliff House, Kingsmead, Farnborough, Hants GU14 7TE. T:01252 544484. Godwins, who started running courses over 16 years ago, offer two-day, non-residential courses at their Farnborough headquarters and at other locations countrywide. Cost (1995), including lunch, is £135 per person; £195 per couple plus VAT. Contact: Mrs Tina Gilchrist, Retirement Consultant at the above address.

Prudential Retirement Counselling Service, Chatham Place, 1 East Harding Street, London EC4A 3PR. T:0171 548 2020. Pre-retirement seminars are offered on an open basis to individuals and their partners every month at a variety of locations around the country. Topics include state and company pension benefits, financial planning, health, moving house, opportunities for further work and leisure pursuits. The (1995) price for a two-day non-residential programme inclusive of literature and luncheon is £193 per person, plus VAT. Senior Management residential seminars are also held regularly at Weybridge in Surrey; price is £405 plus VAT per person. For further information, contact Roy Elms, Retirement Counselling Manager at the above address.

Sedgwick Noble Lowndes, Norfolk House, Wellesley Road, Croydon CR9 3EB. T:0181 686 2466. Runs one-day courses for individuals whose employers do not make in-house arrangements. The main topics covered are finance, health and leisure, together with the social aspects of adjusting to retirement. Price is £160 including VAT per participant; £195 per couple.

Standard Life Assurance Company, PO Box 186, 125 George Street, Edinburgh EH2 2LJ. T:0131 245 0311. Standard Life run about 30 one-day courses each year, which are held in hotels throughout the UK; and also two weekend courses in Cumbria. The courses do not involve high-powered financial topics but include talks on pensions, health, leisure activities, basic finance and personal relationships. The one-day courses cost £90 per person (£150 per couple) plus VAT, inclusive of literature and lunch. The weekend courses cost approximately £190 per person plus VAT, inclusive of literature and full board. Contact Richard Protheroe at the above address.

Other commercial organisations

Aylesbury Industrial Group Training Centre Ltd., Gatehouse Close, Aylesbury, Bucks HP19 3DE. T:01296 81818. Non-residential pre-retirement courses are run five times a year at their Aylesbury headquarters. Courses last two days and include talks on pensions, legal rights, health and fitness, home security and the psychological aspects of retirement. The cost is £250 plus VAT, inclusive of lunches. Spouses are welcomed free of charge. For further information, contact Mr WJS McCunn, Chief Executive, at the above address.

New Life Retirement Services Ltd., 58 Park Road, Chandler's Ford, Eastleigh, Hants SO53 2ES. T:01983 730390. Two-day non-residential courses are held quarterly in Southampton and also in other parts of the country where there is sufficient interest. The programme covers money matters, housing, leisure and health. Cost, including course literature and refreshments, is £95 plus VAT per person; £135 plus VAT per couple.

Prime Time Retirement Services, 63 Lincoln's Inn Fields, London WC2A 3JX. T:0171 831 3141. In partnership with independent financial advisers Chase de Vere, Prime Time offer two-day pre-retirement programmes, and also individual consultations, aimed at professional people and senior executives. The courses focus on the various adjustments following retirement with financial advice to assist individuals in planning a new lifestyle. The price, which includes accommodation, meals and all course literature, is £320 per person; £450 per couple. Non-residential prices are respectively £150 and £250, including lunch. Two-day seminars designed for female groups, *Women – Independence in Retirement*, are also available, priced at £320 per person. All prices are exclusive of VAT. For programme details, contact Miss T Wileman, Conference Manager, at the above address.

Retirement Counselling Service, Turret House, The Avenue, Amersham, Bucks HP7 0AB. T:01494 433553. The Retirement Counselling Service runs about 25 open seminars a year including some specially catering for senior managers and executives. They are non-residential, run over two days and cost £255 (£215 for partners) plus VAT per person, including refreshments and course literature. There are also two-day residential seminars for senior executives. Price is £450 (£400 for partners) plus VAT per person.

Finally two organisations which cater specifically for senior executives:

DPS Consultants Ltd., Dodd's Lane, 27 Preston Street, Faversham, Kent ME13 8PE. T:01795 531472. Three-day courses for small groups of directors and senior managers, and their partners, are held twice a month at Leeds Castle near Maidstone or Ripley Castle near Harrogate. The programme includes a very good introduction to capital management from independent advisers, emphasis on the emotional adjustment to retirement and much practical advice on ways of being active and involved. The tuition fee is £670 single, £985 per couple. Accommodation is extra and costs £535 single, £940 double. Similar two-day middle management courses cost £715 single, £1,100 per couple, including accommodation. All prices exclude VAT.

There is also a three-day residential programme for people in their early-to-mid fifties who, despite taking early retirement, hope to find a new job. Cost is £1,350 plus VAT, with partners free.

Millstream Pre-Retirement Ltd., South Harting, Petersfield, Hants GU31 5LF. T:01730 825711. Millstream were the first to provide retirement courses specially for senior executives and now hold these regularly in the exclusive setting of the Royal Yacht Squadron in Cowes. Small numbers make for a sympathetic approach and partners are encouraged to attend together. Topics covered over the 2½ days include adjusting to retirement, health considerations, leisure activities and new opportunities for the future. All financial planning advice is totally independent and a follow-up service is available. Accommodation, all meals, drinks, newspapers and a number of books are included in the fees which (1995 prices) are £1,140 per person or £1,800 per couple, excluding VAT.

Chapter 14 also contains the names of one or two organisations that run pre-retirement courses as part of their holiday programme.

New focus for the retired

Over the years, a number of organisations have been formed to represent the interests of retired people and to give them a more powerful voice in putting forward their views on issues that affect their lives at both national and local levels. Two of the best known, which in addition to their campaigning role arrange a variety of social and other events, are listed below.

ARP Over 50, (Third Floor), Greencoat House, Francis Street, London SW1P 1DZ. T:0171 828 0500. The Association of Retired Persons is a membership association concerned with promoting the interests of people aged 50 plus. A hundred and thirty Friendship Centres around the country offer a varied programme of social events and take a keen interest in local and national issues. There are two 24-hour emergency helplines (legal and domestic). Among other facilities, members receive the quarterly *050 Magazine* and have access both to a range of shopping discounts and a travel club. Membership costs £18 a year (£23 per couple) by direct debit.

National Pensioners Convention, 4 Stevens Street, Lowestoft, Suffolk NR32 2JE. T:01502 565807. The NPC is an umbrella group for pensioner associations throughout the country, which collectively have a membership of around 1.5 million retired people. While each group is autonomous and so organises its own programme of events, a main aim of all affiliated organisations is to act as a pressure group to improve facilities and opportunities for older people. Local subscriptions range from about 20p to £5 a year. For further information and addresses of local groups, write to Jack Thain, General Secretary of the NPC, at the address above.

Useful reading
The **PRA** compiles an annual directory of pre-retirement courses, price £8. Available from the **Pre-Retirement Association of Great Britain and Northern Ireland,** 26 Frederick Sanger Road, Surrey Research Park, Guildford, Surrey GU2 5YD. A list of courses in individual regions can be obtained on request.

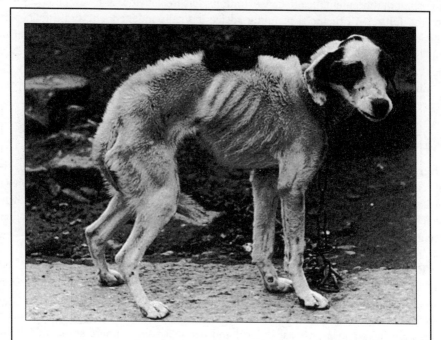

WE ALSO TAKE IN MONEY

Financially, animal rescue is a risky business. The Mayhew Home's experience has served to underline this.

Too often we have been thrown into a crisis of existence by the sheer numbers of abandoned and abused animals.

We desperately need a guarantee of survival. So do the animals. Please help us move toward that goal, by naming us in your will.

Your bequest will be used as a long-term deposit where only the accrued interest will be withdrawn to help pay for the daily running expenses of the home.

And the daily saving of lives.

If you would like more information about our work with animals, and our child education programme, please contact Diane Conrad at the address below.

THE MAYHEW HOME

ONE HUNDRED YEARS OF ANIMAL RESCUE

Trenmar Gardens, Harrow Road, London NW10 6BJ

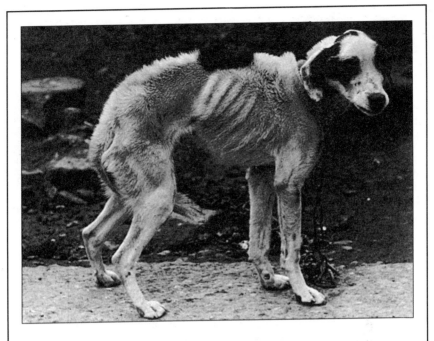

WE ALSO TAKE IN MONEY

Financially, animal rescue is a risky business. The Mayhew Home's experience has served to underline this.

Too often we have been thrown into a crisis of existence by the sheer numbers of abandoned and abused animals.

We desperately need a guarantee of survival. So do the animals. Please help us move toward that goal, by naming us in your will.

Your bequest will be used as a long-term deposit where only the accrued interest will be withdrawn to help pay for the daily running expenses of the home.

And the daily saving of lives.

If you would like more information about our work with animals, and our child education programme, please contact Diane Conrad at the address below.

THE MAYHEW HOME

ONE HUNDRED YEARS OF ANIMAL RESCUE

Trenmar Gardens, Harrow Road, London NW10 6BJ

2 Money in General

For most people approaching retirement, the major concern is money. Some individuals have no worries; they have planned the event for years, made maximum pension contributions, carefully invested their savings, covered themselves and family in insurance policies, budgeted ahead and can even gleefully tell you about the exotic round-the-world trip they intend to take just as soon as their new life begins.

But for a majority of people, however, it is not like that. After years of hardly giving a thought to their pension, panic suddenly sets in as they consider the prospect of no longer drawing a regular salary. The fact that most of their friends who have already retired seem to manage pretty well is of little comfort. Even quite wealthy individuals confess to conjuring up images of going cold and hungry.

Happily, the reality is far rosier than many people imagine. For a start, those retiring today are better off financially than any previous generation. Equally to the point, the spectre of drastic economies that haunts so many men and women is often the result of their having only the haziest idea as to their likely income and expenditure.

Doing the sums

Knowing the facts is the first priority. To make a proper assessment, you need to draw up several lists:

- Expected sources of income on retirement
- Unavoidable outgoings
- Normal additional spending (including holidays and other luxuries).

Stage two, you need to consider a number of options under the following headings:

- Possible ways of boosting your retirement income
- Spending now for saving later
- Cherished plans, if affordable.

Most difficult of all, you will require a third list of variables and unknowns which, while impossible to estimate accurately, must as a matter of prudence be taken into account in any long-term budget planning. The two most important are tax and inflation. A survey of retired people by MORI revealed that nearly half of those questioned said that they had not made sufficient allowance for inflation. Two-thirds of the total cited heating and fuel bills in particular as being more expensive than they had anticipated. Additionally, there are all the possible emergency situations, such as your health, for which, if this ever were to become a problem, you might want to make special provision. Your life expectancy is another consideration, as is that of your partner and any dependants.

Ideally, you should start thinking about at least some of these points, especially those that relate to your pension and to any savings or investment plans, five or even ten years before you retire. When doing the sums, aim to be realistic. Many people make the mistake of basing their calculations on their current commitments and expenditure, without properly realising that some of their requirements will change. To get the figures into perspective, it is a good idea to imagine yourself already retired. The good news is that, while some items will probably take a heftier slice of your budget, others will certainly be cheaper or no longer cost you anything at all.

Possible savings and extra outgoings are discussed below. The most practical way of examining the list is to tick off the items in each column that you expect definitely to apply and, where possible, to write down the expenditure involved in the adjacent box (see Budget Planner, pages 130-135). While inevitably this will be a somewhat rough-and-ready exercise – and obviously there will be gaps – the closer you are to retirement, the more worthwhile it will be.

Possible savings

Going out to work generally involves a fair number of expenses. When you leave your job, you will probably save at least several pounds a week. Items for which you will no longer have to pay include: your travelling costs to work, bought lunches, special clothes; plus all the out-of-pocket incidentals such as drinks with colleagues, trade magazines and collections for presents or the Christmas party.

You will not have to pay any more national insurance contributions and, unless you choose to invest in a private plan, your pension payments will also cease. Additionally, when you retire, you may be in a lower tax bracket.

At the same time you may have reached the stage when your children are now independent, your mortgage is substantially paid off and you have stopped subscribing to a life assurance policy. Moreover, one of the gratifying aspects of attaining state retirement age is that you become eligible for a variety of benefits, for example: concessionary travel, free national health service prescriptions, cheaper theatre and cinema tickets (usually matinees), reduced entrance charges for exhibitions and a wide choice of special holiday offers. Some benefits apply to both men and women from age 60.

Another point worth remembering is that many insurance companies give substantial discounts to mature drivers. With motor insurance zooming in cost, this could give you a valuable saving. In some instances, discounts apply to those aged 50; other companies restrict eligibility to those aged 55 or even 60. Normally, but again this varies, the scheme is terminated when the policy holder reaches 75. Most companies, but not all, extend the cover to a spouse or other named person with a good driving record. At time of writing, average discounts for people over 50 ranged from 10 to 15 per cent with considerable extra savings for drivers with a five-year claim-free record. Best advice is first approach your existing insurance company and ask what terms they will give you. If these appear dullish, it could pay to shop around. Among those that offer special rates for mature drivers are: Commercial Union Assurance, Sun Alliance, Royal Insurance, Guardian Royal Exchange, Legal & General, Norwich Union, Zurich Insurance, Direct Line and The Retirement Insurance Advisory Service.

Altenatively, you could contact **Motor Advice** (T:0171 639 9734) who will advise you where, depending on your personal circumstances, you are likely to obtain the best value insurance. You are only charged if the firm is able to save you money. If so, the fee is 25 per cent of any saving, with a minimum of £5.

Extra outgoings

There is no escaping the fact that when you retire some of your expenses will be heavier than at present.

Firstly, you will probably be spending more time at home, so items like heating and lighting are liable to be costlier.

If you received any perks with your job, such as a company car or health insurance, then unless you have a very generous employer these will have to come out of your own pocket in future. Equally, any business entertaining you enjoyed will largely cease, so any free lunches and the like will have to be paid for instead from the domestic housekeeping.

Another very important consideration is your extra leisure. With more time available, you will understandably be tempted to spend more on outings, your hobbies and on longer holidays from home. To avoid having to stint yourself, these need to be budgeted for in advance. Most people say that in an ideal world they would assume to be spending roughly double on entertainment of all kinds, compared with when they were working. Even voluntary activity is not without its hidden expenses, for example: more use of the telephone, petrol costs, raffle tickets, support of fund-raising occasions and so on.

Looking ahead, as you get older you may want more home comforts. Likewise, you may have to pay other people to do some of the jobs, such as the decorating, that you previously managed yourself.

Anticipating the areas of additional expenditure is not to be pessimistic. On the contrary, it is the surest way of avoiding future money worries. Moreover, when you have sat down and worked out your retirement income in detail, you may even be pleasantly surprised.

Expected sources of income on retirement

Your list will include at least some of the following. Once you have added up the figures in the budget planner, you will have to deduct income tax to arrive at the net spending amount available to you.

- State basic pension
- State graduated pension
- SERPS
- Occupational pension
- Personal pension
- State benefits

Additionally, you may receive income or a capital sum from some of the following:

- Company share option scheme
- Endowment policy
- Investments (stocks and shares, building society etc.)
- Bank deposit account

- National Savings interest
- Other existing income (from a trust, property, family business)
- Sale of business or personal assets

You might also be in receipt of income from an annuity. However, since at this stage you will be unlikely to have purchased one, this really belongs in the category of investment decisions.

Unavoidable outgoings

One person's priority is another person's luxury – and vice versa. For this reason, the divide between 'unavoidable' and 'normal additional spending' (see section following) is fraught with obvious difficulty. For example, readers who do not possess a pet would never include pet food among the essentials, whereas a dog or cat owner unquestionably would.

Almost everyone will want to juggle some of the items between the two lists; or add their own particular commitments or special enthusiasms, omitted by us.

Our suggestions are simply intended as memory joggers – and emphatically not as a guide to what should, or should not, constitute a luxury. What matters is the basic principle behind the exercise. If at some stage budgeting choices have to be made, decisions will be very much easier if you already know: your total outgoings, what you are spending on each individually and those you variously rate as important or marginal.

Whatever your own essentials, some of the following items will certainly feature on your list of unavoidable expenses:

- Food
- Rent or mortgage repayments
- Council tax
- Repair and maintenance costs
- Heating
- Lighting and other energy
- Telephone
- TV licence/rental
- Household insurance
- Clothes
- Domestic cleaning products
- Laundry, cleaners' bills, shoe repair
- Miscellaneous services, e.g. plumber, window cleaner
- Car, including licence, petrol, AA, etc.
- Other transport
- Regular savings and life assurance
- HP/other loan repayments
- Outgoings on health

Normal additional expenditure
This may well include:

- Gifts
- Holidays
- Newspapers/books
- Drink
- Cigarettes/tobacco
- Hairdressing
- Toiletries/cosmetics
- Entertainment (hobbies, outings, video purchase/rental, home entertaining etc.)
- Miscellaneous subscriptions/membership fees
- Charitable donations
- Expenditure on pets
- Other

Work out the figures against these lists. Then in order to compare your expenditure against likely income, jot them down on the Budget Planner (see pages 130-135).

Possible ways of boosting your retirement income

Other than luck – winning the football pools or coming into a legacy – there are three main possibilities for providing you with extra money: your home, work and investment skill.

Your home
Your home offers several different options.

Moving somewhere smaller. You could sell your present home, move into smaller accommodation and end up with the double bonus of pocketing a lump sum and reducing your running costs.

Leaving aside such considerations as whether you would still be able to have your grandchildren to stay and looking at the matter strictly in financial terms, it is as well to realise from the outset that the cash difference on the exchange – in other words, your profit – will invariably be less than you expect. What with removal charges and lawyers' fees, moving home is a very expensive business. Additionally, you will probably have some decorating expenses and there is bound to be a period of overlap when you will be paying two lots of telephone rental, extra electricity bills and so on.

This is not to say that moving may not be an excellent decision; simply that, if money is the main criterion, you need to be thoroughly realistic when calculating the gains.

An important new factor which has upset many people's sums over the past few years has been the state of the property market. There are two aspects to the problem. Firstly, if, as they have been, house sales are still sticking when you come to sell, you may have to accept a lower price than you had hoped to get (although, of course, you may also be able to buy your new property more cheaply). Rather more serious, if you buy a new home before selling your existing one, you could be faced by a bridging loan problem, which despite relatively low interest rates could soon eat into any profits you hope to realise on the exchange. Ideally, you should try to dovetail selling and buying at the same time. If this is not possible (and it usually isn't), the golden advice must be to sell first rather than risk lumbering yourself with the expense of having to borrow for several months or possibly longer.

If you do decide to move, you might consider transferring an existing mortgage to your new property or getting a new one up to £30,000, even if you could afford to buy the property outright. Too old? Not at all. Today mortgages are commonly available to people over retirement age. However, there may be good reasons why a mortgage would not be sensible for you. Also, as you probably know, mortgage interest relief is no longer allowed for basic rate tax but is now restricted to 15 per cent. You will need to do the sums carefully to see whether there is any real gain. If in doubt, consult an accountant or solicitor who will help you work out the various after-tax and other angles.

Taking in lodgers. If your children have left home and you have more space than you need, you could consider taking in lodgers, either as paying guests or, if your property lends itself to the creation of a separate flatlet, in a tenancy capacity.

When assessing the financial rewards, it is wise to assume that there will be times when the accommodation is empty – so you will not be receiving any rent. The good news is that you may be able to keep more of any earnings you make.

Until recently, *any* money you received in rent was counted as part of your taxable income. However, today, people letting out rooms in their home can claim tax relief of up to £62.50 a week (or £3,250 during the year). Any excess rental over £3,250 will be assessed for tax in the normal way. The relief applies only to accommodation that is 'part of your main home', so if you are thinking of creating a *separate flatlet*, you will need to take care that this qualifies and that it is not at risk of being assessed as a commercial let. Since the dividing line is somewhat hazy, check with your architect or other professional adviser that he/she fully understands the technical requirements.

Raising money on your home. A third option is to part-sell your home either for a capital sum or regular payments, under a home income plan, and continue to live in it for as long as you wish. Sounds wonderful? There are both attractions and drawbacks which need to be considered carefully and you would be strongly advised to discuss the matter with your solicitor.

All these possibilities are explored in greater detail in Chapter 8, Your Home. If you think any of the ideas sound interesting, see sections as follows: 'Moving to a new home', 'Letting rooms in your home' and 'Raising money on your home'.

Work

If you would like to continue working, arguably the easiest solution if your employer is agreeable is for you to remain where you are and to defer your pension. See 'Deferring your pension', page 29 in Chapter 3. Alternatively, as many people do, you may look on retirement as the opportunity for a job switch (with perhaps a reduction in hours) or the chance you have always wanted of setting up on your own. When assessing your budget plans, it is as well to err on the cautious side as regards the additional income you will be likely to earn as – although this has been improving – many so called 'retirement jobs' are notoriously badly paid.

If, instead of paid work, you are thinking of becoming self-employed or setting up a business, you will not only have the start-up costs but, as you are probably well aware, very few new enterprises make a profit during the first two or three years.

On the other hand – again, just looking at the economics – while you are working, you will not be spending money on entertainment. Also, particularly if you are self-employed or own a business, there may be certain tax advantages as well as possible scope for improving your pension. Lastly, of course, you may be one of the lucky ones for whom work after retirement really pays. Quite apart from the money, work can be thoroughly enjoyable and rewarding in its own right. For ideas and information, see chapters: 11, Looking for Paid Work and 10, Starting Your Own Business.

Investment

Contrary to what some people believe, you do not need to be very rich; nor for that matter is it too late to start thinking about investing once you are over the age of 55.

As you will see from Chapter 5, investment can take many different forms and among the list of different options there should be something to suit almost everyone. Although you may consider this to be specialist reading, we do suggest that you at least look at it, since maximising your income in retirement could make all the difference between being able to enjoy life or worrying about money.

Spending now for saving later

Although you may normally take the view that there is never a best time for spending money, retirement planning is different in that sooner or later you will need, or want, to make certain purchases – or pay off outstanding commitments, such as a mortgage. Most people's basic list – at least to think about – under this heading includes one or more of the following:

- Expenditure on their home
- The purchase of a car
- The termination of HP or other credit arrangement

Additionally, there may be a number of general domestic or luxury items which you had been promising yourself for some time and the only question is one of actual timing, i.e. determining the right moment to buy. Typical examples might include: a duvet, gardening equipment, a video recorder, a home computer, hobby materials and so on.

To help you decide whether a policy of 'spending now' is sensible, or possibly self-indulgent, there are two very simple questions you should ask:

- Can I afford it more easily now – or in the future?
- By paying now rather than waiting, shall I be saving money in the long run?

True, the issue may be complicated by tax and other considerations but for most choices this very basic analysis helps greatly to clarify the financial arguments on both sides.

Home improvements. If you plan to stay where you are, the likelihood is that at some point you will want to make some changes or improvements: install central heating, insulate the loft, modernise the kitchen or perhaps convert part of the house to a granny flat for an elderly parent who is becoming too frail to live alone.

Conventional wisdom has it that any significant expenditure on your home is best undertaken several years prior to retirement. However, in our experience the matter is less clear-cut and what is right for some is not the solution for others.

As with many other important decisions, the question largely depends on individual circumstances. Some people find it easier, and more reassuring, to pay major household bills while they are still earning. Others specifically plan to use part of the lump sum from their pension to create a dream home.

To arrive at the answer that makes best financial sense, present commitments have to be weighed against likely future expenditure (together with what money you will have available). Equally, as with insulation for example, you will need to work out what long-term savings you could effect by taking the plunge now. There is also the safety aspect: if you have bad lighting or dangerously worn carpet on part of the staircase, waiting for a few years to tackle the problem because it is all part of the grand plan could prove very false economy indeed.

Another very important consideration is how certain you are that you intend to stay in your present home. Investing a fortune and then upping sticks a couple of years later is generally a recipe for being out of pocket. Despite what one or two people may have told you, it is very unusual to recoup all your expenditure by reaping a vast profit when you come to sell.

Though it involves a few minutes' paperwork, a worthwhile exercise is to jot down your own personal list of pros and cons, under the headings: 'spending now' and 'spending later'. If still in doubt, then waiting is normally the more prudent course.

Purchasing a car. There could be two good reasons for buying a new car ahead of your retirement. One is that you have a company car that you are about to lose. The other is that your existing vehicle is on the old side and is beginning (or will probably soon start) to give you trouble. If either of these apply, then it probably makes sense to buy a replacement while you are still feeling relatively flush.

However, on the principle of 'look before you leap', company car owners should first check whether they might be entitled to purchase their present car on favourable terms: many employers are quite happy to allow this. Also, dreary though the suggestion sounds, if economies look like being the order of the day, two-car families might assess whether, come retirement when perhaps husband and wife will be doing more things together, two cars are really such an essential as before.

Paying off HP and similar. In general, this is a good idea since delay is unlikely to save you any money – and may in fact actually cost you more. The only precaution is to check the small print of your agreement, to ensure that there is no penalty for early repayment.

A further exception to the rule could be your mortgage. As already discussed, there could be tax advantages in retaining a mortgage. An accountant would advise you: or, if you are thinking of moving (and the issue is really whether to transfer an existing mortgage – or possibly acquire a new one), include this among the points to raise with your solicitor.

Cherished plans, if affordable

The Budget Planner (pages 130-135) may help you to work out whether the various luxuries and plans of which nearly all of us dream could be affordable or are destined to remain as fantasies.

Fun as it might be to imagine what a 'top twenty' list might include, there would be little real purpose in discussing the practicalities, or otherwise, of going on a cruise, owning a race horse, buying a caravan, flying Concorde or whatever, since not only – even among married couples – would there be wide variations in choice but more particularly, since normal budget wisdom does not apply, any advice would risk being grossly misleading. This does not mean that you should promptly forget the whole idea of noting items which come into this category; but that, as this is such a very personal decision area, only you can really make the assessments.

As a general point, however, if you plan your finances with a specific objective in view, you may find that against expectations a notion that first seemed impossible is actually affordable. Or possibly, when you really think about the choices, some of your earlier priorities will seem less important.

Money – if you become redundant

Much of the information in the earlier part of the chapter is equally valid whether you become redundant or retire in the normal way. However, there are several key points with regard to money which it could be to your advantage to check.

You may be entitled to statutory redundancy pay. Your employer is obliged to pay the legal minimum, which is calculated on your age, length of service and weekly pay. To qualify, you will need to have worked for the organisation for at least two years. The maximum your employer can be required to pay you is £210 a week. For further information, see booklet PL 808, available from Jobcentres.

Ex-gratia payment. Many employers are prepared to be more generous. The Inland Revenue allows individuals to receive up to £30,000 in redundancy pay/benefits, free of tax. Amounts over this are taxed under the PAYE system, so there could be an advantage in requesting that some of the payment be made into your pension scheme. For tax relief to apply, this must be before your departure.

Benefits that are not part of your pay. Redundancy may mean the loss of several valuable benefits, e.g. a company car, life assurance, health insurance. Your employer may let you keep your car as part of your pay-off and might be willing to extend any health/other insurance cover for a few months after you leave. Some insurance companies allow preferential rates to individuals who were previously insured with them under a company scheme.

You could be owed back holiday entitlement for which you should be paid.

Your mortgage. Your mortgage lender should be notified as soon as possible and might agree to a more flexible repayment system. Check whether your mortgage package includes insurance against redundancy. If you have a very low income, you may be able to obtain income support (IS) to help you with your mortgage costs. If your mortgage was taken out before 2 October 1995, IS would be obtainable after eight weeks. If it was taken out after 2 October 1995, you would normally have to wait for about nine months.

Other creditors/debts. Any creditors whom you may have difficulty in paying (electricity, gas, a bank overdraft) should be informed soonest in the hope of agreeing easy payment terms. There could be an argument for paying off credit card bills immediately, even if this means using some of your redundancy pay.

Company pension. Company pension scheme members normally have several choices. See section 'Early leavers' in Chapter 3, Pensions, page 40.

Unemployment benefit. Even if you are hoping to get another job very soon, you should sign on without delay since, as well as the benefit itself (£46.45 a week for people under State pension age, 1995/96) your national insurance contributions will be credited to you. This is important to protect your State pension. Claims cannot be backdated. If you are in poor health, you may be better off claiming sickness benefit. However, check the sums carefully. See leaflet IB 202 *Incapacity Benefit - Information for new customers.*

Jobseeker's Allowance. In April 1996, unemployment benefit is being replaced by jobseeker's allowance. In many respects it is more attractive, as it contains a number of new incentives for those genuinely seeking work. A leaflet explaining the details should be available from Social Security offices early in 1996.

Redundancy helpline. Can answer queries on all aspects of redundancy. Dial free: 0800 848489.

Cheques Act 1992

Over the past few years, there has been growing concern about the number of cheques being stolen in the post. The risks have been somewhat reduced thanks to the 1992 Cheques Act which shifts responsibility to the banks provided all safeguards have been taken.

If you write the words 'Account Payee Only' between the crossings on the cheque, you can be certain that the cheque can only be banked by the person to whom you made it out. Most banks have altered their cheque books accordingly. If your cheques still say 'or order', cross these words out and initial the amendment.

Making a deed of covenant

Making a deed of covenant used to be a popular and tax-efficient way for grandparents to help pay towards their grandchildren's education. However, in the 1988 Budget the Chancellor abolished the tax relief on all inter-personal covenants except those made for charitable purposes. This means that there is no longer any tax advantage in giving money for the benefit of individuals via a covenant. Covenants existing at the time of the 1988 Budget are not affected by the change and can continue as before until their expiry.

Covenants in respect of charities. Contrary to popular belief, it is possible to covenant (that is 'promise') quite small amounts of money to charities you wish to support. Many charities are happy to claim back the tax you have paid from the Inland Revenue for sums as low as £10 per annum. Although slight changes have been made to covenant administration, the principle of committing yourself to giving, for four or more years, remains the same.

For further information plus details of their own very flexible scheme, contact: **Charities Aid Foundation (CAF)**, 48 Pembury Road, Tonbridge, Kent TN9 2JD. T:01732 771333.

Alternatively, as most of the larger charities will have covenant forms, you can approach the charity you wish to help direct.

Payroll giving scheme. Also of possible interest to those attracted by charitable giving is the payroll giving scheme. This scheme allows anyone paying PAYE, either through their earnings or their pension, to give up to £75 a month or £900 a year, free of tax, to charities of their choice. The money is taken out of your *pre-taxed* income, so if you choose to give £10 a month, it will only cost you £7.50 in real terms. Tax is only levied on your remaining earnings.

You will, however, need to know whether your employer/former employer or pension paying organisation has or will be introducing the scheme before you can take part.

For further information, either write to one of the charities you wish to support or contact the **Charities Aid Foundation (CAF)** for details of their own scheme, *Give As You Earn*, at Foundation House, Coach & Horses Passage, The Pantiles, Tunbridge Wells, Kent TN2 5TZ. T:01892 512244.

Gift Aid. This scheme allows individuals to make one-off donations to charities of £250 or more with the benefit of tax relief. The charity will be entitled to claim repayment of the base rate tax from the Inland Revenue which, if you give £250, would mean the charity receiving an extra £83.33.

Personal charity account. The Charities Aid Foundation (CAF) operates an account scheme which can be used for Gift Aid, payroll giving scheme and covenanted donations. The donation, together with the reclaimed tax, is paid into a CAF account from which the donor distributes funds to charities of his or her choice, either by voucher or CharityCard, CAF's special debit card. For further details contact CAF at 48 Pembury Road, Tonbridge, Kent TN9 2JD. T:01732 771333.

Extra income

There are a great many State benefits and allowances available to give special help to people in need. Definition of need covers a very wide range and applies, among others, to problems connected with: health, housing, care of an elderly or disabled relative, as well as widowhood and problems encountered by the frail elderly who for example may require extra heating during the winter.

While many of these benefits are 'means-tested', in other words are only given to people whose income is below a certain level, some, such as disability living allowance, are not dependent on how poor or how wealthy you are. Moreover, even when 'means-testing' is a factor, for some of the benefits income levels are nothing like as low as many people imagine. Because this information is not widely enough known, many individuals, including in particular some 700,000 retired people, are not claiming help to which they are entitled and for which in many cases they have actually paid through their national insurance contributions.

The main benefits and allowances are listed in their appropriate chapters: for example, housing benefit appears in Chapter 8, Your Home; invalid care allowance is briefly described in Chapter 15, Caring for Elderly Parents. For further information about these and some others, such as criminal injuries compensation, obtain a copy of DSS booklet FB2, *Which Benefit?*, available from any Social Security office. Alternatively, telephone DSS Freephone number 0800 666 555.

A number of voluntary organisations also provide assistance to individuals: sometimes in cash or sometimes with facilities, such as special equipment for disabled people. Details are given in the relevant chapters.

For further advice and information, contact your local Social Services Department or Citizens' Advice Bureau. Another very useful source of help is your local Age Concern group.

The national addresses of these organisations are as follows:

Department of Social Security: Richmond House, 79 Whitehall, London SW1A 2NS. T:0171 210 3000.
Freeline: 0800 666 555 operates between 9 a.m. and 4 p.m., Monday to Friday.

Welsh language Freeline: 0800 289 011 operates between 9 a.m. and 4 p.m., Monday to Friday.

Northern Ireland Department of Health and Social Services, Dundonald House, Upper Newtownards Road, Belfast BT4 3SF. T:01232 650111.

National Association of Citizens' Advice Bureaux, 115-123 Pentonville Road, London N1 9LZ. T: 0171 833 2181.

Age Concern

England, Astral House, 1268 London Road, London SW16 4ER. T:0181 679 8000.

Northern Ireland, 3 Lower Crescent, Belfast BT7 1NR. T:01232 245729.

Scotland, 113 Rose Street, Edinburgh EH2 3DT. T:0131 228 5656.

Cymru, 4th Floor, 1 Cathedral Road, Cardiff CF1 9SD. T:01222 371566.

3   Pensions

Those retiring during the 1990s can count themselves lucky. Firstly, State pensions are keeping well up with the cost of living. Additionally, thanks to an increasingly enlightened climate, most occupational schemes have been steadily improving.

Because pensions come in a variety of forms, even many sophisticated people fail to collect all their entitlements or do not understand all the options that are available to them. Since, next to your home, your pension is almost certainly your most valuable asset, it is important to check all the angles well ahead of time to ensure that when you retire you receive the maximum benefit. Incidentally, this applies even to young men and women in their thirties!

State pensions

You can get a pension if you are a man of 65 or a woman of 60, provided you have paid (or been credited with) sufficient national insurance contributions.

In time, the age for women will alter as the Government has published plans to equalise State pension age for men and women at 65. The change will be phased in over ten years, beginning in 2010. This will affect younger women only. Those born before 6 April 1950 have no need to alter their retirement plans.

Your right to a State pension

Your right to a State pension depends on your (or your spouse's) national insurance contributions. Most people have to pay contributions into the national insurance scheme while they are working.

If you are an employee, your employer will have automatically deducted Class 1 contributions from your salary, provided your earnings were above a certain limit (currently £58 a week).

If you are self-employed, you will have been paying a flat-rate Class 2 contribution every week and possibly the earnings-related Class 4 contributions as well.

You may also have paid Class 3 voluntary contributions at some point in your life in order to maintain your contributions record.

If you are over pension age (65 for men and 60 for women) you do not need to pay national insurance contributions.

There may have been times during your working life when you have not, either knowingly or unwittingly, paid national insurance contributions. If you have not paid sufficient NI contributions to qualify for a full rate basic pension you may be entitled to a reduced rate of pension. However, your NI contributions record will have been maintained in the following circumstances:

If you have lived outside Great Britain. If you have lived in Northern Ireland or the Isle of Man, any contributions paid there will count towards your pension.

If you have lived in a European Community country or any country whose social security system is linked to Britain's by a reciprocal agreement,* contributions or residence there may be counted towards your pension depending on the country concerned.

If you have any doubts, you should enquire what your position is at your local Social Security office.

* Countries with reciprocal agreements are: Australia, Bermuda, Canada, Cyprus, Guernsey, Iceland, Israel, Jamaica, Jersey, Malta, Mauritius, New Zealand, Norway, Philippines, Switzerland, Turkey and the USA.

If you have received Home Responsibilities Protection (HRP). If you have not worked regularly at some time since 1978, because you have had to stay at home to care for either a child or a sick or elderly person, you may have protected your right to a pension by claiming HRP. This benefit allows you to deduct the years when you were required to give up work from the normal qualifying period for a basic pension and so, in effect, shorten the number of years when you would otherwise have been required to make contributions.

There are two important points to note. Firstly, if you are a woman and were claiming child benefit, HRP would have been credited to you automatically, whereas a man staying at home to care for a child would have needed to arrange the transfer of child benefit to himself. Secondly, HRP is only available for complete tax years in which earnings were less than 52 times the lower earnings limit.

While HRP can be claimed by both sexes, it predictably applies more frequently to women. For more information, see 'Pensions for women' at the end of the chapter or obtain form CF 411 *Home Responsibilities Protection – How to Protect Your State Retirement Pension*, available from your local Social Security office.

If you have been in any of the following situations, you will have been *credited* with contributions (instead of having to pay them):

- If you were sick or unemployed (provided you sent in sick notes to your Social Security office or signed on at the Unemployment Benefit office);
- If you were a man aged 60-64 and not working;
- If you were entitled to maternity allowance, invalid care allowance or unemployability supplement;
- If you were taking an approved course of training;
- When you left education but had not yet started working.

Married women and widows who do not qualify for a basic pension in their own right may be entitled to a basic pension on their husband's contributions at about 60 per cent of the level to which he is entitled (see 'Pensions for women' at the end of the chapter).

Since the introduction of independent taxation, husband and wife are assessed separately for tax. As a result, a married woman is now entitled to have her section of the joint pension (currently £35.25) offset against her own personal allowance – instead of being counted as part of her husband's taxable income. For many pensioner couples, this should mean a reduction in their tax liability.

Reduced rate contributions note. Many women retiring today may have paid a reduced rate contribution under a scheme which was abolished in 1978. Women who were already paying a reduced rate contribution were, however, allowed to continue doing so. (See 'Pensions for women'.) These reduced rate contributions **do not count** towards your pension and you will not have had any contributions credited to you.

How your pension is worked out

Your total pension can come from three main sources: the basic pension, the additional pension and the graduated pension. There can also be additions, i.e. invalidity addition and age addition.

Anyone wanting to work out what they are due can write to their local Social Security office for a 'pension forecast'. This is normally expressed in percentage terms so, for instance, someone with full contributions will get 100 per cent of pension. You can also get a forecast of the additional earnings related pension to which you are entitled. To obtain a forecast complete Form BR 19.

It is worth getting an early estimate of what your pension will be, as it may be possible to improve your national insurance contribution record by making additional Class 3 voluntary contributions. These can, however, only be paid for six years in arrears, so this concession may not help if you think about it too late.

Basic pension

The full basic pension for a man or woman (April 1995/96) is £58.85 a week, £94.10 for a married couple (unless your spouse is entitled to more than the £35.25 spouse's addition on his/her own contributions, in which case you will receive more). Pensions are uprated in April each year. Up-to-date rates are contained in leaflet NI 196, obtainable from your local Social Security office and main post offices.

All pensions are taxable other than one or two special categories, such as war widows and the victims of Nazism. If, however, your basic pension is your only source of income, you will not have to worry as the amount you receive is below the income tax threshold.

The rate of basic pension depends on your record of NI contributions over your working life. To get the full rate you must have paid (or been credited with) NI contributions for roughly nine-tenths of your working life, although widows can also be entitled to a full basic pension on their husband's contributions. If you are divorced, you may be able to use your former spouse's contributions to improve your own pension entitlement, provided that you have not remarried before reaching pension age.

Your working life, for this purpose, is normally considered to be 44 years for a woman and 49 years for a man (i.e. age 16 until pension age), but it may be less if you were of working age but not in insurable employment when the National Insurance Scheme started in 1948.

Reduced rate pension

If you do not have full contributions but have maintained your contributions record for between a quarter and nine-tenths of your working life, you may get a pension at a reduced rate. The amount is calculated according to the number of years for which you have paid contributions. However, to get any basic pension you must satisfy two conditions. Firstly, you must actually have paid enough full rate contributions in any one tax year, from 6 April 1975, for that year to count as a qualifying year; or have paid 50 flat rate contributions, in any one year, before 6 April 1975. Secondly, your total contributions must be enough to have entitled you to at least 25 per cent of the full basic rate.

Additional pension

This is also known as SERPS, short for the State Earnings Related Pension Scheme. It is worked out on earnings since April 1978 on which you have paid Class 1 contributions as an employee. It is not applicable to the self-employed.

Class 1 contributions are paid as a percentage of earnings between a 'lower' and an 'upper' limit (currently £58 and £440 a week respectively). The lower earnings limit is close to the same level as the basic retirement pension.

How much additional pension you get depends on the amount of your earnings over and above the lower earnings limit for each complete tax year since April 1978. The earnings for each tax year are then increased in line with the rise in national average earnings and added together to produce the total earnings figure on which your additional pension depends.

The current maximum amount of additional pension to which you would be entitled is £92.14 a week. For details on how to apply for a statement of your current savings in SERPS, see Form BR 19 *Pension Forecast Application Form*, obtainable from any Social Security office. Full details and examples of how the additional pension is worked out can be found in leaflet NP 46 *A Guide to Retirement Pensions*.

Although there are plans to scale down the additional pension, this is not expected to affect anyone retiring before 1999 and will only marginally affect those retiring by 2009.

As you will probably know, if you think you can do better by making independent provision, you are not obliged to remain in SERPS but instead can invest in a personal pension. For details, see 'Personal pension schemes' further in the chapter.

If you are a member of a contracted-out occupational pension scheme, you are legally entitled to: either a minimum pension which must be broadly the same as you would have got under the State scheme; or to what are known as protected rights (i.e.

your and your employer's compulsory contributions to your pension together with their accumulated investment growth).

Graduated pension

This pension existed between April 1961 and April 1975. The amount you receive depends on the graduated NI contributions you paid during that period. Anyone over 18 and earning more than £9 a week at that time will probably be entitled to a small graduated pension. This includes married women and widows with reduced contribution liability. A widow or widower whose spouse dies when they are both over pension age can inherit half of the graduated pension based on their late spouse's contributions.

Other additions

Invalidity addition. Your pension will automatically be permanently increased if you were getting invalidity allowance with invalidity benefit (or from April 1995, an age addition with incapacity benefit) within eight weeks before reaching retirement age. The amount you get will be the same as the invalidity allowance/age addition you are already receiving but any additional pension (SERPS) and/or occupational pension will be subtracted from your invalidity allowance with only the balance (if any) being paid to you as invalidity addition.

Age addition. Your pension will be automatically increased when you are aged 80 or over. The current rate is 25p a week.

Other ways to increase your pension

Deferring your pension. Your pension may be increased if you delay claiming it and instead continue working after normal retirement age. This applies between the ages of 65 and 70 for a man and from 60 to 65 for a woman. For every year that you defer retirement, approximately another 7.5 per cent a year will be added to your pension. This extra pension is paid either when you claim your pension or when you reach 70(65), regardless of whether you have retired from work or not. Your local Social Security office could help you work out the figures to see if deferment would be worthwhile.

An exception to the age rule sometimes applies in the case of a married woman over 65 whose pension is based on her husband's contributions. Her pension can continue to increase until such time as her husband gets his pension or reaches the age of 70, whichever is sooner.

For further details obtain leaflet NI 92 *Giving Up Your Retirement Pension to Earn Extra.*

Good news for younger people is that from 2010, i.e. the start date for the phasing-in of equal pension ages, the amount earned by deferring your pension will be increased to 10 per cent a year. Also, the present limit of five years' deferral will be abolished.

Warning. If you plan to defer your pension, you should also defer any graduated pension to which you may be entitled – or you risk losing the increases you would otherwise obtain.

Increases for dependants. Your basic pension may be increased if you are supporting a dependent spouse or children. Most typically, this applies in respect of a non-working wife (or one whose earnings are very low) who is under 60 when her husband retires. However, this also applies for a retired wife supporting a husband dependent by reason of invalidity. The current rates are £35.25 a week for a spouse, £9.85 for the first child and £11.05 each for any other dependent children. The definition of dependent child is one for whom you are receiving child benefit. See leaflet NI 196 obtainable from your local Social Security office.

Income support

If you have an inadequate income, you may qualify for income support which is designed to provide those without sufficient means with enough money to live on. There are special premiums (i.e. additions) for lone parents, disabled people, carers and pensioners.

As a single retired person, you can claim income support to bring your total income to £65.10 a week; for married couples, the amount is £101.05 (April 1995/96 rates). These totals exclude mortgage interest and disregarded income, for example, attendance allowance. Higher sums apply for disabled pensioners and for individuals over the age of 75.

A condition of entitlement is that you should not have capital, including savings, of more than £8,000. To qualify for maximum income support, the capital limit is £3,000. For every £250 of capital over £3,000, individuals are deemed to be getting £1 a week income – so the actual amount of benefit will be reduced accordingly.

A big advantage is that people entitled to income support receive full help with their rent and should also not have any council tax to pay. See 'Housing benefit' and 'Council tax benefit', in Chapter 8, Your Home.

If your only source of income is your basic State pension, you are likely to be entitled to income support. For more information, together with a claim form, see leaflet IS 1 *Income Support*, obtainable from any Social Security office or post office.

Social fund. If you are faced with an exceptional expense you find difficult to pay, you may be able to obtain a Budgeting or Crisis Loan, or Funeral Payment, from the Social Fund. Ask at your local Social Security office.

Working after you start getting your pension

This used to be a problem for many people as a result of the Earnings Rule. At the time, men between the ages of 65 and 69 and women between the ages of 60 and 64 who earned more than £75 a week had their basic State pension reduced. Happily, this does not apply any more and today there is no longer any limit to the amount pensioners can earn.

Early retirement and your pension

Because so many people now retire early, there is a widespread belief that it is possible to get an early pension. While the information is correct as regards a growing number of employers' occupational pension schemes, it does not apply to the basic State pension. If you take early retirement before the age of 60, it may be necessary for you to pay voluntary Class 3 national insurance contributions in order to protect your contributions record for pension purposes. If you are a man over 60, however, you will automatically get contribution credits from the tax year in which you reach 60.

How you get a pension

You should claim your pension a few months before you reach State pension age. The Department of Social Security (DSS) should send you a claim form (BR 1) at the proper time but if this does not arrive, it is your responsibility to contact them. Remember they will send the claim form to the last recorded address they hold for you, so if you have moved and not informed them do make sure they have your new address. You should apply for the form about four months before you are due to retire. If you claim your pension late, you could lose some of the money.

After you claim, you are told in writing exactly how much pension you will get. You will also be told what to do if you disagree with the decision. The information you are given should include the name and address of the organisation responsible for paying you any guaranteed minimum pension.

How your pension can be paid

If you live in the UK, you can choose to have your pension paid either by credit transfer or in order book form.

Credit transfer. This method gives you the choice of having your pension paid direct into a bank or National Giro account; or, alternatively, into an investment account with either the National Savings Bank or with most building societies. Payment will be made in arrears every four weeks, or quarterly, whichever you prefer.

Order book. You receive a book of orders (or pension book) which you can cash at a post office of your choice. Each order is your pension entitlement for one week and is valid for 12 weeks after the date shown on the voucher. If it is difficult for you to get to the post office, the coloured pages in the book explain how someone else can draw the payment for you.

Other situations. If your pension is £2 a week or less, it will normally be paid once a year in arrears by a crossed order which you can pay into a bank or building society account. Payment is made each year shortly before Christmas.

Pensions can be paid to an overseas address, if you are going abroad for six months or more. For further details see leaflets NI 38 *Social Security Abroad* and NI 106 *Pensioners or Widows Going Abroad*, obtainable from your local Social Security office.

If you are in hospital, your pension can still be paid to you. You will receive a reduced amount if you are in hospital for more than six weeks. Leaflet NI 9 *Going Into Hospital* (obtainable from your local Social Security office) provides full information.

Christmas bonus

Pensioners usually get a small tax-free bonus shortly before Christmas each year. The amount and due date will be announced in advance. For the last few years the sum has been £10. The bonus is combined with your normal pension payment for the first week in December, so if you have not received it by the end of that month ask at your local Social Security office.

Advice

If you have any queries or think that you may not be obtaining your full pension entitlement, you should contact your local Social Security office as soon as possible. If you think a mistake has been made, you have the right to appeal and can insist on your claim being heard by an independent Social Security Tribunal. Before doing so, you would be strongly advised to consult a solicitor at the Citizens' Advice Bureau or the Welfare Advice Unit of your local Social Security office. Some areas have special Tribunal Representation Units to assist people to make claims at Social Security Tribunals.

If you are writing to your local Social Security office with a query you should quote either your national insurance number (or your spouse's) or your pension number if you have already started receiving your pension.

DSS Freefone: for free advice on your pension, dial 0800 666 555.

For further information about pensions, see leaflet FB 6, *Retiring? Your Pension and Other Benefits* and booklet NP 46 *A Guide to Retirement Pensions* obtainable from any Social Security office.

Private pensions

The importance of persuading individuals to save for their own pension instead of just relying on the State has been recognised by successive governments. Encouragement has been made through tax incentives, so that pension savings are now one of the most tax effective investments available.

- You get income tax relief on contributions at your highest tax rate.
- The pension fund is totally exempt from income tax and capital gains tax, providing excellent growth prospects for your money.
- Part of the pension can be taken as a cash sum when you retire and that too is tax free.

Private pension schemes fall into two broad categories: those arranged by employers, e.g. company pension schemes, and those you can arrange for yourself.

Company pension schemes

About 10.7 million people, roughly half the employed population, are now participating in company schemes. While these can vary considerably, the following basic features apply to all of them.

Pension fund. Pension contributions go into a pension fund which is quite separate from your employer's company. It is set up under trust and run by trustees, appointed from management and sometimes from staff. It is the job of the trustees to manage the fund and its investments and to ensure that the benefit promises are kept.

Payments into the fund. Your scheme may or may not ask for a contribution from you. For this reason, schemes are known as 'contributory' or 'non-contributory'. If (as is normally the case) you are required to make a contribution, this will be deducted from your pay before you receive it.

Your employer's contributions to the scheme represent the money he is setting aside for your pension and other benefits. In some schemes the amount is calculated as a fixed percentage of your earnings. In others the scheme actuary would estimate the required amount that your employer needs to pay to ensure your (and other members') benefits in the future.

Benefits from the scheme. All pension scheme members should normally be given a booklet describing how the scheme works, what benefits it provides and other information including the address of the Pensions Ombudsman. If you do not receive one, you should ask the person in the company responsible for the pension scheme – this is often the personnel manager – to supply you with a booklet. You can also ask to see a copy of the trust deed as well as the latest annual report and audited accounts.

The key benefits applicable to most pension schemes include:

- A pension due at whatever age is specified by the scheme, usually somewhere between 60 and 65 (although many companies offer early retirement provision)
- Death benefit (sometimes known as lump sum life assurance), paid out if you die before retirement age
- A widow/widower's pension paid for life no matter when you die.

Benefit limits. The Inland Revenue sets limits on pension benefits which members of company schemes can receive. The main ones are:

- The maximum pension you are allowed is two-thirds of your final pay (excluding State pension)
- If you die, the pension can be passed on to someone else but no one beneficiary can receive more than two-thirds
- The tax-free lump sum, if you choose to take it, cannot be more than one and a half times salary. (If you take a lump sum, this will reduce the amount you receive in pension each year.)

The above figures are governed by a ceiling, currently based on £78,600 earnings a year. In other words, the maximum figure allowed for two-thirds of final salary is £52,400 a year; and the maximum tax-free lump sum allowed is £117,900.

The measure is not as draconian as it sounds. Firstly, of course, because it only affects high earners, i.e. those earning more than £78,600 a year. Secondly, because the £78,600 limit is not a static figure but is regularly revalued in line with price increases. Finally, the ruling only applies to members of schemes set up after 13 March 1989, and to new employees joining existing schemes from 1 June 1989. Members of an established company scheme at the time of the 1989 Budget, who remain in the same scheme – or who change schemes within the same group of associated employers – are not affected by the change.

Types of scheme
Most employers' schemes are of the final salary or money purchase type. Other types that exist are average earnings and flat rate schemes.

Final salary scheme. This is the most common. Your pension is calculated as a proportion of your final pay, which could mean literally the last year you work or for example (and this is a requirement for controlling directors and those earning over £100,000) the average of three consecutive years during the last ten.

The amount you receive depends on two factors: the number of years you have worked for the organisation plus the fraction of final pay on which the scheme is based, typically 1/60th or 1/80th. So if you have worked 30 years for a company that has 1/60th pension scheme, you will receive 30/60ths of your final pay – in other words, half.

Final pay schemes can be contracted into or out of SERPS. If a scheme is contracted out of SERPS, it must provide a minimum pension that is at least as good as its SERPS equivalent.

Money purchase scheme. This has been greatly increasing in popularity in recent years and, according to all the forecasts, looks set to become even more widespread. Unlike the other three types of scheme, the amount of pension you receive is not based on a fixed formula but (within Inland Revenue limits) is dependent on the investment performance of the fund into which your own and your employer's contributions on your behalf have been paid.

Although there is an element of gamble with money purchase schemes, in that no one can forecast with certainty how well or badly a pension fund might do, in practice most trustees act very conservatively.

Different schemes have different ways of determining how members' pension entitlements are calculated. You should enquire what the rules are and additionally, to give you a better idea of what size pension you might realistically expect, you could ask for some practical examples – say, over the last five years – of retired individuals in a similar earnings bracket to your own.

An important feature of money purchase schemes is that the bulk of the fund must be used to purchase an annuity that will provide you with a guaranteed income for life. (See 'Compulsory purchase annuities', page 37).

Average earnings scheme. As its name implies, this is based on your average earnings over the total period of time that you are participating in the scheme. Every year, an amount goes into the scheme on your behalf, calculated in accordance with your level of earnings. As your salary increases, so too do your potential benefits. Each year, your 'profits' from the scheme are worked out from a formal table and the total of all these annual sums constitutes your pension.

Flat rate pension scheme. Your level of pay is not a factor. Instead, the same flat rate applies to everyone, multiplied by the number of years in which they have been participants of the scheme. So, for example, if the flat rate is £200 a year of pension and you have been a member of the scheme for 20 years, your pension will be £4,000 a year.

Additional or other schemes. There may be one scheme that applies to everyone in the organisation or there may be a variety of schemes for different grades of employee. For example, there may be a works scheme and a staff scheme operating side by side. It is also quite common for there to be a special pension scheme for executives and directors.

Executive pension plans
These are individual pension plans arranged by an employer for the benefit of some or all executives above a certain grade. In some companies, executive pension plans apply only to directors; in others, they may also include senior and middle management. Equally, there may be a separate policy for each individual or a master policy, covering everyone in the scheme.

One of the attractions of executive pension plans is their potential flexibility. They can be tailored to cater for differing retirement ages as well as for varying contribution levels, which explains why some organisations are able to offer early retirement on very attractive terms.

Historically, executive pension plans are of the money purchase type. Because they are provided by the employer, the maximum benefit allowed is two-thirds of final salary; and, as from the 1989 Budget, the same rules apply as for final salary schemes. Normally, one of the following four types of investment policy is used: with profits, unit linked, deposit administration and non-profit.

These are described in the section on page 53, 'Personal pension schemes'. See also 'Top-up schemes' in the following section.

Focus on high earners
Several changes in the tax treatment of pensions with particular implications for high earners were introduced in both the 1987 and 1989 Budgets. The measures, except

for the rule regarding accelerated accrual rates, are unlikely to affect anyone who has been in a pension scheme prior to March 1987 and remains with the same employer. Individuals on current salaries of £78,600 or more who are thinking of changing jobs and either joining a new scheme or transferring their existing pension to one will need to weigh up the financial consequences.

Maximum tax-free lump sum. Prior to the 1987 Budget, the only restriction that applied was that the maximum was set at one and a half times salary. For the vast majority of individuals this is still the case and they have no need to be concerned about the changes described below.

In the 1987 Budget, a ceiling of £150,000 was imposed on the amount that individuals could take in the form of a tax-free lump sum on retirement. The new rule affected only those on earnings of more than £100,000 who actually joined a new pension scheme after 17 March 1987.

In the 1989 Budget, the Chancellor brought in a new ceiling limit of £90,000, based on earnings of £60,000 to be revalued in line with price increases. The 1995/96 ceiling limit is £117,900, based on earnings of £78,600.

As with the 1987 change, this latest rule affects only members of new schemes (set up after 13 March 1989) or new members joining established schemes after 1 June 1989. Members of an existing scheme prior to these dates who remain with the same employer should not be adversely affected by the change.

Accelerated accrual rates. The proviso whereby it was possible for some individuals to enjoy an enhanced accrual scale to qualify for full pension benefits after 10 years of service was altered in the 1987 Budget – with a new period of 20 years' service being required.

Definition of 'final salary' for high earners. Up until the 1987 Budget, individuals could base their final salary for pension purposes on any one of their last five years' earnings. In March 1987 a new rule was introduced, whereby anyone with earnings of more than £100,000 who joined a new pension scheme was required to base their final salary assessment on their average earnings over any three consecutive years over the last ten.

Two additional changes (also only relevant to joining a new scheme) were brought in at the same time. Firstly, gains from share options in the final year of employment were no longer allowed in the calculation of final salary. Secondly, individuals who were controlling directors were no longer permitted to resign just before retirement to boost their salary but instead had to use the three-year average method of calculation.

These rules still apply with one important difference. Instead of £100,000 being the ceiling limit for tax relief purposes, the maximum final salary allowed is now £78,600 (1995/96). As already stated, the change affects only those joining new pension schemes set up after 13 March 1989 or new members joining existing schemes after 1 June 1989.

Top-up schemes. Employers can still set up 'top-up' pension schemes to provide additional benefits above the new ceiling but such schemes are now taxable. If given any choice in the matter, you should know that funded-in-advance schemes, including FURBS (funded unapproved retirement benefit schemes), offer greater security but are not tax-efficient, as the employee has to make contributions out of his net income. Also lump sums received from offshore FURBS set up after 30 November 1993 are now taxed at an employee's marginal rate; or more precisely, tax is charged on the difference between the amount the employee receives and the contributions to the scheme.

Unfunded 'top-up' schemes, i.e. where the employer does not fund the top-up benefits but simply promises to pay them at retirement, are more tax-efficient but offer less security as you would be dependent on your employer keeping his promise. In the event of a take-over especially, there would be no guarantees.

Compulsory purchase annuities

Everyone with a personal pension, Section 226 policy, retirement annuity, contracted-out company money purchase scheme (COMPS) or AVC arrangement must by law purchase an annuity on retirement.

An annuity is an insurance product which, in exchange for the money invested, guarantees an income for life. You have the choice of using the whole of your accumulated pension fund, or you can first take all, or part, of your tax-free lump sum. If you take your lump sum, this will reduce the size of your annuity and the amount of annual income you receive.

Other important factors that can affect your annuity 'earnings' include: what add-on options you may choose; the timing when you buy your annuity; and the choice of provider to whom you go.

Add-on options. The most typical options that you will be offered include: a spouse's pension; annual increases which may either be fixed at, say, 3 or 5 per cent or may be linked to retail price inflation; a return of some of the capital (either in the form of a lump sum or in annual payments over five or ten years) should you die unexpectedly early. Wise as such options usually are to protect your and your dependants' long-term security, there will almost invariably be some additional cost which, if you were to go for all the possible extras, could reduce the annual income by around 50 per cent.

Timing. The two key factors are what age you are when you purchase an annuity and what the level of interest rates is at the time. As a general rule, the older you are and the higher the level of interest rates, the bigger the annual income you will receive.

While most people have to buy an annuity as soon as they retire, people with personal pensions and members of small self-administered schemes have the option to wait until they are 75. During 1995, the rules were further eased (see para below) to make them more flexible.

Annuity deferral option. People with a tax-approved personal pension, wishing to delay the purchase of an annuity, are allowed to take their tax-free lump sum and withdraw a limited income (i.e. the maximum permitted is broadly equal to the annuity their fund could have provided) during the deferral period.

From April 1996, people with personal pensions who have contracted out of SERPS will also be able to take advantage of the new annuity deferral option. (It is widely believed that before long other people required to purchase a compulsory annuity will be allowed the same deferral choice.)

While the big gain to individuals is that they will be able both to delay purchase of an annuity until interest rates are favourable and obtain their lump sum and an income in the meantime, there are also risks, in particular: the stock market could fall, reducing the value of their capital; or interest rates could be even less favourable when they eventually need to purchase an annuity. Many experts advise that the annuity deferral option is not suitable for anyone with less than £100,000 in their pension fund.

Choice of provider. This is one area above all where expert independent advice is essential. Annuity rates offered by life companies vary by as much as 25 per cent and the difference between the best and worst choice could affect your income by hundreds of pounds a year or more.

There is no obligation to buy your annuity from the company that has been managing your pension plan. Indeed, the best people for pension plans are not usually the most competitive for annuities and while there may be attractions in remaining with the same company (some offer loyalty bonuses), your decision will need to be based on the best all-round terms you can get at the time of purchase. **But** once you have made a choice, it is extremely difficult to switch.

You can take advice from an independent financial adviser, from a pensions consultant or from one of the several companies that specialise in tracking annuity rates.

The Annuity Bureau, for example, monitors the rates on a daily basis and can advise you where you would get the best return. The fee for this is £50 plus VAT. If you would like them to do so, they can also arrange the purchase and deal with the paperwork. For further information, contact the **Annuity Bureau Ltd.**, Enterprise House, 59-65 Upper Ground, London SE1 9PQ. T:0171 620 4090.

Other annuity specialists include: **Annuity Direct**, 32 Scrutton Street, London EC2A 4RQ , T:0171 375 1175; and **Lexis Pension Consultants Ltd.**, 52 Lime Street, London EC3M 7BS. T:0171 283 2828.

Additional voluntary contributions (AVCs)

If, as you approach retirement, you become aware that you are not going to have a big enough pension to live as comfortably as you would like, you might seriously consider the possibility of making additional voluntary contributions. AVCs are a very attractive way of making extra savings for retirement for two special reasons. Firstly, AVCs – as well as the growth of the plan – enjoy full tax relief, so for basic rate taxpayers the Inland Revenue is in effect paying £25 of every £100 invested. A further key advantage for many people is that AVCs allow you to purchase 'added years', to make up any shortfall in your entitlement to benefit under a company scheme.

There should be no difficulty in purchasing AVCs, since all occupational schemes are required by law to provide AVC facilities.

However, as you are probably aware, an option, known as 'free-standing AVCs', is now also on offer. As the name implies, these are not linked to a company scheme but can be purchased independently from: insurance companies, building societies, banks, unit trusts and friendly societies.

Individuals can, if they wish, contribute both to company AVCs and to a free-standing plan or plans. Although the rules only allow the purchase of one new free-standing AVC policy a year, it is possible to purchase a different policy every year, so building up a spread of investments.

The total of all your AVCs plus other contributions to the pension plan is not allowed to exceed 15 per cent of your earnings. In the event of over-funding occurring, whether from a free-standing or company AVC, the surplus will simply be refunded to you in cash, minus the tax relief involved.

Individuals paying less than £2,400 a year in free-standing AVCs will not normally need to involve their employer but just have to certify that they are not paying more than 15 per cent of their earnings in total contributions. Where larger amounts are concerned, the employer will need to become involved but this should not deter you if you believe that the purchase of free-standing AVCs is in your best long-term interest.

Rule changes. Over the years there have been several rule changes of which you should be aware.

- The £78,600 final salary limit applies to AVCs in the same way as to other earnings. It goes without saying that it is not £78,600 in respect of each but the *total* earnings' figure which must not exceed £78,600.
- Previously, individuals had to make a commitment to pay regular contributions for a period of at least five years. This requirement has been abolished and (provided the actual scheme rules permit) both the amount and timing of payments can be varied to suit members according to their personal circumstances.
- Prior to 8 April 1987 AVC plans could be used towards funding an individual's lump sum. Under today's rules, the contributions can only be used for boosting the actual pension itself. These arrangements, however, only affect AVCs that were applied for after the April 1987 deadline. AVCs already entered into are exempt from the 'no commutation' rule.

For most people, the only real problem with AVCs is the sheer enormity of choice. As with any other important investment decision, you would be well advised to take your time, do some basic research into the track record of any policies you might be considering (specialist magazines such as *Money Management* provide a useful starting point) and on no account sign any document without first being absolutely certain that you fully understand all the terms and conditions including the administrative charges. As general wisdom, these are likely to be higher with free-standing contracts than for a collective AVC scheme offered by an employer.

If you have not yet made up your mind between company AVCs and FSAVCs, a question to ask the pension fund trustees is: (a) to give you details of the AVC performance (there are significant variations between the best and the worst) and (b) to explain any early retirement penalties.

Finally, if you are already subscribing to company AVCs, before investing in a new plan check on your present level of contributions and the benefits that these are expected to yield. Your company pension adviser should be only too happy to answer any questions.

Early leavers

In the past, the big problem, as everyone knows, is that early leavers tended to do very badly, due to the heavy financial penalties of withdrawing from a scheme in mid-term. In recent years, however, the Government has introduced new rules which help considerably.

For example, employers can now pay full pension, without actuarial reduction, at any age between 50 and 70, provided an employee has completed 20 years' service with the organisation. Companies are under no obligation to do so but, for those people lucky enough to work for an organisation willing to amend its pension scheme rules accordingly, this provision could make an immense difference to the financial position of early retirees. It has to be said, however, that most employers still apply actuarial reductions (although these are sometimes waived in special cases such as redundancy) so, if you are thinking of taking early retirement it is advisable to work out very carefully how this might affect your pension.

Another very important change concerns what are known as your **preserved rights** – in other words, your financial rights with regard to your pension. Previously you were entitled to these rights only if you had been in an employer's scheme for at least five years. Today, the qualifying period is two years.

If you leave earlier, although there is no obligation, the scheme would usually return the contributions you have paid. But, as you will realise, the amount of money involved is not likely to be very large. There are three choices available to people with preserved rights who leave a company to switch jobs.

Leaving the pension with the scheme. You remain a member of the scheme and receive a pension at the scheme's normal retirement age. If the scheme is a final salary one, the value would probably be calculated on 1/60th (or 1/80th) of your earnings at the time of your leaving and the number of years you have worked for the company. Whereas previously most pensions got frozen, today company schemes are obliged to increase the accrued pension rights by 5 per cent a year or the rate of inflation, whichever is lower. Another advantage of remaining in the scheme is that you keep any benefits – such as a widow's pension and possibly others – that are already included. Also, once you start receiving your pension, you would be entitled to any extra increases that may be given.

In the case of money purchase schemes, your accumulated assets would normally remain invested in the fund, hopefully growing every year to buy you a bigger pension on retirement. You would also be entitled to any benefit that the scheme provided under the rules.

Taking your pension to a new scheme. You do not have to make an immediate decision. You can transfer your pension scheme at any time, provided you do so over a year before you retire. If you wish to switch to a new scheme, this could either be to another company scheme or to a personal pension. Personal pensions are described a couple of pages further along, so if you are interested in taking advantage of this option you should read the section carefully. Here, we explain the various possibilities if you wish to join a scheme run by your new employer.

Early leavers now have the right to move their pension – or more precisely, its transfer value – to a new employer's scheme willing to accept it. The transfer value is the cash value of your current pension rights. Calculating this, however, is fraught with difficulties and early leavers are usually at a disadvantage compared with those who remain in the scheme. For example, if the job change has meant a salary increase, the new scheme will probably be more expensive to buy into as the likelihood is that it will be earnings-related. Any added years will also be calculated in relation to your new salary, so these too will be more expensive.

Your new employer might appear to place a disconcertingly low valuation on your old company pension rights. However, even if 10 years' worth of rights from an old company pension scheme are commuted to no more than two years' worth in your new one, it could still be worth accepting, particularly if your new job is likely to produce rapid pay rises. As your pension is normally ultimately based on the size of your salary when you retire, the two years' worth of added rights could still be worth a tidy amount. When doing the sums high earners will, however, need to take account of the £78,600 cap (see page 36) which applies to anyone joining a new pension scheme.

Joining a new employer's scheme does not necessarily oblige you to transfer your previous benefits. In some circumstances, there may be very good arguments for leaving your existing benefits with your former scheme and joining your new employer's scheme from scratch for the remaining years that you are working. Since you could be at risk of giving up more than you stand to gain by transferring your benefits to a new scheme, expert advice is strongly recommended.

Taking your pension to an insurance company. If neither of the two previous options appeals, or your new company will not accept your old pension value into its own scheme, you can go independent and have the transfer value of your pension invested by a life company into a personal scheme – normally either a Section 32 buy-out or a personal pension. After deducting its charges, the life company would invest the balance of the money in the fund, or funds, of your choice.

Advice. Deciding on your best option is not easy, so before taking action you should at least consult your company pension scheme manager to give you an assessment of the likely value of your pension if you leave it in the scheme. As a result of the improved revaluation changes, explained earlier, this option could be considerably more attractive than it would have been a few years ago. A further point to bear in mind is that your present company scheme may include valuable extras, such as a spouse's pension, life cover and attractive early retirement terms in the event of ill-health.

If you are planning to switch, you will need to decide between a Section 32 buy-out or a personal pension. Although for a majority of employees a personal pension is usually likely to offer a higher return, there are certain limitations and the accepted wisdom seems to be that the older the employee and the larger the transfer value, the more attractive a Section 32 buy-out becomes. Because this is a complex area – and making the wrong decision could prove expensive – independent expert advice is very strongly recommended. Particularly if a large sum of money is involved, it could pay you to get the advice of a pension consultant. For a list of those operating in your area, write to the **Society of Pension Consultants**, Ludgate House, Ludgate Circus, London EC4A 2AB.

Useful reading

The Securities and Investments Board has published two very useful factsheets – *Pension Transfers* and *Pension Opt Outs* – for people thinking of taking a personal pension or leaving their employer's scheme for some other reason. Obtainable free from Citizens' Advice Bureaux; or with 9″ × 7″ sae from: The Publications Department, **Securities and Investments Board**, Gavrelle House, 2-14 Bunhill Row, London EC1Y 8RA.

Becoming self-employed

If, as opposed to switching jobs, you leave paid employment to start your own enterprise, you are allowed to transfer your accumulated pension rights into a new fund. You may have a choice of three options.

The more obvious solution is to invest your money with an insurance company, as mentioned above, or take a personal pension.

Alternatively, if you expect to be in a high earning bracket, you might consider setting up a limited company, even if you are the only salaried employee, rather than launching the same business as a self-employed individual. The company could set up a self-administered pension scheme with attractive loan-back facilities plus other advantages.

However, there are various pros and cons that will need to be weighed up carefully depending on your age, the transfer value of your earlier pension and the anticipated annual amount available for investing in your new scheme. This is rather a complex area, so before taking any action you are strongly advised to consult an accountant.

A third possibility which might be more attractive if you are fairly close to normal retirement age is to leave your pension in your former employer's scheme. See page 40 'Leaving the pension with the scheme'.

Questions on your pension scheme

Most people find it very difficult to understand how their pension scheme works.

However, your pension may be worth a lot of money and, especially as you approach retirement, it is important that you should know the main essentials, including any options that may still be available to you.

If you have a query (however daft it may seem) or if you are concerned in some way about your pension, you should approach whoever is responsible for the scheme in your organisation. If the company is large, there may be a special person to look after the scheme on a day-to-day basis: often this is someone in the personnel department. In a smaller company, the pension scheme may be looked after by the company secretary or managing director.

The sort of questions you might ask will vary according to circumstance, such as: before you join the scheme, if you are thinking of changing jobs, if you are hoping to retire early and so on. You will probably think of plenty of additional points of your own. The questions listed are simply an indication of some of the key information you may require in order to plan sensibly ahead.

Before you join the scheme

- As a basic point, you should enquire whether the scheme is contracted in or out of SERPS and whether the intention is that it should remain so in the future.
- If it is contracted out, what are the criteria for eligibility to become a member of the scheme? For example, there may be different conditions for different grades of staff. There may be an age ceiling for new entrants. Sometimes too, although this is becoming less common, there is a minimum period of service required before you can join. (N.B. Exclusion of part-timers **on grounds of sex** has become unlawful under the sex discrimination legislation.)
- Over the past few years, many companies have set up contracted-out money purchase schemes – or COMPS, as they are known for short – which operate on a different principle from final salary schemes. You should enquire what type of scheme it is that you would be joining and if it is a money purchase one, how in particular members' entitlements are calculated. (See 'Money purchase scheme' page 34.)
- If it is a final salary scheme, what is the exact definition of 'final salary'? This could be very important if the organisation offers phased retirement or the opportunity of a sponsorship in the voluntary sector and, as some employers do, adjusts your remuneration to take account of a shorter working week or less onerous responsibilities.
- Another point, if it is a final salary scheme, is whether guaranteed pension increases are given and, if so, whether these are 5 per cent increases (or higher or lower)? One of the requirements of the 1995 Pensions Act is that, as from 1997, schemes will be obliged to give annual increases of at least 5 per cent or the rate of inflation, whichever is lower.
- Are discretionary increases given (additionally/instead) and, if so, what have these been over the past five years?
- Is anything deducted from the scheme to allow for the State pension?

- At what age is the pension normally paid?
- What is payable if you die within the next year?
- Is there a widow/widower's pension and does it get contractual increases?

If you want to leave the organisation to change jobs

- Can you have a refund of contributions if you were to leave within two years?
- How much will your deferred pension be worth?
- Should you wish to move the transfer value to another scheme, how long would you have to wait from the date of your request? (This should normally be within 12 months.)

If you leave for other reasons

- What happens if you become ill – or die – before pension age?
- What are the arrangements if you want to retire early? Most schemes allow you to do this if you are within about 10 years of normal retirement age but your pension may be reduced accordingly. Many schemes, in fact, operate a sliding scale of benefits with more generous terms offered to those who retire later rather than earlier. The new flexi-age retirement provision is unlikely to help you if you move to a new job, since it applies only to employees of 20 years' standing.
- What are the rules/options regarding pension age for women if, as may well be the case, this has recently been raised to bring it in line with male pension age?

If you stay until normal retirement age

- What will your pension be on your present salary? And what would it be assuming your salary increases by, say, 5 or 10 per cent before you eventually retire?
- What spouse's pension will be paid? Can a pension be paid to other dependants?
- What happens if you continue working with the organisation after retirement age? Normally, any contributions you are making to the scheme will cease to be required and your pension (which will not be paid until you retire) will be increased to compensate for its deferment. Whereas previously, however, by deferring their pension individuals could boost the amount above their two-thirds earnings, under a 1989 Budget change this is no longer allowed. However, existing members of a scheme prior to the change taking effect (i.e. 1 June 1989) are not affected and are still entitled to defer their pension under the old rules, provided their employer is agreeable.
- What are the arrangements if you retire from the organisation as a salaried employee but become a retained consultant or contractor?

What to do before retirement

In addition to understanding your current pension scheme, you may also need to chase up any previous schemes of which you were a member. This is well worth pursuing as you could be owed money from one or more schemes, which will all add to your pension on retirement day.

You may be able to get the information from your previous employer/s. Or, if your previous employer has gone out of business, **OPAS** – see below – may be able to tell you who took over the responsibility for payment of pensions. A free leaflet on the subject is available on application.

Additionally, the Occupational Pensions Board manages a pensions registry and tracing service to assist individuals who need help in tracing their pension rights. All occupational and personal pension schemes including free-standing AVC (FSAVC) schemes are required to register. Applicants can either write to the Registrar giving as much essential detail about the scheme as possible; or alternatively can request a trace application form (PR4) to complete. This is a free service. The address to write to is: **Pension Schemes Registry**, Occupational Pensions Board, PO Box 1NN, Newcastle upon Tyne NE99 1NN.

Other help and advice

If you have any queries or problems to do with your pension, in addition to the registry there are three main sources of help available to you. These are: the trustees or managers of your pension scheme; OPAS; the Pensions Ombudsman.

Trustees or managers. These are the first people to contact if you do not properly understand your benefit entitlements or if you are unhappy about some point to do with your pension. The pensions manager (or other person responsible for pensions) should give you their names and tell you how they can be reached.

OPAS. This is an independent voluntary organisation with a network of 500 advisers throughout the UK. OPAS can give help and advice, other than financial advice of any kind, on all matters to do with any type of pension scheme – except State schemes. The service is available to anyone who thinks they have pension rights including scheme members, existing pensioners, those with deferred pensions and dependants. The usual way of contacting OPAS is via your local CAB. Equally, if you prefer, you can write direct to: **OPAS Ltd.**, 11 Belgrave Road, London SW1V 1RB. T:0171 233 8080.

Pensions Ombudsman. As part of a package of important consumer protection measures, there is now a Pensions Ombudsman. You would normally only approach the Ombudsman if neither the pension scheme trustees nor OPAS are able to solve your problem.

The Ombudsman can investigate: (1) complaints of injustice caused by maladministration by the trustees or managers of an occupational pension scheme (2) disputes of fact or law with the trustees or managers.

He cannot, however, investigate a complaint that is already subject to court proceedings, one that is about a State social security benefit or a dispute that is more appropriate for investigation by another regulatory body. There is also a time limit for lodging complaints which is normally within three years of the act, or failure to act, about which you are complaining.

Provided the problem comes within the Ombudsman's orbit, he will look into all the facts for you and will inform you of his decision, together with his reasons.

There is no charge for the Ombudsman's service. The address to write to is: **The Pensions Ombudsman**, 11 Belgrave Road, London SW1V 1RB. T:0171 834 9144. This is the same address (but different telephone number) as OPAS.

If you have a **personal pension**, contact: **The PIA Ombudsman**, Centre Point, 103 New Oxford Street, London WC1A 1QH; T:0171 240 3838. It is possible he may refer you to the Pensions Ombudsman above but if this is the case, you will be informed very quickly.

New protection for pension scheme members

A number of recent measures have been taken to improve protection for pension scheme members.

As already noted, since the start of 1991 early leavers now get their entire frozen pension uprated and not just, as had been the case, benefits earned after 1985.

In the wake of the Maxwell disaster, the government has published regulations restricting self-investment by occupational pension funds to 5 per cent (a transitional period is allowed in some cases to give schemes time to reduce any existing self-investment). A further welcome change is that in the event of a scheme in deficit being wound up, the deficiency becomes a debt on the employer which the trustees can pursue.

New measures have also been introduced to protect pension scheme members in the event of a company take-over or proposed bulk transfer arrangement.

On a more technical note, pension schemes which are in surplus over the Inland Revenue limit (5 per cent) are no longer allowed to have the money returned to the company unless pension scheme members are first guaranteed certain benefits, namely: pension increases of either 5 per cent a year or the rate of inflation – whichever is lower. The jargon term for these increases is LPI, short for Limited Price Indexation.

In addition to these measures, the 1995 Pensions Act requires all company schemes – as from April 1997 – to index the whole of pensions in payment in line with prices up to 5 per cent a year.

Other reforms in the 1995 Pensions Act, which also come into effect during 1997, include: a minimum solvency requirement to help ensure sufficient funds to pay pensions should a scheme wind up; the appointment of an Occupational Pension Regulator with powers to investigate the way in which schemes are run and to impose sanctions on those who break the law; a right for members to appoint up to a third of the trustees; and the establishment of a compensation scheme, available as a last resort, to help cover losses in the event of fraud.

Personal pension schemes

The self-employed have long been able to make their own pension arrangements. Since July 1988, this option is now available to all. Everyone – whether self-employed or working for an employer – has the choice of continuing as they are or of switching instead to a personal pension.

Although, in general, individuals who have reached their fiftieth birthday are less likely to be tempted than younger people to leave a company scheme for a personal pension or to alter their current self-employed arrangements, if you are thinking of starting your own business, if you are moving to a new job or if you are ineligible to join your company pension scheme, one of the options described below may offer you an attractive solution.

Choices for the self-employed

Personal pensions are largely modelled on the old-style self-employed pensions – with one or two important differences, including in particular the age at which you can retire. As from July 1988, however, the rules for self-employed pensions were also altered to bring them in line with personal pensions. This will not affect anyone who was already contributing to a pension plan prior to July 1988 unless, that is, they actually wish to change.

Differences between Section 226 policies and personal pensions. If you have an existing Section 226 policy (or retirement annuity contract, as it is sometimes also called), then, as you will know, it is an insurance policy designed to invest money for your retirement. It will probably have been sold to you by an insurance broker or insurance company salesman and, at the time of buying, you will have had a choice of four different types of investment policy: with profits, unit linked, deposit administration and non-profit policy.

Under Inland Revenue rules, you are allowed to invest up to 17.5 per cent of your relevant earnings tax free in the policy (with higher limits, rising to 27.5 per cent, if you are over 60). In accordance with the terms of the contract, you can choose to retire at any time after the age of 60, when the policy will buy you a regular pension plus the option of taking part of the money as a tax-free lump sum.

However, as stated a few paragraphs higher, the rules for self-employed pension plans have been altered to bring them in line with other personal pensions. Section 226 policies have been abolished and are no longer available for purchase. In consequence, individuals who wish or need to make their own arrangements will have to buy a new style personal pension (PP).

In practical terms, this change is unlikely to affect many people. For a start, anyone with an existing Section 226 policy has no need, unless they wish to alter their arrangements, to do anything at all. They can continue contributing to the policy on exactly the same terms and conditions as before.

As general wisdom, the view in the pensions industry is that for most people with an existing Section 226 policy there would be little point in changing – and for high earners, in particular, it could be positively detrimental. However, as with most decisions there are advantages and disadvantages on either side and it is important that you should at least know what the choices are.

There are four main differences between Section 226 policies and personal pensions. These concern: the age of retirement, the method of calculating the lump sum, allowable contributions into the plan and the possible size of your pension allowed for tax relief.

- **Age of retirement**. Under a Section 226 policy, retirement cannot be taken before the age of 60. With a new personal pension, you can retire at any time between 50 and 75.
- **Method of calculating the lump sum**. Under Section 226 contracts, this is expressed as three times the residual annuity paid. The PP rules define the amount as 25 per cent (or a quarter) of the total fund excluding your protected rights.
- **Allowable contributions**. A Section 226 policy limits you to a maximum of 27.5 per cent of your earnings. For personal pensions, individuals over the age of 50 can contribute up to 30 per cent, rising (depending on their age) to a maximum of 40 per cent.
- **Size of pension**. For high earners, the £78,600 cap is probably the strongest argument for hanging on to an existing Section 226 policy, since such policies are not affected by the earnings limit. A new personal pension on the other hand would stand to be affected.

For those who might be interested in switching, perhaps because a major aim is to retire before age 60, you should know that whereas at one time insurance companies were virtually the only outlet for buying individual pension plans, today these are also available from banks, building societies, unit trusts, friendly societies and independent financial advisers (IFAs).

For further information, see leaflet PP3 *Personal Pensions for the Self-employed* obtainable by phoning the Pensions Line on 0345 313233 or by writing to Freepost, DSS Pensions, BS 5555/1, Bristol BS99 1BL.

Personal pensions for employees

A main aim behind personal pensions is to give people working for an employer the same freedom as the self-employed to make their own independent pension arrangements, should they wish to do so.

Before making any decision, a basic point to understand is that nearly everyone who pays NI contributions as an employee is already contributing towards an additional pension: either to the State scheme, known as SERPS; or to a contracted-out company pension scheme.

You have the right to take a personal pension (PP) in place of SERPS; or alternatively in place of your employer's scheme (whether this is contracted-in or out).

To judge whether a personal pension is a good idea, you need to understand the advantages and possible limitations of your present arrangements compared with the attractions – but also risks – of a PP.

If you are a member of a good contracted-out final salary scheme – or have the opportunity of joining one – it is very unlikely that a PP would be in your best interest. If, however, your employer does not have a pension scheme, if you are ineligible to join, if the scheme is contracted-into SERPS or if you think you could do better for yourself than your current scheme, then a PP could be worth considering.

A main advantage of a personal pension is that if you change jobs you can take it with you without penalty. There are attractive tax relief benefits. You will have real choice as to how your pension payments are invested. If you have built up a big enough fund, you can retire at any age between 50 and 75. Also, if you change your mind after having taken a personal pension, you can switch back into SERPS; or, if the scheme rules allow it, you can transfer your payments into a company contracted-out scheme.

The big potential drawback of a personal pension, particularly for an older person, is that it may not offer you such attractive benefits as your present scheme. For a start, most employers do not make extra contributions to a personal pension so, other than your rebate from SERPS (see 'Minimum DSS contributions' below), all the investment towards your pension will need to come out of your earnings. You may also lose out on valuable extra benefits that are often included in an employer's scheme, e.g.: a pension before normal age were you to become ill; protection for your dependants should you die; attractive early retirement terms if you were made redundant; any increases in pension payments that the scheme may give to help offset inflation.

A further problem could be the sheer plethora of choice when selecting a pension plan. Not only is there a variety of different types of investment (see next section) but you can obtain a personal pension from any of the following: insurance companies, banks, building societies, unit trusts, friendly societies and independent financial advisers (IFAs).

Knowing what to choose, assessing one policy against another, weighing up the risk factor as well as trying to estimate what this will mean in terms of your standard of living after you retire could be a bit of a gamble even for a financial expert.

Although as a breed pension providers act very conservatively, and moreover, your money would be protected under the strict rules brought in by the Financial Services Act, no one can forecast with total confidence how well or otherwise any particular investment will do. So while it is possible that you could do better with a personal pension, unlike a final salary scheme or SERPS where you have the certainty of a guaranteed figure, you would not know the value of your pension until you come to retire. The amount would depend on: how much money you had paid in, how well it had been invested and how good an annuity you were able to buy (see 'Compulsory purchase annuities', page 37).

Before taking a decision, a first essential is to understand how personal pensions work.

Starting date. You can decide to start a personal pension at any time you want and then, in order to receive all the DSS minimum contributions that will be paid into your pension plan, backdate it to the start of the tax year on 6 April. The formalities involved are very easy.

Contributions into your pension plan. There are three possible ways (previously four, see 'Special Incentive Payments') of building up savings in your pension plan.

- **Minimum DSS contributions**. These will be paid into your new scheme automatically. They are worked out according to the level of national insurance contributions that both you and your employer are required to pay by law. Instead of going into either SERPS or a contracted-out company pension scheme, they will be paid directly into your personal pension plan. The current (1995/96) contribution rebate is 4.8 per cent. However, people over 30 receive an extra 1 per cent, so upping the amount to 5.8 per cent.
- **Extra contributions made by you**. You can make extra contributions into your pension plan. If you do so, you will not only build up more savings for your retirement but you also enjoy full tax relief on these contributions.

  A further advantage is that you will have more flexibility as to when you can retire. If only the minimum DSS contributions are paid, you will have to wait until the normal State retirement age. If you make extra contributions, you can use them to retire whenever you like between 50 and 75.

There are **Inland Revenue rules** as to the amount you can invest, which varies according to your age. Additionally, for the purposes of tax relief, the £78,600 cap (1995/96) applies to all new personal pensions taken out since the 1989 Budget. However, see 'Relating back' below.

- If you are aged 35 or under, you can pay up to 17.5 per cent of your earnings into a personal pension.
- If you are between the ages of 36 and 45, the maximum is 20 per cent.
- If you are between the ages of 46 and 50, the amount is 25 per cent.
- If you are between the ages of 51 and 55, you can pay 30 per cent.
- If you are between the ages of 56 and 60, the maximum is 35 per cent.
- If you are over 60, you are allowed to invest up to 40 per cent of your earnings.

Ages are calculated at the beginning of the tax year.

Relating back. You are allowed to 'relate back' personal pension premiums. This means that a premium paid during a tax year is treated as if it had been paid during the previous tax year; or the tax year before that, if there were no relevant earnings in the previous year. So if a premium is paid before 6 April 1996, it may be treated as having been paid during 1993/94. It is also possible to carry forward unused relief. Your financial adviser will be able to explain how you apply.

- **Voluntary contributions by your employer**. Your employer might decide that he wishes to help you improve your pension by making contributions over and above the statutory national insurance contributions into your pension plan. If you are considering leaving a company pension scheme, this could be one of the questions you should ask as a means of comparing the value of a personal pension against your existing scheme. The Inland Revenue limits described above include any contributions made by your employer, so the total must therefore not exceed the allowed amount.
- **Special Incentive Payments**. An extra 2 per cent payment was given by the government as part of the launch of personal pensions. These payments have now ceased. Anyone who previously received them can look forward to enjoying the benefit when they retire.

Your pension receipts. As with all money purchase schemes, the amount of pension you eventually receive will depend on two main factors: the size of the fund you have been able to build up and the fund's investment performance. As general wisdom, the longer you have been saving towards a personal pension and the bigger the total contributions paid, the larger your pension will stand to be. You have a great deal of choice in the matter but there are also certain rules designed to protect you.

A basic rule concerns what are known as your **protected rights**. These are the DSS minimum contributions (including the value of the extra 2 per cent introductory payment) and tax relief you may have received – together with their accumulated investment growth.

Your protected rights can only be invested in a single contract, in contrast to your/ your employer's extra or voluntary contributions which can be invested in as many different personal plans as you please.

A further point is that your protected rights must be used to purchase the annuity which will pay for your annual pension when you retire; they cannot be used as a contribution towards your lump sum. A point of special interest to women is that annuities by law have now become unisex and so must provide the same rates for men and women alike.

Your lump sum derives from the extra contributions that you and perhaps also your employer have made including (as from the 1989 Budget) the value of dependants' benefits. You can take up to 25 per cent (or a quarter) of this part of the fund. The remainder will be added to your protected rights to purchase a better annuity. (See 'Compulsory purchase annuities', page 37.)

Choosing a pension plan. Personal pensions are offered by insurance companies, banks, building societies, unit trusts, friendly societies and IFAs. Before you make up your mind, you should aim to look at a variety of plans. Furthermore, you should not hesitate to ask as many questions as you want about any points that are unclear or any technical term that you do not fully understand – including in particular any questions you may have about the level of charges.

Understanding the figures has become very much easier than it used to be before 1995. Today, not only are all life and pension policy providers required to state their charges in writing but they must also disclose any salesman's commission – stated in cash terms – in advance of any contract being signed.

These together with other essential 'consumer' information about the policy should be included in what is called the 'key features' document. Advisers must now also state in writing any reasons for any recommendations to you.

Because choosing both the right type of investment and the particular institution with which you are likely to feel happiest is such an important decision, even after you have chosen a scheme you will have a **14-day cooling off period** that gives you a chance to change your mind.

Is a personal pension a wise decision? This is a question that only you, or an adviser who knows your personal circumstances, can answer. As a general rule, if you are in a good company pension scheme the advice is to stay there. However, this does not apply to everyone and those for whom a personal pension might be an advantage are likely to be in the category: under 45 (under 40 for women), high flyer, mobile worker in the sense of being likely to switch jobs and well-off older people who are not covered by company arrangements. Those for whom opting out is likely to be least advised are older people in a good company or public sector pension scheme.

The key issue is how your existing pension arrangements compare with the alternatives. You will therefore need to know what the value of your pension would be if you stay in SERPS or your company scheme, whichever is applicable.

For information about the value of your SERPS rights, complete BR 19 *Pension Forecast Application Form* obtainable from your local Social Security Office.

In the case of an employer's scheme, ask the pensions department or the person responsible for pensions (this could be the personnel manager or company secretary) to provide you with full information about your pension and future benefits, including details of death and disability cover.

Other points you will need to consider include: what type of investment policy would suit you; what size contributions (within Inland Revenue allowed limits) you could realistically afford; and what, after deduction of administrative and other charges, your plan might be worth when you come to retire. This is not to say that taking a personal pension is either a right or a wrong decision. Simply that you need to be aware of all the various factors before opting out of your present arrangements. Since the sums are often very complex, if you are thinking of making a change you would be strongly advised to consult an independent pensions specialist.

Useful reading

Leaflets PP1 *Thinking about a Personal Pension?* and PP2 *Making the Most of Your Personal Pension*, obtainable from your local Social Security office or Citizens' Advice Bureau.

Two excellent factsheets, published by SIB: *Pension Opt Outs* and *Pension Transfers*. Obtainable free from Citizens' Advice Bureaux; or by writing (with 9″ × 7″ sae) to:

The Publications Department, **Securities and Investments Board**, Gavrelle House, 2-14 Bunhill Row, London EC1Y 8RA.

Inland Revenue leaflet IR 78 *Personal Pensions*, obtainable from any tax office.

The Pension Transfer and Opt Out review: What it Will Mean for You. This is another SIB factsheet for people who believe they may have been mis-sold a personal pension. Obtainable free from CABs or, with a 9" x 7" sae, from: Pensions Leaflet, PO Box 701, Basildon, Essex SS14 3FD.

Opting back into SERPS. In recent months, many people have been told by their financial advisers that they might be better off rejoining SERPS. This may well be excellent advice. However, if rather than something you should do immediately, you were advised to consider the matter later on, it may be worth remembering that in 1997 the government is planning to change the present rebate system to one that is age-related – with higher rebates for older people.

Types of investment policy

There are four different types of investment policy: with-profits, unit-linked, deposit administration and non-profit policies. Brief descriptions of each follow.

With-profits policies. These are one of the safest types of pension investments. They guarantee you a known minimum cash fund and/or pension on your retirement and, while the guaranteed amount is not usually very high, bonuses are added at regular intervals, according to how the investments in the fund perform. Additionally, a terminal (or final) bonus is given when the pension policy matures. Over the past couple of years most terminal bonuses have been lower than those paid in the late eighties, reflecting a reduction in interest rates and a disappointing performance by equities. However, an important feature is that once bonuses are given, they cannot later be withdrawn or put at risk due to some speculative investment.

Unit-linked policies. These are less safe than with-profits policies but they offer the attraction of potentially higher investment returns. Unit-linked policies by and large have performed fairly well over the last few years and have consequently been growing in popularity. However, there is always the risk that they might not continue to perform as well in the future and, if there were a down-turn, the size of your pension could obviously be affected. For this reason, many advisers recommend that their clients swop their unit-linked policies to the with-profits type about five years before they retire, provided market conditions are favourable at the time.

The decision as to what is best will very much depend on timing. Clearly, if the stock market is depressed, then cashing in equity based contracts before you need could lose you money, unless of course your adviser takes the view that the stock market is likely to plunge even further. Another factor that will need to be taken into account is the prevailing level of interest rates, since these affect annuity rates.

Deposit administration policies. These lie somewhere between with-profits and unit-linked policies in terms of their risk/reward ratio. They operate rather like bank deposit accounts, where the interest rate is credited at regular intervals.

Non-profit policies. These have lost favour in recent years. Although they provide a guaranteed pension payment, the return on investment is usually very low. As a rule, they tend only to be recommended for people starting a plan within five years of their retirement.

Choosing the right policy. This is one area where it really pays to shop around. Great care is needed when choosing the organisation to invest your pension savings. Once you have committed yourself to a policy, you will not usually be able to move your money without considerable financial penalty.

As a general rule, it is sensible to select a large, well-known company that has been in the market for a long time. Before deciding, you should compare several companies' investment track records. What you should look for is evidence of good, consistent results over a period of 10 to 20 years.

An important point to be aware of is that insurance and other financial companies may give illustrative projections of their investment performance. Projections, however, even when based on a company's own figures – including their charges – (as since 1995 they now have to be) are not the same as guarantees and if, in the event, the results are disappointing you are most unlikely to have any claim.

Information about the administrative and other charges you will have to pay is one of the essential questions you should ask when discussing a personal pension. Until recently, many people did not realise how much they were paying in commission, since this was usually obscured. Today, however, anyone selling personal pensions is required to disclose their commission in advance, stated in cash terms. Normally, the best arrangement to keep the cost down is to pay a series of single premiums at one go or as a 'single recurring premium' contract.

You should aim at very least to talk to two or three financial institutions or independent financial advisers (IFAs) and make it clear to all of them that you are doing so. If you need further advice – and particularly if a large sum of money is involved – there could be a strong argument for consulting an independent pension consultant or IFA who charges fees rather than earns commission. For further information see Chapter 6, Financial Advisers. You might also like to read the section on investor protection at the end of Chapter 5.

Another possibility, not previously mentioned, is to set up your own Self-Invested Personal Pension (SIPP). As the name implies, these are do-it-yourself schemes which among other assets can include directly held shares. Such schemes are only suitable for fairly sophisticated investors who can afford to pay £5,000 or more a year into their plan.

Complaints. If you have a complaint about advice you have received in relation to your personal pension, contact the PIA Ombudsman. For further information, see Chapter 6, 'Financial Advisers', page 122.

If you think you (or a deceased spouse) have been wrongly sold a personal pension, call the special PIA helpline on 0171 417 7001.

A lump sum?

Members of company pension schemes and people with individual pension policies are allowed to take a lump sum of money tax free when they retire. The greatest amount normally permitted is one-and-a-half times your average final salary up to a ceiling of £117,900 (or higher if your pension plan pre-dates the 1989 Budget).

Taking a lump sum reduces the pension you receive but, on the other hand if you invest the money wisely, you could end up with a higher income. Alternatively of course, as many people do, you could use the capital for a worthwhile project such as improving your home; or, if you were planning to give something to your grand-children, this could be an opportune time to settle it on them. Lifetime gifts (in contrast to money left in a will) will normally escape the taxman. The first priority, however, is to ensure that you will have enough income for your own needs.

If you take a lump sum, the amount by which your pension will be reduced is mainly determined by your age. The younger you are, the smaller the reduction. Another consideration is your tax status. Since the lump sum is tax free, as a general rule the higher your top rate of tax after retirement, the greater the advantage in opting for a lump sum. Your life expectancy can also be an important factor. The shorter this is, the more sense it makes to take the lump sum, rather than deny yourself for a longer-term pension that you will not be around to enjoy. If you come from a long line of octogenarians, then clearly you will need to work out the sums on the basis of the next 20 years or longer.

Contrary to what some people believe, it is not an 'all or nothing' decision. You have considerable flexibility and can choose between: not taking a lump sum, taking the maximum amount allowed or taking a portion of it only (whatever sum you decide).

Often the deciding factor when choosing whether to take a lump sum is the problem of investing it. If you have never had to think of it before, the prospect of what to do with several thousand pounds can seem a very daunting challenge. It could be prudent to 'invest' some of it getting good financial advice.

Before consulting an expert, it would be helpful to both of you if you could work out – at least in very general terms – what your financial priorities are. The sort of questions your adviser will ask are: whether you are investing for income now or capital growth in the future; whether you need to go for absolute security with every penny you have or whether you can afford slightly more risky investments in the hope of making more money in the long run; what other sources of income you have, or might expect to receive.

As is normal conservative practice, you will probably find that you will be recommended to spread your lump sum across a mixture of investments. Depending on your circumstances, these might be long- or short-term investments; income or capital producing; or quite likely, a combination of all of them.

An outline of the different types of investment is given in Chapter 5.

Pension rights if you continue to work after retirement age

When you reach normal retirement age, you will usually stop making contributions into your company pension scheme, even if you decide to carry on working. Your employer, of course, would have to agree to your continuing to work, which he is under no compulsion to do. Indeed, some organisations have fixed rules about retirement age and do not allow any exceptions.

If, however, you are allowed to remain, you probably have three options:

- You can continue working, draw your company pension and put some of your earnings into a separate scheme. Once you are over 60, the Inland Revenue allows you to invest up to 40 per cent of your earnings tax free into a pension plan.

Provided you joined your current scheme before 13 March 1989 (or an existing scheme where you were employed before 1 June 1989) you also have the following choices:

- You can leave your pension in the fund where it will continue to earn interest until you retire. In most private schemes, you can expect to receive an extra 9 per cent for every year that you delay retirement. If you continue working, say for an additional five years, your pension will then be 45 per cent higher than if you had started taking it at the normal age. You will also have been earning a salary meanwhile, so you are likely to be considerably better off as a result.
- You can leave your pension in the fund, as described above, and additionally contribute to a personal pension, provided your contributions do not exceed the allowed Inland Revenue limit.

Equal pension age

As a result of recent changes in the law, employers are required to treat men and women equally with regard to retirement and pension issues.

Already for a number of years, employers have not been able to oblige women to retire at an earlier age than their male colleagues but by law must have a common retirement age that applies equally to both sexes.

Now, as a further requirement, employers must also have a common pension age and pension schemes must (with effect from 1990) offer the same benefits to their male and female members.

Most companies have responded by raising the pension age for women, thus – in theory at least – requiring women to work extra years before becoming entitled to their full pension. In practice, however, the majority of employers that have equalised upwards (i.e. instead of reducing the retirement age for men) are at this stage allowing women the option to take their pension early without reductions, instead of obliging those already close to retirement to prolong their working life.

In time the State pension age will also be equalised and, as widely expected, the chosen age is 65. The change will be phased in over 10 years, starting in 2010. Because this is such a long way off, it will only affect younger women. Any woman born before 6 April 1950 will have no need to alter her retirement plans.

Divorce

A long-standing grievance of many divorcees (ex-wives especially) is that the courts do not normally take pension benefits into account when deciding the financial arrangements between the couple. The 1995 Pensions Act goes some way towards remedying this injustice by allowing ex-wives a share in their former husband's occupational or personal pension. However, they will have to wait until their ex-husband is actually in receipt of his pension. N.B. Although the legislation is most likely to be of benefit to women, the rules apply in reverse and allow ex-husbands the right to a share in their former wife's pension.

If sadly you are in the throes of a divorce, this could be a subject to raise with your solicitor.

Part-timers

Many part-timers who were previously excluded from occupational pension schemes can now join as of right and in some cases may even be entitled to back-dated scheme membership for up to two years. In May 1995, the sex discrimination legislation was extended to include access to pension schemes. The new rules are mainly expected to benefit women.

Pensions for women

Women who have worked all their adult lives and paid full Class 1 contributions should get a full basic pension in their own right at the age of 60. The current amount is £58.85 a week. This is up-rated each year in April.

Women who have only worked for part of their adult lives may not have enough contributions to get a full basic pension on their own record. Instead, they may receive a reduced pension or one based on their husband's contributions; or one topping up the other. A wife entitled to a reduced pension on her own contributions can claim it at 60, regardless of whether or not her husband is receiving his pension.

Married women who have never worked are also entitled to a pension on their husband's contributions. In money terms, the value is about 60 per cent of the level of basic pension to which their husband is entitled. There are several important conditions, however.

Firstly, women can only receive a pension based on their husband's contributions if he himself is in receipt of a basic pension. He will have to have reached 65 and must have retired. Additionally, the wife herself must be over 60 to qualify.

If she is still under 60 when her husband claims his State pension and does not work or her earnings do not exceed £46.45, he should be able to obtain a supplement of around £35.25 to his pension, on the grounds of having a wife to support. If the couple are living apart, the earnings limit for the wife is £35.25. Your local Social Security office will be able to advise.

In contrast, if a wife has had her sixtieth birthday but her husband has not yet reached 65 (or has decided to defer his retirement), she must wait until her husband retires to receive her share of the married couple's pension.

An important point to note is that since the introduction of independent taxation, a married woman is entitled to have her section of the joint pension offset against her own personal allowance instead of it being counted as part of her husband's taxable income. For many pensioner couples, this should have the happy result of reducing their tax liability.

If a wife who formerly worked is over 60 and retired but cannot yet get a basic pension on either her own or her husband's contributions, she may be able to qualify for an additional or graduated pension based on her own contributions. These are described a little further on.

But first a word about three other important matters: reduced rate contributions, abolition of the half test and Home Responsibilities Protection.

Reduced rate contribution
Many women retiring today have paid a reduced rate of NI contribution, also known as 'the small stamp'. This option was given to working wives in 1948 and withdrawn in 1978 but women who had already chosen to pay the reduced rate were allowed to continue, provided they did not take more than a two-year break from employment after 1978. If you have never paid anything but reduced rate contributions, you are not entitled to a basic pension in your own right but instead must rely on your husband's contributions for the married couple's pension.

Abolition of the half test
Until a few years ago, married women had to have paid full NI contributions for half the time they were married and working to get anything at all in their own right. This rule, known as the 'half test', has now been abolished. If you were born before April 6 1919 and were a married woman when you reached age 60, having paid full NI contributions while working, you should contact your local Social Security office.

Home Responsibilities Protection (HRP)
Men and women, whether single or married, who have been unable to work regularly because they have had to stay at home to care for children and/or a disabled or elderly person may be able to safeguard their pension by claiming Home Responsibilities Protection. This is a very important benefit, especially for the many single women in their fifties who are sacrificing their career to look after an elderly parent. This measure was introduced in 1978 and protection applies only therefore from this date. The person you are caring for must come into one of the following categories:

- A child under 16 for whom you are getting child benefit

- Someone whom you are looking after regularly for at least 35 hours a week, who is in receipt of attendance allowance, constant attendance allowance or disability living allowance
- Someone – for example, an elderly person – for whom you have been caring at home and in consequence have been getting income support (or supplementary benefit in the past)
- A combination of the above situations

A married woman or widow cannot get HRP for any tax year in which she was only liable to pay reduced rate national insurance contributions. HRP can only be given for complete tax years (6 April to 5 April), so if you simply gave up work for a few weeks in order to help out, you would be unlikely to qualify. Additionally, HRP cannot be used to reduce your total working life to below 20 years. To obtain a claim form, you should ask your local Social Security office for form CF 411.

Since 1978, anyone in receipt of child benefit, supplementary benefit or income support who is caring for someone in one of the eligible categories listed above is automatically credited with HRP. All other claimants should obtain form CF 411 from their local Social Security office.

Graduated pension
This scheme operated between April 1961 and April 1975. Anyone earning over £9 a week and over age 18 at the time would probably have paid graduated contributions and be due a pension. You can only get a graduated pension based on your own personal contributions. However, the pension from the graduated scheme is likely to be small. Further, women were penalised because their pension was calculated at a less favourable rate than for men on account of their longer life expectancy.

Additional pension
The scheme, which is commonly known as SERPS (or State Earnings-Related Pension Scheme) started in 1978. Contributions are earnings related, paid by both employer and employees, as are the pension payments. Women in contracted-out pension schemes are entitled either to a minimum pension, which is broadly equal to its SERPS equivalent; or to what are known as protected rights (i.e. their and their employer's compulsory contributions together with their accumulated investment growth).

Divorced wives
If you have a full basic pension in your own right, this will not be affected by divorce. However if, as applies to many women, despite having worked for a good number of years you have made insufficient contributions to qualify for a full pension, you should contact your local Social Security office, quoting your pension number and national insurance number. It is possible that you may be able to obtain the full single person's pension, based on your ex-husband's contributions.

Your right to use your ex-husband's contributions to improve or provide you with a pension depends on your age and/or whether you remarry before the age of 60. As a general rule, you can use your ex-husband's contributions towards your pension for the years you were married (i.e. until the date of the decree absolute). After that, you are expected to pay your own contributions until you are 60 unless you remarry.

If you are over 60 when you divorce, then whether you remarry or not, you can rely on your ex-husband's contributions. If you remarry before the age of 60, then you cease absolutely being dependent on your former husband and instead, your pension will be based on your new husband's contribution record.

N.B. The same rules apply in reverse. Although it happens less frequently, a divorced man can rely on his former wife's contribution record during the years they were married to improve his basic pension.

Graduated or additional pensions are of no help to a divorced partner of either sex, as these are earnings related and, therefore, only benefit the individual who has earned and paid for them.

For further information, ask your local Social Security office for leaflet CA 10, *National Insurance for Divorced Women*. You should also read leaflet NP 46 *A Guide to Retirement Pensions*.

For changes affecting occupational pension benefits on divorce, see section, headed 'Divorce' on page 57.

Separated wives

Even if you have not lived together for several years, from a national insurance point of view you are still considered to be married. The normal pension rules apply including, of course, the fact that, if you have to depend on your husband's contributions, you will not be able to get a pension until he is both 65 and in receipt of his own pension.

If you are not entitled to a State pension in your own right, you will receive the dependant's rate of benefit, i.e. about 60 per cent of the full rate (or less if your husband is not entitled to a full pension). In such a case, you can apply for income support to top up your income.

Once you are 60, you can personally draw the wife's pension of £35.25 a week, without reference to your husband.

If you are under 60 but your husband has reached 65 and is retired, he may be able to claim a dependency addition of £35.25 for you, provided he pays it to you or is maintaining you to an equivalent amount. He will not be able to claim dependency addition if you are earning more than £35.25 a week.

If your husband dies, you will be entitled to widow's benefit in the same way as any other widow. If there is a possibility that he may have died but that you have not been informed, you can check by writing to or visiting St Catherine's House, where the indexes of registered deaths are filed. The address is: St Catherine's House, 10 Kingsway, London WC2B 6JP. T:0171 242 0262.

Widows

There are three important benefits to which widows may be entitled: widows' payment, widows' pension and widowed mother's allowance. To claim these, fill in Form BW1, obtainable from any Social Security office. You will also be given a questionnaire (BD 8) by the Registrar. It is important that you complete this, as it acts as a trigger to help speed up payment of your benefits. For more information, see leaflet NP 45 *A Guide to Widows' Benefits.*

Widows' payment. This has replaced what used to be known as the Widow's Allowance. It is a tax-free lump sum of £1,000, paid as soon as a woman is widowed provided that: (1) her husband had paid sufficient NI contributions; (2) she is under 60; *or* (3) if she is over 60, her husband had not been entitled to retirement pension. Her claim will not be affected if she is already receiving a State pension, provided this is based on her own contributions.

Widows' pension. There are various levels of widows' pension: the full rate and age-related widows' pension. As with widows' payment, receipt is dependent on sufficient NI contributions having been paid.

Full-rate widows' pension is paid to widows between the ages of 55 and 59 inclusive. The weekly amount is £58.85, which is the same pension as that received by a single person.

Age-related widows' pension is for younger widows, who do not qualify for full rate. It is payable to a widow who is between 45 and 54 inclusive when her husband dies; or when she ceases to receive widowed mother's allowance. Rates depend on age and vary from £17.66 for 45 year olds to £54.73 for those aged 54.

Widows' pension is normally paid automatically once you have sent off your completed form BW 1, so if for any reason you do not receive it you should enquire at your local Social Security office. In the event of your being ineligible, due to insufficient NI contributions having been paid, you may still be entitled to receive income support, family credit, housing benefit or a grant or loan from the social fund. Your Social Security office will advise you.

Widows who remarry, or live with a man as his wife, cease to receive widows' pension unless, that is, they are aged 60 or over in which case they may continue to receive their pension. A widow who has cohabited and loses her entitlement to widows' pension will, if the cohabitation ends, be entitled to claim it again. If she is over 60, the fact that she may be living with a man will not affect her entitlement to a retirement pension, based on her late husband's contribution record.

Widowed mother's allowance. This is paid to mothers with at least one child for whom they receive child benefit. The current value (1995/96) is £58.85 a week. Additionally, widowed mothers receive an extra payment of £9.85 a week for the first or only child; and £11.05 a week for each other dependent child. These allowances are usually paid automatically. If for some reason, although eligible, you do not receive the money, you should inform your local Social Security office. See leaflet NP 45.

Retirement pension. Once a widow reaches age 60, she has the choice of claiming retirement pension or of continuing with widows' pension (until 65, when she no longer has a choice and will receive retirement pension).

If she is over 60 when her husband dies, she will usually receive a retirement pension rather than a widows' pension.

If at the time of death the couple were already receiving the State retirement pension, the widow will continue to receive her share. An important point to remember is that a widow may be able to use her late husband's NI contributions to boost the amount she receives. See leaflet FB 6 *Retiring? Your Pension and Other Benefits*.

Other important points. Separate from the basic pension, a widow may also receive money from her late husband's occupational pension, whether contracted in or out of SERPS. She may also get half of any of his graduated pension.

War widows. The government has changed the rules to help former war widows, whose war widow's pension was withdrawn on remarriage and who – either because of the death of their new husband, divorce or legal separation – have become single again. Women in this position may now have their war widow's pension restored.

4   Tax

Unfortunately, much as we should like to leave this out, the taxman never seems to retire!

Unless you are on a very low income, you will almost certainly be paying income tax and possibly one or two other varieties of tax as well. Paradoxically, however, although over the years you may have been contributing many thousands of pounds to the Inland Revenue, in practice you may have had very little direct contact with the tax system.

The accounts department will have automatically deducted – and accounted for – the PAYE on your earnings as a salaried employee. So unless you have been self-employed or have had other money, not connected with your job, you may never really have needed to give the question very much thought.

Come retirement, even though for most people the issues are not particularly complex, a little basic knowledge can be invaluable. Firstly, it will help you to calculate how much money (after deduction of tax) you will have available to spend: the equivalent, if you like, of your take-home pay. At a more sophisticated level, understanding the broad principles could help you save money, by not paying more in taxation than you need.

The purpose of this chapter, however, is not to suggest clever ways of reducing your liability – although in fact almost everyone has a certain amount of scope to do so without in any way cheating on the system. Apart from some general points, listed here (as well as scattered elsewhere in the book where especially relevant, such as in Chapter 10, Starting Your Own Business), giving tax planning advice is the job for a specialist; and moreover one who is fully conversant with your financial affairs, so that he can advise in the light of your own particular circumstances.

If you are lucky enough to be fairly wealthy or if some of the points mentioned in connection with recent Budget changes give you genuine cause to wonder whether you are taking advantage of the concessions available to you, you should talk to an accountant.

The aim here is simply to remind you of the basics and to draw your attention to some of the new provisions that could have a bearing on your immediate or longer term plans.

Income tax

This is calculated on all (or nearly all) your income, after deduction of your personal allowance; and, in the case of married people, of the married couple's allowance. The reason for saying 'nearly all' is that some income you may receive is tax free: types of income on which you do not have to pay tax are listed a little further on.

Most income, however, counts and you will be assessed for income tax on: your pension, interest you receive from most types of savings, dividends from investments, any earnings (even if these are only from casual work) plus rent from any lodgers, if the amount you receive exceeds £3,250 a year. Many social security benefits are also taxable.

The tax year runs from 6 April to 5 April the following year, so the amount of tax you pay in any one year is calculated on the income you receive (or are deemed to have received) between these two dates.

There are three different rates of income tax: the 20 per cent rate which applies to the first £3,200 of your taxable income; the 25 per cent basic rate tax which applies to the next slice of taxable income between £3,201 and £24,300; and the 40 per cent higher rate tax which is levied on all taxable income over £24,300.

All income tax payers will pay the 20 per cent rate on their first £3,200 of taxable income. Or put another way, for every £100 of your income that counts for income tax purposes up to £3,200, you have to pay £20 to the Exchequer – and are allowed to keep the remaining £80. If you are a basic rate taxpayer, the amount you have to pay the Exchequer increases (after the first £3,200) to £25; and if you are a higher rate taxpayer, it goes up to £40 for every £100 of your taxable income over £24,300.

The different rates sometimes change or, as in the 1992 Budget, a new rate may be introduced. Any changes, whether reductions or increases, are invariably announced in the Budget. This is now held every year around late November, at about the same time as the annual statement giving details of the social security up-ratings.

Tax allowances

Personal allowance
Income tax is not levied on every last penny of your money. There is a certain amount you are allowed to retain before income tax becomes applicable. This is known as your personal allowance. Therefore, when calculating how much tax you will have to pay in any one year, you should first deduct from your total income the amount represented by your personal allowance (plus any additional or other tax allowance to which you may be entitled, see sections following). If your income is no higher than your personal allowance (or total of these allowances), you will not have to pay any income tax.

Calculating your personal allowance used to be fairly complicated, as there were all sorts of variations according to whether individuals were married or single and whether only one partner, or both husband and wife, worked. Happily, since the introduction of independent taxation the system has become very much easier to understand.

Today everyone receives the same basic personal allowance, regardless of whether they are male, female, married or single; and regardless of whether any income they have comes from earnings, an investment, their pension or other source.

- The basic personal allowance (1995/96) is £3,525.

People aged 65 and over may be entitled to a higher personal allowance than the basic, by virtue of their age. Those aged 75 and above may receive even more generous treatment.

The full amount is only given to people whose income does not exceed £14,600. People with higher incomes will have their age allowance reduced by £1 for every £2 of income above the income limit. People with incomes above a certain level do not receive any age allowance. This ceiling is known as the upper limit. But however large your income, your personal allowance can never be reduced below the basic personal allowance.

For those aged 65 (or due to reach 65 before 5 April 1996) to 74:

- personal allowance is increased to £4,630
- the upper limit is £16,810

For those aged 75 (or due to reach 75 before 5 April 1996) and older:

- personal allowance is increased to £4,800
- the upper limit is £17,150.

N.B. Extra allowance linked to age is normally given automatically. If you are not receiving it but believe you should be doing so, you should write to your local tax office (see under Inland Revenue in the telephone directory) stating your age and, if married, that of your partner. If you have been missing out, you may be able to claim back anything you have lost for up to six years and should receive a tax rebate. The amounts have been altered several times since 1989/90, so any rebate would only apply to allowances that would have been due to you at the time.

Married couple's allowance

This is an extra allowance which, provided they live together, is given to all married couples.

Until recently the allowance normally went to the husband unless his income was too low for him to obtain the full benefit – in which case, he could transfer any unused part to his wife.

Today, couples have far greater freedom to decide for themselves how they want the allowance to be used. They can leave it with the husband, choose to divide it equally or, if this is more tax-efficient, allocate the whole allowance to the wife. The wife, if she so wishes, can claim half the allowance as of right. Couples who wish all or half of the allowance to go to the wife will need to arrange the transfer through their tax offices, by completing Form 18. This will need to be done before the start of the tax year, i.e. before 6 April. For the address of your tax office, see Inland Revenue in the telephone directory.

As with the personal allowance, older people enjoy a more generous married couple's allowance. Increases are given when the husband or wife reaches 65, with a bigger increase still at 75. Further details are contained in leaflet IR 81 (see over).

Similar to (age-related) personal allowance, the married couple's age-related increases are subject to a couple's income so it is possible that they might get less than the full addition – or maybe nothing extra at all.

A further point to note is that the option of transferring half, or all, the allowance to the wife only applies to the basic married couple's allowance – and *not* to the age-related addition. Consequently, the income limits are only based on the husband's income. The wife's income is not taken into account in calculating whether their married couple's age allowance would be reduced.

The current (1995/96) married couple's allowance, together with the ceiling limits for the higher allowance, are as follows:

- The basic married couple's allowance is £1,720.
- When the husband or wife reaches 65 (or is due to become 65 before 5 April 1996), the allowance is increased to £2,995.
- The upper limit is £19,360.

- When the husband or wife reaches 75 (or is due to become 75 before 5 April 1996), the allowance is increased to £3,035.
- The upper limit is £19,780.

N.B. Additions for age are normally given automatically. If couples are not receiving any extra but believe they should be, the husband should write to their local tax office stating their ages. If there has been a mistake, he will be given a rebate.

Important change. Since April 1995, married couple's allowance has been restricted to 15 per cent tax relief (previously 20 per cent).

Widow's bereavement allowance

This is an extra allowance, worth £1,720 a year at current rates, specially given to widows to assist them over the first difficult period. The only qualification is that a widow's late husband must have been entitled to the married couple's allowance at the time of his death. The allowance is given both in the tax year she became widowed and in the following tax year.

As with other tax allowances, this is not a cash benefit that can be claimed at the post office. It is an offset against income, before calculation of tax. A widow would therefore be entitled to the total of her personal allowance and widow's bereavement allowance before her income would start to be assessed for tax. She would also be entitled to any unused portion of the married couple's allowance in the year her husband dies. If a widow is aged 65 or over, she may also be able to claim the age-related addition (see 'Personal allowance' above).

- Since April 1995, widow's bereavement allowance has been restricted to 15 per cent tax relief (previously 20 per cent).

Other tax allowances

Extra tax reliefs can also be claimed in a couple of other circumstances.

Additional personal allowance (single parent's allowance). This can be claimed by any parent or guardian bringing up dependent children on their own. The current value of the allowance is £1,720 a year. N.B. A married man whose wife is totally incapacitated can also claim this allowance, in addition to the married couple's allowance, if he has dependent children living at home.

- Since April 1995, the allowance has been restricted to 15 per cent tax relief.

Registered blind people can claim an allowance of £1,200 a year. If both husband and wife are registered as blind, they can each claim the allowance. It is called the Blind Person's Allowance.

If you think you might be entitled to either of the above, you should write to your local tax office (see under Inland Revenue in the telephone directory) with full relevant details of your situation. As with age-related additions, if you were entitled to receive the allowance earlier but for some reason missed out doing so, you may be able to obtain a tax rebate.

Useful reading

For more detailed information about tax allowances and other changes due to independent taxation, see the following Inland Revenue leaflets obtainable free from any tax office (see under Inland Revenue in the telephone directory).

- IR 80 *Income Tax: A Guide for Married Couples*
- IR 90 *Tax Allowances and Reliefs*
- IR 91 *A Guide for Widows and Widowers*
- IR 121 *Income Tax and Pensioners*

Tax relief

Separate from any personal allowances, you can obtain tax relief on the following:

- Interest payments on the first £30,000 of a mortgage paid on your own home (see note below).
- A covenant for the benefit of a charity; or donation under the Gift Aid Scheme.
- Contributions to occupational pensions, self-employed pension plans and other personal pensions.
- Some maintenance payments, if you are divorced or separated.
- Private medical insurance for those aged 60 and over.
- Rental income of up to £3,250 a year from letting out rooms in your home.

Mortgage interest relief. Since April 1995, tax relief on mortgage interest payments has been restricted to 15 per cent. This change affects both existing and new loans used for home purchase. No one loses their right to tax relief on borrowings up to £30,000 for these purposes. It is only the amount of relief granted that has changed.

Loans secured on an older person's (65 years or over) home which are used to purchase a life annuity are not affected and continue to receive tax relief at the basic rate.

Another small good news item that you may have forgotten is that the threshold for stamp duty has been raised from £30,000 to £60,000. This means that anyone buying a property costing £60,000 or less will not be charged stamp duty on the purchase.

Self-employed and other personal pension plans. The rules are not the same for all types of pension plan. In particular, there are important differences between personal pensions (PPs) and retirement annuity contracts. According to your age, you can pay the following amounts into a **personal pension** (PP) scheme and obtain tax relief:

- if you are aged 35 or under, 17.5 per cent of your earnings (up to a ceiling of £78,600)
- between the ages of 36 and 45, 20 per cent of your earnings
- between the ages of 46 and 50, 25 per cent
- between the ages of 51 and 55, 30 per cent
- between the ages of 56 and 60, 35 per cent
- ages 61 and over, 40 per cent

Personal pension schemes started before 1 July 1988 are known as **retirement annuity contracts**. You can pay the following amounts into a retirement annuity and obtain tax relief:

- if you are aged 50 or under, 17.5 per cent of your earnings
- between the ages of 51 and 55, 20 per cent
- between the ages of 56 and 60, 22.5 per cent
- ages 61 and over, 27.5 per cent

Ages are calculated at the beginning of the tax year.

N.B. The £78,600 ceiling on earnings applies to all age groups although in practice, since it is only relevant to high earners, it is more likely to affect senior people. The ceiling only applies to people (with a self-employed/other personal pension plan) who contribute to a personal pension (PP) scheme. It does not affect those who contribute to a retirement annuity contract.

The ceiling also applies to people who joined an occupational pension scheme set up since 14 March 1989; or who joined any occupational scheme from 1 June 1989.

Maintenance payments. The rules were considerably simplified in the 1988 Budget, and, except for previous maintenance arrangements, are now as follows:

- Individuals **receiving** payments are exempted from income tax
- Individuals **paying** maintenance under a legally binding arrangement receive tax relief on the first £1,720 of payments to a divorced or separated spouse; other maintenance payments, including any made directly to children, do not qualify for tax relief. Since April 1995, the relief for spouses has been restricted to 15 per cent (20 per cent for 1994–95).

Maintenance arrangements existing prior to the 1988 Budget remain largely unaffected, other than that *payments received* by divorced or separated spouses are exempt from tax on the first £1,720.

Private medical insurance. People over the age of 60 who are resident in the UK are able to get tax relief, at basic rate, on private medical insurance. The relief is available whether premiums are paid by the insured person or paid by someone else (for example a relative) on their behalf.

For further information, see leaflet IR 103 *Tax Relief for Private Medical Insurance* available from any tax office.

Tax-free income

Some income you may receive is entirely free of tax. It is not taxed at source. You do not have to deduct it from your income, as in the case of personal allowances. Nor do you have to go through the formality of claiming relief on it.

If you receive any of the following, you can forget about the tax angle altogether – at least as regards these particular items:

- Disability living allowance
- Industrial injuries disablement pension
- Income support (in some circumstances, e.g. when the recipient is also getting unemployment benefit or the new Jobseeker's Allowance, income support benefit would be taxable)
- Housing benefit
- Council tax benefit
- Any extra which may be added to your State pension if you support children under 16
- All pensions paid to war widows (plus any additions for children)
- Pensions paid to victims of Nazism
- Certain disablement pensions from the armed forces, police, fire brigade and merchant navy
- Annuities paid to the holders of certain gallantry awards
- £10 Christmas bonus (paid to pensioners)
- National Savings Premium Bond prizes
- SAYE bonuses
- Winnings on the football pools and on other forms of betting.
- People receiving invalidity benefit on 12 April 1995 (i.e. before it was replaced by incapacity benefit) continue – if they are still entitled to benefit – to receive this tax free.

Other tax-free money

The following are not income, in the sense that they are more likely to be 'one off' rather than regular payments. However, as with the above list they are tax free:

- Virtually all gifts (in certain circumstances you could have to pay tax if the gift is above £3,000 or if, as may occasionally be the case, the money from the donor has not been previously taxed).
- Redundancy payment, or a golden handshake in lieu of notice, up to the value of £30,000.
- Lump sum commuted from a pension with (1995/96) a maximum figure of £117,900 allowed. Existing members of pension schemes set up prior to the 1989 Budget or who joined established schemes before 1 June 1989 may not be affected by the rule and may be entitled to a higher tax-free lump sum.
- A matured endowment policy.
- Accumulated interest from a Tax Exempt Special Savings Account (TESSA) held for five years.
- Dividends on investments held in a Personal Equity Plan (PEP).

Income tax on investments

For most investments on which you are likely to receive interest or dividends, basic rate tax will already have been deducted before the money is paid to you.

If you are a basic rate taxpayer, the money you receive will be yours in its entirety and you will not have to worry about making deductions for tax.

If you only pay tax at the 20 per cent rate, you will be able to claim a repayment from the Inland Revenue.

If you pay tax at the higher rate, you will have to pay some additional tax and should allow for this in your budgeting, as its deduction is not automatic. Normally, you will receive a tax demand for the extra tax owing after the end of the year.

Exceptionally, there are one or two types of investment where the money is paid to you gross – without the basic rate tax deducted. These include National Savings income bonds, deposit bonds, capital bonds, the NS Investment Account and also certain specialist types of gilts. As with higher rate taxpayers, you will receive a tax demand for the amount owing.

Abolition of composite rate tax. Since April 1991, non-taxpayers (people whose taxable income is less than their allowances) can request institutions such as banks and building societies to pay any interest owing to them gross, without deduction of tax at source. This is benefiting several million people, including in particular many married women and pensioners, who although not liable for tax, were losing money through the composite rate tax system.

Many people who stand to benefit are still continuing to pay tax unnecessarily. If you are one of those who has been missing out, simply request form R85 from the institution in question, which you will then need to complete. People with more than one bank or building society account will need a separate form for each account. Forms are also included in the Inland Revenue explanatory leaflet IR 110 *A Guide for People with Savings*, obtainable from any tax office or from your bank/building society.

People who have filled in an R85 should automatically receive their interest gross. If your form was not completed in time for this to happen, you can reclaim the tax from your tax office after the end of the tax year in April. Leaflet IR 110 (see above) explains how to do this.

Reclaiming tax overpaid

If your income consists mainly of either taxed investments or bank/building society interest, then you can set your personal allowances against the income. This will normally mean that you are entitled to a tax rebate. To allow for this, there is a special tax form for retired people to reclaim any tax they have overpaid on investment income.

If you think this might apply to you, you should obtain Tax Claim Form R40 from your local tax office (see under Inland Revenue in the telephone directory). Complete the form and return it to the tax office, together with the tax vouchers concerned.

In particular it is estimated by the Inland Revenue that there may be $2^1/_2$ million married women who may be able to claim a repayment of tax on dividend income plus some 3 million pensioners who could claim back tax they have overpaid on bank or building society interest.

If you are claiming a repayment for the first time you should fill in form R95 attached to leaflet IR 110 and send it to your local tax office. A repayment claim form will then be sent to you. The completed claim form should be returned with the certificates showing the amount of tax deducted.

For further information see IR leaflet 110 *A Guide for People with Savings*, obtainable from any tax office.

Mistakes by the Inland Revenue

The Inland Revenue sometimes also makes mistakes. Normally, if they have charged you insufficient tax and later discover the error, they will send you a supplementary demand requesting the balance owing. However, under a provision known as the 'Official Error Concession', allowances are sometimes made and if you have a modest income it is possible that you may not have to pay the full amount. The limits governing the definition of 'modest income' were fairly recently increased to, at their most generous, £40,000 in respect of taxpayers over 65.

Under-charging is not the only type of error. It is equally possible that you may have been over-charged and either do not owe as much as has been stated or, not having spotted the mistake, paid more than you needed to previously. In time the Inland Revenue may notice the error and send you a refund. But equally, they may not. So if you have reason to think your tax bill looks wrong, check it carefully. Then, if you think there has been a mistake, write to your tax office explaining why you think the amount is too high. If a large sum is involved it could well be worth asking an accountant to help you.

As part of the Citizen's Charter, the Inland Revenue has recently appointed an independent Adjudicator to examine taxpayers' complaints about their dealings with the Revenue and, if considered valid, to determine what action would be fair.

Complaints appropriate to the Adjudicator are mainly limited to the way the Inland Revenue has handled someone's tax affairs, for example: excessive delay, errors, discourtesy or how discretion has been exercised. In deciding fair treatment, the Adjudicator has power to recommend the waiving of a payment or even the award of compensation if, as a result of error by the Inland Revenue, the complainant had incurred professional fees or other expenses.

Before approaching the Adjudicator, taxpayers will be expected to have tried resolving the matter with their local tax office or, if this fails, with the Regional Office.

For further information, see IR booklet, Code of Practice 1, *Mistakes by the Inland Revenue*, available from tax offices. Or contact the Adjudicator's office for information about referring a complaint. The address is: **The Adjudicator's Office**, 3rd Floor, Haymarket House, 28 Haymarket, London SW1Y 4SP. T:0171 930 2292.

Tax rebates

When you retire, you may be due for a tax rebate. If you are, this would normally be paid automatically, especially if you are getting a pension from your last employer. The matter could conceivably be overlooked: either if (instead of from your last employer) you are due to get a pension from an earlier employer; or if you will only be receiving a State pension – and not a company pension in addition.

In either case, you should ask your employer for a P45 Form. Then, either send it – care of your earlier employer – to the pension fund trustees; or, in the event of your only receiving a State pension, send it to the tax office together with details of your age and the date you retired. Ask your employer for the address of the tax office to which you should write. If the repayment is made to you more than a year after the end of the year for which the repayment is due – and is more than £25 – the Inland Revenue will automatically pay you (tax free!) interest. The Revenue call this 'Repayment Supplement'.

Useful reading

For further information about income tax, see the following Inland Revenue leaflets, available from any tax office:

- IR 93 *Income Tax – Separation, Divorce and Maintenance Payments*
- IR 92 *Income Tax: A Guide for One-Parent Families*
- IR 34 *Income Tax – Pay As You Earn*
- IR 65 *Giving to Charity – How Individuals Can Get Tax Relief*
- IR 123 *Mortgage Interest Relief: Buying Your Home*

Post-war credits

Post-war credits are extra tax that people had to pay in addition to their income tax between April 1941 and April 1946. The extra tax was treated as a credit to be repaid after the war. People who paid credits were given certificates showing the amount actually paid.

Repayment started in 1946, initially only to men aged 65 or over and to women aged 60 or over, but the conditions for claiming varied over the years until 1972 when it was announced that there would be a 'general release' and that all credits were to be repaid without any further restrictions. In 1972 people who could produce at least one of their post-war credit certificates were invited to claim.

In cases where the original credit holder has died without claiming repayment and the Post War Credit certificate is still available, repayment can be made to the next of kin or personal representative of the estate.

Interest is payable on all claims at a composite rate of 38 per cent. The interest is exempt from income tax.

All claims should be sent to the **Special Post-war Credit Claim Centre** at: Inland Revenue, HM Inspector of Taxes – PWC Centre V, Ty Glas, Llanishen, Cardiff CF4 5TX.

Capital gains tax (CGT)

You may have to pay capital gains tax if you make a profit (or to use the proper term, gain) on the sale of a capital asset, for example: stocks and shares, jewellery, any property that is not your main home and other items of value.

CGT only applies to the actual gain you make, so if you buy shares to the value of £25,000 and sell them later for £35,000 the taxman will only be interested in the £10,000 profit you have made.

Not all your gains are taxable. There is an **exemption limit of £6,000 a year**: so if during the year your total profits amount to £13,000, tax would only be levied on £7,000.

Additionally, **certain items are exempt from** capital gains tax; and others, such as the sale of a family business, get special treatment. Details are given a little further on.

A very important point for married couples to know is that as a result of independent taxation each partner now enjoys his/her own annual exemption of £6,000 instead of, as before, their gains being aggregated (i.e. added together) for tax purposes. This means in effect that, provided both partners are taking advantage of their full exemption limit, a couple can make gains of £12,000 a year free of capital gains tax. However, it is not possible to use the losses of one spouse to cover the gains of the other.

Transfers between husband and wife remain tax free, although any income arising from such a gift will of course be taxed. Income would normally be treated as the recipient's for tax purposes.

Since 1982, the burden of CGT has been eased by the welcome introduction of indexation. This means that any part of an asset's increased value, from 1982 or its subsequent acquisition to its disposal, which is due to inflation is not counted for

CGT purposes. Indexation however can no longer be used to create, or increase, a loss.

A further major reform was introduced in the 1988 Budget, namely: for any disposals on or after 6 April 1988 only increases in value since 31 March 1982 will be brought into account.

Gains are treated as a person's 'top slice' of income and are accordingly taxed at: 20 per cent (the lower rate), 25 per cent (basic rate), 40 per cent (higher rate) or a mixture of rates, i.e. in instances where a gain, or gains, pushes part of an individual's income into a higher rate bracket.

Free of capital gains tax

The following assets are not subject to capital gains tax and do not count towards the £6,000 gains you are allowed to make:

- Your main home (but, see note below)
- Your car
- Personal belongings up to the value of £6,000 each
- Proceeds of a life assurance policy (in most circumstances)
- Profits on British Government stocks (on holdings up to £200,000)
- National Savings Certificates
- SAYE contracts
- Building society savings
- Futures and options in gilts and qualifying corporate bonds
- Personal Equity Plan scheme
- Premium Bond winnings
- Football pool and other bettings winnings
- Gifts to registered charities
- Small part disposals of land (limited to 5 per cent of the total holding, with a maximum value of £20,000)
- Gains on the disposal of qualifying shares within the Enterprise Investment Scheme, provided these have been held for five years.

The Enterprise Investment Scheme has replaced the Business Expansion Scheme (BES). As well as exemption from capital gains tax (provided the shares are held for five years), the scheme provides individuals with income tax relief at 20 per cent on investments of up to £100,000 a year. Losses qualify for income tax or capital gains tax relief. Also, unlike the BES, an investor can become a paid director, provided he/she was not previously connected with the company. For further information, including possible roll-over relief, see Inland Revenue booklet IR 137.

Your home. Your main home is usually exempt from capital gains tax. However, there are certain 'ifs and buts' which could be important.

If you convert part of your home into an office or into self-contained accommodation on which you charge rent, that part of your home which is deemed to be a 'business' may be separately assessed – and CGT may be payable when you come to sell it. (CGT would not apply, if you simply take in a lodger who is treated as family, in the sense of sharing your kitchen or bathroom.)

If you physically vacate some or all of your home and let it for profit – perhaps because you have decided to live permanently with a friend – under tax law, the property would be treated as an investment and subject to certain exemptions would be assessed for CGT when it was sold.

Part of the argument hinges on owner occupation. If you are not living in the property (or a part of it which you have let out for rent), then the house – or that section of it – is no longer considered to be your main home. People who are liable for CGT in these circumstances can apply for special relief of up to £40,000.

If you leave your home to someone else who later decides to sell it, then he/she may be liable for CGT when the property is sold (although only on the gain since the date of death). There may also be inheritance tax implications, so if you are thinking of leaving or giving your home to someone, you are strongly advised to consult a solicitor or accountant.

If you own two homes, only one of them is exempt from CGT, namely the one you designate as your 'main residence'. An exception was sometimes allowed if a second home was occupied by a dependent relative, who lived in it rent free.

This concession was abolished as from 6 April 1988. However, anyone who had a dependent relative living in a second home before that date will continue to enjoy capital gains tax relief. *But* the relief only applies while the dependant is actually inhabiting the property. If he/she moves to more sheltered accommodation and you keep the property as an investment, it will be assessed for capital gains tax purposes from the date of your relative's departure.

Selling a family business. If you sell all or part of your business when you retire, you may not have to pay tax on the first £250,000 of capital gain with a further exemption allowed of one-half of gains between £250,000 and £1,000,000. Relief is on a sliding scale and to get maximum relief, you must be aged 55 or older and when selling shares must have owned at least 5 per cent of the company, either as a working director or employee for 10 years. In general, only trading businesses are eligible. If you are forced to retire early through ill health, the age rules may be applied less stringently and you may still be entitled to retirement relief.

The Chancellor introduced **a new relief for entrepreneurs** in the April 1993 Budget, which allows them to defer paying tax on gains arising from the sale of shares in their own companies, provided the gains are reinvested in other qualifying unquoted companies within three years.

Since then, Re-Investment Relief has been made even more attractive. Firstly, as opposed to simply applying to the sale of shares, the relief has been extended to make it available for all chargeable gains (including importantly the assets of a business). Secondly, the requirement whereby an entrepreneur had to acquire a minimum shareholding of 5 per cent in the new business to qualify for the relief has now been dropped. Other minor changes include the abolition of the 'land rule' and the inclusion of individuals involved in property development or farming as eligible for re-investment relief.

Since this is a very complex field, before either retiring or selling shares, you are strongly recommended to seek professional advice.

Selling shares for gain should not be confused with *giving* part of your family business to the next generation, which was made easier a few years back under the inheritance tax rules. However, the advice about seeking professional help still applies, especially since all disposals including gifts may be liable for CGT.

Useful reading
For further information about capital gains tax, see the following booklets, available from any tax office:

- CGT 4 *Capital Gains Tax – Owner-Occupied Houses*
- CGT 6 *Capital Gains Tax – Retirement Disposal of a Business*
- CGT 11 *Capital Gains Tax and the Small Businessman*
- CGT 13 *The Indexation Allowance for Quoted Shares*
- CGT 14 *An Introduction to Capital Gains Tax*
- CGT 15 *Capital Gains Tax – A Guide for Married Couples*
- CGT 16 *Capital Gains Tax – Indexation Allowance*

Inheritance tax

Inheritance tax (IHT) applies to money and/or gifts with a capital value passed on at time of death (or sometimes before).

The first £154,000 of an individual's estate is tax free. Amounts over this are taxed at a single rate of 40 per cent. However, before any tax is calculated, there are a number of exemptions and other concessions of which perhaps the most important is that there is no tax on gifts or inheritance between spouses. Additionally, most family-owned farms and businesses are exempted from IHT; as are most life-time gifts, providing certain important conditions are met.

There is no immediate tax on lifetime gifts between individuals. The gifts become wholly exempt if the donor survives for seven years. When the donor dies, any gifts made within the previous seven years become chargeable and their value is added to that of the estate. The total is then taxed on the excess over £154,000.

Chargeable gifts benefit first towards the £154,000 exemption, starting with the earliest gifts and continuing in the order in which they were given. Any unused balance of the £154,000 threshold goes towards the remaining estate.

Taper relief – in other words, a tapering rate of tax according to how close to the seven-year limit the death of the donor occurred – reduces the amount of inheritance tax payable on lifetime gifts.Gifts made within three years of death do not qualify for any relief and the tax will have to be paid in full. For gifts made more than three years before death, the rates are as follows:

- Death between 3 and 4 years of gift, IHT reduced by 20%
- Death between 4 and 5 years of gift, IHT reduced by 40%
- Death between 5 and 6 years of gift, IHT reduced by 60%
- Death between 6 and 7 years of gift, IHT reduced by 80%

Gifts or money up to the value of £3,000 can also be given annually free of tax, regardless of the particular date they were given. Additionally, it is possible to make small gifts to any number of individuals free of tax, provided the amount to each does not exceed £250.

Quite apart from IHT, capital gains tax has to be paid (either by your estate or the recipient) on any gain that has built up on an asset you gave away during your lifetime and which is subsequently sold. The appreciation is only calculated from 1982 or subsequent year of purchase and any part of the asset's increased value due to inflation is not counted for tax purposes. Moreover, not surprisingly perhaps, tax specialists say that there are legitimate ways of minimising the liability, for example by putting gifts into a discretionary trust which qualifies them for 'hold-over' relief. Since this is a fairly complex matter, professional advice is essential.

Another important consideration that should not be overlooked is the need to make a will. The rules of intestacy are very rigid and neglecting to make a proper will can have serious consequences for those whom you might wish to benefit. For further information, see 'Making a will', (page 446).

Likewise, if you have already written a will, it is strongly recommended that you have this checked by a professional adviser to ensure that you do not give money unnecessarily to the taxman.

For further information about inheritance tax, see booklets *An Introduction to Inheritance Tax* (IHT 3), *Inheritance on Lifetime Gifts* (IHT 2) and *Alterations to an Inheritance Following a Death* (IHT 8), obtainable from any tax office.

Independent taxation

As most readers will know, independent taxation was introduced on 6 April 1990. Throughout the chapter and elsewhere in the book, the key changes have been described as and where relevant, in particular under the headings 'Personal allowance', 'Married couple's allowance' and 'Capital gains tax' (see pages 64, 65 and 73). However, because this is such a fundamental change, one or two of the essentials are worth repeating.

The switch to independent taxation affects nearly all married couples. As well as allowing married women privacy over their own financial affairs, another major gain is that many couples – especially retired people – are better off financially.

In contrast to the old system, whereby a married woman's income was treated as belonging to her husband for taxation purposes, both husband and wife are now taxed independently on their own income. Each has their own personal allowance and rate band; and each pays their own tax and receives their own tax rebates.

Moreover, independent taxation applies equally to the age-related additions and both husband and wife are now eligible for their own higher tax allowance from the age of 65 (and more generous still after age 75).

Another welcome gain is that couples can now choose whether all the tax relief on the basic married couple's allowance should go to one partner (husband or wife) or whether to split it on a 50-50 basis, whichever they prefer. The wife, if she so wishes, can claim half the allowance as of right. **N.B. This does not apply to the age-related additions for married couple's allowance**.

As explained earlier, a couple's eligibility for age-related increases are based on the husband's income. Consequently, the relief cannot be transferred to the wife. However, if the wife is the older of the two and so attains 65, or 75, before her husband the couple may enjoy the advantage of the age-related addition to the married couple's allowance based on her age. But this would not apply if the husband's income were over the upper limit. (If the wife's income were over the upper limit this would be ignored.)

A further important point for many couples is that independent taxation does not simply apply to income tax but applies equally to both capital gains tax and inheritance tax. As a result, both husband and wife enjoy their own capital gains tax exemption (£6,000 in the 1995/96 tax year) and their own exemption from inheritance tax (£154,000 in the 1995/96 tax year). Property left to a surviving spouse remains, as before, free of inheritance tax.

Useful reading

For further information about independent taxation, see the following Inland Revenue booklets, available from any tax office:

- IR 80 *A Guide for Married Couples*
- IR 90 *Tax Allowances and Reliefs*
- IR 91 *A Guide for Widows and Widowers*
- IR 121 *Income Tax and Pensioners*

Value added tax (VAT)

Unless you are thinking of starting a business or already run one, you do not require any special information about VAT. You pay it automatically on most goods and services, at the flat rate of 17.5 per cent. As a general rule, if you purchase a tangible object, it will be included in the price. For most services, including restaurant bills, it is itemised separately.

Small firms that are not registered for VAT naturally do not charge it. However, even for very small enterprises, there may be definite advantages in registering. If you are planning to become self-employed or start a business after you retire, you should read the VAT section, in Chapter 10, Starting Your Own Business.

The only extra point worth mentioning is that since April 1994, VAT at 8 per cent has become payable on domestic fuel.

Other expenditure taxes

The Chancellor introduced two new taxes which came into effect during 1994.

Insurance Premium Tax (IPT)
Tax is 2.5 per cent and applies to premiums paid on all general insurance. It does not apply to long-term insurance such as life insurance or pensions.

Air passenger duty
Passengers pay a £5 charge on flights within the UK and to other EC destinations. The charge is £10 on flights elsewhere.

Corporation tax

This is a business tax and unless you are involved in running a company, there is nothing you need to know. If you are already engaged in running a small business, you will probably hardly need reminding that the small companies' rate of corporation tax is 25 per cent (instead of the 33 per cent standard rate for larger concerns). The lower and upper limits for the application of marginal relief are £300,000 and £1,500,000 respectively.

Useful reading
Allied Dunbar Tax Handbook published by Pearson Professional, 21-27 Lamb's Conduit Street, London WC1N 3NJ, T:0171 242 2548. Price £23 incl. p&p.
Your Taxes and Savings (1995/96) – published by Age Concern. Price £4.95.

Inland Revenue booklets which could be helpful, especially if you are interested in the possibility of becoming self-employed or starting your own business include:

- IR 28 *Starting In Business*
- IR 52 *Your Tax Office – Why It Is and Where It Is*
- IR 53 *Thinking of Taking Someone On?*
- IR 56/NI 39 *Employed or Self-Employed?*
- IR 57 *Thinking of Working for Yourself?*

Self-assessment
The Chancellor has announced plans to introduce a new system of self-assessment designed to simplify the process of making tax returns for the 9 million or so people who receive them. If your only income is from your salary from which tax is deducted at source you will not be affected by the change. If, however, you have any other income that is not fully taxed under PAYE (e.g. possibly benefits in kind or expenses

payments) or that is not fully taxed at source, you need to notify the Inland Revenue and have to fill in a tax return. One of the reasons for the change which starts from the 1996/97 tax year is to make life easier for the self-employed.

In particular, it is proposed to replace the preceding year basis of income tax with a simpler 'current year' basis (i.e. there will only be need to refer to one period of accounts). Businesses set up after April 1994 will not need to worry about the preceding year method of calculation as they will go (or will already have gone) straight on to the new current year basis.

Self-assesment will be optional. Those choosing to calculate the tax themselves will have until 31 January following the end of the tax year to send in their tax return. Those wishing the Revenue to work out the amount of tax due will need to submit their returns by the earlier date of 30 September. The dates are important, as there is an automatic penalty of £100 if your tax return arrives after 31 January. For further information, see leaflets IR 142, *Self Assessment – An Introduction* and *Self Assessment – A Guide for the Self-employed*, obtainable from any tax office.

Retiring abroad

The stories are legion of people who retired abroad in the expectation of being able to afford a higher standard of living and who returned home a few years later, thoroughly disillusioned. As with other important decisions, this is an area where homework really pays!

Holiday memories of dinner for two complete with bottle of wine for the princely sum of a fiver are, alas, no guide to the cost of actually living in a country – especially if the holiday in question took place five years ago or more. While some services may be cheaper, others may be very much more expensive; and the same goes for any goods you buy in the shops. In particular, if you want to purchase British brands, you can expect to pay considerably more than you do at home. It is crucial to investigate property prices as well as, of course, the cost of health care. As anyone who has ever needed a doctor or dentist abroad knows, the term 'free health service' does not always mean what it says.

While these and similar points are perhaps obvious, a vital question that is often overlooked are the taxation effects of living overseas.

Taxation abroad

Tax rates vary from one country to another: a prime example being VAT, which in some parts of Europe at the time of writing is over 20 per cent on certain items. Additionally, many countries levy taxes that happily do not apply to Britain. Wealth tax exists in quite a few parts of the world. Estate duty between husbands and wives is also fairly widespread.

There are all sorts of property taxes, different from our own, which – however described – are variously assessable as income or capital. Sometimes a special tax is imposed on foreign residents. Some countries charge income tax on an individual's worldwide income, with none of the (by British standards) normal exemptions allowed.

Even so-called tax havens may fail to live up to their privileged reputation. While admittedly not actual taxation, many impose all sorts of conditions on foreigners, effectively excluding all but the super-rich. The terms may vary but could include any, or all, of the following. Only property above a minimum (and pretty exorbitant) price may be purchased. You might have to produce evidence of a sky-high annual income. You may be required to invest in a local business. Or, insultingly, you could be requested to deposit a sum with the government to cover you against repatriation costs, should the necessity arise.

Perhaps even more alarming, many hundreds of Britons in Spain have been landed with vast bills because, unbeknown to them, the developers from whom they purchased their home had taken out a mortgage against the property and then subsequently gone out of business, leaving the British owners with the debt plus interest and legal fees. Although new laws have been introduced in Spain to protect the buyer, it appears that these are not being applied as rigorously as they might.

Apart from the essential of getting first class legal advice when buying property overseas, if you are thinking of retiring abroad the golden rule must be to investigate the situation thoroughly before you take an irrevocable step, such as selling your home.

However, if many people blithely ignore the 'nasties' that may await them overseas, an even more common mistake is to misunderstand their UK tax liabilities after their departure.

Your UK tax position if you retire overseas

Many intending emigrants cheerfully imagine that once they have settled themselves in a dream villa overseas, they are safely out of the clutches of the UK taxman. This is not so, however. You first have to acquire **non-resident status**. If you have severed all your ties, including selling your home, to take up a permanent job overseas, this is normally granted fairly quickly.

But for most retirees, acquiring unconditional non-resident status can take up to three years. The purpose is to check that you are not just having a prolonged holiday but are actually living as a resident abroad. During the check period, the Inland Revenue may allow you **conditional non-resident status**; and if they are satisfied, full status will be granted retrospectively.

Rules. The rules for non-residency are pretty stringent. You are not allowed:

- to spend more than 182 days in the UK in any one tax year
- to spend more than an average of 90 days per year in the UK over a maximum of four tax years.

Even if you are not resident in the UK, some of your income may still be liable for UK taxation.

Income tax

- All overseas income is exempt from UK tax liability

- Income deriving from a UK source is, however, normally liable for UK tax. This includes any director's or consultant's fees you may still be receiving, as well as more obvious income.
- An exception is made if the country in which you have taken up residency has a double tax agreement with the United Kingdom (see below). If this is the case, you may be taxed on the income in your new residence – and not in the UK.
- Additionally, interest paid on certain British Government securities is not subject to tax.
- Non-residents may be able to arrange for their interest on a British bank deposit or building society account to be paid gross.
- Some former colonial pensions are also exempted.

Double tax agreement. A person who is a resident of a country with which the UK has a double taxation agreement may be entitled to exemption or partial relief from UK income tax on certain kinds of income from UK sources and may also be exempt from UK tax on the disposal of assets. The conditions of exemption or relief vary from agreement to agreement. It may be a condition of the relief that the income is subject to tax in the other country.

Capital gains tax

- This is only charged if you are resident or ordinarily resident in the UK; so if you are in the position of being able to realise a gain, it is advisable to wait until you acquire non-resident status.
- An exception to the rule are gains made from the disposal of assets in a UK company. These are subject to normal CGT.

Inheritance tax

- You only escape tax if (a) you were domiciled overseas for all of the immediate three years prior to death (b) you were resident overseas for at least three tax years in your final 20 years of life and (c) if all your assets were overseas. Even if you have been resident overseas for many years, if you do not have an overseas domicile, you will have to pay IHT at the same rates as if you lived in the UK.

Domicile. Broadly speaking you are domiciled in the country in which you have your permanent home. Domicile is distinct from nationality or residence. A person may be resident in more than one country but at any given time he/she can only be domiciled in one.

If you are resident in a country and intend to spend the rest of your days there, it could be sensible to decide to change your domicile. If, however, you are resident but there is a chance that you might move, the country where you are living would not qualify as your domicile. This is a complicated area, where professional advice is recommended if you are contemplating a change.

UK pensions paid abroad

- Any queries about your pension should be addressed to the DSS Overseas Benefits Directorate at Longbenton, Newcastle upon Tyne NE98 1YX.
- Technically your State pension could be subject to income tax, as it derives from the UK. In practice, if this is your only source of UK income, tax would be unlikely to be charged.
- If you have an occupational pension, UK tax will normally be charged on the total of the two amounts.
- Both State and occupational pensions may be paid to any country. (If you are planning to retire to Australia, Canada, New Zealand or Norway, you would be advised to check on the up-to-date position regarding any annual increases you would expect to receive to your pension. Some people have found the level of their pension 'frozen' at the date they left Britain.)
- If the country where you are living has a double tax agreement with the UK, as previously explained your income may be taxed there – and not in Britain. Britain now has a double tax agreement with most countries. For further information, check the position with your local tax office.
- If your pension is taxed in the UK, you will be able to claim your personal allowance as an offset. A married man living with his wife may also be able to claim the married couple's allowance.

Health care overseas. People retiring to another EC country before State retirement age can apply to DSS Overseas Contributions for a form E106 which will entitle them to State health care in that country on the same basis as local people.

An E106 is normally only valid for about 18 months, after which it is usually necessary to take out private insurance cover until State retirement age is reached. Thereafter, UK pensioners can ask the DSS Overseas Benefits Directorate at Newcastle (see under 'Pensions' above) for a form E121, entitling them and their dependants to State health care as provided by the country in which they are living.

Useful reading

Double Taxation Relief (IR 6) and *Residents and Non Residents – Liability to Tax in the UK* (IR 20), available from any tax office.

DSS Leaflet SA 29 *Your Social Security Insurance, Benefits and Health Care Rights in the European Community* contains essential information about what to do if you retire to another EC country. Available from any DSS local office.

The Daily Telegraph Guide to Living Abroad by Michael Furnell, published by Kogan Page, £8.99.

5   Investment

Investment is a subject for everyone. One of your single most important aims must be to make your existing money work for you so you will be more comfortable in the years ahead. The younger you start planning the better. If you are already 65 or over, there is still plenty you can do.

Many articles written on the subject of financial planning for retirement concentrate almost exclusively on ways of boosting your immediate income to compensate for your loss of earnings. Frankly, this is very misleading and short-sighted advice. An equally if not even more critical consideration must be to safeguard your long-term security, even if this means some minor sacrifice to your current standard of living.

The likelihood is that you will live for 20 years or longer after you retire and your partner may live longer still. Your investment strategy must therefore be aimed not just for your sixties but also for your eighties.

Inflation is another essential factor that must be taken into account. People on fixed incomes are the hardest hit when inflation rises and, as happened in the 1970s, many even quite wealthy people were drastically impoverished as a result of their savings being slashed in value.

Even low inflation, as we have today, takes its toll to an alarming extent. For example, if you have an after tax income of £11,000 a year and inflation averages 4 per cent for the next decade, your spending power will be reduced to £7,520. If it averages 6 per cent, it will have dropped still further to £6,580. And if it averages 10 per cent, you will end up with a miserable £4,170 in purchasing power terms.

Sources of investable funds

You do not need to be in the director league to have money for investment. Possible sources of quite significant capital include:

- Commuted lump sum from your pension. The maximum you are allowed to take is one-and-a-half times your final earnings, with a ceiling of £117,900. (Members of existing pension schemes joined prior to the 1989 Budget are allowed a higher tax free lump sum, provided this does not exceed one-and-a-half times final earnings). There is no tax to pay when you receive the money.
- Insurance policies, designed to mature around your retirement. These are normally tax free.
- Profits on your home, if you sell it and move to smaller, less expensive accommodation. Provided this is your main home, there is no capital gains tax to pay.

- Redundancy money, golden handshake or other farewell gift from your employer. You are allowed £30,000 redundancy money free of tax. The same is usually true of other severance pay up to £30,000 but there can be tax if, however worded, your employment contract indicates that these are deferred earnings.
- Sale of SAYE and other share option schemes. The tax rules vary according to the type of scheme, the date the options were acquired and how long the shares have been held before disposal.

General investment strategy

Investments differ in their aims, tax treatment and the amount of risk involved. One or two categories are only suitable for the very rich, who can afford to take more significant risks. Others, such as certain types of National Savings, are only really suitable for those on a very low income.

These two groups apart, the aim for most people should be to acquire a balanced portfolio: in other words, a mix of investments variously designed to provide some income to supplement your pension and also some capital appreciation to maintain your standard of living long term.

Except for annuities and National Savings, which have sections to themselves, the different types of investment are listed by groups, as follows:

- Variable interest accounts
- Fixed interest securities
- Equities
- Long-term lock-ups

As a general strategy, it is a good idea to aim to choose at least one type of investment from each group.

Annuities

Definition. A normal life annuity is a very simple investment to understand. You pay a capital sum to an insurance company and in return are guaranteed a fixed income for life. The money is paid to you at fixed intervals and will remain exactly the same year in, year out. Payments are calculated according to life expectancy tables and for this reason an annuity may not really be a suitable investment for anyone under 70. Other than your age, the key factor affecting the amount you will receive in payments is the level of interest rates at the time you buy: the higher these are, the more you will receive.

An annuity would probably give you more immediate income than any other form of investment. But whether you actually get good value depends on how long you live. When you die, your capital will be gone and there will be no more payments. So if you die a short while after signing the contract, it will represent very bad value indeed. On the other hand, if you live a very long time, you may more than recoup your original capital.

As a precaution against early death, it is possible to take out a capital protected annuity or one guaranteed for a number of years: in other words, an annuity that runs for a specified period. Should you die before the end of the contract, the payments (which can be taken as a lump sum) will go to your partner or other beneficiary. The major drawback to this arrangement is that if you outlive the contract, you will not receive any more annuity income and your capital will have gone along with your security.

There are also other types of annuity, such as capital and income plans (or temporary annuities, as they are sometimes called) which pay you a small income, say, for a 10-year period, at the end of which your capital is returned. These are sometimes taken out, as a kind of holding operation, by people who are too young to obtain sufficiently attractive terms on a normal life annuity. You have to assess whether you could get a better return from another fixed interest security. There are also index-linked annuities, increasing annuities, unit-linked annuities and with-profits annuities.

Annuities, such as those described above, which you choose to buy as a purely optional purchase should not be confused with **pension-linked annuities** which are a required purchase for people with personal pensions (including Section 226 policies or retirement annuities) or with other types of money purchase pension plans. For further information about compulsory purchase annuities, see the 'Pensions' chapter, page 37.

Tax. Income tax on optional annuities is relatively low, as part of the income is allowed as a return on capital which is not taxable. Pension-linked annuities are fully taxable.

How to obtain. You can buy an annuity either direct from an insurance company or via an intermediary, such as an independent financial adviser (IFA). But shop around, since as mentioned above the payments vary considerably. To find an IFA, contact the following organisations: **IFA Promotion Ltd.**, 28 Greville Street, London EC1N 8SU. T:0117 971 1177; **IFA Association**, 12-13 Henrietta Street, London WC2E 8LH. T:0171 240 7878.

Assessment. Safe. Attractive if you live to a ripe old age. But highly vulnerable to inflation. Sacrifice of capital that might otherwise benefit successors.

National Savings

National Savings is one of the biggest savings institutions in the country. It is guaranteed by the government and all investments are backed by the Crown.

It is extremely easy to invest in National Savings, as all you need do is go to the post office. Most types of investment it offers are broadly similar to those provided by banks and other financial bodies. So rather than explain in detail the exact terms and conditions of, say, a National Savings Investment Account, it is easier to suggest that you pick up the relevant leaflet at the post office counter; or telephone the numbers shown a little further down.

National Savings Certificates, of which there are two types – Fixed interest and Index-linked – are free of tax. Although in most cases they do not pay a particularly high rate of interest, any investment that is tax free is of potential interest especially to higher rate taxpayers.

A long-standing feature of National Savings has been that non-taxpayers enjoyed the benefit of income receipts being paid gross, without deduction of tax. Since the abolition of composite rate tax, this now also applies to bank and building society interest. The one advantage, however, that National Savings still offers non-taxpayers is that there is no need for them to complete an Inland Revenue form to receive their money in full, as this is automatic.

The main investments offered by National Savings are:

- *Ordinary Account.* Pays a fairly low rate of variable interest. You can invest between £10 and £10,000. The first £70 of interest each year is free of tax (£140 for joint holdings). Ask for booklet DNS 760 at your post office.
- *Investment Account.* Pays an attractive rate of interest which increases with larger investments. You must give one month's notice if you wish to withdraw money. You can invest between £20 and £100,000. Interest is taxable but paid in full without deduction of tax at source. Ask for booklet DNS 761.
- *Income Bonds.* Pay attractive rates of interest, increasing with larger investments. Interest is taxable, but paid in full without deduction of tax at source. Three months' notice of withdrawal is necessary. You can invest between £2,000 and £250,000. Ask for booklet DNS 767.
- *42nd (current) Issue of National Savings Certificates.* Offers an attractive rate of fixed interest that is tax free. You can invest from £100 to £10,000. (National Savings offers special facilities to purchase up to an additional £20,000 for anyone cashing in earlier issues of certificates they have held for at least five years and re-investing in 42nd issue.) For maximum benefit, you must hold the certificates for five years. Ask for booklet DNS 762.
- *Index-linked Certificates* (8th issue). You can invest from £100 to £10,000. Interest is 3 per cent plus the increase in the Retail Prices Index but, to obtain this rate, certificates must be retained for five years. Interest is tax free. You can buy up to an additional £20,000 if you wish to reinvest earlier certificates held for at least five years. Ask for booklet DNS 763.
- *Gilts.* Can be bought through the National Savings Stock Register. Ask for booklet DNS 766.
- *Capital Bonds.* These offer a guaranteed interest rate, provided you do not withdraw your money before five years.
The one big drawback is that tax on the interest has to be paid annually – with higher bills every year as the interest grows – until you actually receive any money. However, for non-taxpayers especially, it offers an attractive investment as well perhaps as an ideal gift for grandparents to give children. Minimum purchase is £100 and Capital Bonds can be bought over the counter at post offices. Ask for booklet DNS 768.
- *Children's Bonus Bond.* Bonds are sold in multiples of £25 and the maximum total purchase per child is £1,000. Both interest and bonus, which will be paid after five

years, are free of income tax and need not be declared to the Inland Revenue. Interested parents and grandparents should ask for booklet DNS 769 at their local post office.

- *FIRST Option Bond.* Guaranteed growth bond, offering a 12-month fixed rate of interest provided the money is not withdrawn earlier. Come the anniversary date, investors can leave the money in the bond (after deduction of basic rate tax) for a further 12 months – at the then prevailing fixed interest rate – or terminate the arrangement. You can invest between £1,000 and £250,000. Ask for booklet DNS 770.

- *Series 2 Pensioners Guaranteed Income Bond.* A new bond specially for savers aged over 65, offering a guaranteed rate of 7.5 per cent interest per annum for the first five years. The income is paid monthly and, helpful to non-taxpayers, is paid gross. Minimum purchase is £500; the maximum, £20,000. Ask for booklet DNS 773.

The National Savings Sales Information Units offer help during normal office hours. For information about buying National Savings products, telephone: 0645 645000, Monday – Friday, 9 a.m. to 4.30 p.m. (all calls are charged at local rates).

Complaints. No reader has yet complained to us about their dealings with National Savings. However, for information, disputes which cannot be resolved with the Director of Savings can be referred to the independent adjudicator. The address to write to is: **The Adjudicator for National Savings**, Room 106/G, Treasury Chambers, Parliament Street, London SW1P 3AG.

Variable interest accounts

Few people who rely on interest from their savings to provide them with extra income in their retirement will need reminding that interest rates can go down as well as up. In the early nineties, many savers found their income slashed by around a third and, while to some extent this was partly mitigated by the drop in inflation, many older people especially were sorely out of pocket. This is not to say that variable interest accounts should necessarily be avoided (when interest rates were high, they provided one of the best homes for many people's money); but it is essential to understand how such accounts work – together with their advantages and drawbacks.

Recent changes. Over the past few years, most banks and building societies have introduced interest-bearing current accounts. Although an improvement on the standard current account, these do not qualify in anyone's language as a vehicle for investment and, as the banks themselves would be the first to agree, are not a suitable place for anyone to keep large savings for more than a short time. If you are tempted to switch to an interest-bearing current account, you should check very carefully what charges apply if you dip into overdraft. Likewise, you should enquire whether you are being offered 'tiered rates' – those paying the top rate of interest applicable on all your funds; or the less attractive 'banded rates' – those with two levels of interest, with a lower amount paid on, say, the first £500 or £1,000 and the higher rate only on funds above that amount.

A further point to investigate is whether there is a fixed monthly or other charge. This can sometimes change without customers being properly informed. You should check your monthly statement carefully and consider moving your account if you are dissatisfied.

Finally, you should know about TESSAs – or to give them their full name, Tax Exempt Special Savings Accounts – which were first introduced in January 1991. Despite the drop in interest rates since they were launched, TESSAs have remained very popular, due to their attractive tax advantages (see under 'Choosing a Deposit Account ' page 90).

Definition. Other than the interest-bearing current accounts described above, these are all *deposit accounts* (share accounts in building societies) of one form or another, arranged with banks, building societies, the National Savings Bank and with some financial institutions that operate such accounts jointly with banks. They include among others: basic deposit accounts, high interest accounts and fixed term deposit accounts.

Your money collects interest while it is on deposit, which may be automatically credited to your account or for which you may receive a regular cheque. Some institutions pay interest annually, others – on some or all of their accounts – will pay it monthly. If you have a preference, this is a point to check. The rate of interest will vary, up or down, according to the level of national interest rates. While you may get a poor return on your money if interest rates drop, your savings will nearly always be safe as you are not taking any kind of investment risk.

Access. Access to your money depends on the type of account you choose: you may have a cheque book and withdraw your money when you want; you may have to give a week's notice or slightly longer; or if you enter into a term account, you will have to leave your money deposited for the agreed specified period. In general, accounts where a slightly longer period of notice is required earn a better rate of interest.

Sum deposited. It is not usually sensible to consider a deposit account unless you have a minimum of £100. For certain types of account, the minimum investment could be anything from £500 to about £5,000. The terms tend to vary according to how keen the institutions are, at a given time, to attract small investors.

Tax. With the exception both of TESSAs, which are tax-free, and of the National Savings Bank, where interest is paid gross, tax is deducted at source – so you can spend the money without worrying about the tax implications. However, you must enter the interest on your tax return; and if you are a higher rate taxpayer, you will of course have additional liability.

Non-taxpayers can arrange to have their interest paid in full by completing a certificate which enables the financial institution to pay the interest gross. For further information see 'Abolition of composite rate tax' and 'Reclaiming tax overpaid', pages 70-71.

Choosing a deposit account

There are two main areas of choice: the type of deposit account and where to invest your money. The relative attractions of the different types of account and of the institutions themselves can vary, according to the terms being offered at the time. Generally speaking, however, the basic points are as follows:

Basic deposit account. This attracts a relatively low rate of interest. But it is both easy to set up and very flexible, as you can add small or large savings when you like and can usually withdraw your money without any notice. It is a much better option than simply leaving your money in a current account and is an excellent temporary home for your cash if you are saving short term for, say, a holiday. However, it is not recommended as a long-term savings plan.

High interest deposit account. Your money earns a higher rate of interest than it would on an ordinary deposit account. However, to open a high interest account you will need to deposit a minimum sum, which could be of the order of £500 to £1,000. While you can always add to this amount, if your basic deposit drops below the required minimum, your money will immediately stop earning the higher interest rate. If you frequently dip into overdraft, a high interest deposit account is worse than useless.

Fixed term deposit account. You deposit your money for an agreed period of time, which can vary from a few months to over a year. In return for this commitment, you will be paid a relatively star rate of interest.

As with high interest accounts, there is a minimum investment: roughly £1,500 to £5,000. If you need to withdraw your money before the end of the agreed term, there are usually hefty penalties. Before entering into a term account, you need to be sure that you can afford to leave the money on deposit. Additionally, you will need to take a view about interest rates: if they are generally low, your money may be better invested elsewhere.

A further important point is that you should keep a note of the date when the agreement expires. As a rule, your money will no longer earn preferential rates after the term has come to an end (unless of course you renew the agreement). The bank or other institution may not notify you in advance and may, quite legitimately, simply credit you with the normal interest rates after the contract's expiry.

Tax Exempt Special Savings Account (TESSA). TESSAs are special deposit accounts, designed to encourage saving, which, provided you leave the capital untouched for five years, allow you to keep all the interest free of tax. They are widely available from banks and building societies and work as follows.

Anyone over the age of 18 can open a TESSA. The maximum amount you are allowed to put into the scheme is £9,000 over a five-year period. This can either be paid in regular monthly amounts, of up to £150; or savings can be paid in annual sums, as follows: year one, a maximum of £3,000; years two, three and four, up to £1,800 each year; year five, up to £600.

The gross interest earned on the money is credited to the account each year. The capital (i.e. the savings you pay into the account) cannot be withdrawn until the expiry of the scheme at the end of year five, otherwise you lose the tax advantage. People who need some money are, however, allowed to withdraw part of the interest less basic rate tax without penalty – other than the obvious one that if they reduce their 'savings pot', they will lose the extra tax-free interest that could have been generated.

For most people paying tax who can afford to save for five years, TESSAs are an attractive investment. The only point to watch is that, as with any deposit account, interest rates tend to vary from one bank and building society to another, so the usual advice about shopping around applies. When comparing the rates, you should be aware that the sum quoted may be a fixed rate; or, and this is more usual, a variable rate which will alter up or down, in line with the general movement in interest rates.

N.B. If having saved the maximum each year for five years you are thinking of starting a new TESSA, you are allowed to roll over (i.e. reinvest) the whole of the £9,000 capital – but not the interest – from your original TESSA into a new account. You have six months from the date your first TESSA matures to decide. If you wish to continue, you can either keep the money with the same bank/building society or, if you think you can do better elsewhere, switch to another provider.

Information. For banks, enquire direct at your local high street branch. There will be leaflets available, describing the different accounts in detail. Or if you have any questions, you can ask to see your bank manager. You can also investigate the other banks to see whether they offer better terms.

For building societies, enquire at any building society branch or, better still, pop into several as the terms and conditions may vary quite widely.

The **Building Societies Association** at 3 Savile Row, London W1X 1AF offers a free range of helpful leaflets and information sheets, including: *Taxation of Building Society Interest* and a factsheet on investor protection. A *Directory of Members*, giving head office addresses and telephone numbers is also available.

The safety of your investment. No ordinary investor in a UK building society has lost a penny of his or her savings in living memory. Investors are protected by the legislative framework in which societies operate and also by the high standard of prudent management. There is a statutory protection scheme, guaranteeing individual investors with (at maximum) 90 per cent of their investment up to a ceiling of £20,000. Further details about the scheme are explained in the BSA information sheet, obtainable from the above address.

Complaints. As with banks and insurance companies, building societies now also have an Ombudsman. Individual members of building societies who have a complaint can appeal to him direct to investigate the matter, provided that the complaint has already been taken through the particular society's own internal disputes procedure and the matter is within the scope of the Ombudsman Scheme. Broadly speaking, there are five areas where the Ombudsman can intervene: the operation of share and deposit accounts; all kinds of loans and credits including mortgages; banking services; trusteeship; and executorship. The Ombudsman is able to make awards of up to £100,000. The address to contact is: **The Office of the Building Societies Ombudsman**, 16th Floor, Millbank Tower, Millbank, London SW1P 4QZ. T:0171 931 0044.

Details of the Banking Ombudsman are given in the section headed 'Banks' in Chapter 6, Financial Advisers.

Complaints about investment products, such as life assurance and unit trust products, purchased via banks and building societies are handled by the **PIA Ombudsman**, see page 122.

Other accounts

A growing number of unit trusts and other financial institutions now offer interest bearing accounts that are very similar to those run by banks and building societies.

Fixed interest securities

In contrast to variable interest accounts, fixed interest securities offer a fixed rate of interest which you are paid, regardless of what happens to interest rates generally. If you buy when the fixed rate is high and interest rates fall, you will nevertheless continue to be paid interest at the high rate specified in the contract note. However, if interest rates rise above the level when you bought, you will not benefit from the increase. As a generalisation, these securities give high income but only modest, if any, capital appreciation.

The list includes: high interest gilts, permanent interest bearing shares, local authority bonds and stock exchange loans, debentures and preference shares.

Corporate loans, debentures and preference shares

Definition. Companies use fixed interest loan, debenture and preference shares as one of the ways of raising money for expansion. Unlike ordinary shares, bonds and debentures pay a fixed guaranteed rate of interest, usually six monthly, but do not entitle the holder to share in the profits or to vote at the annual general meeting. By contrast, preference shares pay a fixed rate of dividend but this is not always guaranteed.

All are bought and sold on the Stock Exchange and, similar to gilts, their price rises and falls with the market view of future interest rates.

As with other shares, they are backed by the assets of the company and are therefore secure unless the company actually fails. But while your interest payments are virtually guaranteed, you could make a loss when you sell the shares – but equally, of course, a profit.

In theory, you could buy today and sell tomorrow. However, generally speaking it is inadvisable to purchase these shares other than as a long-term holding.

There will be stockbrokers' commission to pay and there is normally about a 10-day delay between selling and receiving the money.

To find a stockbroker, see Chapter 6, Financial Advisers.

Tax. Income tax on your interest is deducted at source. If you make a profit, there could be liability for capital gains tax.

Assessment. Normally pay better interest than gilts – but a more risky investment. There is a chance of a windfall in the event of a takeover. Only really suitable for experienced investors. Specified corporate bonds and preference shares are now allowable for PEPs and enjoy the normal (PEP) tax advantages (see page 100).

Gilt-edged securities
Definition. Usually known as 'gilts', these are stocks issued by the Government which guarantees both the interest payable and the repayment price which is promised on a given date.

The maturity date varies and can be anything from a few months to 20 years or longer. Accordingly, stocks are variously known as: short-dated, medium-dated and long-dated. A further category is undated. Additionally, there are index-linked gilts.

Prices for gilts are quoted per £100 of nominal stock. For example, a stock may be quoted as: 10 per cent *Treasury Stock* 1999, 99 1/2 – 100 1/4. In plain English, this means the following:

- 10 per cent represents the interest you will be paid. The rate is fixed and will not vary, whatever happens to interest rates generally. You will receive the interest payment twice yearly, 5 per cent each time.
- You are buying Treasury Stock.
- The maturity date is 1999.
- To buy the stock, you will have to pay £100.25p (i.e. 100 ¼).
- If you want to sell the stock, the market price you will get is £99.50p (i.e. 99 1/2).

In addition, when buying or selling, regard has to be given to the accrued interest which will have to be added to or subtracted from the price quoted.

Gilts are complicated by the fact that you can either retain them until their maturity date, in which case the Government will return the nominal value in full. Or you can sell them on the Stock Exchange at market value. This accounts for the different buying and selling prices that may be quoted.

Prices are affected by current interest rates. If interest rates are at 6 per cent, a gilt with a guaranteed interest payment of 10 per cent is a very attractive buy – so the price will rise. Conversely, if interest rates are 10 per cent, a guaranteed interest payment of 6 per cent is a poor proposition, so there will not be many buyers and the price will drop. Because gilts are so closely tied to interest rates, the price can fluctuate daily, often by quite big jumps.

Index-linked gilts, while operating on the same broad principle, are different in effect. They are designed to shield investors against inflation: they pay very low interest but are redeemable at a higher price than the initial purchase price, as their value is geared to the cost of living. They are most valuable when inflation is high but are even more sensitive than other gilts to optimum timing when buying or selling.

Tax. Income tax is normally deducted at source. However, this does not apply if you buy gilts on the National Savings Stock Register (NSSR), when instead the interest will be paid to you gross. This does not mean that you avoid paying it, simply that you must allow for a future tax bill before spending the money.

A particular attraction of gilts is that no capital gains tax is charged on any profit you may have made. But equally no relief is allowed for loss.

How to buy. You can buy gilts through banks, building societies, a stockbroker, financial intermediary or through National Savings via your post office. In all cases, you will be charged commission. Prices of gilts are published every day in all the quality newspapers under the heading 'British Funds'.

If you purchase through a stockbroker (see Chapter 6), you will get fairly immediate action. With National Savings you buy and sell by post, so by the time purchase is made for you the price may have changed. The office dealing with gilts makes every effort to carry out buying and selling instructions the same day if these are received by first post; but it cannot undertake to buy or sell at any specified price or on any particular day.

Buying gilts on the National Savings Stock Register may be cheaper especially for smaller purchases but you will not get advice as you would from a stockbroker. It is, however, extremely easy. All you need to do is complete an application form, contained in the booklet DNS 766, and send it with your cheque in the envelope provided. A booklet *Buying Gilts on the National Savings Stock Register* is available from most post offices. Alternatively you can address any queries to **National Savings**, Blackpool, Lancs FY3 9YP; or telephone 01253 766151.

All new issues of gilts can now be registered on the National Savings Stock Register. An advantage of buying a new issue is that there is no commission to pay.

Assessment. Gilts normally pay reasonably good interest and offer excellent security, in that they are backed by the Government. You can sell at very short notice and the stock is normally accepted by banks as security for loans, if you want to run an overdraft. This may not apply if you purchase through the NSSR.

However, gilts are not a game for amateurs as, if you buy or sell at the wrong time, you could lose money; and if you hold your stock to redemption, inflation could take its toll on your original investment. Index-linked gilts, which overcome the inflation problem, are generally speaking a better investment for higher rate taxpayers – not least because the interest paid is very low.

Gilt plans. This is a technique for linking the purchase of gilt-edged securities and with-profit life insurance policies to provide security of capital and income over a 10 to 20-year period. It is a popular investment for the commuted lump sum taken on retirement. These plans are normally obtainable from financial intermediaries, typically members of the PIA.

Useful reading
Investing in Gilts, a free guide for the small investor, available from the Registrar's Department, Bank of England, Southgate House, Southgate Street, Gloucester GL1 1UW.

Permanent Interest Bearing Shares (PIBS)
These are a form of investment offered by some building societies to financial institutions and private investors, as a means of raising share capital.

They have several features in common with gilts, as follows. They pay a fixed rate of interest which is set at the date of issue: this is likely to be on the high side when interest rates generally are low and on the low side when interest rates are high. The interest is paid twice yearly and – again, similar to gilts – there is no stamp duty to pay, nor capital gains tax on profits.

Despite the fact that PIBS are issued by building societies, they are very different from normal building society investments and have generally been rated as being in the high risk category. Anyone thinking of investing their money should seek professional advice. To buy the shares, you would need to go to a stockbroker or financial adviser.

Local authority bonds
Definition. One of the ways local authorities raise money is by selling bonds to the public. These come in two forms: Over the Counter or Tap Bonds, which can be purchased from local authorities direct; and Yearlings, which are bought and sold on the Stock Exchange.

In both cases, you receive a fixed rate of interest, which is usually paid to you automatically every six months. The interest rate offered can vary quite considerably from one council to another.

Tap bonds are similar to term deposit accounts, in that you undertake to keep your money deposited for a specified period, which can be anything from one to ten years. Once bought, they are non-negotiable: in other words, you cannot cash them before the end of the agreed term. Tap bonds are usually issued in units of £1,000 upwards. However, they have been declining sharply in popularity over the past few years with the result that many local authorities have discontinued them.

Yearlings, as the name implies, are one-year bonds. However, because they are traded on the Stock Exchange, you are not locked into your investment and can sell at any time. The minimum investment is usually £1,000. Additionally, you will have stockbrokers' commission to pay.

Tax. Tax on tap bonds is deducted at source so, if you are a basic rate taxpayer, you only need enter the interest on your tax return. Higher rate taxpayers will have the additional tax to pay. Non-taxpayers can reclaim the tax by completing a certificate which enables the financial institution to pay the interest gross. In the case of yearlings, if you make a profit by selling, there may be a liability for capital gains tax.

How to obtain. Apart from yearlings for which you have to go to a stockbroker or your bank manager (see Chapter 6, Financial Advisers), you simply contact the local authority whose bonds you wish to buy. You should ask for the Treasurer's Department.

Assessment. Like gilts, local authority investments can offer reasonably high income. Risk is fairly low but all holdings are vulnerable to inflation and long-term bonds, especially so. Yearlings offer you the possibility of a capital gain. However, although not necessarily a reason to ignore them, local authority bonds have been dwindling in popularity and are less available than a few years ago.

Equities

These are all stocks and shares, purchased in different ways and involving varying degrees of risk. They are designed to achieve capital appreciation as well as give you some regular income. Most allow you to get your money out within 30 days or less. In the past, equities were by and large only considered suitable for a privileged minority. Today, there are an estimated 10 million shareholders and the number is increasing. One reason is that, as the flotation of British Telecom (now BT) demonstrated, equities can be excellent money-spinners. Another is that over the last few years, investment has become very much easier, largely as a result of the growth in the unit trust movement and the increase in the number of telephone share dealing facilities.

Whatever people say, equities are always risky. But for those who believe in caution, the gamble can be substantially reduced by avoiding obviously speculative investments. Equities include: ordinary shares, unit trusts and personal equity plans.

Unit trusts
Definition. Unit trusts offer an alternative to buying shares on the Stock Exchange. Your money is pooled in a fund, run by professional managers, who invest the proceeds in a wide range of shares and other securities. The advantages are that: it is usually less risky than buying individual shares; it is very simple; you get professional management and there are no day-to-day decisions to make. Additionally, every trust is required by law to have a trustee to protect investors' interests.

Over the last twenty years, the number and variety of trusts has increased dramatically. Some specialise in producing high income; some, in maximising capital gains; others are mixed trusts, aiming to combine both virtues. Some of the newer trusts concentrate on particular sectors, such as: money market instruments, convertible shares, European, American, Far Eastern or other overseas markets. There are also cash unit trusts which invest in the money markets and offer rates of interest comparable to those of building society instant access accounts.

The minimum investment in some of the more popular trusts is £500; in others, it can be as high as £10,000. Many trusts allow you to purchase units for smaller amounts on a regular monthly savings plan.

There is often a front end fee of around 5 to 6 per cent to join the trust, although this may be lower for unit trust PEPs. Certain management companies have recently abolished the front end fee, although in some cases this has been replaced with an exit charge when the units are sold.

Investors' contributions to the trust are divided into units, and proportionate to the amount they have invested, all unit holders receive an income distribution – normally paid every six months – or can choose to have their income reinvested.

As with ordinary shares, you can sell all or some of your investment by telling the unit trust managers that you wish to do so. The price you will receive is called 'the bid price'. This is published daily, in respect of all the main unit trusts, in the financial pages of the quality newspapers.

How to obtain. Units are purchased from the management companies, which can be: banks, building societies, insurance companies, stockbrokers, financial intermediaries or specialist unit trust management groups. Some advertise direct in the national newspapers and financial magazines. Some use salesmen or financial intermediaries. The bigger groups tend to use all these techniques.

You will be asked to complete a form, stating how many units you want in which particular trust, and then send it to the company with your cheque.

For a list of unit trusts, you can look in the *Financial Times*. Alternatively, write to the **Unit Trust Information Service** at 65 Kingsway, London WC2B 6TD; or call the Information Service on 0181 207 1361 to obtain a copy of *The Unit Trust Directory*. There is also a range of booklets, obtainable from the Information Service, including: *Unit Trusts and You: an introduction to unit trusts; A User's Handbook: guide on how to choose a unit trust*; and factsheets on PEPS, Emerging Markets and Monthly Savings Schemes.

Tables comparing the performance of the various unit trusts are published in specialist magazines, such as *Money Management, Money Observer and What Investment*.

With over 1,500 trusts from which to choose, it is important to get professional advice. You can ask an independent adviser, your bank, an accountant or solicitor. For further information see Chapter 6, Financial Advisers.

Tax. PEP unit trusts have special advantages (see PEPs, page 100). Otherwise, tax treatment is identical to ordinary shares (see next section).

Assessment. An ideal method for smaller investors to buy stocks and shares: both less risky and easier. Some of the more specialist trusts are also suitable for those with a significant investment portfolio.

Complaints. Complaints about the selling of unit trusts are handled by the PIA Ombudsman. He has power to order awards of up to £50,000 (with discretion to recommend higher amounts).

Before approaching the Ombudsman, you must first try to resolve the problem with the management company direct. All PIA members must have a proper system for handling complaints and it is also obligatory for them to participate in the Ombudsman Scheme. If your complaint is not settled within two months, the company should advise you of your right to refer the matter to the Ombudsman. Whether they inform you or not, the address to contact is: **The PIA Ombudsman Bureau**, Centre Point, 103 New Oxford Street, London WC1A 1QH. T:0171 240 3838.

If, rather than its selling or marketing techniques, your complaint against a unit trust group is about an investment matter, you should contact IMRO (see 'SROs' further in the chapter).

Ordinary shares listed on the Stock Exchange
Definition. Public companies issue shares as a method of raising money. When you buy shares and become a shareholder in a company, you own a small part of the business and are entitled to participate in its profits through a dividend which is normally paid six monthly.

Dividends go up and down according to how well the company is doing and it is possible that in a bad year no dividends at all will be paid. However, in good years, dividends can increase very substantially.

The money you invest is unsecured. This means that, quite apart from any dividends, your capital could be slashed in value – or if the company goes bankrupt, you could lose the lot. Against this, if the company performs well you could enormously increase your wealth.

The value of a company's shares is decided by the stock market. Thousands of large and small investors are taking a view on each company's prospects and this creates the market price. The price of a share can fluctuate daily and this will affect both how much you have to pay, if you want to buy; and how much you will make (or lose), if you want to sell.

To become an investor you can write to the **London Stock Exchange**, Old Broad Street, London EC2N 1HP for a list of brokers who would be willing to deal for you (see Chapter 6, Financial Advisers).

Alternatively, you can go to the securities department of your bank – or to one of the many share shops – who will place the order for you.

Another option which has become increasingly popular are telephone share dealing services, which offer an easy, low-cost way of buying and selling shares over the 'phone. A possible drawback is that most share lines operate an execution-only service – i.e. they accept instructions but do not give advice – which is fine if you know exactly what shares you want to purchase or sell but not so good if you want investment help. However, as part of the service, some share lines are happy to provide factual information. For example, Sharelink has launched a range of publications and a telephone service giving details of analysts' recommendations and other data. For prices and other information, call **Sharelink** on 0121 200 2242.

Whether you use a stockbroker, a share shop or a telephone share dealing service, you will be charged both commission and stamp duty which is $^1/_2$ per cent. You will be issued with a share certificate which you or your financial adviser must keep, as you will have to produce it when you wish to sell all or part of your holding.

It is possible, when approaching a stockbroker or other share-dealing service, that you will be asked to deposit money for your investment up-front or advised that you should use a nominee account. This is because a new 5-day rolling settlement system has been introduced (by which time the transaction, including payment for the shares, must be settled) instead of 10 days as previously. It is planned in the long term to shorten the period to 3-day settlement. Although there are gains in having a shorter transaction period, the expectation is that investors will either end up paying more for the service or will need to opt for a nominee account which usually means missing out on some shareholder rights, such as receipt of the annual report and access to various benefits – including shareholders' perks.

The number of companies offering perks has been increasing over the past few years. Most come in the form of discounts on goods and services including reduced price travel, vouchers for clothes, concessionary prices on hotel and restaurant bills and many others. Among the 1995 crop were a centre court ticket for Wimbledon, 15 per cent off a luxury cruise, premium discounts of 10 per cent on home, motor and travel insurance policies, 20 per cent off the price of certain health screens, a 25 per cent saving on dry-cleaning bills and £600 discount (up to a maximum of £3,000) on every £25,000 spent towards the purchase of a house. In some companies, to be eligible a minimum shareholding is required and/or retention of the shares for a minimum period. Enjoyable as such perks are, it goes without saying that investors should only buy stocks if the share is worthwhile in its own right. A cheaper holiday is no bargain if the price of obtaining it is a dud investment!

If you would like to know what perks are on offer, see *Perks for Shareholders*. Price is £5, obtainable from Henry Cooke, Lumsden, Piercy House, 7-9 Copthall Avenue, London EC2R 7EH.

There are two types of share both quoted on the Stock Exchange that are potentially suitable for small investors. These are investment trusts and convertible loan stocks. Another possibility, but only for those who can afford more risky investments, are warrants.

Investment trusts are companies just like ICI and Shell but, instead of making products to sell, they invest in the shares of other companies, providing a spread of risk. You can buy investment trusts through a saving and investment scheme (offering monthly savings, lump sum investment and dividend re-investment) which is simple, cheap, and gives a choice of over 190 different trusts.

One important group of trusts is known as split capital trusts, which separate capital growth and income growth. These can be mixed and matched to meet your needs during retirement and are well worth investigating.

For a free information pack on investment trusts, saving schemes and PEPs, write to **The Association of Investment Trust Companies**, Durrant House, 8-13 Chiswell Street, London EC1Y 4YY.

Convertible loan stocks give you a fixed guaranteed income for a certain length of time and offer you the opportunity to convert them into ordinary shares. While capital appreciation prospects are lower, the advantage of convertible loans is that they usually provide significantly higher income than ordinary dividends. They are now also allowable for PEPs.

Warrants are issued by companies or investment trusts to existing shareholders either at launch or by way of an additional bonus. Each warrant carries the right of the shareholder to purchase additional shares at a pre-determined price on specific dates in the future. As such, warrants will command their own price on the stockmarket. These are a high-risk investment and professional advice is essential.

Tax. As a result of 1993 Budget changes in the treatment of advance corporation tax, dividend income has generally been cut by 6.25 per cent. Although a problem for higher-rate taxpayers, in practice most basic and lower-rate taxpayers should not be affected. If during the year you make profits by selling shares that in total exceed £6,000, you could be liable for capital gains tax.

Assessment. Although dividend payments generally start low, in good companies they are likely to increase over the years and so provide a first class hedge against inflation. The best equities are an excellent investment. In others, you can lose all your money. Good advice is critical as this is a high risk/high reward market.

Personal equity plan
Definition. The major appeal of a PEP is that dividends and capital gains on shares are exempt from both income tax and capital gains tax.

The scheme works as follows: anyone over the age of 18 can invest up to £6,000 a year in UK or EC shares listed on the Stock Exchange or on the Alternative Investment Market (AIM) or on a recognised stock exchange of any member state of the EC.

If you wish, all the money can be invested in a unit or investment trust, provided that 50 per cent of the holdings of such trusts are in UK/EC equities. In trusts, where the holdings are below 50 per cent, the amount you can invest is limited to £1,500.

In the 1994 budget, the Chancellor extended the range of eligible investments for general PEPs to include specified corporate bonds, convertibles and preference shares.

A further option, if you own shares in your company's 'all employee share scheme', is that you can transfer your holding to a single company PEP with all its tax advantages, provided this is within three months of your receiving the shares. The maximum annual investment in a single company PEP is £3,000.

Alternatively, you could invest £3,000 per annum in the shares of any other single company, bringing your total maximum allowed PEP investment to £9,000 a year.

The money has to be invested through an authorised manager, for example: a stockbroker, bank, building society or financial intermediary.

Tax. PEPS are free of both income tax and capital gains tax. The tax credit on dividends (i.e. 20 per cent) will be claimed on your behalf by the plan manager. Capital gains tax losses incurred on other investments cannot be offset against PEP profits (and vice versa).

Assessment. The inclusion of corporate bonds among the list of eligible investments has made PEPs potentially attractive to many people for whom they were previously unsuitable. Corporate bond PEPs are most likely to appeal to traditional bank and building society savers, as they yield a relatively high income and the risk is much lower than with ordinary PEPs invested in equities. However, they are not totally risk-free, as capital values may fall; also (this is a point to check) charges may be deducted from capital rather than from the income.

Other types of PEPs lost some of their glitter as a result of the 1993 tax credit changes, which have the effect of reducing a PEP's tax benefit. Basic rate taxpayers will need to weigh up carefully whether they might be better off investing their money elsewhere. For higher-rate taxpayers, PEPs are still worthwhile although their value has become eroded by 6.25 per cent. As a general point, shares can go down as well as up. More than ever, the charges could be a critical factor in deciding whether a PEP is a wise buy.

Useful reading
PepGuide: compares details in tabular form of PEP schemes currently available. £12.95 from **Chase de Vere Investments**, 63 Lincoln's Inn Fields, London WC2A 3JX.
IR 89, *Personal Equity Plans (PEPs)*, free from any tax office.

Small businesses

Many people invest in a small business more as a way of providing themselves with a retirement interest than to make money. Although if you are lucky it is possible to achieve both, there is no escaping the fact that investing in small firms is highly risky. Quite apart from the fact that about one in three fails, you may have a problem in realising any profits you make, as – unlike companies listed on the Stock Exchange – most small business shares do not have a ready market.

If despite the warnings the idea of becoming a business angel still appeals, you should know about Capital Gains Tax Re-Investment Relief and also the Enterprise Investment Scheme which offers investors attractive tax relief benefits. See pages 226 and 249.

Another possibility are **Venture Capital Trusts**. These are a new type of investment trust aimed at encouraging more investment in smaller companies. To qualify as a VCT, at least 70 per cent of a Trust's investments must be in unquoted companies and, to give investors an exit route, it must be quoted on the Stock Exchange. In theory at least, it is less risky than investing in just one or two enterprises, which could both fail.

People investing in VCTs will be exempt both: from income tax on their dividends and from capital gains tax on disposal of their shares for investments of up to £100,000 a year provided the shares are held for at least five years. They will also receive roll-over relief on any gains used to invest in the VCT. At time of writing, it was still too early for there to be a list of venture capital companies definitely planning to set up a VCT. Best advice is to watch the 'business pages' or to contact the **British Venture Capital Association (BVCA)**, Essex House, 12-13 Essex Street, London WC2R 3AA. T:0171 240 3846.

Long-term lock-ups

Certain types of investment, mostly offered by insurance companies, provide fairly high guaranteed growth in exchange for your undertaking to leave a lump sum with them or to pay regular premiums for a fixed period, probably 10 years. The list includes: life assurance policies, investment bonds and some types of National Savings certificates.

Life assurance policies
Definition. Life assurance can provide you with one of two main benefits: it can either provide your successors with money when you die or it can be used as a savings plan to provide you with a lump sum (or income) on a fixed date.

In the past, it was very much an 'either – or' situation: you chose whichever type of policy suited you and the insurance company paid out accordingly. In recent years, however, both types of scheme have become more flexible and many policies allow you to incorporate features of the other. This can have great advantages from the point of view of enabling you 'to have your cake and eat it'. But the result is that some of the definitions appear a bit contradictory.

There are three basic types of life assurance: whole life policies, term policies and endowment policies.

Whole life policies are designed to pay out on your death. In its most straightforward form, the scheme works as follows: you pay a premium every year and, when you die, your beneficiaries receive the money.

As with an ordinary household policy, the insurance only holds good if you continue the payments. If one year you did not pay and were to die, the policy could be void and your successors would receive nothing.

Term policies involve a definite commitment. As opposed to paying premiums every year, you elect to make regular payments for an agreed period: for example, until such time as your children have completed their education, say eight years.

If you die during this period, your family will be paid the agreed sum in full. If you die after the end of the term (when you have stopped making payments), your family will normally receive nothing.

Most policies, whether term or otherwise, pay the money in lump sum form. Under term assurance, it is possible, however, to arrange for the benefit to be paid out as regular income. This is known as **family income benefit**. The income payments will cease at the end of the insured term.

There is a fairly widespread view that term and whole life policies, while eminently sensible for people in their thirties or forties, are not really suitable for older people, since: on the one hand death is at some stage inevitable; while on the other, when children grow up, there is less requirement to provide for their security.

Additionally, many people argue that when income is tight, as it often is on retirement, this is one expense that can cheerfully be dropped. While generally true, the thinking could nevertheless prove short-sighted. A major problem for many widows is that, when their husband dies, part of his pension dies with him – leaving them with a significantly reduced income. A lump sum or regular income plan could make all the difference in helping to bridge the gap. Alternatively – and for many this is a more attractive option – whole life or term can be converted into an endowment policy.

Endowment policies are essentially a savings plan. You sign a contract to pay regular premiums over a number of years and in exchange receive a lump sum on a specific date.

Most endowment policies are written for periods, varying from 10 to 25 years. Once you have committed yourself, you have to go on paying every year (as with term assurance). There are heavy penalties if, after having paid for a number of years, you decide that you no longer wish to continue. According to the terms of the policy, you may receive a token lump sum based on the premiums you have paid; or you may receive nothing at all. This is especially likely to apply if you withdraw during the early years. (However, see heading 'Alternatives to surrendering a policy' on page 106.)

An important feature of endowment policies is that they are linked in with death cover. If you die before the policy matures, the remaining payments are excused and your successors will be paid a lump sum on your death.

Endowment policies are a very popular way of making extra financial provision for retirement. They combine the advantages of guaranteeing you a lump sum, with a built-in life assurance proviso. However, the amount of money you stand to receive can vary by literally thousands of pounds depending on the charges you pay. According to an **Office of Fair Trading** report *Fair Trading and Life Insurance Products*, these can vary between 5.8 and 1.4 per cent on 10-year plans and between 2.6 and 0.4 per cent on 25-year plans. At time of writing, the OFT calculated that this could make a difference in pay-out of 30 per cent on a 10-year policy and around 40 per cent on a 25-year policy.

The OFT also provided evidence of the huge sums of money that many people have lost by surrendering their policy early and was highly critical of some companies selling endowment policies. Research shows that, when signing the contract, many people had not properly understood (1) what charges were involved (2) that most of their hoped-for profits only accrue in the 10 final years – so by ceasing payments early they risk losing thousands of pounds. Hopefully, the public should now be much better informed. Since January 1995 life offices are required to show in writing, year by year, what a policy would be worth if it were cashed in early.

Options. Both whole life policies and endowment policies offer two basic options: with profits or without profits. Very briefly the difference is as follows:

Without profits. This is sometimes known as 'guaranteed sum assured'. What it means is that the insurance company guarantees you a specific fixed sum (provided of course you meet the various terms and conditions). You know the amount in advance and this is the sum you – or your successors – will be paid.

With profits. You are paid a guaranteed fixed sum plus an addition, based on the profits that the insurance company has made, by investing your annual or monthly payments. The basic premiums are higher and, by definition, the profits element is not known in advance. If the insurance company has invested your money wisely, a 'with profits' policy provides a useful hedge against inflation. If its investment policy is mediocre, you could have paid higher premiums for very little extra return.

Unit linked. This is a refinement of the 'with profits' policy, in that the investment element of the policy is linked in with a unit trust.

Other basics. Premiums can normally be paid monthly or annually, as you prefer. Size of premium varies enormously, depending on: the type of policy you choose and the amount of cover you want. Also, of course, some insurance companies are more competitive than others. As very general guidance, £35-£40 a month would probably be a normal starting figure. Again as a generalisation, higher premiums tend to give better value as relatively less of your contribution is swallowed up in administrative costs.

As a condition of insuring you, some policies require that you have a medical check. This is more likely to apply if very large sums are involved. More usually, all that is required is that you fill in and sign a declaration of health. It is very important that this should be honestly completed: if you make a claim on your policy and it is subsequently discovered that you gave misleading information, your policy could be declared void and the insurance company could refuse to pay.

Many insurance companies offer a better deal if you are a non-smoker. Some also offer more generous terms if you are teetotal. Women generally pay less than men of the same age because of their longer life expectancy.

How to obtain. Policies are usually available through banks, insurance companies, independent financial advisers (IFAs) and building societies. The biggest problem for most people is the sheer volume of choice. Another difficulty can be understanding the small print: terms and conditions which sound very similar may obscure important differences which could affect your benefit.

An accountant could advise you, in general terms, whether you are being offered a good deal or otherwise. However, if it is a question of choosing a specific policy best suited to your requirements, it is usually advisable to consult an IFA. For help in finding an IFA in your area, contact the following organisations: **IFA Promotion Ltd.**, 28 Greville Street, London EC1N 8SU. T:0117 971 1177; **IFA Association**, 12-13 Henrietta Street, London WC2E 8LH. T:0171 240 7878. See also Chapter 6, Financial Advisers.

As general wisdom, before buying a policy it is sensible to check whether the person selling it to you is an independent financial adviser, or a tied agent who is restricted to selling his/her company's (or institution's) own products. You need not feel in the slightest bit embarrassed to ask the individual concerned since this is a question that most people dealing in financial services expect and are happy to answer (as well as being required to do so by law).

Disclosure rules. Under the new disclosure rules, which came into force during 1995, salesmen must give clients certain essential information before a contract is signed. Although the requirements vary according to different types of product, they normally include a 'key features' document (explaining the product, the risk factors, charges, benefits, surrender value if the policy is terminated early, tax treatment and salesman's commission/remuneration) and a 'reason why' letter, explaining why a particular product/policy is recommended. For further information, see 'Investor protection', page 108.

The **Association of British Insurers (ABI)** have a number of useful information sheets on life insurance. Contact ABI, 51 Gresham Street, London EC2V 7HQ.

Tax. Under current legislation, the proceeds of a qualifying policy – whether taken as a lump sum or in regular income payments (as in the case of Family Income Benefit) – are free of all tax.

Assessment. Life assurance is normally a sensible investment, whether the aim is to provide death cover or the benefits of a lump sum to boost your retirement income. It has the merit of being very attractive from a tax angle and additionally certain policies provide good capital appreciation – although a point to be aware of is that recent bonuses have tended to be considerably lower than their projected amount. However, you are locked into a long-term commitment. So, even more than most areas, choosing the right policy is very important. Shop around, take advice and, above all, do not sign anything unless you are absolutely certain that you understand every last dot and comma.

Complaints. Complaints about life assurance products, including alleged misselling, are now handled by the PIA Ombudsman, instead of as previously by the Insurance

Ombudsman. A major plus is that, whereas before not all life companies needed to join the Insurance Ombudsman Scheme, membership of the PIA Ombudsman Scheme is compulsory.

Before approaching the Ombudsman, you would first need to try to resolve a dispute with the company direct. For further information, contact: **The PIA Ombudsman Bureau**, Centre Point, 103 New Oxford Street, London WC1A 1QH. T:0171 240 3838.

Alternatives to surrendering a policy

As already mentioned, there are heavy penalties if you surrender an endowment policy before its maturity. Some people however, either because they can no longer afford the payments or for some other reason, wish to terminate the agreement – regardless of any losses they may make/or investment gains they sacrifice.

Instead of simply surrendering the policy to the insurance company, people in this situation have two alternative options, both of which stand to yield them a higher return than surrender. The one is to sell the policy by auction; the other to sell it to a market-maker.

Probably the best known specialist auctioneer in this field is H E Foster & Cranfield. They hold fortnightly auctions in London, and once a month outside London, and suggest to clients a reserve price, which by definition would be higher than the surrender value – otherwise they would not accept it on their books. They charge a £50 registration fee plus commission, which is a third of the excess (they make at auction) above the surrender value quoted. While auctioneers can never guarantee a sale, auctioning a policy is a very low risk gamble, since if the policy fails to reach its reserve it can still be surrendered in the normal way. Furthermore, if the policy does not sell at auction, the £50 registration fee would not be payable. For further information, contact: **H E Foster & Cranfield**, 20 Britton Street, London EC1M 5NQ. T:0171 608 1941.

If rather than auction a policy, you prefer to sell it outright, Beale Dobie & Co. Ltd. may be able to help you. They deal in all endowment with-profits life policies (not unit linked) and say, that to be of interest to them, the policy: must have run at least a quarter of its life; have a maximum of 15 years to run before maturity; and must be with a leading life office. Provided these conditions are met, they can often make an immediate cash offer which, if accepted by the vendor, would be paid in the same time-scale as surrender. As with Foster & Cranfield, they would not make an offer unless that offer exceeded the surrender value.

Endowment policies purchased by Beale Dobie are offered for investment as Traded Endowment Policies (TEPs), providing a combination of security with a good potential return. TEPs are proving very popular with people either approaching or upon retirement as an effective way of topping up savings.

For further information, contact: **Beale Dobie & Co Ltd.**, Fullbridge Mill, Maldon, Essex CM9 5FN. T:01621 851133.

For those looking for investment possibilities, second-hand policies could be worth investigating.

A full list of authorised dealers that buy and sell mid-term policies is obtainable from the **Association of Policy Market Makers**. T:0171 739 3949.

Investment bonds

Definition. This is the method of investing a lump sum with an insurance company, in the hope of receiving a much larger sum back at a specific date – normally a few years later.

All bonds offer life assurance cover as part of the deal.

A particular feature of some bonds is that the managers have wide discretion to invest your money in almost any type of security. The risk/reward ratio is, therefore, very high. While bonds can achieve significant capital appreciation, you can also lose a high percentage of your investment.

All bond proceeds are free of basic rate tax but higher rate tax is payable. However, the higher rate taxpayer can withdraw up to 5 per cent of his/her initial investment each year and defer the higher rate tax liability for 20 years or until the bond is cashed in full – whichever is earlier.

Equally, although there is no capital gains tax on redemption of a bond (or on switching between funds), some CGT may be payable by the fund itself which could affect its investment performance.

Companies normally charge a front end fee of around 6 per cent plus a small annual management fee, usually not related to performance.

Some financial institutions – banks, unit trusts, and others – offer investment bonds through their insurance subsidiaries. Accordingly, almost any type of financial adviser will have some knowledge of this area.

The performance of existing bonds is monitored each month in *Money Management* and other specialist magazines.

N.B. Investment bonds should not be confused with corporate bonds which are now allowable for PEPs (see page 100).

Tax. Tax treatment is very complicated, as it is influenced by your marginal income tax rate in the year of encashment. For this reason, it is generally best to buy a bond when you are working and plan to cash it after retirement.

Assessment. This investment is more likely to be attractive to the sophisticated investor, with high earnings in the years before retirement.

Other investment points

In recent years there has been a considerable increase in the number of alternative investments to those which can only be purchased on a recognised investment exchange (such as the Stock Exchange). These include traded options and sponsored securities, some but by no means all of which are also traded on the Stock Exchange.

Under the Financial Services Act, firms which make markets in shares of this type have to be authorised, either by the Securities and Investments Board (SIB) or the

Securities and Futures Authority – see 'Investor protection' below – and have to obey the same stringent conduct of business rules as other authorised companies. In addition, they have to abide by special rules for those transactions which take place outside a recognised investment exchange.

It is important to realise that investments of this kind tend to be more risky than those traded on recognised exchanges. Not only are the companies in whose shares you invest more likely to fail, but also you should remember that if the shares are traded by only one market maker, you may not be able to sell them if the market maker goes out of business or ceases to trade in that particular stock. Advertisements for shares which may not be easily marketable have to include a statement to this effect. Equally, where an adviser recommends such an investment he is obliged to make you aware of the difficulties you may face should you wish to sell.

While these safeguards help to clarify the nature of such investments, it is nevertheless still important for you to be careful in investing your money and to assess the degree of risk you are prepared to bear before committing yourself.

Useful reading

Fair Shares by Simon Rose. A layman's guide to buying and selling stocks. Mercury. Price £5.95.

The Share Book by Rosemary Burr, published by Rosters. Price £5.95.

Investor protection

Over the past few years, we have heard a great deal about investor protection.

Since the Financial Services Act there is now a set of stringent rules on businesses offering investment services and also a powerful watchdog body, namely the Securities and Investments Board (SIB). Additionally, there are a number of Self-Regulating Organisations (SROs) and Recognised Professional Bodies (RPBs), charged with the responsibility of regulating businesses that are 'fit and proper' to operate in the investment field and of monitoring their activities via 'spot checks' and other means.

The main effects of these changes are as follows:

- Investment businesses (including individuals such as accountants or solicitors giving investment advice) are not at liberty to operate without authorisation – or specific exemption from authorisation – from their appropriate SRO or RPB, or from the SIB direct. Operating without such authorisation is a criminal offence.
- Under the polarisation rules, businesses may either promote their own in-house investment plans (unit trusts, insurance policies and so on) or they must act as independent financial advisers (IFAs) and have no vested interest in any product they may recommend. The dual intention is: (1) to enable customers to know the status of an adviser, i.e. whether he/she is a company sales representative, a tied agent or an IFA and (2) to ensure that those who call themselves independent financial advisers, or intermediaries, can legitimately offer 'best advice' by virtue of being free of commercial bias.

- Investment businesses must adhere to a proper complaints procedure with provision for customers to receive fair redress, where appropriate.
- Unsolicited visits and telephone calls to sell investments are for the most part banned. Where these are allowed, (as in the case of unit trusts, life assurance and certain other package products), should a sale result, the customer will have a 14-day 'cooling-off period'. The cooling-off period is to give the customer time to explore other options before deciding whether to cancel the contract or not.
- There is also provision for disclosure of the following information to purchasers of life assurance products: a financial adviser's remuneration including commission (expressed in cash terms); and the company's costs and expenses, also expressed in cash terms, to enable investors to make inter-company comparisons.

  Additionally, certain 'key features' should be provided to investors, including: information on the penalties of early surrender, easier identification of intermediary status and the provision of a 'reason why' letter explaining the rationale on which recommendations are based. Expenses to do with life assurance products should be expressed in actual money terms (i.e. pence in the pound) which people can understand. This product and commission disclosure has been mandatory since 1 January 1995. Work is continuing to bring unit trusts into the current regulatory regime.

In practice, most members of the public are unlikely to require recourse to one of the regulatory organisations since, as already stated, it is the job of SROs and RPBs to authorise membership of any investment business within their appropriate sector and to establish monitoring procedures to check that the investor protection rules are being properly followed. In turn, SROs and RPBs are answerable to the Securities and Investments Board, which itself is directly accountable to the Treasury. If you need to contact SIB, the address to write to is: **Securities and Investments Board (SIB)**, Gavrelle House, 2-14 Bunhill Row, London EC1Y 8RA. T:0171 638 1240.

SROs. Names and addresses of the three Self-Regulating Organisations are as follows:

IMRO (Investment Management Regulatory Organisation), Broadwalk House, 6 Appold Street, London EC2A 2AA. T:0171 628 6022.

PIA (Personal Investment Authority), 7th Floor, 1 Canada Square, Canary Wharf, London E14 5AZ. T:0171 538 8860.

SFA (Securities and Futures Authority), Cottons Centre, Cottons Lane, London SE1 2QB. T:0171 378 9000.

PIA (Personal Investment Authority). Until recently, both FIMBRA and LAUTRO were included in the list of SROs. Both have ceased to exist and the PIA is now the sole regulator for the selling or marketing of personal investment products including unit trusts, life assurance and personal pensions.

As well as making it easier for the public to know whom to contact if they have a query or problem, a further gain is that there is now also a focal point for investors to make a complaint to in the form of the PIA Ombudsman.

RPBs. The following professional bodies have received recognition from SIB:

The Law Society of England and Wales, 113 Chancery Lane, London WC2A 1PL. T:0171 242 1222.

The Law Society of Scotland, The Law Society's Hall, 26-28 Drumsheugh Gardens, Edinburgh EH3 7YR. T:0131 226 7411.

The Law Society of Northern Ireland, Law Society House, 98 Victoria Street, Belfast BT1 3JZ. T:01232 231614.

The Institute of Chartered Accountants in England and Wales, PO Box 433, Chartered Accountants' Hall, Moorgate Place, London EC2P 2BJ. T:0171 920 8682.

The Institute of Chartered Accountants of Scotland, 27 Queen Street, Edinburgh EH2 1LA. T:0131 225 5673.

The Institute of Chartered Accountants in Ireland, Chartered Accountants House, 87-89 Pembroke Road, Dublin 4. T:00 353 1 668 0400.

The Chartered Association of Certified Accountants, 29 Lincoln's Inn Fields, London WC2A 3EE. T:0171 242 6855.

The Insurance Brokers' Registration Council, 15 St. Helen's Place, London EC3A 6DS. T:0171 588 4387.

The Institute of Actuaries, Staple Inn Hall, High Holborn, London WC1V 7QJ. T:0171 242 0106.

Complaints

If you have a complaint against an authorised firm, in the first instance you should take it up with the firm concerned: you may be able to resolve the matter at this level, since all authorised firms are obliged to have a complaints procedure. If, however, you do not receive satisfaction, you can take your complaint to the regulatory body which has authorised the company. Should you still not be satisfied, you can approach the relevant ombudsman or referee who will investigate the matter on your behalf and may even be able to get compensation for you.

For investors, the most likely person to contact would be the PIA Ombudsman. He handles complaints against PIA member firms, namely: unit trusts, life companies (including life assurance arms of banks and building societies), fund management companies and independent financial advisers. The list includes insurance salesman and others selling personal pensions. The Ombudsman can award compensation, including a sum for distress and inconvenience.

As is normal, before approaching the Ombudsman, you first need to try to resolve the dispute with the company, or adviser, concerned.

The address for the Ombudsman is: **The PIA Ombudsman Bureau**, Centre Point, 103 New Oxford Street, London WC1A 1QH. T:0171 240 3838.

Warning

Although the new investor protection legislation should improve standards and help to rid the financial services industry of cowboy operators, as the Securities and Investments Board writes in its published guide: 'All investment carries some degree of risk, whether relating to business or general economic conditions. The existence of SIB no more removes the need for investors to pay attention to where they place their money than the existence of the highway code removes the need to look before crossing the road.'

The existence of SIB and the setting up of the various SROs and RPBs does at least, however, enable you to check on the credentials of anyone purporting to be a financial adviser or trying to persuade you to invest your money in an insurance policy, bond, unit or investment trust, equity, futures contract or similar. If either they or the organisation they represent are not authorised by a relevant SRO, RPB or by SIB, you are very strongly recommended to leave well alone.

Useful reading

Compensation for Investors; Investment Businesses: What to Do if You Need to Complain; How to Spot the Investment Cowboys; The Central Register and *The Background to Investor Protection*; these are all available free from: Securities and Investments Board, Gavrelle House, 2-14 Bunhill Row, London EC1Y 8RA.

Your retirement could last 30 years.

Will your savings make it to extra time?

The fact that more of us are living to a greater age could put a big squeeze on State pensions. So it's all the more important that your own savings will be able to support you in future. What's your best tactic? Talk to an independent financial adviser. He or she will give you expert advice on all your future financial plans. And because that advice will be impartial, you can be sure you'll get the right solution for your own particular circumstances. Call us today on the number below for a free information pack. And start building towards your retirement goals. **0117 971 1177**

It's your future. Take control of it.

The Power of Independent Financial Advice:

- An impartial choice from all the financial options available
- Expertise in savings, investments, pensions, protection
- A review of your individual needs

Wherever you see the blue sign.

6   Financial Advisers

If there is one golden rule when it comes to money matters, it must be: when in doubt, ask. This applies as much if it is a term with which you are unfamiliar, as whether you are wondering how best to invest your savings.

When thinking ahead to retirement planning, it is especially important to get as much advice as possible. Nearly everyone has a certain amount of leeway in budgeting for the future and the difference between an unwise choice and a sensible one could very significantly affect your standard of living.

While a great deal of unnecessary mystique seems to pervade the financial services sector, questions to do with money are often genuinely more complex than they at first appear.

There may be important tax angles to consider. Phrases commonly used in conversation may, when written into a formal document, have legal implications of which you are unaware. The jargon is apt to be confusing: for example, the term 'bond' has a variety of different meanings. Another problem is the volume of propaganda. There are plenty of enticing advertisements seeming to offer the moon which, if you were to take them at face value without being totally sure that you understood the commitment, could prove a sorry mistake.

Moreover, whereas most professional advisers are extremely sound, not everyone who proffers advice is qualified to do so. Before parting with your money, it is essential to ensure that you are dealing with a registered member of a recognised institution.

Checking has become easier. Under the Financial Services Act, not only are those claiming to be specialists required to register with their appropriate professional body and obey its code of conduct but, as a further safeguard, the institutions themselves must comply with the regulations of the Securities and Investments Board, i.e. the government watchdog concerned (see 'Investor protection' page 108).

Even if you have never done so before, there is no cause to feel hesitant about approaching financial advisers. Nor should you feel that because you have asked for advice, you are morally obliged to use a particular individual's services. Indeed, when it comes to investment decisions, you are strongly recommended to shop around in order to compare the many different options on offer.

As someone who may shortly be retiring, you are seen as a very attractive potential client especially if you are a member of a pension scheme with a sizeable commuted lump sum to invest.

However, before making contact, it is generally a good idea to try to sort out your priorities, for example: whether you are looking for capital growth or whether your main objective is to increase your income. Also, if you have any special plans such as helping your grandchildren or if you need several thousand pounds to improve your home, these too should be thought through in advance as they could affect the advice you receive.

A further reason for doing some advance thinking is that, whereas certain types of advisers – for example, insurance brokers – do not specifically charge you for their time, others such as accountants and solicitors charge fees by the hour. Drinking coffee in their office and musing aloud about the future delights of retirement may be a pleasant way of spending the afternoon but it can also work out to be pretty costly!

Choosing an adviser

When choosing an adviser, there are usually four main considerations: respectability, suitability, price and convenience.

Where your money is concerned, you cannot afford to take unnecessary risks. Merely establishing that an individual is a member of a recognised institution, while a basic safeguard, is insufficient recommendation if you want to be assured of dealing with someone who will personally suit you. The principle applies as much with friends, as with complete strangers.

If you are thinking of using a particular adviser whom you do not already know in a professional capacity, you should certainly check on their reputation and, ideally, talk to some of their existing clients. No one who is any good will object to your asking for references. On the contrary, most will be delighted if this means that the relationship will be founded on a basis of greater trust and confidence.

However, quite apart from their general competence, enlisting professional help is very much a question of 'horses for courses'. Just as you would hardly consult a divorce lawyer if you were planning to buy a house, so too in the financial field most practitioners have different areas of expertise. It is, therefore, important to establish that your adviser has the particular capability you require.

This issue is less of a consideration if you choose a sizeable firm, with at least four or five partners, since the likelihood is that between them they will be able to offer a mix of skills. But it can be a problem with the one or two-man band who, though outstanding generalists, may lack the specialist knowledge if you require sophisticated advice in, say, tax planning or investment strategy.

Although some people enjoy bobbing up to London to consult their solicitor, or whoever, generally speaking it makes more sense to choose a firm that is reasonably accessible.

If you live in a part of the country, where the choice of financial advisers is limited, you can approach one of the organisations listed on the following pages that maintain a register of members – or alternatively, you could ask your bank manager to recommend someone suitable.

Finally, you should be aware that some specialist advisers are in the business of selling; or at least stand to gain some financial advantage from persuading you that the investments they market are best for you. In some cases, the commissions are publicly known. In others, they tend to be disguised. Also some brokers and dealers are tied agents for a specific company, so under the Financial Services Act regulations can only promote their own in-house products. To know where you stand, you should ask any agent whom he represents and if it is a single company or group, however excellent the prospect sounds, you should aim to investigate at least two or three other propositions before signing on the dotted line.

Accountants

Accountants are specialists in matters concerning taxation. If there is scope to do so, they can advise on ways of reducing your tax liability and can assess the various tax effects of different types of investment you may be considering. Likewise, they can help you with charitable covenants, the preparation of tax returns and if you are thinking of becoming self-employed or starting your own business, they will be able to assist you with some of the practicalities – such as registering for VAT and establishing a system of business accounts.

Additionally, they may be able to advise in a general way about pensions and your proposed investment strategy. Most accountants, however, do not claim to be experts in these fields and may refer their clients to stockbrokers or other advisers for these more specialised services.

If you need help in locating a suitable accountant, any of the following should be able to assist:

Institute of Chartered Accountants in England and Wales, PO Box 433, Chartered Accountants' Hall, Moorgate Place, London EC2P 2BJ.

Institute of Chartered Accountants of Scotland, 27 Queen Street, Edinburgh EH2 1LA.

Institute of Chartered Accountants in Ireland, Chartered Accountants House, 87-89 Pembroke Road, Dublin 4.

Chartered Association of Certified Accountants, 29 Lincoln's Inn Fields, London WC2A 3EE.

Complaints. Anyone with a complaint against an accountant can write to the Secretary of the Institute's Investigating Committee who, if the complaint is valid, will refer the matter to the Disciplinary Committee.

Banks

Most people need no introduction to the clearing banks since, if they have a bank account, they have probably been popping in and out of their local branch for years.

Yet despite the fact that the counter is usually well decorated with leaflets – and additionally some are apt to come in the post – many customers do not actually realise what a fully comprehensive service their bank can offer.

In addition to the normal account facilities, all the major high street banks offer (either direct or through one of their specialised subsidiaries) investment, insurance and tax planning services, as well as advice on drawing up a will, together with a host of special arrangements for small businesses.

While some of their services are excellent and while approaching your bank manager is also a very convenient solution, especially if you are not very well up on stockbrokers and the like, the banks have tended to be criticised in the past for their rather pedestrian investment advice.

Again as a generalisation, most of their specialist services are not particularly cheap and for certain functions, such as the administration of estates, their fees could be higher than a solicitor's. Also, you should be aware that the banks run their own unit trusts and insurance broking divisions and may direct their clients to these.

Indeed, whereas until recently some clients may not have realised that the bank might be recommending one of its own unit trusts, today there can be no such confusion. Under the Securities and Investments Board (SIB) rules on polarisation, banks are obliged to give 'best advice' and to make it clear whether they are acting as a general broker offering everyone's policies – or whether, by contrast, they are promoting their own in-house products.

Brief information follows on the main clearing banks but there also are other more specialised banks such as Williams and Glynn, Coutts, Hoares and overseas banks that are all part of the UK clearing system and can offer a very good service. The addresses given are those of the head office.

Barclays Bank plc, 54 Lombard Street, London EC3P 3AH. Barclays Bank offers customers a choice of three different current accounts, of which two are interest bearing. In addition to a range of accounts to suit a variety of personal savings requirements, financial planning services are available through various subsidiary companies. These include: Personal Investment Advice, Investment Management, Stockbroking, Unit Trusts, Life Assurance, Pensions, Personal Taxation, Wills and Trusts.

You can either write to the above address or apply through your local branch of Barclays Bank.

Lloyds Bank plc, 71 Lombard Street, London EC3P 3BS. The Lloyds Bank Classic account offers all the facilities traditionally associated with a current account plus interest on credit balances. Classic account holders can apply for a personal overdraft.

For those with an income of £20,000 or more, Lloyds Bank Gold Service offers tiered credit interest at competitive rates, interest being paid monthly to the account. There is also a £250 cheque guarantee facility which is available with the Premier Payment Card. An overdraft facility is also available if required.

Lloyds Private Banking Ltd., Capital House, 1-5 Perrymount Road, Haywards Heath, West Sussex RH16 3SP offers a personalised service tailored to suit the individual's requirements and provides independent advice on the whole spectrum of investments including assistance with taxation, wills and estate planning.

The Asset Management Service offers many features, including a full investment management service and a 'Cash Sweep' facility, whereby any excess cash in your current account is automatically transferred into a high interest-earning account.

Lloyds Bank Personal Equity Plan Centre (also at the Haywards Heath address) provides clients with the opportunity of investing in leading British companies. A proportion of the investment can also be directed into unit trusts managed by Lloyds Bank Unit Trust Managers Ltd. Customers may make their own investment decisions or let Lloyds Bank manage their PEP for them. A single company PEP scheme is also available, as well as unit trust PEPs for lump sum or regular savings.

Lloyds Bank Insurance Direct offers a range of home and other insurance services, T:0800 750750. The Black Horse Financial Services Group includes Black Horse Life Assurance Company Ltd., which offers a variety of life assurance and investment products designed to take account of individual personal circumstances.

The Group also includes Lloyds Bank Unit Trust Managers Ltd., Mountbatten House, Chatham, Kent ME4 4JF which offers a wide range of unit trusts.

Midland Financial Services (Division of Midland Bank plc), Poultry, London EC2P 2BX. Offers a range of stockbroking and personal financial services which can be tailored to individual requirements.

Midland Personal Financial Services has been established to provide customers with a comprehensive choice of financial products ranging from unit trusts and PEPs to life assurance, which are selected according to a customer's requirements by a personal financial planning manager.

Midland Private Banking offers a discretionary Investment Management and Estate Planning Service to clients who prefer to have a local specialist to look after their affairs on a regular basis. Clients would typically have over £100,000 to invest. The Estate Planning Service includes preparation of a will, drawing up trusts and administering customers' estates.

Midland Stockbrokers offers a share dealing and advisory service to those customers who prefer to manage their own portfolios.

Any Midland branch can arrange a meeting if you would like to discuss these services.

National Westminster Bank plc, 41 Lothbury, London EC2P 2BP. NatWest offers a full range of banking services including financial planning for retirement. A meeting with a NatWest adviser can be arranged free of charge. To make an appointment, contact your local NatWest branch or call free on 0800 200400 between 8 a.m. and 8 p.m. weekdays, or 9 a.m. to 6 p.m. Saturdays, quoting reference GRG3.

Royal Bank of Scotland, 42 St Andrew Square, Edinburgh EH2 2YE. The Royal Bank of Scotland offers free banking for customers whose current account is in credit. There is an interest paying current account, a high interest cheque account called the Premium Account, a high interest Gold Deposit Account and a Gold Ninety Account which requires 90 days' notice of withdrawal but pays considerably higher interest.

The Bank's Trustee Division offers free advice in making a will, although the usual legal fees are applicable if you proceed. This is available to customers and non-customers and you should write to The Royal Bank of Scotland, Freepost, PO Box 31, Edinburgh EH2 0BG. You can also write to this address or approach your local branch manager for a personal tax service. The service, again available to customers and non-customers, is charged according to the complexity of the work involved.

The Royal Bank of Scotland offers investment management services through Newton Management and Royal Scottish Assurance; information can be obtained from any branch of the Bank.

New high street banks. As a result of a change in the law, building societies now have the choice to become plcs and to offer the same services as the high street banks. To date, the only one to do so is Abbey National. It seems likely that others may follow. At time of writing, at least three of the biggest building societies were known to be interested.

Abbey National plc, 215-229 Baker Street, London NW1 6XL. Abbey National offers a range of savings, mortgage, pension, current account and insurance products, and also loans for such items as home improvements, a car or money to finance a holiday.

A broad range of savings accounts paying tiered rates of interest are also available. These include: an instant access account that can be opened with £1; and a high yield bond account that requires a minimum deposit of £10,000. There are also TESSAs, PEPs and other accounts.

Additionally, Abbey National IFA (at Prestwood House, Corporation Street, High Wycombe, Bucks HP13 6TQ) offers independent financial planning for those nearing retirement or facing redundancy.

Full details of all Abbey National services can be obtained from any high street branch.

Complaints

The Banking Ombudsman acts as an independent arbitrator, who aims to resolve complaints by individuals and small businesses about banking services from the 43 banks (and 25 designated associates) which come within the scheme. These include all the main high street banks in the UK. His decisions are binding on member banks and he is empowered to award compensation of up to £100,000. The service is free.

Complaints can be handled on most aspects of personal banking, including bank credit cards and other matters normally transacted through bank branches, as well as maladministration or undue delays by banks dealing with wills and trusts. However, except where there has been maladministration, the Ombudsman's powers do not extend to commercial decisions by a bank on the grant of an overdraft or loan.

The address to which to write is: **The Banking Ombudsman**, 70 Gray's Inn Road, London WC1X 8NB. T:0171 404 9944.

For complaints about life assurance and other investment products, sold via banks and building societies, you should contact the **PIA Ombudsman**, see page 122.

Insurance brokers

The insurance business covers a very wide range from straightforward policies – such as motor or household insurance – to the rather more complex areas, including life assurance and pensions. Quite apart from the confusion of the enormous choice of policies available and the importance of ensuring that you understand the conditions laid down in the small print, a further difficulty is the number of different categories of people – agents, salesmen, brokers, independent financial advisers – who may try to sell you insurance.

Although many people think of brokers and independent financial advisers (IFAs) as doing much the same job, IFAs specialise in advising on products and policies with some investment content, whereas brokers deal with the more straightforward type of insurance, e.g. motor, medical, household and holiday insurance. In this section we concentrate on insurance brokers, with IFAs in the section following.

Unless you are already dealing with an insurance company whose advice you value, as a general rule you would be advised to consult an insurance broker. A broker should be able to help you choose the policies that are best suited to you, help you determine how much cover you require and explain any technical terms contained in the documents. He can also assist with any claims and advise you when renewals are necessary. An essential point to check before proceeding is that the firm the broker represents is registered with the Insurance Brokers Registration Council, which operates a code of conduct.

Although a condition of registration is that a broker must deal with a multiplicity of insurers and therefore be in a position to offer a comprehensive choice of policies, most companies pay insurance brokers on a commission basis; so, despite the code of conduct which emphasises that the customer's interest is paramount, it is possible that you could be offered advice that is not totally unbiased. If you are worried about this, you are perfectly entitled to ask a broker how much commission he is receiving.

Generally speaking, you are safer to use a larger brokerage with an established reputation. Also, before you take out a policy, it is advisable to consult several brokers in order to get a better feel for the market. The British Insurance and Investment Brokers Association, which represents nearly 3,000 insurance broking businesses, can put you in touch with a member broker in your area.

Complaints

If you have a complaint against a registered insurance broker you could contact the Insurance Brokers Registration Council. They will investigate the matter and, if they think your complaint is justified, will seek to get redress for you. You should write to the Registrar at: **Insurance Brokers Registration Council**, 15 St. Helen's Place, London EC3A 6DS. T:0171 588 4387.

Also useful to know about is the Association of British Insurers. It represents over 430 companies (as opposed to Lloyd's syndicates or brokers), providing all types of insurance from life assurance and pensions to household, motor and other forms of general insurance. About 90 per cent of the world-wide business done by British insurance companies is handled by members of ABI.

The Association publishes a wide range of information sheets and will, if you are in dispute with one of its member companies, ensure that your complaint is dealt with at top level. There are also regional offices in: Belfast, Birmingham, Bristol, Glasgow, Leeds, Manchester and Norwich. The head office is at: **Association of British Insurers (ABI)**, 51 Gresham Street, London EC2V 7HQ. T:0171 600 3333.

There is also an **Insurance Ombudsman**. He exists to help private policy holders only and cannot take up the cudgels on behalf of commercial organisations, however small. The policy must have been written in the United Kingdom, Isle of Man or Channel Islands. Likewise, those seeking help must have their main residence in one of these locations. However, the Ombudsman is powerless to act if legal proceedings have been started.

A further point is that the Ombudsman can only try to settle a dispute if the company in question is a member of the Ombudsman scheme. You can find this out from: your insurance company, insurance broker, from a Citizens' Advice Bureau – or from the Ombudsman's Bureau direct.

You can only contact the Ombudsman after you have attempted to resolve the difficulty with the company concerned.

The Ombudsman has power to make awards up to £100,000 and while he can advise, adjudicate or arbitrate on most issues, some matters such as third party claims are outside his scope.

You must contact the Ombudsman within six months of the insurance company's final decision on the dispute, giving the details as briefly as possible. Currently, there is no charge for the service. You may accept or reject the Ombudsman's decision. If you reject it, your right to take legal action is not affected. If you want help from the Insurance Ombudsman, you should contact: **The Insurance Ombudsman Bureau**, City Gate One, 135 Park Street, London SE1 9EA. T:0171 928 7600.

Independent financial advisers (IFAs)

IFAs can advise you across the whole spectrum of investment policies and products: endowment policies, personal pensions, life assurance, permanent health insurance, critical illness cover, unit trusts, PEPs and other forms of personal investment such as, for example, mortgages.

Their job is to help you work out whether the type of policy you have in mind would be most suitable and where, depending on your circumstances and objectives, you could obtain best value for money. In other words, they would act as your personal adviser and handle all the arrangements for you.

In order to be able to offer 'best advice', an IFA needs to try to ensure that you would not be at risk of over-committting yourself or taking some other risk that might jeopardise your security. He/she will, therefore, need an understanding of your existing financial circumstances (and future expectations) including, for example: your earnings, employment prospects and any other types of investment you might already have. Your adviser will of course also need to understand what your major aims are, e.g.: to boost your long-term retirement income, to provide money for dependants should you unexpectedly die, to help meet the costs should you develop a critical illness, to start a savings plan that will mature around the time of your retirement or to try to invest your money for capital appreciation.

In turn, you should also ask your adviser a number of questions including – as a first essential – by whom they are regulated. This will probably be the PIA but it could be one of the other regulators such as the Insurance Brokers Registration Council. For a full list see under 'Investor protection' in the Investment chapter (page 108).

As well as enquire about any technical terms or other points in the sales literature which are not crystal clear, you should also ask: what charges are involved; what commission, if any, your adviser will be getting; whether it is possible you could lose money; how soon surrender values will equal premiums paid; and why, in particular, you are being recommended to buy the policy or investment in question. Your adviser should provide you with a 'key features document' and a 'reason why letter', explaining all these points but, if for some reason you do not receive them or if there is anything you do not understand, you should not hesitate to ask.

While commission is still the norm, over the past four or five years a growing number of financial advisers have switched from commission to offering a fee-based service, rather in the manner of an accountant or solicitor. This means, of course, that clients are charged an up-front fee. But against this, they are not forfeiting the often very much larger sum – deducted from their investment – that the IFA would have received. Because of the way some insurance companies operate, fee-charging advisers may still receive the commission in the first instance but will then – depending on the client's preference – either rebate it back to them in cash or (and this could be more sensible) re-invest it on their behalf in the product.

Until recently, the big difficulty for someone wanting to consult a fee-charging adviser was discovering those who actually offered such a service. However, the search should now be very much easier thanks to The Money Management National Register of Fee-based Advisers. Anyone wanting a list of names should write to the Register, enclosing an sae, and will receive back (free of charge) details of at least six local advisers for them to investigate.

The address is: **The Money Management National Register of Fee-based Advisers**, Matrix Database, Freepost, Gossard House, 7-8 Savile Row, London W1X 1AF. T:0117 976 9444.

Two other organisations that will be happy to send you names and addresses of local IFAs are:

IFA Promotion Ltd., 28 Greville Street, London EC1N 8SU. T:0117 971 1177.

IFA Association, 12-13 Henrietta Street, London WC2E 8LH. T:0171 240 7878.

Complaints

If you have a complaint about an IFA, the most likely person to be able to help is the PIA Ombudsman.

Before approaching the Ombudsman, you must first try to settle the dispute with the company or adviser direct. If this fails, the Ombudsman will investigate your complaint and if he finds the complaint justified can award compensation, including a sum for distress and inconvenience. Although he has very wide powers and can adjudicate on such matters as misselling or allegations of 'churning' a policy, he cannot intervene over an actuarial dispute. Nor will he be able to assist if legal proceedings have been started.

For further information, write to the **PIA Ombudsman Bureau**, Centre Point, 103 New Oxford Street, London WC1A 1QH. T:0171 240 3838.

If for any reason the PIA Ombudsman is not the right person (perhaps because your adviser comes under another regulator), the PIA Ombudsman's Office will advise you very quickly and tell you whom to contact.

Other pension advisers

If you have a query to do with your pension, there are other organisations – or professional advisers – who may be able to assist.

Individuals in paid employment

If you are (or have been) in salaried employment and are a member of an occupational pension scheme, the normal person to ask is your company's personnel manager or pensions adviser – or via them, the pension fund trustees.

Alternatively, if you have a problem with your pension you could approach your union, since this is an area where most unions are particularly active and well informed.

If you are in need of specific help, a source to try could be OPAS. It has a network of 500 volunteer advisers who can be contacted through Citizens' Advice Bureaux. OPAS is an independent voluntary organisation that offers help and advice on all matters concerning pension schemes (except State pensions). The service is available to anyone: scheme members, those with deferred pensions, existing pensioners and dependants. Contact: **OPAS Ltd.**, 11 Belgrave Road, London SW1V 1RB. T:0171 233 8080.

As with most other sectors, there is now also a Pensions Ombudsman. You would normally only approach the Ombudsman if neither the pension scheme trustees nor OPAS are able to solve your problem.

Also, as with all ombudsmen, he can only investigate matters that come within his orbit. These are: (1) complaints of injustice caused by maladministration by the trustees or managers of an occupational pension scheme; (2) disputes of fact or law with the trustees or managers. He cannot, however, investigate a complaint that is already subject to court proceedings; one that is about a State social security benefit; or a dispute that is more appropriate for investigation by another regulatory body.

You can write direct to: **The Pensions Ombudsman**, 11 Belgrave Road, London SW1V 1RB. T:0171 834 9144.

Another source of help is the pensions registry and tracing service, managed by the Occupational Pensions Board, which assists individuals in need of help to trace their pension rights. Like the Ombudsman, there is no charge for the service. For further information, write to: **Pension Schemes Registry**, Occupational Pensions Board, PO Box 1NN, Newcastle upon Tyne NE99 1NN.

If, although in paid employment, you have a personal pension rather than an occupational pension and are in dispute with the insurance company or your financial adviser, you should contact the **PIA Ombudsman** (see page 122).

Three other organisations which, while they do not advise on individual cases, are interested in matters of principle and broader issues affecting the pensions debate. These are:

National Association of Pension Funds, 12-18 Grosvenor Gardens, London SW1W 0DH. T:0171 730 0585.

Occupational Pensions Board, PO Box 2EE, Newcastle upon Tyne NE99 2EE. T:0191 225 6414.

Campaign for Equal State Pension Ages (CESPA), Constables, Windsor Road, Ascot, Berks SL5 7LF. T:01344 21167.

Self-employed or running a company

If you are self-employed and want to make pension arrangements, you would probably approach an insurance company or independent financial adviser; or possibly your bank, a building society, unit trust or friendly society. However, in certain circumstances you might be better off to pay for the services of an authorised pension consultant.

The roles are fairly similar. In general, however, pension consultants would normally only be used by employers and by individuals with significant self-employment income.

There are two ways in which the services of a pension consultant are paid for: either in commission or in fees paid directly by the client to the consultant. The position as regards commission is that if advice given by the consultant results in money being invested in an institution, that institution will often pay a commission to the consultant, which may mean that there will be no direct charge to the individual. Fees need no explanation, as they are charged on broadly the same basis as any other professional fees. In order to know where you stand, it is a good idea to enquire from the outset how the consultant will expect to be paid – by you or in commission – and if a fee is involved, what this is likely to be.

Although apparently expensive, the best consultants are independent specialists who can give very valuable advice. Many of them will be members of the Society of Pension Consultants and must comply with its code of conduct.

If you contact the Society, it can supply you with a list of local members. Anyone with a complaint about a member consultant can write to the Secretary. For further information, contact: The Secretary, **Society of Pension Consultants**, Ludgate House, Ludgate Circus, London EC4A 2AB. T:0171 353 1688.

For information about other independent financial advisers who can help with pensions – and also what to do in the event of a complaint – see IFAs, page 120.

Solicitors

Solicitors are professional advisers on subjects to do with the law or on matters that could have legal implications. They can assist with: the purchase or rental of property; drawing up a will; if you are charged with a criminal offence; or if you are sued in a civil matter.

Additionally, their advice can be invaluable in vetting any important document before you sign it, for example: an employment contract, the purchase of a business, a trading arrangement or other form of contract, where either you or the other party is giving an undertaking of some kind.

A solicitor can also help with the legal formalities of setting up a business; trusts; guardianship arrangements or other agreement, where the intention is to make it binding. Likewise, a solicitor would normally be the first person to consult if you were thinking of suing an individual or commercial organisation.

If you do not have a solicitor (or if your solicitor does not have the knowledge to advise on, say, a business matter), often the best way of finding a suitable lawyer is through the recommendation of a friend or other professional adviser, such as an accountant or maybe your bank manager.

If you need a solicitor specifically about a business or professional matter, organisations such as chambers of commerce, small business associations, your professional institute or trade union may be able to put you in touch with someone in your area who has relevant experience.

Another solution is to consult the *Solicitors' and Barristers' Directory and Diary*, available in public libraries and Citizens' Advice Bureaux, which lists the names and addresses of solicitors all over the country, together with brief details about the type of work in which they have experience.

If you want information about your rights, you could approach a Law Centre (sometimes known as a Neighbourhood or Community Law Centre). There are 55 of them up and down the country, mainly in towns and cities. You can get the address by asking at your town hall or Citizens' Advice Bureau. Or you can write to or telephone the Law Centres Federation for the address of your nearest centre. The advice is free. If the matter concerns an area of law that is not dealt with by Law Centres (e.g., conveyancing, probate, divorce, commercial law), the Centre will be able to refer you to a solicitor. **Law Centres Federation**, Duchess House, 18-19 Warren Street, London W1P 5DB. T:0171 387 8570.

Another helpful organisation is the Free Representation Unit (FRU) which represents people at tribunals where legal aid is not available. While all the cases they take on are referred to them by solicitors, CABs or other advice agencies, so there is no point in contacting them direct, it could still be useful to note their name in the event of your advice bureau not thinking about them at the time of your visit. Sadly, FRU's service is limited to London and the South East. The address for your adviser to contact, if appropriate, is: **Free Representation Unit**, 49-51 Bedford Row, London WC1R 4LR.

Legal aid

If you need a legal aid solicitor (or want to find out if you are eligible for legal aid), the place to go is your Citizens' Advice Bureau. Ask for leaflet *A Practical Guide to Legal Aid*, which will tell you about the types of legal aid available and enable you to work out if you qualify for assistance. If you are entitled to legal aid, your CAB will explain what is involved and can help you find a legal aid solicitor. Instead of going through your CAB, if you prefer you can contact the **Legal Aid Board**, Information Section, 85 Gray's Inn Road, London WC1X 8AA. T:0171 813 1000.

Also useful to know about is the *Solicitors Regional Directory* which, among other information, lists solicitors who do legal aid work. A copy should be available at most libraries and town halls.

Complaints

The Law Society is the professional body for solicitors and is responsible for ensuring its members observe proper standards of behaviour when dealing with clients. Formerly, its responsibilities included handling complaints against solicitors but the Law Society has now created an independent arm to manage this function, called the Solicitors Complaints Bureau. The Bureau can investigate such complaints as: failure to reply to letters; delay in dealing with your case; overcharging (see below); wrongly retaining your papers; dishonesty and deception. The Bureau can also deal with complaints which allege 'inadequate professional service (IPS)', that is to say the carrying out of work by your solicitor to an unacceptably low standard, and is able to award compensation up to £1,000.

The Bureau cannot, however, give legal advice or tell a solicitor how to handle a case; nor can it investigate claims of professional negligence. The difference between inadequate professional service (IPS) and negligence is that IPS is substandard work, whereas negligence is a mistake by your solicitor which has lost you money or caused some other loss for which you may be entitled to compensation.

If you believe you have a complaint of negligence, the Bureau will normally be able to help you either by putting you in touch with a solicitor specialising in negligence claims or passing your complaint directly on to the Solicitors Indemnity Fund (where it will be dealt with like any other insurance claim). If the Bureau arranges an appointment for you with a negligence panellist, the panel solicitor will see you free of charge for up to an hour and advise you as to your best course of action.

If you believe that you have been overcharged, you should ask the Bureau to send you a copy of their leaflet *Complaints About Solicitors' Charges*, which explains the procedure for getting your bill checked, the various time limits involved and the circumstances in which you might be successful in getting the fee reduced.

You can ring the Helpline on 01926 822007/8/9 for practical assistance if you are having problems with your solicitor. Alternatively, if you prefer, you can write to the Bureau for a copy of the complaints leaflet and helpform. The address to contact is: **The Solicitors Complaints Bureau**, Victoria Court, 8 Dormer Place, Leamington Spa CV32 5AE. T:01926 820082.

If you are still not satisfied, you can approach the **Legal Services Ombudsman** at 22 Oxford Court, Oxford Street, Manchester M2 3WQ. T:0161 236 9532. You must write to the Ombudsman within three months of being notified of the Bureau's decision.

General queries. For queries of a more general nature, you should approach: **The Law Society**, 113 Chancery Lane, London WC2A 1PL. T:0171 242 1222.

For those in Scotland and Northern Ireland. If you live in Scotland or Northern Ireland, the Solicitors Complaints Bureau will not be able to help you. Instead you should contact the Law Society at the relevant address, as follows:

The Law Society of Scotland, The Law Society's Hall, 26-28 Drumsheugh Gardens, Edinburgh EH3 7YR. T:0131 226 7411.

The Law Society of Northern Ireland, Law Society House, 98 Victoria Street, Belfast BT1 3JZ. T:01232 231614.

Stockbrokers

Stockbrokers buy and sell shares quoted on the London Stock Exchange, on the Unlisted Securities Market (which is due to close at the end of 1996) and on a new market known as the AIM, which is expected mainly to trade in the shares of young and growing companies. These investments include: gilts (government stocks), equities, bonds and investment trusts. The large firms also deal in overseas markets and maintain offices in the major centres including New York, Tokyo and Frankfurt.

Although London is the headquarters of the Stock Exchange in the UK, there are also regional offices in Manchester, Birmingham, Leeds, Glasgow and Belfast. Additionally, there is an Irish Exchange located in Dublin. As well as trading for clients, stockbrokers can advise on the prospects of different companies, help individuals choose the best type of investment according to their financial situation and can also provide a wide range of other financial services including tax planning.

According to your temperament and expertise, you can either give a stockbroker partial or total discretion – or insist that he consults you on every deal. Some people know exactly what investments they wish to make and only want their stockbroker to carry out the transactions for them. Accordingly, a number of stockbroking firms have introduced 'execution-only' services, through which they buy and sell shares for you, without offering any investment advice. This is often considerably cheaper than a full stockbroking service.

Other people do not want to have to keep such a close eye on their money. Instead, they agree a set of guidelines and then leave their stockbroker to make all the investment decisions, just reporting afterwards what has been done. This is known as a 'discretionary service'.

As a half-way house between execution-only and discretionary, there is also an 'advisory' service in which the stockbroker will offer you advice and information but leave you to make the actual investment decisions.

As a result of these different options, it is difficult to be very specific about the cost of using a stockbroker. While some now charge fees in the same way as, say, a solicitor, as a general rule stockbrokers make their living by charging commission on every transaction. Until fairly recently, there was a standard scale rate, varying from 1/2 per cent to 1.65 per cent according to the size of the order but today this no longer applies, so you will need to enquire what the terms and conditions are before committing yourself, as these can vary quite considerably between one firm and another.

Many people still believe that it is pointless to go to a stockbroker unless you have at least £50,000 to invest. This is no longer true. At the present time there are a growing number of small provincial stockbrokers who are happy to deal for private investors with sums from about £5,000. Additionally, nearly all major stockbrokers now run unit trusts and, because through these they are investing collectively for their clients, welcome quite modest investors with around £2,000.

Also good news is that stockbrokers are becoming more accessible. Some firms have formed themselves into national networks, giving them the ability to extend their range of services. Others have been opening share shops in the high streets or linking with banks and building societies to provide convenient retail outlets, where you can buy and sell shares and discuss your investments.

There are several ways of finding a stockbroker: you can approach an individual through recommendation; you can ask the London Stock Exchange to send you their *Regional Brokers List*; or you can write to APCIMS (The Association of Private Client Investment Managers and Stockbrokers) for a full list of stockbrokers and investment managers, together with details of their services and fees. The address is: **APCIMS**, 112 Middlesex Street, London E1 7HY. T:0171 247 7080.

Alternatively, if you are more interested in investment trusts, you can write to the **Association of Investment Trust Companies**, Durrant House, 8-13 Chiswell Street, London EC1Y 4YY, T:0171 588 5347, for their information pack.

You might also like to contact ProShare, which is an independent organisation backed by the London Stock Exchange. As well as giving general advice over the telephone, it produces a wide range of publications including *The Investors' Handbook* which is specially written for first-time investors. Price is £6.95 (p&p free for *Good non-Retirement Guide* readers). To obtain a copy, write to: **ProShare/GnRG**, 13 & 14 Basinghall Street, London EC2V 5BQ. T:0171 600 0984.

Complaints

A Complaints Bureau has been set up by the Securities and Futures Authority and there is also an independent Complaints Commissioner. His role is rather different from that of other financial services ombudsmen, in that he does not handle complaints himself but is responsible for ensuring that the bureau is operating efficiently and fairly. In particular, the bureau offers two arbitration schemes.

In the first instance, however, if you have a complaint, you should put this in writing to the compliance officer of the stockbroking firm involved. If the matter is not satisfactorily resolved, you can then write to the Complaints Bureau which will investigate your complaint. If you are still unsatisfied, instead of going to court, you can use one of the bureau's two arbitration schemes: either the consumer arbitration scheme which, for a fee of £50, handles disputes involving sums up to £50,000; or the full arbitration scheme, which deals with larger amounts but could be more costly as legal advice may be needed. Also, as a condition, both sides must agree to use the full scheme.

The address to write to is: **The Complaints Bureau**, The Securities and Futures Authority, Cottons Centre, Cottons Lane, London SE1 2QB. T:0171 378 9000.

Stock Exchange addresses

London: London Stock Exchange, Old Broad Street, London EC2N 1HP. T:0171 797 1000.

Midlands and Western: London Stock Exchange, Midlands and Western Region, Margaret Street, Birmingham B3 3JL. T:0121 236 9181.

North East: London Stock Exchange, North East Region, Suite 104, Enterprise House, 12 St. Paul's Street, Leeds LS1 2LQ. T:0113 243 0738.

North West: London Stock Exchange, North West Region, 76 King Street, Manchester M2 4NH. T:0161 833 0931.

Scotland: London Stock Exchange, Scottish Region, Stock Exchange House, PO Box 141, 69 St. George's Place, Glasgow G2 1BU. T:0141 221 7060.

Northern Ireland: London Stock Exchange, Northern Ireland Region, Northern Bank House, 10 High Street, Belfast BT1 2BP. T:01232 321094.

Republic of Ireland: Irish Stock Exchange, 28 Anglesea Street, Dublin 2, Eire. T:00 353 1 677 8808.

A note of warning. Despite the safeguards of the Financial Services Act, when it comes to investment – or to financial advisers – there are no cast iron guarantees. Under the investor protection legislation, all practitioners and/or businesses they represent offering investment or similar services need to be authorised by a Self-Regulating Organisation (SRO), a Recognised Professional Body (RPB), a Recognised Investment Exchange or by the Securities and Investments Board (SIB), the watchdog appointed by the Government.

A basic question, therefore, to ask anyone offering investment advice or products is: are you registered and by whom? The information is easy to check by telephoning the organisation concerned.

For further information, see 'Investor protection' at the end of Chapter 5, Investment.

Useful reading

How to Buy and Sell Shares, free from the London Stock Exchange.

How to Spot the Investment Cowboys; Investment Businesses: What to Do if You Need to Complain; Compensation for Investors and *The Central Register*, all free from Securities and Investments Board, Gavrelle House, 2-14 Bunhill Row, London EC1Y 8RA.

7 Budget Planner

Whether you are about to retire tomorrow or not for several years, completing the following Budget Planner (even if there are a great many gaps) is well worth the effort.

If retirement is imminent, then hopefully doing the arithmetic in detail will not only reassure you but will enable you to plan your future life with the confidence of really knowing how you stand financially. Moreover, even at this stage, there are probably a variety of options available to you and just examining the figures you have written down will highlight the areas of greatest flexibility.

An imaginative tip, given to us by one of the retirement magazines, is to start living on your retirement income some six months before you retire. Not only will you see if your budget estimates are broadly correct but since most people err on the cautious side when they first retire, you will have the added bonus of all the extra money you will have saved.

If retirement is still some years ahead, there will be both more unknowns and more opportunities. When assessing the figures, you should take account of your future earnings; and perhaps more to the point, since your pension may well be based on it, what your final salary is likely to be. Also, though it may mean stinting a bit now, you should consider whether you should be paying AVCs and/or making other investments.

Imprecise as they will be, the Budget Planner estimates you have made in the various income/expenditure columns should indicate whether, unless you take action now, you could be at risk of having to make serious adjustments in your standard of living.

To be on the safe side, you must assume some increase in inflation. Equally, everyone should budget for a nest egg, to pay for any emergencies or special events – perhaps a family wedding – that may come along.

1. Possible savings when you retire

Item   *Est. Monthly Savings*

National insurance contributions _____.

Pension payments _____.

Travel expenses to work _____.

Bought lunches _____.

Incidentals at work, e.g. drinks with
  colleagues, collections for presents _____.

Special work clothes _____.

Concessionary travel _____.

Free NHS prescriptions _____.

Mature drivers' insurance policy _____.

Retired householders' insurance policy _____.

Life assurance payments and/or
  possible endowment policy premiums _____.

Other _____.

TOTAL _____.

N.B. You should also take into account reduced running costs, if you move to a smaller home; any expenses for dependent children that may cease; plus other costs, e.g. mortgage payments, that may end around the time you retire. Also the fact that you may be in a lower tax bracket.

2. Possible extra outgoings when you retire

Items   *Est. Monthly Cost*

Extra heating/lighting bills _____.

Extra spending on hobbies and other entertainment _____.

Replacement of company car _____.

Private health care insurance _____.

Life/permanent health insurance _____.

Cost of substituting other perks,
   e.g. expense account lunches _____.

Out-of-pocket expenses for voluntary
   work activity _____.

Other _____.

TOTAL _____.

N.B. Looking ahead, you will need to make provision for any extra home comforts you might want; and also, at some point, of having to pay other people to do some of the jobs that you normally manage yourself. If you intend to take out a covenant for a charity, this too should be included on the list. The same applies to any new private pension or savings plan, that you might want to invest in to boost your long-term retirement income.

Note on Table 3
Many people have difficulty understanding the tax system and you should certainly take professional advice if you are in any doubt at all.

However, if you fill in the following table carefully, it should give you a pretty good idea of your income after retirement and enable you to make at least provisional plans.

Remember, too, that you may have one or two capital sums to invest, such as:

- the commuted lump sum from your pension
- money from an endowment policy
- gains from the sale of company shares (SAYE or other share option scheme)
- profits from the sale of your home or other asset.

3. Expected sources of income on retirement

A. *Income Received Before Tax*

State basic pension ....

Graduated pension ....

SERPS ....

Occupational pension(s) ....

Self-employed or personal pension ....

State benefits ....

Casual or other pre-tax earnings ....

Total ....

Less Personal Tax Allowance and possibly also
    Married Couple's Allowance ....

The 20 per cent rate tax on the first £3,200
    of taxable income ....

....

Basic Rate Tax ....

TOTAL A ....

B. *Income Received After Tax*

Dividends (gilts, unit trusts,

    shares, etc.) ....

Bank deposit account ....

Building society interest ....

Annuity income ....

Other (incl. earnings subject to PAYE) ....

TOTAL B ....

TOTAL A + TOTAL B ....

Less Higher rate tax (if any) ....

Plus Other tax-free receipts ....

Investment Bond withdrawals ....

National Savings interest ....

Other ....

TOTAL NET INCOME ....

4. Unavoidable outgoings

Items   *Est. Monthly Cost*

Food ....

Rent or mortgage repayments ....

Council tax ....

Repair and maintenance costs ....

Heating ....

Lighting and other energy ....

Telephone ....

TV licence/rental ....

Household insurance ....

Clothes ....

Laundry, cleaner's bills, shoe repair ....

Domestic cleaning products ....

Misc. services, e.g. plumber, window cleaner ....

Car (incl. licence, petrol etc.) ....

Other transport ....

Regular savings/life assurance ....

HP/other loan repayments ....

Outgoings on health ....

Other ....

TOTAL ....

N.B. Before adding up the total, you should look at the 'Normal Additional Expenditure' list, as you may well want to juggle some of the items between the two.

5. Normal additional expenditure

Items	*Est. Monthly Cost*
Gifts	
Holidays	
Newspapers/books/videos	
Drink	
Cigarettes/tobacco	
Hairdressing	
Toiletries/cosmetics	
Entertainment (hobbies, outings, home entertaining etc.)	
Misc. subscriptions/membership fees	
Charitable donations	
Covenants	
Expenditure on pets	
Other	
TOTAL	

N.B. For some items, such as holidays and gifts, you may tend to think in annual expenditure terms. However, for the purpose of comparing monthly income versus outgoings, it is probably easier if you itemise all the expenditure in the same fashion. Moreover, if you need to save for a special event such as your holiday, it helps if you get into the habit of putting so much aside every month (or even weekly).

8 Your Home

One of the most important decisions to be taken as you approach retirement is where you will live. To many people, one of the biggest attractions is the pleasure of moving home. No longer tied to an area within easy commuting distance of work, they can indulge their cherished dreams of a wisteria-covered cottage in the Cotswolds or a white-washed villa in some remote Spanish resort. While this could turn out to be everything they hoped for, and more, many people rush full steam ahead without any real assessment of the pros and cons.

It is normally sensible at least to examine the other options, even if you end up rejecting them. An obvious possibility is to stay where you are and perhaps adapt your present home to make it more suitable for your requirements. You might move in to live with family or friends. Or looking further ahead, you could consider buying or renting some form of purpose-built retirement accommodation.

Before you come to any definite decision, first ask yourself a few down-to-earth questions. What are your main priorities? To be closer to your family? To have a smaller, more manageable home that will be easier to run – and less expensive? To realise some capital in order to provide you with extra money for your retirement? To live in a specific town or village, which you know you like and where you have plenty of friends? Or to enjoy the security of being in accommodation that offers some of the facilities you may want as you become older, such as a resident caretaker and the option of having some of your meals catered?

Whatever choice you make is bound to have its advantages and drawbacks but, if you weigh these up, you will be far less likely to take a decision which – while attractive in the short term – you may later regret.

Staying put

While there may be plenty of arguments for moving there are probably just as many for staying where you are. Moving house can be a traumatic experience at the best of times and even more so as you become older, when emotional ties are harder to break and precious possessions more painful to part with, as is usually the necessity especially when moving somewhere smaller.

Although ideally you may want to remain where you are, you may feel that your home is really too large or inconvenient for you to manage in the future. However, before you heave your last sigh of regret and put it on the market, it is worth considering whether there are ways of adapting it to provide what you want. If your house is too big, you might think about re-using the space in a better way. Would it be possible, for example, to turn a bedroom into a small upstairs study? Or perhaps you could convert a spare room into a separate workroom for hobbies and get rid of the clutter from the main living area? Equally, have you thought about letting one or two rooms? As well as solving the problem of wasted space, it would also bring in some extra income.

A few judicious home improvements invested in now could make the world of difference in terms of comfort and practicality. Many of us carry on for years with inefficient heating systems that could be improved relatively easily and cheaply. Stairs need not necessarily be a problem, even when you are very much older, thanks to the various types of stair lifts now on the market. Even so, a few basic facilities installed on the ground floor could save your legs in years to come. Similarly, gardens can be endlessly replanned to suit changing requirements: for example, extending the areas of lawn or paving could spare you hours of exhausting weeding.

For some people, the problem is not so much the size or convenience of their home as the fact that they are unable to buy the freehold, or extend the lease, and so fear for their long-term security. At last there is some hope. The 1993 Leasehold Reform – Housing and Urban Development Act extends the right of enfranchisement to some 750,000 flat leaseholders, variously by giving them the collective right to buy the freehold of their building and the individual right to extend their leases at a market price.

Among other requirements to enfranchise, the original lease must have been held for at least 21 years and at least two-thirds of the eligible tenants in the block must vote in favour of the property being enfranchised. Before proceeding, you will need to obtain a professional valuation as a first step to establishing a fair price to which by law the landlord will be entitled. 'Fair price' is defined as market value which includes at least half the marriage value plus possible compensation to the landlord for any severance losses. If you have a dwindling lease but do not wish to enfranchise, the more straightforward purchase of a 90-year lease extension might be a better option. For further information see Department of the Environment booklet *Leasehold Houses: Your Right to Buy the Freehold of your House or Extend your Lease*, available from housing departments. You might also contact: the **Leasehold Enfranchisement Advisory Service**, 6-8 Maddox Street, London W1R 9PN. T:0171 493 3116.

Moving to a new home

If you do decide to move, the sooner you start looking for your new home the better. There is no point in delaying the search until you retire and then rushing round expecting to find your dream house in a matter of weeks. With time to spare, you will have a far greater choice of properties and are less likely to indulge in any panic buying.

While a smaller house will almost certainly be easier and cheaper to run, make sure that it is not so small that you are going to feel cramped. Remember that when you are both at home, you may need more room to avoid getting on top of each other. Also if your family lives in another part of the country, you may wish to have them and your grandchildren to stay. Conversely, beware of taking on commitments such as a huge garden. While this might be a great source of enjoyment when you are in your sixties, it could prove a burden as you become older.

If you are thinking of moving out of the neighbourhood, there are other factors to be taken into account such as: access to shops and social activities, proximity to friends and relatives, availability of public transport and even health and social support services. While these may not seem particularly important now, they could become so in the future. Couples who retire to a seemingly 'idyllic' spot often return quite quickly. New friends are not always easy to make. So-called 'retirement areas' can mean that you are cut off from a normal cross-section of society and health services are likely to be over-taxed.

After a hard week's wheeling and dealing it is tempting to wax lyrical about exchanging the rat race for a life of rustic solitude. While retiring to the country can be glorious, city dwellers should, however, bear in mind some of the less attractive sides of rural living. Noise, for example low flying aircraft and church bells, can be an unexpected irritant. If you are not used to it, living near a silage pit or farm can also be an unpleasant experience. Prices in village shops are often higher than in city supermarkets and bus services tend to be more infrequent. Finally, would a small village or seaside resort offer sufficient scope to pursue your interests once the initial flurry of activity is over? Even if you think you know an area well, check it out properly before coming to a final decision. If possible take a self-catering let for a couple of months, preferably out of season when rents are low and the weather is bad. A good idea is to limit your daily spending to your likely retirement income rather than splurge as most of us do on holiday.

This is even more pertinent if you are thinking of moving abroad, where additional difficulties can include learning the language, lower standards of health care and the danger of losing contact with your friends. Another problem for expatriates could be a change in the political climate, resulting perhaps on the one hand in your not being so welcome in your adopted country and on the other, in a drop in the purchasing power of your pension. For more information on the financial implications of living overseas, see section 'Retiring Abroad', pages 79-83.

Counting the cost

Moving house can be an expensive exercise. It is estimated that the cost is between 5 and 10 per cent of the value of a new home, once you have totted up such extras as removal charges, insurance, stamp duty, VAT, legal fees and estate agents' commission. If you plan any repairs, alterations or decorations, the figure will be considerably higher. On the other hand, if you move to smaller or cheaper accommodation you will be able to release money for other uses.

A useful annual survey detailing the latest costs of all the unavoidables when moving house is prepared by the Woolwich Building Society based on information from solicitors, estate agents, surveyors and removal firms in 40 towns and cities. For a free copy, contact: Corporate Affairs, Corporate Headquarters, **Woolwich Building Society**, Watling Street, Bexleyheath, Kent DA6 7RR.

A good tip to remember is that stamp duty (which applies to all properties costing more than £60,000) is not levied on fitments such as carpets and curtains. If you are considering a purchase which includes some of these, try to negotiate a separate price for them.

When buying a new home, it is essential to have a full building (structural) survey done before committing yourself. This will cost in the region of £400 for a small terraced house but is worth every penny. In particular, it will provide you with a comeback in law should things go wrong.

If you are buying a newly built house, there are now a number of safeguards against structural defects. Most mortgagors will only lend on new homes with a National House Building Council (NHBC) warranty or its equivalent. The NHBC operates a 10-year warranty scheme under which the builder will remedy any defects which appear in the first two years. For the next eight years, it provides insurance against any major damage due to defects in the load bearing structure.

Many of the problems of buying or selling a house could be eased in time thanks to a logbook called *The House Diary*, which has been devised by the Northern Consortium of Housing Authorities in association with the Building Centre Trust.

Its purpose is to help owners record all the vital information about their property including such technical areas as the foundations and the roof loading, as well as more everyday concerns such as the location of the gas and electricity meters, the essentials of the central heating system and the position of water stopcocks. As well as being of help to both buyers and sellers, the information could also prove invaluable to owners planning a conversion or extension to their home.

The House Diary, which costs £2.25 is available from the **Northern Consortium of Housing Authorities**, Picktree Court, Picktree Lane, Chester-le-Street, County Durham DH3 3SY. T:0191 387 1085.

Also helpful to home-buyers, H.M. Land Registry now allows members of the public to seek information direct about the 15 or so million properties held on its register. There is a small charge for the service, details of which are explained in Leaflet No. 15 *The Open Register – A Guide to Information Held by the Land Registry and How to Obtain It.* To request a copy, write to **H.M. Land Registry**, Lincoln's Inn Fields, London WC2A 3PH; or telephone 0171 917 8888.

Another welcome change is that, thanks to the 1990 Courts and Legal Services Act, conveyancing has become more competitive with banks, building societies, insurance companies and other bodies (as well of course as solicitors) now allowed to offer these services.

Bridging loans

Finally a word about bridging loans which for some unlucky people can end up costing them literally thousands of pounds. Tempting as it may be to buy before you sell, unless you have the money available to finance the cost of two homes – including possibly two mortgages – you need to do your sums very carefully indeed.

To give you an idea of the sort of costs involved, banks usually charge 3 points or more over base rate plus an arrangement or administration fee on top. In other words, if bank rate is

6 per cent, the interest charged on a £100,000 loan works out at £750 a month; or £4,500 if it takes you six months to sell. Although by shopping around the building societies you may get somewhat better terms, you don't need to be a mathematician to work out that if your home is on the market for more than a very short while, the payments can escalate alarmingly.

As an alternative to bridging loans, some of the major institutional estate agents operate chain-breaking schemes and may offer to buy your property at a discount: normally around 10 or 12 per cent less than the market price. In some circumstances this could be worthwhile but a lot of money is involved, so this is not a decision to be taken lightly.

Estate agents

Finding your dream house may prove harder than you think. The grapevine can be effective, so pass the word around about what you are looking for. The property advertisements, especially in local newspapers, may also be worth scanning. Additionally, you could contact a good estate agent in the area to which you want to move.

The National Association of Estate Agents (NAEA), Arbon House, 21 Jury Street, Warwick CV34 4EH. T:01926 496800, runs a service called Homelink, bringing together over 500 agency branches throughout Europe and the UK. Your nearest member of Homelink can get details of houses for sale from a Homelink member in your target area. For names of member agents, telephone the Homelink Hotline: 01926 410785.

Some building societies, banks and insurance companies have created large chains of estate agents and many of these maintain systems for full exchange of information between their branches nationwide. These include: Royal Insurance, General Accident, Black Horse Agencies (linked to Lloyds Bank), Halifax and Woolwich.

All these, together with some 20 of the other large groups, have introduced a Code of Practice and also formed an Ombudsman Scheme in a drive to raise standards within the industry and to provide an independent review service for buyers or sellers of UK residential property in the event of a complaint. The Ombudsman is empowered to make awards of up to £100,000. However, as with most ombudsman schemes, action can only be taken against firms that are actually members of the scheme. For further information write to: **The Ombudsman for Corporate Estate Agents**, Beckett House, 4 Bridge Street, Salisbury, Wiltshire SP1 2LX. T:01722 333306.

A further welcome move to improve standards is the 1993 Property Misdescriptions Act which prohibits estate agents and property developers from making misleading, or inflated, claims about a property, site or related matter.

If you want to contact qualified local estate agents, lists can be obtained from **ISVA**, 3 Cadogan Gate, London SW1X 0AS. T:0171 235 2282. The **Royal Institution of Chartered Surveyors**, 12 Great George Street, Parliament Square, London SW1P 3AD, T:0171 222 7000 can provide names and addresses of chartered surveyors who are estate agents. Contact their Information Centre at the address above.

If you are thinking of retiring abroad, beware of unscrupulous property developers who, it is thought, have swindled hundreds of Britons, many of them pensioners, in Mediterranean tourist resorts. In particular, don't be rushed into a purchase you may later regret by fast-talking salesmen; and ensure that all documents are thoroughly checked by an independent lawyer before you sign anything. Visit the property first and find out what other developments, if any, are planned in the vicinity.

Removals

Transporting your worldly goods from A to B is an exhausting business. Professional help can remove many of the headaches if carried out by a reputable firm. Not only will they heave all the heavy furniture around for you, but they will also wrap your china and ornaments safely in packing cases which they provide as part of the service.

Costs can vary considerably from around £300 to £600 or more for an average three bedroom suburban house, depending on the type and size of furniture and the distance over which it is being moved. Obviously, valuable antiques will cost more to pack and transport than standard modern furniture. It pays to shop around and get at least three quotes from different removal firms. Some may be able to help reduce costs by arranging part or return loads. It is also worth asking whether the firm has a Domestic Removals Seasonal Planner Scheme since, if it is possible for you to plan your move during the slack season, this could reduce the price by up to 20 per cent. Remember, however, that the cheapest quote is not necessarily the best. Find out exactly what you are paying for and whether the price includes packing and insurance.

A useful organisation to contact is: **British Association of Removers**, 3 Churchill Court, 58 Station Road, North Harrow HA2 7SA. T:0181 861 3331.

They will send you a free leaflet advising you what to do when you move house and a list of approved removal firms. (Please enclose sae.)

Moving in with family or friends

This may be accommodation such as a self-contained flat or actually living together as part of the family. It may be possible to get a renovation grant from your local council to help with any conversion costs. Ask about the availability of such grants *before* any work is started.

There are many advantages to such an arrangement. While you are active, you can contribute to the household. Should you become frail or ill, help will be at hand.

Living together can also be fraught with problems, however. You only need to think back to any bachelor flat-sharing days to be reminded of the countless petty arguments – over washing up, noise or bills – that can develop if you are not careful. As a general precaution, try to work out in advance any potential problems or you may have a month of honeymoon and years of regret. Questions worth considering include: whether you will share any meals, social life or transport; whether you will contribute in any practical ways, like baby-sitting, shopping, cleaning or looking after the house during the family's holidays; also, whether you can keep a pet and have friends to stay.

Money is also a common source of dispute. Decide whether you will have your own telephone or whether you will share one. If you will be paying rent, make it a formal arrangement exactly as if you were a normal tenant. You must agree a set figure: what it will cover, how it will be assessed in future and how it will be paid, i.e. weekly, monthly, cash or standing order. If you make a contribution towards the cost of any conversion work, work out beforehand how you would be reimbursed should the arrangement have to be terminated for one reason or another.

Living with family or friends is generally an informal arrangement. However, it is worth having a word with your solicitor or local housing advice centre about how it might affect your rights and obligations as either landlord or tenant. In particular, you should take advice before embarking on any construction work, such as a self-contained 'granny flat', which might affect the property's exemption from capital gains tax in the future.

Sharing with friends

Yet another possibility is to share your own home with one or two friends. For some, this can be a perfect solution but the same pitfalls as living with your family apply, so work out the arrangements carefully beforehand. Legal advice is an absolute 'must' in these circumstances. Your solicitor or housing advice centre will be able to explain any important points that could affect you, as will your building society or bank should you be considering actually buying a property together. When doing the sums, bear in mind that mortgage interest relief is limited to £30,000 on any one property regardless of how many purchasers are involved.

Retirement housing and sheltered accommodation

The term 'retirement' or 'sheltered accommodation' covers a wide variety of housing but generally means property with a resident warden/caretaker, an emergency alarm system, optional meals and some communal facilities such as living rooms, garden and laundry. Guest accommodation and visiting services such as hairdressers and chiropodists are sometimes also available. A number of companies offer extra care and nursing facilities in some of their developments.

Designed to bridge the gap between the family home and residential care, such housing offers continued independence for the fit and active within a secure environment. Much of it is owned and run by local authorities, housing associations and charities. However, there are an increasing number of well-designed, high quality private developments of 'retirement homes' now on the market, for sale or rent, at prices to suit most pockets.

Many of the more attractive properties – and among the most expensive – are in converted country houses of architectural or historic merit or in newly developed 'villages' and 'courtyard' schemes. As a general rule, you have to be over 55 when you buy property of this kind. While you may not wish to move into this type of accommodation just now, if the idea interests you in the long term it is worth planning ahead as there are often very long waiting lists.

Full details on the various types of sheltered accommodation, together with a price guide and some addresses, are given in Chapter 15, Caring for Elderly Parents.

Other options

Boarding houses

At least 30,000 people live in privately run premises such as boarding houses, guest houses, hotels or hostels at which they have accommodation, meals and some services, but not nursing care.

If you are attracted to this idea, make sure you are dealing with a reputable establishment. Following evidence that many retired people were being 'ripped off' by their landlords, anyone offering this type of accommodation to four or more people must now register with the local Social Services Department.

Caravan or mobile home

Many retired people consider living in a caravan or mobile home which they keep either in a relative's garden or on an established site, possibly at the seaside or in the country. You may already own one as a holiday home which you are considering turning into more permanent accommodation. If you want to live in a caravan on your own or other private land, you will require planning permission and a site licence from your local council. Contact your local Housing Development Officer.

If, on the other hand, you want to keep it on an established site, make absolutely sure that the site owner has all the necessary permissions. You should check this with the Planning Department of the local authority.

Find out what conditions the proprietor attaches to any letting agreement (by law this should be a written statement setting out such terms as the services provided, charges and maintenance of the site) as well as your rights regarding security of tenure and resale. Residents normally have the right to sell their unit to a person approved by the site owner, who will be entitled to up to 10 per cent commission on the sale price. The rights of both parties are protected by the 1983 Mobile Homes Act.

In the event of a dispute, either party is free to go to court; or, with the agreement of both sides, to arbitration through the industry-sponsored scheme. If the site resident is unhappy with the express terms of the written agreement, appeal to the court must be within six months of the written terms being received.

It should also be noted that ordinary caravans – as opposed to residential park homes – are not really very suitable as long-term accommodation for the over-sixties. They tend to be damp as well as cramped and what may have been an enjoyable adventure on holiday may soon pall when it is your only option.

Proper residential park homes have the advantage of being more spacious and sturdier but, though usually cheaper than a house of equivalent size, are nevertheless a major expenditure. Moreover, the law regarding such purchases is complex and legal advice is very strongly recommended.

If you do decide to go ahead with the plan, you might like to obtain a copy of *Mobile Homes, A Guide for Residents and Site Owners*, a free housing booklet (No.30) published by the Department of the Environment.

The Park Homes Industry also publishes a *Charter for Mobile Home Residents* which is binding on its members. Copies may be obtained from **COPHI**, Chichester Home, 6 Pullman Court, Great Western Road, Gloucester GL1 3ND.

Self-build

Some 20,000 people a year are now building their own homes and with typical cost savings estimated at between 25 and 50 per cent, the number has been growing. New building methods have been developed which defy the assumption that you need to be a fit young man to undertake such a project and both women and elderly people have successfully become self-builders. No prior building experience is necessary, although this of course helps.

Further good news is that in response to the demand some building societies offer self-build mortgages to enable borrowers to finance the purchase of land plus construction costs.

However, as with any mortgage, it is essential to make sure that you are not in danger of over-committing yourself. Over the past few years, hundreds of people have lost their sites because, due to falling land prices, the size of their loan exceeded the value of the property – and by law building societies cannot make secured loans that are more than 100 per cent of the valuation. Some people were also trapped by being unable to sell their existing home, so found themselves hit twice over by the fall in property and land prices.

Most self-builders work in groups, but individuals who wish to build on their own can make arrangements with an architect or company which sells standard plans and building kits.

Useful addresses include: **Individual House Builders' Association**, 51 High Street, Eton, Berks SL4 6BL. T:01753 621265. The IHBA was set up in 1992 to act as an official industry body and to provide independent information to people interested in self-building. Among other services to members, the IHBA maintains a register of approved suppliers and publishes a regular newsletter.

Walter Segal Self Build Trust, 57 Chalton Street, London NW1 1HU. T:0171 388 9582. This is a charitable trust, named after the architect who pioneered a practical post-and-beam timber frame method of construction particularly appropriate for self-builders with no previous building skills. The Trust provides free advice and information on self-build methods, the costs involved and the financial options available.

There is also a useful publication, entitled *You Build: A Guide to Building Your Own Home* by Ross Fraser and Steve Platt. Price is £17.50 and includes a year's free membership to the Trust.

Centre for Alternative Technology, Machynlleth, Powys, Wales SY20 9AZ. T:01654 702400. Two demonstration energy-efficient houses can be seen at the Centre. Plans are available for the Walter Segal method of self-build. For information and a mail-order catalogue of environment-friendly products, write to the address above.

Making your home more practical

It is sensible to set about any home improvement plans earlier rather than later. For one thing, these are often easier to afford when you are still earning a regular salary. For another, any building work is tiresome and most people find it easier to put up with the mess when they are not living among it 24 hours a day. Thirdly, if you start early, you will enjoy the benefit that much sooner.

A perhaps unnecessary point to mention is that when embarking on changes a specific aim should be to make your home as economic, labour-saving and convenient as possible. A reason for saying this is that many people become so involved with the decorative aspects that they forget to think about some of the longer-term practicalities which, at next to no extra cost, could have been incorporated along with the other work.

Insulation

When you retire, you may be at home more during the day so are likely to be using your heating more intensively. One of the best ways of reducing the bills is to get your house properly insulated. Heat escapes from a building in four main ways: through the roof, walls, floor and through loose-fitting doors and windows. Insulation can not only cut the heat loss dramatically but will usually more than pay for itself within four or five years.

Loft insulation. As much as 25 per cent of heat in a house escapes through the loft. The answer is to put a layer of insulating material, at least 150mm (6 inches) thick, between or over the roof joists. You can lay this yourself quite easily and the materials are readily available from builders merchants. If you prefer to employ a specialist contractor, contact the **National Association of Loft Insulation Contractors**, PO Box 12, Haslemere, Surrey GU27 3AH. T:01428 654011 for a list of their members. Your local Age Concern group or volunteer bureau may also be able to help.

Doors and windows. A further 25 per cent of heat escapes through single-glazed windows, half of which could be saved through double-glazing. There are two main types: sealed units and secondary sashes (that can be removed in the summer).

Compared with other forms of insulation, double glazing is expensive; however, it does have the advantage of reducing noise levels. There are now a number of DIY systems on the market; or as a budget alternative you could tape cling film across the window frames. If using a contractor, make sure that the company you deal with is a member of the **Glass and Glazing Federation**, 44-48 Borough High Street, London SE1 1XB. T:0171 403 7177.

Effective draught-proofing saves heat loss as well as keeping out cold blasts of air. It is also relatively cheap and easy to install. Compression seals, mounted by a variety of methods and supplied in strip form, are the simplest and most cost-effective way to fill the gap between the fixed and moving edges of doors and windows. For draught-proofing older sliding sash windows and doors, wiper seals, fixed with rust-proof pins and screws, need to be used. For very loose fitting frames, gap fillers that can be squeezed from a tube provide a more efficient seal between frame and surround, but this is normally work for a specialist.

If you do fit draught seals, make sure you leave a space for a small amount of air to get through, or you may get problems with condensation. If the house is not well ventilated, you should put in a vapour check to slow down the leakage of moisture into the walls and ceiling. For advice on durable products and contractors, contact the **Draught Proofing Advisory Association**, PO Box 12, Haslemere, Surrey GU27 3AH. T:01428 654011.

Heat loss can also be considerably reduced through hanging heavy curtains (both lined and interlined) over windows and doors. Make sure all curtains cover the window sill or rest on the floor. It is better to have them too long than too short.

Wall insulation. More heat is lost through the walls than perhaps anywhere else in the house: it can be as much as 50 per cent. If your house has cavity walls – and most houses built after 1930 do – then cavity wall insulation should be considered. This involves injecting mineral wool (rock wool or glass wool), polystyrene beads or foam into the cavity through holes drilled in the outside wall.

It is work for a specialist and therefore quite expensive, costing from around £350 for a terraced house up to £725 plus for a detached house. Against this, you could expect a typical saving of around 25 per cent on your heating bill each year so that, in most cases, the initial outlay will be recovered in four years or less. Make sure that the firm you use is on the British Standards Institution's Registered Firms List or can show a current Agrement Certificate for the system and is approved by the BBA. If using a foam fill, the material should comply with British Standard BS 5617 and the installation with BS 5618.

Solid wall insulation can be considerably more expensive, but well worth while, providing similar savings of around 25 per cent of your annual heating bill. Again, this is work for a specialist and involves applying an insulating material to the outside of the wall, plus rendering or cladding.

For further information and addresses of registered contractors, contact:

British Board of Agrement, PO Box 195, Bucknalls Lane, Garston, Herts WD2 7NG. T:01923 670844.

British Standards Institution, PO Box 375, Milton Keynes MK14 6LL. T:01908 220908.

Cavity Foam Bureau, PO Box 79, Oldbury, Warley, West Midlands B69 4PW. T:0121 544 4949. All installers that belong to the Cavity Foam Bureau are registered with the BSI.

Eurisol UK Ltd., Mineral Wool Association, 39 High Street, Redbourn, Herts AL3 7LW. T:01582 794624.

Expanded Polystyrene Cavity Insulation Association, 284 The High Road, North Weald, Essex CM16 6EG. T:01992 522026.

External Wall Insulation Association, PO Box 12, Haslemere, Surrey GU27 3AH. T:01428 654011 – for solid or defective walls.

National Cavity Insulation Association, PO Box 12, Haslemere, Surrey GU27 3AH. T:01428 654011.

Floor insulation. Up to 15 per cent of heat loss can be saved through filling the cracks or gaps in the floorboards and skirting. If you can take up your floorboards, rock wool or glass wool rolls can be extremely effective when fixed underneath the joists. Filling spaces with papier maché or plastic wool will also help especially if a good felt or rubber underlay is then laid under the carpet. Be careful, however, that you do not block up the underfloor ventilation which is necessary to protect floor timbers from dampness and rot. Solid concrete floors can be covered with cork tiles or carpet and felt or rubber underlay.

Hot water cylinder insulation. If your hot water cylinder has no insulation, it could be costing you several pounds a week in wasted heat. An insulating jacket around your hot water cylinder will cut wastage by three-quarters. Most hot water tanks now come ready supplied with insulation. If not, the jacket should be at least 80mm thick and will cost around £25. Jackets come in various sizes, so measure your cylinder before buying. Only purchase one that carries BSI's Kitemark and BS 5615.

Grants
Recipients of income support, family credit, housing benefit, disability working allowance or council tax benefit may be able to get help with insulation costs by applying for a Minor Works Assistance grant. To be eligible, you must either be an owner occupier or a private sector tenant (this includes tenants of housing associations) and payment of the grant is at the discretion of your local authority.

The grant can cover either the cost of labour if a contractor is used and/or the cost of materials, including: loft or floor insulation, draught proofing or the lagging of water tanks and pipes. The maximum amount that can be awarded is £1,080 for each application and the council can pay up to a total of £3,240 in relation to a single property over three years. It is important that you should not start on any work before your application has been approved.

For further information and an application form, you should contact the House Renovation Grants Department of your local council (see Housing Department in your local telephone directory). It is possible that they may recommend that you apply instead for a Renovation Grant. They may also point out that the Minor Works Assistance grant can be used for other home improvement purposes. For further information on both points, see section 'Improvement and Repair Grants' on pages 152-155. Also, when approaching your council, ask for a copy of the Department of the Environment booklet *House Renovation Grants*.

In addition to the above, there is the government Home Energy Efficiency Scheme (HEES) which gives grants to cover the cost of basic home insulation measures and energy efficiency advice. The scheme is open to **all householders aged 60 or over** and also to those in receipt of one of the following: income support, family credit, housing benefit, council tax benefit, disability working allowance or disability living allowance. For further information contact: **Energy Action Grants Agency**, PO Box 1NG, Newcastle upon Tyne NE99 2RP; or telephone freephone 0800 181667.

Heating

It may be possible to save money by using different fuels or by heating parts of your house off different systems. This could apply especially if some rooms are only occasionally used. Your local high street gas and electricity showrooms can advise on heating systems, running costs and energy conservation, as well as heating and hot water appliances. In particular, you might usefully enquire about Economy 7 electricity which provides cheaper rate supplies at night.

Your local office of the **Solid Fuel Advisory Council** (see telephone directory) will also give free advice and information on all aspects of solid fuel heating, including appliances and installation.

If you are in London, a visit to the **Building Centre**, 26 Store Street, London WC1E 7BT, T:0171 637 1022, could save you a lot of leg work. It has a very wide range of appliances on display with experts on hand to give information.

Shopping note. Many people get rushed into expensive purchases on the promise of cheaper energy bills. A point to remember when comparing, say, gas with electricity is that fuel prices are volatile and relative cost advantages are not always maintained. If you have an otherwise adequate system, it could be false economy to exchange it for the sake of a small saving in current heating costs.

Buying and installing heating equipment. When buying equipment, check that it has been approved by the appropriate standards approvals board.

For electrical equipment, the letters to look for are BEAB (British Electrotechnicals Approvals Board) or CCA (Cenelec Certification Agreement), which is the European Community equivalent.

For gas appliances, either buy from a British Gas showroom where all products conform to relevant European or British Standards; or if buying elsewhere, look for the BSI kitemark which denotes performance, reliability and safety. The same applies for domestic solid fuel appliances, which should be approved by the Solid Fuel Appliances Approval Scheme (see sales literature).

When looking for contractors to install your equipment, check that they are enrolled with the relevant inspection council or are members of the relevant trade association. Electricians should be approved by the **National Inspection Council for Electrical Installation Contracting**, Vintage House, 37 Albert Embankment, London SE1 7UJ. T:0171 582 7746. All approved contractors are covered by the NICEIC Guarantee of Standards Scheme and undertake to work to the IEE Wiring Regulations. Any sub-standard work must be put right at no extra cost to the consumer. Names and addresses of local approved contractors can be found in the NICEIC Roll of Approved Contractors kept in local libraries and some CABs; or alternatively can be obtained from NICEIC direct.

An alternative source for finding a reputable electrician is the **Electrical Contractors' Association**, 34 Palace Court, London W2 4HY. T:0171 229 1266. Their members, all of whom have to be qualified, work to national wiring regulations and a published ECA Code of Fair Trading. There is also a Work Bond which guarantees that, in the event of a contractor becoming insolvent, the work will be completed by another approved electrician at the originally quoted price subject to the conditions of the scheme.

Gas appliances can either be installed by British Gas Service or by an installer who is registered with CORGI (Council for Registered Gas Installers). Registration is now compulsory by law. The address for CORGI is: **Council for Registered Gas Installers**, 4 Elm Wood, Chineham Business Park, Crockford Lane, Basingstoke, Hants RG24 8WG. T:01256 707060.

The relevant associations for solid fuel and oil central heating installers are respectively the **Solid Fuel Advisory Service** and the **Approved Coal Merchants Scheme** (see local telephone directory).

Additionally, members of the Heating and Ventilating Contractors' Association can advise on all types of central heating. All domestic installation work done by member companies is covered by a free one-year guarantee. There is also an optional extended warranty scheme. For further information contact the **Heating and Ventilating Contractors' Association**, ESCA House, 34 Palace Court, London W2 4JG. T:0171 229 2488; or call the Home Heating Linkline (all calls charged at local rate) on 0345 581158.

Grants. If you are disabled or on a low income you may be eligible for a grant to assist with improving the heating system to your home. See 'Improvement and repair' on pages 152-155.

Useful reading
Wasting Energy Costs the Earth. A pack of three booklets with advice on insulation and heating systems for the home, which will be of particular interest to those who are

planning home improvements or who have just moved house. Available free from PO Box 200, Stratford-upon-Avon, Warwickshire CV37 9ZZ.

Tips for reducing your energy bills

Energy can be saved in lots of small ways. Taken together, they could amount to quite a large cut in your heating bills. You may find some of the following ideas worth considering:

- Set your central heating timer and thermostat to suit the weather. A saving of half an hour or one degree can be substantial. For example, by setting the thermostat at 1 degree Centigrade lower, heating bills can be cut by about ten pence in the pound.
- A separate thermostat on your hot water cylinder set at around 140 degrees Fahrenheit will enable you to keep hot water for taps at a lower temperature than for the heating system.
- If you run your hot water off an immersion heater, have a time-switch fitted attached to an Economy 7 meter so that the water is heated at the cheap rate overnight. An override switch will enable you to top up the heat during the day if necessary.
- Showers are more economical than baths as well as being easier to use when you become older.
- Reflective foil sheets put behind your radiators help to reduce heat loss through the walls. Similarly, shelves above radiators deflect heat towards the middle of the room.
- Switch off or reduce the heating in rooms not being used.
- Low energy light bulbs can save several pounds a year.
- If you have an open fire, a vast amount of heat tends to be lost up the chimney. A wood-burning stove can help reduce heat loss as well as maximising the amount of heat you get from your wood or solid fuel in other ways. If you dislike the idea of losing the look of an open fire, there are now a number of appliances on the market that are open fronted and fit flush with the fireplace opening. Contact your local Solid Fuel Advisory Service for further information. If you decide to block up a fireplace, don't forget to fit an air vent to allow some ventilation.
- Some small cooking appliances can save energy in comparison with a full-sized cooker. An electric casserole or slow cooker uses only a fraction more energy than a light bulb and is economical for single households. Similarly, an electric frying pan or multi-cooker can be a sensible alternative for people living on their own. Pressure cookers and microwave ovens can save fuel and time.
- Defrosting fridges and freezers regularly reduces running costs.
- Finally, it is a good idea to get in the habit of reading your electricity and gas meters regularly. This will help you keep track of likely bills.

You might like to take advantage of the British Gas 'budget payment' plan which allows customers to spread their gas payments over the year in fixed monthly instalments, based on an estimate of their annual consumption. Estimates are periodically adjusted up or down, depending on actual meter readings. Many of the electricity companies have similar budget plans. If the idea appeals to you, you should enquire via the accounts department or customer services' number listed.

Also of possible interest, British Gas offers discounts to customers paying by direct debit (Direct Pay Scheme). Contact your nearest British Gas public supply office for further details; the telephone number is on your gas bill.

Useful reading

Handy Hints to Save Energy in Your Home and *Do's and Don'ts that Save Money on Your Fuel Bills*. Both available free from: Wasting Energy Costs the Earth, PO Box 200, Stratford-upon-Avon, Warwickshire CV37 9ZZ.

Payment of Gas Bills and other useful guides. British Gas publishes a number of guides, describing their many services, including several specifically aimed at older and disabled customers. Information includes advice on choosing appliances, free safety checks, services for visually impaired people, energy saving tips and other practical help. Available free from your nearest British Gas office.

Other useful addresses

OFFER, Hagley House, Hagley Road, Birmingham B16 8QG. T:0121 456 2100. The interests of electricity customers are represented by the Director General of Electricity Supply and 14 Electricity Consumers' Committees. The Director General, who heads OFFER, and the chairmen of the 14 committees hold quarterly meetings and between them form the National Consumers' Consultative Committee. They have wide-ranging responsibilities to safeguard consumer interests, including monitoring that electricity suppliers abide by Codes of Practice and meet 18 Standards of Performance, some of which are backed by financial penalties.

Should you have any queries or complaints about electricity matters including, for example, threat of disconnection or mistakes in your bill, OFFER advises that in the first instance you should contact your local electricity company (see your electricity bill for address and telephone number).

If you are still dissatisfied you should get in touch with your OFFER regional office (see your electricity bill for address and telephone number) who, if they cannot resolve the problem, may refer it to the local consumers' committee. Your consumers' committee will investigate the matter and if they agree you have a legitimate complaint will take up the matter on your behalf with the electricity company; or if necessary will raise it with the Director General.

Consumers in Scotland should contact **OFFER Scotland**, Regent Court, 70 West Regent Street, Glasgow G2 2QZ. T:0141 331 2678. Consumers in Northern Ireland should contact **OFFER NI**, Brookmount Buildings, 42 Fountain Street, Belfast BT1 5EE. T:01232 311575.

A minicom service for customers with hearing difficulties is available in England, Scotland and Wales on 0345 697128.

Gas Consumers Council, 6th Floor, Abford House, 15 Wilton Road, London SW1V 1LT. T:0171 931 0977. This is the statutory body representing consumers' interests in England, Scotland and Wales.

If you have a query or problem about gas or a gas appliance which you cannot resolve with British Gas, any other gas supplier or with the appliance retailer, you can approach your Regional office of the Gas Consumers Council. The Council has offices in: Birmingham, Bournemouth, Cardiff, Edinburgh, Leeds, Leicester, Letchworth, London, Manchester, Newcastle and Plymouth. For address and telephone number, see the back of your gas bill or look in the telephone directory.

Neighbourhood Energy Action, St. Andrew's House, 90/92 Pilgrim Street, Newcastle upon Tyne NE1 6SG. T:0191 261 5677. A national charity representing organisations which draught-proof and insulate the homes of the elderly, disabled or others on low incomes at risk from the cold.

Useful reading
Age Concern publishes a useful fact sheet, entitled *Help With Heating* (free), available from Age Concern England on receipt of large sae.

Help the Aged runs the 'Winter Warmth Line' on 0800 289404 as part of the government's *Keep Warm, Keep Well* campaign; they also distribute the free booklet of the same title.

Improvement and repair

Building work is notoriously expensive and can be a major deterrent to doing some of the alterations to your home that may be necessary. Before abandoning the idea, it is worth investigating whether you could take advantage of some of the various grants available.

A bank loan may be the simplest way of raising funds for most repairs and improvements.

Many banks and building societies are prepared to offer interest-only mortgages to older people to cover essential repairs and improvements.

If you are unlucky enough to discover dry rot or the like in your home, there is little you can do but try to ensure that the builder you employ does not do a botched job. Unfortunately, insurance cover does not usually extend to damage to your house caused by normal wear and tear, woodworm, rot, insects and vermin. If your house does need structural repairs, contact the Royal Institution of Chartered Surveyors (see 'Useful Addresses' a couple of pages over). They will be able to advise you on your legal position as well as point you in the direction of reputable chartered surveyors.

Improvement and repair grants
Improvements and structural repairs, especially to older houses, often qualify for grants from the local council as does conversion work, such as creating a granny flat.

Most grants are discretionary and are more likely to be given either if the council has a policy of encouraging improvements or if a member of the household is disabled. There are five types of grant as follows. (N.B. In consequence of proposals contained in a recently published Government White Paper, it is possible that there could be some changes during 1996.)

Renovation grant. There are six main eventualities where application for a grant might be successful: (1) to bring a property up to a standard of fitness for human habitation; (2) to replace or repair rotten or defective parts of the structure including, for example, doors, windows, walls, an ineffective damp-proof course or unsatisfactory wiring; (3) for home insulation; (4) to provide heating facilities; (5) for the provision of satisfactory internal arrangements such as improvement of a very steep or winding staircase; (6) for conversions, such as the creation of a self-contained flat.

Other than (1) which is mandatory provided the applicant is eligible for grant, all other claims are at the discretion of the council. Eligibility is means-tested and different tests apply according to whether the applicant is an owner-occupier or tenant or whether he/she is a landlord. An individual's resources are also taken into account in determining the actual amount of grant which, even if mandatory, could only make a tiny contribution to the cost of the works – or might pay for everything.

The property must have been built or converted at least 10 years before the date of application for grant. Second homes do not qualify.

Common parts grant. This is for the improvement or repair of the common parts of a building containing one or more flats. Items that normally count as common parts include the roof, lift, staircase and entrance lobby. Grant is usually discretionary and can be applied for either by a landlord and/or by at least three-quarters of the occupying tenants. As with renovation grant, the applicant's financial resources are taken into account and (where applicable) the property must have been converted at least 10 years previously.

HMO grant. This can only be applied for by a landlord and is for the improvement of Houses in Multiple Occupation; or for the conversion of a property for HMO use. Depending on the requirements, grant may be either mandatory or discretionary. Further information is contained in Housing Booklets Nos. 31 and 32 on HMOs, available from the council.

Disabled facilities grant. This is designed to adapt or provide facilities for a home (including the common parts where applicable) to make it more suitable for occupation by a disabled person. It can cover a wide range of improvements to enable someone with a disability to manage more independently including, for example: work to facilitate access either to the property itself or to the main rooms; the provision of suitable bathroom or kitchen facilities; the adaptation of heating or lighting controls; improvement of the heating system.

Provided the applicant is eligible, grant is mandatory for all the above. Discretionary grant is also available for a variety of other works where these would make a home suitable for a disabled person.

The individual must be registered (or registrable) as disabled and, as with other grants, there is a means test. Additionally, the council will want to check that the proposed work is necessary, appropriate and also reasonable according to the age/condition of the property. The grant can either be applied for by the disabled person or by a joint owner/tenant or landlord, on their behalf.

Eligibility for all the above grants depends on the validity of the proposed work and on the applicant's resources, taking into account their income and any savings over £5,000 (savings below this amount are ignored). There are different calculations according to whether an applicant is an owner-occupier or tenant – or whether he/she is a landlord.

How to apply. Contact the Home Improvement Section of your local council for an application form. Other applications, such as planning permission, may also be necessary; or, in the case of flats, you may need to apply jointly with other tenants.

Before making an application, you should read carefully the Department of the Environment booklet, *House Renovation Grants* (available from the council) which explains the various requirements in detail and also advises of sources such as your Citizens' Advice Bureau and local Home Improvement Agency that can both help you assess your likelihood of qualifying and can advise you of any preliminary steps (such as getting estimates) you need to take. Even if they are highly optimistic of your chances of obtaining a grant, **do not start work until approval has been given to your grant application**.

Minor works assistance. In contrast to the grants described above, Minor Works Assistance is for small but essential works to your home, including: (1) to provide or improve thermal insulation; (2) to repair, improve or adapt a property to enable individuals over 60 to remain in their own home; (3) as 2, if you have an older person coming to live with you permanently; (4) to carry out repairs to a property in a clearance area.

A grant is only available to owner-occupiers and private sector tenants (including housing association tenants) who are in receipt of income support, family credit, housing benefit, disability working allowance or council tax benefit.

Maximum grant is £1,080 per application, up to a total of £3,240 over three years. For further information and application form, contact your Housing Department. If there is a Home Improvement Agency (sometimes known as 'Care and Repair') in your area, it could be useful to ask them to help you assess the likely cost and feasibility of the work. **N.B.** Do not start on any improvement until your council has informed you that your application has been approved.

Community care grant. Income support recipients may be able to obtain a community care grant from the Social Fund to help with repairs. For further information, see leaflet SFL2 *How the Social Fund Can Help You*, obtainable from your local Benefits Agency office.

Grants for the sick and disabled

Your local authority may be able to help with the provision of certain special facilities such as a stair lift, telephone installations or a ramp to replace steps. Apply to your local Social Services Department and, if you encounter any difficulties, ask for further help either from your local Disability Group, local Age Concern Group or from **RADAR (Royal Association for Disability and Rehabilitation)**, 12 City Forum, 250 City Road, London EC1V 8AF, T:0171 250 3222.

Useful addresses

AA Homeline Service, T:0345 383838. The AA has set up a home-care register of approved plumbers, builders, locksmiths, electricians and other trades/craftspeople, available for both normal contract and (24-hour) emergency work. There is an £18.50 annual subscription to become a member. Emergency call-out rates are set by the AA who operate a code of practice and provide an inspection service in the event of dissatisfaction.

Association of Building Engineers and Surveyors, Jubilee House, Billing Brook Road, Weston Favell, Northants NN3 8NW. T:01604 404121. Can supply names of qualified local architects and surveyors.

Association of Master Upholsterers, 102a Commercial Street, Newport, Gwent NP9 1LU. T:01633 215454. Has a list of over 750 approved members throughout the country who specialise in all forms of upholstery including curtains and soft furnishings. Names of those operating in your area can be obtained from the Administrative Secretary.

The Building Centre, 26 Store Street, London WC1E 7BT. T:0171 637 1022. The Centre has displays of building products, heating appliances, kitchen layouts and other exhibits and can give information about building problems. It has manufacturers' lists and other free literature you can take away and there is also a well-stocked bookshop.

Federation of Master Builders (FMB), Gordon Fisher House, 14-15 Great James Street, London WC1N 3DP. T:0171 242 7583. Lists of members are available from regional offices. Warranty Scheme, which insures work in progress and gives up to five years' guarantee on completion of work, is available from some of its members.

Guild of Master Craftsmen, Castle Place, 166 High Street, Lewes, East Sussex BN7 1XU. T:01273 478449. Can supply names of all types of specialist craftsmen including, for example, carpenters, joiners, ceramic workers and restorers.

Institute of Plumbing, 64 Station Lane, Hornchurch, Essex RM12 6NB. T:01708 472791. Can provide a list of registered plumbers; sae appreciated.

National Association of Plumbing, Heating & Mechanical Services Contractors, Ensign Business Centre, Westwood Way, Coventry CV4 8JA. T:01203 470626. Lists of members are available, including approved installers of unvented systems.

The Scottish and Northern Ireland Plumbing Employers' Federation (SNIPEF), 2 Walker Street, Edinburgh EH3 7LB. T:0131 225 2255. SNIPEF is the national trade association for all types of firms involved in plumbing and domestic heating in Scotland and Northern Ireland. It has almost 1,000 member firms and operates a Code of Fair Trading and Guarantee of Work Scheme. Lists of local members can be forwarded on request.

Royal Institution of Chartered Surveyors, The RICS Information Centre, Surveyor Court, Westwood Way, Coventry CV4 8JE. T:0171 222 7000. The RICS will nominate qualified surveyors in your area who can be recognised by the initials ARICS or FRICS after their name. It also publishes a number of useful leaflets, including: *Buying a New Home: Mortgage Valuation Report or Survey?*; *Looking After Your Home*; and *Your House or Flat: Buying the Freehold or Extending the Lease*. (Please send sae).

Royal Institute of British Architects, 66 Portland Place, London W1N 4AD. T:0171 580 5533. The RIBA has a free Clients' Advisory Service which, however small your building project, will recommend up to half a dozen suitable architects. It can also supply you with useful leaflets giving advice on working with an architect.

The British Wood Preserving and Damp-Proofing Association (BWPDA), Building No. 6, The Office Village, 4 Romford Road, Stratford, London E15 4EA. T:0181 519 2588. The Association has over 220 remedial treatment member companies throughout the UK and will advise on anything to do with wood preservation and damp-proofing in the home.

Upkeep – The Trust for Training and Education in Building Maintenance, Apartment 39, Hampton Court Palace, East Molesey KT8 9BS. T:0181 943 2277. The Trust (formerly Building Conservation Trust) has an exhibition centre at Hampton Court which can provide information on just about anything that can go wrong with your home. They will advise on specific technical difficulties and on organisations to contact if you have a problem.

Useful reading
Home Improvement Price Guide (Harper Collins) £7.99. A comprehensive guide to cost and estimated time required for every little job around the home, both if you hire a builder or do-it-yourself. Also describes how to choose builders, the best ways to pay and how to get planning permission and grants.

Older Home Owners – Financial Help With Repairs, free factsheet from Age Concern (please send sae).

Care and repair projects

Local Care and Repair or Staying Put projects exist in an increasing number of areas to help older or disabled house owners repair and adapt their homes. They will help to assess your needs, get a builder, supervise the work, raise the finance, verify the estimate and check the completed job. Contact Care and Repair Ltd. who will be able to advise you about any such schemes in your area.

Care and Repair Ltd., Castle House, Kirtley Drive, Nottingham NG7 1LD. T:0115 979 9091. This is the national co-ordinating body for Home Improvement Agencies. For people in Wales, the address is: **Care and Repair Cymru**, Norbury House, Fairwater, Cardiff CF5 3AS. T:01222 576286.

Anchor Housing Trust, Fountain Court, Oxford Spires Business Park, Kidlington, Oxon OX5 1NZ. T:01865 854000 has 'Staying Put' projects across England which help older people with repair, improvements and adaptations to their homes.

Halifax Building Society, Trinity Road, Halifax, West Yorkshire HX1 2RG. T:01422 333333. The Halifax promotes a range of services for older people who are purchasing a retirement home or adapting their existing home.

Safety in the home

Accidents in the home account for 40 per cent of all fatal accidents, resulting in nearly 5,000 deaths a year. Seventy per cent of these victims are over retirement age and nearly 80 per cent of deaths are caused by falls. A further 3 million people need medical treatment. The vast majority of accidents are caused by carelessness or by obvious danger spots in the home that for the most part could very easily be made safer. Tragically, it is all too often the little things that we keep meaning to attend to but never quite get round to doing that prove fatal.

Steps and stairs should be well lit with light switches at both the top and bottom. Frayed carpet is notoriously easy to trip on and, on staircases especially, should be repaired or replaced as soon as possible. All stairs should have a hand rail along the wall to provide extra support – and on both sides, if the stairs are very steep. It is also a good idea to have a white line painted on the edge of steps that are difficult to see – for instance in the garden or leading up to the front door.

It is perhaps stating the obvious to say that climbing on chairs and tables is dangerous – and yet we all do this. You should keep proper steps, preferably with a hand rail, to do high jobs in the house such as hanging curtains or reaching cupboards.

Floors can be another danger zone. Rugs and mats can slip on polished floors and should always be laid on some form of non-slip backing material. Stockinged feet are slippery on all but carpeted floors and new shoes should always have the soles scratched before you wear them. Remember also that spilt water or talcum powder on tiled or linoleum floors is a number one cause of accidents.

The bathroom is particularly hazardous for falls. Sensible precautionary measures include using a suction-type bath mat and putting handrails on the bath or alongside the shower. For older people who have difficulty in getting in and out of the bath, a bath seat can be helpful. Soap on a rope is safer in a shower, as it is less likely to slither out of your hands and make the floor slippery.

Regardless of age, you should make sure that all medicines are clearly labelled and throw away any prescribed drugs left over from a previous illness.

Fires can all too easily start in the home. If you have an open fire, you should always use a fireguard and sparkguard at night. The chimney should be regularly swept at least once a year and maybe more if you have a wood burning stove. Never place a clothes horse near an open fire or heater and be careful of inflammable objects that could fall from the mantelpiece.

Upholstered furniture is a particular fire hazard, especially when polyurethane foam has been used in its manufacture. If buying new furniture, make sure that it carries a red triangle label, indicating that it is resistant to smouldering cigarettes. Furniture which also passes the match ignition test carries a green label. Since March 1989, the use of polyurethane foam in furniture manufacture has been banned and 'combustion modified foam' which has passed the BS 5852 test now has to be used instead.

Portable heaters should be kept away from furniture and curtains and positioned where you cannot trip over them. Paraffin heaters should be handled particularly carefully and should never be filled while alight. Avoid leaving paraffin where it will be exposed to heat, including sunlight. If possible, it should be kept in a metal container outside the house.

Gas appliances should be regularly serviced by British Gas Service or other CORGI-registered installers. You should also ensure that there is adequate ventilation when using heaters. Never block up air vents: carbon monoxide fumes can kill. **British Gas** publishes a free leaflet *Our Commitment to Your Safety* which includes advice on how to deal with a gas leak as well as how to use your gas appliances safely and effectively. A free safety check on gas appliances is available to anyone living alone who is over the age of 60 or registered disabled; or living with other people where everyone, like themselves, is either over 60 or registered disabled. If additional work needs to be done, you will receive an estimate and may be able to get help with the cost through your local Social Security office or Social Services Department. If you think you might qualify, you must get official approval before any work is started. You can arrange a check by contacting your local district office (look under Gas in your local telephone directory).

More than one in three fires in the home are due to accidents with **cookers**. Chip pans are a particular hazard: only fill the pan one-third full with oil and always dry the chips before putting them in the fat. Or better still, use oven-ready chips which you just pop into the oven to cook. Pan handles should be turned away from the heat and positioned so you cannot knock them off the stove. If called to the door or telephone, always take the pan off the ring and turn off the heat before you leave the kitchen.

Cigarettes left smouldering in an ashtray could be dangerous if the ashtray is full. Smoking in bed is a potential killer!

Faulty electric wiring is another frequent cause of fires, as are overloaded power points. The wiring in your home should be checked every five years and you should avoid using too many appliances off a single plug. Ask an electrician's advice what is the maximum safe number. Only use plugs that conform to the British Standard 1365 and it is a good idea to get into the habit of pulling the plug out of the wall socket when you have finished using an appliance, whether TV or toaster. All electrical equipment should be regularly checked for wear and tear and frayed or damaged flexes immediately replaced. Wherever possible, have electric sockets moved to waist height to avoid unnecessary bending whenever you want to turn on the switch.

In particular, **electric blankets** should be routinely overhauled and checked in accordance with the manufacturer's instructions. It is dangerous to use both a hot water bottle and electric blanket – and never use an underblanket as an overblanket.

Electrical appliances are an increasing feature of labour-saving **gardening** but can be dangerous unless treated with respect. They should never be used when it is raining. Moreover, gardeners should always wear rubber soled shoes or boots and avoid floppy clothing that could get caught in the equipment.

As a general precaution, keep **fire extinguishers** handy and make sure they are maintained in working order. Small hand-held portable extinguishers are now available and easier to use but are only suitable for very small fires. All fire extinguishers should conform to the British Standard BS 5423 or BS 5306 part 3. Many insurance companies now recommend that you install a smoke alarm as an effective and cheap early warning device. Prices start from about £5.

Useful reading

The Association of British Insurers (ABI), 51 Gresham Street, London EC2V 7HQ, has a 22-minute video, *Nobody Told Me*, to alert people to the everyday risks they run at home. It can be borrowed free of charge from the Association by writing to the above address.

Keep Safe: ideas for older people and those with disabilities, a free booklet produced jointly by the Royal Society for the Prevention of Accidents (ROSPA) and Care and Repair; available from Meacham Handlin Centre, PO Box 102, Burton-on-Trent, Staffs DE12 7DR.

Safety in Your Home, Fire, Keep Out the Cold and *Security in Your Home*, free from the Information Department, Help the Aged, St. James's Walk, London EC1R 0BE (A5 sae).

Home security

Nine out of ten burglaries are spontaneous and take less than 10 minutes. However, there is much you can do to protect yourself. The Crime Prevention Officer at your local police station will advise you how to improve your security arrangements and will also tell you whether there is a Neighbourhood Watch Scheme and how you join it. This is a free service which the police are happy to provide.

The most vulnerable access points are doors and windows. Simple precautions such as fitting adequate locks and bolts can do much to deter the average burglar. Prices for a good door lock are about £55 to £80 plus VAT; and prices for window locks, about £11.50 plus VAT, per window.

Doors should have secure bolts or a five-lever deadlock strengthened by metal plates on both sides, a door chain and a spyhole in the front door. Additionally, you might consider outside lights to illuminate night-time visitors and an entry phone system requiring a caller to identify himself before you open the door.

Windows should also be properly secured. Best advice is to fit locks to secure them when partially open. Install rack bolts or surface-mounted security pressbolts on french windows and draw your curtains at night, so potential intruders cannot see in. Both double glazing and venetian blinds act as a further deterrent. If you are particularly worried, you could also have bars fitted to the windows or install old-fashioned internal shutters which can be closed at night.

An obvious point is to ensure that the house is securely locked whenever you go out, even for five minutes. Insist that official callers such as meter men show their identity cards before you allow them inside. If you are going away, even for only a couple of days, remember to cancel the milk and the newspapers. You might also ask the postman for the local number to call for the Royal Mail's new **Keepsafe** service. It will store your mail while you are away and so avoid it piling up and alerting potential burglars to your absence. There is a charge for the service which varies according to the number of weeks you use it. Finally, consider a time switch (cost around £15) which will turn the lights on and off when you are away and can be used to switch on the heating before your return.

If you want to know of a reputable locksmith, you should contact the Master Locksmiths Association who can either give you the name of an approved locksmith in your area over the telephone or will send you a list of their members, classified county by county. Their address is: **Master Locksmiths Association**, Units 4-5, The Business Park, Woodford Halse, Daventry, Northants NN11 3PZ. T:01327 262255.

The Home Office issues a useful booklet, *Your Practical Guide to Crime Prevention.* Available free from your local police station or write to: **The Home Office**, PO Box 999, Sudbury, Suffolk CO10 6FS.

Burglar alarms and safes

More elaborate precautions such as a burglar alarm are one of the best ways of protecting your home. Sophisticated systems can cost upwards of £1,000, but an effective telephone-based unit can be bought for less than £800. For example, Telecom Security Ltd., offers a monitored alarm which, for a flat, costs from £570 to install and £99 annual monitoring fee (incl. VAT). For a house, prices are from £675 and £119 respectively. When triggered, the system automatically sends a signal to Telecom Security's monitoring station, where staff alert the appropriate authority such as fire, police or your own doctor. *Good non-Retirement Guide* readers are offered a 10 per cent discount during 1996. For further details, telephone – free of charge – 0800 010999 and quote ref. GRG.

Many insurance companies will recommend suitable contractors to install burglar alarm equipment. Alternatively, contact: **The National Approval Council for Security Systems (NACOSS)**, Queensgate House, 14 Cookham Road, Maidenhead, Berks SL6 8AJ, T:01628 37512; it will send a free list of its approved contractors in your locality who install burglar alarm systems to British Standard 4737. There are over 600 approved installers and some 800 branches. NACOSS will also investigate technical complaints.

If you keep valuables or money in the house, you should think about buying a concealed wall or floor safe. If you are going away, it is a good idea to inform your neighbours so that if your alarm goes off they will know something is wrong. Burglar alarms have an unfortunate habit of ringing for no reason (a mouse can trigger the mechanism) and many people ignore them as a result. It is advisable to give your neighbours a key so that they can turn off and reset the alarm should the occasion arise.

Insurance discounts

According to recent research seven out of ten householders are under-insured, some of them unknowingly but some intentionally to keep premiums lower. This could be dangerous because in the event of a mishap they could end up seriously out of pocket.

With recent increases in premiums, many readers may feel that this is hardly the moment to be discussing any reassessment of their policy. However, there are two good reasons why this could be sensible: firstly, because the number of burglaries has risen, so the risks are greater; but more particularly, because you may be able to obtain better value than you are getting at present. As you may know, a number of insurance companies now give discounts on house contents premiums if adequate security measures are taken.

For instance, Norwich Union's Home Plus contract offers a 5 per cent discount to householders who fit adequate door and window locks, a further 5 per cent discount if a burglar alarm is fitted as well and a final 5 per cent discount if you join a police-approved Neighbourhood Watch Scheme. The company has also introduced a 55 Plus Policy, covering homes with a maximum of four bedrooms and contents valued up to £30,000, for householders aged 55 or over.

Other insurance companies that offer discounts to householders where proper security precautions have been installed include: General Accident, Eagle Star, Cornhill, Avon, Royal Insurance, Sun Alliance and the Retirement Insurance Advisory Service.

Some insurance companies approach the problem differently and arrange discounts for their policyholders with manufacturers of security devices.

As mentioned above, the police recommend that you join or establish a Neighbourhood Watch Scheme in your area. Large discounts on household insurance are being offered to members of Neighbourhood Watch Schemes by the 1,500 insurance brokers belonging to the Institute of Insurance Brokers (IIB). For the address of your nearest IIB broker, write to: **Institute of Insurance Brokers**, Higham Business Centre, Midland Road, Higham Ferrers, Northants NN10 8DW. T:01933 410003.

See also section headed 'Insurance' a little further along.

Personal safety

Older people who live on their own can be particularly at risk. A number of personal alarms are now available which are highly effective and can generally ease your peace of mind.

A sensible precaution is to carry a 'screamer alarm', sometimes known as a 'personal attack button'. These are readily available in department stores, electrical shops and alarm companies.

Age Concern Aid-Call provides a service which enables anyone living alone to call for help simply by pressing a button. The subscriber wears a small radio transmitter the size of a wristwatch from which a message can be sent, via the telephone, to a 24-hour monitoring centre. The centre alerts a list of nominated relatives and friends and also the local police that something is wrong. There are two ways of paying for Aid-Call: option one consists of an installation and commissioning charge of £175 and a quarterly rental and monitoring charge of £44; option two consists of an installation and commissioning charge of £375 and a yearly rental and monitoring charge of £80. The firm operates a nationwide service and will arrange a demonstration through its head office. For a brochure, contact: **Age Concern Aid-Call**, Linhay House, Ashburton, Devon TQ13 7UP. T:01364 654321.

A telephone can also increase your sense of security. Some families come to an arrangement whereby they ring their older relatives at regular times to check that all is well.

Older people feel particularly vulnerable to mugging. While the dangers are often exaggerated, it must be sensible to take all normal precautions. The police are of the view that many muggings could be avoided if you are alert, think ahead and try to radiate confidence. In particular, don't hesitate to cross the street if you see a group of thugs ahead and, if you are followed, don't lead them to your home.

Insurance

As you near retirement, it is sensible to reassess your building and home contents policy. If the insurance was originally arranged through your building society it may cease when your mortgage is paid off, in which case it will be essential for you to arrange new cover direct. Similarly, when buying for cash – for instance when moving to a smaller house – it will be up to you to organise the insurance and to calculate the rebuilding value of your home. It is advisable to get a qualified valuer to do this for you.

Over the last 20 years the value of your home may have doubled or more and the chances are that the cost of replacing the fabric of your house, were it to burn down, would be significantly greater than the amount for which it is currently insured. Remember – you must insure for the full rebuilding cost: market value may be inadequate. Your policy should also provide money to meet architects' or surveyors' fees as well as alternative accommodation for you and your family if your home were completely destroyed.

If you are planning to move into accommodation which has been converted from one large house into several flats or maisonettes, check with the landlord or managing agent that the insurance on the structure of the total building is adequate. All too many people have found themselves homeless because each tenant only insured their own flat and the collective policies were not sufficient to replace the common parts.

If when buying a new property you decide to take out a new mortgage, contrary to what many people believe, you are under no obligation to insure your home with the particular company suggested by your building society – although this is not to recommend that you necessarily go elsewhere. The point is that, as with all insurance, policies vary and some are more competitive than others.

Many people are woefully under-insured with regard to the contents of their home. Insurance that simply covers the purchase price is normally grossly insufficient. Instead, you should assess their replacement cost and make sure you have a 'new for old' or 'replacement as new' policy.

Most insurance companies offer an automatic inflation proofing option for both building and contents policies. While it is obviously prudent to take advantage of this, many people unthinkingly sign on the dotted line quite forgetting to cancel items such as furniture or jewellery which they may have given away or sold – and so lumber themselves with higher charges than necessary. Equally, many forget to add new valuables they have bought or received as presents. In particular, do check that you are adequately covered for any home improvements you may have added such as an American style kitchen, new garage, conservatory, extra bathroom, swimming pool or other luxury.

Where antiques and jewellery are concerned, simple inflation proofing may not be enough. Values can rise and fall disproportionately to inflation and depend on current market trends. For a professional valuation, contact either **The British Antique Dealers' Association**, 20 Rutland Gate, London SW7 1BD, T:0171 589 4128; or **LAPADA**, The Association of Art and Antique Dealers, 535 King's Road, London SW10 0SZ. T:0171 823 3511, for the name of a specialist.

Photographs of particularly valuable antiques can help in the assessment of premiums and settlement of claims as well as giving the police a greater chance of recovering the items in the case of theft. Property marking, for example with an ultra-violet marker, is another useful ploy as it will help the police trace your possessions should any be stolen.

The **Association of British Insurers**, 51 Gresham Street, London EC2V 7HQ, T:0171 600 3333, will send you information sheets on various aspects of household insurance and loss prevention including *Buildings Insurance for Home Owners, Home Contents Insurance* and *Claiming on Your Home Insurance Policy* which describe what policies you need and indicate the correct amount of cover. Their free factsheet, *Watch Out For Winter*, contains a number of useful tips for preventing or minimising storm damage to your home, burst pipes and the like. It also gives information on household insurance and how to claim if you suffer damage. Enclose an sae.

The **British Insurance and Investment Brokers Association**, BIIBA House, 14 Bevis Marks, London EC3A 7NT, T:0171 623 9043, can send you a list of insurance brokers in your area.

Some insurance companies, including the Prudential and Legal and General, offer Retired Householders Insurance Policies at substantially reduced rates. The rationale behind such schemes is that older people are less likely to leave their homes empty on a regular basis (i.e. 9 to 5) and are therefore less liable to be burgled. In some cases also, policies are geared to the fact that many retired people have either sold or given away many of their more valuable possessions and therefore only need to insure their homes up to a relatively low sum.

Such policies are arranged through **Age Concern Insurance Services**, Garrod House, Chaldon Road, Caterham, Surrey CR3 5YZ; and through **Hill House Hammond Ltd.**, Retired Householders Insurance Department, Freepost, Lewins Mead, Bristol BS1 2BR.

A different kind of contents policy, called Contents Xtra, is offered by the Halifax which works as follows. Premiums are variable according to the number of claims made in a year. If one claim is made, the premium will increase by 15 per cent; two claims, by 25 per cent; and three claims, by 50 per cent. However, increases due to claims are reduced if the householder has a following claim-free year. Other features of the policy include: the option of paying premiums monthly by direct debit; a 10 per cent reduction for people aged 60 or over; and a 5 per cent discount for homes protected by key operated windows and door locks approved by the Halifax. For further details, contact your local branch or write to the head office: **Halifax Building Society**, Trinity Road, Halifax, West Yorkshire HX1 2RG, T:01422 333333.

Commercial Union Assurance, St. Helen's, 1 Undershaft, London EC3P 3DQ, T:0171 283 7500, has a Keyplan Policy offering a 15 per cent premium discount to householders aged over 50. The plan also offers a 15 per cent premium discount if an approved alarm device is installed; or a 5 per cent discount if you live in a Neighbourhood Watch area.

Many other insurance companies give discounts based on age (sometimes applying from as young as 50) and an increasing number, including Avon and Legal and General, offer generous no claims discounts. Another type of discount-linked policy that is becoming more popular is one that carries an excess, whereby the householder pays the first chunk of any claim – say, the first £100 or £250. Savings on premiums can be quite appreciable, so it is certainly worth asking your insurance company what terms they offer. If these are not very attractive, it could pay you to shop around for a better deal.

Raising money on your home

The problem for many retired people is that they are 'asset rich, cash poor', with their main asset being their home. Despite the slide in house prices over the past couple of years, many retired owner-occupiers have substantial amounts of money tied up in their homes while they struggle to make ends meet on reduced incomes. One way round the dilemma is to sell up and move somewhere smaller in order to provide extra income. For those who prefer to stay put, however, there are a number of schemes that enable people to unlock capital without having to move. Generally known as Home Income Plans, these usually fall into one of two categories: mortgage annuity schemes and home reversions. Both are normally more suitable for older people who are already in their seventies or eighties.

Although other types of schemes exist, these are too dangerous and should not be considered. In particular you should avoid any home income plans linked-in with the following: investment bonds, roll-up loans and variable interest mortgages. In the past, many elderly people were unwittingly drawn into debt or even tragically lost their homes as a result of such schemes.

If you were among those who were advised to invest in an investment bond scheme and as a result have suffered financial difficulties, you should contact the **Investors Compensation Scheme** on: 0171 628 8820.

While it is extremely unlikely that you would any longer be offered a high risk plan (as most have been outlawed or voluntarily withdrawn), where your home is concerned you cannot afford to take any chances.

In a welcome move to give individuals better protection, four leading providers – Allchurches Life, Carlyle Life, Home and Capital Trust and Stalwart Assurance – have jointly formed a company called **Safe Home Income Plans (SHIP)**. All abide by a code of practice and undertake to give a full and fair presentation of any plan offered, including what costs are involved and how the plan would affect the value of the person's estate. As a further safeguard, they will not finalise an arrangement without a certificate signed by the purchaser's solicitor, confirming that they have discussed the contract together in detail.

Even 'safe' income plans are not without their drawbacks. The plan may involve a loan repayable on death or may entail your selling all or part of your home at a considerable discount, so either way, the cost to your estate could be substantial. Additionally, there may be fairly hefty setting-up or arrangement charges – as well as the cost of independent legal advice which we recommend as essential.

Mortgage annuity plans

The more popular format tends to be the mortgage annuity which produces a monthly income for life while allowing you to retain ownership of the property. It works as follows: you take out a mortgage on your home and use at least 90 per cent of the money raised to buy an annuity. Part of the income from the annuity goes to pay the interest on the loan (which is tax deductible, at basic rate only, on loans of up to £30,000), while you receive the balance as spending money each month. You still own the house and any increase in the value of the property remains with the family. The amount of money you can raise in this way depends on the lending institution concerned.

The loans are all made on a fixed interest-only basis and are repaid from the proceeds of the sale of the house (or estate) when the owner, or surviving partner, dies. Alternatively, if you decide to sell the property at an earlier date, the loan will be repaid, but the annuity will continue.

Normally these schemes are only available to people over 70 and the older you are the better the annuity payments. If you are married, your combined ages should ideally be at least 150. As with other annuities, the longer you live the greater the benefit. If you survive only a few years, however, the amount of income you receive may nowhere near reach the lump sum you would have sacrificed to buy the annuity. As a safeguard against early death, some schemes offer a 'capital protection' policy, which can be taken in return for lower payments.

Typically, these provide that should you die within one year, only a fifth of the original loan would have to be repaid. This rises to three-fifths within three years. After four years the loan would be repayable in full from the estate.

There are other possible drawbacks, especially for those on low incomes who, as a result of their having the extra money, could risk losing their income support or housing benefit. Income from an annuity is treated partly as tax-free return of capital and partly as the payment of taxable interest. Normally basic rate tax will be deducted automatically by the insurance company. Gross payments may be made to non-taxpayers, but the extra income from this source can push people – especially those who are single – into a tax-paying bracket. Income from the annuity may also affect eligibility for certain means-tested benefits. Finally, annuity payments are often fixed for life, so your return may not look so attractive if inflation shoots up in the future.

Further information about home income plans can be obtained from specialist financial advisers **Hinton & Wild (Home Plans) Ltd.**, 374-378 Ewell Road, Surbiton, Surrey KT6 7BB. T:0181 390 8166.

Fixed annuity-based home income plans are obtainable from:

Allchurches Life Assurance, Beaufort House, Brunswick Road, Gloucester GL1 1JZ. T:01452 526265.

Carlyle Life Assurance Co. Ltd., Home Reversions, 21 Windsor Place, Cardiff CF1 3BY. T:01222 371726.

Home reversion schemes
Many people prefer a cash sum to a regular income, in which case a home reversion plan could be the answer. With these schemes, you sell all or part of your house –

generally at a substantial discount – but retain the right to live in the house for the remainder of your life at a peppercorn rent. You are only likely to receive about 35 to 55 per cent of the market value of your property, as the price paid allows for the fact that it could be many years before the investor sees any return for his money. The proceeds from the sale are received as a lump sum or can be invested in an annuity. You would continue to be responsible for keeping the property in good repair.

While such plans provide a higher initial income than mortgage annuity schemes, they carry a number of disadvantages: the value placed on the house may be disappointing; you lose the benefit of any future increases in the value of the property and you cannot leave the house to your beneficiaries since you no longer own it. Furthermore, your options can be reduced should you wish to move in the future.

New style reversion schemes. Some insurance companies have now come up with a variety of new-style home reversion schemes which aim to get over many of these problems. These schemes not only provide an immediate cash sum for elderly home owners, but also enable them to maintain a share in the future appreciation of their homes.

One variation on the theme is offered by Carlyle Life Assurance Co. Ltd., who have been underwriting Home Income Plans since 1965: you sell your property at a discount in the normal way but, instead of a cash sum, you receive an annuity. Under their 'Reversion 50' scheme, only half the value of the property is used as the basis for the annuity while you retain a 50 per cent equity in your home. In the event of death, your estate receives half of the net proceeds of sale and thus benefits to that extent from any increase in the value of the property. The percentage of equity can be varied as required.

A scheme, offered by Stalwart Assurance, pays a lifetime annuity and also offers the security of a lifetime lease. Future increases in the property value are passed on through an additional income. You also have the option of taking a cash loan of up to 5 per cent of the value of the property placed in the plan. Up to 50 per cent of the increasing value of the house can be retained either for a bequest or conversion to extra income at a later date. A further feature is that there are no restrictions on moving, including moves into sheltered accommodation or a nursing home.

Before committing yourself to a reversion scheme, you are strongly advised to consult a solicitor, especially with a view to guaranteeing your security of tenure. Home reversion plans are offered by:

Carlyle Life Assurance Co. Ltd., Home Reversions, 21 Windsor Place, Cardiff CF1 3BY. T:01222 371726.

Stalwart Assurance, Stalwart House, 142 South Street, Dorking, Surrey RH4 2EU. T:01306 876581.

Home and Capital Trust Ltd., 31 Goldington Road, Bedford MK40 3LH. T:01234 340511.

Useful reading

Extra Income for Life for Elderly Home Owners, free from Hinton & Wild (Home Plans) Ltd., 374-378 Ewell Road, Surbiton, Surrey KT6 7BB.

Safe Home Income Plans: What You Need to Know Before You Take Out a Plan, free from SHIP secretary, Cecil Hinton, of Hinton & Wild above.

Raising Income or Capital from Your Home, free factsheet from Age Concern England (enclose sae).

Using Your Home as Capital, price £4.95 from Age Concern. A useful guide to home income plans, outlining all the details that should be taken into consideration.

Letting rooms in your home

Rather than move, many people whose home has become too large are tempted by the idea of taking in tenants. For some, it is an ideal plan; for others, a disaster. At best, it could provide you with extra income and the possibility of pleasant company. At worst, you could be involved in a lengthy legal battle to regain possession of your property. Before either rushing off to put a card in the newsagent's window or rejecting the idea out of hand, it is helpful to understand the different options together with your various rights and responsibilities.

There are three broad choices: taking in paying guests or lodgers; letting part of your home as self-contained accommodation; or renting the whole house for a specified period of time. In all cases for your own protection it is essential to have a written agreement and to take up bank references, unless the let is a strictly temporary one where the money is paid in advance. Otherwise, rent should be collected quarterly and you should arrange a hefty deposit to cover any damage.

In a move to encourage more people to let out rooms in their home, the government has recently relaxed the tax rules. Previously, any money you received in rent was treated as income for tax purposes. However, you can now earn up to £62.50 a week (or £3,250 a year) free of tax. Any excess rental income you receive over £3,250 will be assessed for tax in the normal way. For further information, see Inland Revenue booklet IR 87 *Rooms To Let*, available from any tax office.

Finally, if you have a mortgage or are a tenant yourself (even with a very long lease), check with your building society or landlord that you are entitled to sublet.

Paying guests or lodgers. This is the most informal arrangement and will normally be either a casual holiday-type bed and breakfast let or a lodger who might be with you for a couple of years.

In either case, the visitor would be sharing part of your home, the accommodation would be fully furnished and you would be providing at least one full meal a day and possibly also basic cleaning services.

There are few legal formalities involved in these types of letting and rent is entirely a matter for friendly agreement. As a resident owner you are also in a very strong position if you want your lodger to leave. Lodging arrangements can easily be ended, as your lodger has no legal rights to stay after the agreed period.

A wise precaution would be to check with your insurance company that your home contents policy would not be affected, since some insurers restrict cover to households with lodgers. Also, unless you make arrangements to the contrary, you should inform your lodger that his or her possessions are not covered by your policy.

Holiday lets. It is a good idea to register with your Tourist Information Centre and to contact the Environmental Health Office at your local council for any help and advice.

Useful reading
Want to Rent A Room? DoE leaflet, available from local libraries, Housing Advice Centres and Citizens' Advice Bureaux.
Letting Residential Property: A Practical Guide by Frances M Way, published by Kogan Page, £8.99.

Letting part of your home
You could convert a basement or part of your house as a self-contained flat and let this either furnished or unfurnished. Alternatively, you could let a room or rooms as bed-sitters with no meals provided.

In general terms, provided you continue to live in the house yourself, you will be in much the same position as if you had a lodger or paying guest. The advice about checking your home contents policy with your insurance company equally applies. The good news, however, is that the 'fair rent' system for new tenancies has been abolished and landlords can now charge market rates. For more details, see housing booklet No. 22 *Letting Rooms in Your Home.*

As a resident landlord, you have a guaranteed right to repossession of your property. If the letting was for a fixed term (e.g. six months or a year), the tenancy will automatically cease at the end of the fixed period. If the arrangement was on a more ad hoc basis with no specified leaving date, you may have to give at least four weeks' notice in writing. The position over notices to quit will vary according to circumstances. For further information, see DoE housing booklet No.24 *Notice That You Must Leave.* Should you encounter any difficulties, it is possible that you may need to apply to the courts for an eviction order.

Tax note. If you subsequently sell your home, you may not be able to claim exemption from capital gains tax on the increase in value of a flat if it is entirely self-contained. It is therefore a good idea to retain some means of access to the main house or flat, but take legal advice as to what will qualify.

Renting out your home on a temporary basis

If you are thinking of spending the winter in the sun or are considering buying a retirement home which you will not occupy for a year or two, you might be tempted by the idea of letting the whole house. In spite of changes in the law, there are plenty of true horror stories of owners who cannot regain possession of their own property, when they wish to return. Laws against harassment and illegal evictions have recently been strengthened.

To avoid many of the problems, you should write the lease under the shorthold tenancy rules, which are designed to protect a landlord's rights and enable repossession of the premises at the end of the fixed term (which must be for at least six months). See housing booklet No.19, *Assured Tenancies*. It is essential to ask a solicitor to help you draw up the agreement. Although this provides for greater protection, especially since the introduction of new accelerated possession procedures to enable landlords to recover their property more quickly and cheaply, you could still have a great deal of hassle if your tenants refuse to leave.

In most circumstances, by far the safest solution is to let your property to a company rather than to private individuals. Before entering into any agreement, you might find it useful to obtain a copy of booklet *Now it's Worthwhile Being a Landlord*, available from your local housing department.

Holiday lets

Buying a future retirement home in the country and renting it out as a holiday home in the summer months is another option worth considering. As well as providing you with a weekend cottage at other times of the year and the chance to establish yourself and make friends in the area, it can also prove a useful and profitable investment.

As long as certain conditions are met, income from furnished holiday lettings enjoys most – but not all – the benefits that there would be if it were taxed as trading income rather than as investment income. In practical terms, this means that you can claim 25 per cent written down capital allowances on such items as carpets, curtains and furniture as well as fixtures and fittings, thereby reducing the initial cost of equipping the house.

Running expenses of a holiday home, including maintenance, advertising, insurance cover and council tax (or business rates, see below) are all largely allowable for tax, excluding that element that relates to your own occupation of the property.

There are also a number of capital gains tax advantages, the most important for those nearing retirement being the fact that furnished holiday lettings qualify as a business asset for capital gains retirement relief. Thus, provided you are aged over 55, or are retiring on the grounds of ill health and have been letting the property for at least one year before the date of sale, some measure of retirement relief will be available, with maximum 100 per cent relief on the first £250,000 of gains if the property has been held for at least ten years; and 50 per cent relief on the next slice i.e., £250,000 – £1,000,000. The maximum relief available is reduced if you have been letting the property for less than 10 years.

If you do not qualify for retirement relief, remember that capital gains over and above the £6,000 exemption are now taxed at the rate that would apply if they were treated as income so you could be liable for capital gains tax at 40 per cent if the gains from the sale of a second or holiday home take your taxable income above the £24,300 upper rate threshold.

With the advent of independent taxation, it would be sensible for a married couple to consider whether the property should be held in the husband's name, the wife's name – or owned jointly. A solicitor or accountant would be able to advise you.

To qualify as furnished holiday accommodation, the property must be situated in the UK, be let on a commercial basis and be available for holiday letting for at least 140 days during the tax year and be actually let for at least 70 days. Moreover, for at least seven months a year, not necessarily continuous, the property must not normally be occupied by the same tenant for more than 31 consecutive days. This still leaves you with plenty of time to enjoy the property yourself as well.

The usual word of warning, however: there is always the danger that you might create an assured tenancy, so do take professional advice on drawing up the letting agreement. Similarly, if you decide to use one of the holiday rental agents to market your property, get a solicitor to check any contract you enter into with the company. The **Royal Institution of Chartered Surveyors**, 12 Great George Street, Parliament Square, London SW1P 3AD, T:0171 222 7000, has a useful set of guidelines for managing agents called *Code of Practice for Management of Residential Property*.

A further point to note is that tax inspectors are taking a tougher line as to what is 'commercial' and that loss-making ventures are being threatened with withdrawal of their tax advantages. To safeguard yourself, it is important to draw up a broad business plan before you start and to make a real effort to satisfy the minimum letting requirements.

Finally, property that is rented 'commercially' (i.e. 140 days or more a year) is normally liable for business rates, instead of the council tax you would otherwise pay. This could be more expensive, even though partially allowable against tax.

Useful reading
Housing Booklet No.22, *Letting Rooms in Your Home*; Housing Booklet No.24, *Notice That You Must Leave*. Both available from Citizens' Advice Bureaux and local authority Housing Departments.

Housing benefit

Provided you have no more than £16,000 in savings, you may be able to get help with your rent from your local council. You may qualify for housing benefit whether you are a council or private tenant or live in a hotel or hostel.

Housing benefit is fairly complicated. The following outline is intended only as a very general guide. For more detailed advice about your own particular circumstances, contact your local authority; or your Citizens' Advice Bureau or Age Concern group.

The amount of benefit you get depends on four factors: your eligible rent; your capital or savings; your income; and your 'applicable amount', which is the amount of money the government considers you need for basic living expenses. These are defined roughly as follows:

Eligible rent. This includes rent and some service charges related to the accommodation but excludes meals, water rates and, as a rule, fuel costs. An amount will generally also be deducted for any adult 'non dependant' (including an elderly relative) living in your household, as it is presumed they will be contributing towards housing costs. This does not apply to commercial boarders or sub-tenants – but any income from a boarder or sub-tenant will be taken into account.

Capital. Any capital or savings up to £3,000 will be disregarded and will not affect your entitlement to benefit. People with savings or capital between £3,000 and £16,000 will receive some benefit but this will be on a sliding scale – with every £250 (or part of £250) over £3,000 assessed as being equivalent to an extra £1 a week of their income. (See para below, starting 'If your income is *higher* than your applicable amount ...'). This is called 'tariff income'. If you have savings of more than £16,000, you will not be eligible for housing benefit at all. 'Capital' generally includes all savings, bonds, stocks and shares and property other than your own home and personal possessions. The capital limits are the same for a couple as for a single person.

Income. Income includes earnings, social security benefits, pension income and any other money you have coming in after tax and national insurance contributions have been paid. While most income counts when calculating your entitlement to housing benefit (N.B. a couple's income is added together), some income may be ignored, for example: all disability living allowance and attendance allowance; the first £5 of earnings (single person), £10 of earnings (couple) or £15 of earnings (if your 'applicable amount' includes a disability premium or working carer's premium or, in special cases, the higher pensioner premium); war pensions are also ignored in part.

Applicable amount. Your 'applicable amount' will generally be the same as the amount of income support you would be eligible for and consists of your personal allowance, personal allowances for any younger children (i.e. normally those for whom you are receiving child benefit), plus any premiums (i.e. additional amounts for pensioners, the disabled and so on) to which you might be entitled. As an indication of the amounts involved, a single pensioner under 75 would be deemed to need an income of £65.10 a week; a married retired couple, £101.05 (1995/96 rates). Higher amounts apply for disabled pensioners and those over the age of 75. Details of allowances and premium rates are contained in leaflet NI 196 from your local Social Security office.

If your income is less than your 'applicable amount' you will receive full 100 per cent housing benefit, covering your eligible rent (less any non-dependant deduction), and you may be eligible for income support if your capital is less than £8,000.

If your income is equal to your 'applicable amount' you will also receive maximum housing benefit.

If your income is higher than your 'applicable amount', a taper adjustment will be made and maximum housing benefit will be reduced by 65 per cent of the difference between your income and your 'applicable amount'. If this leaves you with Housing Benefit of less than 50p a week, it is not paid.

How to claim. If you think you are eligible for benefit (see leaflets RR 1 and CTB 1 available from any Social Security office), ask your council for an application form. They should let you know within 14 days of receiving your completed application whether you are entitled to benefit and will inform you of the amount.

Special accommodation. If you live in a mobile home or houseboat, you may be able to claim benefit for site fees or mooring charges. If you live in a private nursing or residential care home you will not normally be able to get housing benefit to help with the cost. However, you may be able to get help towards both the accomodation part of your fees and your living expenses through income support.

If you make a claim for income support you can claim housing benefit and council tax benefit at the same time. A claim form for these is included inside the income support claim form. When completed, the form is returned to the Social Security office and they pass it on to the local authority.

Useful reading
Leaflet RR2 *A Guide to Housing Benefit and Council Tax Benefit*, free from your council.

Income Related Benefits: Income and Capital and Housing Benefit and Council Tax Benefit, free factsheets from Age Concern England, Astral House, 1268 London Road, London SW16 4ER, on receipt of large sae.

Council tax

Council tax is based on the value of the dwelling in which you live (the property element) and also consists of a personal element – with discounts/exemptions applying to certain groups of people.

The property element
Most domestic properties are liable for council tax including rented property, mobile homes and house boats.

The value of the property is assessed according to a banding system, with eight different bands (A to H): ranging in England from property valued at up to £40,000 (band A) to property valued at over £320,000 (band H). In Wales, the bands run from up to £30,000 (band A) to over £240,000 (band H). In Scotland, the bands run from up to £27,000 (band A) to over £212,000 (band H).

The valuation of each property to determine in which band it falls is administered by the Inland Revenue Valuation Office. The ascribed value is based on prices applying at 1 April 1991. Small extensions/other improvements made after this date do not affect the valuation.

New homes will be banded as if they had already been built and sold on 1 April 1991, in order not to penalise occupants of new dwellings.

Notification of the band is shown on the bill when it is sent out in April. If you think there has been a misunderstanding about the valuation (or your liability to pay the full amount) you have the right of appeal (see 'Appeals' further along).

The personal element

Not everyone pays council tax. The bill is normally sent to the owner, or joint owners, of the property; or in the case of rented accommodation, to the tenant or joint tenants; or in the case of licensed property, to the residents or joint residents.

In some cases, for example in hostels or multi-occupied property, a landlord or owner may pass on a share of the bill to the tenants/residents which would probably be included as part of the rental charge.

The valuation of each dwelling assumes that two adults will be resident. The charge does not increase if there are more adults. However if, as in many homes, there is a single adult, your council tax bill will be reduced by 25 per cent.

There are also a number of other special discounts, or exemptions, as follows:

- People who are severely mentally impaired qualify for a 25 per cent discount;
- Disabled people who require additional space may have their bill reduced to a lower band;
- People on income support should normally have nothing to pay, as their bill will be met in full by the benefit;
- Disabled people on higher rate attendance allowance need not count a full-time carer as an additional resident and therefore may continue to qualify for the 25 per cent single (adult) householder discount; exceptions are spouses/partners and parents of a disabled child under 18 who would normally be living with the disabled person and whose presence therefore would not be adding to the council tax;
- Young people over 18 but still at school are not counted when assessing the number of adults in a house;
- Students living in halls of residence, student hostels or similar are exempted; those living with a parent or other non-student adult are eligible for the 25 per cent personal discount;
- Service personnel living in barracks or married quarters will not receive any bill for council tax.

Discounts/exemptions applying to property

Certain property is either exempt from council tax or is eligible for a discount.

Discounts. Empty property (e.g. second homes) normally gets a 50 per cent discount. There are some exceptions where empty property is treated more generously – see exemptions below.

Exemptions. The most common cases of exemptions include:

- Property in course of being built or undergoing major structural alteration/repair: the exemption will last until six months after the work is completed;
- Property which has been unoccupied and unfurnished for less than six months;
- Home of a deceased person: the exemption lasts until six months after the grant of probate;
- Home that is empty because the occupier is absent in order to care for someone else;

- Home of a person who is/would be exempted from council tax due to moving to a residential home or similar;
- Granny flats that are part of another private domestic dwelling may be exempt but this depends on access and other conditions. To check, contact your local Valuation Office.

Business-cum-domestic property
Business-cum-domestic property is rated according to usage, with the business section assessed for business rates and the domestic section for council tax. For example, where there is a flat over a shop, the value of the shop would not be included in the valuation for council tax.

Transitional arrangements
Transitional arrangements have been introduced in areas including London and the South East where council tax bills might otherwise work out considerably higher than a household's previous community charge. The arrangements will continue to apply until at least April 1996. For further information, see booklet *Council Tax: The Transitional Reduction Scheme*, obtainable from your local council.

Appeals
People who feel they have been wrongly assessed for council tax have the right of appeal.

In the first instance, you should take up the matter with the valuation office (see local telephone directory). If the matter is not resolved, you can then appeal to an independent valuation tribunal. For advice and further information, contact your CAB.

Useful reading
- *Council Tax: A Guide to the New Tax for Local Government*
- *Council Tax: Valuation and Banding*
- *Council Tax: Liability, Discounts and Exemptions*
- *Council Tax: How to Appeal*

All obtainable free from any council office or CAB. Also available in 11 ethnic languages.

Council tax benefit. If you cannot afford your council tax because you have a low income, you may be able to obtain council tax benefit. The help is more generous than many people realise. For example, people on income support are entitled to rebates of up to 100 per cent. Even if you are not receiving any other social security benefit, you may still qualify for some council tax benefit. The amount you get depends on: your income, savings, your personal circumstances, who else lives in your home (in particular whether they would be counted as a 'non-dependant') and on your net council tax bill, i.e. after any reductions which apply to your home. If you are not sure whether your income is low enough to entitle you to council tax benefit, it is worth claiming as you could be pleasantly surprised. If you disagree with your council's decision, you can ask for this to be reviewed. If you still think your council has made a mistake, you can ask for a further review by a local Review Board.

For further information, ask your local Social Security office for leaflet: CTB 1 *Help with the Council Tax*. As well as the English version, this is available in 11 other languages.

Useful organisations

The following should be able to provide general advice about housing and help with housing problems:

• Local authority Housing Departments
• Housing Advice or Housing Aid Centres
• Citizens' Advice Bureaux
• Local authority Social Service Departments if your problem is linked to disability
• Welfare Rights Centres if your problem, for example, concerns a landlord who does not keep the property properly maintained
• Local councillors and MPs

Other organisations that provide a helpful service are:

CHAS, Catholic Housing Aid Society, 209 Old Marylebone Road, London NW1 5QT. T:0171 723 7273. CHAS, which celebrates its 40th anniversary in 1996, serves anyone in acute housing need regardless of race or religion. It provides free advice and information and also an advocacy service. A range of useful leaflets, covering welfare benefits and debt, is available on request.

Federation of Private Residents' Associations Ltd., 62 Bayswater Road, London W2 3PS. T:0171 402 1581. This is a federation of associations of long leaseholders and tenants in private blocks of flats. It advises on setting up residents' associations and provides legal and other advice to its member associations. It issues newsletters and information sheets, publishes a pack on how to form a tenants'/residents' association (price £10 incl. p&p) and acts as a pressure group seeking to influence legislation regarding tenancy and management of flats in the private sector.

Shelter, The National Campaign for Homeless People, 88 Old Street, London EC1V 9HU. T:0171 253 0202. Shelter provides advice to 64,000 badly housed and homeless people each year through a national network of 37 Housing Aid Centres and a London freephone advice line.

Useful reading
The Housing Year Book. This is published annually in the Longmans Community Information Guide series and will be found in most library reference sections. It lists,

among others: all national and local government offices responsible for housing, all national advisory bodies, major house builders, housing associations, professional bodies and trade associations involved with house building. This is an invaluable book for anyone considering the options for retirement housing.

Housing Options for Older People, by David Bookbinder, price £4.95 from Age Concern. Provides a realistic look at all the housing choices for older people.

Your Home in Retirement: An Owner's Guide; £2.50 from Age Concern. Information on repairs and maintenance, heating, security and adaptations for disabled people.

Which? Way to Buy, Sell and Move House. Price £10.99. Describes how to move house painlessly and cheaply, including buying and selling, available p&p free from Consumers' Association, Castlemead, Gascoyne Way, Hertford X, SG14 1LH.

Your Home in Retirement, free Department of the Environment booklet, available from Citizens' Advice Bureaux.

9 Leisure Activities

Whether you are looking forward to devoting more time to an existing interest, resuming an old hobby, studying for a degree or trying your hand at an entirely new pastime, the choice is enormous.

You can do anything from basket-weaving to bridge, archery to amateur dramatics. You can join a music-making group, a Scrabble club, a photographic society or become a beekeeper. There are any number of historic homes and beautiful gardens to visit, as well as museums, art galleries, abbeys and castles.

Almost every locality now has excellent sports facilities and thanks to the efforts of the Sports Council, there is scope for complete novices to take up bowls, golf, badminton and many others. Similarly, there are dancing and keep-fit classes, railway enthusiasts' clubs and groups devoted to researching their local history. Many of the organisations offer special concessionary rates to people of retirement age, as do a number of theatres and other places of entertainment.

This chapter should be read in conjunction with Chapter 14, Holidays, as many of the organisations listed there – such as the Field Studies Council – could apply equally well here. However, to avoid repetition, most are only described once. Those that appear in the Holidays chapter tend in the main either to offer residential courses or would probably involve most people in spending a few days away from home to take advantage of the facilities.

While every effort has been made to ensure that prices are correct, these cannot be guaranteed and those quoted should, therefore, only be taken as a guide rather than gospel. The reason is that most organisations alter their charges from time to time and since there is no set date when this happens, it is impossible to keep track.

In addition to the suggestions contained in this chapter, your library, local authority recreation department and adult education institute will be able to signpost you to other activities in your area.

Given the immense variety of tantalising options on offer, it is perhaps no wonder that many retired people find that they have never been as busy in their lives.

Animals

If you are an animal lover, you will already know about such events as sheep dog trials, gymkhanas and the many wild life sanctuaries around the country. Our list is effectively limited to 'the birds and the bees' with just a couple of extra suggestions for fun.

British Beekeepers' Association, National Agricultural Centre, Stoneleigh, Warwickshire CV8 2LZ. T:01203 696679. The Association runs correspondence courses and practical demonstrations and will be glad to put you in touch with one of the 63 local organisations.

Our Dogs, 5 Oxford Road, Station Approach, Manchester M60 1SX. T:0161 237 1272. If you would enjoy showing a dog, the weekly newspaper *Our Dogs* gives details of local shows, rule and registration changes and also news and addresses of Canine and Breed Societies all over the country. There is an *Our Dogs* diary, which contains feeding and other hints, advice about the Kennel Club and much other useful information. For cat lovers, a similar magazine called *Cats* is available from the same publisher. Should you wish to receive a complimentary copy of either *Our Dogs* or *Cats*, please write, mentioning the *Good non-Retirement Guide* to Sue Jameson at the *Our Dogs* address.

Wildfowl Wetlands Trust, Slimbridge, Gloucester GL2 7BT. T:01453 890333/890065. WWT works to save wetlands and to conserve their wildlife. In addition to Slimbridge, there are centres in Lancashire, Sussex, Tyne & Wear, Cambridgeshire/Norfolk Border, Dumfriesshire, South Wales and Northern Ireland. Membership, which costs £17 (£12 for senior citizens), gives you free entry to all eight WWT centres plus receipt of the biannual magazine. Wheelchair access to reserves and hides.

Adult education

Ever longed to take a degree, learn about computing, study philosophy or do a course in archaeology? Opportunities for education abound with these and scores of other subjects easily available to everyone, regardless of age or previous qualifications.

Adult Education Institutes

There is an Adult Education Institute in most areas of the country. Classes normally start in September and run through the academic year. Many AEIs allow concessionary fees for students over 60.

Choice of subjects is enormous and at one institute alone we counted over 50 options, ranging from Indian history, video production and creative writing to self-defence, calligraphy, dressmaking and drama. Ask at your local library for details. Or in London, buy booklet *Floodlight* (£3.25), available from most bookstalls.

National Adult School Organisation, Masu Centre, Gaywood Croft, Cregoe Street, Birmingham B15 2ED. T:0121 622 3400. National Adult Schools 'Friendship through Discussion' groups meet in members' homes or in halls, weekly or fortnightly. They follow either a national study syllabus or topics of their own choice. Some groups organise social activities and weekend conferences and there is also a national summer school each year. For information about your local group, write to the above address, enclosing sae.

National Extension College, 18 Brooklands Avenue, Cambridge CB2 2HN. T:01223 316644. The NEC is a non-profit making body established to provide high quality home study courses for adults, details of which are listed in their free *Guide to Courses*, available on request. Many of the NEC's most able students are retired and are returning to study after many years. There is a choice of over 100 courses including: GCSE and 'A' level studies, book-keeping, birdwatching, creative writing, modern languages and many others. Some courses specifically help students prepare for the Open University. A student adviser will help you make an appropriate choice. Cost is £50 upwards depending on which course you select, with 15 per cent discount for pensioners on courses costing £86 and over.

Open and Distance Learning Quality Council, 27 Marylebone Road, London NW1 5JS. T:0171 935 5391. If you want to study at home by correspondence, the Council will give you a list of colleges which teach your chosen subject, plus general advice on correspondence courses. Choice of subjects is enormous and, as well as academic and business subjects, includes such options as carpentry, creative writing, graphology, needlework and sailing courses.

Open University, Central Enquiry Service, PO Box 200, Walton Hall, Milton Keynes MK7 6YZ. T:01908 653231. Why not take a degree or a short course through the Open University? Students are all ages – the oldest OU graduate was 92 – no academic qualifications are required and there is a vast range of subjects from which to choose.

Courses normally involve a mix of: correspondence work, radio and TV programmes, audio and video cassettes, contact with local tutors and, in some cases, also a residential school with plenty of opportunities for meeting other students. You can study entirely at your own speed: on average people take up to six or eight years to acquire a degree. However, there is no long-term commitment and it is quite possible to sign on just for one course.

In addition to its degree studies, the Open University offers courses for 'associate' students and study packs in areas of general community and vocational interest. There are also materials designed for use by groups on such subjects as planning for retirement and working with older people. Fees range from under £10 for a study pack to £500 for a degree level course taken as an associate student. (Other courses, designed for professional and technical audiences can be considerably more expensive.) Some local authorities will give financial assistance.

Television and radio
Both the BBC and Channel 4 are very active on the learning front.

BBC Education, 201 Wood Lane, White City, London W12 7TS. T:0181 746 1111. Details of all education and training programmes are available on request. Many have accompanying books, audio and video cassettes.

Channel 4 produces many booklets and leaflets in connection with their programmes, on a wide range of topics from history, the arts and sport to health, disability and politics. There is also a Talking Heads Club for individual viewers who wish to learn by talking about programmes. For further information write enclosing sae to: **Channel 4**, PO Box 4000, London W5 2PA.

University extra-mural departments

Many universities have a Department of Extra-Mural Studies which arranges courses for adults, sometimes in the evening or during the vacation periods. For example, the University of London runs over 1,000 part-time courses through the Centre for Extra-Mural Studies at Birkbeck College, including such subjects as: astronomy, music, philosophy, social studies and history. Classes meet about once weekly and students are encouraged to do reading and written work. Fees vary according to the length of the course. For information about the University of London, write to: **Birkbeck College**, University of London, Centre for Extra-Mural Studies, 26 Russell Square, London WC1B 5DQ. T:0171 631 6633. For other universities, enquire locally.

University of the Third Age, U3A National Office, 1 Stockwell Green, London SW9 9JF. T:0171 737 2541. U3A is a self-help movement for people no longer in paid work, offering a wide range of educational, creative and leisure activities. It operates through a national network of local U3As, each of which determines its own courses and social programmes according to the interests of its members. There is also a national newspaper *Third Age News* which is published four times a year. Individuals may join as Associates for £5 per annum. For a brochure, together with a list of names and addresses of all local U3As, contact the National Office enclosing 6″ x 10″ sae.

Workers' Educational Association, Temple House, 17 Victoria Park Square, Bethnal Green, London E2 9PB. T:0181 983 1515. There are WEA branches in all parts of the country, offering a wide range of adult education courses including education for retirement. There is normally a choice of part-time, day or evening classes. Your library or education authority should be able to put you in touch with your local branch. Alternatively, contact the above address.

Arts

Enjoyment of the arts is certainly no longer confined to London. Whether you are interested in active participation or just appreciating the performance of others, there is an exhilarating choice of events including theatre, music, exhibitions, film-making and so on. Many entertainments offer concessionary prices to retired people.

Regional arts boards and local arts councils

For first-hand information about what is going on in your area, contact your regional arts board; or in the case of those living in Scotland, Wales and Northern Ireland, the national arts council. Most areas arrange an immensely varied programme with musical events, drama, arts and craft exhibitions and sometimes more unusual functions, offering something of interest to just about everyone. Many regional arts boards produce regular newsletters with details of arts events in their area.

Eastern Arts Board, Cherry Hinton Hall, Cherry Hinton Road, Cambridge CB1 4DW. T:01223 215355. For Bedfordshire, Cambridgeshire, Essex, Hertfordshire, Lincolnshire, Norfolk and Suffolk.

East Midlands Arts Board, Mountfields House, Forest Road, Loughborough, Leics LE11 3HU. T:01509 218292. For Derbyshire (excluding High Peak District), Leicestershire, Northamptonshire and Nottinghamshire.

London Arts Board, Elme House, 133 Long Acre, London WC2E 9AF. T:0171 240 1313. For the area of the 32 London boroughs and the City of London.

Northern Arts Board, 9-10 Osborne Terrace, Jesmond, Newcastle upon Tyne NE2 1NZ. T:0191 281 6334. For Cleveland, Cumbria, Durham, Northumberland, Metropolitan Districts of Newcastle, Gateshead, North Tyneside, Sunderland and South Tyneside.

North West Arts Board, 12 Harter Street, Manchester M1 6HY. T:0161 228 3062. For Greater Manchester, High Peak District of Derbyshire, Lancashire, Cheshire and Merseyside.

Southern Arts Board, 13 St. Clement Street, Winchester, Hants SO23 9DQ. T:01962 855099. For Berkshire, Buckinghamshire, Hampshire, Isle of Wight, Oxfordshire, Wiltshire and East Dorset.

South East Arts Board, 10 Mount Ephraim, Tunbridge Wells, Kent TN4 8AS. T:01892 515210. For Kent, Surrey, East Sussex and West Sussex.

South West Arts Board, Bradninch Place, Gandy Street, Exeter EX4 3LS. T:01392 218188. For Avon, Cornwall, Devon, Dorset (except Districts of Bournemouth, Christchurch and Poole), Gloucestershire and Somerset.

West Midlands Arts Board, 82 Granville Road, Birmingham B1 2LH. T:0121 631 3121. For the counties of Hereford and Worcester, Shropshire, Staffordshire, Warwickshire, Metropolitan Districts of Birmingham, Coventry, Dudley, Sandwell, Solihull, Walsall and Wolverhampton.

Yorkshire and Humberside Arts Board, 21 Bond Street, Dewsbury, West Yorkshire WF13 1AX. T:01924 455555. For Metropolitan Districts of Barnsley,

Bradford, Calderdale, Doncaster, Kirklees, Leeds, Rotherham, Sheffield, Wakefield, Counties of Humberside and North Yorkshire.

National arts councils

Scottish Arts Council, 12 Manor Place, Edinburgh EH3 7DD. T:0131 226 6051.

Arts Council of Wales, 9 Museum Place, Cardiff CF1 3NX. T:01222 394711.

Arts Council of Northern Ireland, 185 Stranmillis Road, Belfast BT9 5DU. T:01232 381591.

For those who wish to join in amateur arts activities, public libraries keep lists of choirs, drama clubs, painting clubs and similar activities in their locality.

Films and film making
The cinema continues to flourish as an art form with film societies, opportunities for movie-making, as well as chances to view some of the great performances.

British Federation of Film Societies, PO Box 1DR, London W1A 1DR. T:0171 734 9300. The British Film Institute's *Film and TV Yearbook* lists all film societies in the country and should be available from your local library. Many societies offer reduced rates for senior citizens.

Institute of Amateur Cinematographers, 24c West Street, Epsom, Surrey KT18 7RJ. T:01372 739672. Members can ask for advice on all matters from scripting to animation. There is a library of some of the world's greatest amateur films and also a tape library with illustrated lectures, available to members and groups. The Institute runs an amateur film festival while regional councils organise local competitions, workshops and meetings. Members receive a bi-monthly magazine *Amateur Film and Video Maker*. Cost of joining is £22 a year, with a discount for members over 65.

National Film Theatre, South Bank, London SE1 8XT. T:0171 928 3232. Some 2,000 films are shown a year at the NFT's three cinemas. Membership, which admits up to three guests and costs £11.95 annually, is available from the NFT or from the **British Film Institute**, 21 Stephen Street, London W1P 1PL, T:0171 255 1444.

Music and ballet
Scope ranges from becoming a Friend and supporting one of the famous 'Houses' such as Covent Garden to music-making in your own right.

Friends. If you live close enough to take advantage of the 'perks', subscribing as a Friend allows you a number of very attractive advantages including in all cases priority for bookings.

English National Opera, London Coliseum, St. Martin's Lane, London WC2N 4ES. T:0171 632 8300. As a member of ENO's Premium Mailing List, you can enjoy a Coliseum tour, attend recitals and gain an insight into the creation of opera through a variety of special lunch-time and evening events. There is a magazine and you also receive advance programme information. Membership costs £15 a year.

Friends of Covent Garden, Royal Opera House, Covent Garden, London WC2E 9DD. T:0171 212 9412 or 0171 240 1212. Friends receive regular mailings of news and information, a free copy of the magazine *Opera House* plus opportunities to attend talks, recitals, study days, master classes and certain 'open' rehearsals of ballet and opera. Subject to availability, Friends can buy reduced price tickets one-and-a-half hours before the performance. Annual membership is £45.

Friends of Sadler's Wells, Rosebery Avenue, London EC1R 4TN. T:0171 278 1152. Sadler's Wells has an ever-changing programme of ballet, opera and contemporary dance. Friends are invited to open rehearsals, talks, demonstrations and social events with the resident and visiting companies. They also receive a regular newsletter and ticket concessions. People of retirement age can join the Friends for an annual membership of £12.

Music making
Just about every style of music is catered for, from bell-ringing to recorder playing. There is even an orchestra for retired people. Information about local societies and other groups is contained in the *British Music Education Year Book* and the *British Music Year Book*, both of which should be in the reference section of your library.

Handbell Ringers of Great Britain, 9 Dale Road, Grantham, Lincs NG31 8EF. T:01476 591986. The Society exists to promote the art of handbell tune ringing. It arranges rallies, concerts, workshops and lectures. To contact your local group, write to the above address, enclosing sae.

National Association of Choirs, 21 Charmouth Road, Lower Weston, Bath BA1 3LJ. T:01225 426713. The Association will put you in contact with an amateur choir in your area.

National Federation of Music Societies, Francis House, Francis Street, London SW1P 1DE. T:0171 828 7320. The National Federation can provide you with addresses of some 1,500 affiliated choral societies, orchestras and music societies throughout the country. Most charge a nominal membership fee and standards range from the semi-professional to the unashamedly amateur.

Society of Recorder Players, 15 Palliser Road, London W14 9EB. T:0171 385 7321. The Society has groups in many areas where members play together regularly. The branches welcome players of all standards and ages but do not provide tuition for beginners. There is an annual festival with massed playing, competitions and concerts. Annual subscription which includes a quarterly magazine is £9. Branch subscriptions may differ. Write to the Society, enclosing sae, for a list of addresses.

Poetry

Not so long ago, poetry was very much a minority interest. However, largely thanks to both the media and the Poetry Society, there has been a great upsurge in poetry readings in clubs, pubs and other places of entertainment. Your library should be able to tell you about any special local events.

The Poetry Society, 22 Betterton Street, London WC2H 9BU. T:0171 240 4810. Membership of the Society is open to anyone who enjoys reading, listening to or writing poetry. The Society runs a poetry criticism service where, for an agreed fee, you can have your work assessed. Each year the Society organises a National Poetry Competition with a first prize of £4,000. Additionally, members receive the Society's quarterly magazines *Poetry Review* and *Poetry News*. Annual subscription is £24, £18 for senior citizens. For further information, contact Rachel Bourke.

Television and radio audiences

If you would like to be part of the invited studio audience for a radio or television programme, you can apply to the BBC through the relevant ticket unit for London-based programmes; or for outside London, through the appropriate regional centre. The ticket unit addresses are:

The Ticket Unit, **BBC Television**, Wood Lane, Shepherd's Bush, London W12 7RJ.
The Ticket Unit, **BBC Radio**, Broadcasting House, London W1A 1AA.

For independent television, audience participation in programmes is the responsibility of each programme maker and requests should be channelled to the appropriate contractor for the area. Addresses are as follows:

Anglia Television, Anglia House, Norwich NR1 3JG.

Border Television, The Broadcasting Centre, Durranhill, Carlisle CA1 3NT.

Carlton Television Ltd., 101 St. Martin's Lane, London WC2N 4AZ.

Central Independent Television, Central House, Broad Street, Birmingham B1 2JP.

Channel Television, The Television Centre, St. Helier, Jersey, Channel Islands JE2 3ZD.

Grampian Television, Queen's Cross, Aberdeen AB9 2XJ.

Granada Television, Granada Television Centre, Manchester M60 9EA.

HTV Wales, The Television Centre, Culverhouse Cross, Cardiff CF5 6XJ.

HTV West, The Television Centre, Bath Road, Bristol BS4 3HG.

London Weekend Television (LWT), The London Television Centre, London SE1 9LT.

Meridian Broadcasting Ltd., Television Centre, Southampton SO14 0PZ.

Scottish Television, Cowcaddens, Glasgow G2 3PR.

Tyne Tees Television, The Television Centre, City Road, Newcastle upon Tyne NE1 2AL.

Ulster Television, Havelock House, Ormeau Road, Belfast BT7 1EB.

Westcountry Television Ltd., Western Wood Way, Langage Science Park, Plymouth PL7 5BG.

Yorkshire Television, The Television Centre, Leeds LS3 1JS.

GMTV Ltd., The London Television Centre, London SE1 9TT.

Channel 4 Television Corporation, 124 Horseferry Road, London SW1P 2TX.

S4C, Welsh Fourth Channel Authority, Parc Busnes Ty Glas, Llanishen, Cardiff CF4 5DU.

British Sky Broadcasting, 6 Centaurs Business Park, Grant Way, Isleworth, Middlesex TW7 5QD.

Independent Television News (ITN), 200 Gray's Inn Road, London WC1X 8XZ.

The Network Centre ITV, 200 Gray's Inn Road, London WC1X 8HF.

Teletext Ltd., 101 Farm Lane, London SW6 1QJ.

Data Broadcasting International Ltd., Allen House, Station Road, Egham, Surrey TW20 9NT.

Theatre

Details of current and forthcoming productions, as well as theatre reviews, are contained in the newspapers. As general wisdom, preview performances are invariably cheaper and there are often concessionary tickets for matinees. Listed here are one or two theatres and organisations that offer special facilities of interest, including priority booking and reduced price tickets. Also included is an association for enthusiasts of amateur dramatics.

Arts and Music Club, The Applause Building, 68 Long Acre, London WC2E 9JQ. T:0171 312 1991. Members have the opportunity to attend regular cultural activities as well as special events such as invitations to first nights and private viewings at art galleries and exhibitions. These are often combined with social occasions, for example pre-theatre suppers or drinks after the show, where members can enjoy meeting other like-minded people. There is a club magazine published 11 times a year which, among other information, gives details of discounts, including special prices for travel and hotel bookings.

Most visits are to London but short breaks to Stratford, York, Cheltenham, Bath and other cities are frequently arranged. Annual membership of the Club costs £25.

Barbican Centre, Silk Street, London EC2Y 8DS. T:0171 638 4141 (for information). Box Office: 0171 638 8891. The Barbican Centre combines two theatres, concert hall, art gallery, concourse gallery, cinemas and library. The Centre offers tours of the building, frequent free live musical events in the foyers (including regular Sunday lunchtime jazz), free exhibitions and restaurant facilities. Reduced tickets for senior citizens are available for many concerts and theatre performances on a standby basis and are also given for the cinema and art gallery. For £6 a year (1995), mailing list subscribers receive a monthly diary and enjoy priority booking facilities for concerts and films.

Royal National Theatre, South Bank, London SE1 9PX. T:0171 928 2252 (box office). The Royal National Theatre offers backstage tours, talks by theatre professionals, live foyer music before performances, free exhibitions and restaurant facilities as well as its three theatres. There are group price reductions for most performances and pensioners can buy matinee seats (midweek and Saturday) for £9.50. The Royal National Theatre has a Mailing List Membership (£6.75 a year) which provides: advance information, priority booking and exclusive special ticket offers. For details, contact **Royal National Theatre**, Mailing List, Freepost, London SE1 7BR; or ring 0171 261 9256 (10 a.m. to 6 p.m., Monday to Friday).

Society of London Theatre (SOLT), Bedford Chambers, The Piazza, Covent Garden, London WC2E 8HQ. T:0171 836 0971. The Society co-ordinates a scheme under which senior citizens can get substantial reductions for midweek matinee performances at many West End theatres. Look for the symbol 'M' in *The London Theatre Guide* or the *Independent* listings. Senior citizens can also receive concessionary prices for evening performances or weekend matinees on a standby basis with all listings showing the symbol 'S'. Standby tickets are available approximately an hour before the performance begins.

Concessions are subject to availability and it is always wise to check with the box office to make sure there are tickets before setting off for a performance. When buying tickets on a concessionary basis, you will need to present proof of your senior citizen status at the box office, for example, using a travel pass or pension book. Annual subscription to the *London Theatre Guide* costs £11. Write to the Society at the above address.

The Society presents the annual Laurence Olivier Awards. Members of the general public serve on the judging panels. If you would like to be considered for the Theatre, Opera or Dance panel, write for an application form. Members of the panels receive two complimentary tickets for all nominated productions during the judging period.

You can buy Theatre Tokens from over 150 theatres throughout the UK, including all London West End theatres. Tokens are also available from selected branches of W.H. Smith or through **Tokenline** (24 hours) 0171 240 8800.

Also extremely useful is the Society's *Disabled Access Guide to London West End Theatres* which provides information about special facilities, access for wheelchairs, transport advice and price concessions for disabled theatregoers. Available free from West End theatres or by post from SOLT (please send 38p sae).

Scottish Community Drama Association, 5 York Place, Edinburgh EH1 3EB. T:0131 557 5552. The Association aims to develop amateur drama in the community by offering clubs and societies advice, encouragement and practical help. Individual membership (£10 a year) gives access to the Association's libraries, training courses and script discounts. The Association also runs playwriting competitions and can put you in touch with local dramatic societies. Members receive regular copies of the house magazine *Scene*.

Leicester Square Ticket Booth. The Booth sells tickets to many West End theatres at half-price on the day of performance. It is open to personal callers only Tuesday – Sunday at 12 noon for matinees; Monday – Saturday at 1 p.m. – 6.30 p.m. for evening performances. There is a service charge of £2. Payment in cash only.

Late night trains. Late night trains for theatregoers run from many London stations. For details of services, enquire at your local station.

Visual arts
If you enjoy attending exhibitions and lectures, membership of some of the arts societies offers you a number of delightful privileges.

Contemporary Art Society, 20 John Islip Street, London SW1P 4LL. T:0171 821 5323. The aim of the Society is to promote the collecting of contemporary art and to acquire works by living artists for gift to public galleries. Members can take part in an extensive programme of events including: visits to artists' studios and private collections, previews and parties at special exhibitions, day trips outside London and courses on building up a collection. Membership benefits include a quarterly newsletter and concessionary rates to exhibitions at the Tate Gallery. The annual subscription is £30, £35 per couple.

National Art Collections Fund, Millais House, 7 Cromwell Place, London SW7 2JN. T:0171 225 4800. The National Art Collections Fund raises money to help museums, galleries and historic houses buy works of art to enrich their collections. The benefits of membership include: free entrance to 142 museums and galleries; concessionary admission to many important exhibitions; a countrywide programme of lectures, concerts, private views and other special events including visits to houses not normally open to the public; *The Art Quarterly* magazine plus an illustrated catalogue of the year's acquisitions. There are also art tours at home and abroad led by experts. Subscription (1995) is £25 per year; senior citizens, £15.

National Association of Decorative & Fine Arts Societies, NADFAS House, 8 Guilford Street, London WC1N 1DT. T:0171 430 0730. Member societies of NADFAS have programmes of monthly lectures, museum and gallery visits, as well as guided tours of historic houses. Events are usually held in the daytime (although some take place in the evening) and some societies may be able to help with transport.

Many societies have volunteer groups working in historic houses and galleries and there are also church-recorder groups which make detailed records of the interiors of churches. Details of your local society are available from NADFAS at the above address. Membership of a local society is about £18-£25 a year. It gives access to nationally run study courses, a twice yearly magazine, reduced entry to some galleries plus day events and the opportunity to join organised tours both in the UK and abroad.

Royal Academy of Arts, Piccadilly, London W1V 0DS. T:0171 439 7438. Senior citizens enjoy reduced entrance charges to all exhibitions, including the big annual Summer Exhibition. You can become a Friend of the Royal Academy, which gives you free admission with a companion, saves you from queuing and entitles you to reduced price catalogues. Members may also use the Friends' Room to meet for coffee, are invited to private views and may attend lectures, concerts and go on tours. Subscriptions (1995) are: £37 a year; people over 60, £30. Alternatively, the 'Academy Card', at £15 allows immediate admission to any five exhibitions over an 18-month period.

Tate Gallery, Millbank, London SW1P 4RG. T:0171 887 8000. Recorded Information: 0171 887 8008. The gallery comprises the national collections of British painting and also international 20th century painting and sculpture. Another attraction is the Clore Gallery extension for the Turner Collection. There are free lectures (Tuesday-Sunday) and guided tours every day except Sunday; also special tours for disabled people by prior arrangement. Friends of the Tate enjoy free admission to all exhibitions and may bring two guests on the first Thursday evening of every month. Additionally, they are invited to private views and have opportunities to attend lectures at other galleries. Membership is £30 (£25 senior citizens).

Recent additions include the Tate Gallery, Liverpool, which houses the national collection of 20th century art in the North and the Tate Gallery, St. Ives, which features changing displays of painting and sculpture by artists associated with Cornwall.

Painting as a hobby

If you are interested in improving your own painting technique, rather than simply viewing the works of great masters, contact your local Adult Education Institute for details of courses in your area. Your library may have information about local painting groups, clubs and societies.

Crafts

The vast majority of suggestions are contained in Chapter 14, Holidays, variously under 'Arts and crafts' and 'Special interest holidays', the reason being that most of the organisations concerned make a feature of arranging residential courses or of organising, for example, painting holidays. However, if you are interested in a particular form of craft work and want information or advice, many of the societies and others listed in Chapter 14 should be able to help you. Herewith one or two additional possibilities.

The Basketmakers' Association, Hon. Secretary: Mrs Ann Brooks, Pond Cottage, North Road, Chesham Bois, Amersham, Bucks HP6 5NA. T:01494 726189. The Association promotes better standards of design and technique in the art of basketmaking, chair seating and allied crafts. It arranges day schools, residential courses, demonstrations and exhibitions. There is a quarterly newsletter. Membership costs £10 (£14 family membership, two people).

Crafts Council, 44A Pentonville Road, Islington, London N1 9BY. T:0171 278 7700. As well as holding exhibitions, the Crafts Council runs an information centre and reference library which can give advice on almost everything you could possibly want to know: different craft courses throughout the country, suppliers of materials, addresses of craft guilds and societies, factsheets on business practice for craftspeople as well as details of craft fairs and markets, galleries, shops and other outlets for work. Additionally, the Council has a slide and video library, publishes a bi-monthly magazine, *Crafts*, and maintains both an index of craftspeople and a national register of makers. Admission to the Crafts Council Gallery is free: open, Tuesday to Saturday, 11 to 6; and Sunday, 2 to 6 p.m.

The Embroiderers' Guild, Apartment 41, Hampton Court Palace, East Molesey, Surrey KT8 9AU. T:0181 943 1229. The Guild exists to promote the craft of embroidery to the highest possible standards. Membership is open to all, beginners and experts, with an interest in embroidery and related crafts. Members receive a newsletter twice a year giving information about embroidery activities throughout the country. They can use the Guild's facilities at Hampton Court: visit the collection of embroideries and lace, borrow study folios and attend classes and lectures. There is also a full programme of residential weekends, seminars, exhibitions and tours in the UK and abroad. As well as being an individual member, they can join one of the Guild's 160 local branches which organise lectures, workshops and other activities.

Full membership is £24.50; £16 for those over 60. Branches have their own subscription rates.

Open College of the Arts, Houndhill, Worsbrough, Barnsley, South Yorkshire S70 6TU. T:01226 730495. The OCA, which is affiliated to the Open University, offers courses for those wishing to acquire or improve their skills in drawing, painting, sculpture, textiles, photography, creative writing, garden design, music and art history. Course books are supplied and students have professional tutorial support. Course prices average about £200.

Studio 1 D (Ceramic Restorers), 183 (basement) Ladbroke Grove, London W10 6HH. T:0181 969 8683. This china restoration studio runs two-week courses for beginners, which teach all the basic skills including use of tools and materials to enable you to restore china on your own. Cost is about £385 for two weeks (11 a.m. to 6 p.m. Monday to Friday).

Dance/Keep fit

Clubs, classes and groups exist in all parts of the country, variously offering: ballroom, Old Tyme, Scottish, folk, ballet, disco dancing and others. Additionally, there are music and relaxation classes, aerobics and more gentle keep-fit sessions. Many of the relaxation and keep-fit classes in particular cater for all standards and some are specially designed for older people to tone up muscles and improve their circulation while making friends in an agreeable atmosphere. Best advice is to contact your adult education or sports centre, or alternatively the library, to find out what is available in your area. Listed here are some of the national organisations that can advise you and put you in touch with local groups. There are also some extra names in Chapter 13, Health, see 'Keep fit' section.

British Council of Ballroom Dancing, Terpsichore House, 240 Merton Road, South Wimbledon, London SW19 1EQ. T:0181 545 0085. The Council, which is the governing body of ballroom dancing, can put you in touch with a recognised dance school in your area and can also send you information about the many festivals planned for 1996. Contact the Secretary at the above address.

The Central Council of Physical Recreation, Francis House, Francis Street, London SW1P 1DE. T:0171 828 3163/4. The CCPR will provide information on all sporting activities e.g. badminton, swimming, bowls and offer advice to anyone wishing to become involved in a sport or recreation.

English Folk Dance and Song Society, Cecil Sharp House, 2 Regent's Park Road, London NW1 7AY. T:0171 485 2206. There are some 570 clubs around the country which organise both regular and special events. In addition to ordinary folk dancing, programmes may include: country dancing, morris dancing, 'knees up', clog workshops, musician band sessions, sea shanties, lectures and carol concerts. Membership, which includes journals and use of the library, costs £20 (£30 joint membership); £10 and £17 respectively for members over 60. Contact the Society for details of your nearest branch.

Imperial Society of Teachers of Dancing, Euston Hall, Birkenhead Street, London WC1H 8BE. T:0171 837 9967. Throughout the UK there are some 7,000 teachers offering instruction in virtually all forms of dancing. Many organise classes and events particularly for older people. The Society has lists of teachers in each geographic area. There is no standard charge but dance classes and social dancing tend to be an inexpensive activity.

Keep Fit Association, Francis House, Francis Street, London SW1P 1DE. T:0171 233 8898. The Keep Fit Association has a responsible attitude and emphatically does not believe in 70-year-olds trying to ape Olympic gymnasts. KFA teachers have special training in working with older people. Almost all adult education centres run keep-fit classes in the daytime; many have special classes for keeping fit in retirement. (See also Extend, in Chapter 13, Health.)

Royal Scottish Country Dance Society, 12 Coates Crescent, Edinburgh EH3 7AF. T:0131 225 3854. The Society has members from 16 to 80-plus in its many branches and groups all over the world. It publishes books, records and tapes and holds an annual summer school at St. Andrew's University. The branches offer instruction at all levels and members join in dance events. Information about your local branch/ group can be obtained from the RSCDS Secretary.

For people with disabilities

Happily, there are increasingly fewer activities from which disabled people are debarred through lack of suitable facilities, as will be evident from many of the suggestions listed earlier in the chapter. This section, therefore only deals with one topic not covered elsewhere, namely enjoyment of books which for many blind or partially sighted people can be a special problem.

Calibre, Aylesbury, Buckinghamshire HP22 5XQ. T:01296 432339 (24-hour service) and 01296 81211. Calibre is a lending library of over 4,000 recorded books on ordinary standard cassettes. These are available to anyone who cannot read printed books because of poor sight or physical difficulty. A doctor's certificate/letter is required certifying 'inability to read printed books in the normal way' – a photocopy of the Blind Registration is acceptable. Books include fiction and non-fiction and cover the full range of classifications. Borrowers can keep their books for up to a month – two or more at a time. Members must supply their own cassette players. The library is run almost entirely by volunteers and provides a free service although donations are welcomed. A catalogue (in 4 volumes) of the library's adult books is available at a cost of £2.50 per volume.

National Library for the Blind, Cromwell Road, Bredbury, Stockport, Cheshire SK6 2SG, T:0161 494 0217 (24 hours). The Library lends books – and also music scores – in Braille and Moon free of charge to individual readers (post-free). It also provides large print reading material for people who are partially sighted, through public libraries.

National Listening Library, 12 Lant Street, London SE1 1QH. T:0171 407 9417. The Library loans a special tape player and a wide range of titles to those unable to read due to disability. Annual subscription £25. The visually handicapped are catered for separately by the RNIB.

RNIB Talking Book Service, Mount Pleasant, Wembley, Middlesex HA0 1RR. T:0181 903 6666. This is a library service for anyone who is registered as blind or partially sighted or whose vision is such that they cannot easily read normal print (certified on application form by ophthalmologist, optician or GP).

Application for membership should be made to the local authority Social Services Department or direct to the Library. The charge towards the cost of the service is normally paid by members' local authorities. Books, which are unabridged, are recorded on special cassettes which last about 12 hours and are played back on a special machine supplied on permanent loan. There are more than 10,000 titles from which to choose, covering all categories of books.

Games

Many local areas have their own bridge, chess, whist, dominoes, Scrabble and other groups who meet together regularly, either in a club, hall, pub or other social venue to enjoy friendly games. Competitions are organised and certainly in the case of bridge and chess, district and county teams are usually taken very seriously. Your library should know about any clubs or regular group meetings. Alternatively, you can contact the national organisations listed below.

British Chess Federation, 9a Grand Parade, St. Leonards on Sea, East Sussex TN38 0DD. T:01424 442500. Can provide information about chess clubs and tournaments.

English Bridge Union, Broadfields, Bicester Road, Aylesbury, Bucks HP19 3BG. T:01296 394414. There are over 1,000 affiliated bridge clubs nationwide. Members receive a magazine six times a year which, among other features of interest, contains details of tournaments and bridge holidays at home and abroad. Annual membership costs £11.50 plus county fees (which range from £1 to £4).

Scrabble Clubs UK, Richard House, Enstone Road, Enfield, Middx EN3 7TB. T:0181 805 4848. There are around 250 Scrabble Clubs up and down the country. Some have their own premises and are highly competitive. Others meet in halls or members' houses for a friendly game. Many of them are involved in charitable work, such as raising money for people with disabilities or visiting the housebound. Many competitions are held, including a National Scrabble Championship and a big tournament for clubs. Special tournaments for over-60s are organised on a regional basis. For details of your nearest Scrabble Club, contact Philip Nelkon at the above address.

Gardens and gardening

Courses, gardens to visit, special help for people with disabilities, how to run a gardening association ... these and other interests are all catered for by the organisations listed.

The English Gardening School, at the Chelsea Physic Garden, 66 Royal Hospital Road, London SW3 4HS. T:0171 352 4347. The School teaches all aspects of gardening. Courses which range in length from a day to an academic year are held in the historic lecture room of the Chelsea Physic Garden, the centre for the study of horticulture for over 300 years. Topics include among others: Foliage Borders, the Cottage Garden, Roses Old and New, the Mixed Border and Botanical Drawing. Cost is from about £65 a day.

Gardening for the Disabled Trust & Garden Club, Hayes Farmhouse, Hayes Lane, Peasmarsh, Nr. Rye, East Sussex TN31 6XR. The Trust provides practical and financial help to disabled people who want to garden actively. Their Garden Club publishes a quarterly newsletter, gives answers to horticultural questions and encourages gardeners with disabilities to meet. The annual subscription is £3 (£10 for groups), £25 for 10-year membership.

Henry Doubleday Research Association, Ryton Organic Gardens, Ryton-on-Dunsmore, Coventry CV8 3LG. T:01203 303517. The HDRA is Britain's largest organic gardening organisation. It encourages gardening without artificial fertilisers and pesticides and its centre is open to visitors throughout the year. Members (subscription £15, £9 for senior citizens) receive a magazine, a sales catalogue with discounts, gardening advice and free entry to Ryton Organic Gardens. Members can help by experimenting in their own gardens and joining a network of countrywide local groups.

Horticultural Therapy (HT), Goulds Ground, Vallis Way, Frome, Somerset BA11 3DW. T:01373 464782; 24-hour answerphone service for visually impaired people: 01373 467072. HT helps elderly, disabled or visually impaired people to garden. It runs an advisory service by post and telephone. Members receive a quarterly magazine. There are demonstrations, workshops and meetings. The centre can also advise on special tools and where these can be obtained. In addition HT is developing a network of demonstration gardens which will provide all kinds of opportunities for people to get involved in practical gardening, assisted by full-time demonstrators. These are situated in Battersea Park, Syon Park, North London, Beech Hill, near Reading and Ryton Gardens in Coventry. Contact HT above for details of opening hours.

National Gardens Scheme, Hatchlands Park, East Clandon, Guildford, Surrey GU4 7RT. T:01483 211535. (For England and Wales.) The Scheme covers nearly 3,500 private gardens which are open to the public, perhaps one day a year, to raise money mainly for nurses' benevolent funds, the training of Macmillan Nurses, the Gardens Fund of the National Trust and for retired gardeners and their dependants. Tea is often available, as are plants for sale. Further information plus directions are listed in the Scheme's Yellow Book, *The Gardens of England and Wales* (£3 from booksellers or £3.75 including p&p from the address above). Suitability for wheelchairs is also indicated.

The organisation is always looking for new gardens. Should you wish to offer yours, however small, apply to the county organiser whose address is in the handbook. Sometimes two or more gardens share a group opening, particularly on a village basis.

National Society of Allotment and Leisure Gardeners Ltd., O'Dell House, Hunters Road, Corby, Northants NN17 5JE. T:01536 266576. The Society encourages all forms of horticultural education and the forming of local allotment and gardening associations. It also acts as a national voice for allotment and leisure gardeners.

Annual membership costs £6.45; associate membership for home gardeners, £4.50; and society membership, 44p per member. This gives you access to free help and advice, the right to attend the annual meeting plus receipt of the Society's bulletin. There is also a Seeds Scheme, offering special prices. Leaflets are available on growing vegetables, how to form a gardening association and the running of flower shows.

Royal Horticultural Society, PO Box 313, Vincent Square, London SW1P 2PE. T:0171 834 4333. Members receive free entry to gardens and reduced price tickets to shows, including the Chelsea Flower Show. They can also attend lectures and practical demonstrations both in and out of London. There is a monthly magazine and newsletter and members also have the opportunity of using the famous Lindley Library. Membership of the RHS costs £30 (1995) plus a once only enrolment fee of £7. For further information, contact the Membership Manager at the above address.

Scotland's Gardens Scheme, 31 Castle Terrace, Edinburgh EH1 2EL. T:0131 229 1870. The Scheme supports retired Queen's Nurses, the Gardens Fund of the National Trust for Scotland and other charities through 340 gardens which are open to the public either on one day only or on a regular basis. The booklet giving opening times is £2.50 from bookshops (or £3 from the Scheme to include p&p). The Scheme organises a six-day coach tour of houses and gardens in Scotland (cost is about £600).

Useful reading
Gardening in Retirement by Isobel Pays (£1.95) from Age Concern England, Astral House, 1268 London Road, London SW16 4ER.
Gardening Without Sight, £2.50; *Leisure for all – Opportunities for Visually Handicapped People*, £3.50. Available from RNIB Customer Services, PO Box 173, Peterborough PE2 0WS. T:01733 370777.

History

People with an interest in the past have a truly glorious choice of activities to sample. You can visit historic monuments, including ancient castles and stately homes, in all parts of the country; explore the City of London; study genealogy; research the history of your local area; attend lectures and receptions.

Age Exchange Reminiscence Centre, 11 Blackheath Village, Blackheath, London SE3 9LA. T:0181 318 9105. The Centre features exhibitions recording the life-styles of the 1920s and 1930s. There are also publications, depicting the period, for visitors to enjoy plus a year-round programme of activities including, for example, reminiscence through the arts, music and drama. The Centre is open Monday to Saturday, between 10 a.m. and 5.30 p.m., and admission is free. There is sometimes a small charge for entrance to drama productions and similar. The Centre is fully equipped for disabled access.

Architectural Heritage Society of Scotland, The Glasite Meeting House, 33 Barony Street, Edinburgh EH3 6NX. T:0131 557 0019. The Society promotes the protection of Scottish architecture and encourages the study of Scottish buildings, their furniture and fittings, urban design and designed landscapes. There are six regional groups, covering all of Scotland, which arrange regular events including talks, visits and study trips. Members can also become actively involved in defending Scotland's threatened heritage by joining case panels to assess Listed Building and Conservation Area Consent applications. Membership which includes two newsletters and a copy of the Society's annual journal *Architectural Heritage* is £15; £23 for a family (1995 prices).

British Association for Local History, 24 Lower Street, Harnham, Salisbury, Wilts SP2 8EY. T:01722 320115. The Association exists to promote the study of local history. It will give advice and invite you to seminars and courses. Typical topics include introductory days at the Public Record Office, computers in local history and writing about your local area. Annual membership which includes copies of both *The Local Historian* and *Local History News* is £19.

Cadw: Welsh Historic Monuments, Brunel House, 2 Fitzalan Road, Cardiff CF2 1UY. T:01222 500200. Some 127 castles and historic places in Wales are maintained by Cadw. Most are open summer and winter. Season or single entry tickets can be purchased on site.

City of London Information Centre, St. Paul's Churchyard (South side), London EC4M 8BX. T:0171 332 1456. The City of London offers enough interest to occupy you for a year or longer. The Information Centre acts as a tourist office for the area, giving advice and guidance. Among the many attractions, all of which are open to the public at varying times, are: St. Paul's Cathedral, the Guildhall (open Monday – Saturday, 10 a.m. to 5 p.m., through most of the year, free), Dr. Johnson's House, the Monument, Prince Henry's Room, the Royal Exchange, the Barbican, the Central Criminal Court and several museums. Additionally, there are livery halls, food markets and many interesting examples of London's architecture, both classic and contemporary. Many of the 43 churches give organ recitals and, in the summer, you can enjoy open air concerts. The Centre offers lots of free leaflets including the monthly events list.

English Heritage, (Membership Department), PO Box 1BB, London W1A 1BB. T:0171 973 3400. English Heritage manages many historic properties in England. Members receive a Welcome Pack including guidebook (see below) and map. They enjoy free admission to all English Heritage sites and are sent a quarterly magazine publicising events and developments of conservation interest. Annual subscription (1995) is £18.50, £12.50 for senior citizens, with reductions for couples. *Visitors Guide to English Heritage* indicates which sites have access for wheelchairs.

Federation of Family History Societies, The Benson Room, Birmingham and Midland Institute, Margaret Street, Birmingham B3 3BS. An umbrella organisation for 190 societies throughout the world (130 in the UK) that provide assistance if you are interested in tracing your ancestors. Write to the administrator, Mrs Pauline Saul, at the above address who will be glad to put you in contact with your local society, as well as provide some useful guidelines on how to get started. Please enclose (A4) sae.

Friends of Historic Scotland, Longmore House, Salisbury Place, Edinburgh EH9 1SH. T:0131 668 8999. Membership gives you free access to 330 of Scotland's historic buildings and ancient monuments, a free directory of the sites, special guided tours and a quarterly magazine to keep you up to date with new activities. Membership cost is £17 a year; £11 for senior citizens over 60; £16.50 for retired couples.

Garden History Society, 5 The Knoll, Hereford HR1 1RU. T:01432 354479. The Society is concerned with the importance of historic gardens. It organises visits and lectures for members. An annual summer conference and foreign tours are also arranged. There is a newsletter three times a year and a journal, *Garden History*. Subscriptions are £20 single, £25 joint.

Georgian Group, 37 Spital Square, London E1 6DY. T:0171 377 1722. The Group exists to preserve Georgian buildings and to stimulate public knowledge and appreciation of Georgian architecture and town planning. Activities include day visits, long weekends to buildings and gardens, private views of exhibitions and a programme of evening lectures in London. There are regional groups in South Yorkshire, Shropshire, the South West Peninsula, the West of England, East Anglia, the North West and Wales. The Georgian Group also publishes advisory leaflets and holds courses on alterations to Georgian houses. Membership: £20 a year, £32 for a couple.

Historical Association, 59a Kennington Park Road, London SE11 4JH. T:0171 735 3901. The Association brings together people of all ages and backgrounds who share an interest in and love for the past. Members receive *The Historian* (a fully illustrated quarterly magazine) and may join in a wide variety of activities such as lectures, outings, conferences and tours both at home and abroad conducted by expert lecturers. There are over 80 local branches nationwide offering a programme of social events and monthly talks by top historians. The Association also publishes a number of very useful historical pamphlets. Membership costs £23 a year.

Historic Houses Association, 2 Chester Street, London SW1X 7BB. T:0171 259 5688. Friends of the HHA enjoy free entrance during normal opening hours to nearly 300 HHA-member houses and gardens throughout the country, get the quarterly magazine *Historic House* and receive invitations to lectures, concerts, receptions and other events. Membership (HHA, PO Box 21, Unit 7, Campus 5, The Business Park, Letchworth, Herts SG6 2JF. T:01462 675848): individual £24, double £36 (1995).

Monumental Brass Society, c/o Society of Antiquaries of London, Burlington House, Piccadilly, London W1V 0HS. The Society encourages the preservation and appreciation of monumental brasses. Members attend four General Meetings with lectures and discussions and receive three bulletins, the annual *Transactions*, and an invitation both to the annual excursion and conference. Subscription is £18 a year (1995).

There are many brass rubbing centres around the country where facilities are provided for the craft. Westminster Abbey for example is open Monday to Saturday, 9 a.m.- 5 p.m., where for about £2.50 including materials you can make a rubbing from the replicas which come from all over England.

National Trust, 36 Queen Anne's Gate, London SW1H 9AS. T:0181 464 1111. The National Trust exists to protect historic buildings and areas of great natural beauty in England, Wales and Northern Ireland. Membership gives you free entry to the Trust's many properties and to those of the National Trust for Scotland. You also receive three mailings with an annual handbook, magazines and details of activities in your own region. Hundreds of special events are arranged each year, including guided tours, fairs and outdoor entertainments. The Trust publishes a free annual booklet on facilities for visitors with disabilities; those requiring the help of a companion will be charged admission as normal but their companion will be admitted free of charge on request. The booklet is available on receipt of a stamped addressed adhesive label (minimum postage). Individual membership (1995) which includes a copy of the Handbook is £25.

National Trust for Scotland, 5 Charlotte Square, Edinburgh EH2 4DU. T:0131 226 5922. The National Trust for Scotland cares for over 100 properties and 100,000 acres of countryside. Members also enjoy free admission to any of the National Trust properties in England, Wales and Northern Ireland. Individual membership is £24 a year; for a family, £40. Senior Citizens: single membership is £12 a year; £20 for couples.

Northern Ireland Tourist Board, St Anne's Court, North Street, Belfast BT1 1NB. T:01232 231221. The Tourist Board issues a free information bulletin, *Stop and Visit*, listing 140 historic sites and other places of interest together with opening hours and entrance fees. Another free bulletin, *On the Move*, gives details of special bus trips, rail excursions, lake cruises and pleasure boat trips. Many sites are free and others offer reduced rates for pensioners. Further discounts for those over 55 are listed in the *Holiday Breakaways* brochure. An *Events* leaflet describes a selection of the most important, interesting or new events in Northern Ireland each year, such as music festivals, sporting occasions, agricultural shows and art exhibitions.

Oral History Society, Department of Sociology, University of Essex, Wivenhoe Park, Colchester CO4 3SQ; or National Sound Archive, 29 Exhibition Road, London SW7 2AS. The Society offers support and advice to groups and individuals around the country who record the memories of older people, for projects in community history, schools, reminiscence groups and historical research. It publishes twice yearly journals and runs regular workshops and conferences. It welcomes the help of older people in all these activities. Individual membership is £15 a year.

Society of Genealogists, 14 Charterhouse Buildings, Goswell Road, London EC1M 7BA. T:0171 251 8799. The Society promotes the study of genealogy and heraldry. Lectures are arranged throughout the year and there are also a variety of annual courses, including day and weekend seminars. Members have access to the library and also receive a quarterly magazine. There is a joining fee of £7.50. Annual membership is £30; £21 for country members. Non-members may use the library on payment of hourly, half-daily or daily fees.

Victorian Society, 1 Priory Gardens, Bedford Park, London W4 1TT. T:0181 994 1019. The Victorian Society campaigns to preserve fine Victorian and Edwardian buildings. It organises walks, tours, lectures and conferences through its national office and 11 regional groups. Membership: individual, £20; senior citizens, £12.

Hobbies

Whether your special enthusiasm is stamp collecting or model flying, most of the organisations listed organise events, answer queries and can put you in contact with kindred spirits.

The British Association of Numismatic Societies, Secretary: P H Mernick, c/o Bush Boake Allen Ltd., Blackhorse Lane, London E17 5QP. T:0181 523 6531. BANS is an umbrella organisation that helps to co-ordinate the activities of some 60 local clubs for those interested in the study or collection of coins, medals or similar. It organises two conferences a year, maintains a slide library and will be able to put you in touch with your nearest group.

British Jigsaw Puzzle Library, 8 Heath Terrace, Leamington Spa, Warwickshire CV32 5LY. T:01926 311874. This is a lending library with puzzles usually exchanged by post. The puzzles are wooden and have no guide pictures. They vary in difficulty, style and size and the library tries to suit each member. Subscriptions range from £26 for three months to £65 for a year. Postal charges are extra.

British Model Flying Association, Chacksfield House, 31 St. Andrew's Road, Leicester LE2 8RE. T:0116 244 0028. The BMFA is responsible nationally for every branch of model flying, now the world's most popular aviation sport. It organises competitions, provides guidelines for flying, third party insurance and can put you in touch with clubs in your area from its list of over 550 affiliated clubs. Many older members specialise in indoor free-flight or radio-controlled flying. Membership fee at time of going to press is £17 a year.

Miniature Armoured Fighting Vehicle Association, 15 Berwick Avenue, Heaton Mersey, Stockport, Cheshire SK4 3AA. T:0161 432 7574. The MAFVA is an international society which provides advice and information on tanks and other military vehicles and equipment, issues a bi-monthly magazine *Tankette* and can put you in touch with a local branch or overseas members with similar interests. There are meetings, displays and competitions. Membership in the UK is £7 a year.

National Association of Flower Arrangement Societies, 21 Denbigh Street, London SW1V 2HF. T:0171 828 5145. The Association can put you in touch with local clubs and classes.

National Philatelic Society, 107 Charterhouse Street, London EC1M 6PT. T:0171 251 5040. The Society holds monthly Saturday afternoon meetings for stamp collectors at its premises. These normally consist of an auction and a display with questions to its exhibitor. Members receive a free bi-monthly journal *Stamp Lover* and have use of the Society's library. There is an exchange packet scheme and also an annual competition. Membership costs £21 a year.

Radio Society of Great Britain, Lambda House, Cranborne Road, Potters Bar, Herts EN6 3JE. T:01707 659015. The Society provides advice on how to join the one-and-a-half million amateur radio operators around the world. The introduction of the Novice Licence has made it easier to participate in this hobby.

The Railway Correspondence & Travel Society, 365 Old Bath Road, Cheltenham, Glos GL53 9AH. T:01242 523917. The Society is among the leading railway enthusiast groups, with nearly 4,000 members all over the country. Members receive the monthly magazine, *The Railway Observer*, which includes the Society's fixtures. There are regular meetings at about 30 centres and the Society has a library with postal loan facility. Membership costs £12 a year.

Railway is a magazine for railway enthusiasts. It lists railway preservation events and gives information about local railway societies – including how to contact them. £2.20 monthly.

The Royal Photographic Society, The Octagon, Milsom Street, Bath BA1 1DN. T:01225 462841. The Society promotes photography through meetings, lectures, conferences and exhibitions. There are regional and specialist groups, for example: travel photography, film and video, visual journalism and nature photography. The Society arranges an attractive programme, including workshops, (some of them specially designed for those who have retired), field trips and social events. Membership is open to anyone, amateur or professional. Current annual subscription rates are £69; £50 for over-65s. The Society's centre in Bath is open daily from 9.30 a.m. to 5.30 p.m. Admission to the five exhibition galleries and museum is (1995) £2.50; £1.75 for senior citizens; free for members and disabled visitors.

Museums

Most museums organise free lectures, guided tours, and sometimes slide shows, on aspects of their collection or special exhibitions. As with art galleries and theatres, an increasing trend is to form a group of 'Friends' who pay a membership subscription to support the museum and in return enjoy certain advantages, such as: access to private views, visits to places of interest, receptions and other social activities.

British Association of Friends of Museums, 31 Southwell Park Road, Camberley, Surrey GU15 3QG. T:01276 66617. BAFM which acts as an umbrella organisation supports all Friends' groups around the UK, sharing news, advice, help and good practice. It publishes an annual journal (£2.50) listing all the groups in the Association, a quarterly newsletter (£2) and also a start-up guide (£10). Many museums offer the opportunity, through membership of the Friends' group, of rewarding voluntary activity. If you like the idea, enquire locally or contact the Association to discover what scope exists in your area.

British Museum Society, c/o The British Museum, London WC1B 3DG. T:0171 323 8605. Members enjoy free entry to exhibitions and evening openings as well as information about lectures, study days and 'visits behind the scenes'. A mailing including the events programme and the British Museum Magazine is sent six times a year. Annual membership is £30.

Friends of the Fitzwilliam Museum, Fitzwilliam Museum, Trumpington Street, Cambridge CB2 1RB. T:01223 332900. Friends receive an annual programme listing exhibitions, concerts, lectures and preview parties. Lectures and tours are organised in the Museum and to galleries and historic houses further afield. The Friends welcome help from individual members. The annual (1995) membership fee is £10; £15 double; £8 for senior citizens; £12 double.

Friends of the National Maritime Museum, Greenwich, London SE10 9NF. T:0181 312 6678/6638. The Museum complex, housed in Greenwich Park, comprises the largest maritime museum in the world, Wren's Old Royal Observatory and Inigo Jones's Queen's House. Friends enjoy free entry for themselves and a companion to the buildings and exhibitions as well as: private views, lectures, sailing trips (for all abilities), and visits to exhibitions and places of interest both in Britain and abroad. There are reciprocal arrangements with some other maritime organisations, which includes free entry to the Cutty Sark – also situated in Greenwich. The subscription is £16 a year or £22 for a family membership; £14 each for pensioners and disabled people.

Museum of the Moving Image, South Bank, London SE1 8XT. T:0171 401 2636 (recorded information). MOMI traces the history of the moving image – artistic, social and technical – from Chinese shadow theatre to modern animation; from Charlie Chaplin to the operations of a TV studio. As well as 44 permanent exhibition areas, there are changing exhibitions and also a gift and book shop. Open seven days a week (except 24 – 26 December), 10 a.m. to 5 p.m. (i.e. last admission). Entry (1995) is £5.50; £4 for senior citizens and children.

Friends of the National Museums of Scotland, The Royal Museum of Scotland, Chambers Street, Edinburgh EH1 1JF. T:0131 225 7534. Members are invited to private views, lectures, 'behind the scenes' visits and other events. The subscription is £10 a year, or £200 for life membership. There are reduced rates for pensioners.

Friends of the V & A, Victoria and Albert Museum, London SW7 2RL. T:0171-589 4040. Members enjoy free admission to: the V & A, Apsley House, Bethnal Green Museum and the Theatre Museum in Covent Garden. Membership also entitles you to: free entry to paying exhibitions; thrice yearly mailing of Museum information and Friends' events plus evening access to the Museum for lectures and private views. Annual membership is £30 (£48 double); £24 for over 65s.

Nature and conservation

Many of the conservation organisations are very keen to recruit volunteers and are, therefore, listed in Chapter 12, Voluntary Work, rather than here. By the same token many of those concerned with field studies arrange courses and other special activity interests which, because there is usually a residential content, seem more appropriate in Chapter 14, Holidays. The potential list is enormous. To give you a flavour, herewith a short 'mixed bag', highlighting a range from canals to ecology.

Amenity organisations. If you are interested in conservation and the environment, you might like to join your local amenity society. You should be able to contact it through your public library.

British Ecological Society, 26 Blades Court, Deodar Road, Putney, London SW15 2NU. T:0181 871 9797. Membership is open to all who are genuinely interested in ecology. The BES holds general and special interest meetings and awards grants for ecological projects and expeditions. Membership costs £16 (1995), more if you wish to receive journals.

The Civic Trust, 17 Carlton House Terrace, London SW1Y 5AW. T:0171 930 0914. An environmental charity concerned about the quality of urban living that acts as an umbrella organisation for nearly 1,000 local amenity societies. Publishes quarterly newsletter, *Urban Focus*, with articles on planning, conservation and transport issues. Annual subscription is £10.50.

The Conservation Foundation, 1 Kensington Gore, London SW7 2AR. T:0171 823 8842. For those interested in conservation and protecting the environment, both rural and urban, the Conservation Foundation is a good starting point. Launched in 1982, the Foundation manages a number of conservation award schemes, provides an information and legal advice service and publishes various books and guides. Among recent initiatives, it has set up a databank of Britain's traditional crafts, in the hope of attracting older people with a skill that may be in danger of dying out to pass on their knowledge to younger people. For further information, contact the above address.

Epping Forest Field Centre, High Beach, Loughton, Essex IG10 4AF. T:0181 508 7714. This Field Studies Council Day Centre is easily accessible from London and East Anglia. It runs evening classes, weekend and other field study courses. There are also guided walks and a specially designed wheelchair path.

Forestry Commission, 231 Corstorphine Road, Edinburgh EH12 7AT. T:0131 334 0303. For information on Forestry Commission walks and trails, forest drives, picnic places and visitor centres contact your local Forestry Commission office or the Public Information Division at the above address.

Scottish Inland Waterways Association, 139 Old Dalkeith Road, Edinburgh EH16 4SZ. T:0131 664 1070. The Association co-ordinates the activities of local canal preservation societies and will put you in touch with your nearest group.

The Wildlife Trusts, The Green, Witham Park, Waterside South, Lincoln LN5 7JR. T:01522 544400. There are 47 local Wildlife Trusts and 52 Urban Wildlife Groups which between them care for 2,000 nature reserves, as well as protect our threatened countryside. By joining the Wildlife Trust for your area, you can visit the reserves or even help in their wardening and management. The Trusts run their own activities including arranging talks and organising guided walks along with many other events. Membership fee is £16. For further information, contact the National Office at the above address.

Pen-friends

Despite the telephone, pen-friendship is flourishing. It is an ideal activity for those who have difficulty in getting out and about and many life-long friendships develop this way. Among the organisations that promote pen-friend schemes are:

Friends by Post, 43 Chatsworth Road, High Lane, Stockport, Cheshire SK6 8DA. Makes a real effort to unite correspondents with interests in common. The service is free. Please enclose sae.

National Association of Widows Penclub. Many widows find great comfort in corresponding with others who can share and understand their feelings. Membership is free. For further information, write to the Organiser enclosing note of your interests and other basic details about yourself. Her name is: Barbara Wilkes, 9 Boston Close, Springdale Park, Darlington, Co. Durham DL1 2RF.

Saga Magazine Club, Saga Building, Freepost, Folkestone CT20 1BR. Annual membership of the Club, which includes 10 issues of *Saga Magazine*, is £11.95.

Solitaire Friends Indeed, PO Box 2, Hockley, Essex SS5 4QR. This is a group designed to help women on their own combat loneliness by making new friends. As well as the possibility of becoming a penfriend, members may arrange to meet or stay in contact by telephone. There is also a newsletter. For further details, please enclose sae.

Public library service

Britain's public library service is among the best in the world. It issues about 600 million books free a year, loans records and cassettes and is a source of an enormous amount of information about both local and national activities. Additionally, the reference sections contain newspapers and periodicals as well as a wide selection of reference books which might cover any subject from flower arranging to genealogy.

Many libraries have a mobile service which takes books into villages and/or to senior citizens' clubs, day centres and clinics for elderly and infirm people. Some libraries also have volunteer library visitors who deliver books and materials to housebound people. Among the many facilities on offer, large print books are available at most libraries as are musical scores, leaflets on DSS benefits, consumer information and details of local community activities. Larger libraries have access to computer databases and can provide specialised information from Europe and North America. Some also hold the International Genealogical Index with information on microfiche.

Additionally, all libraries act as a source of information. If the information you require is not available in the library itself, the trained staff will normally do their best to tell you where you might find it.

Sciences and other related subjects

If astronomy fascinates you or you would like to understand more about meteorology (who wouldn't, given our uncertain climate!), there are several societies and associations who would welcome you as a member.

British Astronomical Association, Burlington House, Piccadilly, London W1V 9AG. T:0171 734 4145. The Association is open to all people interested in astronomy. Members' work is co-ordinated in such sections as: Sun, Moon, Terrestrial Planets, Meteors, Artificial Satellites, Historical, Telescope Making and so on. The Association holds meetings both in London and elsewhere and loans instruments to members who may also use the library. Membership costs £31.20 a year; £21.30 for those over 65.

Geologists' Association, Burlington House, London W1V 9AG. T:0171 434 9298. The Association organises lectures, field excursions and monthly meetings at Burlington House. There are varying levels of subscriptions, ranging from about £12.50 to £21. Local groups organise their own programmes. These exist in: Brent, Essex, Farnham, Guildford, Harrow, Ruislip, Oxford, Midlands, Lancashire, Staffordshire, South Wales, Avon, Kent and Cambridge.

Royal Meteorological Society, 104 Oxford Road, Reading, Berkshire RG1 7LJ. T:01734 568500. The Society, which includes among its membership both amateurs and professionals, exists to advance meteorological science. Members and others may attend scientific meetings and receive the monthly magazine *Weather*. Membership costs £34 a year (1995).

Scottish focus

The Saltire Society, 9 Fountain Close, 22 High Street, Edinburgh EH1 1TF. T:0131 556 1836. The Society seeks to improve the quality of life in Scotland through a wide range of activities and also to promote Scotland as a creative force in Europe. Typical branch activities include: musical evenings, Scottish dancing, dinners, excursions, lectures on architecture and history plus many others. There are branches in Aberdeen, Dumfries and Galloway, Dundee, Edinburgh, Helensburgh, Kirriemuir, St. Andrews, Glasgow, Highland and South Fife. The Society has a list of publications and its own Festival Performance Programme. Annual membership is £15; £7.50 for senior citizens and unemployed persons.

Sport

Retirement is no excuse for giving up sport. On the contrary, it is an ideal time to get into trim. Facilities abound and, unlike people with a 9 to 5 job, you enjoy the great advantage of being able to book out of peak hours. The Sports Council publishes information aimed at encouraging people over 50 to become involved in sport. To find out about opportunities in your area, contact your local authority recreational department, or your sports/leisure centre. Both should have the Sports Council's 50-plus leaflets together with information about coaching and medical advice for older people. If you have any difficulties contact the regional office of the Sports Council, address from: The Information Centre, **Sports Council**, 16 Upper Woburn Place, London WC1H 0QP. T:0171 388 1277.

Another useful organisation to know about is: **The Central Council of Physical Recreation**, Francis House, Francis Street, London SW1P 1DE. T:0171 828 3163/4. The CCPR will provide information on all sporting activities e.g. badminton, swimming, bowls and offer advice to anyone wishing to become involved in a sport or recreation.

Angling

The Angling Foundation, Federation House, National Agricultural Centre, Stoneleigh Park, Warwickshire CV8 2RF. T:01203 414999. The Angling Foundation promotes the interests of anglers and angling, including educational and environmental concerns. It can advise on where to find qualified tuition, local tackle dealers and similar information, as well as supply a number of useful leaflets.

Archery

Grand National Archery Society, 7th Street, The National Agricultural Centre, Stoneleigh, Kenilworth, Warwickshire CV8 2LG. T:01203 696631. The Society is the governing body for archery in the UK. It will put you in touch with your nearest club of which there are now over 1,200 around the country. Most clubs provide coaching at all levels including beginners' courses (covered by public liability insurance) for which they supply all equipment. The GNAS organises a full calendar of events and says many archers are still actively competing in their seventies, as the handicap system allows all abilities and disabled people to compete on equal terms. Club membership varies from approximately £25 to £75 a year, including affiliation fees.

Badminton

Badminton Association of England Ltd., National Badminton Centre, Bradwell Road, Loughton Lodge, Milton Keynes, Bucks MK8 9LA. T:01908 568822. Most sports and leisure centres have badminton courts and give instruction, as do many Adult Education Institutes. If you need advice, contact the Association. As well as offering information, it runs a number of short residential courses in several parts of the country.

Bowling

Over the past years, bowling has been growing in popularity. Your local authority may provide facilities. Alternatively contact:

English Bowling Association, Lyndhurst Road, Worthing, West Sussex BN11 2AZ. T:01903 820222. There are almost 3,000 local clubs, including 310 indoor bowling clubs, many of which provide instruction for beginners by qualified coaches. Some clubs have reduced rates for senior citizens. A national competition for 55-plus singles and pairs is organised through clubs each year. If you decide to take up bowls, you are advised not to buy your equipment without advice from the club coach.

English Women's Bowling Association, 2 Case Gardens, Seaton, Devon EX12 2AP. T:01297 21317.

English Indoor Bowling Association, David Cornwell House, Bowling Green, Leicester Road, Melton Mowbray, Leics LE13 0DB. T:01664 481900.

Clay pigeon shooting
Clay Pigeon Shooting Association, 107 Epping New Road, Buckhurst Hill, Essex IG9 5TQ. T:0181 505 6221. The CPSA is an association of individual shooters and a federation of clubs. As a member you have public liability insurance of £2 million, your scores are recorded in the national averages and you can compete in national events. The Association produces its own magazine *Pull!* which is distributed free of charge to all members. There are other specialist booklets available on most aspects of clay shooting. Individual membership is £20 per year and £15 for Veterans (60 and over).

Cricket
Lord's Cricket Ground, St. John's Wood Road, London NW8 8QN. T:0171 266 3825. You can enjoy a conducted tour of Lord's which among other attractions includes the Long Room and MCC Museum, showing the original 'Ashes' as well as a video recording some of the great cricketing performances of the past. Price is £4.95 (£3.95 for pensioners) and tour times are normally at noon and 2 p.m. These times are subject to variation and you are advised to check before making a special visit.

Pensioners can attend the ordinary county matches and the Sunday League games for half-price on production of their pension book. There are no concessions, however, for the Benson and Hedges Cup, NatWest Trophy or Test Matches; early booking for these events is recommended.

National Cricket Association, Lord's Cricket Ground, London NW8 8QZ. T:0171 289 6098. If you want to play, watch or help at cricket matches, contact your local club or send an sae to the above address. The NCA can put you in touch with your county cricket association. It also organises an over-50 County Cricket Championship.

The Foster's Oval Cricket Ground, Surrey County Cricket Club, Kennington, London SE11 5SS. T:0171 582 6660. The Foster's Oval Cricket Ground is home to the Surrey County Cricket Club and one of the main venues for Test and County matches, including a Cornhill Insurance Test, the Britannic Assurance County

Championship, the NatWest Trophy, the AXA Equity and Law League and the Benson and Hedges Cup. All pensioners can get tickets to the county matches at half price and those living within some London boroughs (details from the Club) can gain admittance to the ground on certain county match days. There are also special Club membership rates for pensioners entitling you to a number of benefits including free or reduced price tickets for the Members' Pavilion to watch test and international matches as well as county events.

Croquet
Croquet Association, Tony Antenen, Secretary, Hurlingham Club, Ranelagh Gardens, London SW6 3PR. T:0171 736 3148. A growing number of local authorities as well as clubs now offer facilities for croquet enthusiasts. The Croquet Association runs coaching courses and can advise you about club membership, events, purchase of equipment and other information.

Cycling
Cyclists' Touring Club, Cotterell House, 69 Meadrow, Godalming, Surrey GU7 3HS. T:01483 417217. The CTC is the largest national cycling organisation. It offers members free third party insurance, free legal aid, a handbook, colour magazines, organised cycling holidays and introductions to 200 local cycling groups. There is also a veterans' section. Membership costs £25 a year; £16.50 for retired people.

Darts
British Darts Organisation Ltd., 2 Pages Lane, Muswell Hill, London N10 1PS. T:0181 883 5544/5. Opportunities for playing darts can be found almost anywhere in clubs, pubs and sports centres. Contact the national body should you require further help.

Golf
English Golf Union, 1-3 Upper King Street, Leicester LE1 6XF. T:0116 255 3042.

Golfing Union of Ireland, Glencar House, 81 Eglinton Road, Donnybrook, Dublin 4. T:00 353 1 2694111.

Scottish Golf Union, The Cottage, 181a Whitehouse Road, Barnton, Edinburgh EH4 6BY. T:0131 339 7546.

Welsh Golfing Union, Catsash, Newport, Gwent NP6 1JQ. T:01633 430830.
The National Golf Unions can provide information about municipal courses and private clubs, of which there are some 1,700 in England alone. Additionally many adult education institutes and sports centres run classes for beginners.

Gun target shooting
National Small-Bore Rifle Association, Lord Roberts House, Bisley Camp,

Brookwood, Woking, Surrey GU24 0NP. T:01483 476969. The Association can put you in touch with a local club. It also arranges competitions and publishes a journal called *Rifleman*. Annual membership is £31; £18.50 for people over 65.

Land yachting
British Federation of Sand and Land Yacht Clubs, 23 Piper Drive, Long Whatton, Loughborough, Leicester LE12 5DJ. T:01509 842292. Enthusiast Mike Hampton describes the sport as 'a cross between dinghy sailing and go-karting' and says many people who take it up in retirement prove very good. There are four major clubs and 18 sites (both beach and airfield) in various parts of the country. The going rate for tuition is about £30 for four or five lessons. For addresses and other details, contact the British Federation above.

Rambling
Ramblers' Association, 1-5 Wandsworth Road, London SW8 2XX. T:0171 582 6878. Rambling can be anything from a gentle stroll to an action-packed weekend trek with stout boots and a rucksack. The Ramblers' Association has over 380 local groups throughout the country, many of whom survey and clear footpaths in their area. Membership (1995) is £16 a year; £8 for the retired.

Running
The Running Sixties, 120 Norfolk Avenue, Sanderstead, Surrey CR2 8BS. T:0181 657 7660. Contact: the Secretary. Formed in 1985 to take part in the Great British Fun Run, the Running Sixties extends membership to all men and women over 60 who are interested in running and the comradeship that it can engender. Members have competed every year in the London Marathon since 1986 and of the six finishers in the 1995 event all were in their seventies. The programme of activities includes regular lunch-time handicap runs which cater for all abilities from hares to tortoises. There are also team relay runs which are organised annually in Windsor Great Park and the Isle of Wight. The membership subscription is £6 and in addition to details of events and meetings members receive two newsletters. Part of the money raised every year is donated to the charity Research into Ageing.

Swimming
Amateur Swimming Association, Harold Fern House, Derby Square, Loughborough, Leics LE11 0AL. T:01509 230431. Coaching and 'Learn to Swim' classes are arranged by many authorities who also make the pool available at various times of the week for older people who prefer to swim quietly and unhindered. The Association offers many award achemes to encourage greater proficiency in swimming and as an incentive to swim regularly for fitness and health. Further details on request from the ASA.

Table tennis
English Table Tennis Association, Queensbury House, Havelock Road, Hastings,

East Sussex TN34 1HF. T:01424 722525. Table tennis can be enjoyed by people of all ages and all levels of competence. It is played in community halls, church halls, clubs and many sports centres.

The **Veterans English Table Tennis Society (VETTS)** holds regional and national championships including singles and doubles events for over 40s, 50s, 60s and 70s. These attract increasing numbers of men and women who enjoy playing socially and competitively well into their retirement. Annual membership (1995) is £10; £5 for those over 65. For further information on VETTS contact: Mrs V Murdoch, Membership Secretary, Harwood House, 90 Broadway, Letchworth, Herts SG6 3PH. T:01462 671191.

Tennis

Lawn Tennis Association, The Queen's Club, West Kensington, London W14 9EG. T:0171 381 7000. As with swimming, facilities have been greatly improving and your local authority Recreation Department should be able to inform you. The LTA will be able to put you in touch with your County Association who will advise you about coaching centres or short tennis courses in your area. The LTA Information Department supplies details of residential courses for adult players of all standards at home and abroad.

Veterans' Lawn Tennis Association of Great Britain, c/o Valerie Willoughby, 26 Marryat Square, London SW6 6UA. The Association promotes competitions for 'veterans' in various age groups. The VLTA *Handbook* (£2) lists affiliated clubs as well as tournaments in Great Britain and Europe, including the National Championships for all age levels, held at Wimbledon during August.

Veteran rowing

Amateur Rowing Association, 6 Lower Mall, London W6 9DJ. T:0181 748 3632. Veteran rowing as a sport is fast growing in popularity. Enthusiasts range in age from 31 to well past 80. For those who enjoy a competitive edge, there are special races and regattas with types of craft including eights, fours, pairs as well as single and double sculling. Touring rowing is also on the increase and additionally, there is plenty of scope for those who simply want the exercise and a pleasant afternoon afloat. Nearly all clubs welcome novice veterans, both male and female, and usually the only qualification required is the ability to swim. Coaching is provided and membership is normally in the range of £60 to £100 a year. For information about clubs in your locality, contact the ARA at the above address.

Windsurfing

Seavets, Hon. Secretary, Senior & Veteran Windsurfers Association, 11 Keble Road, Maidenhead, Berkshire SL6 6BB. T:01628 412510. Seavets, which is affiliated to the Royal Yachting Association, aims to encourage the not-so-young of all abilities to enjoy the challenge of windsurfing. Events are organised throughout the country from April to October, providing friendly racing for Seniors, Veterans (50+) and Supervets

(60+). Additionally, Seavets raises money every year for the charity Research Into Ageing, which funds research into the disabilities of old age. Annual membership is £12 (1995).

Yachting
Royal Yachting Association, RYA House, Romsey Road, Eastleigh, Hampshire SO50 9YA. T:01703 627400. There are 1,500 sailing clubs affiliated to the RYA and more than 1,000 recognised teaching establishments. The Association also provides a comprehensive information service for boat owners and can give advice on everything from moorings to foreign cruising procedure. Membership costs £17 a year.

Women's organisations

Although today women can participate in almost any activity on equal terms with men, women's clubs and organisations continue to enjoy enormous popularity. Among the best known are Women's Institutes, the Mothers' Union and Townswomen's Guilds.

Co-operative Women's Guild, 342 Hoe Street, London E17 9PX. T:0181 520 4902. The Guild's objects are to encourage women to play a full part in the co-operative movement and in local, national and international affairs. Branches throughout England and Wales organise their own programme, partly linked to a national theme, which is usually a major topical concern, such as support for carers. Branches also raise funds for a nationally agreed charity. Membership is £7.80 a year; 65p a month.

Mothers' Union, 24 Tufton Street, London SW1P 3RB. T:0171 222 5533. The Mothers' Union is a world-wide organisation which is specially concerned to strengthen and preserve marriage and Christian family life. It is open to any member of the Christian churches who has been baptised and who declares their support for the Union's aims. Members of the MU are involved in a wide range of activities which balance service to the community, learning, worship and recreation – a mixture of faith, fun and fellowship. Members who are housebound are linked through prayer circles.

National Association of Women's Clubs, 5 Vernon Rise, King's Cross Road, London WC1X 9EP. T:0171 837 1434. There are 300 Women's Clubs with a membership of 12,500. They are open to women of all ages and interests. Each club is self-governing, choosing its own meeting times and programme. Typical activities include: crafts, home-making, beauty and health care, music, dancing, drama and keep fit. There are outings to theatres and exhibitions and visits to places of interest and many clubs arrange holiday groups in Great Britain and abroad. Some do voluntary service in their communities for the sick and elderly. A number run co-operative shopping ventures and mutual self-help projects. Membership is £3.50 a year to head office plus a small membership fee to the local club.

National Federation of Women's Institutes, 104 New King's Road, Parsons Green, London SW6 4LY. T:0171 371 9300. The Women's Institute has 280,000 members in 8,500 WIs throughout England, Wales, the Channel Islands and the Isle of Man. The WI is a democratically controlled organisation for women, providing its members with the opportunity to work together to improve the quality of life locally and nationally and to develop their individual skills and talents. Denman College, which runs short recreational and educational courses, the monthly magazine *Home & Country* and WI Markets, with an annual turnover of more than £10 million, are all part of WI life. Membership is £12 per annum.

Scottish Women's Rural Institutes, 42 Heriot Row, Edinburgh EH3 6ES. T:0131 225 1724. This is the Scottish counterpart of the Women's Institute movement. There are 35,000 members of all ages who enjoy social, recreational and educational activities. There are talks and demonstrations, classes in arts and crafts and discussions on matters of public interest. You can be put in touch with your local institute via the headquarters office.

If you live in Northern Ireland, contact the **Federation of Women's Institutes of Northern Ireland**, 209-211 Upper Lisburn Road, Belfast BT10 0LL, T:01232 301506/601781.

National Women's Register, 3A Vulcan House, Vulcan Road North, Norwich, Norfolk NR6 6AQ. T:01603 406767. The NWR is a nationwide organisation of women who meet in each others' homes to take part in informal discussions on subjects outside the domestic sphere. It promotes friendship and self-confidence, giving women from whatever background an opportunity to learn from each others' points of view.

There are about 11,000 members in some 700 groups. Many additionally arrange other activities, for example: theatre outings, book clubs and the chance to participate at conferences and workshops. The NWR also has a house exchange scheme and an international register of members covering 23 countries. The annual subscription is £9.

Townswomen's Guilds, Chamber of Commerce House, 75 Harborne Road, Edgbaston, Birmingham B15 3DA. T:0121 456 3435. The Townswomen's Guilds is an organisation committed to advancing the social awareness of all women, irrespective of race, creed or political affiliation. It has around 100,000 members throughout the UK who meet to exchange ideas, learn new skills and take part in a wide range of activities. There are regular monthly meetings plus a programme of local, regional and national events. Annual subscription is £8.50. A monthly journal, *Townswoman* is available at 44p per copy.

Other information

The Dark Horse Venture, Kelton, Woodlands Road, Liverpool L17 0AN. T:0151 729 0092. The Dark Horse Venture seeks to encourage retired people into discovering exciting new challenges. Participants are free to choose any activity under whichever of the following headings they would enjoy: giving and sharing; learning and doing; exploring and exercising; generations working together.

To obtain an award certificate, they must devote approximately 100 hours over a minimum 12-month period to their chosen pursuit, under guidance of an adviser or assessor with whom they must agree their personal targets. Participants are also required to keep a journal of their progress. There is an optional payment of £5 on completion of the project. For further details and ideas write to the Administrator at the above address.

Public transport. One of the big gains of reaching retirement age is the availability of cheap travel. Most local authorities offer concessionary fares to senior citizens during the off-peak periods. Coaches too very often have special rates for older people and, as everyone knows, British Rail Senior Railcards, available to men and women over 60, offer wonderful savings. Details of these are given in Chapter 14, Holidays.

10 Starting Your Own Business

Running a small business can be one of the most satisfying retirement occupations. There are hundreds of success stories of those who took the plunge at 55-plus to build a company that provided involvement, fun and income plus a legacy for their children. However, a word of warning. For every success story there is a failure and your money will disappear fast if you set up in big company style. Small business is all about cutting costs, doing it yourself and driving second-hand cars until you are making profits with a positive cash flow. If you are married, your partner's attitude is probably crucial. Even if he or she is not directly involved they will have to accept the loss of a sitting room as an office, the out-of-hours phone calls and the suddenly cancelled social engagement.

If you have a skill to offer, the drive to sell it and the health to support your ambition, this chapter will give you the information you need to set up or buy into a small concern and join the ranks of other successful entrepreneurs.

Legal structure of business

If you are thinking of starting a business, you have three main choices as to the legal form it can take. You can operate as: a sole trader, a partnership, or a limited company.

Sole trader
This is the simplest form of trading, with virtually no start-up expenses and minimal bureaucracy involved. If you trade under your own name then, apart from informing the Inland Revenue and the Department of Social Security, there are no legal formalities. If you use another name, you must indicate on documents such as letterheads that you are the owner (see 'Business names', page 218).

Even if you employ others, you will be treated as self-employed for both tax and national insurance purposes and will be liable to pay personal income tax on your profits, after deducting allowable expenses. You will also be required to pay national insurance contributions on your earnings.

Very small businesses, defined at time of writing as those with a total turnover from business and rental income of under £15,000, are spared the expense of supplying full accounts and instead are able to submit a three-line statement showing: income, expenses and profit. Proper records will nevertheless need to be kept in the event of a query or investigation by the tax office. Businesses with a higher total turnover will need to prepare proper trading accounts with full details of their expenditure and income. However, new concessions have been introduced which greatly simplify accounting procedures and the most you are likely to require (unless your turnover exceeds £350,000) is an accountant's report confirming that your records are accurate.

The main disadvantage of operating as a sole trader – and it is a major one – is that it carries unlimited liability so you would be personally liable for all business debts. Should the business fail, your own assets as well as your business ones would be at the disposal of your creditors – and if the worst came to the worst, you could be made personally bankrupt.

Partnership

A partnership is a business with two or more proprietors. Similar to operating as a sole trader, a partnership can be formed without any legal formalities or documentation other than informing the Inland Revenue and DSS.

To avoid any possible future misunderstanding however, it is advisable to have a formal partnership agreement drawn up at the outset, covering such points as: distribution of profits (equal or unequal shares), voting rights, control of the bank account and arrangements for admitting new partners. While it is a simple matter to form a partnership, it can be very irksome to settle the affairs of one that has gone wrong. A few legal expenses at the beginning could prove a worthwhile investment.

As with sole traders, partners are treated as self-employed for both tax and national insurance purposes. Profits are divided and taxed as the personal income of individual partners. However, if one partner fails to pay his/her share the other partners will be called upon to meet the shortfall. Similarly, each partner carries unlimited liability for all the debts of the business.

An exception to this rule – although rare today – is that of a limited partnership. This has to be registered at Companies House and at least one partner has to incur unlimited liability. The limited partners (sometimes known as sleeping partners) cannot take part in the running of the business in any way and their liability is limited to their share of the partnership capital. Accounts need to be prepared at least once a year, but they do not need to be published.

In common with sole traders, partnerships with a turnover limit of £15,000 (1995/96) can enter in their tax returns a three-line statement showing their income, expenses and profit instead of having to submit full accounts.

Limited company

A limited company is a legal entity in its own right. As its name implies, liability for the company's debts in the event of insolvency is limited to the amount invested in the business by each shareholder.

As a director of a limited company, you will be treated for tax and national insurance purposes as an employee of the business, paying income tax under the PAYE system. Corporation tax will also be payable on the profits of the company.

The main disadvantage of a limited company is the bureaucracy. The government has been reducing the red tape for small firms but not surprisingly there are still a number of legal requirements that must be fulfilled, both before and after trading starts. A limited company must be registered by Companies House (or, in Scotland, by the Registrar of Companies for Scotland): this involves the filing of both a Memorandum of Association and the Articles of Association (see below). The company's accounts have to be audited once a year by a firm of qualified accountants and a set showing, among other details, a profit and loss account must be filed annually with Companies House, together with basic information about the company and its directors, all of which are open to public inspection.

N.B. Companies with a turnover of less than £90,000 are no longer required to have a statutory audit. Similarly, those with a turnover of between £90,000 and £350,000 must prepare proper trading accounts but only require to obtain an independent accountant's report confirming that the accounts accurately reflect the company's books.

Registering a limited company. Although you can register a limited company yourself, it is advisable to get a professional accountant, solicitor or company registration agent to do it for you. Charges vary considerably, but are likely to start from around £150 upwards.

To register a limited company, you need to fill in: Form 10, *Notification of First Directors and Secretary and Location of Registered Office* and Form 12, *Declaration of Compliance*. These must be sent to the Registrar of Companies together with the *Memorandum of Association* (stating the company's name, registered office, share capital and nature and scope of the business arrangements, including the extent of liability) and the *Articles of Association* (stating the internal rules of the company).

All the necessary forms can be got either from law stationers or from Companies House at the Cardiff address (see below). Specimen memoranda and articles can only be obtained from law stationers.

Fees. There are two scale rates: the normal service, which costs £20 to register (plus an additional £18 per year, payable when the annual returns are sent in for public display); or the same-day incorporation service, which costs £200.

To take advantage of the same-day service, it is necessary to present the completed documents at Companies House by 3 p.m. If you use the standard service, registering a new company will take five working days from the receipt of correct documents at Companies House.

'Off the Shelf'. Another possibility, if you are not too fussy about the company name is to buy a previously registered company 'off the shelf' from a company registration agent. This will cost, on average, about £130 for all the documentation, including the company books. There will be a further charge of around £75 should you decide to change the name and a charge of around £25 to change the Articles of Association. If you simply need to change the name, which is not a difficult matter, you could do it direct with the Registrar. The cost in this case will be £20. For more information, contact the **New Companies Section**, Box 717, Companies House, Crown Way,

Cardiff CF4 3YA. T:01222 380801; or **The Registrar of Companies for Scotland,** Companies House, 37 Castle Terrace, Edinburgh EH1 2EB. T:0131 535 5800.

Workers' co-operative

This is another possible form of business structure. Co-operatives are basically owned and controlled by the workers according to international co-operative principles – for instance, all members have equal voting rights irrespective of financial involvement, profits are distributed in proportion to members' participation in the activities of the business, and all workers qualify for membership after a suitable probationary period.

Co-operatives provide their members with limited liability, by registering either as Companies Limited by Guarantee (requiring a minimum of two founder members) or as Industrial and Provident Societies (requiring a minimum of seven founder members). The Scottish Co-operatives Development Committee also has a Company Limited by Shares Model.

Most new workers' co-operatives adopt Model Rules for registration. There are a number of different models available from the three national support bodies, ICOM (Industrial Common Ownership Movement), the Wales Co-operative Development and Training Centre and the Scottish Co-operatives Development Company.

Registration will usually cost £300-£400 if Model Rules are used; alternatively ICOM provides a 'tailor-made' service where a group has special requirements, costing from £420. In addition, many areas of the country are now served by local Co-operative Development Agencies which can advise and assist on the establishment of a new co-operative venture; of these some also have loan funds available to provide start-up capital.

For more information, contact **The Wales Co-operative Development and Training Centre**, Llandaff Court, Fairwater Road, Cardiff CF5 2XP. T:01222 554955; **The Scottish Co-operatives Development Company**, Templeton Business Centre, Templeton Street, Bridgeton, Glasgow, Scotland G40 1DA. T:0141 554 3797.

Industrial Common Ownership Movement (ICOM), Vassalli House, 20 Central Road, Leeds LS1 6DE, T:0113 246 1737/8. ICOM publishes a number of useful books, including *A Guide to Co-operative* and *Community Business Legal Structures* (£5.50 incl. p&p).

Business names

It is no longer necessary to register a business name. However, where a sole trader uses a business name that is different from his real name, or where a partnership trades under a name that differs from those of all the partners, or a limited company trades other than under its full corporate name, then certain legal requirements have to be met. All business stationery – including letterheads, order forms, invoices and receipts – must contain the real name(s) of the sole trader, partner or company, together with the official address of the business. These details must also be prominently displayed on all business premises. Failure to do so is a criminal offence, punishable with a fine of up to £400.

There are also certain regulations governing the words that may be used in a business or company name 'without justification'. Prohibited words include: those considered offensive or those that imply connection with the Crown, the Government or a local authority, e.g. British, National, European.

Other prohibited categories are titles like Society or Institute which suggest a representative status or words which imply a specific function such as insurance or banking. In all such cases, approval must be sought from the appropriate government department or governing body that the use of such words is justified. The Registrar of Companies will also refuse to register a company name that is identical to one already on the register, even if it is your own name.

For more information see *Choosing a Company Name* (CHN2); *Business Names and Business Ownership* (CHN11); *Sensitive Words and Expressions* (CHN3), available from Companies House. T:01222 380568.

Alternative ways of getting started

Rather than start a new business, you could buy into one that is already established or instead, consider franchising.

Buying a business

Buying an established business can be an attractive route to becoming your own boss, as it eliminates many of the problems of start-up. The enterprise is likely to come equipped with: stock, suppliers, an order book, premises and possibly employees. It is also likely to have debtors and creditors.

Take professional advice before buying any business, even one from friends. In particular, you should consider why the business is being sold. It may be for perfectly respectable reasons – for instance, a change of circumstances such as retirement. But equally, it may be that the market is saturated, that the rent is about to go sky high or that major competition has opened up nearby.

The value of the company's assets will be reflected in its purchase price, as will the 'good will' (or reputation) that it has established. For more information, contact **Christie & Co.**, the agents specialising in small businesses, at 2 York Street, London W1A 1BP. T:0171 486 4231; or look in the telephone directory for the address of one of its 12 UK offices.

Before parting with your money, make sure that the assets are actually owned by the business and get the stock professionally valued. You should also ensure that the debts are collectable and that the same credit terms will apply from existing suppliers. Get an accountant to look at the figures for the last three years and have a chartered surveyor check the premises. It is also advisable to ask a solicitor to vet any legal documents, including staff contracts: you may automatically inherit existing employees. See Education and Employment Department booklet PL 699 *Employment Rights on the Transfer of an Undertaking*.

Franchising

Franchising has become an increasingly popular form of distribution, with attractions for both franchisor and franchisee. The franchisor gains in that it enables an ambitious group to expand very quickly. The advantage to the franchisee is that there are normally fewer risks than starting a business from scratch.

A franchisee buys into an established business and builds up his own enterprise under its wing. In return for his investment plus regular royalty payments, he acquires the right to sell its products or services within a specified geographic area and enjoys the benefits of the organisation's reputation, buying power and marketing expertise. Examples of well known franchises include Burger King, Budget Rent-a-Car and ServiceMaster.

As a franchisee you are effectively your own boss. You finance the business, employ the staff, and retain the profits after the franchisor has had his cut. You are usually expected to maintain certain standards and conform to the broad corporate approach of the organisation. In return, however, the franchisor should train you in the business, provide management support and give you access to a wide range of back-up services.

Cost. The amount of capital needed to buy a franchise varies enormously according to the type of business and can be anywhere between £2,000 and £500,000 or more. The franchisee is normally liable to pay:

- an initial fee, covering both the entry cost and the initial support services provided by the franchisor, such as advice about location, market research and so on. The British Franchise Association estimates that on average this represents roughly 5 to 10 per cent of total setting-up costs. Advice should be taken as to whether the fee will be partially or wholly allowable for tax purposes;
- recurring fees or royalties, which are usually based on a percentage of gross sales (typically 11 per cent), exclusive of VAT. Sometimes, where the franchisor supplies his own exclusive products, he may derive his income from the usual mark-up on the sale of products to you.

Length of agreement. The length of the agreement will depend both on the type of business involved and the front end fee. Agreements can run from three to 20 years, with five years being average. Many franchisors include an option to renew the agreement, which should be treated as a valuable asset.

Raising the finance. Franchising has now built up a good track record with a relatively low rate of business failures, so raising the money for a franchising venture is rarely a major difficulty. Most of the leading high street banks operate specialist franchise loan sections.

Franchisors may also be able to help in raising the money and can sometimes arrange more advantageous terms through their connections with financial institutions.

Unemployed people starting a business under a franchise arrangement can also apply to their local TEC to receive the Business Start-up Scheme allowance (see heading 'Government grants and loans' page 252).

The British Franchise Association (BFA) represents 'the responsible face' of franchising and its members have to conform to a stringent code of practice. The BFA publishes a *Franchisee Information Pack* (£18) which provides comprehensive advice on buying a franchise together with a list of BFA member franchisors and affiliated advisers.

It is well worth visiting one of the two annual National Franchise Exhibitions – held in London during the spring and in Birmingham during the autumn – where you can see and compare the various franchise options on offer.

A good franchisor will provide a great deal of invaluable help. However, some franchisors are very casual in their approach, lacking in competence, or even being downright unethical. Points to look out for include overpricing of exclusive stock and lack of back-up services. Make careful enquiries before committing any money: as basic information, you should ask for a bank reference together with a copy of the previous year accounts. Also check with the BFA whether the franchisor in question is a member and talk to some of the other franchisees to find out what their experience has been. Before signing, seek advice from an accountant or solicitor.

For more information, contact **The British Franchise Association**, Thames View, Newtown Road, Henley-on-Thames, Oxon RG9 1HG. T:01491 578049.

Developing an invention

Inventors looking for a manufacturing outlet for their ideas should consider contacting Inventorlink, a London-based company which, for a fee, specialises in helping inventors find suitable manufacturers. Few inventions, however, get anywhere near the market. After strict vetting of projects – and only a fraction of those submitted are accepted – between 60 and 90 potential makers of the product are mailed. Usually about 10 per cent reply of which one or two may end up being genuinely interested. Inventions are also publicised in the company's own newsletter, sent to 8,000 manufacturers and distributors. Financial rewards eventually depend on demand for the product. Manufacturers normally pay an upfront fee of between £5,000 and £25,000 and then pay a royalty on sales ranging from about 7.5 to 10 per cent. For more information, contact **Inventorlink**, 5 Clipstone Street, London W1P 7EB. T:0171 323 4323.

For information about patenting an invention, telephone the **Patent Office**, T:0645 500505.

Taxation

Taxation arrangements vary considerably according to whether you are operating as a sole trader, partnership or limited company. As you will know, tax rates, bands and allowances are revised annually and take effect at the beginning of the financial year in April. Figures quoted in this section apply to the 1995/96 financial year.

Sole trader or partnership

As soon as you start work on your own account, you should inform your local Inspector of Taxes. To do so, you should obtain Form 41G from your local Inland Revenue office (see telephone directory for address) and return it, when completed, together with your Form P45 which your employer will have given you when you left.

Income Tax. As a sole trader or member of a partnership, you are treated as self-employed for tax purposes. Profits are aggregated with any other personal income and are taxed at the normal rates of income tax. After allowing for the 20 per cent rate on the first £3,200, the basic rate of 25 per cent extends to the first £24,300 of taxable income, with all income in excess of this subject to the higher rate of 40 per cent.

Not all your income is taxable. In common with everyone else, you get a personal tax allowance (currently £3,525); and if you are a married man living with your wife, you will also receive the married couple's allowance (currently £1,720). Additionally, as a self-employed person (Schedule D), you are allowed certain other reliefs. As a general guideline, the following expenses and allowances are tax deductible:

- *Business expenses*: these must be incurred 'wholly and exclusively' for the purposes of the trade. Professional publications would probably qualify; however, your 'wages', national insurance contributions and any business entertaining would not. Bad debts are usually allowable. Certain expenses incurred in advance of getting the business started are also permitted, for example: necessary travelling, printing costs and telephoning.
- *Partially allowable expenses*: these mainly apply if you are working from home. They include such items as that part of your rent, heating, lighting and telephone usage that you devote to business purposes; also possibly, some of the running expenses on your car, if you use your car for your business.
- *Spouse's wages*: if you employ your partner in the business, his/her pay (provided this is reasonable) qualifies as a legitimate expense, in the same way as any other employee's, but must of course be accounted for through the PAYE system.
- *Pension contributions*: depending on your age, you are allowed to invest between 17.5 per cent and 40 per cent of your earnings in a pension plan, free of tax. However, for pension plans taken out after 1 June 1989, the relief only applies on earnings up to an Inland Revenue determined ceiling, currently (1995/96) £78,600.
- *Capital allowances*: a percentage of the cost of some items is 'allowed' for tax relief, for example, an annual allowance of 25 per cent (on the reducing balance) of the cost of plant and machinery, including office furniture, computer software and cars. Certain items of plant and machinery qualify for 40 per cent relief during the first year. For further information, see Inland Revenue leaflet IR 106 *Capital Allowances for Vehicles and Machinery*.
- *Interest on loans*: tax relief is given on money borrowed to invest in a small firm, in most normal circumstances.

Some other advantages include:

- *Basis of assessment*: the first year's trading results will normally be used as the basis for tax assessments for up to three years. This can be an advantage if low profits are earned in the first 12 months. (N.B. See also 'Making a Tax Return' on page 224).
- *Tax losses*: any tax losses in the first four years may enable you to recover PAYE from your last three years in employment. A tax loss made by the business can also be set against any other income the proprietor may have.

Because of these reliefs, being a sole trader or partner can offer substantial tax advantages. As a result, the Inland Revenue has become increasingly strict about the definition of self-employed. If you work as a consultant or freelance and most of your income derives from one employer, your Inspector of Taxes may argue that you are an employee of that firm – and not a self-employed person. For more information, see leaflet IR 56/NI 39 *Employed or Self-Employed?* available from your local tax office.

Capital gains tax. Sole traders or partners are liable to capital gains tax (indexed against inflation) levied at their own marginal rate of income tax (25 per cent or 40 per cent) if they sell the company or any of its assets. Capital gains above the individual's annual tax-free allowance of £6,000 are taxed at the rate that would apply if they were treated as the 'top slice' of someone's income, so they could push a basic rate taxpayer into the higher tax bracket. Since the introduction of independent taxation, in the case of a married couple, both husband and wife are taxed independently on their capital gains and each enjoys his/her own separate annual exemption. Tax may not be payable if the proceeds are re-invested within three years in another business (or business assets). Assets bought the previous year might also qualify. This is normally referred to as roll-over or reinvestment relief.

If the owners want to give part of their business (or its assets) to their family, capital gains tax need not be payable until a sale to a third party occurs. This is called hold-over relief. Alternatively, retirement relief is available on a sliding scale up to 100 per cent for all gains up to £250,000 and on one-half of any gains between £250,000 and £1,000,000 from the disposal of a business or of shares in a family company on retirement at age 55, or earlier on health grounds.

Another valuable relief allows trading losses to be offset against capital gains tax. Proprietors of unincorporated businesses who make a loss (and do not have enough income in the year to offset that loss in full) can make a claim to set the unused loss against capital gains of the same year – with any excess of loss carried forward against capital gains of the year following.

For further information, see Inland Revenue leaflet CGT 11 *Capital Gains Tax and the Small Businessman*, CGT 6 *Capital Gains Tax – Retirement: Disposal of a Business* and CGT 15 *A Guide for Married Couples*.

Inheritance tax. Most small family-owned businesses can be passed on to the next generation free of inheritance tax. Although since the 1992 Budget tax planning has become much easier for small business owners, you would nevertheless be strongly advised to speak to an accountant.

Preparation of accounts. Accounts must be submitted annually to the Inland Revenue. These are normally in two parts: the trading account and profit and loss account, which provide a summary of the year's trading transactions; and the balance sheet, which shows the assets and liabilities of the business at the end of the year.

The accounts of a sole trader or partnership do not have to be audited by an independent qualified accountant. However, whether you draw up the accounts yourself or engage professional help, full and accurate records must be kept from the start. While not essential, there is a very strong argument for having a qualified accountant to help you, since his/her advice is likely to prove invaluable in a whole range of matters. For assistance in finding a local accountant, contact: **The Institute of Chartered Accountants**, PO Box 433, Chartered Accountants Hall, Moorgate Place, London EC2P 2BJ, T:0171 920 8682.

Very small businesses, i.e. those with a turnover of less than £15,000 a year, are no longer required to submit full accounts but are simply required to provide the Inland Revenue with the following information:

1. details of their total takings;
2. details of their expenses;
3. their profits.

For further information, obtain a copy of leaflet IR 104 *Simple Tax Accounts*, from any tax office.

Making a tax return. As an employee, you will have had income tax deducted from your gross pay automatically under the PAYE system. When you become self-employed, you become responsible for the payment of tax and are required by law to make a true return of your income each year.

Until recently, tax has usually been payable in two equal instalments: on 1 January and 1 July on the preceding year's profits. However, the Government is in process of changing the system from assessment of the preceding year profits to a 'current year' basis, which should be both simpler and more straightforward. The timing of the change is in stages. Businesses and self-employed people who started trading after 5 April 1994 come under the new system from the start. Businesses existing prior to April 1994 have a transitional period before switching fully into 'current year' assessment during 1996/97. A further change is that from 1998 the payment dates will be 31 January and 31 July, instead of the first day of the month.

Whichever system applies to your business, the Inspector of Taxes will send you annual tax return forms and formal notices of assessment to tax. If you have an accountant, arrangements can be made for copies of the assessments to be sent to him direct. Normally, no assessments will be made until you have completed 12 months' trading. If you disagree with the amount of taxable profits given in the notice of assessment, you have 30 days in which to appeal.

For further information, see *A Guide to the Current Year Basis*, obtainable from any tax office.

Self-assessment

The Chancellor has announced plans to introduce a new system of self-assessment designed to simplify the process of making tax returns for the 9 million or so people who receive them, including among others the self-employed. The new system will come into effect in April 1996, at the start of the 1996-97 tax year.

As an employer, self-assessment might affect you personally and it might also affect some of your employees and/or co-directors. People who work for (or with) you who receive a tax return will require certain information from you – mainly about PAYE, benefits in kind and expenses payments. Details are contained in *Self-assessment – What it will mean for employers*, obtainable free from tax offices.

There is no obligation on anyone to switch to the new system, as self-assessment will be optional. However, both in your own capacity and as an employer, you need to be aware of the different timings that apply.

Those choosing to calculate the tax themselves will have until 31 January following the end of the tax year to send in their tax return. Those wishing the Revenue to work out the amount of tax due will need to submit their returns by the earlier date of 30 September. The dates are important, as there is an automatic penalty of £100 if your tax return arrives after 31 January. For further information, see leaflets IR 142 *Self Assessment – An Introduction* and *Self Assessment – A Guide for the Self-employed*, obtainable from any tax office.

Useful reading

For more information about the tax position of sole traders and partnerships, see Inland Revenue booklet, IR 28 *Starting in Business* (obtainable from any tax office).

Limited company

The Inland Revenue will be automatically notified when a limited company is formed and will contact the directors in due course. However, to avoid delays it is sensible for you to contact the Revenue as soon as the company is incorporated.

Corporation tax. A company pays corporation tax on its taxable profits. The main rate of corporation tax (1995/96) is 33 per cent. This applies to companies with taxable profits over £1,500,000. A small companies' rate of only 25 per cent applies to companies with taxable profits of less than £300,000. There is marginal relief due if the profits are between £300,000 and £1,500,000.

As a director of a limited company, the business will pay your salary (which will be subject to PAYE) out of its trading income. Allowable expenses, similar to those for sole traders and partnerships, are also deductible before corporation tax is charged. Directors' expenses may however be disallowed, in whole or in part, if the Inland Revenue takes the view that these benefited directors personally – as opposed to being a legitimate business expense. Such expenses may be taxed as a personal benefit.

The Inland Revenue does not allow unlimited payments into pension schemes, particularly those designed to benefit directors. The limits depend, among other factors, on the age of the individuals concerned: it is advisable to discuss this with the company's accountants.

Relief for losses. If your company makes a loss, the directors cannot offset this against their personal taxable income. The losses can, however, be offset against both future and past profits made by the company – with trading losses carried back for up to three years.

Relief for pre-trading expenditure. The period for tax relief for expenditure incurred before the start of trading has been extended from five to seven years.

Preparation of accounts. Limited companies are required to file annual accounts, which have been audited by an independent qualified accountant, within twelve months of their year end. These accounts will normally form the basis of the Revenue's tax assessment. As stated earlier, however, companies with an annual turnover of £350,000 or less are no longer required to have a statutory audit. Instead, the most they will need is a report from an independent accountant confirming that the accounts accurately reflect the company's books.

Capital gains tax. When a company sells an asset at a profit, such as a building, it will pay corporation tax on the chargeable gain (25 per cent for small firms). If the company itself is subsequently sold, there would be capital gains tax to pay on the profit realised from the sale of the shares. Advance corporation tax (which companies pay on dividends to their shareholders) can be offset against tax due on profits including any gains. As a result, there are advantages in issuing dividends to shareholders in order to extract value from a company before it is sold.

Hold-over, roll-over or reinvestment relief are available to individuals in certain circumstances.

Re-investment relief allows entrepreneurs to defer paying tax on gains arising from the sale of shares in their own companies, provided the gains are re-invested in a qualifying unquoted company within three years of the shares' disposal. The relief is also available to managerial or technical employees who have owned more than 5 per cent of the shares in their company for at least a year.

Previous rules, which restricted eligibility for relief and which have now been abolished, include: the requirement to acquire a minimum 5 per cent shareholding in the new business; the former 'land rule', which limited the proportion of land/ buildings a company could hold; and the exclusion from relief of property development and farming companies.

Individuals engaged in running a family business are entitled to **retirement relief** on sale of the business, or their shares, when they retire. Relief applies to the first £250,000 of gains plus half of further gains between £250,000 and £1,000,000.

Unless retirement is on grounds of ill-health, individuals must be aged at least 55 and to obtain full relief must have worked in the business for 10 years. In the case of a married couple, both husband and wife may each be able to claim.

If you are planning to sell a major asset, you should consult your accountant to avoid the possibility of a double tax payment.

Tax offset. If your company makes a trading loss, this can be used as an offset against profits made on the sale of assets, provided the sale takes place in the same or previous year.

Inheritance tax. Since 1992 most small family-owned businesses have been taken out of the inheritance tax net and can be passed on to the next generation free of tax. There are, however, one or two exceptions, such as where an owner has holdings of 25 per cent or less without control in an unquoted company (or one quoted on the AIM).

In cases such as these plus a couple of others (i.e. where the controlling shares are in a fully quoted company; and where certain assets are owned by partners or by controlling shareholders and are used in their respective businesses), there is tax relief of 50 per cent.

Although inheritance tax planning has now become much easier for small business owners, you would nevertheless be strongly advised to speak to an accountant.

Useful reading
Inland Revenue leaflet IR 105 *How Your Profits are Taxed*, obtainable from any tax office.

Value added tax (VAT)
Value added tax is imposed on most business transactions. The legal structure of the enterprise does not in general affect the issue.

Registration. Consult your local Customs and Excise Office (see telephone directory) about registration for VAT.

Registration is required if your annual 'taxable turnover' exceeds £46,000 (for financial year 1995/96). 'Taxable turnover' applies to the gross turnover of goods or services which are made or supplied by the business. You have 30 days to notify Customs and Excise if you become liable to register. Businesses may de-register from VAT, if they so choose, if their taxable turnover falls below £44,000.

Charging and paying VAT. You collect VAT from your customers by including it in, or adding it to, the price you charge (output tax). Similarly, you will be charged VAT by your suppliers on the goods and services you buy (input tax). When you receive a VAT return your input tax is subtracted from your output tax and the difference is paid to Customs and Excise. If the input tax is greater than the output tax, you can claim a refund on the difference.

Businesses with an annual turnover of less than £350,000 enjoy two special options. Firstly, they can opt to submit a VAT return once a year instead of quarterly. A condition is that they must make monthly payments by direct debit, based on estimates agreed with Customs and Excise – with a balancing adjustment made when the annual return is submitted. Secondly, they can opt for cash accounting for VAT, enabling them to delay paying the VAT on their sales to Customs and Excise until they have actually received payment for these. The scheme should help the cash flow of small firms with tardy customers and provide automatic VAT relief for bad debts. Bad debts can be written off for the purpose of claiming VAT relief after six months. A debtor no longer has to be declared formally insolvent for relief to be allowed.

Taxable supplies and exempt supplies. Most transactions are liable to VAT at either the standard rate (currently 17.5 per cent) or the zero-rate (nil).

Zero-rated supplies include: most food (but not catering), books and newspapers, sales of new buildings, young children's clothing and footwear, protective boots and helmets meeting EC safety standards, export of goods, dispensing of prescriptions and the supply of many aids for disabled persons, mobile homes and houseboats. Zero-rated suppliers have to complete and return a VAT form, even though they are not liable to pay this tax.

Exempt supplies include: insurance, betting, gaming and lotteries, provisions of credit, certain education and training, services of doctors and other medical specialists, certain supplies by undertakers. Such suppliers do not have to complete regular VAT returns but must complete form VAT 1 when they apply for exemption. If you are granted exemption, you will not be able to reclaim the VAT you pay on goods and services for your business.

Since the November 1994 budget the 'de minimis' limit for partly exempt businesses has been raised to £7,500 a year. To qualify for partial exemption, VAT incurred on the exempt supplies must not exceed 50 per cent of total input tax. For further information, see Budget Notice 51/94.

Below the VAT registration limit. If you are not registered for VAT, any expenditure which you incur which includes a charge for VAT should be entered in your records, inclusive of VAT. Even if you do not have to register at present, you may have to do so in the future if your taxable turnover increases. There could be an argument for early registration, as you would be able to offset the VAT the business has to pay to its suppliers. Another advantage is that VAT usually helps in establishing well-kept accounts. For more information, see C & E booklet *Should I Be Registered for VAT?*, obtainable from any C & E office.

How to register. Fill in Form VAT 1 (or the Welsh equivalent Form VAT 20). If the business to be registered is a partnership you will also need Form VAT 2. If you have acquired a business as a going concern you may be able to have the registration number of the previous owner reallocated to you. See VAT leaflet *Selling or Transferring a Business as a Going Concern.*

N.B. Don't delay. If you do not notify within the 30-day limit once you are liable to be registered, you may have to account for tax which you have not collected, together with penalties for late payment. You should start keeping VAT records and charging VAT to your customers as soon as you know you are required to be registered. You will have to account for VAT from this date whether or not you have included VAT in your prices.

Penalties. The VAT penalty rules were relaxed a couple of years ago in order to bear less harshly on small businesses.

Benefits in kind

The rules affecting benefits in kind apply to all directors and to employees earning £8,500 or more a year (including the value of benefits in kind). Any tax payable is deducted via the PAYE system. Two items of particular interest to many smaller businesses are company cars and mobile telephones.

Company cars. As all company car owners will know, the rules were changed in April 1994. Instead of the benefit value being taxed according to engine size, owners are now taxed at their marginal rate on 35 per cent of the original list price of their car. There is a one-third discount for those driving more than 2,500 business miles a year and two-thirds discount for those driving more than 18,000 business miles. A further one-third discount is given for cars that are already four years old at the end of the tax year. For further information, see leaflets IR 133 *Income Tax and Company Cars from 6 April 1994: Guide for Employees* and IR 132 *Taxation of Company Cars from 6 April 1994: Employers' Guide*, obtainable from any tax office.

Employers have to pay national insurance contributions on the provision of cars for private use by employees as well as on the fuel consumption they enjoy. (See leaflet *Cars and Fuel – A Manual for Employers*, available from your local Contributions Agency office.) Some companies are finding it a better and cheaper solution to give employees a loan to buy their own car. (Beneficial loans up to £5,000 are not assessed as a taxable benefit.)

Individuals using their own cars on company business can receive the following mileage rates tax free:

	Cars up to 1000cc	Cars 1001 to 1500cc	Cars 1501 to 2000cc	Cars over 2000cc
Up to 4000 miles	27p	34p	43p	60p
Over 4000 miles	15p	19p	23p	32p

N.B. Since August 1995, businesses are able to recover VAT on cars bought wholly for business use.

Mobile phones. A standard tax charge is now payable by employees on mobile phones, provided by their employer, against their private use of the phone. The amount of tax payable is calculated on the basis of the individual having received £200 extra pay. The charge applies to each phone an employee receives, so if he has one in his car plus another portable model there will be tax to pay on £400 of assumed income.

National insurance

As with tax, your liability for national insurance contributions will depend on whether you are self-employed (sole trader or partner) or whether you are a director of a limited company.

Self-employed

If you are self-employed, you will have to pay flat rate Class 2 contributions – currently £5.75 a week – unless:

- you are over 65 for men; 60 for women (even if you have not retired from work)
- you are entitled to pay married women's or widow's reduced rate Class 1 contributions
- you have been granted 'a certificate of exemption' because your earnings are likely to be less than £3,260 a year (see leaflet CA 03 *National Insurance Contributions for Self-Employed People Class 2 and 4*, available from Social Security offices).

If your annual profits or profit share are above £6,640, you will also have to pay Class 4 contributions of 7.3 per cent on profits between £6,640 and £22,880, unless you are in one of the following categories:

- partner not resident for income tax purposes in the UK
- trustee, executor or administrator of wills and settlements (there are, however, exceptions)
- sleeping partner, taking a profit but not active in the business.

N.B. There is no additional NI liability on profits that exceed £22,880 and the maximum payable is £1,185.52 a year.

How to pay. Class 2 contributions can be paid either by direct debit from your bank, see leaflet CA 04; or by the quarterly billing system which has replaced the traditional NI stamps. If you prefer quarterly billing, the Contributions Agency should automatically advise you of the amount owing for the previous quarter, which is payable through banks or at all post offices via Girobank.

Class 4 contributions are normally assessed and collected by the Inland Revenue, together with PAYE or Schedule D income tax. As they will be paid retrospectively, remember to keep the necessary cash ready and not spend it as part of your monthly salary. See leaflet CA 03.

Husband and wife. As with independent taxation, husband and wife are assessed separately for Class 4 contributions.

Further information about Schedule D tax assessments and related Class 4 national insurance contributions can be obtained from your local Inspector of Taxes. For help on deferment or refund of Class 4 contributions, contact: Contributions Agency, Deferment Group, **Department of Social Security**, Longbenton, Newcastle upon Tyne NE98 1YX.

Double income. If you are self-employed but also receive a salary you may have to pay NI contributions on both incomes. However, there is an overall limit of £2,086.08 (1995/96) above which contributions are not payable. If too much has been deducted in total you can reclaim the excess or ask for a reduction of Class 2 and/or Class 4 contributions. See leaflet CA 01 *National Insurance Contributions for Employees*, available at Social Security offices.

Limited company
If you trade as a limited company, the company will pay employer's Class 1 contributions and you will suffer the same deductions from your salary as any other employee. If you control the company, you will in effect be paying both the employer and the employee's share of NI contributions on your own account.

If you are a director of several companies, you may be liable for multiple NI contributions: see leaflet CA 44 *National Insurance Contributions for Company Directors*, available from Social Security offices.

National insurance benefits
Different classes of contributions qualify you for different types of benefit.

Class 2 contributions count for:

- incapacity benefit (leaflets IB 201 and IB 202)
- basic retirement pension (leaflet NP 46)
- basic widow's benefit (leaflet NP 45)
- basic maternity benefit (leaflet NI 17A)

Class 1 contributions entitle you to all the above and additionally to unemployment benefit (or after April 1996, the new jobseeker's allowance), should the need ever arise. They also count towards the additional pension (i.e. SERPS).

Class 3 contributions. These may be paid voluntarily to help you qualify for some benefits, if your contribution record is insufficient. A flat rate of £5.65 a week is payable. See leaflet CA 08, available from your local Social Security office.

Pensions

Sole traders and partners are self-employed for pension as well as tax purposes and must make their own arrangements. Directors of limited companies are treated as employees and may be included in their company's pension scheme or may run their own self-administered pension schemes.

Self-employed pensions

Depending on their age, the self-employed can invest between 17.5 per cent and 40 per cent of their earnings in a personal pension plan and can claim tax relief on the contributions at their top rate of tax. In particular, for those between the ages of 51 and 55, the amount is 30 per cent; for those aged between 56 and 60, 35 per cent; and for those aged 61 and over, 40 per cent.

If the full relief is not used in any one tax year, it can be carried forward for up to six years. Similarly, it may be possible to offset the premium against the previous year's earnings if there are no taxable profits in the current year. For further information, see Chapter 3, Pensions, under heading 'Personal pension schemes'.

Loan-back facilities

Almost all old-style self-employment pension plans carry loan-back facilities which can provide a useful and tax-efficient line of credit for small businesses. Such loans can take one of two forms: either the self-employed can borrow up to the accumulated value of the pension fund, or the loan can be calculated as a multiple of the annual premiums paid.

In both cases, suitable security is required as collateral. You can usually delay the repayment of the loan (but not the interest) until you receive your tax-free lump sum on retirement. There are no restrictions on the purposes for which the loans can be used. However, under rules which came into effect in July 1988 'loan-back' facilities are not allowed on new personal pensions.

Directors

Company pension schemes have limits on the maximum level of benefits they can provide: for instance, the maximum pension is limited to two-thirds of an employee's final salary. For anyone joining a new pension plan post-June 1989, the maximum pensionable final salary is one of £78,600. This figure is regularly adjusted to reflect changes in the RPI. However, unlimited contributions can be pumped into the fund by the company and written off against corporation tax so long as these maximum benefits are not exceeded. The employee (i.e. director) can make additional voluntary contributions up to a total of 15 per cent of his salary (provided these do not take him/her over the £78,600 ceiling) and offset the premiums against his top rate of tax. Members of an existing pension scheme, before the rule changes came into effect, are not affected by the £78,600 limit.

Company pension schemes can either be effected through an insurance company in much the same way as for self-employed schemes; or set up as a self-administered scheme, run mainly by its members and one independent 'pensioneer trustee'. The investment of the funds is almost entirely a matter for the trustees, subject to certain limitations imposed by the Inland Revenue to prevent abuse. Investments may include the company's own property, loans to the company and the company's own shares.

Company loan-back facilities

Loans by a company pension scheme to its members are not normally allowed; loans to director-controlled companies are the exception, where a direct loan-back of up to 25 per cent of the fund is permitted. After the fund has been in operation for two years, the amount allowed is increased to 50 per cent. Such funds can therefore provide useful working or development capital in a tax-efficient way. Cash can be transferred into a tax-exempt fund and written off against corporation tax. The company can then borrow back up to 25 per cent (50 per cent after the two years), claiming tax relief on the interest payments. The fund receives the interest net of tax and then claims the tax back from the Inland Revenue. The loans can similarly be used to finance property developments. All loans must be for a specific purpose and be made on a commercial basis with the approval of the independent pensioner trustee.

Your responsibilities as an employer

Many people starting a business wisely limit recruitment to the minimum in the early days, until they are sure that they can afford the cost of having permanent staff. Once you become an employer, you take on responsibilities. As well as paying the salaries, you will have to account for PAYE, keep national insurance records and conform with the multiple requirements of employment legislation. While this may sound rather daunting – and information is given for those who want to do it themselves – the good news is that your bank and possibly your accountant are likely to offer a full payroll service which will cost you money but will take the worry off your shoulders.

PAYE

If you employ someone in your business (including your wife/husband) you are responsible for deducting income tax under the PAYE arrangements and accounting for it to the Collector of Taxes.

Contact your local Inland Revenue office for a copy of booklet *Employer's Guide to PAYE* (P7). You will also be provided with tax tables and working sheets. The tax office will then notify you of the various PAYE tax codes in respect of your employees and explain how to use the tax table to work out the deductions.

If an employee does not have an existing P45, you should ask him/her to complete a Starting Certificate Form P46, obtainable from the tax office.

An individual is liable for tax after deduction of their personal allowance and various reliefs. As a rough guide, for those only in receipt of the personal allowance (£3,525), this would be after earnings of £68 a week. Even if an employee's pay is less than the threshold, there could still be PAYE implications, as he/she may have other earnings. Employers whose average monthly payments of PAYE and NIC total less than £600 can make quarterly payments rather than monthly. The due dates for quarterly payments are: 19 July, 19 October, 19 January and 19 April. For more information, see Inland Revenue booklet IR 53 *Thinking of Taking Someone On*.

National insurance for employees

The national insurance threshold is £58 a week. With one or two exceptions, in particular persons over State retirement age, anyone earning this amount or over will be liable for national insurance. You are responsible for the payment of both the employer's and employee's contributions but are entitled to deduct the employee's share from his/her earnings.

National insurance is payable on a graduated scale for both employers and employees. In the case of employees, two different rates apply: 2 per cent on earnings of £58 a week and then 10 per cent on earnings between £58 and £440. Employees earning more than £440 are not liable for extra contributions. Employers' contributions also vary according to earnings: starting at 3 per cent on earnings of £58, rising in stages to 10.2 per cent on earnings of £205. There is no ceiling limit, so as an employer you will be liable to pay 10.2 per cent on the total earnings of staff whose gross pay is £205 weekly or more.

Where employees are contracted out of the State earnings-related pension scheme (SERPS) the rates are reduced by 1.8 per cent for employees and by 3 per cent for employers on earnings between the lower and upper earnings limits.

Contact your local Social Security office for booklet CA 28 *Employer's Manual on National Insurance Contributions*. The staff will explain to you how the system works and answer any queries.

You will be sent a payslip booklet by the Collector of Taxes, together with official Deductions Working Sheets P.11 and P.14. Payments must be made within 14 days of the end of each income tax month.

Contribution holiday. From April 1996, employers will get an NI contribution 'holiday' for up to 12 months for anyone they take on who has been out of work for two years or more.

Statutory Sick Pay

Employers are responsible for paying Statutory Sick Pay (SSP) to their employees for up to 28 weeks of sickness absence. The rate and earnings thresholds are subject to review annually. The current (1995/96) SSP rate (until April 1995 there were two different rates) is £52.50; it applies on earnings of £58 or more. SSP is subject to deduction of income tax and NI contributions in the same way as ordinary pay. The previous special measures to help small businesses have been abolished and have been replaced by a new scheme which allows employers to recover SSP costs in any month where these exceed 13 per cent of their NI liability for that month. The amount that can be reclaimed is the excess over 13 per cent. Full details are contained in leaflet CA 32 *Statutory Sick Pay Small Employers' Relief*, available from Social Security offices.

Statutory Maternity Pay

The requirements for maternity pay were recently changed to bring benefits in line with European requirements. Under the new rules, any woman who has been in the same job for 26 weeks is entitled to the following rates: 90 per cent of earnings for the first six weeks of maternity leave; a flat-rate payment of £52.50 – on weekly earnings of £58 and above – (1995/96) for the remaining 12 weeks. Small employers whose gross annual national insurance contributions (NICs) are £20,000 or less are fully reimbursed. Those paying more than £20,000 a year in gross NICs receive back 92 per cent of SMP costs.

N.B. Although a woman must have worked in the same job for 26 weeks to qualify for SMP, an employer can no longer request her to leave – however short a period she has been in a job (even one day) – on grounds of pregnancy.

Advice note. Most of what you need to know is contained in the *Quick Guide to NI Contributions Class 1A, SSP and SMP Contributions*, CA 27, obtainable from Social Security offices.

If you have any queries about these or other DSS matters, you can telephone the Social Security Advice Line for Employers. Dial freephone 0800 393539. Lines are manned weekdays from 9 a.m. to 4.30 p.m. (4 p.m. on Fridays).

Personnel Records

Many businesses find it useful to keep personnel records, covering such information as national insurance numbers, tax codes, merit appraisal reports and so on. If using any of the computerised systems on offer, you may need to register with the Data Protection Registrar. For advice and information, contact: **Data Protection Registrar**, Wycliffe House, Water Lane, Wilmslow, Cheshire SK9 5AF. T:01625 535711 (Administration); 01625 535777 (Enquiries).

Employment legislation

As an employer, you have certain legal obligations in respect of your staff. The most important cover such issues as: health and safety at work, terms and conditions of employment and the provision of employee rights including, for example, maternity leave, trade union activity and protection against unfair dismissal. Very small firms are exempted from some of the more onerous requirements and the government is taking steps to reduce more of the red tape. However, it is important that you understand in general terms what legislation could affect you.

Health and safety at work. The Health and Safety at Work Act applies to everyone in a business whether employer, employee or the self-employed. It also protects your neighbours and the general public who may be affected by your business activity. The Health and Safety Executive publishes a number of useful free leaflets and also has a public enquiry point which is open between 9 a.m. and 5 p.m. Contact: **Health and Safety Executive**, Information Centre, Broad Lane, Sheffield S3 7HQ. T:0114 289 2345.

A model safety policy entitled *Writing Your Health and Safety Policy Statement*, with blank sections for an employer to fill in and step-by-step notes for guidance is available from HSE Books and all good bookshops, price £2.50.

Discrimination. An employer – however small his business – may not discriminate against someone on the grounds of sex, race or marital status. This applies to all aspects of employment, including training, promotion, recruitment, company benefits and facilities. The law now also applies to partnerships. If you have more than 20 employees, you are also required to employ a small quota of disabled people. For more information, contact the **Equal Opportunities Commission**, Overseas House, Quay Street, Manchester M3 3HN, T:0161 833 9244, or the **Commission for Racial Equality**, Elliot House, 10-12 Allington Street, London SW1E 5EH. T:0171 828 7022.

Contract of employment. A contract of employment exists as soon as an applicant accepts a job, whether or not the offer and acceptance are made in writing. Within two months of the job starting, the employer must normally give the employee either a written contract or a written statement highlighting the key terms and conditions of the job together with a general description of the duties.

There is a useful guide prepared by the Education and Employment Department, PL 700 *Written Statement of Employment Particulars*, available free from your local Jobcentre. Further information can also be obtained from Citizens' Advice Bureaux or a solicitor.

Main sources of advice

The Department for Education and Employment can provide advice on all aspects of employment legislation and also supplies several free pamphlets. The most handy place to obtain these is your local Jobcentre and, while picking them up, you could take the opportunity of introducing yourself to the manager and discussing any recruitment needs. You may also telephone the Department for Education and Employment on 0171 925 5000 (ask for the Public Enquiry Point).

Disputes

If you find yourself with a potential dispute on your hands, it is sensible to approach the **Advisory, Conciliation and Arbitration Service (ACAS)**, which also operates an effective information and advisory service for employers and employees on a variety of workplace problems including employment legislation and industrial relations. Contact: **ACAS**, 27 Wilton Street, London SW1X 7AZ, T:0171 210 3613, or one of its regional offices (see local telephone directory).

Useful reading

Employing People: The ACAS Handbook for Small Firms. A useful guide which can be used as a quick reference to most problems of employment law such as industrial relations, health and safety, pay, trade union law and employment protection. Price £1.50, available from: ACAS Reader Ltd., PO Box 16, Earl Shilton, Leicester LE9 8ZZ.

Trading regulations

Trading regulations laying down your obligations to your customers are contained in various Acts of Parliament, such as the Fair Trading Act, Trade Descriptions Act, Sale of Goods Act, Consumer Credit Act and the Consumer Protection Act. For free advisory literature, contact: **Office of Fair Trading**, Room 306, Field House, 15-25 Bream's Buildings, London EC4A 1PR. T:0171 242 2858. Solicitors are also qualified to advise on such matters.

Licences

Certain types of business require a licence or permit to trade, including: pubs, off-licences, nursing agencies, pet shops, kennels, mini-cabs or buses, driving instructors, betting shops, auction sale rooms, cinemas, hairdressers, street traders and, in some cases, travel agents and tour operators. You will also require a licence to import certain goods.

Your local authority Planning Office will advise you as to whether you require a licence and in many cases your council will be the licensing authority.

The Consumer Credit Act 1974 also imposes a licensing requirement on various types of business that offer credit and hire facilities. The Act is administered by the Office of Fair Trading (see above), which publishes a helpful booklet *Do You Need a Credit Licence?*.

Another useful source of information is the **Department of Trade and Industry Import Licensing Branch**, Queensway House, West Precinct, Billingham, Cleveland TS23 2NF. T:01642 364333.

Finding suitable premises

A few years ago, finding premises was often a real problem for small firms. Today, however, thanks to the relaxation of many planning regulations, together with an increase in small workshops, it has become very much easier. The sources to tap when you start looking include:

Newspapers. There are property pages in publications such as *Dalton's Weekly*, *Exchange & Mart* and the *Estates Gazette*. Evening and local newspapers also carry advertisements for industrial, commercial and retail property.

Estate agents. Ask for the department dealing with commercial premises. You will have to pay commission, which may be structured in various ways. Check carefully on the terms and conditions.

Local authorities. Councils often maintain a list of vacant properties including a register of small units. Many authorities own and manage workshop developments. If you are thinking of building your own premises, your District Council will also have information on sites earmarked for development and will be able to advise you on the planning implications. Contact the Industrial Development Officer.

Chambers of commerce. These are often an excellent source of information about vacant premises, as they have wide contacts with local businesses and others.

Enterprise agencies. Again, a first class contact point. Some agencies run managed workshops. Their premises often provide shared facilities such as typing, fax and photocopying. For addresses of local enterprise agencies (enterprise trusts in Scotland), contact **Business in the Community**, 8 Stratton Street, London W1X 5FD, T:0171 629 1600, who can put you in touch with your nearest EA/ET.

Business Links. Your local Business Link will almost certainly have knowledge of available small business premises – or at least should be able to advise you whom to contact. For further information, see page 256.

Railtrack Property. Vacant railway arches, small shops, offices and other commercial property throughout England, Wales and Scotland are available to rent from: **Railtrack Property**, Fitzroy House, 355 Euston Road, London NW1 3AG. T:0171 830 5501.

Rural Development Commission

The Rural Development Commission can provide assistance to expanding businesses in the Commission's designated rural development areas. It can give grants to help convert redundant buildings into workspace; it also builds its own workshop and small factory units for rent in particularly remote areas where workspace supply is limited. For further information, contact your nearest office (see local telephone directory) or write to: **Rural Development Commission**, 141 Castle Street, Salisbury, Wiltshire SP1 3TP. T:01722 336255.

Enterprise Zones

Enterprise Zones have been set up in various parts of the country, with the intention of winning business to these areas. The major attraction is that EZs are exempt from industrial and commercial rates and are also largely free of planning controls, although the normal health and safety regulations apply. The rates holiday only lasts for 10 years from an EZ's designation date, so in some cases, only a relatively short time remains. EZs are currently located in the following places: Lower Swansea Valley, North West Kent, Inverclyde, Sunderland and North Lanarkshire (Ravenscraig). New EZs are proposed in the East Midlands, Dearne Valley (S Yorks) and East Durham.

Contact the relevant local authority or your nearest regional office of the **Department of the Environment** or Scottish/Welsh offices, (see telephone directory), for further information.

New Town Development Corporations

There are five New Town Development Corporations in Scotland (Cumbernauld, East Kilbride, Glenrothes, Irvine and Livingston) all of which have industrial estates. For more information contact the Industry section of the appropriate Development Corporation. For new towns in England (Basildon, Bracknell, Central Lancashire, Corby, Crawley, Harlow, Hatfield, Hemel Hempstead, Milton Keynes, Northampton, Peterborough, Redditch, Skelmersdale, Stevenage, Telford, Warrington and

Runcorn, Washington and Welwyn Garden City) contact the **Commission for the New Towns**, Saxon Court, 502 Avebury Boulevard, Central Milton Keynes MK9 3HS. T:01908 696300.

Assisted Areas

A wide range of industrial and commercial property is available for rent or sale in the Assisted Areas. Premises can often be built or converted to suit your specific requirements. Many of the leases are very flexible, with short in-out options, to allow for the changing needs of expanding small firms.

In England, contact your local Regional Government Office (for addresses, see page 254).

For Wales, Scotland and Northern Ireland contact, as appropriate: **Welsh Development Agency**, **Highlands and Islands Enterprise** and **LEDU, The Small Business Agency**. See below for addresses.

Scotland

Highlands and Islands Enterprise, Bridge House, 20 Bridge Street, Inverness IV1 1QR. T:01463 234171. HIE builds advance factories and workshops for sale or lease. Rents are generally lower than in other parts of the country and in some circumstances, premises can be made available on a rent-free basis for a period of up to two years.

Clyde Workshops, Fullarton Road, Glasgow G32 8YL. T:0141 641 4972. Clyde Workshops is the job creation arm of British Steel plc. The workshops provide commercial, office and industrial premises on flexible leasing terms for new-start businesses.

Wales

Welsh Development Agency, Pearl House, Greyfriars Road, Cardiff CF1 3XX. T:0345 775577 (English enquiry line); 0345 775566 (Welsh enquiry line). The WDA is one of the largest developers of industrial property in the UK and has a comprehensive range of business premises, varying in size from 1,000 to 50,000 sq.ft. It also offers a wide range of business services.

Development Board for Rural Wales, Ladywell House, Newtown, Powys SY16 1JB. T:01686 626965. Call freefone: 0800 269300. The Development Board offers a similar service to the WDA but is responsible for mid-Wales. Units vary in size, typically from 750 sq.ft. to 10,000 sq.ft. Some units have retail showrooms attached. Competitive rents and financial help are also available.

Northern Ireland

LEDU, The Small Business Agency, LEDU House, Upper Galwally, Belfast BT8 4TB. T:01232 491031. LEDU can put you in touch with local enterprise agencies which have units suitable for start-up and existing small businesses.

Get expert advice

However impeccable the organisation offering you property for lease or sale, you should always consult a solicitor before you sign a contract. If you are thinking of buying either a long lease or freehold, you are strongly advised to get a surveyor's report. Though you will have to pay for the service, it could save you a fortune if you otherwise later discovered dry rot, rising damp or worse.

Planning permission

If you intend to build or convert property, use a mobile shop or change the use of existing business premises, from say an office to a workshop, you will need to get planning permission from your local authority. This often used to take months and months but the procedure has now been greatly speeded up, especially where small businesses are concerned. Tempting as it is to take a chance or to install workmen before you have officially received the 'go-ahead', this is very unwise because in the event of permission not being granted, you could be ordered to restore the property to its original condition, which could be hugely expensive if you have knocked down the odd wall.

In rural areas, the Rural Development Commission can often be of assistance when preparing a planning application. As general advice, it recommends that before an application goes to a planning committee, every effort should be made to sound out local opinion, explain what the intention is and allay any fears. The blessing of the Parish Council can often tip opinion in your favour. The department to contact is your District Council Planning Office.

Other permissions

Depending on the nature of your business, other permissions may also need to be obtained, including those of the police, the environmental health department, licensing authorities and the fire prevention officer. In particular, there are special requirements concerning the sale of food and safety measures for hotels and guest houses. Your local authority will advise you what is necessary.

Working from home

Many people quietly 'set up shop' from home and there are no questions asked. There could, however, be trouble if in consequence of your business, there was an increase in traffic on your street, noise, smells or other inconvenience caused to your neighbours. Even more likely, unless you own the freehold of your home, you could have problems with your landlord if the tenancy agreement states that the accommodation is for domestic use only. If you simply use your home as a telephone base, this will probably not be an issue but if you have a stream of callers and a van parked outside, you could be accused of violating the lease. You may have to pay business rates (in addition to your council tax) on that part of your home you use as business premises.

Another possible down-side of working from home is that this could have capital gains tax implications should you ever want to sell the property.

As working out the various financial pros and cons has become rather a complex matter, before taking any decision you would be advised to take professional advice.

Useful reading

The Department of the Environment publishes a free booklet, *Planning Permission for Small Businesses: A Step by Step Guide*, explaining the planning system, and giving clear guidance on working from home. Copies can be obtained from your local authority or ordered from: **Department of the Environment**, PO Box 151, London E15 2HF.

Insurance

Insurance is more than just a wise precaution. It is essential if you employ staff, have business premises or use your car regularly for commercial purposes. Many insurance companies now offer 'package insurance' for small businesses that cover most of the main contingencies in a single policy. This usually works out more cheaply than buying a collection of individual policies. If you buy a package, check that it contains whichever of the following are relevant to your needs.

- **Employers' liability**. This is compulsory if you employ staff. It provides indemnity against liability for death or bodily injury to employees and sub-contractors, arising in connection with the business.
- **Product and public liability**. Insures the business and its products against claims by customers or the public. It could also cover legal expenses and the cost of complying with enforcements or judgements.
- **Professional indemnity**. Now essential for all businesses offering investment advice in whatever form. Also highly recommended for doctors, architects, consultants and other professionals who might be sued personally – or whose business might be sued – if a client suffered a mishap, loss or other damage in consequence of advice or services received. With the recent growth in litigation, many professional bodies are recommending that cover should continue after retirement in the event of an individual – or their estate – being sued for work done some years previously.
- **Material damage risk**. Covers against fire or other risk to the property, damage to equipment and theft. You can also be insured against loss of money or goods in transit.
- **Loss of profits or business interruption risk**. Insures the business against loss of profits in the event of your having to cease or curtail trading for a time, due to material damage. The two policies are normally linked. It should also cover the risk of break-down of a key item of machinery.
- **Motor risks**. Compulsory for all motor vehicles.
- **Life assurance**. Essential should you wish to provide for your own or key employees' families or to ensure that funds are available to pay off any debts or to enable the business to continue in the event of your death.
- **Permanent health insurance**. Otherwise known as 'income protection', it provides insurance against long-term loss of income as a result of severe illness or

disability. Most income protection plans are pretty flexible and can be tailored to individual needs.

- **'Key man' insurance**. Applies to the loss of a key man or woman through prolonged illness as well as death. In small companies where the success or failure of the business is dependent upon the skills of two or three key executives, 'key man' insurance is increasingly being written into investment deals as part of the necessary security demanded by banks, financial institutions and private investors. Remember, however, that whereas life insurance benefits your family, key man insurance only benefits the company.
- **Jury service insurance**. Business people cannot seek automatic exemption from jury service even though prolonged absence from work could severely disrupt their business. Insuring against the risk of being called for jury service is therefore worth considering.

Insurance when working from home. If you are self-employed, you may need to extend your existing private policies to cover your commercial activities. A fire at home could destroy business products as well as your domestic possessions. Likewise your motor insurance may not be sufficient for business purposes, if the loss of your car could cause serious interruption to your trading. You should discuss these points with your insurance company or a broker.

Insurance brokers. To find an insurance broker, contact: **British Insurance and Investment Brokers Association**, BIIBA House, 14 Bevis Marks, London EC3A 7NT. T:0171 623 9043.

Useful reading
The **Association of British Insurers**, 51 Gresham Street, London EC2V 7HQ, publishes a useful free booklet: *Insurance Advice for Small Businesses*.

Marketing

Unless you were employed in sales or marketing, you may suspect that this is likely to be a weak point in your business plan. The essence of good marketing is very simple. Find out what the customer wants and then try to supply it rather than design a product or service and hope that buyers will come flocking to your door. You have to sell the sizzle as well as the sausage. The points you need to consider are:

- what kinds of individuals (or companies) are likely to be your customers, including their age group and sex
- whether you are competing with existing suppliers or are offering a genuinely new concept (including for example, a delivery service which other local shopkeepers do not supply)
- whether the market is expanding or contracting with particular emphasis on how many potential customers live close by

- finally, how you can inform the potential market that your new product or service is available.

This sort of preliminary thinking is essential. The following organisations may be able to help you formulate a realistic marketing plan. Your local library will probably have trade directories and *Yellow Pages* from which you can see how many other organisations already offer a similar local service. It may also have copies of trade magazines relevant to the industry you plan to enter. In particular look out for *Business Monitors*, of which there are now some 200, carrying production, sales, trade and other industrial statistics for most sectors of British industry.

Your local council will have information on the population and demographic profile of the area and will be able to give you details of any development plans that could affect customer potential.

Your chamber of commerce should be able to offer practical advice and training in marketing techniques and may also be able to assist with useful contacts.

Your local Enterprise Agency, TEC and Business Link exist to help small businesses and should be able to offer valuable marketing advice.

National organisations that may be useful include:

The Chartered Institute of Marketing, Moor Hall, Cookham, Maidenhead, Berkshire SL6 9QH. T:01628 524922. Runs courses for non-members who need general marketing advice and, for an appropriate fee, can offer practical consultancy advice on setting up or developing your business.

Central Statistical Office, Cardiff Road, Newport, Gwent NP9 1XG. T:01633 812973. Holds information on many aspects of the economy, including sales by UK manufacturers and imports/exports of specific products.

Institute of Management, Management House, Cottingham Road, Corby, Northants NN17 1TT. T:01536 204222. Runs an extensive management information centre which non-members can visit with the agreement of the Institute.

Market Research Society, 15 Northburgh Street, London EC1V 0AH. T:0171 490 4911. The MRS can put you in touch with a research company which could mount a research exercise on your behalf. Cost could range from a couple of hundred pounds to several thousand.

BSI (British Standards Institution), 389 Chiswick High Road, London W4 4AL. T:0181 996 7111 (enquiries). Will provide technical help to ensure that products comply with standards laid down by the UK and EC governments.

Data Protection Registrar, Wycliffe House, Water Lane, Wilmslow, Cheshire SK9 5AF. T:01625 53577. If you maintain a database for marketing purposes, you may need to register with the Data Protection Registrar above.

Promotion

Once you have assessed where your market lies, you have to decide how to promote yourself. Methods of advertising your product (service) might include:

- direct mail shots and leaflet drops
- advertising in specialist publications or local newspapers with a potentially high readership among your target market
- exhibitions and local displays at functions such as school prize givings, agricultural shows or local sporting events
- telephone sales, perhaps with the help of a small team
- editorial coverage in the press, on local radio programmes or TV.

You are likely to succeed better with any of these techniques if you discuss your plans with a professional consultancy. The names of local practitioners should be available from:

Institute of Public Relations, The Old Trading House, 15 Northburgh Street, London EC1V 0PR. T:0171 253 5151.

The Chartered Institute of Marketing, Moor Hall, Cookham, Maidenhead, Berkshire SL6 9QH. T:01628 524922.

Public Relations Consultants Association Ltd., Willow House, Willow Place, Victoria, London SW1P 1JH. T:0171 233 6026.

Competitors

It is useful to know who your competitors are and what they are doing. One way is to get copies of their annual reports, by writing to the companies concerned who will usually be glad to supply them free of charge; alternatively, these are available for a fee from the **Postal Search Section**, Companies House, Crown Way, Cardiff CF4 3UZ. T:01222 380691. When writing, it would be helpful if you could quote the company number of those businesses whose annual reports you want. All companies should have this listed on their letterhead. It is also sensible to attend trade shows of the industries within which you are planning to compete. Your local library will probably hold a directory listing what shows are held each year.

Exports

Completion of the Single European Market does not mean that doing business in the rest of Europe is as easy as doing business in the UK. DTI's *Business in Europe* service offers information, advice and practical assistance to help you compete successfully. Telephone the 24-hour Hotline on 0117 9444888 and ask for the free *Business in Europe* brochure.

Additionally, a network of 26 European Information Centres has been set up in the UK which can be reached on the following numbers: Belfast (01232 491031); Birmingham (0121 454 6171); Bradford (01274 754262); Bristol (0117 973 7373);

Cardiff (01222 229525); Exeter (01392 214085); Glasgow (0141 221 0999); Hove (01273 326282); Hull (01482 465940); Inverness (01463 702560); Leeds (0113 282 3600); Leicester (0116 255 9944); Liverpool (0151 298 1928); London (0171 489 1992); Maidstone (01622 694109); Manchester (0161 236 3210); Mold (01352 704748); Newcastle (0191 261 0026); Norwich (01603 625977); Nottingham (0115 962 4624); Sheffield (0114 253 2126); Slough (01753 577877); Southampton (01703 832866); Stafford (01785 59528); Telford (01952 588766); Worcester (01905 765335).

The Centres can also offer to connect enquirers to the EC Business Co-operation Network (BC-Net) which helps firms liaise with other companies in Europe to establish partnerships or other contacts.

If you are considering an export business, you should also contact the Department of Trade and Industry 'Overseas Trade Services'.

The DTI/FCO *Overseas Trade Services* operation provides practical help, advice and financial support to exporters at each stage of the exporting process. Assistance ranges from help in doing the groundwork of market research through to establishing a presence in the market. For further information contact your nearest Regional Office of the DTI, Scottish Office, Welsh Office or the IDB in Northern Ireland.

A number of Business Links now have Export Development Counsellors to offer advice to smaller companies hoping to develop overseas markets.

Press & Pictures Division, Central Office of Information, Hercules Road, London SE1 7DU. T:0171 261 8448. The Press and Pictures Division of COI may be able to help you promote your products overseas.

Institute of Export, 64 Clifton Street, London EC2A 4HB. T:0171 247 9812. The IOE offers technical help and advice on international trading matters and provides education and training through its short course programme. Fees and membership subscription details available on request.

Export Market Information Centre (Department of Trade and Industry), Ashdown House, 123 Victoria Street, London SW1E 6RB. T:0171 215 5444. Open to personal users for whom exporting is a genuinely viable proposition, Monday to Friday from 9 a.m. to 8 p.m. (last admission 7.30 p.m.); and Saturday, 9 a.m. to 5.30 p.m. Short enquiries can be dealt with by telephone. Free access to comprehensive collection of foreign statistics and trade directories.

Your local **chamber of commerce** should have first class information on some of the problems you might encounter and your **bank** will also have up-to-date information on the market conditions in most overseas countries, which it will supply free of charge.

Raising finance

Before you approach anyone for money, you must have a proper business plan. This means that you are bound to spend some time researching your business ideas and producing a realistic projection of cash flow needs. Your business plan should be brief and to the point but must contain the following items:

- a clear statement of what product or service you plan to offer
- sales and marketing projections, based if possible on some research or knowledge of the market
- your initial investment plus on-going cash flow requirements
- basic information concerning premises, staff, equipment and development plans
- profit and loss projections, showing when you expect the business to start making money.

It is a good idea to ask an accountant to vet your business plan. Some high street banks offer the same service for a low fixed fee. The different types of finance now available to small businesses through traditional sources such as banks and other institutions are more extensive than most people realise. They fall into four broad categories: overdrafts, commercial and bank loans, equity finance and government loans and grants.

Overdrafts

You will be familiar with overdrafts from your private banking arrangements. The bank allows you to borrow money up to a predetermined limit but only charges you interest on the amount outstanding. If you trade as a limited company the bank will almost certainly require a personal guarantee, which will make you liable for the overdraft if the company fails. Although overdrafts are theoretically repayable at a day's notice, in practice the banks will normally review the arrangement with you once a year. That said, over the past few years banks have been tightening up considerably and, if you think you might have a problem, the earlier you discuss this with your bank manager the more likely you are to avoid trouble. At very least, by putting your bank manager in the picture, you will know where you stand and may be able to buy extra time to make alternative arrangements, if necessary.

Interest on overdrafts fluctuates in line with bank base rate and you will usually have to pay a premium of between 2 per cent and 5 per cent over this level.

Loans

There are various types of loans including: bank loans for a fixed period; leasing and hire purchase arrangements; credit factoring and invoice discounting; stock financing; and the loan guarantee scheme.

In each case, your loan will be for a specific period but interest will normally fluctuate as it does with overdrafts. Most loans are made against the security of a specific asset, such as vans, office equipment, your debtors, or stock. Lenders will generally ask for a personal guarantee, which you should resist unless there is clearly no other way of obtaining the money.

Bank loans. Unlike an overdraft, the bank undertakes to lend you money for a fixed period, say, five years. You will be required to repay a percentage of the loan each year and before lending the bank will want to check your business plan to see that the agreed repayments are realistic. Quite apart from the interest charges, there may be an arrangement fee and the bank may also ask for a debenture which gives it security over all the assets of your business but does not involve you in pledging personal possessions such as your house.

Leasing and hire purchase. These are both methods of using equipment or vehicles and paying for them by instalments. Leasing is normally slightly cheaper, as the supplier owns the asset and benefits from the relevant tax allowances. As an alternative to negotiating an agreement with the supplier, it may be cheaper to ask your bank or other lender to arrange the necessary finance for you. Interest is usually fixed at the start and will remain at the same level throughout. This has the advantage that you know what your commitment is. However, such agreements tend to be expensive.

Bills of exchange, invoice discounting and credit factoring. Bills of exchange are possibly the simplest method of smoothing cash flow. The bill of exchange is sent by the supplier to the customer who signs indicating that it will be paid on maturity at some specific time in the future – say two months. The bill is then exchanged for cash in advance against the bill by a bank, minus a discount equivalent to an interest charge. The discount is usually lower than the interest charged on a bank loan or overdraft and therefore cheaper, but the bank will probably require you to 'back' your customer's bill giving recourse against you if the client does not pay.

Invoice discounting is somewhat similar but is only useful if you deal with prestigious companies whose credit is good. You sell selected invoices for about 75 per cent of their face value for immediate cash. You retain full responsibility for collecting the money and in the event of your customer defaulting have to repay the sum involved. In effect, you are paying a high premium for cash up front.

Credit factoring is a continuous financial arrangement whereby the trade debts of a business are sold to a factoring company as they arise. In return, you immediately receive about 80 per cent of the debt, less the factoring company's charges, and the balance of the money when your customer pays. A potentially useful aspect of factoring is the provision by the finance company of a full sales ledger, credit control, cash collection and bad debts service. Although this service sounds marvellous, it does not come cheap and can also be extremely complicated if your customers are not well known companies with good credit rating.

Both factoring and invoice discounting are offered by specialist companies within the major banking groups.

Stock financing. This is a means of helping small manufacturing businesses finance their stock of raw materials and finished products. The finance company purchases and sells back to the manufacturer, say, £30,000 of stock. The financier pays the manufacturer an immediate cheque, less his charges, and takes out a 90-day bill of exchange.

This can be a useful method of financing working capital if your high street bank will not lend you money against the security of your stock. Although more expensive than ordinary bank borrowing, it is less expensive than borrowing through a finance house.

Loan guarantee scheme. Exists to help supply loan finance for businesses which would not normally be able to raise a loan because they cannot offer adequate security or do not have a proven track record. The government provides a guarantee of 85 per cent of the money borrowed, up to a maximum of £250,000. Much smaller loans are also possible and one of the attractions of the scheme is that streamlined arrangements exist for dealing with loans under £15,000. The scheme is run through the high street banks who charge an arrangement fee plus a small premium over their normal lending rate. Additionally, there is a small government premium on the loan. Although theoretically personal security is not required, the banks like to see some backing for the 15 per cent not covered by the government guarantee and will always require the business assets to be pledged. Loans are available to both start-up and established firms, excluding certain types of businesses, such as financial services and property development.

The most usual way of arranging loan guarantee finance is through your normal clearing bank. Some other financial institutions including certain merchant banks sometimes also offer this facility.

Equity finance

With equity finance, as opposed to simply borrowing money, you are taking in a financial partner who will own part of your business. For this reason most small businessmen have traditionally been reluctant to accept equity investment. However, this is changing as the value of venture capital as well as the practical contribution of investors are increasingly becoming appreciated. Unlike loans, equity investment is permanent capital. If a shareholder wishes to sell out, the proprietor is not bound to buy back his shares but sometimes has an option to do so.

The most likely sources of equity finance are friends or family, business angels or venture capital specialists. The Enterprise Investment Scheme offers another possibility.

Friends and family. You may know people who would like to back you when you are starting a business. It is important that both sides should understand the risks and commitments involved and be aware that these may affect your normal relationship. However close you are, it is sensible to ask an accountant or solicitor to advise you on a formal agreement. There are specific percentages of shareholdings, such as 25 per cent, that normally carry legal rights; it is important to understand what these are and to decide whether you wish them to apply. If an investor owns more than 10 per cent of your company, he/she would usually expect to be a director and maybe also play an active part in the business.

Business Angels. You may need or want to find an investor outside your circle of family and friends. This has become considerably easier than a few years ago, partly because the new Enterprise Investment Scheme (see below) offers attractive tax relief to individuals investing in unquoted companies but also because several organisations run introductory services to put firms seeking funds in contact with potential investors – or business angels as they are often called.

One of the best known is **LINC (Local Investment Networking Company)**, consisting of 12 member agents around Britain, which distributes a monthly bulletin of business opportunities to its investors. The agents also run local meetings, where entrepreneurs seeking finance can make presentations to potential investors. For further information, contact: **LINC**, 4 Snow Hill, London EC1A 2BS. T:0171 236 3000.

Another possibility is The Capital Exchange newsletter which is distributed to some 4,000 members who subscribe to the service as a means of sourcing investment openings in small firms. Cost to a company seeking an entry is £200. Firms interested in being included are required to submit a business plan for vetting before acceptance is given. For further details, contact: **The Capital Exchange**, PO Box 127, Hereford HR4 0YN. T:01432 342484.

There is also **Venturenet**, which is an on-line national database providing information to business angels about small firms – typically seeking funding of between £20,000 and £½ million. Businesses applying must adhere to recognised quality standards. Costs involved are £90 for database listing; £250 for an (optional) independent assessment of the proposal. Contact: **Enterprise Adventure Ltd.**, The Enterprise Pavilion, Cross Lanes, Guildford GU1 1UG. T:01483 458111.

Other sources of business angels include: **3i** (T:0171 928 3131); **NatWest Angels Service** (T:0171 454 2236); **Capital Match**, covering Surrey, Sussex and Hants (T:01273 833881); **Halo**, covering Dorset (T:01202 448834); **Investors Forum**, covering Tyneside (T:0191 261 4838); and **TechInvest**, covering Cheshire, the Wirral and Merseyside (T:01606 734308).

Accountants are also worth approaching, as are your local TEC and Business Link.

Enterprise Investment Scheme. This has replaced the Business Expansion Scheme. Although the basic purpose remains the same, namely to encourage more equity investment in small companies, a number of welcome new rules have been introduced. Particular attractions for individuals investing in unquoted companies include: 20 per cent tax relief on investments up to £100,000 a year; exemption from capital gains on sale of shares providing these are held for five years; roll-over relief from CGT provided gains arising from a disposal are reinvested for shares under the EIS in a period beginning one year before and ending three years after the disposal; relief against income tax or CGT on losses. A further big plus, of particular appeal to many retired business angels, is that outside investors (i.e. not previously connected with the business) can play an active part as paid directors.

Companies can raise up to £1 million under the scheme. Best bets for tracking likely investors are the same as for business angels plus also some venture capital companies. See Inland Revenue booklet IR 137.

Venture capital. There are now over 114 venture capital firms in the UK that make long-term unsecured equity investments in new and expanding businesses. These investors normally look for a company with high growth potential and will take a minority stake in it. They usually expect to have a representative on the company's board, with the aim of helping the business to maximise its performance.

Sources of venture capital. Your accountant may be able to recommend a venture capital company. Alternatively, contact: **British Venture Capital Association (BVCA)**, Essex House, 12-13 Essex Street, London WC2R 3AA, T:0171 240 3846. BVCA represents every major source of venture capital and produces a free annual directory listing all its members together with their varying investment criteria. Other useful BVCA publications, all free, are: *A Guide to Venture Capital; Business Plans and Financing Proposals; Sources of Business Angel Capital.*

Although most venture capital funds invest from £250,000 upwards, the following are prepared to consider investments of £50,000 or under:

No Minimum	*Telephone*
Fleming Investments Ltd.	0171 638 5858
Industrial Development Board for Northern Ireland	01232 233233
Lancashire Enterprises plc.	01254 692692
Larpent Newton & Co Ltd.	0171 251 9111
Loxko Venture Managers Ltd.	0171 836 1225
Northern Venture Managers Ltd.	0191 232 7068
Minimum £5,000	
Seed Capital Ltd.	01491 579999
Welsh Development Agency	01222 222666
Yorkshire Enterprise Ltd.	0113 237 4774
Minimum £10,000	
Lothian Enterprise Ltd.	0131 220 2100
Prelude Technology Investments Ltd.	01223 423132
Minimum £25,000	
British Coal Enterprise Ltd.	01623 826833
Cornwall Enterprise Board Investments Ltd.	01872 223883
Transatlantic Capital Ltd.	0171 224 1193
Minimum £35,000	
Baring Venture Partners Ltd.	0171 290 5000

Minimum £50,000

Abel Venture Managers Ltd.	01372 470373
Cambridge Capital Management Ltd.	01223 312856
Derbyshire Enterprise Board Ltd.	01246 207390
Enterprise Equity (NI) Ltd.	01232 242500
Korda & Co Ltd	0171 253 5882
Scottish Enterprise	0141 248 2700
The South West Scotland Investment Fund Ltd.	01387 61769
Ulster Development Capital Ltd.	01232 246765

Additionally **Midland Enterprise Funds** which are run by regional fund managers consider investments ranging from £5,000 to £150,000. Numbers to contact and minimum investment figures are: East Anglia, from £20K, T:01767 651920; East Midlands, from £5K, T:0115 967 8400; Greater London, from £5K, T:0171 935 6123; North East, from £5K, T:0191 233 1892; North West, from £5K, T:01772 203020; South East, from £25K, T:01273 835455; South West, from £5K, T:0117 931 1318; Thames Valley and Chilterns, from £20K, T:01767 651920; West Midlands, from £5K, T:01922 58200; Yorkshire/Humberside, from £5K, T:0113 237 4774; Wales, from £5K, T:01222 230490.

Venture Capital Trusts. These are a new type of investment trust aimed at encouraging more investment in smaller companies. To qualify as a VCT, at least 70 per cent of a Trust's investments must be in unquoted companies and, to give investors an exit route, it must be quoted on the Stock Exchange. People investing in VCTs will be exempt both: from income tax on their dividends and from capital gains tax on disposal of their shares for investments of up to £100,000 a year. They will also receive roll-over relief on any gains used to invest in the VCT. At time of writing, it was still too early for there to be a list of venture capital companies definitely planning to set up a VCT. Best advice is to watch the 'business pages' or to contact the **British Venture Capital Association (BVCA)**, Essex House, 12-13 Essex Street, London WC2R 3AA. T:0171 240 3846.

Other useful organisations

Enterprise Boards. The Yorkshire, West Midlands and Greater London Enterprise Boards, originally set up by local authorities in the early 1980's, have been emerging as important regional sources of venture and development capital, concentrating on equity investments in local small firms. Contact:

Yorkshire Enterprise Ltd., St Martins House, 210-212 Chapeltown Road, Leeds LS7 4HZ. T:0113 237 4774.

West Midlands Enterprise Board Ltd. (WMEB), Wellington House, 31-34 Waterloo Street, Birmingham B2 5TJ. T:0121 236 8855.

Greater London Enterprise (GLE), 63-67 Newington Causeway, London SE1 6BD. T:0171 403 0300.

Useful reading

Venture Capital Report publishes a monthly magazine in which they appraise companies which need additional investment and management expertise. VCR vets the companies to make sure that their claims and plans are realistic. Potential investors subscribe to the report (£350 p.a.) and contact companies of interest to them direct. Companies use VCR to raise sums from £5,000 to £500,000, or sometimes more. It costs £350 to be included in the VCR report plus a success fee of £1,000 plus 2.5 per cent of the funds raised. For further information, contact VCR at: Magdalen Centre, Oxford Science Park, Oxford OX4 4GA. T:01865 784411.

Government grants and loans

There is a vast range of public sector financial assistance available from local authorities, government sources and the EC. Small firms could benefit from loans, grants or possibly the Business Start-up Scheme. Most major firms of accountants and also the banks produce comprehensive publications listing all such resources currently available.

An example is the *Small Business Information Directory* offered free by the NatWest Bank. For ease of reference information is classified according to local post codes. Application forms to receive the directory are contained in the *Business Start-up Guide* which is obtainable free from all NatWest branches.

The types of fund listed below are among the most potentially useful to smaller firms.

Business Start-up Scheme (formerly Enterprise Allowance). This scheme is designed to help unemployed individuals run their own business by paying them a weekly allowance while they get started. Depending on the particular enterprise in question, the sum can vary between £20 and £90 a week and can be given for between 26 and 66 weeks.

The scheme is administered by the Training and Enterprise Councils (TEC) in England and Wales; and by the Local Enterprise Companies (LEC) in Scotland. Each will have its own slightly different criteria for eligibility. As a general rule, however, all applicants will need to be unemployed and starting a new business which they are planning to run themselves.

For further information about the scheme, together with the address of your local TEC (or LEC), contact your nearest Jobcentre.

The **Midland Bank** offers free banking services for all those on the scheme. For further information, contact your local branch.

Local authority assistance. Local authorities are now playing a much fuller role in co-ordinating the advice and financial resources available to small companies in their area. Many have developed their own loan and grant schemes. In particular, councils can offer generous mortgages to buy or improve land or buildings and can provide rent and/or rates relief. With government agreement, they can sell land below market value, provide improvement grants, build advance factories and give employment subsidies. Contact your local authority Planning Department or alternatively, where appropriate, the Industrial Development Department.

Grants for development and other assisted areas. Small firms in selected areas of Great Britain may be eligible for one of the available Regional Enterprise Grants. These are divided into two elements:

Regional investment grants. These are available to firms employing up to 25 people in all Development Areas and designated localities affected by colliery closures. The grant is 15 per cent of the cost of fixed assets of a project up to a maximum of £15,000.

Regional innovation grants. These are available to firms employing up to 50 people in all Development, Intermediate, City Challenge, Taskforce, EC Objective 2 Areas and designated localities affected by colliery closures; they are also available in certain Scottish urban areas. These grants help qualifying businesses to develop new or improved products or processes. The grant is 50 per cent of the agreed project costs up to a maximum of £25,000.

In the wider Assisted Areas, which include the Intermediate Areas as well as the Development Areas, Regional Selective Assistance Grants may also be available to both manufacturing and some service companies. To qualify for assistance, the project must be commercially viable, create or safeguard employment, demonstrate a need for assistance, and offer a distinct regional or national benefit. The level of grant will be the minimum necessary for the project to proceed.

Development Areas are as follows:
In England: Barnsley, Birmingham (part of), Bishop Auckland, Doncaster, Falmouth, Hartlepool, Helston, Liverpool, Mansfield, Middlesbrough, Morpeth and Ashington, Newcastle upon Tyne, Newquay, Penzance and St. Ives, Redruth and Camborne, Rotherham and Mexborough, South Tyneside, Stockton-on-Tees, Sunderland, Thanet, Wigan and St. Helens, Wirral and Chester, Wolverhampton.
   In Scotland: Arbroath, Bathgate, Cumnock and Sanquhar, Dunfermline, Forres, Girvan, Glasgow, Greenock, Irvine, Kilmarnock, Kirkcaldy, Lanarkshire, Newton Stewart.
   In Wales: Aberdare, Blaenau, Gwent and Abergavenny (part of), Fishguard, Haverford West, Holyhead, Merthyr and Rhymney, Pontypridd and Rhondda, South Pembrokeshire.

Intermediate Areas are as follows:
In England: Alfreton and Ashfield, Alnwick and Amble, Barnstaple and Ilfracombe, Barrow-in-Furness, Bideford, Birmingham (part of), Blackburn, Bodmin and Liskeard, Bolton and Bury, Bridlington and Driffield, Bude, Castleford and Pontefract, Chesterfield, Clacton, Coventry and Hinckley, Dorchester and Weymouth

(part of), Dover and Deal, Dudley and Sandwell, Durham, Folkestone, Gainsborough, Great Yarmouth, Grimsby, Harwich, Hastings, Heathrow (part of), Hull, Isle of Wight, London (part of), Louth and Mablethorpe, Manchester (part of), Newport, Oldham, Plymouth, Retford, Rochdale, Sheffield, Sittingbourne and Sheerness, Skegness, St. Austell, Torbay, Wakefield and Dewsbury, Walsall, Whitby, Widnes and Runcorn, Wirral and Chester (part of), Wisbech, Workington, Worksop.

In Scotland: Ayr, Alloa, Campbeltown, Dumbarton, Dundee, Dunoon and Bute, Falkirk, Invergordon and Dingwall, Lochaber, Skye and Wester Ross, Stranraer, Sutherland, Thurso, Western Isles, Wick.

In Wales: Bangor and Caernarfon, Blaenau Gwent and Abergavenny, Bridgend, Cardiff (part of), Cardigan, Llanelli, Neath and Port Talbot, Newport (part of), Pontypool and Cwmbran, Pontypridd and Rhondda (part of), Porthmadoc and Ffestiniog, Pwllheli, Shotton, Flint and Rhyl (part of), Swansea, Wrexham (part of).

EC Objective 2 Areas include all or part of:
In England: Accrington and Rossendale, Alnwick and Amble, Ashfield, Barrow-in-Furness, Bishop Auckland, Birmingham, Blackburn, Bolton and Bury, Bradford, Burnley, Burton-on-Trent, Castleford and Pontefract, Chesterfield, Cleveland, Coventry and Hinckley, Darlington, Doncaster, Dudley and Sandwell, Durham, Greater London, Grimsby, Hartlepool, Hull, Liverpool, Manchester, Mansfield, Morpeth and Ashington, Newcastle upon Tyne, Nottingham, Pendle, Plymouth, Scunthorpe, South Yorkshire, Stoke, Sunderland, Telford and Bridgnorth, Thanet, Tyne and Wear, Wakefield and Dewsbury, Walsall, Whitehaven, Wigan and St. Helens, Widnes and Runcorn, Wirral and Chester, Wolverhampton, Workington, Worksop.

In Scotland: Alloa, Ayr, Bathgate, Cumnock and Sanquhar, Dumbarton, Dundee, Dunfermline, Edinburgh, Falkirk, Girvan, Glasgow, Greenock, Irvine, Kilmarnock, Kirkcaldy, Lanarkshire, Midlothian, Stirling.

Regional Government Offices. The Government has recently established ten new regional offices which bring together under one roof the former local departments for Trade and Industry, Employment, Transport and the Environment. Two particular benefits of this reorganisation are that services can be tailored in a more integrated fashion to the needs of the community and that business people now have a single port of call for all enquiries. Addresses are:

Eastern Region: Heron House, 49-53 Goldington Road, Bedford MK40 3LL. T:01234 363161.

East Midlands: Cranbrook House, Cranbrook Street, Nottingham NG1 1EY. T:0115 935 0602.

London: Millbank Tower, 21-24 Millbank, London SW1P 4QU. T:0171 217 3000.

Merseyside: Graeme House, Derby Square, Liverpool L2 7SU. T:0151 224 6300.

North East: Wellbar House, Gallowgate, Newcastle upon Tyne NE1 4TD. T:0191 201 3395.

North West: Sunley Tower, Piccadilly Plaza, Manchester M1 4BE. T:0161 952 4054.

South East: Charles House, 375 Kensington High Street, London W14 8QH. T:0171 605 9000.

South West: Tollgate House, Houlton Street, Bristol BS2 9DJ. T:0117 987 8488 or: Phoenix House, Notte Street, Plymouth PL1 2HF, T:01752 221891.

West Midlands: Five Ways Tower, Frederick Road, Edgbaston, Birmingham B15 1SJ. T:0121 626 2000.

Yorkshire and Humberside: City House, New Station Street, Leeds LS1 4JD. T:0113 280 0600.

The main offices for small business enquiries in Scotland and Wales are:

Scottish Office Industry Department, Meridien Court, 5 Cadogan Street, Glasgow G2 6AT. T:0141 248 4774.

Welsh Office Industry and Training Division, Cathays Park, Cardiff CF1 3NQ. T:01222 823976.

Regional Agencies. If you are planning to start a business in Scotland, Wales or Northern Ireland, these agencies (or in the case of Wales, the Industry and Training Division) offer financial facilities that may be of assistance to you. All finance is discretionary and to be eligible, your business would almost certainly either have to increase job opportunities, offer export potential, reduce the need for imports or hold promise of significant expansion. You are more likely to get finance – which could be a grant or loan – if you are willing to locate in an area of high unemployment.

Depending on the area, priority may be given to enterprises involved in: tourism, manufacturing, new technology and, in the Highlands and Islands, fisheries. In the main, retailing is unlikely to receive assistance. For further information, contact the appropriate agency:

Scottish Enterprise, 120 Bothwell Street, Glasgow G2 7PJ, T:0141 248 2700.

Highlands & Islands Enterprise, Bridge House, 20 Bridge Street, Inverness IV1 1QR, T:01463 234171.

LEDU, The Small Business Agency, LEDU House, Upper Galwally, Belfast BT8 4TB, T:01232 491031.

Rural Development Commission. The Rural Development Commission can provide top-up loans to businesses located in the Commission's rural development areas. These loans are intended to cover any shortfall between the total cost of an eligible project and the amount that can be raised from the applicant's own resources and private sector lenders. Contact your nearest office (see local telephone directory) or: **Rural Development Commission**, 141 Castle Street, Salisbury, Wiltshire SP1 3TP. T:01722 336255.

Loans from the European Investment Bank. The European Investment Bank has arranged credit facilities for a number of UK banks and financial institutions to help promote financing for capital investment by small and medium-sized businesses (those with fewer than 500 employees, net fixed assets of less than £50 million and with capital investment projects of up to £20 million).

Loans are available direct from the EIB for capital investment projects of £20 million and over in industry and related services, infrastructure, communications, environmental protection, energy and meeting European Union priorities. The EIB may finance up to half the gross investment cost. For further information contact: **European Investment Bank**, London Office, 68 Pall Mall, London SW1Y 5ES, T:0171 839 3351.

Advice and training

Never has small business been so well served when it comes to general help and training. A number of organisations offer free advice and low-cost consultancy, as well as a variety of training schemes ranging from general information on setting up and developing a business to more specialised courses.

Training and Enterprise Councils (TECs)
These are independent companies run by business leaders whose aim is to stimulate economic growth within their area by assisting local enterprises to compete effectively – in particular by providing appropriate training to meet local requirements.

Over 80 TECs have been established in England and Wales. In Scotland, there is a network of 22 similar organisations called Local Enterprise Companies (LECs).

While the particular courses and other programmes offered by the TECs will inevitably vary according to what the local priorities are, in general terms their key functions are: to promote training in accordance with employer needs (courses include business start-up training and management training for owner/managers); to provide a comprehensive advisory service for small and start-up businesses; to manage the Business Start-up Scheme; and to run a co-ordinated information service.

For further information, including the address of your local TEC, contact your nearest Jobcentre.

Business Links
A network of Business Links is being formed by the DTI to provide smaller

businesses with a one-stop access point to the full range of advisory and support services (both government and private) in their area.

The Links are largely funded and run by local business organisations with teams of advisers to assist firms with their development plans and to put them in direct contact with marketing specialists, venture capitalists or other sources of help as relevant.

By the end of 1995, the DTI was aiming to have 200 Business Links operating across all parts of England. For further information, contact your nearest Regional Government Office, TEC or chamber of commerce.

Department of Trade and Industry: Diagnostic and Consultancy Service

The Diagnostic and Consultancy Service provides subsidised consultancy support for small and medium-sized enterprises. The service is divided into two distinct elements: an in-depth diagnosis of a business's strengths and weaknesses; and full strategic consultancy. The service is available only through the Business Link network.

Eligibility and cost. Most independent firms or members of groups with fewer than 250 employees based in England are eligible to apply. Subsidy rates of up to 50 per cent are available for each element of the service with a maximum grant of £2,000 for a diagnostic project and £10,000 for a consultancy project. For further information contact your nearest Government Office or Business Link.

Support for innovation and technology

The Government provides a package of measures to help businesses innovate and make better use of technology. Several of the schemes are specifically directed at smaller firms, including in particular: Regional Enterprise Grants of up to £25,000; SMART, an annual competition designed to stimulate innovative technology, with valuable awards given to entrants producing the best commercially viable ideas; and SPUR, a scheme providing grants for the development of new products and processes which involve a significant technological advance.

For further information about these and other available schemes, contact your nearest Regional Government Office; or the Scottish or Welsh Office; or alternatively, ring the Freephone Innovation Enquiry Line on 0800 442001.

Other Government schemes

Managing in the 90s Programme. The programme aims primarily to assist small and medium-sized enterprises become more competitive to meet the challenges of the '90s. It provides information and advice on the adoption of best practice with regard to: marketing, design and product development, management of information, purchasing and materials management, production and quality.

The programme provides information through seminars, a roadshow, a demonstration company scheme and a range of literature. Other sources of advice are also signposted.

For further information contact your nearest Regional Government Office, Scottish Office or Welsh Office (for addresses, see page 254).

Skills for Small Business. This is a three-year programme, launched during 1995, which is aimed to help firms with fewer than 50 employees improve their skills. Key workers are given training to assist them to pass on their knowledge to colleagues via delivery of in-house training. The scheme is limited to one key worker per firm. For further information, contact your local TEC.

Adult Education Centres

Short courses in specific business skills are run by business schools and colleges of higher and further education. Various trade and professional associations also run courses. Enquire through your local education authority (see telephone directory).

Rural Development Commission

The Rural Development Commission aims to promote jobs and communities in rural England. Through its local office network it runs a wide variety of advisory and training services for businesses in its designated Rural Development Areas. The Commission also offers technical training to practising craftsmen and their trainees in a selected range of disciplines for which training courses are limited or difficult to access. For further information, contact your nearest office or: **Rural Development Commission**, 141 Castle Street, Salisbury, Wiltshire SP1 3TP. T:01722 336255.

Regional agencies

These organisations are designed to assist the development of industrial activity in their areas and all have small business divisions that will be only too glad to offer any assistance they can.

Scottish Enterprise. Scottish Enterprise operates through a network of 13 Local Enterprise Companies, in lowland Scotland, offering a wide range of services to start-up and expanding businesses. For further information, contact the **Scottish Business Shop**, 120 Bothwell Street, Glasgow G2 7JP. T:0800 787878 who will put you in touch with your nearest regional office.

A Euro Info Centre has been set up in Strathclyde to provide companies with information on European business law and EC Initiatives in business development. T:0141 221 0999.

Highlands and Islands Enterprise. The HIE network covers the Northern and Western parts of Scotland, as well as the Scottish Islands. It offers a free counselling service to small firms and to those considering setting up in these areas. This includes advice on recruitment, rates of pay, labour availability and other employment issues. Financial assistance may be given to meet training expenses but this does not normally exceed 50 per cent of the cost. The HIE network runs specific training courses on: tourism, fish farming, forestry and agriculture. For further information, contact: **Highlands and Islands Enterprise**, Bridge House, 20 Bridge Street, Inverness IV1 1QR. T:01463 234171.

The Development Board for Rural Wales. Offers help on setting up a business in the mid-Wales area. Schemes available include an advisory service on all aspects of business and training courses targeted to meet the specific needs of different groups of people. For further information, telephone (Newtown) 01686 626965 or call free on 0800 269300.

LEDU, The Small Business Agency. LEDU offers an extensive range of advisory and financial services suitable for businesses at all stages, from pre-start-up to growth and development. Help is given with research and development, marketing, accountancy systems and total quality systems. For further information, contact: **LEDU,** Upper Galwally, Belfast BT8 4TB, T:01232 491031.

For list of addresses in England, see page 254.

Other regional agencies
Various other regional agencies, usually established as partnerships between the public and private sectors, now operate in different parts of the country.

Part development agency, part enterprise agency and part enterprise board, they generally offer a wide range of help for businesses in the region. Some useful addresses include:

Lancashire Enterprises plc., Enterprise House, 17 Ribblesdale Place, Preston PR1 3NA, T:01772 203020.

Northern Development Company, Great North House, Sandyford Road, Newcastle upon Tyne NE1 8ND, T:0191 261 0026.

West Midlands Development Agency, 1500 Solihull Parkway, Birmingham Business Park, Birmingham B37 7YD. T:0121 717 0909.

Non-government sources of advice and training

Many enterprise agencies, chambers of commerce, business institutes and small business clubs, scattered around the country, provide counselling services, together with, in some cases, more formal training.

Enterprise agencies (Enterprise trusts in Scotland)
These are partnerships between local businesses, the professions, chambers of commerce, local authorities and others, designed to stimulate the start-up and expansion of small businesses by providing advice and counselling.

There are more than 300 LEAs/ETs now operating in the U.K., offering varying facilities which often include: free business advice, provision and management of small business workshops, enterprise training and the facilities of a small business club.

Enterprise agencies operate closely with Business in the Community who can put you in direct contact with your nearest EA. For further information, contact: **Business in the Community (BIC)**, 8 Stratton Street, London W1X 5FD, T:0171

629 1600 or **Scottish Business in the Community (SBC)**, Romano House, 43 Station Road, Corstorphine, Edinburgh EH12 7AF, T:0131 334 9876.

London Enterprise Agency (LEntA). An example of a fully comprehensive service is provided by LEntA. This Enterprise Agency offers:

- help in developing a business plan for presentation to banks; this includes advice on which banks might sensibly be approached and what to do if your proposal is rejected
- general advice on market research, marketing strategy and techniques such as direct mail
- a patenting and licensing technical service
- a 'marriage bureau' service for introducing investors to companies seeking funds
- courses in starting up and developing a business, held during the evenings and at weekends as well as during the working day.

For further advice, contact: **LEntA**, 4 Snow Hill, London EC1A 2BS, T:0171 236 3000.

Enterprise trusts. There are now also many Enterprise trusts, including some 44 throughout Scotland, under the umbrella of SBC.

Chambers of commerce. Chambers specialise in providing on-going help, general business advice and training. Examples of regular courses, offered by many, include telephone sales and data preparation for computers. Costs vary but average £50 a day for non-member companies. Chambers provide informal networks of contacts with other businessmen who may well need the products/services you plan to offer. Addresses are listed in the local telephone directory. Alternatively, contact: **Association of British Chambers of Commerce**, 9 Tufton Street, London SW1P 3QB. T:0171 222 1555.

Institute of Business Counsellors. IBC is a non-profit making professional institute with over 1,600 members nationwide who offer advice based on practical business experience. Topics covered include accounting, marketing, production, taxation and exporting. Counselling for a new business can usually be arranged free of charge through your local TEC, LEC or Enterprise Agency. If you are unable to locate a suitable Business Counselling service locally, write to: Brian L Dunsby, Chief Executive, **The Institute of Business Counsellors**, PO Box 8, Harrogate, North Yorkshire HG2 8XB.

Institute of Directors Business Information and Advisory Services (IAS). Staffed by experienced people, IAS gives information, advice and counselling on the more complicated problems of business life from whether a redundancy settlement is fair to advice on raising finance, export marketing or operating a group of companies. General information on such things as the Retail Prices Index can also be supplied, often over the telephone. Each of the advisers specialises in certain areas, including: finance, tax and small businesses; personnel management, retirement, redeployment and conditions of service; exports and marketing; company secretarial practice and company commercial and employment law. The service, which is exclusive to members, is free. Contact IAS, Institute of Directors, 116 Pall Mall, London SW1Y 5ED. T:0171 839 1233 for an appointment; or to discuss your problem over the telephone with an adviser.

Lawyers for Your Business, Law Society, Chancery Lane, London WC2A 1SX. T:0171 405 9075. A legal advisory service set up by Business in the Community and the Law Society with the aim of encouraging smaller businesses to seek the advice of a solicitor at an early stage in the hope of avoiding future problems. Applicants are offered an initial free consultation at which they can discuss – and may often resolve – any queries. Further consultations, if these are required, are charged at normal rates. Leaflets about the service together with a list of participating solicitors are obtainable from libraries, enterprise agencies, TECs and similar.

British Steel (Industry) Ltd. Established to help create jobs in steel closure areas, British Steel (Industry) can offer a package including small premises, finance and advice for businesses setting up or expanding in one of the 19 locations that come within its orbit. For further information, contact: **British Steel (Industry) Ltd.**, Canterbury House, 2-6 Sydenham Road, Croydon CR9 2LJ, T:0181 686 2311.

British Coal Enterprise Ltd. Provides a similar service to the above in UK coal mining areas. Loan finance is available, as is business assistance. Help is also given with finding premises and provision includes a number of managed workspaces. For further information, contact: **British Coal Enterprise Ltd.**, Edwinstowe House, Edwinstowe, Mansfield, Notts NG21 9PR. T:01623 826833.

Trade associations

Virtually all industries have a trade association that provides advice and other services to members. If you are considering purchasing or starting a business in a particular trade sector, ask at your local library for the name and address of the relevant trade body. Examples are: National Federation of Retail Newsagents, British Institute of Interior Design, the Institute of Employment Consultants and the Booksellers Association.

Hotels and catering

Many retired people plan to run a hotel, restaurant or other type of catering business. While some make a success of it, the evidence suggests that for many more the dream turns to disaster – leaving them with debts and their savings gone.

Tourism officials in the West Country have been so dismayed by the number of hotels that shut down after only a season or two that they have started an advice service called **Operation Fresh Start** to impress on starry-eyed novices the financial and other business realities involved. For further information, contact: Development Department, **West Country Tourist Board**, 60 St. David's Hill, Exeter EX4 4SY. T:01392 76351.

Another very useful source is the **Hotel and Catering Training Company** which can provide information on setting up and running a hotel/restaurant. Contact: HCTC, Capital House, 9 Logie Mill, Edinburgh EH7 4HG. T:0131 557 4677.

Pubs. If you are interested in running a pub, see page 290 in Chapter 11, 'Looking For Paid Work'.

Tourist boards

There are many opportunities for mature people to start tourism-related businesses, especially if they live or plan to retire to one of the major tourist areas. Advice about the development and marketing of tourist attractions and amenities is available from the tourist boards, as follows:

English Tourist Board, Thames Tower, Black's Road, London W6 9EL, T:0181 846 9000.

Wales Tourist Board, Brunel House, 2 Fitzalan Road, Cardiff CF2 1UY. T:01222 499909.

Scottish Tourist Board, 23 Ravelston Terrace, Edinburgh EH4 3EU. T:0131 332 2433.

Northern Ireland Tourist Board, St. Anne's Court, 59 North Street, Belfast BT1 1NB. T:01232 231221.

The English Tourist Board publishes a selection of guides for people branching out in a tourism-related business. Titles include: *Starting a Bed and Breakfast Business?*, *Starting a Caravan Business?*, *Starting a Self-Catering Business?* and *Funding a Tourism Business* (with information about financing the above types of enterprise). The guides are £10 each (or £30 for the set), available from: **English Tourist Board**, Department D, Thames Tower, Blacks Road, London W6 9EL.

Rural Development Commission, 141 Castle Street, Salisbury, Wiltshire SP1 3TP, T:01722 336255, also provides a comprehensive advisory service including tourism.

Local authorities are closely involved in the development of tourism in their area. Contact the Tourism Development Officer at your County or District Council.

In certain designated areas, tourism and leisure projects may be eligible for:

- a grant towards the conversion of a redundant building to provide tourist amenities and facilities

- a loan towards the acquisition of accommodation and equipment.

For more information, contact the Rural Development Commission.

Agriculture

If you already live or plan to retire to the country, you may be considering starting some form of agricultural enterprise such as fish farming, organic farming or cheese making. The Rural Development Commission has published a useful booklet, *Action for Rural Enterprise*, detailing all the assistance available to businesses in rural areas. To obtain a copy, write to: **Rural Development Commission**, Freepost SA122, Salisbury SP1 3BR.

The following organisations can also provide useful advice and/or training:

ADAS. ADAS is an Executive Agency of the Ministry of Agriculture, Fisheries and Food (MAFF). It is a comprehensive consultancy organisation providing research and advisory services to agriculture and its associated industries. This includes advice on various forms of agricultural production and on the options for diversification. Its services are provided mainly on a fee-paid basis. For further information contact **ADAS**, Oxford Spires, The Boulevard, Kidlington, Oxon OX5 1NZ. T:01865 842742.

Farm Retail Association. Farm shops can provide a useful outlet for your own and neighbouring farmers' produce as can Pick-Your-Own farms. Many are quite small, concentrating on one fruit or vegetable such as strawberries, raspberries or asparagus. Some of the essentials you would need to know are described in *A Guide to Good Hygienic Practice for Farm Shops*, available from the Association (free to members, £5 to non-members). For more information and advice on planning requirements contact: The Secretary, **Farm Retail Association**, 22 Long Acre, Covent Garden, London WC2E 9LY. T:0171 235 5077.

Also useful is *Farm Gate Sales to the Public*, which is a legal guide (£5.50 to NFU and FRA members, £10.95 to non-members) available from Shaw & Sons, 21 Bourne Park, Crayford, Kent DA1 4BZ.

Useful organisations

The following are the key organisations representing small business interests. Some act as pressure groups, conduct research and also provide a service to their members:

Confederation of British Industry, Smaller Firms Council, Centre Point, 103 New Oxford Street, London WC1A 1DU. T:0171 379 7400.

Federation of Small Businesses Ltd., 140 Lower Marsh, London SE1 7AE. T:0171 928 9272.

Forum of Private Business, Ruskin Chambers, Drury Lane, Knutsford, Cheshire WA16 6HA. T:01565 634467.

Institute of Directors, 116 Pall Mall, London SW1Y 5ED. T:0171 839 1233.

Useful reading
Starting and Running Your Own Business available from your local TEC; or in Scotland, Local Enterprise Company.

A list of books for small and start-up businesses published by Kogan Page is available from 120 Pentonville Road, London N1 9JN. T:0171 278 0433.

11 Looking for Paid Work

Far from thinking of putting your feet up when you retire from your present job, perhaps like many other people today one of your ambitions is to continue working in some form of paid employment. If so, then despite present unemployment levels, prospects are improving all the time as more and more employers are actively seeking to recruit older people. However, before dashing off a shoal of application letters, it helps to think through some of the practicalities. Start by asking yourself a few basic questions.

Firstly, what is your main motive in wanting to work? The wish to supplement your income? The companionship? Fear of boredom? The desire for mental stimulation? The need to have a sense of purpose? Or the lurking suspicion that without a job, friends and social acquaintances will be less interested in hearing your views?

The answer may well be a combination of factors but you should at least try to pinpoint your priorities to avoid drifting into a job that does not satisfy your main aims. The stories are legion of people whose prime reason for seeking work was to get out of the house to make new friends and who then plumped for a solitary occupation working from home. Likewise, one frequently hears of those whose real purpose was financial but who somehow signed on instead for unpaid voluntary work.

Another fundamental consideration is how many hours you are thinking of committing per week. A full Monday to Friday? Or just a couple of half-days? And while on the subject of time, is working a long-term goal or simply a pleasant occupation to fill in the next year or so?

What about distance? Would you be prepared to commute or are you aiming for a job that is strictly local? Was there anything, for example the travel, that you particularly disliked about your previous employment and that you are determined to avoid in your future job?

Also very much to the point, are you planning to seek an opening in a similar field, where your experience and contacts would come in useful? Or do you want to do something entirely different? And if so, were this to help, would you be willing to do a training course?

Moreover, have you considered the important economic questions? It may sound stupid when you have been working most of your life but factors such as your age, your total weekly earnings, your pension and other income, as well, of course as any out-of-pocket expenses you incur, could mean that at the end of the day the sums look rather different from what you had supposed.

Financial considerations

Until October 1989 one of the big flies in the ointment was a provision known as the Earnings Rule, whereby any man between the ages of 65 and 69 and any woman between the ages of 60 and 64 who was earning more than £75 a week had their State pension reduced. Happily the earnings rule has been abolished; so today, regardless of your age or how much you earn, there is no longer any forfeit to your State pension, although of course you may have to pay tax on your additional income.

In the past as a means of getting round the earnings rule, we used to recommend that consideration be given to deferring your State pension. Although the earnings rule no longer applies as a reason for this, if you are working close to a full-time week and/or have enough money to live on, there could still be an advantage in asking the DSS to defer your pension as this will entitle you to a bigger pension in the future. Your local Social Security office could advise whether this would be worthwhile. Each year of deferral earns an increment of about 7.5 per cent of the pension.

Decisions concerning your occupational pension could also arise, particularly if you are not so much looking for a retirement job, as a last big move before you retire. Most (though not all) pension schemes apply actuarial reductions for early retirement and joining a new pension scheme in late middle age, though not impossible, can present difficulties or impose certain limitations, especially for very high earners who could be affected by the £78,600 earnings cap on entitlement for tax relief. For further information, see section 'Early leavers' in the Pensions chapter.

National Insurance is another consideration. Unless you are over State retirement age or earning less than £58 a week (1995/96 rates), in which case you can forget about NI contributions, you will be liable for the normal Class 1 contributions. If, as many early retirers do, you work for two or more different employers you will have to pay Class 1 in respect of each. The maximum you would have to contribute is £2,086.08 (1995/96). To avoid being billed for more, fill in the form attached to leaflet CA 01, available from Social Security offices.

If you obtain work through an agency (e.g. catering, nursing, exhibition work), you are usually regarded as an employee of the agency for national insurance purposes and the agency is responsible for the payment of Class 1 contributions on your behalf. However, this does not apply if: you do the work from home; are not subject to anyone's direct supervision; or are in the entertainment business. See leaflet CA 25.

If you are over retirement age and have a job, the only requirement is that you obtain an exemption card to give to your employer. See Form CF 384 (Certificate of Exception), also from any Social Security office.

If you do freelance or other assignment work (unless virtually all your earnings come from one employer, in which case the Inland Revenue would argue that you are an employee of the organisation), you are officially considered to be self-employed for both national insurance and taxation purposes (see Chapter 10, Starting Your Own

Business). For further information, you might find it helpful to read leaflet IR56/ NI39 *Employed or Self-Employed?* available from any tax office.

Two other leaflets, issued by the DSS which you might like to read are: FB 30 *Self-Employed?* and CA 03 *National Insurance Contributions for Self-Employed People Class 2 and 4*; available from Social Security offices.

Unemployment benefit. Even if you are in your sixties and already receiving an occupational or personal pension, you are entitled just like anyone else to claim unemployment benefit, although if you are over 55, unemployment benefit will be abated by the amount by which your occupational/personal pension exceeds £35 (£50 under the new Jobseeker's Allowance, see below).

Provided you satisfy the conditions and have paid sufficient national insurance contributions, you can continue claiming until such time as you find a job or receive an equivalent benefit, e.g. as a result of doing an approved training course, till you reach the age of 70.

To qualify however, you must genuinely be available for work and moreover be able to prove that you are actively seeking a job. Claimants are advised to keep a proper record on a week-by-week basis of what steps they have taken in their quest for employment (including for example copies of job application letters they have written) and are told that their endeavours may be checked from time to time by Claimant Advisers.

A further condition is that claimants are not allowed to turn down a job offered to them via the Employment Service without good reason. Lower pay would not normally be accepted as a reason although, that said, there is a 'permitted period' up to a maximum of 13 weeks when individuals are allowed to restrict their job search to openings that take advantage of their skills, experience and reasonable salary expectations.

The rules also allow 'employment on trial', when you can try out a job for between 6 and 12 weeks (provided you work at least 16 hours a week and have been unemployed for at least 6 months) without risking disqualification for receiving unemployment benefit if you decide to leave. N.B. The new Jobseeker's Allowance will allow employment on trial after only 3 months' unemployment. Also the minimum trial period, if individuals decide to leave, is being reduced from 6 weeks to 4 weeks.

The current (1995/96) rates of unemployment benefit are as follows: £46.45 a week for people under State pension age; £58.85 a week for people over State pension age (i.e. 60 for women, 65 for men). A higher rate of benefit is paid to those with responsibility for dependants. The additional rate for a dependent adult is: £28.65 for people under State pension age; £35.25 for those over State pension age.

For further details about unemployment benefit, see leaflet NI 12 *Unemployment Benefit* and FB 9 *Unemployed?*, available from any Social Security office.

Jobseeker's Allowance. In April 1996, unemployment benefit is being replaced by the new Jobseeker's Allowance. Although most of the same conditions apply, there are several important changes (in addition to the couple noted above). Some are tougher; others, a big improvement.

The only drawback, which is difficult to argue, is that Jobseeker's Allowance is limited to people under State retirement age. A further new condition of eligibility is that applicants must agree an action programme with the Employment Services to help them maximise their chances of finding a job.

Highly welcome new measures include: (1) the fact that everyone receiving the allowance will get a national insurance credit for the work they do (at present people working over 8 hours lose their credit); (2) partners of those getting Jobseeker's Allowance will be able to work up to 24 hours a week (currently 16) without loss of benefit to the household; (3) jobseekers and their partners who work part-time will get credits, enabling them to build up a lump sum bonus of up to £1,000 which they can cash when they move off benefit.

A leaflet explaining Jobseeker's Allowance in detail should be available from Social Security offices early in 1996.

If you work but are not earning very much, there are two benefits which could be helpful: *Family Credit* and *Disability Working Allowance.*

Family Credit. This is a tax-free weekly payment for families who, despite the fact of one or both parents working, still have a low income. To be eligible for benefit, the claimant must work at least 16 hours a week and have at least one child under 16 (or under 19 if in full-time education). Although means-tested, benefit levels are more generous than many people realise – with the average payment being around £47 a week. Furthermore, not all your income is taken into account in calculating entitlement to Family Credit. These disregards include: child benefit; one parent benefit; the first £15 of any maintenance payments you receive; plus certain child care costs (up to £40 a week) which are allowed against earnings.

A claim pack FC 1 can be obtained from your local Social Security office or post office; or for further information, telephone the Family Credit freephone number: 0800 500222.

Disability Working Allowance (DWA). This is a tax-free benefit for people – including those already over pension age – with an illness or disability. The benefit is means-tested and additionally to qualify, you would need to work at least 16 hours a week, either as an employee or in a self-employed capacity.

Similar to Family Credit, the benefit amount depends on your income, savings and size of your family – but could be worth around £50 a week. A further attraction is that people taking a job with the help of DWA automatically qualify for free prescriptions and free dental charges. For further information obtain leaflet DS 703, available from your local Social Security office, or ring the Benefit Enquiry Line free on 0800 882200.

Bigger payments. People working 30 hours a week or more receive an extra £10 on top of the normal weekly benefit in recognition of their longer hours. This applies both to those in receipt of Family Credit and Disability Working Allowance.

Redundancy. If you have just been made redundant, or fear this is a possibility, see information in the 'Money in General' chapter, page 20.

Assessing your abilities

Some people know exactly what they want to do. They have planned their action campaign for months, done their research, prepared a CV, followed up selective openings and are just waiting for their present employment to come to an end before embarking on a new career. But for most of us, it is not like that. Having merrily announced our intention to find a job, there comes a moment of truth when the big question is what?

Knowing what you have to offer is an essential first step. Make a list of everything you have done, both in your formal career and ordinary life, including your outside interests such as: local politics, Rotary, hobbies, voluntary work and even jobs around the home – decorating, gardening, carpentry or cooking. In particular, consider any practical or other skills, knowledge or contacts that you have acquired through these activities which may now prove useful, for example: public speaking, fund-raising, committee work, conference organisation, use of mini-computers, production know-how or fluency in a foreign language.

As a result of writing everything down, most people find that they have far more to offer than they originally realised.

Add too your personal attributes and any special assets you can offer an employer. The list might include: health, organising ability, a good telephone manner, communication skills, the ability to work well with other people, use of a car and willingness to do flexible hours.

Maturity can also be a positive asset. Many employers prefer older people as being more reliable and less likely to be preoccupied with family and social demands. Also, in many small firms in particular, a senior person's accumulated experience is often rated as especially valuable.

By dint of looking at yourself afresh in this fashion, you may get a clearer idea of the sort of job that would suit you. Although there is an argument for keeping a fairly open mind and not limiting your applications too narrowly, the worst mistake you can make is to answer scores of advertisements indiscriminately – and inevitably end up with a sackload of rejections.

Of course, offers do sometimes turn up out of the blue; and in some cases in a field that it would never have occurred to you to look. But as a general rule when job-hunting, it helps to know at least in broad terms what you are seeking before you start.

Many people find this extraordinarily difficult. After years of working in one occupation, it takes quite a leap in imagination to picture yourself in another role – even if it is in the same or a related area. If you intend to do something completely different, it will be harder still, as your knowledge of what the job entails will probably be second-hand. Also quite apart from deciding what you would enjoy, in many parts of the country the issue may be more a matter of what is available.

Talking to other people helps. Friends, family, work colleagues or business acquaintances may have useful information and moreover will quite likely be able to appraise your abilities more objectively than you can yourself. It could also be sensible to consult outside experts, who specialise in adult career counselling and whose advice may be more realistic than that of friends in the context of current employment opportunities.

Job counselling

This is usually a mixture of helping you to identify your talents in a vocational sense combined with practical advice on successful job-hunting techniques. Counsellors can assist with such essentials as writing a curriculum vitae, preparing for an interview and locating job vacancies. They can also advise you of suitable training courses. Counselling is offered both by government agencies and private firms.

Government services
There are six services that could be helpful to adult jobseekers. In all cases, for further information, contact your local Jobcentre.

New Restart Programme. Everyone who has been unemployed for six months or more is offered a Restart interview at which Employment Service advisers discuss what job vacancies, training courses or other programmes might be suitable. Part-time Restart courses lasting two weeks give practical help with job-hunting, including: letter-writing and other ways of applying for a job; interview technique; information on vacancies and training opportunities available locally.

Jobclubs. Give advice on job-search techniques including, for example, applying for a job on spec and practice interviews. Members attend part-time, usually over four days per week. Among other resources, they have use of the telephone and free postage for job appplications. To join, it is normally necessary to have been out of work for six months. However, certain groups, such as people with disabilities and victims of designated large-scale redundancies, are exempt from this requirement.

Job search seminars. Provide those who have been unemployed for 13 weeks or more with expert advice on the best way to search out and apply for jobs. The seminars last four days, spread over five weeks.

Job review workshops. These are for unemployed people, who are unlikely to return to their normal occupation or who are looking to broaden their job search, make an informed choice of alternatives. The two-day workshops are particularly suitable for those with professional, executive and managerial backgrounds who have been unemployed for around 13 weeks.

Jobplan workshops. Designed to help people who have been unemployed for over a year focus on clear and realistic job goals. Workshops last five days and include computer skill-match, a one-to-one assessment with an adviser, group discussions and counselling on how to get started. For further details, see leaflet *Give Your Jobhunting a Lift*, available from Jobcentres.

Jobcentres. Can give general advice about local employers, training opportunities and other openings. Some Jobcentres have a small library of careers guidance books. It is a good idea to ring beforehand to make an appointment.

Private counselling

Job counselling has become a growth industry in the private sector. Some people find it extremely helpful; others, an expensive waste of time. Best advice is to obtain brochures from a variety of agencies and study the literature carefully to see exactly what you are being offered. You could ask for a list of former clients and then speak to one or two of them direct, to find out whether they found the service useful. Some of the better known organisations include:

Career Analysts, Career House, 90 Gloucester Place, London W1H 4BL. T:0171 935 5452. Their Career Review service caters specifically for those in the 35-60 age group, who need to consider carefully what they plan to do for the remainder of their working lives. The Review involves filling in a detailed questionnaire about yourself at home and then spending a day at Career House, completing a number of aptitude, interest and personality tests. This is followed by in-depth counselling and practical guidance. You receive a full report with recommendations as to the best options for you to pursue, including references for employment or suitable courses – as well as help with preparation of a CV. Career Analysts like to keep in touch and will send a follow-up document for completion after two years. Fees are £275 plus VAT.

Career Counselling Services, 46 Ferry Road, London SW13 9PW. T:0181 741 0335. Individual counselling is staged over a number of sessions, lasting 12-14 hours in all. The service includes various tests and questionnaires which are used as a basis for discussion. A tape recording of this discussion is given to you. Price is £360 plus VAT. A service to help with job-hunting is also available at £140 plus VAT.

Career and Educational Guidance, 4 Cadogan Lane, London SW1X 9EB. T:0171 631 1209. Offers a combination of tests with a detailed follow-up interview and a written report. Price is £245 incl. VAT.

Those living out of London should look in the *Yellow Pages* under the word 'Career' or 'Vocational'.

Training opportunities

Knowing what you want to do is one thing. But before starting in a new job, you may want to brush up existing skills or possibly acquire new ones. Most professional bodies have a full programme of training events, ranging from one-day seminars to proper courses lasting a week or longer. Additionally, the Department for Education and Employment offers a number of schemes – available nationally – which may be of interest.

Open and flexible learning. The main purpose of the Government's Open and Flexible Learning Scheme is to expand the range and flexibility of vocational education and training opportunities available to individuals of all ages. The courses are designed to increase the scope for participants to learn at a time, place and pace best suited to their own particular circumstances. For further information on the full range of open learning opportunities, ask to see a copy of the *Open Learning Directory* at your local Training and Enterprise Council (TEC).

Training for work. This scheme is aimed at helping people of any age between 18 and 63 who have been unemployed for six months get a job and/or gain vocationally relevant qualifications. People with disabilities and victims of large-scale redundancies may not need to wait six months. For more details contact your local Jobcentre or TEC.

Meeting local needs. Training and Enterprise Councils, or TECs as they are more generally known, offer a variety of training courses. These are specifically tailored to local employment requirements and therefore offer participants a good chance of finding a job in their area. In Scotland, they are called Local Enterprise Companies. For further information, together with an address and name of individual to contact, ask at your local Jobcentre.

Help with finding a job

The ideal is to find a job for your retirement while you are still at work. Quite apart from it being more difficult to summon the energy to start looking around after a period of being idle, employers tend to give preference to those they see as being busy and involved, rather than those whom they suspect as having got out of the habit of the normal disciplines of work.

However, whether you leave it a while or start hunting well in advance, this will not affect the approach you probably adopt. The only extra tip if you have been retired for some time is to consider doing some voluntary work, or a short course, so you have a convincing answer to the inevitable question: what have you been doing?

There are four basic ways of finding a job; through contacts; by following up advertisements; by applying to an agency for suitable introductions; or by direct approaches to suitable employers. As general wisdom, the more irons you have in the fire, the better.

Make sure all your friends and acquaintances know that you are in the market for work – and include on the list your present employer. Some firms actually encourage consultancy links with former executives, or at least are prepared to respond to a good idea. A greater number are more than happy to take on previous employees over a rush period or during the holiday season.

Another obvious move, if you are a member of a professional institute, is to inform them of your availability. Many institutes keep a register of members seeking work and, the encouraging part is, receive a fair number of enquiries from firms seeking qualified people for projects, part-time or temporary work, or sometimes even for permanent employment.

A further source of very useful contacts is the local Chamber of Commerce, CBI or Institute of Directors. Likewise, if you are a member of a Rotary Club, it can only be useful to spread the word; and the same applies to, say, a golf club, political association where you are active, any committee you sit on or other group with which you are involved. Often the most unlikely person turns out to be the one who helps you most.

If you intend to follow up advertisements, selectivity is the name of the game. Rather than write around to all and sundry, limit your applications to those that sound genuinely promising. You will save yourself a lot of stationery, not to mention disappointments when another 'sorry' letter arrives – or you fail to hear anything at all. As well as national and local newspapers, remember that the trade press often offers the best bet of all. Some local radio programmes broadcast a regular weekly 'job spot'; it could be useful to check when this is scheduled.

Agencies will invariably have more applicants than vacancies, except where skill shortages exist. However, most of them clearly place a fair number of people (or they would be out of business) and, as with other endeavours, keenness counts. People who simply register their name and then sit back and wait tend to be forgotten. The moral is telephone frequently to enquire what opportunities have arrived; or if you live close-by, pop into the office from time to time. Being on the spot at the right time is nine-tenths of success. A selection of agencies that specialise in appointments for people aged 50-plus is listed at the end of the chapter.

A direct approach to likely employers is another option. Study the business press and talk to your colleagues for ideas of firms that might be interested in employing someone with your abilities. Always find out who the appropriate person is to whom you should be writing – a properly addressed letter is far more likely to get noticed than one merely marked 'For the attention of the Personnel Manager'.

Regardless of whether you use contacts, advertisements or agencies – or preferably all three – a prime requirement will be to have a well presented CV, suggestions for which follow overleaf.

CV writing

This is your personal sales document. It should contain:

- your name
- address
- telephone number
- age (optional)
- brief details of your education

- a summary of your work experience including: dates, employers, job titles and outline of responsibilities
- other achievements
- key outside interests

Ideally, it should not be longer than two pages of A4 and it must be typed.

There are a number of firms that specialise in providing assistance with the writing of CVs, who advertise their services regularly in *The Times* and other serious newspapers. While some are highly professional, a common fault tends to be the production of over-lengthy CVs, which can be definitely counter-productive. An all-purpose CV can also put off employers. Wherever possible, you should try to gear your CV specifically to the job on offer, emphasising those elements of your experience and skills that are relevant. If you are thinking of using a specialist service, check the price first as charges can be on the hefty side. As with other purchases, you should do a bit of price comparison before making a decision. The price will normally include a batch of immaculately typed copies of your CV, ready for you to distribute.

A far cheaper option is to take advantage of the Government Jobclubs, which are run by Jobcentre staff or other agencies on the Department for Education and Employment's behalf to assist those who have been out of work for six months or more (people with disabilities can apply as soon as they wish). As part of the service, help is given with CV preparation and free facilities are provided including telephone, typewriter and photocopying equipment. Contact your Jobcentre for details.

Women's Job Change, operating as part of the Skills Development Services of the charity Birmingham Settlement, offers a similar wide-ranging and free service to unemployed women. Help and advice can be obtained on matters relating to finding a job, education and retraining opportunities.

Further information from: **Women's Job Change** (Skills Development Services), Birmingham Settlement, 318 Summer Lane, Newtown, Birmingham B19 3RL. T:0121 359 3562.

Interview technique

If you have worked for the same employer for a number of years, your interview skills are liable to be a little rusty. It is a good idea to list all the questions you expect to be asked, (including those you hope won't be brought up) and then get a good friend to rehearse you in your answers.

In addition to questions about your previous job, be prepared for some or all of the following: what you have done since leaving employment; why, if you are now seeking a job, you retired earlier than you might have done; whether your health is good – this may take the form of a polite enquiry as to whether you would not find the hours or travelling too much of a strain; why you are particularly interested in working for them as an employer; and given the job requirements, what you think you have of special value to offer. You may also be asked what you know about the organisation. If the answer is likely to be 'very little', it could pay you to do a bit of research – such as obtaining a copy of the annual report.

Obvious mistakes to avoid are: claiming skills/knowledge that you do not possess; giving the impression that you have a series of stock answers to problems; criticising your former employer; or by contrast, drawing comparisons which could be interpreted as being faintly disparaging of the organisation where you are attending for interview.

Possibly the most difficult subject of all to come up may be the question, how much money would you expect? As a sad generalisation, most jobs for retired people – including early retirers – pay less than their previous employment, so you may have to strike a balance between what you want and the risk of pricing yourself out of the market.

Part-time openings

Another reason why the pay may appear low is that the work is part-time. For some people, of course, this is the ideal arrangement. Others may regard it as very second best. However, do not sniff at part-time work if the opportunity is available. Firstly, it is a way back into the market and many part-time or temporary assignments develop into full-time jobs in due course. This is especially true in small firms, which may of necessity be cautious about recruitment while the business is in the early development stage.

Additionally, far-reaching changes are happening in the job market, with temporary, or project-based, professional and executive assignments becoming increasingly common. For example, freelance accountants are in growing demand, as are project-based computer staff and personnel specialists with particular knowledge of, say, pensions or performance pay. Proficient temporary secretaries are again high on the 'wanted list'. Likewise, there are a growing number of part-time and other openings for older people to work in supermarkets, chain stores, hotels, conference centres and other outlets connected with the tourist industry.

Part-time or freelance work can to all intents and purposes become a full-time occupation in its own right. Ask any retired businessman who has taken on half a dozen such appointments and the likelihood is that he will tell you that he is working harder than he has ever done in his life. The only real note of caution is that many employment rights do not apply to part-timers and those working less than 16 hours a week are particularly vulnerable.

Employment ideas

Going the established routes – agencies and so forth – while obviously recommended, may not suffice. Many of the best jobs are never advertised, either because people obtain them through personal recommendation or because – and this is becoming more frequent – individuals have been partially instrumental in creating their own opportunities.

One clear-cut way of doing so is to use a bit of initiative when spreading the word of your availability, by actually suggesting work you could usefully perform. Consultancy is very much a case in point.

Consultancy

Many retired executives make a tidy income by hiring themselves back to their former employer in a consultancy guise. As opposed to being paid a regular salary and working full time, they undertake specific projects for which they are paid a fee. This may be structured as a lump sum, for example £5,000 for devising and helping implement a merit appraisal scheme; or as many consultants do, they may negotiate a day-rate.

Likewise, an idea that has been copied by some other employers is a scheme started by IBM, called Skillbase, which as well as unblocking promotion lines has the big advantage to the company of retaining valuable skills that would otherwise be lost. As an alternative to full early retirement, individuals are invited to join Skillbase which guarantees them 90 days' work per annum for two years on very attractive pay rates.

Consultancy, by definition, is not limited to a single client. By using your contacts judiciously plus a bit of marketing nous, it is quite possible to build up a steady list of assignments on the basis of your particular expertise.

Marketing skills are always in demand, as is computer knowledge, experience in pensions, and personnel-related subjects and, increasingly today, public relations know-how.

Small firms are often a good bet for consultants, as they cannot afford to employ specialists full-time, so normally buy in expertise, as and when it is required. Any contacts with the chamber of commerce or similar could prove fruitful avenues for promoting your services.

Many established consultancies retain a list of associates – a sort of freelance register – whom they call on, on a horses-for-courses basis, to handle suitable assignments. The Institute of Management Consultants (IMC) which publishes a number of useful booklets might be able to assist if you are looking for names to contact. The address is: **Institute of Management Consultants**, 5th Floor, 32-33 Hatton Garden, London EC1N 8DL. T:0171 242 2140.

Also worth knowing about is the Temporary Executive Service, run by the CBI in association with P-E International. It places senior executives with companies on a temporary basis, essentially to bridge management gaps or to provide a specialised service. Projects normally last anything from two to three months up to two years. Contact: Sue Shortland, **Temporary Executive Service**, Employment Affairs Directorate, CBI, Centre Point, 103 New Oxford Street, London WC1A 1DU. T:0171 379 7400.

Executives in Scotland should write to: The Assistant Director, CBI Scotland, Beresford House, 5 Claremont Terrace, Glasgow G3 7XT. T:0141 332 8661.

Similarly, the Institute of Directors runs a Temporary Executive Service called Executive Reserve as an adjunct to its Board Appointments Service. Openings are mainly for specific project work, such as perhaps a marketing or manufacture assignment; or for regular part-time work, normally involving from 4 to 12 days a month. Client companies tend to be smaller or medium-sized businesses across a wide range of sectors. Contact: **Board Appointments, Institute of Directors**, 116 Pall Mall, London SW1Y 5ED. T:0171 839 1233.

Another possible source of work is your local Training and Enterprise Council (TEC) – or in Scotland, Local Enterprise Company – some of whom retain business counsellors to assist small and start-up firms to develop successfully. Applicants need to have entrepreneurial and/or senior management experience and ideally also training in business counselling skills. Pay and conditions vary but with a normal range of about £80 to £120 a day. For address of your local TEC, contact the Jobcentre.

A useful organisation to know about is the Institute of Business Counsellors which, with a membership of over 1,600 nationwide, has contact with all Business Links, TECS, Enterprise Agencies and similar organisations seeking counsellors qualified to advise small, start-up and medium-sized businesses. A code of conduct and professional standards of competence have been established and substantial business experience is a prerequisite of membership.

There is a registration fee of £25 and annual subscriptions (1995/96) are as follows: Associate, £59; Member (MIBC) £79; Fellow (FIBC) £99. A professional indemnity insurance scheme is available for members. For further information, contact: Brian L Dunsby, Chief Executive, the **Institute of Business Counsellors**, PO Box 8, Harrogate, North Yorkshire HG2 8XB. T:01423 879208.

Interim management

Interim management has been one of the biggest growth areas in recruitment over the past couple of years.

The term covers an enormously wide range, from a temporary manager engaged to cover in an emergency or to handle a specific job such as the closure of a plant, to an outside specialist recruited short-term to implement a particular assignment – for example, a marketing campaign or the installation of a new computer system.

The growth is largely due to two factors: the down-sizing of personnel by large organisations and the requirement of many small companies for specialist skills that they cannot afford to employ full-time. Either way, what it means is an upsurge in temporary job opportunities for experienced managers and/or those with particular expertise to offer – with many of the plum jobs going to those who have recently taken early retirement or been made redundant.

Most of the organisations that specialise in such placements have more candidates on their books than vacancies but all agree that this is a growth industry with opportunities set to increase.

As in consultancy, fees vary enormously. While the going rate for senior people is around £250 to £350 a day, some managers command double or even more. However, as with any temporary or freelance situation, there will inevitably be days when you will not be working and, in contrast to a permanent job, very few interim assignments offer the normal executive perks. Typical assignments last between six and nine months and may be full-time or simply involve one or two days' work a week.

Several of the organisations listed above offer what is in effect an executive leasing register, by another name.

There is now also an association representing those engaged in executive leasing and interim management, known as **The Association of Temporary and Interim Executive Services**, ATIES, 36-38 Mortimer Street, London W1N 7RB, T:0171 323 4300. Member organisations are:

Albemarle Interim Management Services Ltd., 18 Marlborough Street, London W1V 1AF. T:0171 437 3611.

Barton Interim Management, Bere Barton, Bere Ferrers, Yelverton, Devon PL20 7JL. T:01822 840220.

Ernst & Young Temporary Executive Service, Rolls House, 7 Rolls Buildings, Fetter Lane, London EC4A 1NH. T:0171 931 1054.

Executive Standby (South) Ltd., 27 Preston Street, Faversham, Kent ME13 8PE. T:01795 590119.

IEMIT Ltd., 4 Tanners Yard, London Road, Bagshot, Surrey GU19 5HD. T:01276 452288.

Interim Management (UK) Ltd., 8 Bloomsbury Square, London WC1A 2LP. T:0171 404 6772.

P-E International/CBI Temporary Executive Service, Park House, Wick Road, Egham, Surrey TW20 0HW. T:01784 434411.

Praxis Executive Taskforce Ltd., Norfolk House, The Courtyard, Gorsey Lane, Coleshill, Birmingham B46 1JA. T:01675 466812.

Russam GMS Ltd., 48 High Street North, Dunstable, Beds LU6 1LA. T:01582 666970; **GMS Consultancy North Ltd.**, Delaunay House, Scoresby Street, Bradford BD1 5BJ. T:01274 723151; **GMS Consultancy West Ltd.**, Maggs House, 78 Queen's Road, Bristol BS8 1QX. T:0117 926 6531.

Other firms (not members of ATIES) that could be worth contacting are:

Executive Interim Management, Devonshire House, Mayfair Place, London W1X 5FH. T:0171 629 2832.

Touche Ross Management Consultants, Stone Cutter Court, 1 Stone Cutter Street, London EC4A 4TR. T:0171 936 3000.

Triple A Group Ltd., 18 Lawrence Avenue, New Malden, Surrey KT3 5LY. T:0181 335 3135.

W & S Interim and Project Management Ltd., Hanover House, 14 Hanover Square, London W1R 0BE. T:0171 499 7599.

Executive Resourcing Service, The Chartered Institute of Marketing, Moor Hall, Cookham, Maidenhead, Berkshire SL6 9QH. T:01628 524922. Specialises in placing marketing and sales executives in both full-time and interim posts.

Openings via a company or other reference

Just as your company could turn out to be your best customer for consultancy services, it could also open other doors. If you are still a couple of years off retirement, you could broach your employer about seconding you to an enterprise agency or charity, where you would be helping small businesses or a worthwhile voluntary organisation in your local community. Secondment can be part-time for a few hours a week or full-time for anything from a few weeks to two years. It can also often lead to a new career.

Normally only larger employers are willing to consider the idea since, as a rule, the company will continue to pay your salary and other benefits during the period of secondment. However, the concept has been gaining increasing popularity and more companies are giving the idea sympathetic consideration, especially since the Inland Revenue now allows companies to offset any secondee's employment costs against tax. Also, employers gain by having an 'ambassador' in the community and by the media attention secondees usually attract.

The major organisation specialising in co-ordinating secondments is Action: Employees in the Community. It is the leading consultant to companies on secondment policies and practice, as well as the main agency arranging all forms of secondment to community organisations. For further information, contact: **Action: Employees in the Community**, 8 Stratton Street, London W1X 5FD. T:0171 629 2209.

Public appointments

Opportunities regularly arise for individuals to be appointed to a wide range of public bodies, such as tribunals, commissions and consumer consultative councils. Many appointments are to local and regional bodies throughout the country, including Scotland, Wales and Northern Ireland. Some are paid but many offer an opportunity to contribute to the community and gain valuable experience of working in the public sector on a part-time expenses-only basis.

Self-nomination and nomination of others who are willing to be considered for public appointments are always welcome. Short application forms are available from the **Public Appointments Unit**, Cabinet Office (OPSS), Horse Guards Road, London SW1P 3AL. T:0171 270 6210/6217.

The Public Appointments Unit is not the only gateway to nomination and those with particular interests may also wish to make their availability known to an individual government department, or to a chairman of a public body for which they feel they have suitable qualifications.

Additionally, both the TUC and CBI are consulted on some appointments. If you are active on either, there is nothing to lose by letting it be known that you could be interested in a public appointment.

Non-executive directorships

Many retiring executives see this as the ideal. The problem, whichever way you look at it, is: either that more executives want appointments than there are directorships available; or that not enough companies have yet recognised the merits of having outside directors on their board.

The old idea that such appointments are a pleasant sinecure is distinctly out of date. In the past few years a more exacting business climate has developed, coupled with more onerous demands made on all company directors by recent legislation. If you are able, committed and have the necessary experience the key organisations to which you might apply are:

Promotion of Non-Executive Directors (PRO NED), Devonshire House, Mayfair Place, London W1X 5FH. T:0171 493 4567. PRO NED maintains a register of candidates for non-executive directorships in companies ranging from the very large to small family businesses. The main requirements for inclusion on the register (which, PRO NED explains, are determined by the demands set by client companies) are that you should have served on the main board of a quoted public limited company (plc) and that you are below the age of 60. PRO NED, which was founded by the Bank of England and others, has now been acquired by Egon Zehnder International.

Institute of Directors, Board Appointments, 116 Pall Mall, London SW1Y 5ED. T: 0171 839 1233. The IOD runs a Board Appointments service. Membership of the IOD is not a necessary requirement. However, only high-calibre candidates with the necessary experience and judgement are accepted. Openings, including appointments for part-time chairmen, occur in companies of all sizes.

Independent Direction, Cadsden House, Cadsden Road, Princes Risborough, Bucks HP27 0NB. T:01844 274575. Specialises in board appointments for smaller/ private companies. To be included on the register, candidates must have several years' board experience at the top level of an organisation, large or small.

Prowess, 118 Eaton Square, London SW1. T:0171 245 6153. Handles a wide mix of both private and public sector board appointments. Candidates must have held director level responsibilities. Prowess is particularly pleased to have placed a substantial number of women as well as high-calibre ethnic minority candidates.

The 3i Independent Director Programme, 91 Waterloo Road, London SE1 8XP. T:0171 928 3131. Essentially interested in candidates who run, or have run, their own business.

Barton Independent Directors, Bere Barton, Bere Ferrers, Yelverton, Devon PL20 7JL. T:01822 840220. Also runs a non-executive directors' register, specifically for small to medium-sized companies.

Another route to becoming a part-time director which might appeal is to join the growing number of business angels by taking a stake in one or several smaller companies. For further information, see Chapter 10, page 249.

Market research

In addition to the normal consultancy openings in marketing, there is also scope for those with knowledge of market research techniques. The work covers a very broad spectrum, from street or telephone interviewing to data processing, designing questionnaires, statistical analysis and sample group selection.

Many of the specialist market research agencies employ researchers and analysts on a freelance basis. However, as with other fields, supply exceeds demand so there is a certain amount of luck involved, as well of course as ability, in finding regular work.

For further details together with a list of market research companies that employ freelance interviewers, contact: **Market Research Society**, 15 Northburgh Street, London EC1V 0AH. T:0171 490 4911.

Paid work for charities

Although charities rely to a very large extent on voluntary workers, most charitable organisations of any size have a number of paid appointments. Other than social workers and other specialists that particular charities may require for their work, the majority of openings are for general managers/administrators, fundraisers and for those with financial skills. Secretarial vacancies also exist from time to time.

Salaries have been improving but in general are still considerably below the commercial market rate. A further point is that, unlike the big company world, managers cannot expect to find a battery of support staff and must be willing to turn their hand to the more menial jobs such as adding up the petty cash and fixing the photo-copier – as well as handling meetings, building up good media relations and sustaining the enthusiasm of volunteers and paid staff alike.

It is essential therefore that anyone thinking of applying for a job in a charity must be in sympathy with its aims and style. Agencies specialising in charity recruitment advise that it is a good idea to do a stint as a volunteer before seeking a paid appointment, as not only will this provide useful experience but will help you to decide whether you would find the work satisfying.

Most of the serious newspapers carry charity job advertisements – the *Guardian* on Wednesday is especially fertile hunting ground – as do some of the weeklies and monthlies including *Community Care* and *New Statesman and Society*. Other possibilities are to approach a charity direct or to register with one of the agencies below.

Charity Appointments, 3 Spital Yard, Bishopgate, London E1 6AQ. T:0171 247 4502. Helps other charities fill their key jobs – for example, chief executive, finance director and fundraiser – and also finds trustees who are unpaid. If you are interested in putting your name on the register, you should send a CV with a brief covering letter indicating the type of job you are seeking, together with any preferences re salary or location.

Charity Recruitment, 40 Rosebery Avenue, London EC1R 4RN. T:0171 833 0770. An appointments service specialising in recruiting paid staff for work in charities. It caters for jobs at all levels from directors and fundraisers to senior secretaries. CR advises regretfully that it is more difficult to place candidates over 60. Olga Johnson, Chief Executive, would be pleased to answer any queries and CVs can be sent to her in confidence.

Sales

If you are a whizz salesperson, you will hardly be reading this chapter. You will have already used your contacts and flair to talk yourself into a dozen jobs, with the only problem being which one to choose. Almost every commercial firm in the country is crying out for people with that particular brand of authority, charm and persuasiveness to win extra orders.

Many people who have never thought of sales could be excellent in the job, because of their specialist knowledge in a particular field combined with their enthusiasm for the subject. Educational and children's book publishers for example are often keen to recruit ex-teachers to market their books to schools and libraries.

There is an almost insatiable demand for people to sell advertising space and if you are an avid reader of a particular publication, for example a specialist motoring or gardening magazine, you might find the work fun and be very successful.

Another possibility where star performers can do exceptionally well is insurance selling. Standards have been considerably tightened up since the furore over personal pensions with the result, which can only be a good thing, that far more attention is being given to training than used to be the case. Another gain is that earnings are becoming less commission-dependent – with instead proper basic salaries being paid by a growing number of companies.

Selling today is not just standing in a shop or trudging the rounds of sceptical customers. Over the past few years telephone selling has caught on in a big way and, like mail order, is used by a vast array of very different businesses; so if you have a good telephone voice, this could be for you.

Additionally, many firms employ demonstrators in shops or at exhibitions for special promotions. The work is usually temporary or freelance by definition; and while pay is normally good, the big drawback is that you could be standing on your feet for long periods of the day.

The big 'beware' are firms that pay on a commission-only basis. Far from merely earning a pittance, you could end up distinctly out of pocket.

If the idea of selling appeals, either study the newspaper advertisements or, better still, approach firms direct that you reckon could make genuine use of your special knowledge. If the idea makes you quail, the likelihood is that selling is not for you. If it fires you with enthusiasm, you could actually find yourself making more money in your retirement than ever before.

Sales distributor

Some companies employ softer-sell methods, using distributor agents who call on their neighbours with a catalogue or arrange parties at which it is possible to buy a range of merchandise.

Betterware which recruits some 30,000 distributors a year – including many retirees – says the essence is building up friendly relationships, noting down orders and delivering the goods a few days later. There is no financial outlay, the hours are totally flexible and most agents can reckon on earning £4 to £6 an hour.

Other big name companies employing freelance distributors include Avon, Tupperware and Amway and, while their terms and conditions all vary slightly (e.g. some encourage distributors to purchase samples or charge them a nominal amount for catalogues), all have frequent openings for both permanent and temporary work.

For further information, contact the companies direct or write to the Direct Selling Association, requesting a list of all member companies together with their advice sheet, listing points to check before signing on as a distributor. Addresses are:

Direct Selling Association, 29 Floral Street, London WC2E 9DP. T:0171 497 1234.

Amway (UK) Ltd., Snowdon Drive, Winterhill, Milton Keynes, Bucks MK6 1AR. T:01908 679888.

Avon Cosmetics Ltd., Nunn Mills Road, Northampton NN1 5PA. T:01604 232425.

Betterware UK Ltd., Stanley House, Park Lane, Castle Vale, Birmingham B35 6LJ. T:0121 693 1000.

The Tupperware Company, Chaplin House, Moorhall Road, Harefield, Uxbridge, Middlesex UB9 6NS. T:01895 826400.

Tourist guide

An extrovert personality is also needed for tourist guide work. The London Tourist Board whose exam qualifies for the coveted *Blue Badge*, is discouraging of the prospects of anyone much over 35, on the basis of the exam being very tough to pass and of the difficulty experienced by qualified older people in finding work.

However, while this may be true of the big London tour operators, not all provincial operators put such a high premium on youth and we know of a number of decidedly middle-aged men and women who act as guides in and around their own area. All have obtained a locally recognised qualification (involving six months' to a year's hard study); all speak at least one foreign language and all are blessed with bags of stamina and a real liking for people. The pay is not particularly scintillating and moreover the work is largely seasonal, so the probability is that there would be several months of the year when you would not be employed.

If despite the obvious drawbacks you are determined to go ahead, approach your local tourist board or tourist information centre to investigate what openings exist. It may also be worth contacting local coach and tour operators who, if nothing else, may have a freelance register you could join.

Aspiring London guides should not be totally disheartened. **Guide Training (London)** which runs the two-year course leading to the Blue Badge says, despite the fierce competition, some older people do manage to make a success. For information about the course and annual pre-entry test, write to: **Guide Training (London)**, 33 Greencroft Gardens, London NW6 3LN.

Another possibility is to sign on as a lecturer with one of the growing number of travel companies offering special interest holidays. To be eligible you need real expertise in a subject, the ability to make it interesting and an easy manner with people. Pay is usually fairly minimal, although you may receive tips plus of course the bonus of a free holiday.

While the number of openings is fairly limited, two of my own friends have got on the circuit – the one lecturing on tours around India, the other running painting classes in Italy. The Holidays chapter gives names of operators that make a feature of special interest programmes. The travel pages of most newspapers should also give you plenty of ideas.

Other tourist work

You might like to consider courier work. Holiday firms are increasingly looking to recruit people in their fifties and early sixties, in part due to the decline in the number of students but equally because they are finding that their clients often prefer having more mature people in charge.

Some jobs take you overseas, others not. Not very long ago, for example, a major camping and mobile home travel company ran a campaign to recruit around 1,000 individuals in middle life to look after visitors at their caravan and camp sites.

It is demanding work that calls for a calm, unflappable personality. If the idea appeals, watch the classified columns for vacancies or, if there is a travel company you particularly admire, you might try approaching them direct.

If you live in a popular tourist area, there is a whole variety of seasonal work, including: jobs in hotels, restaurants, shops and local places of interest. Depending on the locality, the list might also include: deckchair attendants, play leaders for children, caravan site staff, extra coach drivers and many others.

Teaching and training skills

If you have been a teacher at any stage of your career, there are a number of part-time possibilities:

Coaching

With examinations becoming more competitive, demand has been increasing for ex-teachers with knowledge of the public examination system to coach youngsters in preparation for 'A' level, GCSE and common entrance. Contact local schools or a specialist educational consultant such as **Gabbitas Educational Consultants Ltd.**, Carrington House, 126-130 Regent Street, London W1R 6EE. T:0171 734 0161. Gabbitas provides a wide range of recruitment and consultancy services to independent schools in Great Britain and for English-speaking schools overseas. It also maintains an extensive register of teachers seeking appointments. It is also worth looking in the *Yellow Pages* under 'Coaching', 'Tutoring' and 'Education'.

Specialist subjects

Teachers are in demand for mathematics, physics, chemistry, technology and modern languages. People with relevant work experience and qualifications may be able to teach or give tuition in these subjects. A formal teaching qualification is, however, required to teach in state maintained schools.

The **Teacher Training Agency**, Information Section, Portland House, Stag Place, London SW1E 5TT, T:0171 925 5880, has a range of publications about entry into teaching.

School inspector

Men and women with a professional background in education, including actual teaching experience, might like to consider applying to become a school inspector. A particular attraction is that there is no upper age limit. Also vacancies exist nationwide, especially for primary school inspectors. Most openings are for freelance work, with fees – which vary around the country – generally quoted as £200, or more, per day.

In the first instance, it is necessary to submit a CV to the Scrutiny Panel. Successful applicants are then required to attend four tutorial days over several weeks, with assignments in between, followed by a final assessment. Cost is about £300.

For further information, write to: Registration Team, **OFSTED**, 1st Floor, Alexandra House, 33 Kingsway, London WC2B 6SE. T:0171 421 6800.

English as a foreign language

Over the past decade, there has been a mini-explosion of new schools teaching English to foreign students. These tend to be concentrated in London and the major academic cities such as Oxford, Cambridge, Bath and York. The basic requirement for people entering the profession is the RSA/Cambridge Certificate in Teaching English as a Foreign Language to Adults, which can be studied for either part-time or full-time. A list of colleges offering the course can be obtained from: **University of**

Cambridge Local Examinations Syndicate, TEFL Unit, 1 Hills Road, Cambridge CB1 2EU. T:01223 553311.

Other. Adult Education Institutes and Colleges of Further Education may sometimes have part-time vacancies.

Working in the third world

There are various opportunities for suitably qualified people to work in the developing countries of Africa, Asia, the Caribbean and the Pacific on a semi-voluntary basis. Skills most in demand include: civil engineering; mechanical engineering; water engineering; architecture; urban, rural and regional planning; agriculture; forestry; medicine; teaching English as a foreign language; maths and physics training; and economics. All air fares, accommodation costs and insurance are usually covered by the organising agency and pay is limited to a 'living allowance' based on local levels. As a general rule, there is an upper age limit of 65 and you must be willing to work for a minimum of two years. The following are the major agencies involved in this kind of work. Fuller details are contained in Chapter 12, Voluntary Work.

VSO (Voluntary Service Overseas), 317 Putney Bridge Road, Putney, London SW15 2PN. T:0181 780 2266.
Skillshare Africa, Recruitment/Selection, 3 Belvoir Street, Leicester LE1 6SL. T:0116 254 0517.
International Co-operation for Development, Unit 3, Canonbury Yard, 190a New North Road, London N1 7BJ. T:0171 354 0883.
United Nations Association International Service, Suite 3A, Hunter House, 57 Goodramgate, York YO1 2LS. T:01904 647799.

Publishing

Publishers are increasingly using freelance staff with appropriate experience for: proof-reading, copy-editing, design, typography, indexing and similar work as well as for writing specialist copy. For a list of firms that could be interested, your local reference library should have a copy of *Cassell's Directory of Publishing* which catalogues businesses by the type of publishing they do. Alternatively, *The Bookseller* (available through newsagents) carries classified advertisement columns, useful for advertising your own skills as well as for finding work.

Freelance journalism

This is a highly competitive field with very limited scope and other than for professionals, should really be included in the hobbies section. Best bet if you remain undaunted is to approach specialist magazines direct, where you have a real knowledge of the subject. It is normally a waste of time sending articles 'on spec'.

Instead, telephone the editor with a list of suggestions – and find out exactly what the magazine wants, including number of words and so on.

Caring for other people

There are a number of opportunities for paid work in this field. Mature women or couples are often preferred.

Fostering elderly people

An increasing number of local authorities run fostering schemes, whereby an elderly person lives with a family as an ordinary member of the household, receiving whatever care and special assistance is necessary. As with child fostering, enormous trouble is taken by social workers in matching families with their foster guest. Pay varies from one area to another but averages around £100-£197 a week for every elderly person fostered.

Since April 1993, anyone providing personal care for a non-relative who is living in their home, is required to register with their local authority.

Ask at your Social Services Department whether there is a fostering or 'boarding out' scheme to which you could contribute.

Domestic work

A number of private domestic agencies specialise in finding temporary or permanent companions, housekeepers, caretakers, emergency mothers and extra care help for elderly and disabled people or for those who are convalescent. Many of these jobs are particularly suitable for retired people or couples. Pay generally starts at around £175 or more a week plus travelling expenses (£100 a week for caretakers). Agencies worth contacting include:

Care Alternatives, 206 Worple Road, Wimbledon, London SW20 8PN. T:0181 946 8202.
Consultus, 17 London Road, Tonbridge, Kent TN10 3AB. T:01732 355231.
Country Cousins and Emergency Mothers, 10a Market Square, Horsham, West Sussex RH12 1EX. T:01403 210415. Also branches in Plymouth and Lutterworth (Leics.).
Easymind: Home Care Services, 3 Oakshade Road, Oxshott, Surrey KT22 0LF. T:01372 842087.
Universal Aunts Ltd., PO Box 304, London SW4 0NN. T:0171 738 8937.

Another possibility worth pursuing is to contact the United Kingdom Home Care Association which represents over 1,000 member agencies and organisations that provide home care. For further information, contact: **UKHCA**, 42 Banstead Road, Carshalton Beeches, Surrey SM5 3NW. T:0181 288 1551.

Local agencies will be listed in *Yellow Pages* under 'Domestic', 'Employment' or 'Care Agencies'.

Home helps
Local authorities sometimes have vacancies for home helps, to assist disabled or elderly people in their own home by giving a hand with the cleaning, light cooking and other chores. Ask at your local Social Services Department.

Childminding
If you already look after a grandchild during the day, you might consider caring for an additional couple of youngsters. You will need to be registered with the local Social Services Department who will explain all the requirements.

Nursing
Qualified nurses may be able to find work at their local hospital or alternatively through one of the many nursing agencies. See *Yellow Pages*. Family Planning clinics could also be worth approaching.

Those with suitable experience although not necessarily a formal nursing qualification could apply to become a Care Attendant for the national charity Crossroads, which provides regular short-term relief for carers of sick or disabled people in their own homes. For information on local schemes, contact: **Crossroads**, Caring for Carers, 10 Regent Place, Rugby CV21 2PN. T:01788 573653.

Chiropody
Chiropody offers two major advantages as a possible new career. Firstly, there is a national shortage of chiropodists; and secondly, chiropody is one of the few professions where there is no upper age limit for training.

No-one in their late forties or fifties, however, should think of signing on for a course without first researching the prospects for building up a successful practice. Clearly your chances will be better if you live in an area with a large elderly population, where all the local chiropodists have long waiting lists.

The reason for caution is that the training is expensive and normally takes between one and two years. Also, once qualified, you will have setting-up costs, including purchase of your equipment plus marketing expenses to get yourself known. Against this, the going rate for chiropody services (depending on where you live) is between £12 and £25 per half-hour treatment so, even working part-time, it should be possible to make a fairly good income.

The two best known courses for mature entrants are those run by the SMAE Institute, leading to membership of the British Chiropody and Podiatry Association and the Scholl Chiropody course, qualifying you for membership of the Institute of Chiropodists.

Both are a mix of home-learning and practical, with the practical part (which must be taken at the SMAE or Scholl School) variously lasting between two weeks and two months. Cost, depending on which of the several options you select, varies from about £1,500 to £3,000 excluding VAT.

For further information, contact: the **SMAE Institute**, The School of Chiropody and Podiatric Medicine, The New Hall, Bath Road, Maidenhead, Berkshire SL6 4LA. T:01628 21100; the **Scholl Chiropody Course**, 475 Capability Green, Luton LU1 3LU. T:0345 125342.

Homesitting

Homesitting means taking care of someone else's home while they are away on holiday or business trips. Mature, responsible people, usually non-smokers with no children or pets, are in demand for this type of work. More like a paid holiday, you could expect to receive anything from about £40 to £100 a week (extra if care of pets is involved), depending on the responsibilities and on the size of house or flat. Food and travelling expenses are normally also paid. It is useful to have your own car. Firms specialising in this type of work include:

Home and Pet Care, Green Rigg Farm, Caldbeck, Wigton, Cumbria CA7 8AH. T:01697 471515.

Homesitters Ltd., Buckland Wharf, Buckland, Aylesbury, Bucks HP22 5LQ. T:01296 630730.

Housewatch, Little London, Berden, Bishops Stortford, Herts CM23 1BE. T:01279 777412.

Universal Aunts, PO Box 304, London SW4 0NN. T:0171 738 8937.

Cashing in on your home interests

Cooking, gardening, home decorating, dressmaking and DIY skills can all be turned into modest money-spinners.

Cooking

Scope includes: catering other people's dinner parties, selling home-made goodies to local shops and cooking for directors' lunches. Other than top class culinary skills, requirements are: a large deep-freeze, a car (you will normally be required to do all the necessary shopping) and plenty of stamina.

Notify your friends, advertise your services through the local newspapers, chamber of commerce or local businessmen's club or, if you are really serious about it, enrol with one of the specialist catering agencies. See *Yellow Pages.*

Gardening

Small shopkeepers and florists sometimes purchase flowers or plants direct from local gardeners, in preference to going to the market. Alternatively, you might consider dried flower arrangements or herbs for which there has been a growing increase in demand. However, before spending any money, check around to find out what the sales possibilities are. If you are willing to tend someone else's garden, the likelihood is that you will be inundated with enquiries. Spread the word among friends, acquaintances, local shops and in the pub. For information on all aspects of herbs including growing techniques, contact: **The Herb Society**, 134 Buckingham Palace Road, London SW1W 9SA. T:0171 823 5583.

Dressmaking and home decorating
If you are happy to do alterations, the chances are that you could be kept busy from dawn to dusk. Many shops are desperate for seamstresses. Likewise, many individuals and families would love to know of someone who could alter clothes, as well as dressmake properly. Perhaps to a slightly lesser extent, the same goes for curtains, chair covers and other soft furnishings. Often a good move is to approach firms selling materials for the home, who may be only too glad to put work out to you. Alternatively, put up a card in newsagents' shops or run a small advertisement in the local paper.

DIY
Competition is more intense, as many small builders offer this service. However, elderly people often require small jobs, as do women who do not have a handy-man around the house. Advice for getting your services known is the same as for gardening.

Pubs and paying guests
Many people dream of running a pub in their retirement – and many people live to regret it. A less strenuous option which others may like is offering bed and breakfast accommodation in their own home.

Running a pub
Running a pub is more a way of life than a job and one that requires a great deal of stamina. Anything less like a quiet retirement would be hard to imagine. You are on your feet for most of the day, the hours are long and when you are not pulling pints or preparing bar snacks, you will be dealing with the paperwork plus all the other day-to-day business requirements.

You can either buy your own 'free' house outright or become the tenant or lessee of a brewery or pub-owning company. Prices vary according to the length of lease, location and so on but, as a rough guide, you would need at least £10,000 in order to get started as a tenant; and between £60,000 and £250,000 – or even more – for a 'free house'. Big free houses in London can fetch over £1 million today. On top of all this, as with any other business, you will need to budget for operating capital.

If you are over 50, some experience of self-employment or the leisure industry is vital in order to be considered for a tenancy or long-term lease and even then, you may need to convince the company that you are not making the mistake of imagining that running a pub is a congenial way of easing into retirement.

Tenancy packages vary and may include the range of products you sell as well as repairs and decorations. As a self-employed business person, a tenant or leaseholder has responsibility for the hiring and firing of any staff, compliance with the fire regulations and with the other laws of the land. As a licensee, he is also required to know and enforce the licensing laws.

Information on training courses can be obtained from the **British Institute of Innkeeping**, Wessex House, 80 Park Street, Camberley, Surrey GU15 3PT. T:01276 684449. Details of tenancies and pubs for sale are contained in *The Licensee and Morning Advertiser* and in *The Publican* (available from newsagents).

Useful reading

Thinking of Running a Pub, free brochure available from the Brewers and Licensed Retailers Association, 42 Portman Square, London W1H 0BB.
Successful Pubs and Inns by Michael Sargent and Tony Lyle, Butterworth Heinemann, £12.95.
Handbook for the National Licensee's Certificate, obtainable from the British Institute of Innkeeping; £6.45 incl. p&p.

Bed & breakfast

Tourist areas, in particular, offer scope for taking in bed and breakfast visitors. However, unless you want to make a regular business of it, it is advisable to limit the number of guests to a maximum of five otherwise you will be subject to stringent fire regulation precautions requiring special doors and other expensive paraphernalia. To be on the safe side, contact the local Environmental Health Officer (see telephone directory or enquire at the town hall) who will advise you of anything necessary you should do. You should also register with your local Tourist Information Centre. See the section headed 'Letting rooms in your home' in Chapter 8, Your Home.

Agencies and other useful organisations

Jobhunting through agencies is very much a question of luck. People can be on their books for months and months and not be sent to a single interview. Someone else can walk through the door and within 48 hours be fixed up with an ideal job.

Applicants normally greatly exceed vacancies and the majority of jobs, especially for the over-60s, tend to be on the modest side: clerical, security work, gardening, domestic services and similar. However, more challenging opportunities are sometimes registered and one or two of the organisations listed below specialise in executive appointments. Retired accountants in particular are almost always in demand, as are people with fund-raising skills.

A positive attitude – with agencies as well as with prospective employers – unquestionably helps. People are often their own worst enemy when it comes to jobhunting and sadly this is especially true of older people, who may give the impression of half expecting to be turned down on the grounds of age. While you may be asked to state your date of birth (in which case it is usually better to be honest), there is no need to volunteer the information unless requested – least of all at the start of an interview.

Equally, there is no need to limit your applications to agencies that specialise in placing older candidates. If you are serious about finding work, you need to cast your net as widely as possible. So check the *Yellow Pages* and keep an eye on the local papers for other agencies in your area. Depending on what you are looking for, several of the following organisations may be able to help.

Jobcentres. It is easy to forget the obvious. Jobcentres have changed their image considerably over the last few years and now carry a wide range of vacancies for all levels of ability. In particular, many small firms use them for recruitment in preference to the more expensive private employment agencies. There are around 1,000 Jobcentres throughout Great Britain which, between them, handle about 2 million vacancies a year. They also act as a gateway to many of the training courses and advisory services. See local telephone directory for address.

Other organisations
Age Concern. Age Concern runs employment bureaux for people over 60 in a few areas around the country. They deal mainly in fairly unskilled part-time work, such as: shop and office cleaning, messengers, clerks, home help for elderly people and manual jobs. Contact your local Age Concern group (see telephone directory).

Careers (Cont'd), 14 Trinity Square, London EC3N 4AA. T:0171 680 0033. Specialises in catering for job-hunters aged 40 to 60 plus. Full, part-time and temporary openings are available. Jobs are essentially office orientated including accounts, secretarial, administrative and other professional skills. Also messenger, reception, switchboard and occasional hall portering positions. Work is mainly in the Central London area.

Corps of Commissionaires, Market House, 85 Cowcross Street, London EC1M 6BP. T:0171 490 1125. Offers full or part-time work to ex-servicemen and women, police, prison officers, firemen, coastguards and merchant seamen. Jobs cover a fairly broad range from managerial and administrative posts to others that require the wearing of the Corps' uniform, for example: commissionaires, security staff, ushers at sporting or official events. Maximum age is normally 60 for permanent jobs; 70 for temporary work. The Corps is not an employment agency as such, but operates as a membership association and charges a fee to employers for its services. All applicants are invited to an interview and are required to provide references.

Executive Standby Ltd., 310 Chester Road, Hartford, Northwich, Cheshire CW8 2AB. T:01606 883849; and sister agency **Executive Standby (South) Ltd.**, 27 Preston Street, Faversham, Kent ME13 8PE. T:01795 590119. Both agencies specialise in placing executives of proven competence in management or similar posts in industry, commerce and voluntary organisations. These include both temporary and permanent positions, as well as occasional openings abroad where there is usually an upper age limit of 65.

Extend, 22 Maltings Drive, Wheathampstead, Herts AL4 8QJ. T:01582 832760. Extend runs recreational exercise-to-music classes for the over-sixties and for people with disabilities of all ages. The organisation is constantly looking for potential group teachers. Training courses last 8 to 12 days spread over several weeks and cost about £350. There are written and practical assessments on completion. At the present time, eight training teams operate in different parts of the UK and Ireland. Details can be obtained from the above address, on enclosure of sae.

HERA, 2 Valentine Place, London SE1 8QH. T:0171 928 6141. Job-seekers receive a weekly bulletin of vacancies in the field of housing with jobs throughout the country, ranging from management to secretarial. HERA also offers careers counselling relevant to jobs in housing.

Manpower plc., International House, 66 Chiltern Street, London W1M 1PR. T:0171 224 6688. Manpower is a major supplier of temporary and contract staff. Skills in particular demand include: engineering (PC maintenance, communications and cabling); IT, both programming and software engineering; secretarial and clerical experience; nursing; driving and assembly/manufacturing.

Officers' Association, Employment Department, 48 Pall Mall, London SW1Y 5JY. T:0171 930 0125. The Association maintains an employment department, which operates in conjunction with the Forces Resettlement Service. Eligibility to register is restricted to candidates who have held a commission in the armed services, who must be under 60 and currently unemployed. A wide range of vacancies is handled in industry, commerce, high technology and in the professional and charitable institutions. There are regional offices in Scotland and Eire.

Part-Time Careers Ltd., 10 Golden Square, London W1R 3AF. T:0171 437 3103. Specialises in permanent part-time secretarial jobs as well as accountancy and book-keeping.

Campaign Against Age Discrimination in Employment (CAADE), 395 Barlow Road, Altrincham, Cheshire WA14 5HW. T:0161 941 2902. This is a lobby organisation which, as its name implies, was set up to campaign against age discrimination in matters affecting employment. Its core philosophy is that individuals should have choice and that age – whether 17 or 70 – should not be a barrier.

Local job-finding agencies. A number of specialist recruitment agencies, concentrating on the over-40s or 50s have recently been springing up in different parts of the country to assist unemployed people in their middle years back into work. Most concentrate on fairly local vacancies – with range of jobs very much a question of what is needed in the area. Enquire at your library, TEC or Jobcentre for any useful names and addresses.

Useful reading

Just the Job, free Government booklet, available from Jobcentres and TECs.

12 Voluntary Work

There are probably as many different kinds of voluntary work that need to be done, as there are organisations that need your help. The range of tasks and the variety of groups are both enormous. Perhaps this is one reason why some people simply steer clear of the whole area, fearing that the commitment may get out of control and that they may find themselves involved to a greater extent than they wish. Though this may be true in a few cases there are probably many thousands more who, starting in a small way, find themselves caught up in the enthusiasm for their cause and immensely rewarded by the contribution they feel able to make and by the new friends that it has brought them.

Very broadly, voluntary help falls into four main categories: clerical/administrative, fund-raising, committee work, and direct work with the public.

Clerical. Any active group is likely to need basic administrative help from typing and stuffing envelopes to answering the telephone and organising committees. This may involve a day or so a week or simply occasional assistance at peak times.

Fund-raising. Every voluntary organisation needs more money and their ingenuity in raising it seems boundless. Jumble sales, coffee mornings and flag days are probably still the most common, but sponsored events of all kinds are growing in popularity and negotiating contributions from local or national businesses may test anyone's diplomatic skill.

Committee work. This can cover anything from very occasional help to virtually full-time commitment as branch treasurer or secretary. People with business skills or financial or legal backgrounds are likely to be especially valuable in this area.

Direct work. Driving, delivering 'meals on wheels', doing counselling work, visiting the housebound, working in a charity shop, helping with a playgroup, giving the mother of a sick child a chance to get out of the house for an hour or so ... the list is endless and the value of the work incalculable.

It will be clear from the above that while certain skills and experience – financial, legal, nursing, social work – have particular value in some circumstances, there is a multitude of interesting and useful jobs for those without special training or with relatively ordinary abilities like driving or typing.

Similarly, the time commitment can be varied to suit both helper and organisation. It is far better to give just one morning a month and be reliable than to promise more time than you can spare and end up always being late or having to cancel at the last minute. Equally, as with a paid job, before you start you should be absolutely clear about all the terms and conditions.

- What sort of work is involved?
- Who will be working with you?
- What is expected?
- When will you be needed?
- Are expenses paid? What for? How much? (See tax note.)

If you straighten all this out in the beginning there will be less chance of any misunderstandings and you will find that voluntary work is not only very rewarding in its own right but also allows you to make a real contribution to the community.

Tax note. Volunteer drivers who receive a motor mileage allowance and who make a small profit, in that the allowance exceeds their actual incurred expenses (i.e. petrol and maintenance), are taxed on any profit they make. For further information, see leaflet IR 122 *Volunteer Drivers*, obtainable from any tax office.

Choosing the right voluntary work

It is one thing to decide that you would like to do some kind of voluntary work; quite another to discover what is available in your area and what particular outlet would suit you. For this reason we have included a list of organisations, arranged in broad categories of interest, indicating the types of activities for which they are seeking volunteers. But no such list can be complete – there are literally thousands of voluntary groups, national and local, which need help in some way or other. For further information on needs and opportunities in this sector there are several other major sources to which you can turn:

REACH, Bear Wharf, 27 Bankside, London SE1 9ET. T:0171 928 0452. REACH was set up over 15 years ago to place retired, or redundant, men and women with business or other professional skills in voluntary organisations, throughout Great Britain. It finds only part-time, voluntary jobs, but with out-of-pocket expenses paid. REACH is itself a registered charity and makes no charge to either the volunteer or voluntary organisation. Many jobs are waiting to be filled so there is a good chance of finding an opening that makes real use of your particular talents.

Scottish Corps of Retired Executives (SCORE), sponsored by Scottish Business in the Community, Romano House, 43 Station Road, Edinburgh EH12 7AF. T:0131 334 9876. The Scottish Corps of Retired Executives has been set up by SBC to help community, voluntary and charitable organisations and also to assist under-resourced new small businesses. Similar to REACH, members are retired business men and women who wish to offer their skills to the community on a voluntary basis according to the time they have available. If you would like to help please contact the Administrator.

Trustee Register, 114 Peascod Street, Windsor, Berkshire SL4 1DN. T:01753 868277. The Register acts as an introductory service in finding trustees and committee members for established charities. Interested candidates are asked to complete a short form, giving information about themselves and any strong preferences they may have regarding type of charity to which their name may be forwarded. Commitment varies but averages about a day a month. Travel expenses may sometimes be paid.

Volunteer Bureaux. Usually listed in the telephone book under 'V'. Most towns have a body of this kind which seeks to match up volunteers with local organisations seeking help. Alternatively, see the *Volunteer Bureaux Directory*, which is available at most libraries or can be obtained direct from **The National Association of Volunteer Bureaux**, St. Peter's College, College Road, Saltley, Birmingham B8 3TE, T:0121 327 0265. Price of the 1996 Directory is expected to be about £7.50 incl. p&p. The Association is happy to put enquirers in touch with their nearest local Bureau.

The Volunteer Centre UK, Carriage Row, 183 Eversholt Street, London NW1 1BU. T:0171 388 9888. The Volunteer Centre UK can provide information if you want to volunteer for the first time or if you are already involved and want to know more. As well as offering advice as to what openings might suit you, the Centre can send you a computer print-out ('Signposts') of current volunteer opportunities in your area.

Volunteer Development Scotland, 80 Murray Place, Stirling FK8 2BX. T:01786 479593. Can put you in touch with a local organisation which could assist you with volunteering in your area. Also publishes leaflet *Volunteering in Retirement in Scotland*, (please enclose two first class stamps).

Wales Council for Voluntary Action, Llys Ifor, Crescent Road, Caerphilly, Mid Glamorgan CF8 1XL. T:01222 869224. This is the umbrella body for voluntary activity in Wales. If you are interested in volunteering, it would be glad to put you in contact with an organisation that would welcome your help.

Citizens' Advice Bureau. Your local CAB will also have information on local needs and groups to contact.

If you have a good idea for a new voluntary project, it is worth contacting: **New Horizons Trust**, Paramount House, 290-292 Brighton Road, South Croydon, Surrey CR2 6AG. T:0181 666 0201. New Horizons Trust is a registered charity offering grants of up to £5,000 to groups of retired people who wish to start a new voluntary project drawing on their own knowledge and experience for the benefit of their local community. To qualify, there must be at least 10 people in the group, half of whom must be over the age of 60. Schemes may improve local amenities or fill identified gaps in social services. Examples of projects around the country which have been helped by the Trust include: a laundry for pensioners, a community activity group, a workshop for refurbishing old furniture for those in need, another workshop where retired craftsmen can pass on their skills to young people and the restoration of a disused windmill.

General

The scope of the work of the British Red Cross, WRVS and Citizens' Advice Bureau is so broad that they almost justify a category to themselves.

British Red Cross, 9 Grosvenor Crescent, London SW1X 7EJ. T:0171 235 5454. The Red Cross is the world's largest humanitarian organisation. It needs volunteer help from men and women for first aid, health and social care, therapeutic beauty care and welfare services. Training is always provided. It also requires fund-raisers, publicity officers, drivers for escort work and people with teaching, clerical, administrative and management skills. Expenses are paid. Volunteers may give as little or as much time as they choose. Contact the local branch (under 'British' or 'Red Cross' in the telephone book) or write to the National Volunteer Co-ordinator at the London headquarters.

Women's Royal Voluntary Service, 234-244 Stockwell Road, London SW9 9SP. T:0345 595555. The WRVS works with the local authority and Social Services to cover almost the complete range of needs in the community. It particularly welcomes offers of help from people with time during the working day. Activities are too numerous to list but include: meals on wheels, shopping for elderly people, helping in playgroups and organising children's holiday schemes, running canteens in prisons and courts, providing transport in rural areas, running hospital shops and assisting with catering and welfare services in emergencies. No special qualifications are required.

Citizens' Advice Bureau (See telephone book for your local branch.) First founded in 1939, the service has continued giving invaluable help and advice for over 50 years. Throughout the country, it deals with over 7 million enquiries a year. Apart from being an excellent source of information on other voluntary organisations needing help, the CAB itself has over 15,000 volunteer helpers working in its 1,000 or so branches throughout the country.

The work involves interviewing and advising clients on a wide range of questions from welfare benefits and legal rights to local events and community schemes. No formal qualifications are required but it is essential that the applicant is able to master and explain a considerable amount of complicated and detailed information. Training is given (usually two days a week for about six weeks followed by a period of in-service training and appraisal) and volunteers are then expected to work a minimum of six hours a week in their Bureau. Contact the Manager at your nearest CAB for further details.

Another well known organisation which functions across a more general spectrum is: **Community Service Volunteers**, 237 Pentonville Road, London N1 9NJ.

T:0171 278 6601. CSV operates a nationwide scheme called the Retired and Senior Volunteer Programme (RSVP) for people over 50 years of age who want to be involved in their community. Each group plans its own activities which might include working with elderly people locally, using their business experience to advise young people starting out on their own and going into schools to help pupils and support teachers. Local volunteer organisers provide guidance and suppport. For further details, contact Janet Atfield.

Animals

Cinnamon Trust, Poldarves Farm, Trescowe Common, Germoe, Penzance, Cornwall TR20 9RX. T:01736 850291. The Cinnamon Trust is a registered charity which seeks to relieve the problems of elderly pet owners who, owing to illness or some other emergency, are temporarily unable to care for their pets. It also offers a long-term haven to animals whose owners have died.

Animal lovers throughout the country assist in a voluntary capacity, either by fostering a pet in their own home or helping out on a daily basis, for example walking a dog, feeding it, cleaning out a bird cage or similar. Likewise, long-term homes are required for pets who have lost their owners. For further details, write to Mrs. Averil Jarvis at the above address (enclosing sae).

Pet Fostering Service Scotland. T:01674 810356. The service provides short-term foster care for the pets of elderly people who, owing to some emergency such as going into hospital, are temporarily unable to manage. Volunteers may either look after a pet in their own home until the owner is able to take it back or provide some other caring service, such as walking a dog. Food, cat litter and any vet's fees that may be incurred are paid for by the owner. If you live in Scotland, have a love of pets and would like to help out in a crisis, telephone the above number.

PRO Dogs, Rocky Bank, 4 New Road, Ditton, Maidstone, Kent ME20 6AD. T:01732 848499. PRO Dogs is a national charity which originated the PAT Dog Hospital visiting scheme. To bring both an extra interest and an outlet for petting and affection into the lives of those in institutional care, dog owners visit long stay hospital wards and residential homes together with their pets. An essential is that the dogs are of suitable temperament and well behaved. At present, there are over 8,000 volunteers throughout the country making regular visits. If you would like to join them, it is necessary to become a PRO Dogs member to be covered by their insurance scheme. Annual subscription is £10.

Royal Society for the Prevention of Cruelty to Animals, Causeway, Horsham, West Sussex RH12 1HG. T:01403 264181. The RSPCA works to promote kindness and to prevent cruelty to animals. Operating through its team of 300 Inspectors, it is concerned with the welfare of all animals and with education of the general public – especially children – by campaigning in the media and through its wide range of promotional material. It also works for the cause of animal welfare abroad. Volunteers are needed to help with fund-raising at local level. Contact headquarters for the address of your nearest branch.

Royal Society for the Protection of Birds, The Lodge, Sandy, Bedfordshire SG19 2DL. T:01767 680551. The RSPB is Europe's largest wildlife conservation charity with over 860,000 members and 132 nature reserves around the UK. Volunteers have a valuable contribution to make and are regularly needed to undertake biological surveys, assist with the management on nature reserves, work with visitors and young people or carry out administrative tasks in regional offices around the country. Volunteer opportunities range from a few days to a few weeks. No particular expertise is required nor, if you would like to help, is it necessary to become a member. For those who would like to join, annual membership (1995) costs £20 single, £25 joint.

Wildfowl Wetlands Trust, Slimbridge, Gloucester GL2 7BT. T:01453 890333/890065. WWT works to save wetlands and to conserve their wildlife. As well as Slimbridge, it has centres in: Lancashire, Sussex, Tyne & Wear, Cambridge/Norfolk border, Dumfriesshire, South Wales and Northern Ireland. All have a network of volunteers who give valuable help, variously: attending the information desk, dealing with visitor enquiries, conducting guided tours and assisting staff with administrative work. There is no minimum commitment but most volunteers come in for a few hours, one day a week. For further information, contact Sandy Prax at the above address.

Bereavement

Cruse – Bereavement Care, Cruse House, 126 Sheen Road, Richmond, Surrey TW9 1UR. T:0181 940 4818. Cruse, which has over 190 branches throughout Britain, is the national organisation for people who have been bereaved. It provides counselling, practical help and organises social programmes to counter loneliness. Volunteers are needed in the branch offices to help with all these services. Training for counselling is given.

Children and young people

Barnardo's, Tanners Lane, Barkingside, Ilford, Essex IG6 1QG. T:0181 550 8822. Barnardo's provides services for children who face disability or disadvantage. Projects throughout the country include work with families, day care centres, community projects, playgroups, play buses and holiday schemes. Two major areas require help:

Fund-Raising. Thousands of people work as voluntary fund-raisers for Barnardo's. Activities may include helping in a charity shop or with local flag-days and events. Write to the National Appeals Director at the above address who will pass on your application to your regional branch.

Child Care Programme. This usually involves befriending a young person with a disability, perhaps to give the mother a much-needed break. Write to the Child Care Administration Officer at the above address.

Action for Sick Children, Argyle House, 29-31 Euston Road, London NW1 2SD. T:0171 833 2041. The Charity supports sick children and their families and advocates that health services be planned to cater for their special needs. Local branches give practical help to parents and professionals in the hospitals.

Work is organised through local branches which can be contacted through the London headquarters. Although different branches may operate slightly different schemes, most will welcome voluntary help, for example:

Help with transport. Either driving, where a mileage charge is payable, or accompanying mothers with young children.

Help with volunteer play schemes, on wards or in out-patients' departments.

Help with fund-raising for more parents' and children's facilities in hospital.

Save the Children, Mary Datchelor House, 17 Grove Lane, London SE5 8RD. T:0171 703 5400. SCF works to achieve lasting benefits for children within the communities in which they live. Volunteers are very much welcomed to assist with fund-raising via the charity's network of some 750 branches throughout the UK. Helpers are also needed to work in SCF shops. Check the local telephone directory for the nearest branch or contact the head office.

Scout Association, Baden-Powell House, Queen's Gate, London SW7 5JS. T:0171 584 7030. The Scout Association encourages the physical, mental and spiritual development of young people through an enjoyable programme of activities. There is a multitude of opportunities for voluntary help, either as a Leader or Commissioner, an Administrator or Committee member, or as a member of a District Scout Fellowship. Administrators have important responsibilities in the management of the property as well as for the equipment and finances of the movement. Members of the Fellowship help to organise events, contribute to training (e.g. vehicle maintenance, map reading, first aid), maintain camp-sites, raise funds, work in a Scout shop or edit a District Newsletter.

Sea Cadet Corps, 202 Lambeth Road, London SE1 7JF. T:0171 928 8978. The Sea Cadet Corps is a youth organisation which offers boys and girls aged 12-18 challenging new experiences and adventure. Emphasis is placed on waterborne activities, with encouragement given to those who wish to pursue a career at sea. Units exist throughout the UK and welcome volunteer help either as administrators or specialist instructors. Details may be obtained by contacting the national headquarters above.

The Children's Society, Edward Rudolf House, Margery Street, London WC1X 0JL. T:0171 837 4299. The Children's Society offers comprehensive child care services to children and families in need. It runs over 100 projects which include safe houses for young runaways, family and community centres, special needs adoption and fostering and respite care for young people with disabilities. Virtually every parish in the country has an Honorary Local Secretary who is mainly concerned with fund-raising. There are also more than 144 charity shops, run entirely by volunteers. Contact may be made either through the London headquarters or the local office, which may be listed in the telephone book.

Volunteer Reading Help, Room 438, High Holborn House, 49/51 Bedford Row, London WC1V 6RL. T:0171 404 6204. The purpose of the scheme is to assist children in the age group 6 to 11 who need help and encouragement with their reading. Volunteers undertake to give two hours, twice a week during term time, by going into a local school and devoting half an hour's individual attention to three children on a regular one-to-one basis. No formal qualifications are needed but volunteers must like children, have plenty of patience, possess a sense of humour and be willing to commit themselves for at least a year. A short training of about six hours, spread over three sessions, is provided. As well as London, the scheme operates in: Berkshire, Bolton, Bradford, Bristol, Dorset, Kent, Leeds, Liverpool, Northampton, Nottingham, Oxfordshire and Surrey. Other branches are planned.

Youth Clubs UK, 11 St. Bride Street, London EC4A 4AS. T:0171 353 2366. Youth Clubs UK is the biggest youth organisation in the country, supporting both youth clubs and special projects for around 700,000 young people. A large number of the youngsters are disadvantaged in some way – whether physically disabled, homeless or involved with drugs or crime – and a key aim of the work is to give them the skills and information they need to manage their lives more positively. Volunteers of all types are needed to assist in their area. For further information, contact Fiona Davidson at the above address.

Conservation

Architectural Heritage Society of Scotland, The Glasite Meeting House, 33 Barony Street, Edinburgh EH3 6NX. T:0131 557 0019. The Society promotes the study and protection of Scottish architecture. As well as enjoying events such as talks and visits, members can play an active part in defending Scotland's threatened heritage by joining case panels for which volunteers are always needed. The work involves visiting and assessing listed building and conservation area consent applications. Membership of the Society, which includes a free copy of its annual journal *Architectural Heritage*, is £15 a year; £23 for families (1995).

BTCV (British Trust for Conservation Volunteers), 36 St. Mary's Street, Wallingford, Oxfordshire OX10 0EU. T:01491 839766. BTCV plays a leading role in encouraging volunteers from both town and country to improve the environment. Over 600 working holidays are organised nationally and over 1,600 local groups run community projects at weekends and sometimes mid-week. Typical projects include planting trees, cleaning ponds, restoring footpaths, protecting valuable habitats for wildlife, creating urban nature areas and assisting with woodland management. Not all of them involve heavy work but a reasonable degree of fitness is required. Volunteers are also needed to help the local offices with administration, fund-raising and publicity. Membership costs £12 (£6 for retired people).

Council for the Protection of Rural England (CPRE), Warwick House, 25 Buckingham Palace Road, London SW1W 0PP. T:0171 976 6433. CPRE works to protect and enhance the countryside. Voluntary helpers act as local watchdogs within CPRE's county branches, assessing and reporting threats to the environment and sometimes representing the Council at enquiries. There is also a need for help with fund-raising which is carried out by local groups.

Friends of the Earth, 26-28 Underwood Street, London N1 7JQ. T:0171 490 1555. Friends of the Earth is one of the leading environmental pressure organisations in the UK, aiming to conserve and protect the resources of the planet. Over 250 groups run local campaigns and fund-raising projects. These can be contacted through the London office which can also use help with the administration and with answering enquiries. Travelling expenses and a lunch allowance are paid. Most volunteers work between one and three days a week. People with scientific training may also be able to help on specific research projects.

Greenpeace, Canonbury Villas, London N1 2PN. T:0171 354 5100. An international environmental pressure group which campaigns to protect the natural environment against pollution. Volunteers are needed both to help in the London office and also for fund-raising by local groups across the country.

Ramblers' Association, 1-5 Wandsworth Road, London SW8 2XX. T:0171 582 6878. The aims of the Ramblers' Association are to keep footpaths open and to protect the countryside. Each of its 50 area offices needs help with administration and with walking over and checking the condition of local footpaths. The time involved is whatever you can manage.

Scottish Conservation Projects Trust, Balallan House, 24 Allan Park, Stirling FK8 2QG. T:01786 479697. SCP offers training in conservation skills and opportunities to work as a volunteer for as little or as much time as you can spare. There are 7-14 day conservation projects, called 'Action Breaks', in all parts of Scotland as well as weekend and single day events. Type of work includes fencing, footpath construction, small traditional building restoration and habitat management. Individuals pay for their own fares, as well as a contribution to board and lodging (£4 a day). Volunteers are also welcomed to help with administration, fund-raising and publicity. Annual membership is £15 (£8 for pensioners). For further information, contact SCP at the above address.

The elderly

Abbeyfield Society, 53 Victoria Street, St. Albans, Herts AL1 3UW. T:01727 857536. Local volunteers acquire or build houses to provide independent accommodation for older people who are on their own. The aim is to achieve a family atmosphere but preserve the privacy of each resident. There are also 'extra care' schemes for older people who can no longer look after themselves without some help. Voluntary help needed may vary from shopping for a resident, standing in for the housekeeper, gardening, typing or organising a fund-raising event to giving specialist financial and legal advice with regard to the purchase of new Abbeyfield houses. There are 600 local Abbeyfield Societies nationwide involving some 12,000 volunteers.

Age Concern England, Astral House, 1268 London Road, London SW16 4ER, T:0181 679 8000; **Age Concern Scotland**, 113 Rose Street, Edinburgh EH2 3DT, T:0131 228 5656; **Age Concern Wales**, 4th Floor, 1 Cathedral Road, Cardiff CF1 9SD, T:01222 371566; **Age Concern Northern Ireland**, 3 Lower Crescent, Belfast BT7 1NR. T:01232 245729. The aim of Age Concern is to promote the welfare of older people. It does this by campaigning on their behalf and by organising services to meet their needs. Local groups, using over 250,000 volunteer helpers, operate all over the country and services include day care, lunch clubs, home visiting, over-60's clubs and, in some areas, specialist services for physically and mentally frail elderly people. Fund-raising activities in all their variety are also organised by the local groups which may be contacted through the central offices listed above.

Carers National Association, 20-25 Glasshouse Yard, London EC1A 4JS. T:0171 490 8818. CNA is a mine of information for those who care for elderly or infirm people at home. With over 115 local branches, it provides a postal advisory service, campaigns for better social security benefits and domiciliary services, supports holiday and sitter-in help for carers and organises conferences. Help is needed to organise carers' groups, to enable them to meet occasionally to discuss mutual problems. Contact the Information Department at the above address for details of your local branch.

Contact the Elderly, 15 Henrietta Street, Covent Garden, London WC2E 8QH. Freephone: 0800 716543. Contact the Elderly offers a way of making new friends and at the same time providing much needed companionship for lonely elderly people living nearby. Nearly two-and-a-half thousand Contact volunteers keep a personal link with isolated elderly people by taking them on one Sunday afternoon each month to have tea in the home of a volunteer host. Help is needed with driving (one Sunday a month) and/or hosting a tea-party for about 10 elderly people once or twice a year. No expenses are paid. There are 152 Contact groups, nationwide. The name and address of the nearest local organiser can be got from the above address.

Help the Aged, St. James's Walk, London EC1R 0BE. T:0171 253 0253. Help the Aged aims to improve the quality of life for elderly people here and overseas. In the

UK, it funds day centres and day hospitals, community transport, home safety devices, emergency alarm systems and sheltered housing. It also produces a range of advice leaflets and operates a freephone advice line on 0800 289404. Overseas, it advises on social policy for elderly people and supports projects in combating destitution and ill-health. Help the Aged is a major fund-raising charity. Volunteer help is needed to staff charity shops and to assist local organisers in their work. Contact the Volunteer Co-ordinator at the above address for further details.

The family

Catholic Marriage Care Ltd., Clitherow House, 1 Blythe Mews, Blythe Road, London W14 0NW. T:0171 371 1341. The CMC runs pre-marriage courses and also provides a professional counselling service for anyone with relationship problems. Help is required in running and administering its 80 centres. For local addresses, contact the headquarters above.

Family Service Units, 207 Old Marylebone Road, London NW1 5QP. T:0171 402 5175. Twenty local Units work to prevent the breakdown of family and community life by running services for disadvantaged communities, deprived families and children. They carry out welfare counselling, community work and social work with families. The Units, which are professionally staffed, are managed by voluntary committees and help is needed on these as well as with administration and fund-raising. From time to time local Units need to recruit honorary treasurers.

Relate: National Marriage Guidance, Herbert Gray College, Little Church Street, Rugby, Warwickshire CV21 3AP. T:01788 573241. Relate works to support marriage and family life. There are about 130 local Relate centres which offer counselling to anyone with relationship problems and also undertake education work in schools. Volunteers who would like to become counsellors receive training. There are also openings to serve on committees and help in the office. The work is most likely to appeal to people who have been previously involved with social or community activity of some kind.

Soldiers', Sailors' and Airmen's Families' Association (SSAFA), 19 Queen Elizabeth Street, London SE1 2LP. T:0171 403 8783. SSAFA provides a welfare and advisory service for the families of service and ex-servicemen and women. There are 7,000 volunteers in over 1,000 branches throughout the UK and also professionals overseas wherever service families are stationed. Case workers deal with every kind of problem – domestic, financial, legal and compassionate. Training is given and although there is no minimum time commitment it is obviously critical to see a case through to the end. Help is particularly needed in inner cities. There is also a requirement for assistance in the counties as chairman, treasurer or administrative helper. A service background may be helpful but is not necessary.

Health

British Heart Foundation, 14 Fitzhardinge Street, London W1H 4DH. T:0171 935 0185. The British Heart Foundation funds research into the causes, prevention, diagnosis and treatment of heart disease. Its educational role is to inform the medical and scientific community of the results of its research and to pass on this information to the general public. BHF also provides life-saving cardiac care equipment to hospitals and ambulance services and helps support rehabilitation centres and heart support groups.

With a national network of over 500 branches BHF helps fund this vital work through a wide variety of fund-raising schemes. For details of your local branch please contact head office.

British Ski Club for the Disabled, Springmount, Berwick St. John, Shaftesbury, Dorset SP7 0HQ. T:01747 828515. The aim of the Club is to encourage people with a disability to learn or continue to enjoy the fun of skiing and the self-confidence gained from participating in an exhilarating sport. Volunteers, who must be competent parallel skiers, are needed to act as teachers and guides both on artificial slopes around the country and skiing holidays abroad. The Club runs its own instructor courses. Small subsidies are available for guides accompanying individuals on holiday.

Calibre, Cassette Library for the Blind and Handicapped, Aylesbury, Bucks HP22 5XQ. T:01296 432339 or 81211. Calibre is a national lending library of recorded books on ordinary standard cassette tapes for use by 'anyone unable to read'. Volunteers are needed to help run the library, which is maintained entirely from donations. Publicity and fund-raising help are also required. Contact the General Secretary, Mr A F C Montgomery.

Cancer Research Campaign, 10 Cambridge Terrace, London NW1 4JL. T:0171 224 1333. The aim of the Campaign is to defeat cancer. It supports research at centres throughout the United Kingdom on the recommendation of its Scientific and Education Committees. Money for this is raised by about 1,000 voluntary local committees, hundreds of honorary organisers and through its 230 shops throughout the country. If you would like to help, see 'Cancer Research Campaign' in the telephone directory for the address of your local group.

Imperial Cancer Research Fund, 61 Lincoln's Inn Fields, London WC2A 3PX. T:0171 242 0200. Imperial Cancer Research Fund carries out research into the causes, prevention and treatment of cancer and funds one-third of all cancer research in the UK. Over 20,000 volunteers help in the Fund's shops (sorting, serving, pricing, ironing, mending and similar) or assist with general office work in the Fund's various Regional Centres. All offers of help are greatly appreciated. Look in the *Yellow Pages* for the phone number of your nearest Regional Centre.

Leonard Cheshire Foundation, 26-29 Maunsel Street, London SW1P 2QN. T:0171 828 1822. The Leonard Cheshire Foundation works for the care, well-being and rehabilitation of people with physical, mental or learning disabilities or with a mental health problem. Each of its 128 UK homes and services are supported by local people, who make an enormous contribution. There are endless practical ways in which you can lend a hand. This might include driving, gardening, painting and decorating, shopping and writing letters. Or you might help with fund-raising through jumble sales and similar events. Contact the London office above for the address of your nearest Cheshire Home.

Mental Health Foundation, 37 Mortimer Street, London W1N 8JU. T:0171 580 0145. The Mental Health Foundation plays a vital role in pioneering new approaches to the prevention, treatment and care of mental illness and in helping people with learning disabilities. Its work includes: allocating grants for research and community projects, contributing to public debate, educating healthcare professionals and striving to reduce the stigma attached to mental illness. Volunteers are needed for fund-raising: either helping with the annual Mental Health Action Week or organising fund-raising in their local area. For further information, please write to the Director at the above address.

MIND (National Association for Mental Health), Granta House, 15-19 Broadway, London E15 4BQ. T:0181 519 2122. MIND works to promote the interests of people who are diagnosed as mentally ill and campaigns for their right to lead an active and valued life in the community. There are seven regional offices and some 250 local associations throughout England and Wales. MIND provides an information service and guidance on legal rights and also publishes a range of books and leaflets as well as a bi-monthly magazine. The local associations, which can be contacted through the national office, vary in size and in the scope of their work. While all will be involved in fund-raising, their activities also include running social clubs, day centres and an advice and information service as well as offering support and help to individuals.

National Association of Leagues of Hospital Friends, 2nd Floor, Fairfax House, Causton Road, Colchester, Essex CO1 1RJ. T:01206 761227. The Association acts as the national support and advice centre for over 1,000 Leagues of Hospital and Community Friends which operate throughout England, Scotland, Wales and Northern Ireland. Each League is autonomous and all work to improve the health, comfort and dignity of patients.

New volunteers, of whatever age, are always welcomed. Opportunities for voluntary work vary but all Leagues are concerned with both service to patients and fund-raising. The National Association will be pleased to provide names and addresses of local Leagues to contact.

National Back Pain Association, 16 Elmtree Road, Teddington, Middlesex TW11 8ST. T:0181 977 5474. The NBPA funds research into the causes and treatment of back pain. It teaches children and adults how to use their bodies sensibly and runs a network of local self-help branches. The NBPA needs volunteers to start local branches and to provide practical help for back pain sufferers. Particular activities include: organising exercise and hydrotherapy classes, arranging talks and demonstrations and running social and fund-raising events. For further information, contact the Branches Officer at the above address.

Riding for the Disabled Association, Avenue R, National Agricultural Centre, Kenilworth, Warwickshire CV8 2LY. T:01203 696510. The Association aims to help provide opportunities for riding for disabled children and adults. You do not have to be horsey to help with the administration in one of the 727 local groups or with fund-raising to support it. Legal and financial knowledge is particularly valuable in connection with the opening of new groups and with keeping the accounts. For those with experience of horses (which may be supplemented by training courses) the main jobs are leading or walking beside the ponies while they are being ridden and accompanying parties on riding holidays. Write to the head office above for the address of your nearest group.

Royal National Institute for the Blind, 224 Great Portland Street, London W1N 6AA. T:0171 388 1266. RNIB aims to help blind and partially sighted people lead full and independent lives. Among many other initiatives, it runs schools for blind children, provides careers advice, offers training and assists with finding suitable employment. It also manages two rehabilitation centres and special homes; has a welfare advisory service; sells specially designed or adapted goods to make life easier and safer for visually impaired people; publishes books and magazines in Braille and Moon and runs the Talking Book Library.

Help is mostly required with fund-raising: by lending a hand on flag days; or by placing and emptying RNIB collecting tins. Additionally, volunteers are needed all over the country to service talking book players on a regular basis, two or three times a month. London office will put you in touch with your nearest local group.

SCOPE, 12 Park Crescent, London W1N 4EQ. T:0171 636 5020. Contact the Information Officer. SCOPE (formerly the Spastics Society) provides a range of services including schools, colleges and residential care homes for people with cerebral palsy. There is also a Helpline information service (0800 626216) and a monthly newspaper *Disability Now*, as well as over 200 local groups throughout the country.

Helpers are needed particularly with transport – either driving or assisting with wheelchairs – with running open days and events and with fund-raising and street collections.

St. John Ambulance, 1 Grosvenor Crescent, London SW1X 7EF. T:0171 235 5231. Best known for their first aid role at public events, St. John Ambulance volunteers also carry out care within the community. Volunteers receive a seven-hour induction course, followed by a more specialised training in one of the following: care, transport, communications or first aid. Scope for volunteers is hugely varied and includes such activities as vehicle maintenance, fund-raising, public relations and community care as well, of course, as first aid. For further information contact your county office or the national headquarters at the above address.

Heritage and the arts

Arts Council of England, Information Department, 14 Great Peter Street, London SW1P 3NQ. T:0171 333 0100. There is scope for becoming involved in the arts in a volunteer capacity through community arts projects, arts centres, local arts councils and other arts activities associated with special groups such as, for example, the youth services or people with disabilities. All kinds of abilities are needed from painting and other creative skills to accounting and clerical know-how. Additionally, local arts councils which seek to promote the arts in their areas especially welcome people with experience of communications and marketing. To find out about your local arts council, contact your local authority or library. The Arts Council of England can supply you with a list of the ten regional arts boards in England, all of whom will be able to give you news of arts events in their area.

Council for British Archaeology, Bowes Morrell House, 111 Walmgate, York YO1 2UA. T:01904 671417. Various archaeological excavations take place throughout the UK, mainly from March to September. The work will probably involve lifting, stooping and wheeling barrows so is not suitable for people with bad backs. No training is necessary. A two-week stay is the average. Accommodation will vary according to the site but may be pretty basic. Information on the various digs is given in *British Archaeology News* (£18 annual membership subscription, from the above address). The Council will also supply the address of the nearest local Archaeological Society (enclose sae).

National Trust, 33 Sheep Street, Cirencester, Glos GL7 1QW. T:01285 651818. The National Trust involves volunteers in many aspects of the work of conservation in the great houses open to the public and on 239,000 hectares of coast and countryside properties. Inevitably, the needs will vary according to the location and time of the year. However, last year, over 28,000 volunteers worked alongside Trust staff in the regions. If you are interested, contact the Volunteers Office at the address above.

There is also a separate programme of working holidays in outdoor conservation, including a series of projects especially for the over-50s. For a brochure, please send a large sae (with two 2nd class stamps) to: **The National Trust Working Holidays**, PO Box 538, Melksham, Wilts SN12 8SU.

Society for the Protection of Ancient Buildings, 37 Spital Square, London E1 6DY. T:0171 377 1644. The SPAB promotes the preservation and conservation of ancient buildings. It organises courses, scholarships, seminars and lectures and also gives advice on the repair and reconditioning of ancient buildings. There is a need for a small number of volunteers to help on a part-time basis in the London office and also for people with specialist qualifications as architects, surveyors and engineers to work on particular projects.

The needy

DGAA Homelife, 1 Derry Street, London W8 5HY. T:0171 369 6700. DGAA Homelife assists people from professional or similar backgrounds either financially or with nursing and care in a number of residential homes. There is a network of county committees as well as committees based on each home. Work involves general fund-raising and also visiting patients and helping to organise outings and entertainments for them.

International Voluntary Service (IVS), Castlehill House, 21 Otley Road, Headingley, Leeds LS6 3AA. T:0113 230 4600. IVS runs international work camps in Britain and Europe (including Eastern Europe). Assignments normally last from two to four weeks and involve work such as helping in a psychiatric hospital, assisting with holidays for handicapped children, running children's play schemes and working with minority groups. There are also environmental and conservation work projects. No experience is needed – but motivation is. The Summer work camp list which comes out in April is obtainable from the above address (price £5).

OXFAM, Oxfam House, 274 Banbury Road, Oxford OX2 7DZ. T:01865 311311. Oxfam aims to relieve poverty, distress and suffering in any part of the world. Over 30,000 volunteers are involved in all parts of the UK and Ireland. One of the major areas of need is to help with the running of Oxfam shops: jobs range from the day-to-day management to sorting and pricing, selling and window display. Other volunteers organise fund-raising events, give administrative help and support the educational or campaigns aspect of Oxfam's work. Travel expenses and meals can be reimbursed. For further information, contact your local Oxfam shop or office (see telephone directory) or write to the above address.

Quaker International Social Projects (QISP), Friends House, Euston Road, London NW1 2BJ. T:0171 387 3601 ext 2255. QISP organises residential projects in Britain and Northern Ireland, lasting one to three weeks, where volunteers undertake a variety of community work activities, for example: play schemes, hospital and social work. Food and basic accommodation are provided. Individuals are asked to meet their own travel costs. Volunteers can apply through QISP for placements abroad.

Royal British Legion, Poppy Appeal, Aylesford, Kent ME20 7NX. T:01622 717172. The Royal British Legion was founded to help needy ex-service men and women and also their dependants. Today, with over 3,000 branches in the UK, it: runs convalescence and care homes; maintains sheltered workshops for the disabled; gives pension counselling; provides training for jobseekers; offers advice and friendship, and through its welfare service, gives financial help. It also organises pilgrimages to war graves overseas and has a small business advice service.

The Royal British Legion's most important fund-raising activity for all this work is the Poppy Day Appeal. Its most pressing need is to recruit more voluntary organisers and helpers to assist with the Appeal by sparing a few hours for street or home-to-home collections. If you would like to help, please write to – or telephone – Pat Reger at the above address.

The Samaritans, 10 The Grove, Slough, Berks SL1 1QP. T:01753 532713. The Samaritans aims to offer emotional support to the suicidal and the despairing. Much of the work is done on the telephone so that, while no special qualifications are required, good hearing, an unshockable disposition and complete reliability are essential qualities in a volunteer. Training is given – often at weekends – and those who qualify will be expected to attend further courses from time to time. The minimum time commitment is about 12 hours a month plus a few all-night duties each year. Some expenses are paid. Apart from this work, there is need for fund-raising help from anyone with a little time and a lot of enthusiasm.

Offenders and the victims of crime

NACRO (National Association for the Care and Resettlement of Offenders), 169 Clapham Road, London SW9 0PU. T:0171 582 6500. NACRO promotes the care and resettlement of offenders in the community and community involvement in the prevention of crime. It runs housing, employment, youth training, education and advice projects for offenders as well as providing information and training services for people concerned with offenders and the criminal justice system. Opportunities for voluntary work, which are organised on a local basis, are limited to a small number of projects such as arranging education for unemployed adults and running activities for young people. For further information, contact the Information Department.

Society of Voluntary Associates (SOVA), 350 Kennington Road, London SE11 4LH. T:0171 793 0404. SOVA promotes the work of volunteers with offenders, ex-offenders, their families and young people at risk. It recruits, trains and deploys volunteers to the probation and social services. The work may be with children, in the adult literacy scheme, prison visiting or helping ex-offenders. The necessary training is given by SOVA and the volunteer then works in a Probation Service or Befrienders' Scheme.

Work after work

Association of British Chambers of Commerce, 9 Tufton Street, London SW1P 3QB. T:0171 222 1555. Chambers of commerce, the organisations representing the local business community, are highly active in a wide range of projects to promote local economic development and renewal in the wider community. Many chambers, for example, take the lead in initiatives for inner city regeneration, crime prevention, industry/education links, training schemes and similar and very much welcome input from retired business people to contribute to their special working parties. There are also opportunities for involvement in the representational role of chambers on behalf of business, as a committee or panel member looking into such areas as transport, the environment and industrial affairs. For further information, contact your local chamber direct (see telephone directory) or get in touch with the Association at the above address.

Business in the Community, 8 Stratton Street, London W1X 5FD. T:0171 629 1600. For executives and managers who would like to continue to work in business after retirement, Business in the Community may be the answer. Set up as a partnership between government, employers, trade unions and the voluntary sector it aims to encourage the greater local involvement of businesses in the communities in which they operate. In practice the work will involve advising and helping new small firms at the start-up stage and as they further develop. Time involved is likely to be of the order of one day a week. Expenses are paid. Contact can be made through your nearest local Enterprise Agency (listed in the telephone book), via the London head office above; or for Enterprise Trusts (as they are known in Scotland) through SBC, Romano House, 43 Station Road, Corstorphine, Edinburgh EH12 7AF, T:0131 334 9876.

Free Representation Unit, 49-51 Bedford Row, London WC1R 4LR. T:0171 831 0692. The Free Representation Unit (FRU) is a registered charity providing legal representation at tribunals in London and the South-East for which legal aid is not available. Cases which are referred by agencies such as Citizens' Advice Bureaux and Law Centres cover a very broad spectrum, including for example: medical and disability appeal tribunals, criminal injuries compensation boards, industrial tribunals and housing benefit review boards. Most representation is undertaken by volunteers who, in addition to a legal qualification, will normally be expected to attend a FRU training session and to cover one or two cases with an existing representative. Volunteers can take on as many or few cases as they can handle. Once involved, however, they become responsible for all further procedural steps and negotiations. For further information contact the Administrator, Kathleen McGivern, at the above address.

Politics

You may not immediately think of political parties in the context of voluntary work but all of them use vast numbers of volunteer helpers. Between elections the help is mostly required with fund-raising, committee work and staffing the constituency offices. At election time activity is obviously intense: delivering literature, addressing and stuffing envelopes, recording canvas returns, driving elderly and disabled people to the polls, and, for the politically informed, canvassing. Contact your constituency office which will be listed in the telephone book or, if you have difficulty in finding it, contact the national party headquarters. The addresses of the major parties are:

Conservative Central Office, 32 Smith Square, Westminster, London SW1P 3HH. T:0171 222 9000.

Labour Party Headquarters, 150 Walworth Road, London SE17 1JT. T:0171 701 1234.

Social and Liberal Democrats, 4 Cowley Street, London SW1P 3NB. T:0171 222 7999.

Plaid Cymru, 51 Cathedral Road, Cardiff CF1 9HD. T:01222 231944.

Scottish National Party, 6 North Charlotte Street, Edinburgh EH2 4JH. T:0131 226 3661.

Green Party, 1A Waterlow Road, London N19 5NJ. T:0171 272 4474.

Social Democratic and Labour Party (SDLP), Cranmore House, 611c Lisburn Road, Belfast BT9 7GT. T:01232 668100.

Ulster Unionist Party, 3 Glengall Street, Belfast BT12 5AE. T:01232 324601.

Long-term volunteering

If you are thinking of a long-term, probably residential, commitment there are a number of organisations both in the UK and abroad in need of voluntary help for a wide variety of projects. Some require specialist skills, such as engineering or medicine; others essentially need people with practical qualities, common sense and enthusiasm.

For those with a serious interest, a guide well worth reading is *Volunteer Work*, published by the Central Bureau. It contains information on over 100 organisations recruiting volunteers in the UK and countries worldwide including organisations specifically seeking one-time executives or those on early retirement. Price £8.99 from the **Central Bureau**, Seymour Mews House, Seymour Mews, London W1H 9PE. T:0171 486 5101.

As an indication of the kinds of opportunities that exist, we have listed below some of the main bodies in the sector.

Overseas

There are four major groups all of which require a two-year minimum period of service. General conditions are similar for all of them, i.e. travel is paid plus a living allowance/salary which is based on local levels rather than on expatriate rates; couples without dependent children are welcome as long as both have the necessary skills; national insurance contributions are provided and a resettlement grant is paid on completion of the tour.

VSO (Voluntary Service Overseas), 317 Putney Bridge Road, Putney, London SW15 2PN. T:0181 780 2266. VSO places nearly a thousand volunteers a year to work in developing countries in Africa, Asia, the Pacific and the Caribbean in order to help local people acquire more skills. It is particularly keen to recruit retired men and women with a professional or practical background in education, health, agriculture, technical trades and engineering, business, communications and social development. For further information, contact the Enquiries Unit at the above address.

Skillshare Africa, Recruitment/Selection, 3 Belvoir Street, Leicester LE1 6SL. T:0116 254 0517. Skillshare Africa co-ordinates volunteers to work on a variety of projects in Botswana, Lesotho, Swaziland and Mozambique. You must be qualified with at least two years' relevant experience. The range of jobs to be done is very diverse and technical, educational, medical, agricultural, business and social work skills are all required. All applicants are required to pass a medical examination. There is an upper age limit of 65.

International Co-operation for Development, Unit 3, Canonbury Yard, 190a New North Road, London N1 7BJ. T:0171 354 0883. ICD (a department of CIIR) provides technical assistance for community projects which tackle the causes of poverty. It operates in Latin America, Africa and the Yemen. The programme is open to professionally qualified and technical people with several years' experience. ICD has vacancies in the field of health, agriculture and education. Most jobs involve training local people in new skills and some knowledge of Spanish or Arabic would be useful. A preliminary orientation course is arranged with training sessions and thorough briefings.

United Nations Association International Service, Suite 3A, Hunter House, 57 Goodramgate, York YO1 2LS. T:01904 647799. UNAIS is a voluntary body which sends skilled personnel to work in the Third World (West Africa, Latin America, Occupied Palestinian Territories) on projects aiming to achieve a fundamental change in the distribution of wealth and power. Third World and community work experience are an advantage and it is essential to have either knowledge of the local language or the ability and willingness to learn. Recent vacancies have been for people with a wide range of skills from nurses and agronomists to water engineers and community development workers. There is a one-month orientation course plus language training as necessary.

An organisation which operates on a rather different, less long-term basis is **British Executive Service Overseas (BESO)**, 164 Vauxhall Bridge Road, London SW1V 2RB. T:0171 630 0644. BESO is an independent charity whose primary objectives are to aid development, trade and employment in developing and emerging economies abroad.

Mature volunteers with a skill or professional qualification are particularly sought to help on projects in over a hundred countries. Assignments vary in length from two weeks to six months. Executives receive neither salary nor fee but their marriage partner may accompany them. Travel, insurance and incidentals are met by BESO. Accommodation, subsistence and local transport are paid for by the requesting organisation.

In UK

Although the groups which we have listed in this section are primarily concerned with schemes requiring volunteer help for between two weeks and six months, many of them also need shorter term help with administration and fund-raising.

Children's Country Holidays Fund, 1st Floor (Rear), 42-43 Lower Marsh, Tanswell Street, London SE1 7RG. T:0171 928 6522. Contact: The Director. The purpose of this charity is to give disadvantaged London children aged between five and twelve a country or seaside summer holiday, either in private homes or camps. Suitable host families are needed as are country representatives who undertake to find local hostesses willing to welcome one or two children into their home. There are also opportunities for: London organisers; camp supervisors; train marshals to escort parties of youngsters to and from holidays; people to co-ordinate the travel arrangements at stations; volunteer office helpers and fund-raisers.

MENCAP (Royal Society for Mentally Handicapped Adults and Children), Holiday Services, 119 Drake Street, Rochdale OL16 1PZ. T:01706 54111. Volunteers help on holidays for people with learning disabilities. They work in groups of four or five looking after a similar number of guests, usually for a two-week period. After the holiday, volunteering can be continued by helping at a Gateway Club, which is a leisure time youth club for people with mental handicaps, or by working at weekends at a hostel or hospital. Board and lodging on the holidays is free for volunteers and a travel allowance up to £25 is also paid.

Sue Ryder Foundation, Sue Ryder Home, Cavendish, Sudbury, Suffolk CO10 8AY. T:01787 280252. Contact: Mr K Wilkinson. Sue Ryder Homes cater for the sick and disabled. They are run fairly informally and as far as possible as family homes in the true sense of the word. Volunteers are needed for work in a variety of jobs including the general running of the homes or headquarters. Those with secretarial skills are particularly sought for weekend work. Board and lodging is provided.

The Winged Fellowship Trust, Angel House, 20-32 Pentonville Road, London N1 9XD. T:0171 833 2594. Volunteers of all ages are needed most times of the year at the five holiday centres run by the Trust for people with severe physical disabilities. No formal qualifications are required. The work involves caring and providing companionship for guests. Stay is for one or two weeks. Free board and lodging are offered and fares are refunded for travel within the UK.

Useful reading

Work After Work, by Judy Kirby, £2.95 from Quiller Press, 46 Lillie Road, London SW6 1TN.

The Volunteer Centre UK, Carriage Row, 183 Eversholt Street, London NW1 1BU. T:0171 388 9888, produces a free magazine about volunteering from your workplace called *Working Out* and also a free booklet called *An Invitation to Volunteer*.

Directory of Social Change, 24 Stephenson Way, London NW1 2DP. T:0171 209 5151. The Directory publishes a number of useful guides, including the *Directory of Volunteering and Employment Opportunities (£9.95)*, and also organises seminars and training courses in fund-raising, financial management and communications.

A lasting and living memorial to your generosity

ALMSWORTH COMMON, EXMOOR. PHOTOGRAPHY BY BRIAN HARRIS FOR CPRE

The English countryside has been the delight of countless generations – yet this very heart of our national heritage is constantly under threat from damaging development.

Working at national and local level since 1926, CPRE has played a major part in the creation and protection of National Parks, the provision of Green Belts around cities and in establishing firm planning controls. Important contributions are also being made to agricultural, forestry, water and transport policies and hedgerow protection. CPRE's success is based on solid research, constructive ideas and reasoned argument.

CPRE is ever-vigilant but its work as a small but cost-effective charity is totally dependent on public support. By making a bequest or a donation to CPRE, you can help to ensure that England's Green and Pleasant Land is enjoyed by future generations. Remember, a legacy to a registered charity like CPRE is exempt from Inheritance Tax.

If you would like further information about remembering CPRE in a will, write to David Conder, Room 14, Council for the Protection of Rural England, Warwick House, 25 Buckingham Palace Road London SW1W 0PP

PATRON HM THE QUEEN

PRESIDENT JONATHAN DIMBLEBY

CAMPAIGNING FOR THE COUNTRYSIDE

CPRE

REGISTERED CHARITY NUMBER 233179

Look forward to a healthier future. With PPP healthcare.

Immediate treatment
At PPP healthcare, we'll help you look after your health. If you ever need hospital treatment, you won't have to wait.

Your Personal Adviser
Friendly, helpful, reassuring – your Personal Adviser is someone to talk to whenever you have a query or need to make a claim.

Free 24-hour Healthline
You can't always speak to your doctor, but you can talk to our understanding nurses and pharmacists at any time, any day.

Tax relief
There's a choice of affordable plans. And if you're over 60, you get tax relief on payments for you and your spouse.

Instant quote – call now
For a no-obligation, personal quotation call 8am-8pm weekdays, 9am-1pm Saturdays.

Apply today and get your FIRST MONTH FREE

0800 33 55 55
Please quote reference 4916.
Or write to PPP healthcare, FREEPOST
PPP house, Upperton Road, EASTBOURNE,
East Sussex BN21 1BR.
Quoting reference 4916.

with you at every step™

PPP healthcare™

13 Health

How often have you enviously commented when meeting a recently retired friend: 'Goodness, he looks a different man. Fit, relaxed, contented – retirement must suit him.' And why not? Perhaps more than any other period since your twenties, retirement is a time for positive good health! You have more chance to be out in the fresh air and take up a favourite sport again. You won't have to rush your meals so much and, without the need for business lunches or sandwiches day after day, will probably knock off a few pounds without any effort at dieting. At the same time, there will be less temptation to pop into the pub on the way home so you will feel brighter and more alert at the start of the evening.

A major gain is that there will be no more fighting your way to work on buses and trains, jam-packed with people all coughing and sneezing; or sitting in traffic, raising your blood pressure. Also, once free of the strains and pressures that are part of any job, you will feel less harassed, look better, maybe cut down on smoking and, best of all, have the energy to devote to new interests and activities.

People can get aches and pains of course as they become older but, as any doctor will tell you, this is far less likely if you remain physically and mentally active. In other words, the days for putting out the carpet slippers and equating retirement with the onset of old age are definitely attitudes of the past.

Today's retirement brigade – younger in age, looks and behaviour than any previous generation – can legitimately look forward to many healthy years ahead.

As with anything else, however, bodies do require a modicum of care and attention if they are to function at their best and, just as cars need regular servicing, routine checks such as eye testing and dental appointments are obviously sensible.

Also moderation, middle-aged as it may sound, is generally a wiser policy than excess. Don't get it wrong! This has nothing to do with treating yourself as a premature geriatric – quite the reverse. It means enjoying small vices without paying the penalty for over-indulgence, keeping trim instead of getting out of shape and looking good when you take exercise rather than puffing like the proverbial grampus.

Keeping fit

Exercise plays an important part in keeping you healthy. It tones up muscles, improves the circulation, reduces flab, helps ward off illnesses such as heart disease and, above all, can be a great deal of fun.

The experts' motto is: little and often. For those not accustomed to regular exercise, it is essential to build up gradually. If you are planning to run a marathon, win the local tennis competition, start playing your son at squash or recapture the sporting feats of your youth, do check with your doctor before jumping into your track suit.

The Sports Council has been running a campaign aimed at the 50-plus age group, to encourage men and women to get back into the sporting habit. Training in a whole range of activities is available around the country, with beginners particularly welcome. Details of some of the many facilities, together with other keep-fit options are listed in Chapter 9, Leisure Activities.

In addition to some of the more exotic choices, swimming has long been recognised as one of the best forms of exercise. Some swear that there is nothing to beat a good brisk walk. Gardening is also recommended. With the explosion of sports clubs, leisure centres and adult keep fit classes run by local authorities, opportunities have never been better for athletes of all ability levels – and none.

At the very plush end of the market, there are Health Clubs managed by Fitness for Industry in conjunction with Forte Hotels where, in addition to facilities such as gymnasiums, swimming pools and sauna, qualified staff advise on – and supervise – personal fitness programmes. Information from: **Fitness for Industry Ltd.**, Riverview House, Beavor Lane, Hammersmith, London W6 9AR. T:0181 748 7755.

Similar facilities are provided by commercial organisations up and down the country, often combined with massage and various beauty treatments. However, at a fraction of the price, many local authority leisure centres offer a marvellous range of sports as well as training classes in everything from self-defence to badminton.

Equally, emphasis on more leisurely keep fit is also on the increase and a welcome innovation is the growing number of opportunities for older people as well as for those with disabilities. The town hall should be able to tell you what local provision exists. Additionally, the following organisations may be able to help you.

Extend, 22 Maltings Drive, Wheathampstead, Herts AL4 8QJ. T:01582 832760. Extend aims to enhance the quality of life for over-sixties and disabled people of all ages by providing structured recreational movement sessions to music. Write to the above address for information about classes in your area. (Please enclose stamps to the value of £2.)

Health and Beauty Exercise, 52 London Street, Chertsey, Surrey KT16 8AJ. T:01932 564567. A national organisation whose aim is to promote fitness in an atmosphere of 'happy informality'. Emphasis is on exercise and movement to music with special regard to individual ability. There are classes suitable for all ages with some participants in their seventies and older. Membership (including joining fee) is around £5. Classes cost from about £1.50 to £3.

Medau Society, 8b Robson House, East Street, Epsom, Surrey KT17 1HH. T:01372 729056. Medau Rhythmic Movement was evolved in Germany at the beginning of the century. Recreational movement classes aim to provide enjoyable lessons which improve posture and muscle tone, while developing suppleness, strength and stamina. There are also special breathing exercises, influenced by yoga, which are designed to aid respiration and stimulate the circulation. Classes are held all over the country. For further information, send large sae to the address above.

Relaxation for Living, 168-170 Oatlands Drive, Weybridge, Surrey KT13 9ET. T:01932 831000. A registered charity which promotes the teaching of stress management and physical relaxation to combat strain and anxiety and to increase confidence and well-being. There are usually between six and ten in a class and courses run over several weeks. Prices are very roughly in the bracket £25 to £55, depending on area, length of course and whether classes are sponsored by the local authority. A correspondence course with tapes is available to those who are out of reach of a teacher. For addresses of local classes, tapes and leaflets for sale, write to the above address enclosing large sae.

Yoga

The number of yoga enthusiasts is increasing year by year and it is estimated that over half a million people in Britain regularly practise yoga as a means of improving fitness and helping relaxation. Classes are provided by a great many local authorities. There are also a number of specialist organisations. Three which arrange courses in many parts of the country are:

British Wheel of Yoga, 1 Hamilton Place, Boston Road, Sleaford, Lincs NG34 7ES. T:01529 306851. Runs classes suitable for all levels of ability. Fees vary according to class size and area of the country but average about £25 to £30 a term. Some classes have special rates for retired people. For further details and addresses of local teachers, write to the secretary at the above address.

Iyengar Yoga Institute, 223a Randolph Avenue, London W9 1NL. T:0171 624 3080. The Institute runs classes at all levels, including remedial for those with medical conditions. Of special interest is the 59-plus class for people who would like to start gently. Fees begin at £2.50; membership is £12 a year. For further information and addresses for local classes contact the Institute's headquarters above.

Yoga for Health Foundation, Ickwell Bury, Biggleswade, Bedfordshire SG18 9EF. T:01767 627271. This is a registered charity with clubs and teachers around the country. Additionally, residential programmes are provided at the Foundation's headquarters near Biggleswade. Cost includes full board and for five days would be around £198. There are also special courses for senior citizens. National membership is £14 a year (£19 for couples), which includes a quarterly journal.

Sensible eating

A trim, well kept body is one of the secrets of a youthful appearance, whereas being fat and out-of-condition adds years to anyone's age. Regular exercise is one-half of the equation, sensible eating the other. Not to put too fine a point on it, more than one in five adults in Britain is obese – in other words, overweight. No one is going to fuss about two or three pounds but half a stone or more, as well as looking unsightly, starts to become a health risk. In middle-aged men in particular, it increases the possibility of a heart attack, can lead to other illnesses, makes operations more difficult – and, in older people, is one of the causes of restricted mobility.

No one should go on a serious diet without first consulting their doctor. However, medical advice is not necessary for knocking off: sweets, cakes, sticky buns, deep-fried foods, alcohol and rich sauces. Healthy foods which most people (except of course those on a special doctor's diet) can eat in almost unlimited quantities are: fruit, salad, vegetables, fish and white meat such as chicken.

Excessive cholesterol (fatty deposits that collect in the arteries) is another concern and, whereas it often goes with overweight, slimmer people can also be affected. The basic health message is: eat more of the foods listed above; include plenty of roughage such as wholemeal bread in the diet; cut down on dishes with a high sugar, salt and animal fat content – including cream, butter and too much red meat.

As every health magazine advises, crash diets are no solution for long-term fitness – not least because, unless individuals re-educate their eating habits, the weight creeps back on; or more frequently, gallops back within a few days.

However, most of us need a boost to get ourselves started. One increasingly popular method is sponsored dieting for charity. Another possibility, which some people swear by and others rubbish, is going to a health farm. As opposed to starvation, the emphasis today is on a few days' general fitness eating (but usually enough to avoid being hungry). If nothing else, the experience is very relaxing, albeit expensive, with average costs being in the region of £95 to £150 a day. Magazines such as *Vogue* carry regular advertisements.

Cheaper and arguably more successful for long-term slimmers are Weight Watchers' meetings, of which there are now some 5,000 a week across the British Isles. The aim of Weight Watchers is to help members establish a permanent way of healthy eating so that they 'lose weight without hunger by eating three balanced meals a day, giving a lower calorie intake and being nutritionally sound'.

Undoubtedly part of Weight Watchers' success is the help and encouragement members receive by belonging to a group where everyone else is trying to shed a few pounds. More important than the initial weight loss, the organisation sets store by teaching members how to maintain their desired weight. Initial registration is £9 and meetings are £3.95 each. Prices for senior citizens are £7.50 registration; £2.95 per meeting. For further details and local addresses, contact: **Weight Watchers (UK) Ltd.**, Kidwells Park House, Kidwells Park Drive, Maidenhead, Berkshire SL6 8YT. T:01628 777077.

As an initiative to help those unable (or unwilling) to attend meetings, Weight Watchers have introduced Weight Watchers 'At Home'. Participants follow an eight-week programme and, as well as the material which includes a food and exercise plan, they are given a telephone link with a consultant who will answer any queries as they go along. Price (1995) for the standard course is £36.50 or £41.50 for a premium pack (p&p £2). If wanted, it is possible to enrol either for a continuation or weight maintenance course. For further details, telephone 0191 296 2200; or write to **Weight Watchers At Home**, Freepost, North Shields, Tyne and Wear NE2 6BR.

Of particular interest to women, the Women's Nutritional Advisory Service maintains that many of the problems associated with the menopause can be alleviated without recourse to hormone replacement therapy (HRT) by healthy eating and exercise. The organisation runs clinics in London and Sussex (initial consultation about £55, subsequent visits £25) and also has a four-month postal course which costs £98. For further information and a free explanatory leaflet, write enclosing sae plus four first class stamps to the **Women's Nutritional Advisory Service**, PO Box 268, Lewes, East Sussex BN7 2QN. T:01273 487366.

As a rule chubby people tend to be those who enjoy rather too many good meals in the company of others. People living on their own, however, sometimes also get weight problems: either because they cannot be bothered to cook for themselves, so snack off the wrong kinds of food such as jam sandwiches and chocolate biscuits; or because they neglect themselves and do not take enough nourishment.

Elderly ladies, in particular, sometimes quite literally hardly eat enough to keep a bird alive and, in consequence, not only undermine their health but because of their general frailty are more susceptible to falls and broken bones. Two excellent stocking fillers for anyone living alone or for couples whose family has flown the nest are: *More Easy Cooking for One or Two* and *Easy Cooking in Retirement*, both by Louise Davies. Penguin, £5.99 each.

Other useful reading includes: *Eight Guidelines to a Healthy Diet*, obtainable free from: **Food Sense**, London SE99 7TT.

Self-help to avoid trouble is one thing. But anyone who suspects that they could have something wrong should not hesitate to consult a doctor.

Food safety

No discussion about food would be complete without a word or two on the subject of food safety. As most readers will know it is inadvisable for anyone to eat raw eggs, whether consumed steak tartare fashion or used in uncooked dishes such as mayonnaise and mousses. To be on the safe side, elderly people as well as the very young should probably also avoid lightly cooked eggs. Likewise, if as was the case several summers ago, there is an official warning about certain seafood, then it is only common sense to refrain from eating the items in question.

However, when it comes to food poisoning, eggs and seafood are far from being the only culprits. A recent survey revealed that two-thirds of us shop only once a week for perishable food, so are running the risk of eating items that are no longer as fresh as they should be. 'Cook-chill' foods in particular, including ready-cooked chickens and pork pies, are a breeding ground for bacteria especially in the summer, when many foods – even vegetables – are liable to deteriorate more quickly.

Storage and cooking also play a major part in warding off the dangers of food poisoning. The government leaflet *Food Safety* recommends the following basic advice:

- Keep all parts of your kitchen clean
- Aim to keep your refrigerator temperature at a maximum of 5°C
- Keep raw and cooked foods separate and use within the recommended dates
- Cook foods thoroughly
- Do not reheat food more than once and don't keep cooked food longer than two days.

The leaflet is recommended reading for all households. Free copies are obtainable from **Food Sense**, London SE99 7TT.

Drink

Most doctors cheerfully maintain that 'a little bit of what you fancy does you good'. The majority of healthy adults can enjoy a drink at a party or a glass of wine with dinner without any ill effects and retirement is no reason for giving up these pleasures. Moreover, in small quantities, it can be a very effective nightcap and can also help to stimulate a sluggish appetite. However, where problems begin is when people fancy more than is good for them. Alcoholism is the third great killer after heart disease and cancer.

The condition is far more likely among those who are bored or depressed and who, perhaps almost without realising it, drift into the habit of having a drink to cheer themselves up or to pass the time when they have nothing else to do. The trouble is the habit can become insidious and, though at the beginning it does not feel that way, individuals can quite quickly start becoming dependent on drink. Because the early symptoms appear fairly innocuous, the danger signs are apt to be ignored but these include: needing a drink as a confidence boost; having 'just one more' out of misplaced conviviality at the end of a party; drinking in the morning to cure a hangover; drinking on your own; keeping a spare bottle 'just in case'; and having sneak drinks when you think no one is noticing.

Whereas most people are sensible enough to be able to control the habit themselves, others may need help. The family doctor will of course be the first person to check with for medical advice. But additionally, for those who need moral support, the following self-help groups may be the answer.

Alcoholics Anonymous, PO Box 1, Stonebow House, Stonebow, York YO1 2NJ. T:01904 644026/7/8/9. AA has over 3,000 autonomous groups all over the country, designed to help those with a serious alcohol problem learn how to abstain. Through friendship and mutual support, sufferers assist each other in trying to kick the habit which is made easier by meeting others with the same problem. Meetings take two forms. Some are for members only, where everyone is anonymous and participants can discuss their feelings in strictest confidence. Others are open to relatives and friends, where discussion of the wider family problems is welcomed. Membership is free, although a collection is taken towards the cost of renting meeting rooms. For addresses of local groups: either see telephone directory or contact the national headquarters.

Al-Anon Family Groups UK & Eire, 61 Great Dover Street, London SE1 4YF. T:0171 403 0888 (24-hour confidential service). Al-Anon Family Groups offer support and understanding where a relative or friend's drinking is causing concern. Of possible interest to worried grandparents, Alateen, a part of Al-Anon, is specifically for teenagers aged 12-20 whose lives are or have been affected as a result of someone else's drinking. There are over 1,080 groups throughout the UK and Eire. Please write or telephone for details of local meetings.

Alcohol Concern, Waterbridge House, 32-36 Loman Street, London SE1 0EE. T:0171 928 7377. Alcohol Concern is a charity which aims to promote better understanding of alcohol-related problems and to improve services for those in need of help. It publishes a quarterly magazine, has a library and a small bookshop and can supply addresses of local advice and information centres.

Useful reading
Why Spoil a Good Time? Price 10p, from The Scottish Council on Alcohol, 5th Floor, 137-145 Sauchiehall Street, Glasgow G2 3EW. T:0141 333 9677.

Smoking

Any age is a good one to cut back on smoking or preferably give up altogether. The dangers are so well known that only idiots (like this author) continue puffing, when it is obvious lunacy. The gruesome facts are that smokers are 20 times more likely to contract lung cancer. They are at more serious risk of suffering from heart disease, particularly coronary thrombosis; and additionally are more liable to chronic bronchitis as well as various other ailments.

Most people agree that is easier to give up completely than attempt to cut back since, as every smoker knows, after the first cigarette of the day you can always think of a thousand excuses for lighting another. Aids to will-power include: travelling in non-smoking carriages in the train; leaving your cigarettes behind when you go out; not buying cigarettes for guests to smoke in your home, which they leave but you take; and refusing as a personal point of honour to cadge off friends. Many hardened smokers also swear by nicotine patches, available from most chemists.

Working out how much money you could save in a year and promising yourself a holiday or other reward on the proceeds could help. Thinking about your health in years to come should be an even more convincing argument.

Dozens of organisations concerned with health publish leaflets giving the facts, including the harm you can do to non-smokers. To list just a few, you can obtain literature from:

BUPA Health Screening Centre, 300 Gray's Inn Road, London WC1X 8DU.

ASH, 109 Gloucester Place, London W1H 3PH. A report *As Time Goes By: Smoking and The Older Woman* is obtainable from ASH, price £3.50 (incl. p&p).

Quitline, Victory House, 170 Tottenham Court Road, London W1P 0HA. T:0171 487 3000. Offers information, advice and counselling for smokers and ex-smokers alike. Lines are open from 9.30 a.m. to 5.30 p.m., weekdays.

Smokeline (Scotland only), T:0800 848484. Offers free advice, counselling and encouragement to those wishing to give up smoking. Available noon to midnight, seven days weekly.

Accident prevention

One of the most common causes of mishap is accidents in the home including, in particular, falls and incidents due to faulty electrical wiring. The vast majority could be avoided by taking normal common-sense precautions, such as repairing worn carpets and installing better lighting near staircases. For a list of practical suggestions, see 'Safety in the home', in Chapter 8, Your Home.

If you are unlucky enough to be injured in an accident, whether in the street or elsewhere, the Law Society offers a free service called **The Accident Line** to help you decide whether you can make a claim. You will be entitled to a free consultation with a local solicitor specialising in personal injury claims who will inform you whether you have a good case, how to go about claiming and how much you might claim. Should you decide to pursue the matter, you are under no obligation to ask the same solicitor to act for you. For further information, telephone: Freeline 0500 192939.

Aches, pains and other abnormalities

There is nothing about becoming 50, 60 or even 70 that makes aches and pains an inevitability. Age in itself has nothing to do with the vast majority of ailments. However, a big problem is that many people ignore the warning signs when something is wrong, on the basis that this symptom or that is only to be expected as one becomes older. More often than not, treatment when a condition is still in its infancy can either cure it altogether or at least help to delay its advance.

The following should always be investigated by a doctor, to be on the safe side:

- any pain which lasts more than a few days
- lumps, however small
- dizziness or fainting
- chest pains, shortness of breath or palpitations
- persistent cough or hoarseness
- unusual bleeding from anywhere

- unnatural tiredness or headaches
- frequent indigestion
- unexplained weight loss.

Health insurance

An increasing number of people are covered by private health insurance or provident schemes during their working lives. If you wish to continue this benefit, and you are unable to remain in your company scheme after retirement, you will normally be welcomed as an individual client by most of the main groups provided you are under the age of 70 (or in some cases, even older). You can then renew your membership when you do reach 70.

Even if you have not previously been insured, it is not too late to consider doing so. Firstly, because a number of low-cost schemes for older people have recently been introduced; secondly because tax relief is allowable on private health insurance payments for people aged 60 and over who are resident in the UK. Provided the scheme is an eligible policy (permanent health insurance plans, i.e. those that pay a cash benefit of more than £5 a night, do not qualify), the tax relief is given to whoever actually makes the payment: the individual concerned or their grown-up children (or other relative/friend) buying insurance on their behalf. Relief is restricted to the basic rate of tax and is deducted at source in the same way as mortgage interest relief. For further information, see IR booklet 103 *Tax Relief for Private Medical Insurance*, available from tax offices.

Terms and conditions of the different schemes offered by health insurance groups vary to some extent but all the major ones offer to pay all or the greatest part of the costs of in-patient accommodation, treatment and medical fees as well as out-patient charges for specialists, X-rays and similar services. They do not normally cover GPs' costs.

Subscription levels largely depend on area and on the type of hospital to which you choose to be admitted. The top figure is usually based on charges in private hospitals in London; the next is based on private hospitals outside London; and the lowest rate is based on charges in NHS paybeds and some private hospitals.

Other factors that can substantially affect the price are: your age, the extent of the cover offered and the various restrictions – or exclusions – that may apply. Many insurers have recently introduced a range of budget policies which, while they have the advantage of being less costly, are naturally also less comprehensive. For example, some policies confine cover to surgery or only cover certain specified procedures. Particular illnesses, or conditions, may be excluded as may out-patient treatment. There may be an annual cash limit or the policy may include an excess – i.e. the subscriber pays a fixed amount of every claim, typically the first £150 or £250. Another popular saving are policies which restrict private care to cases where the wait for NHS treatment would exceed six weeks. As with all types of insurance the small print matters, so look carefully at all the plans available before selecting the scheme that best suits your needs.

Although the NHS has an excellent record in dealing with urgent conditions and accidents, it sometimes has a lengthy waiting list for the less urgent and more routine operations such as hip replacements and hernias. By using health insurance to pay for private medical care you will probably get faster treatment as well as greater comfort and privacy in hospital. The major organisations are:

BUPA, Provident House, Essex Street, London WC2R 3AX. T:0800 600500. BUPA, the largest of the provident associations, offers a choice of four schemes.

BUPACare provides the most extensive cover and this is open to new subscribers up to the age of 75, who can renew thereafter. It offers three different scales of cover, according to the particular grading of hospitals and the category of accommodation. It may be possible to obtain a discount, either as an ex-member of your company scheme or as a member of an organisation such as the Royal Automobile Club (RAC) which receives a 10 per cent discount.

Other schemes are: BUPA EssentialCare, which excludes out-patient treatment; BUPA LocalCare, which is restricted to various selected hospitals; and BUPA Local HospitalCare, which is a budget mix of both schemes.

Examples of subscription costs shown below are all for the most popular – i.e. lowest – scale rates.

	BUPACare	**BUPA LocalCare**	**BUPA Local HospitalCare**
	Scale C*	*Scale C**	
	£/month	*£/month*	*£/month*
Age 60-64:			
Single	54.20	29.70	20.93
Married	103.84	59.40	41.86
Age 65-69:			
Single	68.36	38.00	26.98
Married	136.71	76.00	53.96
Age 70-74:			
Single	81.78	52.18	37.30
Married	163.56	104.36	74.60
Age 75 plus:			
(renewal only)			
Single	97.88	69.54	50.08
Married	195.76	139.08	100.16

*includes tax relief at 25 per cent available to people aged 60 and over.

The cost of subscriptions can be further reduced by electing to take an excess option where you pay the first part of any claims you make in a year. There are five levels of excess: £100, £150, £200, £250 and £500. You pay this excess only once in the subscription year, not every time you make a claim.

Private Patients Plan, PPP House, Upperton Road, Eastbourne, East Sussex BN21 1LH. T:01323 410505. PPP offers several different plans to meet the cost of private treatment. The brief descriptions below outline the benefits and monthly subscriptions (April 1995) of three of these. For further details and current subscription rates, contact Gina Ryan on freephone 0800 335555. If you quote the *Good non-Retirement Guide*, Reference ED4338, PPP will be pleased to give you a special 15 per cent discount; this has already been included in the prices quoted, as has the tax relief for over 60s.

Premier. This plan provides substantial cover for the cost of in-patient and out-patient treatment. There are four subscription scales, according to which hospital band you choose. New applicants may join at any age and renew thereafter, although subscriptions increase as you get older. There is only a single rate, with married couples each paying according to age.

As an indication of charges, the most popular hospital band at time of writing costs:

Age	Band C
	£
60-64	63.65
65-69	88.72
70-74	100.40
75-79	106.55
80-plus	112.40

These figures can be reduced by up to 30 per cent, if you take one of the three 'Excess' options available.

Secure 60+. This is designed to give immediate access to private treatment when the NHS waiting list is longer than six weeks. If you cannot be admitted within that time, the plan will allow you to arrange private treatment immediately. You may join at any age and renew thereafter. Monthly subscriptions including tax relief at 25 per cent are:

Age	Rate per person
	£
60-64	17.76
65-69	26.75
70-74	36.05
75-79	48.28
80-plus	63.65

Value. This operates on a similar basis to Secure 60+ but has set levels of benefits payable to surgeons and anaesthetists. Monthly subscriptions including 25 per cent tax relief are:

Age	£
60-64	17.84
65-69	22.30
70-74	27.14
75-79	36.59
80-plus	48.05

Both Secure 60+ and Value offer an excess option to enable you to reduce your subscription.

Other benefits offered by PPP include: cover for travelling abroad; international emergency medical cover worldwide; special discounts for health screening; and reduced charges for home nursing care arranged through the BNA (British Nursing Association).

Western Provident Association Ltd., Rivergate House, Blackbrook Park, Taunton, Somerset TA1 2PE. T:01823 623330. This provident association is smaller than the other two and its rates are competitive. New applicants can join up to the age of 75 and renew thereafter. To take advantage of the allowed tax relief for those over 60, WPA has a choice of four schemes – Beech, Senior Maple, Walnut and Senior Elect.

Beech, which is the most comprehensive of the four, offers full refunds on hospital charges, home nursing and specialist out-patient services. *Senior Maple* offers the same range of cover **but** with the important difference that hospital stay is restricted to private beds in NHS hospitals; an advantage is that the premiums are lower.

Walnut is more modestly priced than either of the above schemes – but also less comprehensive. Cover is limited to a maximum of £20,000 in any one year (except in the event of there being unforeseen medical complications during treatment, in which case the limit is £40,000) and in all cases claimants are required to pay the first £100 on each new claim out of their own pocket. Additionally, neither home nursing care nor the cost of a private ambulance are included among the benefits and specialist services for out-patient care are limited to £100 per annum.

Senior Elect provides cover for 17 specified conditions, i.e. those that normally make up the majority of NHS waiting lists including hip replacements, cataracts and varicose veins. Providing the problem is not already known at time of enrolment (in which case it is automatically excluded), the policy insures patients for the full cost of all consultations, out-patient treatment, hospital charges and surgeons' fees.

Charges for all schemes depend on your age. *Beech* and *Senior Maple* are also partially based on where you live with London, not surprisingly, being the most expensive area. The 1995 annual rates below, with figures net of tax relief, should give you an idea of the costs.

	Beech	Senior Maple	Walnut	Senior Elect
	£	£	£	£
Ages 60-64				
Single	662.07	407.92	261.90	166.97
Married	1,324.14	815.85	523.81	333.93
Ages 65-69				
Single	808.38	489.51	374.00	238.20
Married	1,616.76	979.02	748.01	476.43
Ages 70-74				
Single	986.48	571.10	442.62	281.40
Married	1,972.96	1,142.19	885.24	562.79

In the case of *Beech* and *Senior Maple*, subscription rates are based on urban areas, other than London.

WPA Health Contract. WPA has also launched a special scheme, known as the Health Contract, which is open to new subscribers up to the age of 101. Only applicants in relatively good health are accepted and before you are able to join, WPA will first want to see a medical report (which they pay for) from your GP. Single rates for those in the age bracket 75 to 80 start at £529.60; for those in the age bracket 80 to 101, at £605.90.

Bristol Contributory Welfare Association Ltd., Bristol House, 40-56 Victoria Street, Bristol BS1 6AB. T:0117 929 3742. BCWA, the fourth largest of the provident associations, offers two recently launched schemes.

Preferential gives comprehensive cover providing full refund benefits in respect of in-patient, day-patient and out-patient treatment. It also includes BCWA Assistance which provides a package of services for hospital treatment abroad as well as a 24-hour assistance helpline and repatriation cover. Excess levels are available, ranging between £50 and £400, which give a saving of between 8 and 30 per cent.

Vital Private Health Cover provides slightly less comprehensive cover by only meeting in full the cost of in-patient and day-patient treatment (not out-patient).

The annual subscription figures below are inclusive of tax relief for people over 60.

	Preferential £	Vital £
Ages 60-64		
Single	405.77	258.67
Married	791.25	504.41
Ages 65-69		
Single	513.77	327.52
Married	1,001.84	638.66
Ages 70-74		
Single	581.71	370.82
Married	1,134.32	723.11

Exeter Friendly Society, Beech Hill House, Walnut Gardens, Exeter, Devon EX4 4DG. T:01392 75361. Exeter is an old established non-profit-making friendly society with subscribers throughout the UK. Its private health insurance scheme has three major distinguishing features that may make it particularly attractive to people of retiring age:

● it accepts new subscribers of any age up to 79 and thereafter renewal is guaranteed regardless of age
● it does not increase subscription rates on account of age, which is a big advantage if income is tight in retirement
● the subscription rates for older people are considerably lower than for most other schemes.

Examples of monthly rates (1995), taking into account the tax relief for those aged 60 and over, are:

	London Scale £	Provincial Scale £
Single aged 60	63.03	39.39
Couple both aged 60	126.06	78.78
Couple 65 and 60 years	133.50	83.43
Couple 70 and 63 years	149.10	93.18

Although some benefits may be marginally smaller, cover in general is very comparable with the other main schemes and the substantially lower annual subscription may more than compensate for any differences.

Other groups that offer health insurance plans relevant to people over retirement age include:

Prime Health Ltd., Wey House, Farnham Road, Guildford, Surrey GU1 4XS. T:01483 440550.

Sun Alliance, Richmond Hill, Bournemouth BH2 6EQ. T:01202 292464 (or contact your local branch – see telephone directory).
Lloyds Bank Healthcover, 205 Brooklands Road, Weybridge, Surrey KT13 0PE. T:01932 821052.
Norwich Union Healthcare Ltd., Chilworth House, Hampshire Corporate Park, Templars Way, Eastleigh, Hants SO5 3RY. T:01703 266533.
Provincial Insurance Company (contact your local branch – see telephone directory).

Help with choosing a scheme
With so many plans on the market, selecting the one that best suits your needs can be quite a problem. If you would welcome advice, you can either ask an independent financial adviser for help or approach a specialist insurance broker.

Sedgwick Noble Lowndes Healthcare Ltd. operates a telephone advice line and, as a follow-up service, will send you details of plans that are most likely to be of interest. T:0117 988 7546 (Mon – Fri, 9 a.m. to 5 p.m.). Or you could contact **Private Health Partnership** who will send you a questionnaire and then help you match your key requirements to the most suitable scheme. Charge is £10 (plus VAT). For further information, telephone helpline: 01943 851133. Although there is no obligation, both services will arrange the purchase of the policy for you.

Private patients – without insurance cover
If you do not have private medical insurance but want to go into hospital as a private patient, there is of course nothing to stop you doing so provided your doctor is willing and you are able to pay the bills. The choice is between the private wings of NHS hospitals, hospitals run by charitable or non-profit-making organisations (such as the Nuffield Hospitals) and those run for profit by private companies.

Long-term care insurance
An emergency operation is one thing; long-term care because an individual can no longer cope unaided, quite another. Over the past few years, a number of insurance companies have launched policies designed to help meet the costs in the event of a person needing to stay long-term in a nursing home or requiring a carer to look after them in their own home.

With State support now limited to people whose total assets (including the value of their home) are £8,000 or less, some provision against long-term care must be worth considering.

However, although a godsend in case of need, none of the policies is exactly cheap and in most cases the criteria for paying out are pretty stringent. Cover normally only applies if an illness is diagnosed after joining and while some plans cover a wide range of eventualities, others specifically exclude some of the critical illnesses such as cancer.

The premiums vary considerably, as of course does the amount of financial assistance given. In all cases, the charges are largely determined by the subscriber's age at time of first joining and, as you would expect, are very much cheaper at 55 than 75.

To avoid wrangles over eligibility for benefit, most of the schemes have adopted a system, known as Activities of Daily Living (ADLs). ADLs typically include: bathing/washing; dressing; feeding; going to the lavatory; getting in and out of a bed/chair. The higher the number of these an individual is unable to manage on their own, the greater their benefit entitlement.

Companies offering long-term care policies include: Prime Health, Commercial Union, Eagle Star, PPP Lifetime, Clerical Medical, Hambro Assured and Scottish Amicable European.

A possible alternative to a conventional long-term care policy is **critical illness insurance** which pays a lump sum if you are unfortunate enough to be struck by one of a specified number of dread diseases, such as cancer or a stroke. Companies selling this type of plan include: PPP Lifetime, Axa Equity & Law, Norwich Union and Sun Life.

Deciding on your best option is not easy, since quite apart from the cost, all such policies are restrictive in one way or another. As with anything to do with insurance, you are strongly advised to shop around and to read the small print extremely carefully before signing. If, as may be suggested, you are thinking of investing some of your lump sum to pay for the policy, it would be sensible to ask a lawyer or financial adviser to check the policy for any hidden drawbacks.

Permanent Health Insurance
PHI should not be confused with other types of health insurance. It is a replacement of earnings policy for people who are still in work and who, because of illness, are unable to continue with their normal occupation for a prolonged period and in consequence suffer loss of earnings. While highly recommended for the self-employed, many employees have some protection under an employer's policy. Either way, if you are close to retirement, PHI would be unlikely to feature on your priority list.

Health screening
Prevention is better than cure and most of the provident associations offer a diagnostic screening service to check general health and to provide advice on diet, drinking and smoking if these are problem areas. These tests show that roughly a quarter of patients aged over 55 have an unsuspected problem which can often be treated quickly and easily.

Screening services normally recommend a check-up every two years and centres are usually available to members of insurance schemes and others alike.

BUPA. There is a network of BUPA health screening centres up and down the country. The cost of a full health screen and consultation is: Men, £342; Women, £366. Some of the most vital checks for women – for instance, mammography and breast examination and pelvic examination plus smear – are available separately from a full health screen. The Well Woman screen is £142 with mammography and £125 without mammography.

The BUPA breast screen, including mammography instruction on breast examination and an explanatory video, is £79.

The centres are located in: London, Birmingham, Blackpool, Bournemouth, Brentwood, Bristol, Bushey, Cambridge, Cardiff, Colchester, Edinburgh, Gatwick, Glasgow, Harpenden, Leeds, Leicester, Lincoln, Maidstone, Manchester, North Cheshire, Norwich, Nottingham, Portsmouth, Redbridge, Sawbridgeworth, Scarborough, Southampton, Southend, Sutton Coldfield, Torquay, Wirral and Worcester. For further details, see relevant telephone directory; or call BUPA on 0800 616029.

Healthlinx, backed by BMI Health Care and PPP, has screening centres in: London, Beckenham, Birmingham, Blackburn, Blackheath, Bolton, Canterbury, Chertsey, Enfield, Glasgow, Great Missenden, Harrow, Kings Lynn, Manchester, Nottingham, Rochdale, Sheffield, Winchester and Windsor. Screening programmes include: Health Screen Plus (£400 for men, £423 for women); Health Screen (£306 for men, £329 for women); Heart Screen (£306); Wellman (£173); Wellwoman (£156). For further information contact: Customer Services, Healthlinx, BMI Health Services, International House, Ealing Broadway, London W5 5DB. T:0181 840 3335.

WPA. Centres are located in: Birmingham (T:0121 441 1212); Taunton (T:01823 623330); Harrogate (T:01423 562276); Leicester (T:0116 255 1318) and London (T:0171 495 4880).

BCWA. Offers a rebate of £14 for a health check at an approved medical centre and £7 for breast screening.

National Health Service. The NHS offers several different screening services of particular relevance to those aged 50-plus. Two are especially for women and the others are more general. Firstly, all adults are entitled to regular 'life-style' check-ups, giving you a relaxed opportunity to discuss any health problem that may be worrying you; to seek advice if, for example, you are trying to lose weight; and to have one or two simple tests such as checking your blood pressure. Individuals over 75 are now offered a special health assessment cum check-up every year, which can either be done in their own home or at the practice premises. As well as general health, attention will be devoted to such matters as failing eye sight, hearing difficulties, trouble with your feet and similar problems.

The special women's tests are to screen for cancer of the cervix and breast. These are now available in all parts of the country. All women between 20 and 64 years will be offered a smear test at least every five years; and all women between 50 and 64 years will be invited for screening by breast X-ray every three years. (Women over 64 can request a mammography test every three years.)

You should automatically receive invitations for screening if you are registered with a GP. If not, ask your GP for details or enquire at your local health authority.

For further information, see leaflets *The Cervical Smear Test – Why You Need It* and *NHS Breast Screening – The Facts*, both obtainable from GPs and health centres.

Hospital cash plans

These schemes provide a cash sum for every night the insured person spends in hospital. Premiums start from 50p a week, giving a payment of about £10 a day. By buying multiple premiums, you can build up quite a significant sum which can be used to substitute for loss of earnings or to meet additional bills such as transportation costs for family visits. All benefits are tax free.

About 30 organisations offer such schemes as well as a wide range of other health insurance including cover for optical and dental treatment. A full list can be obtained from: **British Health Care Association**, 24a Main Street, Garforth, Leeds LS25 1AA. T:0113 232 0903.

National Health Service

Most readers will need no introduction to the National Health Service. However, there are one or two scraps of information that you may not know – or possibly have forgotten – that may come in useful around retirement.

One area is the range of professionals, including district nurses and occupational therapists, who can provide invaluable support if you are caring for an elderly relative or if a member of the household requires to go into hospital. Most of what you need to know is described in Chapter 15, Caring for Elderly Parents.

Choosing a GP

If you move to a new area, you will need to find a new doctor. The best way is normally by recommendation but if you do not know whom to ask you can write to, or call into, your local **Family Health Services Authority (FHSA)**, see telephone directory for address.

You could ask to consult the local medical directory, where you will find details of GPs' qualifications and special areas of knowledge. This could be useful if someone in the household has a particular health problem and you would feel happier with a doctor who has more specialised experience.

Additional points you may want to consider are: how close the doctor is to your home; whether there is an appointments system; whether it is a group practice and, if so, how this is organised. All GPs must now have practice leaflets, available at their premises, with details about the service. The information should include: names, addresses, sex, year of qualification and type of qualifications along with essential practice information such as surgery hours, services provided and arrangements for emergencies and night calls.

Having selected a doctor, you should take your medical card to the receptionist in order to have your name registered. This is not automatic as, firstly, there is a limit to the number of patients any one doctor can accept. Also, some doctors prefer to meet potential patients before accepting them on their list. If you do not have a medical card, you will need to fill in a simple form.

If you want to change your GP, you go about it in exactly the same way. If you know of a doctor whose list you would like to be on, you can simply turn up at his/her surgery and ask to be registered; or you can ask the Family Health Services Authority, or Health Board in Scotland, to give you a copy of their directory before making a choice. You do not need to give a reason for wanting to change and you do not need to ask anyone's permission. Two useful publications to read are:

- *The NHS Reforms and You*
- *You and Your GP*

Available free from libraries, FHSAs and doctors' surgeries.

Help with NHS costs
People in receipt of Income Support, Family Credit or in some cases Disability Working Allowance (N.B. see below) have an automatic right to free: NHS prescription charges, NHS dental treatment, NHS wigs and fabric supports and an NHS sight test. They are also entitled to the maximum value of an optical voucher to help towards cost of glasses or contact lenses and payment of their travel costs for treatment to and from hospital. N.B. Entitlement for recipients of Disability Working Allowance only applies to those with capital of £8,000 or less when DWA was claimed.

Even if you do not have an automatic right to the above benefits, you and your partner may be entitled to some help on the grounds of low income. To find out, fill in claim form AG1 – obtainable from any Benefits Agency office as well as many hospitals, dentists, opticians and GPs – and send it to the Health Benefits Division (the address is on the form).

If you are eligible for help, you will be sent a certificate which is valid for 6 months. Depending on your income, you may receive an AG2 certificate, which entitles you to full help with NHS costs; or alternatively, an AG3 certificate which will entitle you to partial help.

For more details see leaflet AB 11 *Help with NHS Costs* (available from Benefits Agency offices and Post Offices).

Benefits
If you are on income support and have a disability, you may be entitled to certain premiums on top of your ordinary Income Support allowance. There are four rates: £19.80 (single); £28.30 (couple) for the generally disabled; £35.05 for the severely disabled; £70.10 if both partners qualify as severely disabled.

Various social security benefits are also available to those with special problems because of illness. These include:

- *Severe Disablement Allowance,* see leaflet NI 252
- *Attendance Allowance,* see leaflet DS 702

- *Disability Working Allowance,* see leaflet DS 703
- *Disability Living Allowance,* see leaflet DS 704
- *Incapacity Benefit,* see leaflets IB 201 and IB 202

All the above leaflets are obtainable from any Social Security office.

Incapacity Benefit
Sickness and Invalidity Benefit were abolished in April 1995 and have been replaced by Incapacity Benefit.

People who cannot work because of an illness or disability and were receiving either sickness or invalidity benefit immediately before 13 April 1995 continue to receive their benefit in the same way as before, provided they continue to remain unfit for work (this need not necessarily be their former job but any type of work). Meanwhile they must send in valid medical certificates. For further information, see leaflet IB 201 *Incapacity Benefit – A Guide for People Getting: Sickness Benefit, Invalidity Benefit, Severe Disablement Allowance, the Disability Premium paid with Income Support, Housing Benefit, or Council Tax Benefit.*

The situation for people first claiming after April 1995 is as follows. There are three basic levels of payment: two for short-term incapacity – a lower and higher rate; and one for long-term incapacity. Benefit payments quoted below are for 1995/96. There are also certain additions, for example for age, which might entitle you to extra.

The lower rate short-term payment is for people (including the self-employed and those without a job) who are unable to get Statutory Sick Pay from an employer, who are sick for more than four days in a row and who are unable to do their normal job. The decision of 'incapacity for normal work' is dependent on a medical certificate from a doctor and an adjudication officer's decision. The benefit is £44.40 a week and is payable for up to 28 weeks of sickness.

The higher short-term rate is for people who are still unable to work after the first 28 weeks. The 'incapacity test' is more stringent and applies, not just to your normal occupation, but to a wider range of jobs. You will be sent a questionnaire and may also be requested to have a medical examination. This higher rate is payable from week 29 to the remainder of the year (week 52). Payment is £52.50 a week.

Long-term Incapacity Benefit is for those who, due to an illness/disability, are still unable to work after a year. Individuals receiving the highest rate component of Disability Living Allowance and those who are terminally ill may be entitled to benefit paid at the long-term rate after only 28 weeks, instead of having to wait for a year. Payment is £58.85 a week.

In all cases, eligibility for Incapacity Benefit is restricted to people under State pension age or to those whose illness began before ages 65 (men) or 60 (women).

People in this latter category who have since reached pension age may be able to get the short-term benefit – paid at the retirement pension rate – for up to a year of incapacity.

Another important point to note is that, other than short-term benefit paid for the first 28 weeks, Incapacity Benefit is normally taxable. N.B. People receiving Invalidity Benefit before 13 April 1995 are not liable for tax on their Incapacity Benefit.

For further information, including the special concessions for part-time, voluntary and therapeutic work, see leaflet IB 202 *Incapacity Benefit – Information for new customers*, available from any Social Security office.

Prescriptions

Men – as well as women – aged 60 and over are now entitled to free NHS prescriptions. Additionally, certain other groups, including those on low income (see 'Help with NHS costs', page 339) and people who suffer from a specified medical condition, are also entitled to free prescriptions. For further information, see leaflet P 11 *NHS Prescriptions*, obtainable from Benefits Agency offices, pharmacists and GPs.

People who do not qualify but who require a lot of prescriptions could save money by purchasing 'a season ticket'. This costs £27.20 for four months; or £74.80 for a year. A season ticket will work out cheaper if you are likely to need more than five prescription items in four months, or more than 14 items in 12 months. Obtain Form FP 95 (EC 95 in Scotland) from a post office, pharmacy, Benefits Agency office or your Family Health Services Authority.

Going into hospital

Stories abound of people who wait months and months for an operation because of shortage of beds. But while waiting lists for a hernia or hip replacement may stretch from here to eternity in one area, hospitals in another part of the country may have spare capacity. Many patients are unaware that they can ask their doctor to refer them to a surgeon anywhere in Britain.

Finding out which hospitals have beds has become very easy. A Government Health Information Service has been established in each region which, among other information, can advise you which hospitals have the shortest waiting lists. Ring freephone: 0800 665544.

The College of Health operates a similar telephone helpline service to advise which hospitals have the shortest waiting lists for particular operations. The list includes: general surgery, orthopaedic, ear, nose and throat, gynaecology, ophthalmology, oral surgery, urology, cardiac surgery, neurosurgery and plastic surgery. Either you or your doctor can telephone the National Waiting List Helpline, which is open Monday to Friday, between 10 a.m. and 5 p.m. The number to ring is: 0181 983 1133.

Before you can become a patient at another hospital, your GP will of course need to agree to your being referred and may also need to check that money can be allocated from the district budget; but with more and more doctors becoming fundholders, the bureaucracy is fast diminishing.

A further useful point to know is that the Patient's Charter sets out a maximum waiting time of 18 months for admission to hospital once a consultant has decided hospital treatment is required. While according to the Department of Health almost half of all patients are treated within five weeks of being placed on a waiting list, if you are one of the unlucky ones there is no longer any reason to suffer in silence. See 'Complaints', below.

Those likely to need help on leaving hospital should speak to the Hospital Social Worker, who will help make any necessary arrangements.

Help is sometimes available to assist patients with their travel costs to and from hospital. This applies: if you receive income support or family credit; get a war or MOD disablement pension; or if you have to travel an exceptionally long way to get to hospital, as could be the case if you live in the Isles of Scilly or the area covered by Highlands and Islands Enterprise. Claims for help with travelling costs can also be made on the grounds of low income. For detailed information, see leaflet H 11 NHS *Hospital Travel Costs*.

If you go into hospital, you will continue to receive your State pension as normal for six weeks. After that, it will be reduced. Certain social security benefits are also affected if you or a dependant have to go into hospital. For further information, see leaflet NI 9 *Going Into Hospital?*, obtainable from any Social Security office.

If you have any complaints while in hospital, in the first instance you should speak to the specially appointed officer within the hospital who is there to deal with complaints; or if the matter is more serious, you should write to the general manager of the hospital. In turn they may refer your complaint to the Regional Director of Public Health. If you are still unhappy, you can take the matter up with the Health Service Ombudsman – see addresses and other information below.

Complaints

The Patient's Charter establishes the right to have any complaint about NHS services investigated and to receive a full and prompt written reply from the senior person in authority.

If you have a complaint about a GP, dentist, optician or chemist, you should contact your local Family Health Services Authority (or in Scotland, your local Health Board). The address should be on your medical card. Alternatively, look in the telephone directory or ask at your Citizens' Advice Bureau. Complaints should be made in writing and submitted within the proper time limits (see below).

If you have a complaint about Hospital or Community Health Services (HCHS), you can either complain direct to the Chief Executive of the Hospital or NHS Trust or you can ask your local Community Health Council (in Scotland, Local Health Council) to help you. These councils represent the interests of patients with regard to the health service in general. The address is listed under 'Community' in the telephone directory.

If you are still dissatisfied, then the Health Service Ombudsman (known formally as the Health Service Commissioner) might be able to help. His job is to investigate complaints of failure in service or maladministration by health authorities of the NHS. He cannot, however, take up legal causes on a patient's behalf nor investigate complaints about a clinical judgement or about Family Health Service Practitioners. Addresses to write to are:

Health Service Commissioner (Ombudsman) for England, Millbank Tower, Millbank, London SW1P 4QP. T:0171 276 2035.
Health Service Commissioner (Ombudsman) for Wales, 4th Floor, Pearl Assurance House, Greyfriars Road, Cardiff CF1 3AG. T:01222 394621.
Health Service Commissioner (Ombudsman) for Scotland, 1 Atholl Place, Edinburgh EH3 8HP. T:0131 225 7465.

If you have a complaint you should get on to the matter fairly speedily while events are still fresh in your mind. Time limits require you to register complaints with Family Health Services Authorities within 13 weeks of the incident. If you are on a course of treatment under a doctor, so the problem takes longer to notice, you have a limit of six months. For the Ombudsman, the time limit is a year from when the problem first came to your notice. If you delay, you may find that your complaint is out of time and that no one will be able to help you. (Occasionally, if there is an extremely good reason, the time limit may be extended).

For a complaint about a dentist, the time limit is 6 months after the end of the treatment or 13 weeks after the cause of the complaint came to your notice, whichever is sooner.

Finally, if you think your rights under The Patient's Charter are being denied, you can write to: Mr Alan Langlands, Chief Executive of the NHS, **Patient's Charter Unit**, NHS Executive HQ, Room 4N34B, Quarry House, Quarry Hill, Leeds LS2 7UE.

Rather than proceed through the formal channels described above, an alternative approach – which of course does not prevent you from also applying to the Ombudsman or to anyone else – is to get in touch with **The Patients Association**, 8 Guilford Street, London WC1N 1DT. T:0171 242 3460. This is an independent advice centre which offers guidance to patients in the event of a problem with the health service. The Association also publishes a selection of useful leaflets, a directory of self-help groups and a journal *Patient Voice*.

Alternative medicine

Alternative medicine remains a very controversial subject. Some doctors dismiss it out of hand. Many patients claim that it is of great benefit. We list here some of the better known organisations.

British Acupuncture Association and Register, 34 Alderney Street, London SW1V 4EU. T:0171 834 1012. Treatment, which is by needles, is claimed to be effective for: migraine, lumbago, arthritis, high blood pressure and other conditions. The Association can provide a register of its members (£2.50 incl. p&p).

British Chiropractic Association, Equity House, 29 Whitley Street, Reading RG2 0EG. T:01734 757557. Practitioners specialise in mechanical disorders of the spine and joints and the effects on the nervous system. Treatment is mainly by specific manipulation without drugs or surgery. For a register of members, write to the Association enclosing a 9″ x 6″ sae plus a cheque or postal order for £2.

British Homoeopathic Association, 27a Devonshire Street, London W1N 1RJ. T:0171 935 2163. Homoeopathy is essentially natural healing which follows the principle of looking at the whole person rather than just the illness. Homoeopathy is available on the NHS but as yet not many doctors are trained in this branch of medicine. The Association can supply a list of practising GPs as well as the names and addresses of pharmacies that stock homoeopathic medicines (please send sae).

Patients wanting NHS treatment can only apply to GPs in their catchment area or get a letter of referral to one of the homoeopathic hospitals. Otherwise, patients can be treated anywhere by doctors on a private basis. Membership of the BHA costs £15 a year and includes six issues of their magazine and use of their extensive library.

British Hypnotherapy Association, 67 Upper Berkeley Street, London W1H 7DH. T:0171 723 4443. Hypnotherapy is sometimes sought by people with phobias, emotional problems, anxiety, migraine or relationship difficulties. For details of the nearest registered trained hypnotherapist, including qualifications and fees, write to the Association stating your age and the nature of the problem. You will also be sent a pamphlet answering common questions about hypnotherapy. A number of other publications are also available (enclose sae for list).

Incorporated Society of Registered Naturopaths, Kingston Coach House, 293 Gilmerton Road, Edinburgh EH16 5UQ. T:0131 664 3435. Naturopaths are concerned about the underlying conditions that may cause illness including, for example: diet, general fitness, posture, stress and the patient's mental outlook on life. A list of registered practitioners can be obtained from the Society.

Institute for Complementary Medicine, PO Box 194, London SE16 1QZ. T:0171 237 5165. This is a charity which aims to promote the use and knowledge of natural therapies. It holds the British Register of Complementary Practitioners and can put you in touch with qualified specialists in the fields of: homoeopathy, osteopathy, Chinese medicine, aromatherapy, reflexology and others. For information please send sae plus three loose first class stamps.

National Institute of Medical Herbalists, 56 Longbrook Street, Exeter, Devon EX4 6AH. T:01392 426022. The practice of herbal medicine aims to offer the sufferer not just relief from symptoms but an improved standard of general health and vitality. For further information and a register of practitioners, write to the above address enclosing large sae.

Osteopathic Information Service, 56 London Street, Reading, Berkshire RG1 4SQ. T:01734 512051. Osteopathic treatment is often appropriate for those with back problems or with muscle or joint disorders. Advice sheets and leaflets are available on request (please send sae); or you can telephone for a list of osteopaths in your area.

Wessex Healthy Living Foundation, Beekay House, 6c St. Catherine's Road, Southbourne, Bournemouth BH6 4AA. T:01202 422087. The Foundation is a non-profit-making registered charity which, as well as having an educative purpose, runs a clinic where all natural therapies are available under one roof. Annual membership of the Foundation is £10; £15 for families. Members enjoy the benefit of reduced clinic fees and also receive a bi-annual newsletter and information leaflets. For further details, write enclosing sae.

Eyes

It is advisable to have your eyes checked at least every two years. You can get a free NHS sight test if: you are registered blind or partially sighted; are prescribed complex lenses; are diagnosed as having diabetes or glaucoma; if you are over 40 and are a close relative of someone with glaucoma; (i.e. parent, child, brother or sister); or if you are a patient of the Hospital Eye Service and have been referred to an optometrist by your doctor. You also qualify for a free sight test if you or your partner are getting income support, family credit or, in some cases, disability working allowance (i.e. if you had capital of £8,000 or less when DWA was claimed).

Even if you do not belong to any of these groups but are on a low income, you may be entitled to a voucher to help pay for the test. To find out whether you qualify for assistance, you should fill out claim form AG1 which you can obtain from Social Security offices, hospitals and opticians together with an envelope addressed to the Health Benefits Unit in Newcastle. You should hear from the Unit within a few weeks and if you qualify for help you will receive a certificate AG2 or AG3 entitling you to a voucher. Wait until you hear before having a sight test, as it is difficult to claim the money back afterwards.

People with mobility problems can arrange a domiciliary visit to have their eyes examined at home. This is free for those with an AG2 certificate. People with a (partial help) AG3 certificate can use the benefit towards a private home visit by their optician.

The going rate for sight tests if you do have to pay is about £16. Many opticians, however, charge less for people who are retired or run special promotions at various times of the year. Even if this is not advertised in the window, you have nothing to lose by asking before booking an appointment.

As you probably know, you do not need a doctor's referral to have your eyes tested. Simply book an appointment with a registered ophthalmic optician or ophthalmic medical practitioner. If you qualify for free testing, remember to take your AG2 or AG3 certificate with you to give to the optician. The sight test should establish whether or not spectacles are required and should also include an eye examination to check for signs of injury, disease or abnormality.

Whether you have to pay or not, the optician must either give you a prescription identifying what type of glasses you require or alternatively give you a statement confirming that you have no need of spectacles. The prescription is valid for two years. If you do not use it straight away, you should keep it carefully so that it is handy when you need to use it. When you do decide to buy spectacles or contact lenses, you are under no obligation to obtain them from the optician who tested your eyes but can buy them where you like.

The voucher system also applies to the purchase of spectacles. If you are on a low income or if you require exceptionally powerful lenses, you are likely to qualify for a voucher to help towards the cost of your glasses or contact lenses. The cash value of the voucher, which currently (1995/96) ranges from £26.40 to £118, will depend on your circumstances and optical prescription: it might be sufficient to pay for your spectacles outright or it may only make a small contribution towards the cost. Part of the equation will depend on the frames you choose. You will not be tied to any particular glasses: you can choose specs that cost more than the value of the voucher and pay the difference yourself. For further details, together with an application form, see leaflet G 11 *NHS Sight Tests and Vouchers for Glasses*, obtainable from any optician, NHS hospital or Benefits Agency office. People who are registered blind are entitled to a special tax allowance of £1,200 a year.

A great deal of practical help can be obtained by contacting the Royal National Institute for the Blind. In addition to giving general advice and information it can supply a range of special equipment, details of which are listed in a free catalogue. There are also a number of leaflets relating to visual impairment. For information, contact the **Royal National Institute for the Blind**, 224 Great Portland Street, London W1N 6AA, T:0171 388 1266.

Many elderly people with failing sight suffer from macular degeneration which affects their ability to distinguish detail. Although there is no known cure individuals can be helped to make the most effective use of their sight by special magnifiers and other aids, such as clip-on lenses that fit over normal spectacles. For further information contact: **The Partially Sighted Society Sight Centre**, Dean Clarke House, Southernhay East, Exeter EX1 1PE, T:01392 210656. There is also a centre in London.

Another helpful organisation is the National Library for the Blind, which lends books and music scores in Braille and Moon free of charge, and post-free, to any blind reader who registers with the service. It also provides large print reading material for people who are partially sighted, through public libraries. For information, contact: **National Library for the Blind**, Cromwell Road, Bredbury, Stockport, Cheshire SK6 2SG, T:0161 494 0217 (24 hours).

Another special library is the **Talking Book Service**, Mount Pleasant, Wembley, Middlesex HA0 1RR, T:0181 903 6666.

A regular tape of a local newspaper is available free from Talking Newspaper Groups, of which there are now 528 around the country. Also, for an annual membership fee of £15, listeners can enjoy a choice of any one of a selection of national newspapers and magazines on cassette tapes. For further information, contact: Susanne Campbell, **Talking Newspaper Association of the United Kingdom (TNAUK)**, National Recording Centre, Heathfield, East Sussex TN21 8DB. T:01435 866102.

For gardening enthusiasts, there is the **Cassette Library for Blind Gardeners**, which is offered as an auxiliary service to subscribers of the *Come Gardening* magazine. The information is also available in Braille. Inclusive annual subscription £3. For further information, contact: **Horticultural Therapy**, Goulds Ground, Vallis Way, Frome, Somerset BA11 3DW. T:01373 467072 (24-hour answerphone).

Also worth knowing, all the main banks will provide statements in Braille; and Barclaycard now also issues credit card statements in Braille, on request. Additionally, several institutions offer large print cheque books or templates for cheque books as well as other facilities, such as a taped version of their annual report. There is no extra charge for these services.

Finally, BT has introduced a free directory enquiry service for blind and disabled customers. To use the service you first need to register with BT who will issue you with a personal identification number. For an application form and other information, call the free Linkline on: 0800 800150.

Feet

Many people forget about their feet until they begin to give trouble. Corns and bunions if neglected can become extremely painful and ideally everyone, especially women who wear high heels, should have chiropody treatment from early middle age or even younger.

One of the problems of which chiropodists complain is that because many women wear uncomfortable shoes they become used to having painful feet and do not notice when something is more seriously wrong. The result can sometimes be ingrowing toenails or infections.

Chiropody is available on the National Health Service without referral from a doctor being necessary but facilities tend to be very over-subscribed, so in many areas it is only the very elderly or those with a real problem who can get appointments.

Private chiropodists are listed in the *Yellow Pages*. Alternatively, you can write to the Society of Chiropodists and Podiatrists which is the professional association for State registered chiropodists, asking for some local names off their list. In addition to keeping a list of members, the Society can supply a number of free leaflets on foot health. The address to contact is: **Society of Chiropodists and Podiatrists**, 53 Welbeck Street, London W1M 7HE, T:0171 486 3381.

Help the Aged have produced a helpful leaflet called *Fitter Feet* which advises on how to avoid problems, gives tips on buying shoes and provides information on where to go for further help and treatment. Available free from: The Information Department, **Help the Aged**, St. James's Walk, London EC1R 0BE.

Hearing

As they grow older, a great many people suffer some deterioration in their sense of hearing. Should you begin to have difficulty in hearing people speak clearly or find that you are having to turn up the television, it is probably worth having a word with your doctor.

Your GP may well refer you to a consultant who will advise whether a hearing aid would be helpful; or alternatively may refer you direct to a hearing aid centre for examination and fitting.

You can either obtain a hearing aid and batteries free on the NHS or you can buy them privately. Either way, you may like to read a booklet entitled *How to Use Your Hearing Aid* (HAG 2), available free from BAPS, Health Publications Unit, DSS Distribution Centre, Heywood Stores, Manchester Road, Heywood, Lancs OL10 2PZ.

There are many other aids on the market that can make life easier. BT, for example, has a variety of special equipment from louder bell tones to flashing light systems. You can either try out the gadgets at one of BT's Aids Centres or, for further information, dial BT free on 0800 800150.

Disabled Living Foundation, 380-384 Harrow Road, London W9 2HU, T:0171 289 6111, collects information on equipment (excluding hearing aids) designed to help people who are hard of hearing.

Additionally, there are a number of specialist organisations that can give you a lot of help, both as regards hearing aids and other matters.

Hearing Concern (British Association of the Hard of Hearing), 7-11 Armstrong Road, London W3 7JL. T:0181 743 1110 (voice and Minicom). Hearing Concern, which administers the Sympathetic Hearing Scheme, publishes a selection of practical leaflets, including: *Choosing a Hearing Aid, Getting Used to a Hearing Aid, Lip Reading*, as well as information for the family on communicating with the hard of hearing. It also publishes a quarterly magazine, free to members, and has 150 local social clubs throughout the UK. Membership is £8 a year or £21 for three years.

Royal National Institute for Deaf People, 105 Gower Street, London WC1E 6AH. T:0171 387 8033 (voice); 0171 383 3154 (Minicom). The RNID publishes a comprehensive range of free leaflets and factsheets for deaf and hard-of-hearing people. Titles include: *The Ear and How it Works; Hearing Aids: Questions and Answers* and *Questions About Tinnitus*. The RNID also publishes a monthly magazine called *See Hear!*, annual subscription, £13. Additionally a range of services is provided through the RNID's network of regional offices.

British Tinnitus Association, Room 6, 14-18 West Bar Green, Sheffield S1 2DA. T:0114 279 6600. Tinnitus is a condition that produces a sensation of noise, for example hissing or ringing, in the ears or head. The BTA helps to form self-help groups and provides information through its quarterly journal *Quiet*. Annual membership costs £5. Sae with enquiries appreciated.

British Deaf Association, 38 Victoria Place, Carlisle CA1 1HU. T:01228 48844 (voice/text). The BDA aims to help those who are profoundly deaf or who use British Sign Language as their preferred language. It has branches that organise social activities in most cities and towns. The Association also arranges holidays and courses both in this country and overseas.

Friends and family can do a great deal to help those whose hearing is less good, including in particular the profoundly deaf. The BDA believes that attending a course to learn Sign Language is the most useful thing you can do. For those less severely deaf, the essentials are not to shout but to speak slowly and distinctly. You should always face the person, so they can see your lips; avoid speaking with your hand over your mouth or when smoking.

Teeth

Everyone knows the importance of having regular dental check-ups. Many adults, however, slip out of the habit which could result in their having more trouble with their teeth as they become older.

Dentistry is one of the treatments for which you have to pay under the NHS, unless you have a low income. Charges are based on 80 per cent of the cost up to a maximum of £300. If you are receiving income support or believe you may be entitled to reduced charges because your income is about the same level as that of income support, obtain a copy of leaflet D 11 *NHS Dental Treatment* (from any NHS dentist or Benefits Agency office) which explains the eligibility conditions. If you think you qualify, you should obtain forms AG5 and AG1 from your local Benefits Agency office and return them, when completed, to the address indicated. Even though most people have to pay for treatment under the NHS, going as an NHS patient is normally cheaper than going as a private patient. To avoid any nasty surprises when the bill comes along, it is important to confirm with your dentist before he treats you whether you are being treated under the NHS. This also applies to the hygienist should you need to see one. Best advice is to ask in advance what the cost of your treatment is likely to be.

Denplan. For those who like to be able to budget ahead for any dental bills, a scheme called Denplan Care could be of interest. Described as 'a low cost maintenance plan for dental health', the idea is that you pay a fixed amount each month which entitles you to normal treatment as and when required.

Among other benefits, membership of Denplan entitles you to registration with International SOS for emergency treatment worldwide, insurance cover of up to £5,000 per claim for accidental damage and access to a 24-hour UK helpline. Monthly fees are calculated according to your dental history and the state of your teeth and gums at time of joining, with £10.50 (£126 a year) being about average. Registration must of course be with a Denplan Care dentist but as over a quarter of dentists in the UK participate this should not be a problem.

Denplan also offers a separate package (Denshield) for those who only want cover against dental accidents and emergencies. For further information, contact: **Denplan Ltd.**, Denplan Court, Victoria Road, Winchester, Hampshire SO23 7RG. T:01962 866662.

Two other companies offering similar schemes but with, as yet, fewer dentists on their books are: **CDC**, 115 Station Road, Hayes, Middlesex UB3 4BX. T:0181 848 1028 and **Norwich Union Healthcare**, Pinnacle House, 23-26 St Dunstan's Hill, London EC3R 8HL. T:0800 515876.

A list of other schemes offering insurance cover for dental treatment is obtainable from the **British Health Care Association**, 24a Main Street, Garforth, Leeds LS25 1AA. T:0113 232 0903.

Prevention is always better than cure. The British Dental Health Foundation is a registered charity and publishes a range of information on most aspects of dentistry. Topics include: *Dental Care for Elderly People; Oral Hygiene; Partial Dentures and Bridges;* and *Dentures and Cosmetic Dentistry*. Personal enquiries will be answered. Write, enclosing sae to: **British Dental Health Foundation**, Eastlands Court, St. Peter's Road, Rugby CV21 3QP. T:01788 546365.

Another useful free factsheet is: *Dental Care in Retirement* from Age Concern England, Astral House, 1268 London Road, London SW16 4ER. (Please enclose 9" x 5" sae).

Personal relationships

Retirement is a bit like getting married again. It involves a new life style, fresh opportunities and inevitably, as with marriage, a few adjustments for both husband and wife to make. He will have to accustom himself to no longer going to a regular job. She will have to start thinking about another meal to prepare and may possibly feel that she will have to reorganise her domestic or working routine. Alternatively, of course, it may be the other way round with the wife giving up her job and the husband, who has long acted as household chef, sighing at the prospect of a regular gourmet lunch to produce.

After years of perhaps hardly seeing each other for more than a few hours a week except for weekends, suddenly almost the whole of every day can be spent together. He may feel hurt that she does not appear more delighted. She may feel guilty about wanting to pursue her normal activities especially if, as more and more women are, she is still working after her husband has retired. Even in the most loving marriages, the first weeks of retirement – for either partner – can produce tensions, which may even affect their sex life, that neither had anticipated.

Normally with good will and understanding on both sides any difficulties are quickly resolved and an even deeper, more satisfying relationship develops. However, for some couples it does not work out so easily and it may be helpful to seek skilled guidance.

Relate: National Marriage Guidance, Herbert Gray College, Little Church Street, Rugby CV21 3AP. T:01788 573241. Relate offers a counselling service to people who are experiencing difficulties in their marriage or other personal relationships. Their clients are all ages. Some have been married twice or even three times. Many are in the throes of actually seeking a divorce but are trying to prevent the bitterness that can develop. Some come for advice because of upsets with their stepchildren. Others may have sexual problems.

Sometimes couples come together. Sometimes, either the husband or wife comes alone. Often, the emphasis is not on a particular crisis but instead because couples are seeking to make their marriage more positively enjoyable, as at retirement.

Relate offers counselling through some 130 centres around the country. You can either find the address in the local telephone directory under 'Relate' or 'Marriage Guidance' or by contacting the national headquarters above. Each counselling session costs about £25 and at the initial interview counsellors will discuss with clients what they can reasonably contribute. However, no one is turned away if they cannot afford to make a contribution.

The address of the equivalent organisation in Scotland is: **Marriage Counselling Scotland,** 105 Hanover Street, Edinburgh EH2 1DJ. T:0131 225 5006.

Catholic Marriage Care Ltd. offers a similar service for those who are having problems with their marriage. Addresses are: **Catholic Marriage Care Ltd.,** Clitherow House, 1 Blythe Mews, Blythe Road, London W14 0NW. T:0171 371 1341; for Scotland, 196 Clyde Street, Glasgow G1 4JY. T:0141 204 1239; for Ireland, Accord, All Hallows College, Drumcondra, Dublin 9. T:00 353 1 371151.

Two other organisations that may be of interest are:

Albany Trust, Counselling, Psychotheraphy & Training Services, Sunra Centre, 26 Balham Hill, Clapham South, London SW12 9EB. T:0181 675 6669. Offers counselling for people with difficulties in relationships or psychosexual problems. The initial interview, which is partially an assessment session, is £30 (£40 for couples), after which fees are determined according to the length of time and frequency of counselling required. As well as London, counselling can be arranged throughout the home counties.

SPOD, 286 Camden Road, London N7 0BJ. T:0171 607 8851. SPOD is a registered charity, largely funded by the Department of Health, that offers a telephone counselling service to people with a disability (or whose partner has a disability) who are experiencing sexual or relationship problems. In particular, it can usually put individuals in touch with a professional counsellor in their area and also publishes a wide range of leaflets. The telephone line above is open at the following times: Wednesdays: 1.30 to 4.30 p.m.; Tuesdays and Thursdays: 10.30 a.m. to 1.30 p.m.

Help for grandparents

A sad result of today's divorce statistics is the risk to grandparents of losing contact with their grandchildren. While some divorcing parents lean over backwards to avoid this happening, others – maybe through force of circumstance or hurt feelings – deny grandparents access or even sever the relationship completely.

Until 1991 grandparents had very few rights. However, following the introduction of the Children Act, grandparents may, with the leave of the court, seek an order for contact with the child or for residence so that the child may live with them. Generally, a fee is payable to the court for the making of such applications unless the grandparent is in receipt of full civil legal aid.

In reaching a decision the paramount consideration for the court must be what action, if any, is in the best interest of the child. If the court feels that the child is of sufficient age and understanding it will take into account his or her views in reaching a decision.

Recourse to the law is never a step to be taken lightly and should obviously be avoided if there is the possibility that a more conciliatory approach could be successful. An organisation with considerable experience of advising grandparents is **Children Need Grandparents**, 2 Surrey Way, Laindon West, Basildon, Essex SS15 6PS. (Please enclose sae.)

Depression

Depression can be first cousin to marriage and other relationship problems. It is fairly common after bereavement, can be caused by worries or may occur after an operation. Sometimes too, as a number of retired people find, it develops as a result of loneliness, boredom or general lack of purpose. Usually people come out of it of their own accord: either as time heals sorrow or the scars of a relationship that has gone wrong; or in the case of those who are temporarily bored and fed up, as they find new interests and outlets for their talents.

If the condition persists for more than a few days, a doctor should always be consulted as depression can create sleeping difficulties as well as affect the appetite and lead to an overall feeling of physical malaise. The sufferer can be caught in a vicious circle of being too listless to enjoy anything, yet not having done enough during the day to be able to sleep at the proper time.

Another reason for consulting a doctor is that depression may be due to being physically run down, as after 'flu, and all that is required is a good tonic – or perhaps a holiday.

Sometimes, however, depression persists and it may be that rather than medicines or the stimulus of a new activity, individuals may feel they need to talk to someone outside the family circle who has a deeper understanding of what they are experiencing. There are several organisations that may be able to help.

Depression Alliance, PO Box 1022, London SE1 7QB. T:0171 721 7672 (answerphone). This is a self-help organisation, run by people who themselves have suffered from the effects of depression at some stage of their lives. There are local groups across the country, where individuals can meet to provide mutual support and advice. Pen-friendships are encouraged. There is also a quarterly newsletter plus a range of leaflets dealing with such subjects as: tablets and depression, self-help and advice to carers. For further information, write to the headquarters enclosing 9" x 7" sae or phone the above number for information pack.

The Samaritans, 10 The Grove, Slough, Berkshire SL1 1QP. T:01753 532713. The Samaritans are available at any time of the day or night, every single day of the year. They are there to talk or listen for as long as an individual needs or wants to be able to speak to another person. Although most people think of the Samaritans as being a telephone service for those who feel they may be in danger of taking their own lives, anyone who would like to can visit their local branch. You do not need to feel positively suicidal before contacting the Samaritans; if you are simply very depressed, they will equally welcome your call. The service is free and completely confidential. For your local branch, see telephone directory under 'S' or call T:0345 909090.

MIND, Granta House, 15-19 Broadway, London E15 4BQ. T:0181 519 2122. MIND is a national charity that aims to help both individuals who are mentally ill and also their families. There is a wide network of local groups throughout the country as well as day centres, social clubs, friendship schemes and self-help projects. Services also include counselling and MIND publishes a large range of pamphlets and books. For further information, either contact your local branch (see telephone directory) or the above address.

Some common afflictions

Quite probably you will be one of the lucky ones and the rest of this chapter will be of no further interest to you. It deals with some of the more common afflictions, such as back pain and heart disease, as well as with disability. However, if you are unfortunate enough to be affected, or have a member of your family who is, then knowing which organisations can provide support could make all the difference in helping you to cope.

Arthritis and rheumatism

Although arthritis is often thought of as an older person's complaint, it accounts for the loss of an estimated 70 million working days a year in Britain.

Arthritis Care, 18 Stephenson Way, London NW1 2HD. T:0171 916 1500. Arthritis Care is a registered charity and national welfare organisation working with, and for, people with arthritis. It encourages self-help and has over 600 local branches offering practical support including transport and social activities as well as a visiting service for housebound people. Arthritis Care also provides specially adapted holiday centres and self-catering units, runs a residential home for severely disabled people and publishes various free leaflets and booklets. Membership, including quarterly newspaper *Arthritis News*, is £4 a year. For address of local branch, contact the central office above.

The Arthritis & Rheumatism Council, Freepost, Chesterfield, Derbyshire S41 7BR. T:01246 558033. In addition to funding a major research programme, ARC publishes a large number of free booklets on understanding and coping with arthritis. To receive information pack, please send 9″ x 6″ sae.

Back pain

Four out of five people suffer from back pain at some stage of their lives. While there are many different causes, doctors agree that much of the trouble could be avoided through correct posture, care in lifting heavy articles, a firm mattress and chairs that provide support in the right places. Whether you have problems or are hoping to prevent them, the following two organisations could be helpful.

The Back Shop, 24 New Cavendish Street, London W1M 7LH. T:0171 935 9120. A shop and mail order business that sells medically approved products that help prevent back trouble or may provide relief for those who suffer. The shop is staffed by assistants with specialised knowledge of back pain and related problems. A free mail order catalogue is available on request.

National Back Pain Association, 16 Elmtree Road, Teddington, Middlesex TW11 8ST. T:0181 977 5474. The NBPA is a registered charity that funds research into the causes and treatment of back pain and also publishes a range of free leaflets and fact sheets to help back pain sufferers. The Association has local branches around the country which organise talks, lectures and exercise classes as well as social activities and fund-raising events. Membership, which includes copies of the quarterly magazine, *Talkback*, is £15. For further information, write enclosing large sae.

Cancer

One of the really excellent trends in recent years is a far greater willingness to talk about cancer. Quite apart from the fact that discussing the subject openly has removed some of the dread, increasingly one hears stories of people who have made a complete recovery. Early diagnosis can make a vital difference. Doctors recommend that all women should undergo regular screening for cervical cancer and women over 40 are advised to have a routine mammography to screen for breast cancer at least once every three years. Computerised cervical screening systems for women aged 20 to 64 and breast cancer screening units for women aged 50 to 64 are available nationwide. Anyone with a lump or swelling, however small, should waste no time in having it investigated by a doctor.

There are a number of excellent support groups for cancer sufferers. Rather than list them all, we have only included three as BACUP, as well as its own services, can act as an information service about other local cancer support groups.

BACUP (British Association of Cancer United Patients), 3 Bath Place, Rivington Street, London EC2A 3JR. BACUP offers a free and confidential telephone information service to help people with cancer and their families. Calls are answered by a nurse who has the time, knowledge and understanding to answer your questions and listen to how you may be feeling. Call freephone: 0800 181199. Alternatively you can write to the above address.

A London and Glasgow based one-to-one counselling service is also available which is free to anyone affected by cancer. If travelling is difficult, BACUP can put you in contact with local counsellors. Call 0171 696 9000 or 0141 553 1553. BACUP publishes over 40 booklets on different types of cancer and their treatment. A publications list is available on request.

Breast Cancer Care, Kilm House, 210 New King's Road, London SW6 4NZ. Freeline: 0500 245345. Offers practical advice, information and emotional support to women who have, or fear they have, breast cancer or benign breast disease. Its services include helplines, free leaflets, a prosthesis fitting service and one-to-one support from volunteers who have themselves experienced breast cancer, or whose partner has been affected.

Women's Nationwide Cancer Control Campaign, Suna House, 128-130 Curtain Road, London EC2A 3AR. T:0171 729 4688/1735. A health education charity, offering advice and information on screening and on questions that may arise following a smear test or mammography. The WNCCC operates a helpline (0171 729 2229) which is open Monday to Friday and can also supply a number of free leaflets, such as for example *Health Care for the Older Woman*.

Chest and heart diseases
The earlier sections on smoking, diet, drink and exercise list some of the most pertinent 'dos and don'ts' that can help prevent heart disease. The advice is not to be taken lightly.

Latest statistics from the Office of Health Economics reveal that English death rates from heart disease are among the highest in the world, killing over 160,000 people annually in the UK, with coronaries in particular accounting for 40 per cent of deaths among men aged 45 to 64. Although middle age is identified as the peak danger period, about one man in four over the age of 65 is at risk of suffering a heart attack and the evidence suggests that women are fast beginning to catch up with men. In an effort to reduce the casualty rate, the Government has launched the 'Look After Your Heart' programme, run jointly with the Health Education Authority, designed to create greater awareness of how heart disease can best be avoided through healthier living.

Also helpful is the **Heartline** run by Network Scotland, which offers information and counselling on reducing the risk of heart disease and on coping if you already have problems. T:0800 858585 (Monday to Friday, 12 noon to 5 p.m.).

Useful reading
Helpful factsheets, free from the **Coronary Prevention Group**, Plantation House, Suites 5/4 D&M, 31-35 Fenchurch Street, London EC3M 3NN. T:0171 626 4844. Enclose large sae with 19p stamp.

Free leaflets on heart disease and related problems are available from the **British Heart Foundation**, 14 Fitzhardinge Street, London W1H 4DH. T:0171 935 0185.

Diabetes

Diabetes is caused by too much sugar in the blood. It can sometimes be treated by diet alone; sometimes medication or insulin may also be needed. Diabetes can be diagnosed at any age, although it is common in the elderly and especially among individuals who are overweight.

British Diabetic Association, 10 Queen Anne Street, London W1M 0BD. T:0171 323 1531. Careline: 0171 636 6112. The BDA offers a comprehensive information and advisory service for all diabetics and their families covering such subjects as: diet and recipes, exercise, insurance, employment, driving and travel. There are over 440 local groups throughout the UK which offer support and also hold regular meetings and social activities. For details of local groups contact Head Office. BDA membership which includes a regular magazine *Balance* costs £12 (£3 for reduced rate members) per year.

Migraine

Migraine affects over 6 million people in Britain. It can involve head pains, nausea, visual disturbance and speech problems.

The Migraine Trust, 45 Great Ormond Street, London WC1N 3HZ. T:0171 278 2676. The Trust funds and promotes research, holds international symposia and runs an extensive support service which includes a helpline, free information pack and regular newsletters.

Osteoporosis and menopause problems

Osteoporosis is more commonly known as the 'brittle bone' disease, which causes loss of height, spine curvature and broken limbs and kills more women than cancer of the ovaries, cervix and uterus combined. It often starts around the onset of the menopause when the body begins to lose calcium more rapidly and at least one in three women (as well as about one in twelve men) are affected in some way.

The National Osteoporosis Society, PO Box 10, Radstock, Bath BA3 3YB. T:01761 471771. The Society offers help, support and advice on all aspects of osteoporosis. It operates a medical helpline staffed by specialist nurses and publishes a free leaflet about the ailment (send sae). Membership, which is optional but which would entitle you to free newsletters and publications as well as attendance at annual meetings, is £10. All donations gratefully received.

Women's Health Concern (WHC), 83 Earl's Court Road, London W8 6EF. T:0171 938 3932. WHC is a national charity, founded in 1972 to offer advice and counselling to women with gynaecological and hormonal disturbance problems, in particular with the menopause and proper use of HRT. As well as distributing literature to some 70,000 women a year, it runs a telephone counselling service and also sees patients face-to-face at its centres in Peterborough, Newcastle, Surbiton and London. As a charity, WHC charges no fee but donations are very much appreciated. For further information, contact the above address.

Stroke

Over 100,000 people in the UK suffer a stroke each year. Stroke is like a heart attack in the brain. It is unpredictable in its effects which may include muscular paralysis or weakness on one side, loss of speech or loss of understanding or language, visual problems or incontinence. Prevention is similar to the prevention of heart disease.

The Stroke Association, CHSA House, Whitecross Street, London EC1Y 8JJ. T:0171 490 7999. The Stroke Association works to prevent stroke illness and helps stroke patients and their families. It produces a wide range of publications and provides advice and welfare grants to individuals through its London office and regional centres. Its Community Services, Dysphasic Support and Family Support help stroke sufferers through home visits and more than 500 stroke clubs provide social and therapeutic support. A free information pack and details of local groups are available from the London office above.

Aids

If you are concerned about the possibility of Aids and do not feel able to consult your doctor, there are a number of helpful organisations to which you can turn for advice. Among those with telephone helplines are:

National Aids Helpline. T:0800 567123. Free service, available 24 hours a day.

Terrence Higgins Trust Ltd. T:0171 242 1010. Hours are 12 noon to 10 p.m. every day.

London Friend. T:0171 837 3337. This is a befriending and counselling agency for gay and bi-sexual men and women. It has branches in most major cities in the UK. Details of these can be obtained from the above number. The helpline is open every evening between 7.30 p.m. and 10 p.m. There is a special women's line, on Sunday to Thursday evenings from 7.30 p.m. to 10 p.m., call 0171 837 2782. London Friend also runs a number of social support groups and offers face-to-face counselling where requested.

'Health-Lines' or 'Aids-Lines', as they are sometimes called, have been set up in a number of local areas. Ask telephone directory enquiries for the number of your nearest centre.

GUM Clinics. Genito-urinary-medicine clinics exist in all NHS hospitals. You can get telephone numbers from your local health authority. Or look in the telephone directory under 'Venereal' or 'Sexually transmitted diseases'.

Disability

Disability is mainly covered in Chapter 15, Caring for Elderly Parents, so if you or someone in your family has a problem, you may find the answer you need there. In this section, we list some of the key organisations that can help you and include one or two other points that may be useful for younger people.

Local authority services

Social Services Departments (Social Work Department in Scotland) provide many of the services which people with disabilities may need, including:

- practical help in the home, perhaps with the support of a home help
- adaptations to your home, such as a ramp for a wheelchair or other special equipment for your safety
- meals on wheels
- provision of day centres, clubs and similar
- issue of orange badges for cars driven or used by people with a disability (in some authorities this is handled by the Works Department or by the Residents' Parking Department)
- advice about other transport services or concessions that may be available locally.

In most instances, you should speak to a social worker who will either be able to make the arrangements or signpost you in the right direction. He/she will also be able to tell you of any special facilities or other help provided by the authority.

Occupational therapists, who can advise about special equipment and help teach someone with a disability through training and exercise how best to manage, also come within the orbit of the Social Services Department.

Health care

Services are normally arranged either through a GP or the local authority health centre. Key professional staff include:

- health visitors: qualified nurses who, rather like social workers, will be able to put you in touch with whatever specialised services are required
- district nurses: will visit patients in their home
- physiotherapists: use exercise and massage to help improve mobility, for example after an operation
- medical social workers: employed at hospitals and will help with any arrangements before a patient is discharged.

Employment

The Disablement Resettlement Officer helps and advises people looking for work and can also give information about any available grants, for example towards the cost of fares to work and for special equipment that may make work life easier. Ask at your nearest Jobcentre.

Council tax
If someone in your family has a disability, you may be able to claim a reduction on your council tax. If you have an orange badge on your car, you may get a rebate for a garage. You would normally apply to the Housing Benefits Officer but different councils employ different officers to deal with this. Either ask a councillor or enquire at the town hall whom you should approach.

Equipment
If you have temporary need of, say, a wheelchair, you will normally be able to borrow this from the hospital or your local British Red Cross branch. If you want equipment including aids for the home on a more permanent basis, the best source of information is the Disabled Living Foundation Equipment Centre where all sorts of equipment can be seen and tried out by visitors. Qualified therapists are on hand to demonstrate the material and to give advice. An appointment is essential to enjoy the most benefit from a visit. Contact: **Disabled Living Foundation**, 380-384 Harrow Road, London W9 2HU, T:0171 289 6111.

If it is not possible for you to come to London, the **Disabled Living Centres Council** (T:0171 700 1707) will be able to recommend a centre nearer your home.

Another extremely useful organisation to contact for advice on equipment and home adaptations is RADAR – see 'Helpful organisations' below.

Finally, BT supplies more than 70 aids to enable people with disabilities to use the telephone more easily. These are illustrated in a booklet entitled *BT Guide for People Who Are Disabled or Elderly*. For further information, dial BT free on 0800 800150.

Helpful organisations
Fount of all knowledge on almost every topic to do with disability is: **Royal Association for Disability and Rehabilitation (RADAR)**, 12 City Forum, 250 City Road, London EC1V 8AF. T:0171 250 3222.

RADAR can give help and advice across a very wide spectrum including: statutory and voluntary services, access and mobility issues, holidays, employment and housing. It publishes a monthly bulletin with sections on aids and equipment and other helpful information for people with disabilities.

RADAR also helps with the National Key Scheme for Toilets for Disabled People. About 300 local authorities throughout the country have fitted standard locks to their loos – and issue keys to disabled people – so that the facilities can be used by them, even when these would normally be locked against vandalism. RADAR supplies keys at a charge of £2.50 incl. p&p for those who are unable to obtain an NKS key in their own locality. Applicants must state their name and address together with a declaration of disability. There is also a *National Key Scheme Guide*, listing the location of NKS toilets throughout the UK; price is £5 incl. p&p. For all further information and RADAR's publications list, contact the above address.

Health Education Authority, Hamilton House, Mabledon Place, London WC1H 9TX. T:0171 383 3833. The HEA runs 'Look After Your Heart: Look After

Yourself' programmes nationwide which include safe exercise, sensible eating, stress management and simple relaxation techniques. For further details, write to: HEA Business Unit, 64 Burgate, Canterbury, Kent CT1 2HJ.

Age Concern England, Astral House, 1268 London Road, London SW16 4ER. T:0181 679 8000. Age Concern England runs the Ageing Well UK pilot programme. A number of local projects recruit 'senior health mentors' – older volunteers trained to encourage people of their own generation in healthy living. The programme is supported nationally by the Department of Health, the Health Education Authority and others. For further information, contact the above address.

Disability Alliance Educational and Research Association (DAERA), 1st Floor, Universal House, 88-94 Wentworth Street, London E1 7SA. T:0171 247 8776; Rights Advice Line: 0171 247 8763 (both Minicom access). Provides advice over the telephone on social security benefit issues. Also publishes a number of guides including the annual *Disability Rights Handbook* which is packed with information about benefits and services both for people with disabilities and their families. Price is £8.95 (post free); £5 for customers in receipt of any benefit.

Disability Scotland, Princes House, 5 Shandwick Place, Edinburgh EH2 4RG. T:0131 229 8632. Disability Scotland is a national voluntary organisation for people throughout Scotland with disabilities. The Information Department is available to answer queries by letter or telephone or alternatively, visitors are welcome at Princes House.

Health Education Board for Scotland, Woodburn House, Canaan Lane, Edinburgh EH10 4SG. T:0131 447 8044. The HEBS has an excellent library and can provide leaflets and information on all aspects of positive health.

Disability Action, 2 Annadale Avenue, Belfast BT7 3JH. T:01232 491011. Disability Action provides a forum for disability organisations in Northern Ireland, as well as practical help and information for individuals. Transport services can be arranged and there is a driving school for disabled people. Information and assistance is available in respect of access, employment, benefits, services and other aspects of disability. The organisation produces a monthly diary of events and a range of free fact sheets. Full details from the Information Officer at the above address.

Disability Wales/Anabledd Cymru, Llys Ifor, Crescent Road, Caerphilly, Mid Glamorgan CF8 1XL. T:01222 887325. DW works to promote the rights, recognition and support of people with disabilities. It provides a comprehensive information service as well as training and also help with problems such as access difficulties.

Greater London Association of Disabled People, 336 Brixton Road, London SW9 7AA. T:0171 274 0107 (voice and minicom). GLAD provides an information service on disability issues (non-medical). It also produces a monthly newsletter, a fortnightly bulletin and (send large sae with 79p stamp) the *Free London Disability Guide*.

DIAL UK (National Association of Disablement Information and Advice Lines), Park Lodge, St. Catherine's Hospital, Tickhill Road, Balby, Doncaster, South Yorkshire DN4 8QN. T:01302 310123. Offers information on all aspects of disablement through a network of local disability advice centres. Telephone the above number for details of your nearest centre.

Disablement Income Group, Unit 5, Archway Business Centre, 19-23 Wedmore Street, London N19 4RZ. T:0171 263 3981. DIG promotes the financial welfare of disabled people through a programme of advice, advocacy, fieldwork, information, research, training and publications.

Help the Hospices, 34-44 Britannia Street, London WC1X 9JG. T:0171 278 5668. Help the Hospices is the umbrella organisation dedicated to ensure that the best possible care is available for the terminally ill in all Hospices and Day Care Units throughout the country. Over 30,000 patients of all ages, as well as their families, are helped each year. For a list of independent hospices and other information contact the above address.

Mobility Advice and Vehicle Information Service (MAVIS), Transport Research Laboratory, Old Wokingham Road, Crowthorne, Berkshire RG45 6AU. T:01344 770456. Run by the Department of Transport, MAVIS is an information service advising on all aspects of mobility – in particular, problems associated with driving. Its services include assessment of elderly motorists wishing to return to driving after a stroke or other disabling illness and advice on low-cost adaptations to relieve the pain of arthritic joints or other conditions that make driving uncomfortable. While general information is free, charges for more specialised services are as follows: full assessment of individuals who have suffered a disability, £60; consultation and advice on car adaptations, £40; vehicle familiarisation session, £15 an hour.

Motability, Customer Services Department, Gate House, West Gate, Harlow, Essex CM20 1HR. T:01279 635666. Motability is a registered charity set up to assist recipients of the higher rate mobility component of disability living allowance (formerly mobility allowance) get maximum value for money when obtaining a car or wheelchair. Motability can provide you with a list of manufacturers with whom they have negotiated special discounts. Additionally, they offer hire purchase facilities and in certain circumstances can also give help from their charitable fund to meet costs that are not covered by the allowance.

Wellbeing. A free health information service, essentially for people in Scotland. Answers calls 24 hours a day and can put individuals in touch with over 1,000 organisations. T:0141 248 1899.

Useful reading

Health and Well-Being: A Guide for Older People. Department of Health booklet, obtainable by writing to Health Publications Unit, No. 2 Site, Heywood Stores, Manchester Road, Heywood, Lancs OL10 2PZ.

Your Health in Retirement by Dr J A Muir Gray and Pat Blair, £4.50. Published by Age Concern England, Astral House, 1268 London Road, London SW16 4ER.

14 Holidays

Holidays can be even better when you retire! You do not have to plan months ahead in order to fit in with colleagues. You can avoid the peak periods which are almost invariably more expensive and crowded. You can also enjoy real flexibility, in a way that is usually not possible when you are working, by taking several mini breaks when you feel like it or going away for an extended period.

Additionally, one of the great things about retirement is the availability of concessionary prices, including in particular the possibility of cheaper fares and reduced charges for hotel accommodation.

Apart from these benefits, the fact of being retired makes very little difference. You can ride an elephant in India, take a caravan around Europe, sail on the Norfolk Broads, go bird-watching in Scotland, combine a holiday with a special interest such as painting or music, enrol for summer school, exchange homes with someone in another country or sign on for a working holiday, such as voluntary conservation activity or home-sitting, for which you get paid.

The choice is literally enormous. The list of suggestions which follows is by no means exhaustive. You can go to any travel agent and collect further ideas by the dozen. However, the two main criteria we adopted in deciding which, among the thousands of possibilities, to include, were: variety and holidays which, one way or another, offer some special attraction or specifically cater for those aged 50 and above.

Some of the options verge on the exotic, with prices to match; others are extremely reasonable in cost. There are suggestions which are only suitable for the really fit and active; at the other extreme, there are a number of inclusions which would only be of interest to individuals in need of special care. Some of the choices may strike you as mad, risky, humdrum, too demanding – or simply not your style. But retirement is a time for experimentation and trying something entirely different is half the fun.

For ease of reference, entries are listed under such headings as 'arts and crafts', 'sport', 'self-catering holidays' and so on. Inevitably, some organisations criss-cross several sections but to avoid repetition, the majority are only featured once in what, hopefully, is the most logical place.

At the end of the chapter, there is a general information section with brief details about insurance, concessionary fares and other travel tips.

Prices and some of the other detailed information, while accurate at the time of writing, may be slightly out of date as programmes change (sometimes at very short notice) and it is impossible to keep track. The intention is to provide an indication of fairly typical events together with an idea of price bracket.

Art appreciation

The choice ranges from visiting Classical Greece to two days exploring Shakespeare's England. It also includes the music and drama festivals held in many parts of the country, as well as some of the famous festivals overseas.

British Museum Tours, 46 Bloomsbury Street, London WC1B 3QQ. T:0171 323 8895. The British Museum organises cultural tours, accompanied by their own specialist lecturers, to visit the sites of some of the great civilisations of the past. Parties are limited to a maximum of 25 people and hotels are normally of a high standard. The 1995 programme included: Jordan, Jericho and Jerusalem (10 days, £1,495); Classical Greece (13 days, £1,685); Byzantine Italy (8 days, £935); New York and Boston Museums and Art Galleries (9 days, £1,055), and many more.

National Association of Decorative & Fine Arts Societies, NADFAS House, 8 Guilford Street, London WC1N 1DT. T:0171 430 0730. NADFAS is an organisation of over 280 UK societies. It organises tours at home and abroad to places of interest to its members. Recent tours in Britain have included: Roman Day in London (£10), Shakespeare's England (2 nights, £272) and Artists in Lakeland (4 nights, £316). Some tours abroad have been Spring Festival in Prague (4 nights, £925) and The Tropical Island of Sri Lanka (13 nights, £1,585). For information about your local Society, write to NADFAS at the above address.

Specialtours, 81a Elizabeth Street, London SW1W 9PG. T:0171 730 2297. Specialtours arranges holidays in many countries of the world for tour groups from the National Art Collections Fund and other prestigious societies. Destinations planned for 1996 include among others: The Czech Republic, France, Holland, Hungary, Israel, Italy, Jordan, Madeira, Spain, Turkey and the USA. The costs include flight, hotels and meals, travel within the country, guides, entrance fees and insurance. Prices start from about £900. Non-members are welcome but are required to pay the subscription fee to the sponsoring society before the tour begins.

Festivals

A veritable feast of music, drama and the arts. The most famous are those held at Edinburgh and Aldeburgh. Over the years the number of festivals has been growing and these are now a regular feature in many parts of the country. To find out what is going on where, you should contact the Arts Council or your Regional Arts Association. **The British Federation of Music Festivals** publishes a Year Book, which should be in your local reference library, listing festivals around the country. The major events, especially at the bigger festivals, tend to get booked well in advance, so early application for tickets is advisable.

Aldeburgh Foundation, High Street, Aldeburgh, Suffolk IP15 5AX. T:01728 452935. Box Office: 01728 453543. The Aldeburgh Festival of Music and the Arts is

held annually during June (Forty-ninth Festival 7-23 June 1996). A varied programme of concerts at Snape Concert Hall, local churches and country houses is
complemented by exhibitions, talks, walks and films. In addition there is a year-round
programme of concerts and master classes which are open to the public. For further
details contact the Aldeburgh Foundation at the above address.

Edinburgh International Festival, 21 Market Street, Edinburgh EH1 1BW.
T:0131 226 4001. The 1996 Edinburgh International Festival will be held from 11 to
31 August. A detailed programme of music, theatre, dance and other events is
available from early April, from the above address.

Arts and crafts

The focus here is on taking courses or just participating for the pleasure, rather than
viewing the works of others. The choice includes wood carving and other crafts,
painting and music. Further suggestions are also given in Chapter 9, Leisure
Activities.

Artscape Painting Holidays, Suite 4, Hamlet Court Business Centre, 18 Hamlet
Court Road, Westcliff-on-Sea, Essex SS0 7LX. T:01702 435990. Artscape runs
tutored painting holidays in Britain, Spain, Italy, Crete, France, Morocco and the
USA. Prices are from £395 for a week covering accommodation, tutoring and meals.

Benslow Music Trust, Little Benslow Hills, Hitchin, Herts SG4 9RB. T:01462
459446. Benslow Music Trust provides opportunities for the study and practice of
music for people of all ages. There are weekend and other courses all year for amateur
players and singers. The programme covers chamber music, choral and solo singing,
theory of music, Alexander Technique, jazz, solo wind, orchestras, brass ensembles
and early music. The standard fee for a weekend or two-day course is £95 with full
board or £76 non-resident.

Crafts Council, 44A Pentonville Road, Islington, London N1 9BY. T:0171 278
7700. The Council keeps a list of organisations that run their own short craft courses
or that can provide information on where similar courses are being held.

Summer Music, 22 Gresley Road, London N19 3JZ. T:0171 272 5664. Despite its
name, Summer Music organises a series of day and weekend courses throughout the
year, for among others: cello, guitar, string quartets, choirs and trumpet.
    There is also an eight-day summer school in Berkshire during August and a
Christmas house party for singers and string players at Hitchin. The charges vary, but
a weekend with full board costs about £95.

West Dean College, West Dean, Chichester, West Sussex PO18 0QZ. T:01243
811301. West Dean College, housed in a beautiful mansion surrounded by

landscaped gardens and parkland, organises short residential courses in arts, crafts and music – variously lasting a weekend, five or seven days. A typical programme includes: stained glass, calligraphy, textile design, woodcarving, picture framing, music appreciation, photography, upholstery, blacksmithing, sculpture, drawing and painting, jewellery, cane and rush seating and many more. Prices, which include board and lodging, range from about £142 for a weekend to £339 for a five-day course.

There are also longer courses, including one and two years' Diploma courses in the restoration of antiques run in conjunction with the British Antique Dealers' Association.

Coach holidays

Some of the coach companies organise holidays proper, as distinct from simply offering a mode of transport. Advice note from other holidaymakers: before embarking on a lengthy coach tour, try a few shorter excursions to see how you cope with the journey. Some people swear by the comfort, others find coach travel very exhausting.

Frames Rickards Coach Tours, 11 Herbrand Street, London WC1N 1EX. T:0171 837 3111. Frames Rickards operate a comprehensive range of coach tours in the UK. Prices cover: travel in reclining-seat coach; full breakfast and dinner; rooms with private bath or shower and all sightseeing. 1995 examples included: The Best of Scotland, six days from £435; Devon and Cornwall, three days from £185; English Lakes, four days from £235.

National Express, 4 Vicarage Road, Birmingham B15 3ES. T:0121 456 1102. Provides a scheduled coach network to over 1,300 destinations across England, Scotland and Wales and also a wide choice of Bargain Break holidays. An attractive example are London Theatre Breaks from £64, including one night's accommodation with continental breakfast, return coach travel, theatre ticket and Bargain Break card offering discounts to many attractions and restaurants. There are also Breaks to Paris and Amsterdam. Over-55s with a National Express discount coach card are entitled to 30 per cent reduction on all scheduled services as well as discounts on Bargain Breaks. For further information contact the above address or your local National Express office, or agent, for details.

Field studies

The number and variety of courses arranged by National Parks and Field Centres almost deserves a special publication of its own. In addition to wildlife studies, the choice, which varies from one centre to another includes: archaeology, landscape painting, spinning and weaving, ecology, folklore, yoga, silk screen printing and many others.

National Parks are located in Northumberland, Lake District, Yorkshire Dales, North York Moors, Peak District, Snowdonia, Pembrokeshire Coast, Brecon

Beacons, Exmoor, Dartmoor and the Norfolk and Suffolk Broads. To give you a flavour of the varied programmes that are on offer in the parks, a mini description of typical events in the Peak District follows.

Peak National Park Centre, Losehill Hall, Castleton, Derbyshire S30 2WB. T:01433 620373. Weekend and week-long special interest breaks include: photography, painting and illustration, historic houses, natural history and rambling. All courses are led by experts. Losehill Hall is set in beautiful country with comfortable single and twin-bedded en-suite accommodation. Prices start from £110 for a weekend and are fully inclusive of meals, accommodation, transport and tuition.

Field Studies Council, (GRG), Central Services, Preston Montford, Montford Bridge, Shrewsbury SY4 1HW. T:01743 850674. The Council manages Field Centres in England and Wales offering a wide variety of courses categorised as follows: General Interest, Natural History and Conservation, Flowers and Other Plants, Birds and Other Animals, Geology, Landscape and Climate, History and Architecture, Painting and Drawing, Photography and Crafts.

The Centres are based near Colchester, Pembroke, Taunton, Settle, Haverfordwest, Keswick, Shrewsbury, Dorking, Kingsbridge and Betws-y-Coed. Each Centre organises its own programme and usually includes one or two courses featuring local attractions. For example, Flatford Mill Field Centre in Suffolk offers 'Weekends in Constable Country', Juniper Hall runs courses on Surrey Churches, while Preston Montford in Shropshire arranges weekends entitled 'In the Footsteps of Brother Cadfael'.

The Council publishes a free brochure giving details of all courses (there are over 500) at their 10 residential Centres. Many last for a week (Friday to Friday) and the average cost is from about £240 which includes tuition, full board and lodging plus transport during the course. Weekends are from around £90.

The Council also organises courses overseas. A few examples of those planned for 1996 include: visits to Poland, Guatemala and the Canadian Arctic. Membership of the Field Studies Council, which is optional, costs £8 a year and entitles members to various benefits.

Scottish Field Studies Association, Kindrogan Field Centre, Enochdhu, Blairgowrie, Perth PH10 7PG. T:01250 881286. The Centre runs a range of courses in natural history and the countryside covering most aspects of the environment. Examples include: Mountain Flowers, Fungi, Highland Birds, Botanical Illustration and Highland Rambles. Cost is about £255 for a week including tuition, board and lodging. An annual programme can be obtained from the centre.

Historical holidays

Holidays with a particular focus on history are becoming increasingly popular. The choice includes: battlefield and other overseas tours, exploring historic parts of Britain and the highly imaginative 'production' at Kentwell Hall.

Historical Association, 59a Kennington Park Road, London SE11 4JH. T:0171 735 3901. The Association organises tours with expert lecturers. 1996 foreign trips include the Bay of Naples (eight days, £675) and Ghana (ten days, £1,000). Home tours include: Norwich and South Norfolk (eight days, £420); and The Northern Isles (eight days, £250). All prices are approximate and subject to change. Membership costs £23 a year.

Holts' Battlefield Tours Ltd., 15 Market Street, Sandwich, Kent CT13 9DA. T:01304 612248. Holts' offer a choice of over 50 battlefield, historical and archaeological tours to some 20 countries worldwide. All are accompanied by a specialist guide-lecturer and local experts are also used. Highlights of the 1996 programme include: World War One (four-day introductory tour, about £300); Waterloo (four days, about £350); China and Hongkong (14 days, about £2,350).

Most tours are half board in good standard hotels with private bathrooms. Every effort is made to cater for single travellers, many of whom are ladies. Special group tours can be arranged.

Kentwell Hall, Long Melford, Suffolk CO10 9BA. T:01787 310207. Every summer Kentwell Hall recreates a living panorama of what life was like during the Tudor period. Participants are required to provide their own costumes and to enter into the role of a character living at the time: for example, this could be a 16th-century cook or hay-maker. You are expected to prepare yourself by reading and there are Open Days at Kentwell with briefing sessions. The event lasts for four weeks and participants can stay for one, two, three or four complete weeks. The only cost involved is the provision of a suitable costume. All meals are provided free and there is camping space available. Those requiring more comfort can book into one of the many local bed and breakfast hotels.

Middlebrook-Hodgson Battlefield Tours, 48 Linden Way, Boston, Lincolnshire PE21 9DS. T:01205 364555. Military historians, Martin Middlebrook and Michael Hodgson, organise coach tours for small groups (about 26 people) to visit World War One and Two battlefields. Recent tours (variously between two and five nights) were to the Somme, Ypres, Loos, Verdun, Normandy and Arnhem. The cost is from about £140 for all travel, bed and meals, local tours and guiding.

Should you wish to visit a particular grave, the **Commonwealth War Graves Commission**, 2 Marlow Road, Maidenhead, Berkshire SL6 7DX, T:01628 34221, will tell you where it is.

People interested in making a pilgrimage to war graves or battlefields should contact **The Royal British Legion**, The Pilgrimage Department, The Royal British Legion Village, Aylesford, Kent ME20 7NX, T:01622 716729/716182. The Pilgrimage Department is the recognised authority in this field and each year visits are organised to about 30 different countries in the Far East, Africa and Europe. Approximate prices, which include all travel, full board, accommodation in a good standard hotel and excursions (including a non-denominational Service of

Remembrance in one of the Commonwealth War Graves Commission Cemeteries) are from £229 for a three-day pilgrimage to France/Belgium; £595 for an eight-day visit to Italy; and £1,550 for a nine-day pilgrimage to Malaysia/Indonesia.

Under the Government's War Widows Grant-in-Aid Scheme, run by the Legion, war widows can apply for a government grant to cover seven-eighths of the cost of one visit.

Language courses

If you are hoping to travel more when you retire, being able to speak the language when abroad will greatly add to your enjoyment. Quickest and easiest way to learn is in the country itself. There are attractive opportunities for improving your French, German, Italian and Spanish.

The British Institute of Florence, Palazzo Lanfredini, Lungarno Guicciardini 9, 50125 Florence, Italy. T:(from England) 00 39 55 284031. The Institute, an officially sponsored joint Anglo-Italian institute of over 75 years' standing, runs two- to four-week graded Italian language courses throughout the year for learners of all ages and levels. There are also courses in history of art, drawing, opera and cooking. Various events such as lectures and concerts are arranged by the Institute for students and local people. Two-week summer courses are available near the Tuscan coast.

Accommodation can be arranged in local homes, *pensioni* and hotels: cost is from about £14 a day. Teaching takes place in a 13th-century palazzo. Tuition fees vary according to the length and intensity of the course you choose: for example, £235 for 10 lessons a week for four weeks. The Florentine Renaissance courses (in English) last four weeks and cost £155. Specially packaged courses are available for groups and discounts are given to members of the University of the Third Age.

En Famille (Overseas), The Old Stables, 60b Maltravers Street, Arundel, West Sussex BN18 9BG. T:01903 883266. The Agency arranges short or long stays with host families for people who want an insider's view of a European country. There is a registration fee of £25 plus a selection fee of £25. You pay travel costs and about £185-£265 a week full board; or £160-£220 demi-pension. En Famille matches your background and interests to the families on their register and sends you details of a selection of host families from which to choose. The Agency also runs some homestays in France combined with language courses. Older people are very welcome on these holidays.

Eurocentres, 56 Eccleston Square, London SW1V 1PQ. T:0171 233 9888. Eurocentres run language learning courses in France, Italy, Japan, Switzerland, Spain, Germany and Russia for adults of all levels. The courses last from a couple of weeks to about six months and are set in the life and culture of the host country. Most people live with families but Eurocentres will also arrange hotels.

A 12-week French course in Paris with accommodation (single room) and half board costs about £3,800; a two-week course in Florence with half board costs about £620. In all cases, fares are additional.

Estudio General Luliano, c/o John Galleymore, 25 High Street, Portsmouth PO1 2LZ. T:01705 824095. The Estudio runs two- to three-week Spanish courses in Majorca for adult English students of all levels of proficiency. Classes are held in the morning in small groups. The fee is about £130 for a fortnight with accommodation in private houses or beach hotels; with full board the cost comes to about £350 inclusive for the two weeks. Air travel can be arranged.

Goethe Institut, Helene-Weber Allee 1, Postfach: 190419, D-80604 Munchen, Germany. T:00 49 89 159 21 200/206. For German courses in Britain: **Goethe Institute,** 50 Princes Gate, Exhibition Road, London SW7 2PH. T:0171 411 3451. The Goethe Institute offers one-, two-, four- or eight-week German language courses, for beginners to examination level, at 16 centres in Germany. The instruction is designed so that you can follow from one level to another in all centres. Price of a four-week course in Germany averages DM 1,420. Bed and breakfast, staying with a family or in a hostel, costs about DM 650 for the whole month. Course fees sometimes include such items as excursions and cultural events as well as the help of course assistants.

Useful reading
Study Holidays, price £8.99 from the **Central Bureau,** Seymour Mews House, Seymour Mews, London W1H 9PE. T:0171 486 5101. Just about everything you need to know on language and study courses all over Europe, including those where language learning is part of wider studies on art, literature and civilisation. The guide also offers practical information on accommodation and travel.

Other people's homes

Living in someone else's home for free is one of the cheapest ways of enjoying a holiday. There are two ways of arranging this. You can exchange your home with another person, in this country or abroad. The onus is on you to select a suitable property and to decide whether the person with whom you are swapping is likely to care for your home properly. The alternative is to become a homesitter and, for a modest payment, mind someone else's property while they are away.

Home exchange
Unless you are lucky enough to hear about someone through personal recommendation, probably the easiest method of finding a swap (and of advertising your own home) is through a specialised directory. In most cases, this is not an introduction service as such. The exchanges are normally arranged direct between the two parties concerned, who agree the terms between themselves. Some people even exchange their cars and pets.

Green Theme International Home Exchange Holiday Service, Little Rylands Farm, Redmoor, Nr Bodmin, Cornwall PL30 5AR. T:01208 873123. Publishes a directory of home exchange listings three times a year featuring properties worldwide. There is a registration fee of £35 plus optional 'personalised matching' service at an extra cost of £25. Airline ticketing and travel insurance are offered. Green Theme also publishes a UK-only list.

Home Base Holidays, 7 Park Avenue, London N13 5PG. T:0181 886 8752. Publishers of the annual guide *Bed & Breakfast in the United States & Canada* (£7.50 incl. p&p), Home Base Holidays also operates a home exchange agency specialising in the USA, but also covering Canada, Australia and Europe. Accommodation varies from small city apartments to large country homes complete with swimming pool. Annual registration costs £38 and includes an introductory brochure (with advice on arranging a satisfactory swap) plus three directories throughout the year – one with published details of your own home. Home Base Holidays does not get involved in the actual arrangements but is happy to give advice. Information pack, including sample listings, sent on request.

Homelink International, Linfield House, Gorse Hill Road, Virginia Water, Surrey GU25 4AS. T:01344 842642. Publishes five directories a year, containing in the region of 9,000 listings covering 50 countries throughout the world. Annual membership costs £49 and entitles members to feature their home in one of the directories (December, February, April, May or June) but to receive all five books if they wish to do so. There is a supplement of £9 for inclusion of a photograph of the property. A special UK-only exchange book is published in March and costs £8.

Intervac International Home Exchange, 3 Orchard Court, North Wraxall, Wiltshire SN14 7AD. T:01225 892208. Publishes four holiday directories a year, with around 9,000 listings, covering 50 countries worldwide. Choice of accommodation ranges from bedsitters to mansions. Cost of an entry is £65 and detailed hints are provided on points to check before agreeing an exchange. Attractive discounts are available on holiday insurance.

Worldwide Home Exchange Club, 50 Hans Crescent, London SW1X 0NA. T:0171 823 9937. Publishes a directory which is mailed out in January each year and a supplement mailed out in April. These two publications contain approximately 1,500 listings in 35 countries. Annual subscription is £29 and includes option of having your home listed or not, as you prefer. All subscribers receive both publications. Especially good for America, as the club has an office in Maryland.

Useful reading
Home from Home, price £8.99 from the **Central Bureau**, Seymour Mews House, Seymour Mews, London W1H 9PE. As well as advice about home swaps, it includes a section on staying in other people's homes where you live as a member of the family.

Homesitting

Retired people are generally considered ideal. Homesitting means that you provide a caretaking service and get paid for doing so. Duties variously involve: light housework, plant watering, care of pets and sometimes tending the garden. First class references are naturally required.

Home and Pet Care, Green Rigg Farm, Caldbeck, Wigton, Cumbria CA7 8AH. T:01697 478515. Although Home and Pet Care get some requests for simply caring for a property while the owners are away, they specialise in offering pet care as part of the service. Predictably, most requests are for dogs and cats. However, they cheerfully accept any type of pet from a baby alligator to a mynah bird. Pay varies according to both the species of the pet in question and what household duties are involved but averages about £80 a week.

Homesitters, Buckland Wharf, Buckland, Aylesbury, Bucks HP22 5LQ. T:01296 630730. Homesitters are looking for mature, responsible people with no children or pets, usually non-smokers, and it is useful to have your own car. Assignments may be for short or long periods. Pay is from £38 a week depending on responsibilities, plus food and travel expenses. With agreement, a Homesitter can take their partner. The houses can be anything from a city centre apartment to an isolated country mansion.

Housewatch, Little London, Berden, Bishops Stortford, Herts CM23 1BE. T:01279 777412. Housewatch sitters variously: offer a holiday care service, provide long-term specialised care (as, for example, if a property is vacant during probate) or will care for a home and any pets if the owner has to go into hospital. They will also visit the patient, take in mail and generally keep them in touch with domestic events during their absence. Pay, depending on duties, averages about £80 a week.

Universal Aunts, PO Box 304, London SW4 0NN. T:0171 738 8937. Universal Aunts organise a home and pet sitting service for absent owners and recruit single or pairs of mature, responsible people for this work. Payment is £119 a week plus travelling expenses (whether you go alone or with a partner). All applicants for the home sitters panel are interviewed before acceptance on the list.

Overseas travel

Many of the big tour operators make a feature of offering special holidays, designed for the over 55s. For fun, we have also included companies that specialise in arranging cruises and packaged motoring holidays; and also information about time-sharing. For up-to-date details, you should check the brochures.

Explore Worldwide Ltd., 1 Frederick Street, Aldershot, Hants GU11 1LQ. T:01252 344161. Explore takes small groups of people on holidays off the tourist track, designed to give travellers a real flavour of the country and its way of life.

Examples of recent journeys include: Discovering Wildlife on the Galapagos Islands (12 days from £1,390); Experiencing the Festive Culture of Bhutan (22 days from £2,395); Travelling the Silk Road in China (25 days from £2,095) and Big Game Viewing in Namibia and Botswana (17 to 22 days from £1,335). Accommodation is mostly fairly simple and fully trained leaders accompany every tour. Prices quoted include return air flights from London.

Farthing Holidays, Holiday House, Weir Road, Kibworth, Leics LE8 0LQ. T:0116 279 6060. This company specialises in group travel worldwide. Group size is usually about 30 but smaller groups are catered for (particularly when travelling by air rather than coach). Travel can be arranged from any location in Britain. If you belong to a group which wants to arrange a trip together, tell Farthing your proposed destination, dates and numbers and they will suggest itineraries and prices.

Portland Holidays, 218 Great Portland Street, London W1N 5HG. T:0171 388 5111; Manchester: 0161 228 1188; Bristol: 0117 9226144; Birmingham: 0121 233 2211. Holidays in Spain, Majorca, Tenerife, Cyprus, Algarve, Madeira and Tunisia, November-April for one to four weeks, for over-55s, arranged under Portland's Home and Away programme. Prices, which include entertainments and other extras, start at £129 for 7 nights half board.

Relais de Silence. These are a French group of independently owned hotels with a network of about 300 hotels throughout Europe and about 15 in Britain. They offer tranquil, rural settings in 2, 3 and 4-star comfort at reasonable prices with good food and a family-like atmosphere. For more information, contact the **French Government Tourist Office**, 178 Piccadilly, London W1V 0AL. Please enclose self-addressed label and stamps to the value of £1. Or telephone 0891 244123 (premium rate).

Saga Holidays Ltd., Saga Building, Freepost, Folkestone, Kent CT20 1BR. T:Reservations: 0800 300500; Brochures: 0800 300456. Saga specialises in holidays for over-50s and offers a varied choice of options both in Britain and overseas. The list includes: coach tours, cruises, short breaks, long-stay winter holidays and multi-centre touring vacations plus a selection of special interest holidays including, for example, dancing, fitness, bridge and bowls.

For further information, obtain Saga brochures: *Travellers World, Europe and the Mediterranean, Great British Resorts, Universities and Study Breaks, Cruise Book* and *Special Interest Selection*, available from the Folkestone address above.

Thomson Young at Heart, Greater London House, Hampstead Road, London NW1 7SD. T:0171 707 9000. Short and long-stay winter sunshine holidays in hotels and apartments for people over 55, accompanied by special Young at Heart Representatives. The resorts are in: Spain, Portugal, Madeira, Malta, Tenerife, Tunisia, Cyprus, Italy and Egypt. Special interest holidays include walking weeks, sequence dancing and bowls competitions. All holidays include a free excursion and there are entertainments at all hotels. A number of hotels do not charge single room supplement.

Cruises

Cruises seem to become more exotic by the year. Among the programmes that we particularly liked are those arranged by:

Fred. Olsen Travel, Olsen House, White House Road, Ipswich, Suffolk IP1 5LL. T:01473 292222. Operates an attractive worldwide choice of cruises including Mississippi, Caribbean, Hawaii, Norwegian Fjords, Mediterranean and Canary Islands. Prices range from £345 for a 3-night Mississippi cruise to £5,645 for a 30-night Caribbean cruise from the UK.

Norwegian Cruise Line, Brook House, 229-243 Shepherd's Bush Road, London W6 7NL. T:0171 408 0046. Fly-cruise and stay holidays in the Caribbean. Eight days from £1,200; also Alaskan cruises with hotel stay, 9 nights, from £1,445.

P & O Cruises, 77 New Oxford Street, London WC1A 1PP. T:0171 800 2345. P & O has three separate cruising programmes:

P & O Cruises (T:0171 800 2222) offer a wide range of destinations including two Round World Cruises, the Mediterranean, Atlantic Isles, Scandinavia and the Caribbean;

Princess Cruises (T:0171 800 2468) has nine ships cruising to Alaska, the Far East and Australia, the Caribbean, Panama Canal, Mexico, South America, Hawaii and the South Pacific, New England, the Mediterranean and Scandinavia;

Swan Hellenic Cruises (T:0171 800 2300) runs East and West Mediterranean, Red Sea and Black Sea cruises for lovers of art and archaeology; also Nile, Rhine and bulbfield cruises.

Page and Moy Cruise Ltd., PO Box 155, Leicester LE1 9GZ. T:0116 251 3377. Choosing the cruise most likely to offer what you want no longer entails elaborate detective work thanks to a comprehensive *Weekly Cruise Hot List* published by travel agents Page and Moy. Discounts are offered on every booking and there are also many exclusive special offers. Cruise specialists are available seven days a week to give assistance.

Motoring holidays abroad

A number of organisations – for example, the AA and some ferry operators – offer 'packages' for the motorist which include ferry crossings, accommodation and insurance. While these often provide very good value, some people prefer to make all their own arrangements in order to give them exactly what they want. Whatever your preference, if a main concern is carefree motoring, maybe one of the options suggested below could provide a happy solution.

Automobile Association, PO Box 128, Copenhagen Court, New Street, Basingstoke RG21 1DT. T:01256 493878. The AA's shops, located in many large towns throughout the UK, will be pleased to arrange a continental motoring holiday tailored to suit your requirements. A package can include some or all of the following: ferry bookings, AA Five Star service plus accommodation in holiday centres or hotels. Prices vary enormously according to time of the year and how luxuriously you want to stay. Alternatively, instead of fixed bookings, you can go-as-you-please using the AA's Driveaway France and Europe service to help discover typically regional hotels that are recommended for their food and hospitality. For further details, ask at your nearest AA shop or telephone the above number.

Brittany Ferries (through all good travel agencies). Brittany offer short-break holidays in France and Spain linked to their own ferries. The choice includes: four nights' bed and breakfast in Rouen from £110, inclusive of ferry return by car; seven-night à la carte tour of the Loire Valley in two- or three-star hotels including bed and breakfast and ferry crossing, from £240; nine-day tour of Spain staying in Spanish paradors (good hotels) from £386. Prices quoted are for 1995.

RAC Travel Services, RAC House, Brighton Road, South Croydon, Surrey CR2 6XW. As well as providing a range of travel insurances for motorists holidaying in Europe, the RAC also offers a route planning service and can supply maps and guides plus international driving permits, camping cards and other essential documents. For a copy of the travel services' brochure, call free on 0800 765711.

Tips when motoring abroad. All basic common-sense but, given the tales of woe one hears, many holiday-makers forget the obvious precautions:

- have your car thoroughly serviced before you go;
- take the following with you: a tool kit, manual for your car, a rented spares kit, a gallon can, a mechanic's light which plugs into the cigarette lighter socket and at least one extra set of keys;
- always lock your car and park it in a secure place overnight (nearly 75 per cent of luggage thefts abroad are from cars).

Unless you are taking one of the packages which include insurance, you should contact your insurance company or broker well ahead of time to arrange special insurance cover. ABI leaflet *Holiday Insurance and Motoring Abroad* summarises the essentials you need to know when taking your car overseas. Obtainable free from the **Association of British Insurers**, 51 Gresham Street, London EC2V 7HQ. A further possibility is to contact either the AA or RAC overseas travel department. Both have facilities for helping you if you become stranded and welcome non-members.

Another well-recommended organisation is **Europ Assistance**, Sussex House, Perrymount Road, Haywards Heath, West Sussex RH16 1DN. T:01444 442211.

Advice from seasoned travellers is to have information about garages, spare parts and the legal rules of the country through which you are driving.

If your main purpose in taking your car is to enjoy the freedom it offers when you reach your destination, rather than the journey itself, it is worth looking at the Motorail facilities to Southern France and Italy and the long-range ferries to Spain and Portugal which save on wear and tear and may be no more expensive than the extra cost of petrol plus overnight stays.

If instead of taking your own car, you plan to hire a car or motor scooter overseas, you will probably have to buy special insurance at time of hiring the vehicle. Make sure that this is properly comprehensive and that at very least it gives you adequate third party cover. If in any doubt, you would be recommended to seek advice from the local motoring organisation as to the essential requirements – including any foreign words or terms you particularly need to understand before signing.

Short breaks

A very large number of organisations offer short break holidays all year round with special bargain prices in spring, autumn and summer. Many British hotels have winter breaks from November to April when full board can be considerably cheaper than the normal rates. Likewise, many overseas travel operators slash prices during the off-peak seasons. While the brochures contain plenty of suggestions, including some glorious city breaks, for very best value (and often all the more fun for being unplanned) see the newspapers for last minute bargains.

Timesharing

Timesharing is an investment in long-term holiday accommodation and, as with other investments, should not be undertaken lightly. The idea is that you buy the use of a property for a week or longer, either for an agreed term or in perpetuity. Your timeshare can be lent to other people, sub-let or left eventually in your will. Most timeshare schemes allow you to swap your property for one in other developments throughout the world for your annual holiday.

A week's timeshare will cost from under £3,000 to more than £15,000 depending on the location, the size of the property, the time of year and the facilities of the resort. The average is around £6,500 for one bedroom (peak season). Maintenance charges could cost another £170 or so a week and you should always check that these are linked to some form of cost of living index such as the RPI and ascertain – item by item – precisely what the charges cover. Another useful point to check is that there is an owners' association linked to the property.

While the great majority of people enjoy very happy experiences, stories about unscrupulous operators still occur. You should be on your guard against dubious selling practices which, despite efforts by the European Timeshare Federation, have not been entirely stamped out. In particular, you should beware invitations to collect glittering prizes and likewise avoid the lure of enticing promotional gifts such as a 'free' holiday flight to visit the property (it may end up costing you more than a normal package to the same destination). Above all, do not be stampeded into signing any commitment – even if described as an option – until you have had the validity of all aspects of a proposed contract thoroughly checked by a solicitor.

Thanks to the 1992 Timeshare Act buyers now have 14 days 'cooling off' period after signing a contract. This only applies, however, to contracts signed in the UK (there is also a 14-day cooling-off period for contracts signed in Portugal/Madeira), with no protection at present for the many UK buyers signing a contract outside these areas. The situation is due to improve. In accordance with the 1994 Timeshare Directive, all EU member countries will need to enact legislation to provide for a 10-day cooling-off period; the final deadline for this is April 1997.

Among the points you need to be specially careful about are the future management/maintenance charges (these have been known to sky-rocket within a year or so of purchase) and the potential resale value of a property which sometimes has been found to be very substantially below the initial purchase price. Also timeshare owners in Spain could be liable for a property tax.

Although you cannot be too careful, there are hopeful signs that the industry is tightening itself up by the imposition of more self-regulation and stricter vetting procedures.

The Timeshare Council (TTC) is the regulatory body dedicated to promoting the interests of all with a legitimate involvement in the industry. It offers potential buyers free advice and information. Contact **The Timeshare Council**, 23 Buckingham Gate, London SW1E 6LB. T:0171 821 8845 (please enclose sae).

Most reputable companies also belong to one of two world-wide exchange organisations:

RCI Europe Ltd., Kettering Parkway, Kettering, Northants NN15 6EY. T:01536 310111. Membership of RCI (£94 for 2 years) gives access to more than 2,900 holiday resorts in over 80 countries. Their travel club can book flights, insurance and car hire and also offers a special programme of short breaks and cruises.

Interval International Ltd., Spring Gardens, 4 Citadel Place, Tinworth Street, London SE11 5EG. T:0171 820 1515.

Your Place in the Sun is a checklist for those considering purchasing a timeshare, issued by the Department of Trade and Industry and available free from Room 415, 10-18 Victoria Street, London SW1H 0NN; also obtainable by telephoning 0171 215 3344.

Existing owners wishing to sell their property should be on their guard against unknown resale agents contacting them 'on spec' and offering, in exchange for a registration fee, to act on their behalf. While some may be legitimate, The Timeshare Council has received complaints about so-called 'agents' taking money and doing nothing further. A telephone call to the TTC will establish whether the company is a member body. If not, leave well alone. If you are actually seeking an agent, the TTC can provide you with a list of reputable resale companies (please enclose sae).

Retreats

Some people want to have no more than peace and quiet for a few days. If you would welcome the idea of a retreat you might like to contact:

The National Retreat Association, Liddon House, 24 South Audley Street, London W1Y 5DL. T:0171 493 3534. The NRA's annual journal *The Vision* gives details of 200 retreat houses in Britain and Ireland, together with their programmes.

Another publication listing more than 300 retreats in the UK, Ireland, France and Spain is *The Good Retreat Guide* by Stafford Whiteaker (Rider, £12.99).

Self-catering and other low-budget holidays

If you cannot quite manage to survive on a tenner a day, some of the suggestions in this section need hardly cost you very much more. This applies especially if you are camping, caravanning or renting very simple accommodation with friends. The list includes: farm cottages, hostels, university accommodation, forest cabins and other rentals of varying degrees of sparseness or comfort. There are also one or two hotels that offer specially attractive rates.

British Universities Accommodation Consortium, Box 1240, University Park, Nottingham NG7 2RD. T:0115 950 4571. Contact: Carole Formon, General Secretary. Over 60 universities provide bed and breakfast and self-catering accommodation during the student vacations for individuals, families and groups. Some provide facilities throughout the whole year and many also offer study and activity breaks. BUAC publishes a brochure describing the facilities in detail, together with tariffs and booking dates.

Camping & Caravanning Club, Greenfields House, Westwood Way, Coventry CV4 8JH. T:01203 694995. Members may use the network of around 80 full facility club sites all over Britain, as well as enjoy access to nearly 5,000 other sites. These are listed in the annual *Your Place in the Country* and in the *Big Sites Book* which are sent to all members along with an Ordnance Survey map and free copies of the monthly magazine *Camping and Caravanning*. The Club also offers insurance, special terms for membership of the Royal Automobile Club (RAC) and a full foreign touring service including reservations on continental sites. Senior citizen members pay reduced site fees on club sites. Membership costs £25 plus £4 joining fee.

CampusHotels, PO Box 808, Edinburgh EH14 4AS. T:0131 449 4034. The Scottish Universities Accommodation Consortium which is marketed under the name of CampusHotels provides holiday letting in Scotland's eight universities. Between them, they offer 10,500 beds in: Aberdeen, Dundee, Edinburgh, Glasgow, Heriot-Watt, St. Andrews, Stirling and Strathclyde. Average cost of bed and breakfast is about £20 a night.

Connect, 36 Collegiate Crescent, Sheffield S10 2BP. T:0114 268 3759. Connect is a network of 80 universities and colleges that let residential accommodation in the vacation periods. A few let rooms throughout the year and some have self-catering flats. Group facilities can also be provided. Charges start from about £10 for bed and breakfast; £40 per person, per week for a self-catering apartment. A free holiday brochure, giving full details, is sent to all enquirers.

The English Tourist Board publishes a selection of *Freedom* guides featuring a wide range of caravan parks around Britain, all of which have been inspected and quality graded. Available free from: **Caravan Holiday Home Campaign**, Dept. 855, PO Box 26, Lowestoft NR32 3LM.

English Country Cottages Ltd., Grove Farm Barns, Fakenham, Norfolk NR21 9NB. T:01328 864041 (brochures). T:01328 851155 (bookings – all UK).

Welsh Country Cottages. T:01328 851341 (brochures).

Country Cottages in Scotland. T:01328 864011 (brochures).

The 'cottages' range enormously in size, style and location and are variously capable of sleeping between 2 and 25. Many are available for long or short breaks all year round, with low out-of-season prices from September to May. Apply for the free brochure which gives full details and photographs of all properties.

Farm Holiday Bureau UK Ltd., National Agricultural Centre, Stoneleigh Park, Warwickshire CV8 2LZ. T:01203 696909. Many farms take paying guests, let holiday cottages or run sites for tents or caravans. Farm Holiday Bureau members offer a range of high quality accommodation, all Tourist Board inspected, plus a glimpse of life on a farm. The Farm Holiday Bureau Guide *Stay on a Farm* contains information on over 1,000 good value farm holidays all over Great Britain and Northern Ireland. Bed and breakfast facilities are normally from about £12 upwards. Many farms provide an evening meal, if required. Self-catering cottages start at around £100. The Guide is available from bookshops, Tourist Information Centres and from the Farm Holiday Bureau, £5.95.

Forestry Commission, 231 Corstorphine Road, Edinburgh EH12 7AT. T:0131 334 0303/2576. The Forestry Commission lets fully equipped log cabins and holiday houses in Scotland, Cumbria, Yorkshire and Cornwall. These all sleep from five or six people and cost from about £125 a week per cabin in low season. The Commission also runs 29 camp and caravan sites throughout Britain.

Gites de France Ltd., 178 Piccadilly, London W1V 9DB. T:0171 493 3480. Gites de France are privately owned properties in France which have been modernised with the help of government grants and are supervised by the National Federation of Gites. A gite may be a small cottage, a flat in a farm house or manor, or a restored barn. Most are 'off the beaten track'. Details are given in the annual *Gites de France Handbook* available from the above address. All gites holidays are offered on an inclusive gite-plus-ferry-crossing basis, but if you prefer you can make your own travel arrangements.

Hilton National, PO Box 137, Millbuck House, Clarendon Road, Watford, Herts WD1 1DN. T:01923 246464. Hilton National arranges weekend breaks at over 20 hotels throughout Britain. There are numerous Special Interest Weekends organised around a variety of subjects, including: gardening, antiques, wine appreciation, history, health and beauty, bridge, walking and needlecraft. Prices, which include full board, start at around £130 per person.

Hoseasons Holidays Abroad, Sunway House, Lowestoft, Suffolk NR32 2LW. T:01502 500555. Hoseasons offer self-catering holidays in villas, gites and cottages throughout France and Spain. There is also a good choice of accommodation in purpose-built holiday villages, providing a wide range of entertainments and leisure activities, in Holland, Germany and Belgium. Prices vary widely, depending on number of people and time of the year, but average costs for family parties of four to six are from £100 per person a week including ferry crossings.

Hoseasons also have holiday homes in Britain which are listed in their *Hoseasons Holiday Homes* brochure each year. For information, ring: 01502 500500.

Landmark Trust, Shottesbrooke, Maidenhead, Berkshire SL6 3SW. T:01628 825925. The Trust owns buildings of special architectural interest all over Britain, which out of peak season can be rented for less than a week. Sample prices are: £390 per week for a four-bed mill in Derbyshire, during April; £628 per week for a six-bed castle in Wales, in May or October; £35 per person, per night, for a fisherman's cottage on Lundy Island between January and March. The Trust has a 150-page Handbook which is fully illustrated and contains room plans and location maps, price £8.50 (refundable against your next booking) from the above address.

Lee Abbey, Lynton, North Devon EX35 6JJ. T:01598 752621. Lee Abbey is a holiday and conference centre, run by a Christian community. Set in a 275-acre coastal estate, accommodation is either in the house or in self-catering units. Depending on the time of the year, visitors can stay for either a short break weekend or up to a fortnight. There is a Christian content to the holidays and guests can be involved as much or as little as they please. Costs vary according to season: a week in the summer is from about £200 full board. There are reductions for clergy and their families.

M P Associates, 262a Wellingborough Road, Northampton NN1 4EJ. T:01604 230505. Specialises in low-cost, long winter holidays (three or four months) in Spain, Portugal and Tenerife. Accommodation varies from one-bed apartments to four-bed villas. Rents are reasonably nominal but in exchange visitors are expected to maintain the properties as they would their own homes. For further details, send large sae (47p).

National Trust Holiday Cottages. The National Trust has a wide variety of holiday cottages and flats in many areas of England, Wales and Northern Ireland with varying accommodation for 2 to 10 people. Although heavily booked in the high holiday seasons, there are usually plenty of vacancies at other times of year and enquiries from older people are welcomed. A brochure, including information as to suitability for people with disabilities, is available from major National Trust Shops or by writing to PO Box 536, National Trust Enterprises, Melksham, Wilts SN12 8SX. Please enclose £1 to cover p&p costs.

For cottages in Scotland and free copy of *Information About Trust Properties for Disabled Visitors*, contact the National Trust for Scotland, 5 Charlotte Square, Edinburgh EH2 4DU.

Scottish Farmhouse Holidays, 51 Drumtenant, Ladybank, Fife KY15 7UG. T:01337 830451. Over 100 farms and crofts in all areas of Scotland which take guests for two nights or longer. The cost is from £20 per night for dinner, bed and breakfast or from £14 per night bed and breakfast. SFH can offer holiday insurance cover, car rental and ferry crossings. Free brochure available.

Vacances en Campagne, Bignor, Near Pulborough, West Sussex RH20 1QD. T:01798 869411. Vacances en Campagne specialise in letting country houses in rural areas of France and Corsica. Properties vary widely in size, amenities and price: from £135 a week for a studio flat to over £1,000 for a four-bedroomed house or chateau with a swimming pool at the height of the summer, sleeping eight to ten. Competitive ferry prices. Also motorail and fly/drive facilities.

Vacanze in Italia, Bignor, Near Pulborough, West Sussex RH20 1QD. T:01798 869421. Farmhouses, villas and apartments in Umbria, Apulia, Florence, Tuscany, Lake Garda, Argentario, Sicily and Amalfi coast. All comfortably furnished, some with swimming pool. Rentals from £150 a week. Full flight and travel facilities if required.

Youth Hostels Association, Trevelyan House, 8 St. Stephen's Hill, St. Albans, Herts AL1 2DY. T:01727 855215. **Scottish YHA**, 7 Glebe Crescent, Stirling FK8 2JA. T:01786 51181. Despite the name, YHA hostels welcome people of all ages. Membership is £9 a year or £120 for life membership. This gives you access to 240 hostels in England and Wales and over 5,000 more throughout the world.

Hostels are simple and inexpensive; but also clean, tidy and comfortable. Beds are usually in single-sex dormitories with communal washrooms. Most have a lounge and many have recreational facilities and a shop. Most provide meals and also self-catering facilities. Overnight charges vary according to the facilities and location of hostel: prices range from £5.35 to £12.42, excluding breakfast. The *YHA Accommodation Guide* describes the hostels in England and Wales (£2.99). Membership of the Scottish YHA gives you the same access to hostels.

P.S. Watch the Sunday newspapers. From about early January, the classified section begins to fill up with advertisements for rentals both in this country and overseas. Later in the season, this is the column to watch for slashed prices and other last minute bargains.

A useful book describing modestly priced accommodation in pleasant places is *Staying off the Beaten Track* by Elizabeth Gundrey (Arrow, price £8.99).

Special interest

This is the longest section – and a real mixed bag. It includes weekend courses and more formal summer schools, between them offering a huge range of subjects including: pottery, cooking, computer studies, drama, video techniques, wildlife, creative writing and many others. It also includes holidays in the more conventional sense, both in Britain and abroad, but with the accent on a hobby such as: bridge, folk dancing, photography, antiques, public speaking, model making and other pastimes. There are one or two pre-retirement courses included in the holiday programme. They are impossible to categorise other than alphabetically because many of the organisations offer a veritable bran-tub of choices.

Centre for Alternative Technology, Machynlleth, Powys, Wales SY20 9AZ. T:01654 702400. Set in magnificent scenery in the mountains of Mid-Wales, the Centre is a working exhibition of the possibilities of alternative technology with displays of wind, solar and water power, organic gardens and high-insulation houses. The Centre is open daily to the public throughout the year. Short residential courses are held frequently, ranging from two to five days, and subjects covered include renewable energy systems, organic gardening, vegetarian cookery, crafts and many others. Accommodation is in simple but comfortable two- to six-person bedrooms; there are also a few single rooms. Fees range from £80 to around £250, including full board and all tuition fees. Pensioners and those on low incomes pay a reduced rate.

Opportunities also exist for voluntary work. For a week or fortnight volunteers live and work as members of staff, helping with all the tasks of running a busy, experimental visitor centre. Volunteers pay about £4 a day towards bed and board.

Countrywide Holidays, Birch Heys, Cromwell Range, Manchester M14 6HU. T:0161 225 1000. Countrywide Holidays aims to provide warm hospitality, comfortable accommodation and sensible prices for holidays throughout the year. Many include walking or offer other activities, such as: folk dancing, bridge, photography, literature, singing and many more. The cost varies from about £195 per week in winter to £240 in summer including full board. There are special Vintage Holidays for people who enjoy more gentle walking and excursions, as well as traditional house parties over Christmas and New Year costing from £235 for five nights at Christmas and from £185 for four nights over the New Year.

Denman College (National Federation of Women's Institutes), Marcham, Abingdon, Oxfordshire OX13 6NW. T:01865 391991. Denman College is the WI's residential adult education college. It runs over 600 courses for WI members, their husbands and friends each year. These take place during the week and over weekends and cost about £56 a day including full board and tuition. Over half the accommodation is in single rooms. Courses cover such subjects as: antiques, art, the countryside, dance, drama and the theatre, food and wine, gardening, social history, literature, public speaking and many others.

Earnley Concourse, Earnley, Chichester, Sussex P020 7JL. T:01243 670392. A residential centre near Chichester which holds weekend and week-long courses throughout the year on such subjects as: arts and crafts, music, drama, wildlife, computer studies, cookery, keep fit, yoga and others. Charges are from £140 for a weekend.

HF Holidays Ltd., Imperial House, Edgware Road, London NW9 5AL. T:0181 905 9556; for brochures, T:0181 905 9388. HF Holidays offers walking and special interest holidays in a wide range of locations throughout Britain and abroad. The choice of activities includes, among others: golf, bridge, bowls, ballroom dancing, yoga, egg decorating, painting, photography, music making, birdwatching and British Heritage. There are also discovery coach tours and holidays, with gentle rambles and excursions, for those who want a more leisurely break. Prices start from £249 full board. The walking holidays range from easy walking to rock scrambling. A week's walking in Dorset costs from £261 full board. A week in Austria costs from £439 half-board. Other overseas destinations include: France, Switzerland, Italy, Canada, USA and New Zealand.

Holiday Club Pontin's, PO Box 100, Sagar House, The Green, Eccleston, Chorley, Lancs PR7 5QQ. T:01257 452452. Organise Hobby Holidays at the majority of their locations. These include such activities as: darts, snooker, bridge, bowling, model making, music, dancing and retirement planning. Average 1995 prices (which varied according to date, location and activity), for full board, were £200 including VAT per person per week.

Millfield School Village of Education, Street, Somerset BA16 0YD. T:01458 445823. The Village of Education operates during August, offering over 300 courses including: painting, pottery, bridge, tennis and other sports. Prices for board, lodging and tuition are from £220 a week. There is a 5 per cent reduction for senior citizens and previous visitors.

National Institute of Adult Continuing Education (NIACE), 21 De Montfort Street, Leicester LE1 7GE. T:0116 255 1451. Special interest weekend and summer school courses are offered by many colleges and universities throughout the country. Choice of subjects is enormous ranging from yoga to astronomy, creative writing to video techniques. Prices vary very roughly from about £25 to £35 a night, including full board and tuition. Probably the easiest way to find out what is available is to obtain a copy of *Time to Learn*, published twice a year by NIACE. Price £4.25 including p&p.

Old Rectory, Fittleworth, Pulborough, West Sussex RH20 1HU. T:01798 865306. The programme is tilted at those nearing retirement with the aim of stimulating new interests and opportunities. Typical courses, which last 3 to 7 days, include: painting, crafts, music and singing, bridge, writing, theatre, complementary therapies and many others. Prices start at £105 for a weekend residential course.

Summer Academy, School of Continuing Education, The University, Canterbury, Kent CT2 7NX. T:01227 470402/823473. Offers summer study courses at British and Irish universities. Prices range from £340 to £390 and cover full board for six/ seven nights, tuition fees and course-related excursions. Study topics include: heritage, the arts, the countryside and personal development. Accommodation is in single rooms in university halls of residence.

Vegi-Ventures, Castle Cottage, Castle Square, Castle Acre, Norfolk PE32 2AJ. T:01760 755888. A holiday tour company that specialises in catering for vegetarians, offering an attractive range of destinations in Britain, Europe and wider afield. Accommodation is chosen very much with the food in mind and is variously in hotels, special guest houses and villas with own cook. A flavour of 1995 holidays includes: house parties (three nights, from £135); a week's walking and sightseeing in the Lake District including half board and guided walks (seven nights, £225); three weeks 'journey of a lifetime' in Peru with tour guide and half board (£1,295). Flights are willingly arranged but are not included in prices quoted above.

Workers' Educational Association, Temple House, 17 Victoria Park Square, Bethnal Green, London E2 9PB. T:0181 983 1515. The WEA runs weekend schools and residential summer schools or study tours at home and abroad. Participants can include all ages from 18 to over 80. Subjects cover a very wide range including: local history, literature, music appreciation, natural history and others. There are cultural visits to various parts of Europe. Facilities for people with disabilities are available at some of the summer schools in this country.

Useful reading
Activity Holidays 96, published in association with the English Tourist Board, £4.95 from all good bookshops.

Sport

Holidays with on-site or nearby sporting facilities exist all over the country. However, if sport is the main objective of the holiday, it is often more difficult to know where to apply. The list that follows is limited to organisations that can advise you about organised residential courses or can offer facilities, rather than simply put you in touch with, say, your nearest tennis club. For wider information, see Chapter 9, Leisure Activities, which lists some of the many national sports associations.

Scottish Sports Council, Caledonia House, South Gyle, Edinburgh EH12 9DQ. T:0131 317 7200. The Council runs three national sports centres which offer courses for all levels in sports such as golf, hill-walking, skiing and sailing. Contact the above address for further information and free *Activity* newsletter.

YMCA National Centre, Lakeside, Ulverston, Cumbria LA12 8BD. T:015395 31758. Despite the youth connotation, the YMCA runs Adventure Holidays suitable for all ages including a special programme entitled '50-plus Activity'. Choice of activities includes, among many others: rock climbing, canoeing, orienteering, archery, country crafts and fell walking. There are also excursions to places of interest as well as talks and films in the evening.

The Centre is in a superb setting on Lake Windermere. The accommodation is in twin bedded or single rooms with toilet and shower en suite. Cost for four nights inclusive of full board and programme is about £175.

Boating

One or two ideas for holidays afloat are included as well as organisations that offer serious sailing instruction.

Royal Yachting Association, RYA House, Romsey Road, Eastleigh, Hants SO50 9YA. T:01703 627400. The RYA can supply you with a list of recognised sailing and windsurfing schools which offer approved courses.

Blakes Holidays Ltd., Wroxham, Norwich NR12 8DH. T:01603 782141. Reservations: 01603 782911. Blakes hire out yachts, cruisers, houseboats and cottages for holidays in various parts of Britain, Ireland and France. Basic boating tuition is provided for novices. Costs vary according to season, size and type of accommodation. For example, a weekend boating on the Broads during the spring and autumn months costs around £180 a couple. Boats for two to four people in France start at about £400 a week. Pets are normally allowed on British holidays. For holidays abroad, Blakes will quote an inclusive price with travel arrangements.

French Government Tourist Office, 178 Piccadilly, London W1V 0AL. T:0891 244123. Can provide information about houseboats and other craft for hire in France.

Hoseasons Boating Holidays, Sunway House, Lowestoft, Suffolk NR32 2LW. T:01502 501010 (UK holidays); 01502 500555 (overseas boating holidays). Hoseasons arrange boating holidays on the Norfolk Broads, the canals, the Thames and in Scotland as well as holidays in France and Holland. There are holidays at lower prices in April and September and special reductions if you start mid-week. Ferry-inclusive package to Holland, based on a party of four, costs from £155 to £260 per person, depending on season.

Cycling

Cycling for Softies, Susi Madron's Cycling Holidays Ltd., 2 & 4 Birch Polygon, Rusholme, Manchester M14 5HX. T:0161 248 8282. Offers over 50 holiday options in nine regions of France from 7 to 14 nights, cycling between a network of small country hotels, with terrain varying from very easy to quite a few hills. The cost (£450-£915) includes: ferry or air fares, transfer to hotel, dinner, bed and breakfast, bicycles, equipment and information packs.

Cyclists' Touring Club, Cotterell House, 69 Meadrow, Godalming, Surrey GU7 3HS. T:01483 417217. The CTC organises cycling tours in Britain and overseas and can also provide a great deal of extremely helpful information for cyclists wishing to organise their own holiday, including advice on accommodation and scenic routes. Organised UK cycle tours cost about £150 a week with hostel accommodation or £300 a week bed and breakfast with evening meal. Overseas tours vary from about £250 for a fortnight's camping in Southern France to about £1,000 for three weeks in South Africa. The CTC also offers members: free third-party insurance, free legal aid, a handbook and introductions to local cycling groups. Membership costs £25 a year; £16.50 for retired people.

Just Pedalling Cycling Holidays, 9 Church Street, Coltishall, Norfolk NR12 7DW. T:01603 737201. If you can ride a bike and are reasonably healthy, you can take a cycling holiday at your own pace. Just Pedalling arranges tours including bed and breakfast accommodation, a multigear hybrid bike with puncture-proof tyres, maps and a free river trip in the summer. The cost is about £140-£150 a week depending on season.

Windmill Ways, 50 Bircham Road, Reepham, Norfolk NR10 4NQ. T:01603 871111. Offers both standard and individually tailored cycling and walking holidays in Norfolk. Itineraries are planned according to how far you want to go each day and the particular places of interest you would like to visit. Baggage is transported and for the less energetic a car can drive you to your next stop. Cost is inclusive of accommodation, full English breakfast, maps, information pack and cycles. Average prices for seven nights are: cycling, £346.50; walking, £276.50.

British Rail. Cycles are normally allowed on trains, although some have strict limits as to the number they will accept especially during rush hours when they may be completely prohibited. On most services, advance registration is required with a charge payable. Around South-East England cycles are still generally carried free. Leaflets giving full details are available at railway stations.

Golf

Many clubs will allow non-members to play on weekdays when the course is less busy, on payment of a green fee. (A telephone call to the Secretary before arrival is normally advisable.) Better still, if you can spare the time, many hotels around the country offer special golfing weekends and short-break holidays. If you fancy a golfing holiday overseas, both **BA Holidays** (T:01293 723131) and **Thomson Holidays** (T:0171 707 9000) offer a wide choice, with favourite destinations including Florida, Spain and the Algarve in Portugal. The travel ads in newspapers and golfing magazines should also give you plenty of ideas. See also the Tourist Board activity booklets.

Rambling

Rambling features on many special interest and other programmes as one of the options on offer. Three organisations that specialise in rambling holidays are described below.

Alternative Travel Group Ltd., 69-71 Banbury Road, Oxford OX2 6PE. T:01865 310244. Forget staying in cheap hostels and lugging around a rucksack with all your possessions for a week. Rambling Alternative Travel style means staying in the most comfortable hotels in the area, having your luggage transported and enjoying the option of a ride on days when you feel like taking it easy. The emphasis is on visiting places of historical or artistic interest, exploring the scenic highlights and dining out on the best local cuisine.

Groups are limited to a maximum of 16 and most holidays last between 8 and 11 days, with Italy a favourite destination. Other choices include France, Sicily, Portugal and Spain.

Prices are not cheap and in 1995, exclusive of flight, mostly ranged from £975 to £1,245 (with longer-stay trips in Camino de Santiago and Path to Rome, more expensive). There are also tailor-made walking and cycling holidays for those who prefer to travel more independently yet who welcome the services of a local representative including having their luggage transported.

Ramblers Holidays Ltd., PO Box 43, Welwyn Garden, Herts AL8 6PQ. T:01707 331133. Ramblers Holidays, in conjunction with the Ramblers' Association, organise guided walking tours at home and abroad, ranging in choice from just four or five hours a day relatively gentle exercise to maybe nine hours a day hard mountain trekking. Some trips focus on a special interest such as bird-watching or flowers or make a particular feature of visiting places of cultural interest. There is a huge choice of destinations including New Zealand, North America, China, the Far East and most of Europe. Prices start from £200 for a week in Britain inclusive of all meals and VAT; and from about £340 for a week in Europe including flights and half board.

Waymark Holidays, 44 Windsor Road, Slough SL1 2EJ. T:01753 516477. Choice of walking holidays throughout the year, graded to your level, from about four hours a day in: Europe, North and South America, Asia and Africa. Accommodation in hotels and guesthouses. Cost for half board is from about £350 for seven nights, depending on the country and time of year. Cross-country skiing holidays are also offered during the winter.

Skiing

Ski Club of Great Britain, 118 Eaton Square, London SW1W 9AF. T:0171 245 1033. The Ski Club runs skiing holidays in Austria, France, Switzerland and the USA for over-50s who have some basic skiing experience. The cost is from about £650 a week for half board, travel and a qualified leader who accompanies each group and will ski with you and offer advice, if wanted. Two weeks are also available.

A disability, including blindness or even an amputated leg need no longer be a bar to skiing, thanks to the availability of special equipment and the efforts of two charities who have specially trained guides to assist. For further information, contact **British Ski Club for the Disabled**, Springmount, Berwick St. John, Shaftesbury, Dorset SP7 0HQ. T:01747 828515; and the **Uphill Ski Club**, 12 Park Crescent, London W1N 4EQ. T:0171 636 1989.

Many artificial slopes in England and Wales have reserved sessions with specialist instructors for people with disabilities. A list can be obtained from the British Ski Club for the Disabled.

Tennis

The Lawn Tennis Association, The Queen's Club, West Kensington, London W14 9EG. T:0171 381 7000. The LTA Information Department can supply details of residential courses at home and abroad.

For **other sporting holidays** see 'Tourist Boards' (page 394). Their publications list scores of suggestions for golfing, sailing and fishing holidays, pony trekking in Wales, skiing in Scotland and many others.

Wine tasting

Wine-tasting holidays are becoming more popular every year. The best guided tours ensure plenty of variety with a mix of visits, talks, convivial meals, free time for exploring and memorable tastings.

Arblaster & Clarke Wine Tours, Clarke House, Farnham Road, West Liss, Nr Petersfield, Hants GU33 6JQ. T:01730 893344. Operates tours to France, Spain, Portugal, Italy, California, Australia and South Africa. Most of the chosen regions are places of interest in their own right, famous for their historic buildings or picturesque scenery. Guides accompany every tour and though groups can be as large as 36, every effort is made to give personal attention and to create a friendly, informal atmosphere. A flavour of 1995 visits included: Aix-en-Provence (four days during festival, £699); Verona (three days including opera evening, £669); plus a variety of barge-and-wine holidays. Supplementary charge for single rooms.

Wine Journeys, 69-71 Banbury Road, Oxford OX2 6PE. T:01865 310244. Wine Journeys, part of the Alternative Travel Group, offers a range of wine tours in France and Italy, variously lasting from five to eight days. All are limited to a maximum of 16 bookings and are led by wine experts, most of whom are Masters of Wine. Prices start from £695.

Working holidays

There is scope for volunteers who would like to engage in a worthwhile project during their holidays. Activities vary from, for example, helping run play schemes to conservation work. In order to avoid repetition, only a couple of suggestions are listed here. For more information and ideas, see Chapter 12, Voluntary Work.

BTCV (British Trust for Conservation Volunteers), 36 St. Mary's Street, Wallingford, Oxfordshire OX10 0EU. T:01491 839766. Anyone, from 16 to 75, who would like a working holiday can become a conservation volunteer. BTCV organises over 600 Natural Break holidays each year throughout England, Wales and Northern Ireland. Projects usually last a week and the work can vary from creating wildlife habitats and nature gardens to improving access to the countryside. No experience is necessary, only plenty of enthusiasm plus reasonable fitness. From around £28 a week including food and accommodation you can enjoy good company, fresh air and beautiful countryside. International conservation working holidays are also available. Membership costs £12; £6 for retired people.

Scottish Conservation Projects Trust, Balallan House, 24 Allan Park, Stirling FK8 2QG. T:01786 479697. SCP offers training in conservation skills and opportunities to work as a conservation volunteer, when and where you want, for as much or as little time as you can spare. There are 7- to 14-day conservation projects called 'Action Breaks' as well as weekend and single-day events. Type of work varies from conservation proper – drystone dyking, fencing, foot path conservation, historic building restoration and habitat management – to jobs such as office skills, cooking and driving. Cost of Action Breaks is £4 a day, plus your fare. All participants are required to join the Trust which gives them access to Action Breaks and courses elsewhere in the UK. Annual subscription is £15; £8 for pensioners.

TOC H, 1 Forest Close, Wendover, Aylesbury, Bucks HP22 6BT. T:01296 623911. TOC H organises short residential projects throughout the year in Britain and Germany, normally lasting between a weekend and three weeks. Scope for volunteers includes running play schemes, activities with disabled people, conservation and manual work. There is a £5 registration fee; accommodation and food, however, are usually free. The projects programme, available from the above address, is published in March and September.

Useful reading
Working Holidays. Contains information on thousands of paid and voluntary seasonal opportunities, in 70 countries, for people of all ages. Comprehensive details on each

country cover: entry regulations, work and residence permits, medical insurance and passport requirements plus travel, accommodation and tourist information. Price £8.99 from the **Central Bureau**, Seymour Mews House, Seymour Mews, London W1H 9PE. T:0171 486 5101.

Holidays for singles

Many people would rather not go on holiday if it means travelling alone. Until recently single people, especially women over 50, were virtually ignored by the holiday industry. For a start, tour operators arranging group parties would often impose an age limit with the aim of keeping the sexes roughly in balance. There was (and still is) almost invariably a supplement for single rooms. And worst of all was the prospect of dining alone or of receiving unwanted attentions which could become embarrassing.

Over the past few years however, the outlook has been improving considerably. Many of the 'special interest holidays' listed on pages 383-385 are ideal for those without a partner, as are some of the 'working holidays' – see section above and also in Chapter 12, Voluntary Work. Additionally, one or two organisations are now springing up that cater specifically for solo holiday-makers.

Odyssey International, 21 Cambridge Road, Waterbeach, Cambridge CB5 9NJ. T:01223 861079. Odyssey is a nationwide club, with members aged 17 to 80, which can put you in touch with a like-minded travel companion, whether you are planning a short break or long, either in England or overseas.

You will be sent a brief questionnaire, requesting details of your preferred travel plans, particular interests (and dislikes), age group of companion sought and similar information. There are also a number of organised weekend breaks and other holidays throughout the year which are focused around an activity such as walking trips, cycling or painting. Prices for weekend breaks start at £40. As well as providing an introduction service, Odyssey operates a members' advice line for budgeting and other queries, produces a quarterly newsletter and offers discounted travel insurance. A year's membership subscription is £20.

Travel Companions (UK) Ltd., 110 High Mount, Station Road, London NW4 3ST. T:0181 202 8478. An organisation for individuals aged 25 to 75 seeking a congenial companion with whom to go on holiday. All applicants complete a form listing their special interests, the type of destination they have in mind, as well as other requirements, and Travel Companions will then put them in contact with like-minded people. All personal information is handled in strict confidence. Travel Companions emphasises that it is not a dating service and makes the point that people often prefer to travel with someone of their own sex. Cost is £40, entitling you to at least three introductions a year from the time you join. Should none of these result in a holiday in that year, your fee covers you for a further period.

Travelmate, 52 York Place, Bournemouth BH7 6JN. T:01202 431520. Travelmate is an introduction service for travellers. Members seeking a holiday companion are sent a list of possible individuals, who approximately fit their requirements according to age, sex and planned destination. A minimum of six introductions is guaranteed, although with a membership of around 2,000, Travelmate assured us that most applicants received far in excess of this number. The organisation takes no responsibility for screening members but is happy to offer advice as to the kind of questions that should be explored before any commitment is made. Annual membership costs £35.

Women's Travel Advisory Bureau, Lansdowne, High Street, Blockley, Glos GL56 9HF. T:01386 701082. A travel information service focused on, and for, women. Among other helpful material, there is a travel pack (£6.25) with advice on such essential know-how as assertiveness and staying healthy, together with holiday recommendations and contact addresses. One-day seminars are held in various parts of the country for women thinking of travelling alone or in groups. Charge is £20, including tea/coffee.

Holidays for those needing special care

Over the past few years, facilities for infirm and disabled people have at last been improving. More hotels are providing wheelchairs and other essential equipment. Transport has become easier. Specially designed self-catering units are more plentiful and of a higher standard. As a result of these improvements, many people with disabilities can now travel perfectly normally, stay where they please and participate in the entertainment and sightseeing without disadvantage. This section lists general sources of advice plus one or two organisations that arrange special care holidays.

Travel and other information

If you need help getting on and off a train or plane, inform your travel agent in advance. Arrangements can be made to have staff and, if necessary, a wheelchair available to help you at both departure and arrival points. If you are travelling independently, you should ring the airline and/or local station: explain what assistance you require, together with details of your journey in order that facilities can be arranged at any interim points, for example if you need to change trains.

A useful free leaflet is *British Rail & The Disabled Traveller*, available from mainline stations.

Highly recommended are two very comprehensive books, published by RADAR. Both are annual guides to accommodation and facilities available to disabled holidaymakers: one deals with the UK, the other with travel overseas. *Holidays in the British Isles*, £7; *Holidays and Travel Abroad*, £5. Available from: **Royal Association for Disability and Rehabilitation**, 12 City Forum, 250 City Road, London EC1V 8AF.

Two other helpful books are: *AA Guide for the Disabled Traveller*, £3.99 (free to disabled members at AA shops); and *Door to Door: a Guide to Transport for People with Disabilities*, £3.95, available from Department of Transport office, T:0171 271 5252.

A useful organisation to contact could be: **The Holiday Care Service**, 2 Old Bank Chambers, Station Road, Horley, Surrey RH6 9HW. T:01293 774535; Minicom: 01293 776943. This is a central information and advice service on holiday opportunities in the UK and abroad for elderly and disabled people and their companions. The service is free. Details are available on transport and attractions, together with a range of leaflets (one for each region) listing inspected hotels with accessible accommodation. Holiday insurance advice is offered, as is a reservations service which as well as handling the booking for you can obtain special discounts at many of the UK hotels on their list. The HCS also organises low-cost holidays for people with special needs through the Tourism For All Holidays Scheme.

If rather than simply point you in the right direction you are looking for an agency that can make all the practical arrangements, get on to ATS Travel which specialises in organising tailor-made holidays for people with disabilities. Among other services, they will arrange the journey from door-to-door, book suitable accommodation according to your requirements, organise the provision of special equipment and generally take care of any other details to make your holiday as enjoyable and trouble-free as possible. For further information, contact **ATS Travel**, ATS House, 1 Tank Hill Road, Purfleet, Essex RM16 1SX. T:01708 863198.

Also worth knowing about is **Carefree Holidays**, 64 Florence Road, Northampton NN1 4NA, T:01604 34301. This is a tour operator, offering package holidays (mainly within the UK) that has built up a reputation for the quality of its service in assisting older travellers including people with disabilities.

Many local Age Concern groups are a mine of information. They can often put individuals in touch with organisations that assist with, say, transport; or that organise special care holidays, as do a number of Age Concern branches themselves. Age Concern England also publishes a free factsheet *Holidays for Older People*. See telephone directory for the address of your local group or write to the headquarters enclosing large sae: **Age Concern England**, Astral House, 1268 London Road, London SW16 4ER.

Another source to contact is your local Social Services department. Some local authorities arrange holidays or give financial help to those in real need.

Examples of special holidays
John Grooms Association for Disabled People, 10 Gloucester Drive, London N4 2LP. T:0181 802 7272. Provides a variety of holiday accommodation including two award winning hotels and a number of self-catering flats, bungalows and caravans.

Winged Fellowship Trust, Angel House, 20-32 Pentonville Road, London N1 9XD. T:0171 833 2594. Caters for people who would not otherwise have a holiday because of their physical disability, in purpose-built centres with one-to-one care provided 24 hours a day. There are plenty of activities in which to take part including theatre outings and other excursions. The Trust also organises holidays abroad. Cost is from about £180 per week.

Many voluntary organisations and others provide special holidays for those with a particular disability.

Arthritis Care, 18 Stephenson Way, London NW1 2HD. T:0171 916 1500. Runs five holiday centres and 18 self-catering units adapted for people with arthritis. Holiday centre accommodation available to members costs £80-£185 a week; units £60-£165 depending on the time of year. Specialist holidays include painting weeks, whist, Scrabble and birdwatching. Family weeks are also a feature.

British Diabetic Association, 10 Queen Anne Street, London W1M 0BD. T:0171 323 1531. Advice on holidays is given and foreign travel guides are available for various destinations.

Royal National Institute for the Blind, 224 Great Portland Street, London W1N 6AA. T:0171 388 1266. Has three seaside hotels, specially catering for blind and partially sighted people. Additionally, RNIB can provide advice about suitable hotels, self-catering holidays, accommodation in London, outdoor activity and educational holidays.

Multiple Sclerosis Society of Great Britain & Northern Ireland, 25 Effie Road, London SW6 1EE. T:0171 736 6267. Runs several respite care and holiday homes throughout the UK. Additionally, some local branches have adapted self-catering accommodation for family holidays.

Parkinson's Disease Society, 22 Upper Woburn Place, London WC1H 0RA. T:0171 383 3513.

Stroke Association, CHSA House, Whitecross Street, London EC1Y 8JJ. T:0171 490 7999.

Tourist boards

England's Regional Tourist Boards and the Scottish and Wales Tourist Boards are the main sources of information for all aspects of holidays in their areas. They can advise about: accommodation, transport, highlights to see, special events and festivals, sporting facilities, special interest holidays – in short, almost everything you could possibly want to know. All produce excellent leaflets and guide books.

Scottish Tourist Board, 23 Ravelston Terrace, Edinburgh EH4 3EU. T:0131 332 2433. *Touring Guide to Scotland* (£4.95 incl. p&p). Free brochure: *Scotland: The Main Guide for 1996.* There are also guides to hotels and guest houses, bed and breakfast, self-catering accommodation and camping and caravanning sites.

Wales Tourist Board, Brunel House, 2 Fitzalan Road, Cardiff CF2 1UY. T:01222 499909. *The Wales Holiday Brochure (free).*

Regional Tourist Boards. Addresses of England's 11 regional tourist boards are:

Cumbria Tourist Board, Ashleigh, Holly Road, Windermere, Cumbria LA23 2AQ. T:015394 44444.

East Anglia Tourist Board, Toppesfield Hall, Hadleigh, Suffolk IP7 5DN. T:01473 822922. Covering Cambridgeshire, Essex, Norfolk, Suffolk, Hertfordshire and Bedfordshire.

East Midlands Tourist Board, Exchequergate, Lincoln, LN2 1PZ. T:01522 531521. Covering Derbyshire, Leicestershire, Lincolnshire, Northamptonshire and Nottinghamshire.

Heart of England Tourist Board, Woodside, Larkhill, Worcester WR5 2EQ. T:01905 763436 (24 hours). Covering Gloucestershire, Herefordshire, Shropshire, Staffordshire, Warwickshire, West Midlands and Worcestershire.

London Tourist Board, 26 Grosvenor Gardens, London SW1W 0DU. T:0171 730 3488.

Northumbria Tourist Board, Aykley Heads, Durham DH1 5UX. T:0191 384 6905. Covering Cleveland, Durham, Northumberland and Tyne & Wear.

North West Tourist Board, Swan House, Swan Meadow Road, Wigan Pier, Wigan, Lancashire WN3 5BB. T:01942 821222. Covering Cheshire, Greater Manchester, Lancashire, Merseyside and High Peak of Derbyshire.

South East England Tourist Board, The Old Brew House, Warwick Park, Tunbridge Wells, Kent TN2 5TU. T:01892 540766. Covering East and West Sussex, Kent and Surrey.

Southern Tourist Board, 40 Chamberlayne Road, Eastleigh, Hampshire SO5 5JH. T:01703 620006. Covering Hampshire, Northern and Eastern Dorset, South Wiltshire, the Isle of Wight, Berkshire, Buckinghamshire and Oxfordshire.

West Country Tourist Board, 60 St. David's Hill, Exeter, Devon EX4 4SY. T:01392 211171. Covering Avon, Cornwall, Devon, Somerset, Western Dorset, Wiltshire and the Isles of Scilly.

Yorkshire and Humberside Tourist Board, 312 Tadcaster Road, York, North Yorkshire YO2 2HF. T:01904 707961 (707070 24 hours). Covering North, South and West Yorkshire and also Humberside.

Long-haul travel

The two specialist organisations below can offer a great deal of practical information and help, as well as assist in obtaining low-cost fares, if you are planning to travel independently. Round-the-world air tickets are an excellent buy. Most airlines offer their own fares or travel agents can put together routes using various carriers.

Trailfinders Travel Centre, 194 Kensington High Street, London W8 7RG. Long-haul flights: 0171 938 3939. European and transatlantic flights: 0171 938 3232. First and business class flights: 0171 938 3444. Will work out an itinerary for you to any destination worldwide, obtain the necessary visas and arrange comprehensive travel insurance. Trailfinders has a reference library and information centre, medical advisory and immunisation centre and also a map and bookshop.

Wexas International, 45 Brompton Road, London SW3 1DE. T:0171 589 3315. As well as providing a comprehensive travel service for independent holidaymakers, Wexas also offers a variety of trips to long-haul and unusual destinations including such places as the Antarctic, China and the Nile Valley. Members enjoy flight, hotel and car hire discounts and receive the *Traveller* magazine. Membership costs £39.58.

Insurance

Even the best laid holiday plans can go wrong. It is therefore only sensible to take out proper insurance cover before you depart.

Many tour operators insist that, as a condition of booking, you either buy their inclusive insurance package; or alternatively, make private arrangements which are *at least as good*. While this suggests that they are demanding very high standards, terms and conditions vary greatly; so before signing on the dotted line, you should read the small print carefully to ensure that the package you are being offered meets all the eventualities and provides you with adequate cover should you make a claim.

If you are travelling independently, if anything it is even more important to be properly insured, since you will not be protected by the normal compensation that the reputable tour operators provide for claims for which they could be held liable in the event of a mishap.

Holiday insurance should cover you for:

- personal accident leading to injury or death
- medical expenses including: hospital treatment, cost of ambulance, emergency dental treatment plus expenses for a companion, who may have to remain overseas with you should you become ill (see 'Medical Insurance' page 398)
- additional hotel and repatriation costs resulting from injury or illness
- loss of deposit or cancellation: check what emergencies or contingencies this covers
- cost of having to curtail your holiday because of serious illness in the family
- compensation for inconvenience caused by flight cancellations or other travel delays
- cover for baggage and personal effects and for emergency purchases should your baggage be delayed

- cover for loss of personal money
- personal liability cover, should you cause injury to another person or property
- extra insurance in respect of your car, if you are taking it abroad (see earlier 'Motoring holidays abroad' page 373); or fully comprehensive insurance cover (which you may need to purchase while on holiday) if you are planning to hire a car or motor scooter overseas.

Before lashing out on new insurance, check whether any of the above items are already covered under an existing policy. This might well apply to your personal possessions and to medical insurance. Even if the policy is not sufficiently comprehensive for travel purposes, it would probably still be cheaper to pay a small supplement to give you the extra cover you need than to buy a holiday insurance package from a tour operator. This could be especially true if you are over 65, as many travel agents load premiums against older holidaymakers.

Although many travel agents would like you to believe otherwise, unless the insurance is an intrinsic part of a special holiday offer (in which case the offer may be rather less of a bargain than the discount suggests), you are under no obligation to buy insurance off a travel company.

When assessing holiday insurance, and especially inclusive packages, it pays to do a bit of mental arithmetic. Although at first glance the sums look enormous, the likelihood is that should you have to claim you will end up being out of pocket. A sum of £750 or even £1,000 in respect of lost baggage might well be insufficient if, as well as your clothes, you had to replace your watch, camera and other valuables.

A recent checklist in the Consumers' Association magazine *Which?* suggested the following guidelines in respect of the amount of cover holidaymakers should be looking for in their policy:

Cancellation or curtailment of holiday: the full cost of your holiday, as well as the deposit and any other charges paid in advance.
Money and travel documents: £500.
Luggage/belongings: minimum £1,500. (N.B. check the limit on single articles.)
Delayed baggage: £75 for emergency purchases in case luggage is lost en route and arrives late.
Delayed departure: £20 per hour after the first 12 hours; and full cost of your holiday if you cancel after the first full 24 hours' delay.
Personal liability: up to £1 million (£2 million for the USA).

It is essential that you take the insurance documents with you, as losses or other claims must normally be reported immediately. You will also be required to quote reference number and/or other details, given on the docket. Failure to report a claim within the specified time limit could nullify your right to compensation.

Be sure to get a receipt for any special expenses you incur – extra hotel bills, medical treatment, long-distance phone calls and so on. You may not get all the costs reimbursed but if your insurance covers some or all of these contingencies, you will need to produce evidence of your expenditure.

The Association of British Insurers (51 Gresham Street, London EC2V 7HQ, T:0171 600 3333) publishes a free information sheet on holiday insurance and motoring abroad, explaining the key points you should know in simple language.

The Association of British Travel Agents (55-57 Newman Street, London W1P 4AH, T:0171 637 2444) operates a code of conduct for all travel agents and tour operators who are members of ABTA and also runs a consumer advisory service for holidaymakers on how to seek redress if they are dissatisfied with their travel company.

ABTA's code of conduct has been revised, offering greater protection to travellers. For example, if you have an accident due to negligence by one of the tour operator's suppliers (e.g. trip over a frayed carpet and break your ankle in the hotel), your tour operator must now accept responsibility with you in making a claim and pay the legal expenses involved (up to a limit of £5,000).

Also highly welcome is the Denied Boarding Regulation which entitles passengers who cannot travel because their flight is overbooked to some immediate cash payment, even if the airline puts them up in a hotel or books them on to an alternative flight a few hours later. To qualify, passengers must have a confirmed reservation and have checked in on time. Also, their flight must have been booked from an EC member state and/or through an EC travel agent. Charter flights are excluded.

Compensation for a flight of up to 2,175 miles is Ecu 150 (about £120); and double for longer journeys. For short delays, two to four hours, compensation is normally half. Not all airlines volunteer the information – so if you want the compensation, it may be up to you to ask!

Medical insurance

This is one area where you should never skimp on insurance. Although many countries now have reciprocal arrangements with Britain for emergency medical treatment, these vary greatly both in quality and generosity. Some treatments are free, as they are on the National Health Service; others, even in some EC countries, may be charged for as if you were a private patient.

Department of Health leaflet *Health Advice for Travellers* (T5) explains what is entailed and what forms you should obtain. In particular you should get a Form E111 which is a certificate entitling you to free or reduced-cost emergency treatment throughout the European Economic Area. An application form is contained in the T5 leaflet. You can pick up a copy at any main post office which will process the paperwork and stamp your Form E111 for you on the spot.

However, even the very best reciprocal arrangements may not be adequate in the event of a real emergency; and they certainly will not cover you for any additional expenses you may incur, such as: the cost of having to prolong your stay; extra hotel bills if a companion has to remain with you; special transport home, should you require it, and so on. Additionally, since in an emergency you may need or want private treatment, you would be advised to insure for this – even if you are going to a country where good reciprocal arrangements exist.

As a general rule of thumb, the further from Britain you are going the higher the cover you need. This applies especially to Third World countries, where the risk of falling ill is greater and where medical facilities away from the big towns may be basic in the extreme; and also to America, where the cost of medical treatment is literally astronomic. *Which?* recommends the following levels of cover: £250,000 for Europe; £1 million for all other parts of the world.

Most insurance companies impose various terms and let-out clauses as a condition of payment. You should read these very carefully because, whereas some are obviously sensible, others may be very restrictive or, for whatever reason, you may not be able to satisfy the requirements: for example, if you have a chronic heart condition.

Although there is no upper age limit if you want to take out medical insurance, many companies request a note from a qualified medical practitioner stating that you are fit to travel if you are over 75.

Another common requirement is that the insured person should undertake not to indulge in any dangerous pursuits, which is fine in theory but in practice (depending on the company's interpretation of 'dangerous') could debar you from any activity that qualifies as 'strenuous'.

Travel and other concessions

Buses, coaches, some airline companies and especially the railways offer valuable concessions to people of retirement age. Some of the best-value savings which are available to anyone aged 60 and over are provided by British Rail. These include:

Senior Railcards. These cost £16 and entitle you to: one-third off most fares including cheap day singles and returns; Savers and Supersavers returns and most Rail Rover tickets; first class single and return tickets; and one-day Travelcards subject to a minimum fare. Discounts are also available on some ferry services.

Disabled Persons Railcard. This costs £14 and entitles the holder and companion accompanying him/her to reduced rates by train. Details and conditions are described in the British Rail brochure.

Network Cards. These normally cost £14 (£17 for two people) but are available to anyone aged 60 or over for £10 (£12 for two). They are available only in South-East England. They give a one-third reduction on most standard fares after 10 a.m., Monday to Friday, (any time at weekends or bank holidays). Up to four adults (including the cardholder/s) can travel at a discount and up to four children can travel with them for £1 each.

Rail Europe Senior Cards. Available to retired persons from age 60 who are also BR Senior Railcard holders. They cost £5 and entitle you to savings of up to 30 per cent on 1st and standard/2nd Class full fares from London to most parts of Europe, including Eurostar Services through the Channel Tunnel.

Reductions on Cross Channel jetfoils, seacats and ships are only allowed if these services are part of rail/sea combined tickets to or from the Continent. The cards also allow you to purchase tickets at a discount within 18 European countries.

Rail Europe Senior Cards can be obtained from selected British Rail stations, British Rail International appointed travel agencies or from the International Rail Centre, Victoria Station, London SW1V 1JY (telephone enquiries: 0171 834 2345; credit card telephone: 0171 828 0892).

Buses and coaches

There are often reduced rates for senior citizens on long-distance buses and coaches. For example, discounts of 33 per cent apply on National Coaches on both ordinary and Rapide services. If you are planning to travel by coach, *Good non-Retirement Guide* readers have advised that it is worth shopping around to find out what bargains are available.

Airlines

Several of the airlines offer attractive discounts to older travellers. The terms and conditions vary, with some carriers offering across-the-board savings and others limiting them to selected destinations. Likewise, in some cases the qualifying age is 60; in others, it is a couple of years older. A particular bonus is that concessions are often extended to include a companion travelling at the same time.

These discounts are not particularly widely advertised and may well not be suggested by airline staff, often because they do not know a passenger's age. Best advice is to ask your travel agent at time of booking what special discounts, if any, are offered.

Overseas

Many countries offer travel and other reductions to retired holidaymakers including, for example, discounts for: entry to museums and galleries, day excursions, sporting events and other entertainment. As in Britain, provisions are liable to change and for up-to-date information probably the best source to contact is the national tourist office of the country to which you are travelling. Herewith, however, a flavour of reductions current at time of writing. The rail discounts are available in each case to holders of a Rail Europe Senior Card purchasing international rail travel tickets and are applicable to both first and second class travel.

All EC countries – as well as Norway, Hungary, the Czech Republic, Slovakia and most lines in Switzerland – give 30 per cent reductions on rail fares. Additionally, extra concessions apply in the following countries:

Austria: most museums and galleries are free at weekends.

Denmark: most museums offer pensioner discounts.

Eire: CIE Rambler Tickets give unlimited travel by rail and bus at discounted prices. Most museums are free and most entertainments offer concessionary prices to people of retirement age.

Finland: there are 30 per cent reductions on internal weekday Finnish airline flights and also on coaches for people over 65. Additionally, many museums offer reduced entrance charges.

France: there are lower entrance charges at most museums as well as at some theatres and cinemas.

Luxembourg: discounts up to 30 per cent on coaches and buses.

Netherlands: reduced prices on internal KLM flights; also cheaper entrance charges at museums.

Sweden: 30 per cent reductions on some coaches; off peak flat rate fare for internal flights; concessionary entry to museums and entertainment.

Switzerland: for a full list of concessions, see *Season for Seniors* – information from the Swiss National Tourist Office.

If you are expecting to travel extensively by train while abroad, it could be worth considering a Euro-Domino ticket, a Freedom Pass or an Inter-Rail Europe ticket. Explanatory leaflets about each are available from most main line stations.

Plans are afoot to increase the range of discounts for retired holidaymakers throughout the EC. Ask, when booking, what information your agent has – or can find out for you.

Air Travel Advisory Bureau. T:0171 636 5000. Advises on low-cost fares to all parts of the world. If you are looking for good value fares, it is well worth giving them a ring rather than shopping around. There is a free helpline which advises on all aspects of travel including visas, passports, inoculations, insurance and so on.

Holiday saving schemes
More and more institutions, in particular banks and building societies, are offering discount schemes and/or bonus payments to customers who book their holidays through them. At time of writing, most offers are in the region of £50 to £500, depending on the institution concerned and the actual price of the holiday itself.

As far as we can ascertain, there are no particular strings attached. Holidaymakers can use most of the major tour operators, booking through their credit card or building society travel club. While the savings may not be enormous, even an extra £50 spending money is certainly worth enjoying, particularly when it is offered for the selfsame holiday you had chosen, with the only difference being that bookings are normally by telephone rather than face-to-face.

Health tips for travellers

Most are plain common sense – but worth repeating for all that.

- Remember to pack any regular medicines you require: even familiar branded products can be difficult to obtain in some countries.
- Take a mini first aid kit, including: plaster, disinfectant, tummy pills and so on.

- If you are going to any developing country, consult your doctor as to what pills (and any special precautions) you should take.
- One of the most common ailments among British travellers abroad is an overdose of sun. In some countries, it really burns, so take it easy, wear a hat and apply plenty of protective lotion.
- The other big travellers' woe is 'Delhi belly', which unhappily can apply in most hot countries, including Italy and Spain. Beware the water, ice, salads, seafood, ice cream and any fruit which you do not peel yourself. Department of Health advice is only to eat freshly cooked food which is both hot and thoroughly cooked.
- Always wash your hands before eating or handling food, particularly if you are camping or caravanning.
- Travelling is tiring and a sudden change of climate more debilitating than most of us admit: allow plenty of time during the first couple of days to acclimatise before embarking on an activity programme that would exhaust a 17-year-old.
- Have any inoculations or vaccinations well in advance of your departure date.
- When flying, wear loose clothes and above all comfortable shoes as feet and ankles tend to swell in the air. On long journeys, it helps to drink plenty of fruit juice and remember the warning that 'an alcoholic drink in the air is worth two on the ground'. If you have a special diet, inform whoever makes your booking: most airlines, especially on long-distance journeys, serve vegetarian food.
- Department of Health leaflet T5, *Health Advice for Travellers*, contains essential information and advice on what precautions to take when you travel abroad, how to cope in an emergency and what vaccinations may be required. Available from any main post office or Health Centre or by ringing 0800 555777 (call free). Prestel 50063 has updated information.
- Should some disaster befall you, there are air-ambulance services which will fly you home with a doctor and nurse in attendance. One such is **Heathrow Air Ambulance**, PO Box 279, Iver, Bucks SL0 0BQ, T:0181 897 6185/6/7.
- Finally, the old favourite, don't drink and drive.

Keep fit and have a wonderful holiday!

15 Caring for Elderly Parents

Most of us sooner or later have some responsibility for the care of elderly parents. Although an increasing number of people live well into their eighties and beyond, the vast majority manage with a little help to remain in their own homes rather than go into residential care. While there is no hiding the fact that with a very elderly person this can impose strains, most families cope exceedingly well. Moreover, since the evidence shows that this is the undoubted preference of most older people themselves, the main bias of this chapter is towards helping aged parents remain as independent as possible.

Knowing what facilities are available, what precautions you can take against a mishap occurring and whom you can turn to in an emergency can make all the difference, both to you and to parents who may fear becoming a burden. Over the last few years provision has enormously improved and ranges from simple gadgets such as alarm systems which can buy peace of mind to full-scale nursing care, should this become necessary.

A basic choice for many families is whether parents should move in with them or continue to live on their own. While the decision will depend on individual circumstances, in the early days at least the majority choice on all sides is generally in favour of 'staying put'. Although later in the chapter we cover sheltered housing, which some people see as the best of all worlds, an alternative solution to any move may be simply to adapt the home to make it safer and more convenient.

Ways of adapting a home

Many even quite elderly people will not require anything more complicated than a few general improvements, such as: better lighting, especially near staircases; a non-slip mat and grab-rail in the bathroom; safe heating arrangements; and perhaps the lowering of some kitchen and other units to place them within easy reach.

Another sensible plan worth considering is to convert a downstairs room into a bedroom and bathroom, in case managing the stairs should later become a difficulty. These and other common-sense measures are covered in more detail in Chapter 8, Your Home.

For some people, however, such arrangements are not really sufficient. In the case of a physically handicapped or disabled person, more radical improvements will usually be required. Far from presenting a major problem as used to be the case, today these are normally fairly easy to organise.

Local authority help

Local authorities have a legal duty to help people with disabilities and, depending on what is required and the individual's ability to pay, may assist with the cost.

Your parents can either approach their GP or contact the Social Services Department direct. A sympathetic doctor will be able to: advise what is needed; supply any prescriptions such as for a medical hoist; suggest which unit or department to approach; and can make a recommendation to the Housing Department, should rehousing be desirable.

The Social Services Department may be able to supply kitchen, bathroom and other aids for the home, arrange an appointment with an occupational therapist and support an application for a housing grant, should major adaptations be required.

If only relatively small changes are necessary, e.g. a hand-rail on the stairs or ramp for a wheelchair, the occupational therapist may arrange for these to be done by the local authority. This can take months however, so if your parents cannot wait and want the work done privately, the Occupational Therapist will give you names of local firms.

Care and repair schemes

Also known as 'Staying Put' schemes, these are voluntary and/or local authority projects aimed at helping older or disabled home owners to repair and adapt their homes. They help to assess your needs, get a builder, supervise the work, raise the finance, verify the estimate and check the completed job. Contact the national body for information about local schemes: **Care and Repair Ltd.**, Castle House, Kirtley Drive, Nottingham NG7 1LD. T:0115 979 9091.

Housing grants

There are several grants available, in the event of more substantial adaptations being required. The three most likely to be of interest are: renovation grant, disabled facilities grant and minor works assistance. All are means-tested and most types of work for which grant is given are at the discretion of the council, so it is very important not to commence any work until grant application has been approved.

More detailed information as to the criteria for eligibility and other points is given in Chapter 8, Your Home (see section headed 'Improvement and repair grants', page 152). Also, it could be useful to contact your local Citizens' Advice Bureau, Age Concern group or Care and Repair service who would be able to advise you of any preliminary steps you need to take, such as obtaining estimates, before completing the application form.

Renovation grant. There are six eventualities where application for a grant might be succesful: (1) to bring a property up to a standard of fitness for human habitation; (2) to replace or repair rotten or defective parts of the structure including, for example, doors, windows, walls, an ineffective damp-proof course or unsatisfactory wiring; (3) for home insulation; (4) to provide heating facilities; (5) for the provision of satisfactory internal arrangements such as improvement of a very steep or winding staircase; (6) for conversions, such as the creation of a granny flat.

Disabled facilities grant. This is designed to adapt or provide facilities for a home (including the common parts where applicable) to make it more suitable for occupation by a disabled person. It can cover a wide range of improvements to enable them to manage more independently including, for example: work to facilitate access either to the property itself or to the main rooms; the provision of suitable bathroom or kitchen facilities; the adaptation of heating or lighting controls; improvement of the heating system; plus various other works where these would make a home suitable for a disabled person.

How to apply
For both the above, contact the Home Improvement Section of your local council for an application form. At the same time, you might usefully request a copy of the Department of the Environment booklet *House Renovation Grants*.

Minor works assistance. In contrast to the grants described above, Minor Works Assistance is for small but essential works to your home, including: (1) to provide or improve thermal insulation; (2) to repair, improve or adapt a property to enable individuals over 60 to remain in their own home; (3) as 2, if you have an older person coming to live with you permanently; (4) to carry out repairs to a property in a clearance area.

Grant is only available to owner-occupiers and private sector tenants (including Housing Association tenants) who are in receipt of income support, family credit, housing benefit, disability working allowance or council tax benefit.

Maximum grant is £1,080 per application, up to a total of £3,240 over three years. For further information and application form contact your Housing Department.

Other sources of help
The Disabled Living Foundation, 380-384 Harrow Road, London W9 2HU. T:0171 289 6111. This is a national charity concerned with the practical problems of disability including infirmities of age. As well as running a letter enquiry service, DLF has an Equipment Centre where gadgets of all kinds can be demonstrated and tried out by visitors.

The range includes: special equipment for the bathroom, kitchen, bedroom and living room; hoists, wheelchairs and gadgets to assist reading and writing. None of the items is for sale but the Centre can provide information on suppliers and prices.

The Centre is staffed by therapists who show visitors round and discuss individual needs. It is advisable to make an appointment as the Centre is sometimes closed to the public for the running of training courses. Opening hours are: 10 a.m. to 4 p.m., Mondays to Fridays.

The Royal Association for Disability and Rehabilitation (RADAR), 12 City Forum, 250 City Road, London EC1V 8AF. T:0171 250 3222. RADAR can help and give advice across a very wide spectrum, including: statutory and voluntary services, access and mobility issues, holidays, employment and housing. It publishes a useful monthly bulletin and can supply names and addresses of the many Disabled Living Centres (as can the co-ordinating body for the DLC, i.e. the **Disabled Living Centres Council**, 286 Camden Road, London N7 0BJ) which are now being established throughout the country. These exist in: Belfast, Birmingham, Blackpool, Caerphilly, Cardiff, Dudley, Edinburgh, Leeds, Leicester, Liverpool, Macclesfield, Manchester, Middlesbrough, Newcastle upon Tyne, Paisley, Portsmouth, Sheffield, Southampton, Stockport and Swindon.

Both the **British Red Cross** and **Age Concern** (see local telephone directory) may loan equipment in the short term and may also be able to advise on local stockists. Larger branches of Boots, for example, sell a wide range of special items for people with disabilities, including: bath aids, tableware, grips and wheelchairs.

Smith & Nephew Homecraft Ltd., Sidings Road, Low Moor Industrial Estate, Kirkby-in-Ashfield, Notts NG17 7JZ. T:01623 754047. Stocks a very wide variety of practical equipment to help older people cope with everyday life including: 'reachers' (to help lift down items beyond reach); walking aids; stair rails; bed raisers; bath seats and kitchen aids, such as tin openers and tap turners as well as special gardening utensils and other leisure items. There is also a mail order service called Chester-care, telephone: 01623 757955.

Keep Able, Fleming Close, Park Farm, Wellingborough, Northants NN8 6UF. A mail order service with gadgets galore from shower chairs to needle threaders to make life easier for disabled and elderly people. The catalogue is extremely well laid out and there is an advice line – telephone 01933 679426 – to answer queries or assist with choosing a product to meet customers' particular requirements. Those lucky enough to live within convenient reach of either Brentford or Brierley Hill can visit a Keep Able Centre and examine the vast range of equipment on offer. Addresses are: 2 Capital Interchange Way, Brentford, Middlesex TW8 0EX. T:0181 742 2181; Sterling Park, Pedmore Road, Brierley Hill, West Midlands DY5 1TB. T:01384 484544. There is also a small showroom at the Wellingborough office and a retail shop at the Sheldon Precinct, Coventry Road, Sheldon, West Midlands B26 3JB. T:0121 722 3747.

REMAP, Hazeldene, Ightham, Sevenoaks, Kent TN15 9AD. T:01732 883818. Can often help design or adapt goods to suit individuals, where there is no commercially available product to meet their particular needs.

The Centre for Accessible Environments, Nutmeg House, 60 Gainsford Street, London SE1 2NY. T:0171 357 8182. Runs an architectural advisory service and can recommend local architects with experience of designing for people with disabilities. When writing, you should give broad details of the type of work required. The Centre also offers an information service on accessible design and additionally will check architects' drawings to confirm their suitability for a proposed project. Cost for the checking service is £75 an hour (1995) but could prove invaluable for people planning to adapt their home either for their own retirement or for, say, a parent coming to live with them. A publications list is available on request.

BT supplies some 70 devices to assist those with hearing difficulties, visual handicap, impaired mobility and other problems that make using a telephone more difficult. For details see the *BT Guide for People who are Disabled or Elderly*, available from local BT offices. A home visit can sometimes be arranged for those who are housebound. For further information, dial BT free on 0800 800 150.

Another useful body to know about is **DIEL**, which provides independent advice to the telecommunications industry about the needs of disabled and elderly people. Its secretariat, financed by OFTEL, will take up complaints if you are not satisfied with the phone company's response and can also tell you about special equipment and services. DIEL produces a handy free folder of information on services and facilities which can benefit elderly or disabled telephone users. The address to contact is: **DIEL**, 50 Ludgate Hill, London EC4M 7JJ. T:0171 634 8770 (speech) or 0171 634 8769 (minicom).

Other helpful sources of advice include:

Disability Scotland, Princes House, 5 Shandwick Place, Edinburgh EH2 4RG. T:0131 229 8632.

Disability Wales/Anabledd Cymru, Llys Ifor, Crescent Road, Caerphilly, Mid Glamorgan CF8 1XL. T:01222 887325.

Disability Action, 2 Annadale Avenue, Belfast BT7 3JH. T:01232 491011.

Useful reading
Equipment for Disabled People. A series of 14 books which give full details of the wide range of available equipment and self-help devices for those with a disability or for those who are no longer as active as they once were. Available from: **The Disability Information Trust**, Mary Marlborough Centre, Nuffield Orthopaedic Centre, Headington, Oxford OX3 7LD, T:01865 227592. Prices are between £4.25 and £10.50. Stocked by many public libraries.

Electrical Controls by Tessa Palfreyman contains advice on the safe location of switches and controls for use by elderly and disabled people plus information on specialist equipment such as visual door bells and smoke alarms; price £4. Obtainable from the **Centre for Accessible Environments**, Nutmeg House, 60 Gainsford Street, London SE1 2NT. T:0171 357 8182.

Alarm systems

Alarm systems have become very much more widespread in recent years. The knowledge that help can be summoned very quickly in the event of an emergency is not only reassuring in its own right but in practical terms can enable many elderly people to remain independent far longer than would otherwise be sensible. Some local authorities have alarm systems that now allow people living in their own homes to be linked to a central control. Types of alarm vary greatly. Some have a telephone link, enabling personal contact to be made; others simply signal that something is wrong. In other areas, a relative or friend who has been nominated will be alerted; or sometimes, the police. To find out whether your parents' local authority operates such a system, contact the Social Services Department.

Commercial firms
A number of firms install and operate alarm systems. Price, installation cost and reliability can vary quite considerably. For general advice plus a list of suppliers, write to: The Information Service, **Disabled Living Foundation**, 380-384 Harrow Road, London W9 2HU.

Community alarms
Telephone alarm systems operated on the public telephone network can be used by anyone with a direct telephone line. The systems link into a 24-hour monitoring centre and have a pendant which enables help to be called even when the owner is some distance from the telephone. Grants may be available in some cases to meet the costs. For further information, contact: The Community Alarms Department, **Help the Aged**, St. James's Walk, London EC1R 0BE or telephone 0171 253 0253.

Age Concern Aid-Call
This is another highly recommended alarm system. The subscriber wears a small radio transmitter from which a message can be sent via the telephone to a 24-hour monitoring service. The centre then alerts a list of nominated relatives or friends and the local police that something is wrong, and help can be on its way in a matter of minutes. (See Chapter 8, Your Home, for details of costs). Contact: **Age Concern Aid-Call**, Linhay House, Ashburton, Devon TQ13 7UP. T:01364 654321.

Main local authority services

Quite apart from any assistance with housing, local authorities supply a number of services which can prove invaluable to an elderly person. The two most important are meals on wheels and home helps. Additionally, there are social workers and various specialists concerned with aspects of health.

Since the introduction of Community Care, local authority Social Services Departments have taken over all responsibility for helping to assess and co-ordinate the best arrangements for individuals according to their particular requirements.

Meals on wheels
The meals on wheels service is sometimes run by local authorities direct and sometimes by voluntary organisations, such as the Women's Royal Voluntary Service

or the British Red Cross, acting as their agents. As you will know, the purpose is to deliver a hot lunch to individuals in their own home. Different arrangements apply in different areas and schemes variously operate from two to seven days a week. Cost also varies: from about 35p to £1.75 a day, with the norm about £1. For further information, contact the Social Services Department.

Home helps
Local authorities have a legal obligation to run a home help service to help frail and housebound elderly people with such basic household chores as shopping, tidying up, a little light cooking and so on. In many areas the service is overstretched, so the amount of help actually available varies considerably, as does the method of charging. Different local authorities have different policies and while some may charge nothing or just a small weekly amount, as a rule people are means-tested according to their ability to pay. If your parents could afford to do so, this could mean paying the full cost. Apply through the Social Services Department. Some of the larger authorities have a special telephone number which may be listed either as 'Home Help Services' or 'Domiciliary Services'.

Specialist helpers
Local authorities employ a number of specialist helpers, variously based in the Social Services Department or Health Centre, who are there to assist.

Social workers. Normally the first people to contact if you have a problem. They can put you in touch with the right person, if you require a home help, meals on wheels, have a housing difficulty or other query and are not sure whom to approach. Often, even if ultimately it is the responsibility of another department, a social worker may come and discuss the matter with you – or with your parents direct. You should ring the local Social Services Department; in Scotland, this is normally referred to as the Social Work Department.

Occupational therapists. Have a wide knowledge of disability and can assist individuals via training, exercise, or access to aids, equipment or adaptations to the home. Ring the Social Services Department.

Health visitors. Qualified nurses with broad knowledge both of health matters and of the various services available through the local authority. Rather like social workers, health visitors can put you in touch with whatever specialised facilities are required. Contact through the local Health Centre.

District nurses. Fully qualified nurses who will visit a patient in the home: change dressings, attend to other routine nursing matters, monitor progress and help with the arrangements if more specialised care is required. Contact through the Health Centre.

Physiotherapists. Use exercise and massage to help improve mobility and strengthen muscles, for example after an operation or to alleviate a crippling condition. Normally available at both hospitals and health centres.

Medical social workers. In the old days, used to be known as almoners. Are available to consult, if patients have any problems – whether practical or emotional – on leaving hospital. MSWs can advise on coping with a disablement, as well as such practical matters as transport, after-care and other immediate arrangements. Work in hospitals and an appointment should be made before the patient is discharged.

Good neighbour schemes
A number of local authorities have an organised system of good neighbour schemes. In essence, these consist of individuals contracting with the authority to act as good neighbours to one or several elderly people living close by. Depending on what is required, they may simply pop in on a daily basis to check that everything is all right; or they may give more sustained assistance such as providing help with dressing, bathing, shopping or preparing a light meal. In some authorities, the service may largely be run by volunteer organisations. In others 'good neighbours' are paid by the authority, according to the number of hours they commit. To find out whether such a scheme exists locally, enquire at the Social Services Department or at your Citizens' Advice Bureau.

Key voluntary organisations

Voluntary organisations complement the services provided by statutory health and social services in making life easier for elderly people living at home. The range of provision varies from area to area but can include:

- Lunch club
- Day centres and clubs
- Aids such as wheelchairs
- Transport
- Good neighbour schemes
- Advice and information
- Holidays and short-term placements
- Friendly visiting
- Odd jobs and decorating
- Gardening
- Prescription collection
- Family support schemes.

The particular organisation providing these services depends on where you live but the Citizens' Advice Bureau will be able to advise you whom to contact. The following are the key agencies:

Age Concern Groups may provide any or all of the voluntary services listed above. Most groups recruit volunteers to do practical jobs and provide friendship. They also give advice and information and when necessary refer enquirers to a more appropriate agency. Their addresses and telephone numbers are in the local phone book. Alternatively you can telephone **Age Concern Greater London** (T:0171 737 3456) for London addresses; or contact the national headquarters for addresses outside the capital: **Age Concern England,** Astral House, 1268 London Road, London SW16 4ER. T:0181 679 8000.

Headquarters in Scotland, Wales and Northern Ireland are:

Age Concern Scotland, 113 Rose Street, Edinburgh EH2 3DT. T:0131 228 5656.

Age Concern Cymru, 4th Floor, 1 Cathedral Road, Cardiff CF1 9SD. T:01222 371566.

Age Concern Northern Ireland, 3 Lower Crescent, Belfast BT7 1NR. T:01232 245729.

Women's Royal Voluntary Service runs a number of invaluable services:

- Meals on wheels
- Lunch clubs
- Day centres
- Books-on-wheels
- Transport
- Home visiting
- Shopping outings
- Children's holiday schemes

Look in the phone book for the address of the local office or contact the national headquarters: **Women's Royal Voluntary Service,** 234-244 Stockwell Road, London SW9 9SP. T:0171 416 0146.

British Red Cross supplies some important services to elderly people. The principal ones available from many branches include:

- Acting as a link between hospital and home after discharge
- Visiting
- Escorting sick, disabled or frail people when travelling
- Loaning equipment for sick or convalescent patients at home, e.g. wheelchairs and commodes
- After-care and home visiting (including practical help in such tasks as hair washing, shopping, changing library books)
- Sitting-in with elderly people and those with disabilities
- Providing transport for the housebound
- Organising stroke clubs
- 'Signposting' sick people and those with disabilities towards the statutory or voluntary services from which their needs may best be met
- Therapeutic beauty care service for patients with long-term illness.

The following activities are also carried out by the Red Cross in co-operation with or on behalf of statutory authorities:

- Clubs
- Lunch clubs
- Day centres
- Christmas shopping
- Holidays and holiday homes for people with disabilities

To contact your local British Red Cross branch, see telephone directory, or write to: **British Red Cross**, 9 Grosvenor Crescent, London SW1X 7EJ. T:0171 235 5454.

St. John Ambulance comprises 70,000 volunteers who are examined annually in first aid; and sometimes nursing as well. They help in hospitals and will also come to people's homes to assist with various practical tasks such as shopping, collecting pensions, staying with an elderly person for a few hours or providing transport to and from hospital. It is emphasised, however, that the kind of help which the volunteers can provide (if any) varies enormously from county to county and depends on the local resources available. In some areas loan of equipment such as wheelchairs, can be arranged.

St. John give advice on caring and run courses locally for carers looking after elderly people. Anyone wishing to enlist the help of St. John Volunteers should contact their St. John Ambulance County headquarters: ask your local Citizens' Advice Bureau for the address, see telephone directory or enquire at the national headquarters: **St. John Ambulance**, 1 Grosvenor Crescent, London SW1X 7EF. T:0171 235 5231.

Other sources of help and advice

Counsel & Care, Twyman House, 16 Bonny Street, London NW1 9PG. T:Advice Line (10.30 a.m. – 4 p.m.) 0171 485 1566; Appeals 0171 485 4513. Provides a free confidential advisory service, which is used by thousands of elderly people and their relatives each year. Advice-workers liaise with all the statutory services, private and voluntary organisations as well as with charities and benevolent funds in order to inform you of the various options. There is a range of factsheets. Limited funds are also available to help with an exceptional needs payment.

Central Council for Jewish Community Services, Stuart Young House, 221 Golders Green Road, London NW11 9DW. T:0181 458 1035. CCJCS is an umbrella organisation for Jewish community services and has over 60 affiliated member organisations. It publishes a Directory of Jewish Social Services, listing facilities throughout the UK. Price is £4.75.

Services for elderly Jewish people in London and the South East are carried out by **Jewish Care**, located at the same address as the Central Council above. Principal facilities include:

Kosher meals service, operates in: City of Westminster, Tower Hamlets, Muswell Hill and Highgate, Enfield, Barnet, Brent, Chelsea and Kensington, Lambeth and Watford. Charges range from about 50p to £1 per meal. Enquire through the local authority Social Services Department or Jewish Care direct.

Day centres, of which there are four in the London area for elderly or disabled Jewish people. Individuals are sometimes referred by a hospital but can apply direct and will be invited to be a guest for one or two days. Charges average about £2 a day.

Other services include domiciliary care, hostels and a day care centre for those recovering from mental illness. There are also 12 residential homes in London and the South East.

Outside London, contact:

Leeds Jewish Welfare Board, 311 Stonegate Road, Leeds LS17 6AZ. T:0113 268 4211.

Manchester Jewish Blind Society, Nicky Alliance Day Centre, 85 Middleton Road, Crumpsall, Manchester M8 4JY. T:0161 740 0111.

Brighton & Hove Jewish Welfare Board, c/o 2 Modena Road, Hove, East Sussex BN3 5QJ. T:01273 722523.

Merseyside Jewish Welfare Council, Shifrin House, 433 Smithdown Road, Liverpool 15. T:0151 733 2292.

Help the Aged, St. James's Walk, London EC1R 0BE. T:0171 253 0253. Runs SeniorLine, a free national information service, and can put enquirers in contact with an appropriate local organisation. There is also a range of free advice leaflets on money matters, home safety and health. Telephone 0800 650065, 10 a.m. – 4 p.m., Monday to Friday.

Civil Service Retirement Fellowship, 1b Deals Gateway, Blackheath Road, London SE10 8BW. T:0181 691 7411. The Fellowship runs a home visiting service for those who are housebound or living alone and has an extensive network of branches and local groups throughout the country which offer a wide range of social activities for retired civil servants and their families.

The Forces Help Society and Lord Roberts Workshops, 122 Brompton Road, London SW3 1JE. T:0171 589 3243. Through its countrywide network of voluntary workers the Society, in association with SSAFA, provides whatever help may be needed to retired people who have served at any time in HM Forces. This may typically include advice on pensions and benefits or the provision of a grant for a special need, which the Society may be able to arrange either from its own resources or from Service or Regimental funds.

The Society also has two residential care homes and maintains cottages for ex-servicemen and their wives, who are not charged rent but only a modest maintenance payment. Additionally, the Forces Help Society builds specially designed cottages in various parts of the country for disabled ex-servicemen or women and their partners and has bungalow-style apartments in the Isle of Wight, providing holidays for disabled ex-service people and those who care for them.

For further information, write to the above headquarters or contact the Society's local representative, whose name and address is obtainable from post offices, libraries and Citizens' Advice Bureaux.

Disability Alliance Educational and Research Association (DAERA), 1st Floor, Universal House, 88-94 Wentworth Street, London E1 7SA. T:0171 247 8776;

Rights Advice Line: 0171 247 8763. Gives advice over the telephone on social security benefit issues. Also publishes an annual *Disability Rights Handbook* which is packed with information on benefits and services for all people with disabilities and for their families. Price £8.95, post-free (£5 for customers in receipt of any benefit).

Transport

The difficulty of getting around is often a major problem for elderly and disabled people. In addition to the facilities run by voluntary organisations already mentioned, there are several other very useful services.

Voluntary and Community Schemes Database. Produced by the Department of Transport, the database lists details of hundreds of transport schemes around the country helpful to elderly and/or disabled people, including those needing to use a wheelchair. Individuals can request either local or nationwide information. For further details, contact Lena Hanen, T:0171 271 5252 (voice and minicom).

London Taxi Card Service.
A scheme whereby disabled people can incur taxi fares up to £10.80 but only pay £1.50. Normal extras, however, such as weekend charges, are payable by the cardholder. The fleet includes taxis capable of accommodating wheelchairs. Leaflets and application forms are obtainable from local authority Social Services Departments or the **London Accessible Transport Unit** (T:0181 748 7272). The prices quoted above are valid until March 1996, when they may possibly change.

Mobility Advice and Vehicle Information Service (MAVIS), Transport Research Laboratory, Old Wokingham Road, Crowthorne, Berkshire RG45 6AU. T:01344 770456. Run by the Department of Transport, MAVIS is an information service advising on all aspects of mobility – in particular, problems associated with driving. Its services include assessment of elderly motorists wishing to return to driving after a stroke or other disabling illness and advice on low-cost adaptations to relieve the pain of arthritic joints or other conditions that make driving uncomfortable. While general information is free, charges for the more specialised services are as follows: full assessment of individuals who have a disability, £60; consultation and advice on car adaptations, £40; vehicle familiarisation session, £15 an hour.
   Door to Door: a Guide to Transport for People with Disabilities. A Department of Transport publication. Price £3.95. T:0171 271 5252.

Driving licence renewal at age 70
All drivers aged 70 are sent a licence renewal form and have to pay a £6 fee to have their licence renewed. The licence has to be renewed (and £6 paid) at least every three years. Depending on the individual's health, including in particular their eyesight, the driver might be sent a new form to complete after only one or two years. If this applies, the form must be completed honestly but no extra charge will be made.

Holidays

Many people in their late seventies and older travel across the world, go on activity holidays, see the great sights in this country and abroad without any more difficulty than anyone else. They will find ideas galore in Chapter 14, including information about how to obtain assistance at airports and railway stations. However, some elderly people, especially those who are in any way disabled, need special facilities if a stay away from home is to be possible. A number of organisations can help.

ATS Travel, ATS House, 1 Tank Hill Road, Purfleet, Essex RM16 1SX. T:01708 863198. ATS Travel specialises in arranging holidays for people with disabilities, whether travelling alone, with a companion or in a group. It will fix all the necessary arrangements to make travel, whether in the UK or overseas, as easy as possible, including: organising the journey, booking suitable accommodation, ensuring the availability of special diets, arranging for the provision of aids or equipment that may be needed together with any other requirements.

Holiday Care Service, 2 Old Bank Chambers, Station Road, Horley, Surrey RH6 9HW. T:01293 774535; minicom: 01293 776943. Runs an information service providing details of holiday facilities, both in the UK and abroad, for people with special needs including the frail elderly and those with disabilities. The service is free. There is also a UK reservations service, through which attractive discounts at many hotels can be obtained.

John Grooms Association for Disabled People, 10 Gloucester Drive, London N4 2LP. T:0181 802 7272. Provides a variety of holiday accommodation including two award-winning hotels and a number of self-catering flats, bungalows and caravans and also a centre in South Wales, which is designed to provide holidays with 24-hour care.

A number of the specialist voluntary organisations run holiday centres or provide specially adapted self-catering accommodation. In some cases, outings and entertainment are offered; in others, individuals plan their own activities and amusement. Guests requiring assistance usually need to be accompanied by a companion, although in a few instances care arrangements are inclusive. Most of the organisations can advise about the possibility of obtaining a grant or other financial assistance. For further details, contact the following:

Arthritis Care, 18 Stephenson Way, London NW1 2HD. T:0171 916 1500.

Multiple Sclerosis Society, 25 Effie Road, London SW6 1EE. T:0171 736 6267.

Royal National Institute for the Blind, 224 Great Portland Street, London W1N 6AA. T:0171 388 1266.

Parkinson's Disease Society, 22 Upper Woburn Place, London WC1H 0RA. T:0171 383 3513.

Winged Fellowship Trust, Angel House, 20-32 Pentonville Road, London N1 9XD. T:0171 833 2594. Offers respite care and holidays throughout the year at their five centres. Full care is provided and guests can come alone or with their carer. A number of weeks are kept specially for people with Alzheimer's Disease.

There are also several extremely useful publications, listing a wide choice of holiday venues, where disabled travellers can go in the normal way but with the advantage of having special facilities provided.

AA Guide for the Disabled Traveller. Lists over 600 hotels, guest houses, inns and other accommodation suitable for those confined to wheelchairs together with advice on travelling in Europe. £3.99 from bookshops (free to disabled members at AA shops or by calling 0800 262050).

Holidays in the British Isles, £7; Holidays and Travel Abroad, £5. Both from RADAR.

Goldenrail Short Breaks and Holidays brochure indicates a number of hotels with special facilities for physically handicapped guests. Available free from most travel agents.

Finally, a number of organisations provide rent-assisted (or sometimes, free) holidays for the financially needy. Local Citizens' Advice Bureaux, Age Concern groups and county branches of the British Red Cross will often know what, if anything, is available to residents in the area.

Power of attorney

Around the late-60s, many perfectly fit men and women wonder whether it might be sensible to give power of attorney to someone they trust. This involves authorising another person to take business and other financial decisions on their behalf, on the basis that any such decisions would reflect the action that they themselves would have taken. Until a few years ago, the power was only valid where the individual was unwilling rather than incapable of acting for him/herself. So in effect just at the time when the power was most needed it ceased to exist. However, thanks to a law known as the Enduring Powers of Attorney Act, the power is not automatically revoked by any subsequent mental incapacity but can now continue, regardless of any decline, throughout the individual's life.

To protect the donor and the family, the Act clearly lays down certain principles which must be observed; and furthermore calls for the power to be formally registered, with both sides signing a declaration that they understand the various rights and duties involved. As any lawyer would explain, the right time to give power of attorney is when the individual is in full command of his or her faculties, so that potential situations that would require decisions can be properly discussed and the donor's wishes made clear.

There are two ways of drawing up an enduring power of attorney: either through a solicitor, or by buying a standard form published by the **Solicitors' Law Stationery Society Ltd.** (ref. Con 36E). Available by phone from: **Oyez Stationery Ltd.**, 7 Spa Road, London SE16 3QQ. T:0171 232 1000; or Third Avenue, Denbigh West

Industrial Estate, Bletchley, Milton Keynes MK1 1TG. T:01908 371111; or from any Oyez shop. It is sensible for people without a legal background to consult a solicitor.

Temporary living-in help

Elderly people living alone can be more vulnerable to 'flu and other winter ailments. They may have a fall; or, for no apparent reason, may go through a period of being forgetful and neglecting themselves. Equally, as they become older, they may not be able to cope as well with managing their home or caring for themselves. In the event of an emergency or if you have reason for concern – perhaps because you are going on holiday and will not be around to keep a watchful eye – engaging living-in help can be a godsend. Most agencies tend inevitably to be on the expensive side, although in the event of a real problem often represent excellent value for money. A more unusual and interesting longer-term possibility is to recruit the help of a Community Service Volunteer.

Community Service Volunteers, 237 Pentonville Road, London N1 9NJ. T:0171 278 6601. The Volunteers are young people, between 16 and 35, involved in community service through a range of nationwide projects. CSV's Independent Living Projects match full-time helpers with individuals and families who need a high degree of support. The volunteers are untrained and work for periods of 4 to 12 months away from home.

They take their instructions from the people for whom they are working but are not of course substitutes for professional carers. In general they provide practical assistance in the home including, for example: shopping, light cooking, tidying up, attending to the garden and sometimes also decorating jobs. They also offer companionship.

Usually a care scheme is set up through a social worker, who supervises how the arrangement is working out. Volunteers are placed on a one month's trial basis. There is an annual retainer of £1,764 that can be paid in monthly instalments (in case of real financial need, the social worker would assess whether the local authority could pay the costs). Other charges include: fares; accommodation; full board or a weekly food allowance of £27; pocket money of around £22.50 a week; plus one week's paid holiday, after four months. Contact your parents' local Social Services Department; or approach CSV direct, at the address given above.

Agencies

Most of the agencies listed specialise in providing temporary help, rather than permanent staff. Charges vary, but in addition to the weekly payment to helpers, there is normally an agency booking fee. As a rule payment is gross, so your parents will not be involved in having to work out tax or national insurance.

Consultus, 17 London Road, Tonbridge, Kent TN10 3AB. T:01732 355231.

Country Cousins Employment Bureau, 10a Market Square, Horsham, West Sussex RH12 1EX. T:01403 210415.

Easymind: Home Care Services, 3 Oakshade Road, Oxshott, Surrey KT22 0LF. T:01372 842087.

Universal Aunts Ltd., PO Box 304, London SW4 0NN. T:0171 738 8937.

For a further list of agencies, see *Yellow Pages* under heading 'Employment' or 'Care' agencies.

Nursing care

If one of your parents needs regular nursing care, their doctor may be able to arrange for a community or district nurse to visit them at home. This will not, of course, be a sleeping-in arrangement but simply involves a qualified nurse calling round when necessary.

If you want more concentrated home nursing you will have to go through a private agency. Both Consultus and Easymind (see above) can sometimes supply trained nurses. Additionally, there are many specialised agencies, which can arrange hourly, daily or live-in nurses on a temporary or longer-term basis.

Terms of employment vary considerably. Some nurses will literally undertake nursing duties only – and nothing else; and may even expect to have their meals provided. Others will do light housework and act as nurse-companions. Fees vary throughout the country, with London inevitably being most expensive.

BNA, a private agency which has over 115 branches throughout the UK, quotes inclusive costs from £6.07 to £9.57 an hour (weekdays) for trained nurses; or from £524.25 to £689.10 for a live-in nurse, Monday to Sunday.

Fees for nursing auxiliaries and care assistants are from £5.04 to £7.78 an hour, weekdays; £363 to £560.20 for a live-in care assistant for a full week.

N.B. In both cases, the fees quoted for residential care are for guidance only and are negotiable according to the circumstances.

Private health insurance can sometimes be claimed against part of the cost but this is generally only in respect of qualified nurses, not auxiliaries and care assistants. Address of the head office is: **BNA**, North Place, 82 Great North Road, Hatfield, Herts AL9 5BL. T:01707 263544. For branch addresses, see telephone directory under BNA.

One of the more flexible schemes we have come across is WPA's 'Home Independence'. It is designed to provide short-term home nursing care for older people when they come out of hospital after an illness or accident. Cover can be bought for a week, three weeks or 35 days with subscriptions ranging – according to the number of hours' nursing – from £44.15 to £223 a year. To qualify, patients must be under the age of 85 and must have spent at least four nights in hospital. Also a doctor must confirm that home nursing is necessary and claims cannot be made within the first three months of the policy being taken out. For further information, ring Freecall: 0500 414243; or write to **Home Independence**, WPA, BS 481, Freepost, Taunton, Somerset TA1 2BR.

Permanent living-in help

There may come a time when you feel that it is no longer safe to allow one of your parents to live entirely on their own. One possibility is to engage a companion or housekeeper on a permanent basis but such arrangements are normally very expensive: the going rate for housekeepers in London is anything between £130 and £250 a week clear. However, if you want to investigate the idea further, many domestic agencies (see the *Yellow Pages*) supply housekeeper-companions. Alternatively, you might consider advertising in *The Lady*, which is probably the most widely read publication for these kinds of posts.

Permanent help can also sometimes be provided by agencies (such as those listed under 'Temporary living-in-help'), who will supply continuous four-weekly placements. This is an expensive option and the lack of continuity can at times be distressing for elderly people, particularly at the change-over point. But it can also lead to a happier atmosphere as the housekeeper comes fresh to the job and neither party has time to start getting on each other's nerves.

Au pairs are cheaper: roughly £35 to £65 a week with full board and lodging. A drawback, however, is that most au pairs speak inadequate English (at least when they first arrive); and, as they are technically students living 'en famille', they must by law be given plenty of free time to attend school and study. An alternative solution for some families is to engage a reliable daily woman who, in the event of illness or other problem, would be prepared to stay overnight.

Flexible care arrangements

One of the problems for many elderly people is that the amount of care they need is liable to vary according to the state of their health and other factors including, for example, the availability of neighbours and family. Whereas after an operation the requirement may be for someone with basic nursing skills, a few weeks later the only need may be for someone to act as a companion – or simply to pop in for the odd hour during the day to cook a hot meal and check all is well. Few agencies cater for all the complex permutations that may be necessary in caring for an elderly person in their own home but two that aim to offer a genuinely flexible service are Care Alternatives and Cura Domi – Care at Home. Equally worth knowing about is the United Kingdom Home Care Association; and also CareQuest.

Care Alternatives, 206 Worple Road, Wimbledon, London SW20 8PN. T:0181 946 8202. Care workers and professional nurses can be engaged by the hour, day, weekend, to sleep in overnight or in a temporary/permanent residential capacity. All are competent in basic home nursing care and, while not available to undertake heavy cleaning, will assist with such tasks as the shopping, cooking and light housework. There is an on-call service to deal with emergencies day or night and qualified nurses are available for advice in every branch. Care Alternatives takes up references and interviews all staff before placing them on their books.

Not suprisingly charges are fairly hefty. There is a £15 non-returnable registration fee and, while prices vary according to the requirements, to give you an idea: hourly rates are £7.54 (daytime); sleep-in cost is £32.05 per night; and temporary residential care is £294.91 a week. All these prices include VAT. Branches cover: Greater London, much of Middlesex, Surrey and Kent (0181 946 8202); Portsmouth, South East Hants and the Isle of Wight (01983 406808). Additionally, residential carers can be supplied all over the country and will also go abroad as escorts.

CareQuest, Barrington Road, Orwell, Cambs SG8 5QP. T:01223 208300. Offers a comprehensive and very sympathetic advisory service to help individuals and their families decide which among the various care options available to them would be most suitable. All possible solutions – from gadgets for the home to residential care – are discussed at a meeting, including what they would cost and the means of arranging them. The recommendations are confirmed in writing together with appropriate contact addresses.

Consultations are held in Cambridge (£85 plus VAT) and in Central London (£115 plus VAT). For further information, contact Primrose Taylor at the above address.

Cura Domi – Care at Home, Guildford House, 8 North Street, Guildford, Surrey GU1 4AF. T:01483 302275. Carers undertake all or any of the tasks traditionally managed by a reliable housekeeper-companion: shopping, cooking, attending to the chores around the home, helping an elderly person bath or dress, reading aloud and generally providing whatever assistance may be needed. Where appropriate, carers can also provide all intimate care and help needed with such problems as incontinence and dementia. Depending on what is required, they will come in for the hour or live in full-time for a few days, few weeks or longer. Great care is taken to try to match clients with a carer who possesses the right skills and temperament and all carers are backed by a team of RGN care managers on 24-hour call, seven days a week.

There is a once-only non-returnable registration fee of £21.15 with a list of varying prices according to whether the job is weekday, weekend, day-time, night-time or live-in. For example: hourly rates are £7.10 weekdays, £9.88 weekends; overnight charges are £35.20 weekdays, £43.67 weekends; live-in fees (minimum 48-hour booking) are £53.52 a day. Additionally, there are travelling expenses (16p a mile or coach/train fare) plus the option of a home assessment or consultation. All prices quoted are inclusive of VAT. At the present time daily care is only available in the Surrey and Hampshire areas. Live-in care, however, can be arranged anywhere in the country.

United Kingdom Home Care Association, 42 Banstead Road, Carshalton Beeches, Surrey SM5 3NW. T:0181 288 1551. Represents over 1,000 agencies throughout the country specialising in providing care for elderly and/or disabled people. All requirements are catered for including temporary and permanent posts, residential, daily, overnight and hourly work. UKHCA runs a Helpline which can refer enquirers to a local member agency committed to upholding the Association's Code of Practice.

Although any of these suggestions can work extremely well, many families find them either too expensive or haphazard – or both. So, sooner or later the decision may come down to a choice between residential care and inviting a parent to live with you.

Most families, to their credit, choose to care for an elderly parent in their own home; or sometimes, particularly in the case of a daughter, to move into their parents' home.

Emergency care for pets

For many elderly people a pet is a most important part of their lives, providing companionship and fun as well as stimulating them into taking regular outdoor exercise. But in the event of the owner having to go into hospital or due to some other emergency being temporarily unable to care for their pet, there can be real problems including concern for the welfare of the animal and considerable distress to the owner.

To overcome these problems, two highly imaginative schemes have been set up, one operating throughout the UK and the other just in Scotland. Depending on what is required, volunteers will either simply feed or exercise the animal or will care for it in their own home until the owner can manage again.

Cinnamon Trust, Poldarves Farm, Trescowe Common, Germoe, Penzance TR20 9RX. T:01736 850291. As well as the above services, Cinnamon also offers permanent care for pets whose owners have died. Some animals stay at the Trust's haven in Cornwall. Others are found alternative loving homes with a new owner. Either way, every effort is made to help pets adjust. Familiar possessions, such as the animal's basket or favourite toy, are very much encouraged and as far as possible 'families' of pets are kept together to avoid the further distress of separating them from their companions. Emergency services can be called 24 hours a day. The Trust makes no charge but donations, or a bequest, are very much appreciated.

Pet Fostering Service Scotland. T:01674 810356. The focus is on temporary care. The only charges are the cost of pet's food, litter – in the case of cats – and any veterinary fees that may be incurred during fostering. In the main the service caters for dogs, cats and birds but some volunteers are willing to care for more exotic species such as snakes. If help is needed telephone the above number.

Practical help for carers

If your parent is still fairly active – visits friends, does his/her own shopping, enjoys some hobby which gets him/her out and about – the strains and difficulties may be fairly minimal. This applies particularly if your home lends itself to creating a granny flat, so everyone can retain some privacy and your parent can continue to enjoy maximum independence. However, this is not always possible and in the case of an ill or very frail person far more intensive care may be required.

If you have to go out to work, need time to attend to other responsibilities or quite understandably feel that if you are to remain human you must have time for your own interests, it is important to know what help is available and how to obtain it.

The many services provided by local authorities and voluntary agencies, described earlier in the chapter, apply for the most part equally to an elderly person living with their family as to one living alone. If there is nothing in the list that solves a particular problem you may have, it is sensible to talk to the Citizens' Advice Bureau and Social Services Department, as there may be some special local facility that could provide the solution.

In particular, you might ask about **day centres and clubs**. Activities and surroundings vary, so you might wish to investigate. However, a responsible person will always be in charge and transport, to and from the venue, is often provided.

You could also ask the local Age Concern group and WRVS. These organisations will be able to tell you about the possibility of **voluntary sitters**: people who come in and stay with an elderly person for a few hours (or sometimes overnight), to prevent them being on their own. Other sources to try include: the local branch of the British Red Cross, St. John Ambulance and the Volunteer Bureau (see local telephone directory).

In response to the Government's Community Care scheme, most areas now have, or are planning, **respite care facilities** to enable carers to take a break from their dependants from time to time. Depending on the circumstances, this could be for just the odd day or possibly for a week or two to enable carers who need it to have a real rest. A particularly welcome aspect of respite care is that many schemes specially cater for, among others, elderly people with dementia. For further information, contact your local health or Social Services Department.

Another service well worth knowing about is **Crossroads**. This is a national organisation which arranges for attendants to care for very frail or disabled people in their own home, while the regular carer is away. They will come in during the day, or stay overnight, and provide whatever practical help is required. Arrangements are planned very much on an individual basis and are tailored to meet particular family circumstances. There is no charge but donations are welcomed. Demand for the service is very high, so priority is given according to the strain imposed on the carer.

Both the Citizens' Advice Bureau and Social Services Department should be able to give you the address of the local branch. Alternatively, you could contact Crossroads direct: **Crossroads**, Caring for Carers, 10 Regent Place, Rugby, Warwickshire CV21 2PN. T:01788 573653, for information on local schemes throughout the UK.

More help should be on the way. The **Princess Royal Trust for Carers** is aiming to help set up at least one carer centre or information network in every social services area in the UK in order to give carers advice and practical support. Centres in 41 places have already been established with a further 25 planned to open shortly. Existing centres are in: Aberdeen, Avon, Banbury, Basildon, Belfast, Borders,

Camden, Dundee, Falkirk, Glasgow, Greenwich, Gwynedd, Hackney, Herts, Highlands, Kennet, Kettering, Lanarkshire, Leeds, Leicester, Lincoln, Lothian, Maldon, Mid Glamorgan, Newry & Mourne, North Tyneside, Nottingham, Orkney, Perth, Peterborough, Powys, Reading, Sandwell, Sefton, Sheffield, Stirling, Sunderland, Sutton, Swindon, Wandsworth and Winchester. For further information, ask at your local Social Services Department.

Holiday breaks for carers

There are various schemes to enable families with an elderly relative to go on holiday alone or simply to enjoy a respite from their caring responsibilities.

A number of local authorities run **fostering schemes**, on similar lines to child fostering. Elderly people are invited to stay in a neighbour's home and live in the household as an ordinary family member. Lasting relationships often develop. There may be a charge or the service may be run on a voluntary basis (or be paid for by the local authority). Schemes are patchy around the country. The Citizens' Advice Bureau and Social Services Department will advise you if anything exists.

Some voluntary organisations, in particular the WRVS, Age Concern groups and sometimes the Mothers' Union, organise **holidays for older people** to give relatives a break. Different charities take responsibility according to the area where you live: the CAB, Volunteer Bureau or the Social Services Department should know whom you should approach. As with most types of provision, priority is given to families in greatest need.

You might also usefully contact Holiday Care Service which, as well as advising on holidays for elderly and disabled people, can also advise carers who need a holiday about suitable provision for their dependent relative while they are away. Write to or telephone **Holiday Care Service**, 2 Old Bank Chambers, Station Road, Horley, Surrey RH6 9HW. T:01293 774535.

Another solution is a **short stay home**, which is residential accommodation variously run by local authorities, voluntary organisations or by private individuals which cater specifically for elderly people. Style and facilities vary from the very luxurious to the frankly decrepit. The different types of home are described in more detail under the heading 'Residential care' further in the chapter. For information about local authority provision, ask the Social Services Department. For information about other names, contact: **Counsel and Care** (for Greater London area only), Twyman House, 16 Bonny Street, London NW1 9PG. T:0171 485 1566 (10.30 a.m. – 4 p.m.).

If, as opposed to general care, proper medical attention is necessary, you should consult your parent's GP. Many **hospitals and nursing homes** offer short-stay care arrangements as a means of relieving relatives and a doctor should be able to help organise this for you.

Fount of almost all knowledge on anything to do with caring is:

Carers National Association, 20-25 Glasshouse Yard, London EC1A 4JS. T:0171 490 8818 (general); 0171 490 8898 (Carers Line, Mon – Fri, 1 p.m. – 4 p.m.). The CNA, which was set up specifically to assist those caring for a friend or relative at home, is able to advise on all aspects of caring. It has over 115 local branches which are run for and by carers. There is a bi-monthly magazine called *The Carer*. Annual membership is £5.

Jewish Care, 211 Golders Green Road, London NW11 9DQ. T:0181 458 3282. Runs a number of carers' groups, mostly in London.

Useful reading
Caring for Someone?, published by the Benefits Agency. Available free from Social Security offices.
Taking Good Care, £6.95 published by Age Concern.
Help at Hand: The Home Carers' Survival Guide, by Jane Brotchie. Price £6.95 from Plymbridge Distributors Ltd., Estover Road, Plymouth PL6 7PZ (cheques payable to Plymbridge Ltd.).

Benefits and allowances

There are a number of benefits/allowances available to those with responsibility for the care of an elderly person and/or to elderly people themselves.

Entitlements for carers
Home responsibilities protection. A means of protecting your State pension if you are unable to work because of the necessity to care for an elderly person. For further details, see under 'State pensions' at the start of Chapter 3 or ask for form CF 411 at any Social Security office.

Invalid care allowance. Men and women up to the age of 65 who do not work full-time because of the need to care for a severely disabled person (i.e. someone who gets Attendance Allowance, Constant Attendance Allowance or, the two higher care components of Disability Living Allowance) may qualify for ICA. You do not need to be related to the person; nor do you need to live at the same address. Current ICA payment (1995/96) is £35.25 a week and counts as taxable income. Carers who receive income support, housing benefit or council tax benefit are entitled to a special £12.60 premium. If caring ceases, for whatever reason, the carer premium continues to be paid for a further eight weeks.

To be eligible for ICA, it is necessary to spend at least 35 hours a week looking after a severely disabled person. Claimants may earn up to £50 a week after deduction of allowable expenses without loss of benefit. For further details, together with a claim form, obtain claim pack DS 700 from your local Benefits Agency.

Entitlements for elderly/disabled people
Higher personal allowance. People over 65 receive a higher personal allowance –

£4,630 for those aged 65-74 and £4,800 for those aged 75 and over – compared with the basic personal allowance of £3,525 (1995/96). The full amount is only given to people whose income does not exceed £14,600. People with higher incomes will have the age-related element of their personal allowance reduced by £1 for every £2 of income above the income limit. For further information, see Inland Revenue leaflet IR 121 *Income Tax and Pensioners*, available from any tax office.

Higher married couple's allowance. A higher married couple's allowance is similarly available to those couples where the elder partner is over 65. The current (1995/96) amounts are: £2,995 for ages 65-74 and £3,035 for ages 75 and over, compared with the basic married couple's allowance of £1,720. However, as with higher rate personal allowance (see above), the full amount is only given to people whose income does not exceed £14,600. All married couples' allowances are restricted to 15 per cent tax relief. For further details, see Inland Revenue leaflet IR 80 *Income Tax – A Guide for Married Couples*, available from any tax office.

Attendance allowance. This is paid to people aged 65 or over who are severely disabled, either mentally or physically, and have needed almost constant care for at least six months. (They may be able to get the allowance even if no-one has actually given them that help.) An exception to the six months' qualifying period is made in the case of those who are terminally ill, who can receive the allowance without having to wait.

There are two rates of allowance: £46.70 a week for those needing 24-hour care; and £31.20 for those needing intensive day or night-time care. The allowance is tax free and is generally paid regardless of income (although payment might be affected by entering residential care). For further details, together with a claim form, obtain leaflet DS 702 from your local Social Security office.

Disability Living Allowance (DLA). This benefit is paid to people up to the age of 65 inclusive who become disabled. It has two components – a mobility component and a care component. A person can be entitled to either one or to both components.

The level of benefit depends on the person's care and/or mobility needs. There are two rates for the mobility component and three rates for the care component.

The higher rate mobility component, i.e. for people who are unable or virtually unable to walk, is £32.65 a week; the lower rate, i.e. for those who due to physical or mental disability need guidance or supervision in getting around, is £12.40.

The three rates for the care component are: higher rate, £46.70; middle rate, £31.20; lower rate, £12.40.

Disability Living Allowance is tax free and is generally paid regardless of income (although payment might be affected by entering residential care).

Except in the case of people who are terminally ill who can receive the higher rate care component of DLA immediately, there is a normal qualifying period of three months.

For further information see leaflet DS 704, obtainable from any post office, Citizens' Advice Bureau or Social Security office. The leaflet contains a reply slip, which you should complete and return as soon as possible in order to obtain the necessary claim pack. The pack includes a questionnaire with space for you to explain how the disability is making your life more difficult.

Cold weather payments. These are designed to give particularly vulnerable people extra help with heating costs during very cold weather. Anyone aged 60 and over who is in receipt of income support qualifies automatically. The payment is made by post as soon as the temperature in an area is *forecast* to drop – or actually drops – to zero degrees celsius (or below) for seven consecutive days, so people can turn up their heating secure in the knowledge that they will be receiving extra cash help. The amount paid is £8.50 a week and those eligible should receive it without having to claim. In the event of a problem, contact your local DSS office.

Financial assistance

A number of charities give financial assistance to elderly people in need. These include:

Counsel and Care, Twyman House, 16 Bonny Street, London NW1 9PG. T:0171 485 1566 (10.30 a.m. – 4 p.m.). Advice can be given to those in need of nursing care who wish to remain in their own homes. Single needs payments are sometimes available to help towards holidays, special equipment, telephone installations and other priority items.

DGAA Homelife, 1 Derry Street, London W8 5HY. T:0171 396 6700. Provides grants to enable people to remain in their own home or in the care home of their choice. Also runs both residential and nursing homes.

Guild of Aid for Gentle People, 10 St. Christopher's Place, London W1M 6HY. T:0171 935 0641. Can assist those 'of gentle birth or good education' who want to stay in their own home and who cannot call on any professional/trade body. The Guild will also consider long-term help with fees in residential and nursing homes.

Independent Living 93 Fund, PO Box 183, Nottingham NG8 3RD. T:0115 942 8191. This is a trust fund set up with Government backing to assist people, aged 16 to 65, with severe disabilities, pay for domestic or personal care to enable them to remain in their own homes.

To become eligible, applicants must first approach their local authority for assistance under the community care scheme and be successful in obtaining care services to the value of about £200 a week. The Trust may top this up by up to an extra £300, provided: (1) they are living on their own or with someone who is unable to provide all the care they need (2) they are receiving income support (or have a similar level of income once care has been paid) and also the highest rate care component of Disability Living Allowance.

Motability, Customer Services Department, Gate House, West Gate, Harlow, Essex CM20 1HR. T:01279 635666. This is a registered charity set up to assist recipients of the higher rate component of DLA (formerly mobility allowance) get maximum value for money when purchasing a car or wheelchair. Among other useful help, it can provide you with a list of vehicle manufacturers with whom it has negotiated special discounts.

Royal United Kingdom Beneficent Association (RUKBA), 6 Avonmore Road, London W14 8RL. T:0171 602 6274. Provides life-time annuities to persons in need from a professional or similar background. It is sometimes also possible to obtain help with residential home fees.

SSAFA (Soldiers', Sailors' and Airmen's Families Association), 19 Queen Elizabeth Street, London SE1 2LP. T:0171 403 8783. Assistance is restricted to those who have served in the armed forces and their families. Grants can be made to meet immediate need including rent, wheelchairs and similar essentials. Contact via the local branch is preferred (see local telephone directory for address or ask at Citizens' Advice Bureau).

The Royal Agricultural Benevolent Institution, Shaw House, 27 West Way, Oxford OX2 0QH. T:01865 724931. Supports retired or disabled farmers, farm managers and their families who are in need. Assistance includes a wide range of grants, help towards fees in residential, convalescent and nursing homes and advice on Government support. RABI has two residential care homes and flats at Bury St. Edmunds and Burnham-on-Sea and nomination rights to other homes across England.

Wireless for the Bedridden Society, 159A High Street, Hornchurch, Essex RM11 3YB. T:01708 621101. Loans on a permanent basis radios and televisions to elderly housebound people who cannot afford sets. Application should be made through a health visitor, social worker or officer of a recognised organisation.

Useful reading
For other sources of financial help, ask your library for: *A Guide to Grants for Individuals in Need*, published by the Directory of Social Change; also *The Charities Digest*, published by the Family Welfare Association.

Helpful guidance
For many people one of the main barriers to getting help is knowing which of the many thousands of charities to approach.

Charity Search exists to help elderly people in need overcome the problem by putting them in contact with those charities most likely to be able to assist. Write to:

The Secretary, **Charity Search**, 25 Portview Road, Avonmouth, Bristol BS11 9LD. T:0117 982 4060.

A book written by the founder explains the different criteria charities use in deciding grants. *Charity Made Clear* by Auriel James £4.95 (cheques payable to Petal Publishing) is available post free from the above address.

Special accommodation

Retired people who need particular support, assistance or care may choose or need to move to accommodation where special services are provided. This can either be sheltered housing or a residential home. Both terms cover an enormous spectrum, so anyone considering either of these options should make a point of investigating the market before reaching a decision.

An all too common mistake is for people to anticipate old age long before it arrives and to move into accommodation that is either too small or quite unnecessarily 'sheltered', years before they have need of the facilities. By the same token, some individuals buy or rent sheltered housing with a minimum of support services, only to have to move a few months later because they need rather more help than is available.

Choosing the right accommodation is critically important, as it can make all the difference to independence, life style and general well-being. It can also of course lift a great burden off families' shoulders to know that their parents are happy, comfortable, in congenial surroundings and with help on tap, should this be necessary.

Sheltered housing

As a general description, sheltered housing is usually a development of independent, purpose-designed bungalows or flats within easy access of shops and public transport. They generally have a warden, an alarm system for emergencies and often some common facilities, such as: a garden, possibly a launderette, a sitting room and a dining room with meals provided for residents, on an optional basis, either once a day or several days a week.

Residents normally have access to all the usual range of services – home helps, meals on wheels – in the same way as any other elderly person.

Sheltered housing is available for sale or rental, variously through private developers, housing associations or local authorities. It is occasionally also provided through gifted housing schemes; or on a shared ownership basis.

Sheltered housing for sale

During the early part of the nineties, anyone looking to purchase sheltered accommodation was very much in a buyers' market. Not only was there a wide choice of property but due to the recession prices actually dropped.

While there were bargains to be had, the downside was that some developers went into receivership. Many others either froze all new work or cut back dramatically on the number of new properties they were planning.

The result is that, with sales now picking up again, there are fears of a shortage with some buyers having to go on a waiting list. Although this is emphatically not a reason for rushing into a decision you might regret, if you were hoping to move in the fairly near future it could be as well to start looking sooner rather than later.

There are around 40 companies offering sheltered housing for sale – with standards and facilities varying enormously. Many now also provide residential and nursing care as an adjunct to their retirement home schemes.

Flats and houses are usually sold on long leases (99 years or more) for a capital sum, with a weekly or monthly service charge to cover maintenance and resident care services.

Should a resident decide to move, the property can usually be sold on the open market, either through an estate agent, or through the developer, provided the prospective buyer is over 55 years of age. Most developers impose a levy of 1 per cent of the sale price for checking the credentials of incoming residents, irrespective of whether the property is sold through them. Look carefully at any schemes that enable you to buy the property at a discount as many such schemes entitle the developer to retain a proportion of the equity on resale.

Occupiers normally have to enter into a management agreement with the housebuilder and it is important to establish exactly what the commitment is likely to be before buying into such schemes. Factors that should be considered include: who the managing agent is; the warden's duties; what the service charge covers; the ground rent; the arrangements for any repairs that might prove necessary; whether there is a residents' association; whether pets are allowed; what the conditions are with regard to reselling the property – and the tenant's rights in the matter.

Prices. The range of prices is very wide – between approximately £40,000 and £250,000 – depending on size, location and type of property. Weekly service charges vary between roughly £12 and £25, with £18-£25 being the norm.

The service charge usually covers: the cost of the warden, alarm system, maintenance, repair and renewal of any communal facilities (external and internal) and sometimes the heating and lighting costs. It may also cover insurance on the building (but not the contents). A particular point to watch is that the service charge tends to rise annually, sometimes well above the inflation level. Be wary of service charges that seem uncommonly reasonable in the sales literature, as these are often increased sharply following purchase. Owners of sheltered accommodation have the same rights as other leaseholders and charges can therefore be challenged in the courts.

A further safeguard is the Sheltered Housing Code operated by the **National House Building Council** (Chiltern Avenue, Amersham, Bucks HP6 5AP. T:01494 434477), which has now become mandatory for all registered housebuilders. The Code, which applies to all new sheltered dwellings in England and Wales registered on or after 1st April 1990, has two main requirements: (a) that every prospective purchaser should be given a Purchasers Information Pack (PIP), clearly outlining all essential information that they will need to enable them to decide whether or not to buy; (b) that the builder and management organisation enter into a formal legal agreement giving purchasers the benefit of the legal rights specified in the Code. An independent advice service is run in association with Age Concern.

For those on lowish incomes, it may also be possible to get housing benefit to meet some or all of the service charge. The local authority Housing Department will advise on this.

The following organisations can provide information about sheltered housing for sale:

Sheltered Housing Services, 8-9 Abbey Parade, North Circular Road, London W5 1EE. T:0181 997 9313. Independent company which, acting in association with the New Homes Marketing Board, offers information and advice on most current sites and resales countrywide. Cost of making an enquiry, plus up-dating service for one year, is £7.50.

Elderly Accommodation Counsel, 46a Chiswick High Road, London W4 1SZ. T:0181 995 8320. A registered charity with a nationwide computer register – covering some 500,000 dwellings – that for a £5 fee (waived in cases of limited income) supplies detailed information on accommodation to suit individual requirements, in area of choice, within requested price range.

Sheltered Housing Advisory and Conciliation Service (SHACS), Walkden House, 3-10 Melton Street, London NW1 2EJ. T:0171 383 2006. Operating in association with Age Concern, SHACS offers advice and help to anyone with problems living in private sector sheltered housing. Guidance is also offered to those thinking about buying on points to check before signing any contract.

Useful reading
A Buyer's Guide to Sheltered Housing, published by Age Concern England/National Housing and Town Planning Council, price £2.50. An excellent guide to the sort of questions you should ask before committing yourself. Also useful information on the financial aspects of buying a sheltered home. Available from Age Concern England, Astral House, 1268 London Road, London SW16 4ER.

Private companies with sheltered housing for sale
New developments are constantly under construction. Properties tend to be sold quickly soon after completion, so it pays to find out about future developments and to get on any waiting lists well in advance of a prospective purchase. Firms specialising in this type of property include:

Beechcroft Developments Ltd., 1 Church Lane, Wallingford, Oxfordshire OX10 0DX. T:01491 834975. Two-, three- and four-bedroom cottages situated in market towns in: Berkshire, Buckinghamshire, Oxfordshire, Wiltshire, Hampshire, Gloucestershire and Dorset. Prices range from £150,000 to £250,000. Videos can be loaned on request.

Bovis Retirement Homes, The Brew House, Castle Bromwich Hall, Castle Bromwich, Birmingham B36 9DF. T:0121 749 4411. Mostly one- and two-bedroom apartments in very sheltered housing – in Cheshire, Merseyside and the West Midlands – with prices ranging from £79,950 to £175,000. There are also warden-controlled apartments in Cornwall, with prices starting at £45,000.

English Courtyard Association, 8 Holland Street, London W8 4LT. Freephone: 0800 220858. Architecturally award-winning 'courtyard-style' schemes in the South and South-West. Two- and three-bedroom cottages and flats for sale on 150-year leases. Latest developments at Halstead, Ickenham, Ilminster, Mytchett, Stanford in the Vale and Tattenhall. Prices range from £95,000 to £235,000.

Home Housing Association, Ridley House, Regent Centre, Gosforth, Newcastle upon Tyne NE3 3JE. T:0191 285 0311. Sites throughout the country with varying levels of independence/management. Prices up to £60,000.

McCarthy & Stone (Developments) Ltd., Homelife House, 26-32 Oxford Road, Bournemouth, Dorset BH8 8EZ. T:01202 292480. Builds approximately 1,500 new retirement apartments a year in all parts of the country including Scotland and Wales. Prices start at around £42,000 for a 125-year lease. Also has retirement cottages on various sites with prices from around £67,000.

Pegasus Retirement Homes plc., 105-107 Bath Road, Cheltenham, Glos GL53 7LE. T:01242 576610. Wide choice of one-, two- and three-bedroom apartments and cottages in Avon, Berkshire, Bucks, Cheshire, Devon, Dorset, Glos, Hampshire, Lancs, Northants, Oxon, Wales and Worcs. Prices are from £69,000.

Retirement Care Group plc., Tubs Hill House, London Road, Sevenoaks, Kent TN13 1DB. T:01732 460664. A major management company involved in retirement estates in all parts of England and Wales.

Springshire Holdings plc., Cranmer Mount, St. Anns Hill, Nottingham NG3 4LA. T:0115 985 7236. Retirement communities created within period country houses and their grounds. Luxury accommodation in self-contained flats and cottages, often with access to associated nursing and rest-homes. Current developments include: Henford House, Warminster and The Firs, Nottingham. Prices range from about £40,000 to £85,000.

Westbury Retirement Homes, Westminster House, Mercia Road, Gloucester GL1 2SQ. T:01452 527123. Retirement developments including cottages and apartments in Wiltshire and West Midlands. Prices from about £44,995 to £59,995.

Also of interest: **Country Houses Association**, 41 Kingsway, London WC2B 6UB. T:0171 836 1624. The Association provides one- to three-room apartments in houses of historic or architectural interest. Residents loan the Association a fixed sum, based on the apartment chosen, which is refunded – less 3 per cent a year – when they leave. Additionally, there are monthly charges for: all meals, heating, cleaning, resident staff and other overheads. Loans range from £25,000, plus monthly charge from £750, for one bedroom and bathroom to £75,000, plus monthly charge of up to £1,850, for a three-room apartment.

Housing associations with sheltered housing for sale

Housing associations build sheltered housing for sale and also manage sheltered housing developments on behalf of private construction companies.

Guardian Housing Association, Fountain Court, Oxford Spires Business Park, Kidlington, Oxon OX5 1NZ.T:01865 854000. Flats, bungalows and cottages on long leases at prices ranging from £25,000 to £115,000.

Hanover Property Management Ltd., 1st Floor, Maylands House, Maylands Avenue, Hemel Hempstead, Herts HP2 7DE. T:01442 242419. Most of the property is built by private developers. Prices start below £40,000 for flats on 125-year leases and £60,000 for freehold bungalows.

James Butcher Leasehold Housing Association, James Butcher House, 39 High Street, Theale, Reading RG7 5AH. T:01734 317200. Apartments and houses in the South on 99-year leases, starting at around £35,000 (shared ownership).

Retirement Lease Housing Association, 2nd Floor, 1 Pickford Street, Aldershot, Hants GU11 1TY. T:01252 318181/2. Bungalows and flats on 99-year leases from around £50,000 and upwards in the South East. Shared ownership purchase available in some cases.

Rented sheltered housing

This is normally provided by local authorities, housing associations and certain benevolent societies. As with accommodation to buy, quality varies.

Local authorities. This is usually only available to people who have resided in the area for some time. There is often an upper and lower age limit for admission and prospective tenants may have to undergo a medical examination, since as a rule only those who are physically fit are accepted. Should a resident become infirm or frail, alternative accommodation will be found. Apply to the local Housing or Social Services Department or via a Housing Advice Centre.

Housing associations. Housing associations supply much of the newly built sheltered housing. Rents, which may sometimes be inclusive of service charge, vary very roughly from £35 to £110 a week. The **National Federation of Housing Associations** expects the average to be about £55 during 1996. In case of need, income support may be obtained to help with the cost.

Before signing an agreement, a point you should be aware of is that some charitable housing associations, including the Abbeyfield Society, offer a licensee arrangement which does not provide the same security of tenure as some other tenancy agreements. Where this is the case, you are strongly advised to have the proposed contract checked by a lawyer to ensure you properly understand your rights – and those on the other side.

Citizens' Advice Bureaux and Housing Departments often keep a list of local housing associations. You can look in the *Yellow Pages* telephone directory. Or alternatively, you can contact either Age Concern or the Housing Corporation, at the following addresses:

Age Concern England, Astral House, 1268 London Road, London SW16 4ER. Has lists of housing associations with rented accommodation for older people. Letters should be addressed to the Housing Information Officer and a large sae enclosed.

Housing Corporation, 149 Tottenham Court Road, London W1P 0BN. T:0171 393 2000. Will send you a list of their regional offices who will be able to supply you with addresses of housing associations in their area.

For Scotland, Wales and Northern Ireland, contact:

Housing for Wales/Tai Cymru, 25-30 Lambourne Crescent, Llanishen, Cardiff CF4 5ZJ. T:01222 747979.

Scottish Homes, Thistle House, 91 Haymarket Terrace, Edinburgh EH12 5HE. T:0131 313 0044.

Northern Ireland Federation of Housing Associations, Carlisle Memorial Centre, 88 Clifton Street, Belfast BT13 1AB. T:01232 230446.

A few of the very many housing associations include:

The Abbeyfield Society, 53 Victoria Street, St. Albans, Herts AL1 3UW. T:01727 857536; and 15 West Maitland Street, Edinburgh EH12 5EA. T:0131 225 7801. Abbeyfield has nearly 1,000 supportive houses nationwide providing independent accommodation, a resident housekeeper and main meals of the day. Also over 40 houses providing 24-hour 'extra care' facilities.

Anchor Housing Association, Fountain Court, Oxford Spires Business Park, Kidlington, Oxon OX5 1NZ. T:01865 854000. Provides over 22,000 flats for older people whose existing housing is poor and who for pressing social, health and financial reasons need the security and support of sheltered housing. The flats are in towns and cities all over England and each scheme has a guest room and laundry. There are also special Anchor Housing-with-Care flats for very frail people who need more help with everyday living. Applicants must have strong links with the area.

Central and Cecil Housing Trust, 2 Priory Road, Kew, Richmond, Surrey TW9 3DG. T:0181 940 9828. Provides a range of sheltered housing and also residential care homes in London. Priority is given to those in greatest need with a local connection. Current charges for sheltered accommodation start at £83 per week and at £309 for residential care.

Fellowship Houses Trust, Clock House, Byfleet, Surrey KT14 7RN. T:01932 343172. Sheltered housing schemes in southern England.

Habinteg Housing Association, 10 Nottingham Place, London W1M 3FA. T:0171 486 3519; 145a Merton Road, Wimbledon, London SW19 1ED. T:0181 545 0510; and Ground Floor, Prospect House, Tong Street, Dudley Hill, Bradford, West Yorkshire BD4 9LY. T:01274 682215. Habinteg builds accessible houses for rent, suitable for both able-bodied people and those with disabilities. Most have emergency cover for elderly people, and others, for whom an extra degree of security would be welcome.

Hanover Housing Association, Hanover House, 18 The Avenue, Egham, Surrey TW20 9AB. T:01784 438361. Provides managed sheltered accommodation for rent throughout England. Applicants must be over 60.

James Butcher Housing Association, James Butcher House, 39 High Street, Theale, Reading RG7 5AH. T:01734 317200. Sheltered housing schemes in southern counties. Priority given to those with connections in the areas. Certain schemes offer a residential care facility where all meals and residential care are provided.

JBG Housing Society Ltd., 221 Golders Green Road, London NW11 9DW. T:0181 458 3282. Some 300 warden-controlled flatlets primarily for Jewish people in housing need, in and near London.

Oaklee Housing Association Ltd., Murray House, Murray Street, Belfast BT1 6DN. T:01232 325175. Forty sheltered housing schemes in Northern Ireland.

Servite Houses, 2 Bridge Avenue, London W6 9JP. T:0181 563 7090. Some 4,000 flatlets with resident warden in and around London, the West Midlands and Merseyside. Rent (incl. service charges) is about £50 per week. There are also 10 residential care homes for frail elderly people in the London region and two in the West Midlands.

Benevolent societies. These all cater for specific professional and other groups.

Housing 21, PO Box 32, St John's Road, Penn, High Wycombe, Bucks HP10 8JF. T:01494 813771. A charitable housing association with over 12,000 flats in 350 sheltered housing schemes throughout England, mainly for active elderly people.

Royal Alfred Seafarers' Society, Weston Acres, Woodmansterne Lane, Banstead, Surrey SM7 3HB. T:01737 352231. Residential homes in Banstead and Eastbourne for retired mariners, their widows and those closely connected with the sea. Nursing care is provided at Banstead, as is sheltered housing under assured tenancy terms. For further details, contact the General Secretary at the above address.

SSAFA (Soldiers', Sailors' and Airmen's Families Association), 19 Queen Elizabeth Street, London SE1 2LP. T:0171 403 8783. Works with the Abbeyfield Society to provide sheltered accommodation for retired ex-service people.

Teachers' Benevolent Fund, Hamilton House, Mabledon Place, London WC1H 9BE. T:0171 465 0499. Retirement homes for school teachers and their dependants in Elstree (Herts), Trentham (Staffs), Scarborough and Birmingham. Nursing and convalescent care are available in all their homes, as are respite care and holiday accommodation for those with special needs.

Alternative ways of buying sheltered accommodation
For those who cannot afford either to buy into sheltered housing outright or through a mortgage, there are a variety of alternative payment methods:

Shared ownership and 'Sundowner' schemes. Part-ownership schemes are now offered by a number of developers. Would-be residents who must be over 55 years part-buy/part-rent, with the amount of rent varying according to the size of the initial lump sum. Residents can sell at any time but they only recoup that percentage of the sale price which is proportionate to their original capital investment, with no allowance for any rental payments made over the intervening period.

'Investment' and gifted housing schemes. Some charities and housing associations operate these schemes (sometimes called 'leasehold schemes'), for which a capital sum is required to obtain sheltered accommodation. They work as follows. The buyer puts in the larger share of the capital, usually 50 to 80 per cent, and the housing association puts in the remainder. The buyer pays rent on the housing association's share of the accommodation and also service charges for the communal facilities.

Gifted housing schemes differ in that an individual donates his/her property, usually to a registered charity, in return for being housed and cared for in their own home or, if necessary, in one of the charity's sheltered homes. The attraction is that the owner can remain in his or her own property with none of the burden of its upkeep.

However, it is advisable to consult a solicitor before signing anything, because such schemes have the big negative of reducing the value of the owner's estate with consequent loss for any beneficiaries.

One of the better known organisations to offer both kinds of scheme is the charity, Help the Aged. Its investment type accommodation is in: Chester, Luton, Woking, Rustington, Salcombe, Lowestoft, Corbridge, Huddersfield, Colchester and Lindfield. With the gifted housing scheme, Help the Aged becomes responsible for the building's external maintenance, insurance and rates. Their alternative sheltered accommodation consists of private apartments in large houses; or modern purpose-built flats and bungalows, set in the grounds of the main house. Contact: **Help the Aged**, Housing and Care Department, St. James's Walk, London EC1R 0BE. T:0171 253 0253.

For further information on such schemes, send for a copy of Age Concern's free factsheet *Housing Schemes for Older People Where a Capital Sum is Required*, available from: the Information Department, Astral House, 1268 London Road, London SW16 4ER (enclose sae).

Almshouses
The term 'almshouse' describes sheltered housing for elderly people of reduced means, which is administered by a charitable trust. There are now over 2,500 groups of almshouses providing about 30,000 dwellings. Although many are of considerable age, most of these have been modernised, and new ones are being built. Rents are not charged but there may be a maintenance contribution towards upkeep and heating.

A point you should be aware of is that, similar to Abbeyfield and some other charitable housing associations, almshouses do not provide the same security of tenure as some other tenancies. You would be well advised to have the proposed agreement checked by a lawyer or other expert to ensure you understand exactly what your rights are.

There is no standard way to apply for an almshouse since each charity has its own qualifications for residence. Some housing departments and advice centres keep lists of local almshouses; or write to: **The Almshouse Association**, Billingbear Lodge, Wokingham, Berkshire RG40 5RU. T:01344 52922.

Granny flats
A granny flat or annexe is a self-contained unit attached to a family house. A large house can be converted or extended for this purpose, but planning permission is needed. Enquire at your local authority planning department. Some councils have houses to rent with granny flats, particularly New Towns.

Housing for ethnic groups
ASRA Greater London Housing Association Ltd., 239-41 Kennington Lane, London SE11 5QU. T:0171-820 0155. Provides sheltered housing for Asian elders, single women and families.
ASRA Leicester, 78 Burleys Way, Leicester. T:0116 255 8121. Offers a similar service to the above.

Salvation Army homes
The Salvation Army has 27 eventide homes in various parts of the British Isles offering residential care for elderly men and women unable to manage independently in their own homes. Christian caring is given within a family atmosphere, in pleasant surroundings, but the homes are not nursing homes. Fees are within the DSS scale.

For more information contact: **The Salvation Army Social Services Headquarters**, 105-109 Judd Street, King's Cross, London WC1H 9TS. T:0171 383 4230.

Very sheltered schemes
A number of organisations which provide sheltered accommodation also have extra care sheltered housing, designed for those who can no longer look after themselves without assistance in their own rooms. Priority would normally be given to existing tenants but others can apply. Cost is in the region of £210 a week; and about £280 in London. Although expensive, it is cheaper than most private residential homes and often more appropriate than full-scale nursing care. A possible problem is that tenants of some of these schemes do not have security of tenure and could therefore be asked to leave if more intensive care were required.

Among the housing associations that provide these facilities are Abbeyfield and Servite Houses. Additional names should be obtainable from the various regional offices of the **Housing Corporation**, 149 Tottenham Court Road, London W1P 0BN.

Community Care
Since the start of Community Care in April 1993, anyone needing help in arranging suitable care for an elderly person should contact their local Social Services department.

Before making suggestions, the department will assess what type of provision would best meet the needs of the individual concerned. This could be either services or special equipment to enable them to stay in their own home; residential home accommodation; or a nursing home. If residential or nursing home care is necessary, the department will arrange a place – either in a local authority or other home – pay the charge and seek re-imbursement from the individual according to their means. (See 'Financial Assistance for Residential and Nursing Home Care', page 440).

The general range of choices is the same as for an individual making their own private arrangements, which of course anyone – providing they can afford it – is free to do.

Residential homes
There may come a time when it is no longer possible for an elderly person to manage without being in proper residential care. Sometimes known as rest homes, the accommodation usually consists of a bedroom plus communal dining rooms, lounges and gardens. All meals are provided, rooms are cleaned and staff are at hand to give whatever help is needed. Most homes are fully furnished, though it is usually possible to take small items of furniture. Except in some of the more expensive private homes, bathrooms are normally shared. Intensive nursing care is not usually included.

Homes are run by private individuals (or companies), voluntary organisations and local authorities. All private and voluntary homes must be registered with the Social Services to ensure minimum standards. Any unregistered home should not be considered!

No home should ever be accepted 'on spec'. It is very important that the individual should have a proper chance to visit it and ask any questions. Before reaching a final decision, it is a good idea to arrange a short stay to see whether the facilities are suitable and pleasant.

Private homes. Private rest homes tend either to be converted houses, taking up to about 30 people; or, as more companies move into the market, purpose-built accommodation which may include heated swimming pool and luxury facilities. The degree of care varies. If a resident becomes increasingly infirm, a rest home will normally continue to look after them if possible although it may be necessary at some point to arrange transfer to a nursing home or hospital. Fees cover an enormous range: from about £250 a week to over £1,000. The average is about £350.

Voluntary rest homes. These are run by charities, religious bodies or other voluntary organisations. Eligibility may be determined by age, background or occupation, depending on the criteria of the managing organisation. Income may be a factor, as may general fitness and individuals may be invited to a personal interview before acceptance onto the waiting list. Priority tends to be given to those in greatest need. Homes are often in large converted houses, with accommodation for under 10 people or up to 100. Fees normally start at around the £197 mark with top charges, about £400 – and even higher for Greater London.

Local authority homes. These are sometimes referred to as 'Part III Accommodation' and admission would invariably be arranged by the Social Services department. If someone does not like the particular accommodation suggested, they can turn it down and ask the department what other offers might be available. Weekly charges vary around the country, starting from about £197. In practice, however, individuals are only charged according to their means.

Nursing homes

Nursing homes provide medical supervision and fully qualified nurses, 24 hours a day. Most are privately run with the remainder being supported by voluntary organisations. All nursing homes must be registered with the local Health Authority which keeps a list of what homes are available in the area.

Private. They normally accommodate between 15 and 100 patients. Average fees are between £325 and £500 a week; in London, they start at around £350 – rising in some of the plusher nursing homes to over £1,000 weekly; in many other parts of the country, charges can reach £500 or even more if intensive nursing is required. For information about private nursing homes in the UK, contact the following: **Elderly Accommodation Counsel**, 46A Chiswick High Road, London W4 1SZ. T:0181 742 1182; **The Registered Nursing Home Association**, Calthorpe House, Hagley Road, Edgbaston, Birmingham B16 8QY. T:0121 454 2511.

Voluntary organisations. There are normally very long waiting lists and beds are often reserved for those who have been in the charity's rest home. Charges in Greater

London start at around £325 but are calculated according to means. Voluntary organisations which run residential and nursing homes include:

British Red Cross, 9 Grosvenor Crescent, London SW1X 7EJ.
Crossways Trust Ltd., 11 South Road, Brighton, Sussex BN1 6SB.
DGAA Homelife, 1 Derry Street, London W8 5HY.
Friends of the Elderly and Gentlefolk's Help, 42 Ebury Street, London SW1W 0LZ.
Jewish Care, 221 Golders Green Road, London NW11 9DQ.
Quaker Social Responsibility and Education, Friends House, 173-177 Euston Road, London NW1 2BJ.
Royal United Kingdom Beneficent Association, 6 Avonmore Road, London W14 8RL.
Women's Royal Voluntary Service, 234/244 Stockwell Road, London SW9 9SP.
Catholic Old People's Homes, are listed in the *Catholic Directory*, available in libraries.

Financial assistance for residential and nursing home care

Under the Community Care arrangements people needing to go into a residential or nursing home may receive help from their local authority Social Services department.

As explained earlier, the department will make the arrangements direct with the home following their assessment procedure and will seek reimbursement from the person towards the cost, according to set means-testing rules.

People who were already in a residential or nursing home before April 1993 have what is known as 'preserved rights' and continue receiving special levels of income support as before. The maximum amount they can get depends on the type and level of care they receive. The current maximum weekly amount (1995/96) for residential care homes is between £197 and £267 (£34 higher in London); and for nursing homes, between £296 and £331 (£39 higher in London).

People who had been or are currently paying for themselves but can no longer afford to do so may have the right to claim help, now or in the future, if they qualify on grounds of financial need – for example if their savings fall to £8,000.

For more information, see leaflet IS 50 *Income Support: Help for People who Live in Residential Care Homes or Nursing Homes* from your local DSS office.

Age Concern also publishes some useful factsheets: *Local Authority Charging Procedures for Residential and Nursing Home Care* and *Preserved Entitlement to Income Support for Residential and Nursing Homes*, available on receipt of large sae.

Further information

Key sources of information about voluntary and private homes are: the *Charities Digest* (available in libraries, Housing Aid Centres and Citizens' Advice Bureaux) and the *Directory of Independent Hospitals and Health Services* (available in libraries).

Elderly Accommodation Counsel, 46a Chiswick High Road, London W4 1SZ. T:0181 995 8320. Has a nationwide computer register with details of all types of accommodation suitable to meet the needs of retired or elderly people including sheltered housing for sale or rent, residential care, nursing homes and hospices. Use of the service costs £5 (fee waived in cases of limited income). The Counsel can advise on possible sources of top-up funding for those requiring help in meeting the fees in a home.

Grace, 35 Walnut Tree Close, Guildford, Surrey GU1 4UL. T:0800 137669. Provides a comprehensive advisory service for elderly people seeking residential or nursing home accommodation. Grace advisers personally match accommodation with a client's needs – whether for permanent or short stay – from their wide knowledge of homes. Experienced representatives assess homes annually and also on change of ownership. There is a registration fee of £25.

Cinnamon Trust, Poldarves Farm, Trescowe Common, Germoe, Penzance, Cornwall TR20 9RX. T:01736 850291. Maintains a register of residential and care homes that allow pets to be kept.

Social Services Departments keep lists of both voluntary and private homes as does (but only in the Greater London area where it visits all homes every year) **Counsel & Care**, Twyman House, 16 Bonny Street, London NW1 9PG. T:0171 485 1566.

Useful reading
Finding Residential and Nursing Home Accommodation. Free factsheet obtainable from Age Concern England, Astral House, 1268 London Road, London SW16 4ER. Please enclose large sae.

Some special problems

A minority of people, as they become older, suffer from special problems which can cause great distress. Because families do not like to talk about them, they may be unaware of what services are available so may be missing out both on practical help and sometimes also on financial assistance.

Hypothermia
Elderly people tend to be more vulnerable to the cold. If the body drops below a certain temperature, it can be dangerous because one of the symptoms of hypothermia is that sufferers no longer actually feel cold. Instead, they may lose their appetite and vitality and may become mentally confused. Instead of doing all the sensible things like getting a hot drink and putting on an extra sweater, they are liable to neglect themselves further and can put themselves at real risk. Although heating costs are often blamed, quite wealthy people can also be victims by allowing their home to become too cold or not wearing sufficient clothing. For this reason, during a cold snap it is very important to check up regularly on an elderly person living alone.

British Gas, Electricity Companies and the Solid Fuels Advisory Service are all willing to give advice on how heating systems can be used more efficiently and economically. (See telephone directory for nearest branch or ask at the Citizens' Advice Bureau.)

Another very useful source of help is the **Winter Warmth Line**, run by Help the Aged on behalf of the Department of Health. This is a freephone advice service which – as well as offering practical information on beating the cold – can, if there is a particular problem, refer you to a relevant help agency in your area. The telephone number to dial is 0800 289404. Help the Aged also distributes a useful Government booklet *Keep Warm, Keep Well*, available free by calling the Winter Warmth Line.

Insulation can also play a very large part in keeping a home warmer and cheaper to heat. There are various grants available to assist with this. See heating and insulation sections in Chapter 8, Your Home.

Additionally, elderly and disabled people in receipt of income support may receive a cold weather payment to help with heating costs during a particularly cold spell, i.e. when the temperature is forecast to drop to zero degrees celsius (or below) for seven consecutive days. The amount paid is £8.50 a week. Those eligible should receive the money automatically. In the event of any problem, ask at your local DSS office. In the event of any emergency, such as a power cut, contact the Citizens' Advice Bureau or local Age Concern group.

Incontinence

Incontinence can cause deep embarrassment to sufferers as well as inconvenience to relatives. It can occur in an elderly person for all sorts of reasons and a doctor should always be consulted, as it can often be cured or at least alleviated by proper treatment. To assist with the practical problems, many local authorities operate a laundry service which collects soiled linen, sometimes several times a week. In many areas the service is free and the person to talk to is the Health Visitor or District Nurse (telephone your local Health Centre) who will be able to advise about this and other facilities.

InconTact (National Action on Incontinence) offers information and support to people whose lives are affected by bladder and bowel problems. An Incontinence Information Helpline, staffed by nurses with a special understanding of these conditions, operates Monday to Friday from 9 a.m. to 6 p.m. T:0191 213 0050.

Useful reading
In Control: Help with Incontinence by Penny Mares. Price £4.50 available from Publications Unit, Age Concern England, Astral House, 1268 London Road, London SW16 4ER.

Free booklets on continence care are available from Coloplast Ltd., Freepost, Peterborough Business Park, PE2 6BR.

Dementia
Sometimes an elderly person can become confused, forgetful, suffer severe loss of

memory or can have violent mood swings and at times be abnormally aggressive. It is important to consult a doctor as soon as possible as the cause may be due to depression, stress or even vitamin deficiency, all of which can be treated and often completely cured. If dementia is diagnosed, there are ways of helping a sufferer to cope better with acute forgetfulness and other symptoms. As well as a doctor, it is usually a very good idea to talk to the Health Visitor, as she will know about any helpful facilities that may be available locally and can also arrange appointments with other professionals, such as the Community Psychiatric Nurse and Occupational Therapist.

The charity, MIND, can often also help. Addresses to contact are:

MIND (National Association for Mental Health), for England, Granta House, 15-19 Broadway, London E15 4BQ, T:0181 519 2122; for Wales, 23 St. Mary Street, Cardiff CF1 2AA. T:01222 395123.

Scottish Association for Mental Health, Atlantic House, 38 Gardners Crescent, Edinburgh EH3 8DQ. T:0131 229 9687.

Northern Ireland Association for Mental Health, 80 University Street, Belfast BT7 1HE. T:01232 328474.

Two other helpful organisations giving support to people with dementia and their carers are:

Alzheimer's Disease Society, for England and Wales and Northern Ireland, Gordon House, 10 Greencoat Place, London SW1P 1PH. T:0171 306 0606.
Alzheimer's Scotland – Action on Dementia, 8 Hill Street, Edinburgh EH2 3JZ. T:0131 225 1453. The Society has local groups throughout the country; for addresses and other information, contact the London or Edinburgh office.

Useful reading
Caring for the Person with Dementia, published by the Alzheimer's Disease Society, £3.50 incl. p&p.

The 36-Hour Day – Caring at Home for Confused Elderly People. Co-published with Age Concern England by Hodder & Stoughton and available from all good bookshops. Price £9.99.

Coping with Caring, by Brian Lodge. Published by MIND and available from MIND Publications Mail Order Service, at the address listed above. Price £2.65 incl. p&p.

16 No One is Immortal

In Bali death is celebrated with glorious processions, merry-making and days of feasting. In Western society, we go to the other extreme. Many couples never even discuss death or the financial practicalities, in the subconscious belief perhaps that to do so would be tempting fate. For the same reason, many people put off making a will or rationalise that it does not really matter, since in any case their possessions will eventually go to their family. However, as every widows' organisation would testify, a great deal of heartbreak and real financial worry could be avoided if husbands and wives were more open with each other.

Wills

Anyone who is married, has children or is over the age of 35 should make a will. At very least, should anything happen, this will ensure that their wishes are known and properly executed. But also very important, it will spare their family the legal complications that arise when someone dies intestate. A very major problem if someone dies without leaving a will is that the surviving husband or wife will usually have to wait very much longer for badly needed cash, as the legal formalities are more complex. There will be no executor. Also, the individual's assets will be distributed according to a rigid formula, which may be a far cry from what he or she had intended and may perversely result in their partner's security being quite unnecessarily jeopardised.

Laws of intestacy
The rules if you die without leaving a will are as follows:

- If there are **no surviving children, parents, brothers, sisters or direct nephews or nieces** of the deceased, the widow/widower inherits the whole of the estate.
- If there are **children but no surviving spouse**, the estate is divided equally among the children. If one child has died, his/her share would go to his/her own children.
- If there is a **spouse and children**, the partner receives: all personal possessions, £125,000, plus a life interest in half of the remainder. The other half goes to the children, who will also inherit their mother or father's half on his/her death.
- If there are **no children** but other close members of the family still living (parents, brothers, sisters, direct nephews or nieces), the surviving partner receives: all

personal possessions, £200,000, plus half of the remainder of the estate. The other half is divided between the rest of the family.

- **Common law spouses** have no legal rights of inheritance (unless it can be proved that they were being supported by the deceased).
- If a **couple are separated,** but not divorced, they are still legally married and, therefore, the separated partner would in all probability be the major beneficiary.

Making a will

You have three choices: you can do it yourself; you can ask your bank to help you; or you can use a solicitor.

Doing it yourself

Homemade wills are not generally recommended. People often use ambiguous wording, which while perfectly clear to the individual who has written it, may be less patently obvious to others. This could result in the donor's wishes being misinterpreted and could also cause considerable delay in settling the estate.

You can buy forms from W.H. Smith and other stationers which, while helpful, are not perfect and still leave considerable margin for error. Alternatively you could purchase the *Which?* Action Pack entitled *Make Your Will*, which, in addition to a number of forms, contains guidance on inheritance tax and other helpful information. The text is based on the law as it applies in England and Wales and is therefore not pertinent to residents of Scotland and Northern Ireland. Price of the pack is £10.99, obtainable from **Consumers' Association**, Castlemead, Gascoyne Way, Hertford X, SG14 1LH.

For individuals with sight difficulties, RNIB has produced a comprehensive guide to making or changing a will which is available in large print size, Braille and on tape, as well as in standard print size. This is obtainable free by contacting Sebastian Wilberforce at **RNIB**, 224 Great Portland Street, London W1N 6AA. T:0171 388 1266.

Two witnesses are needed and an essential point to remember is that beneficiaries cannot witness a will; nor can the spouses of any beneficiaries. In certain circumstances, a will can be rendered invalid. A sensible precaution for anyone doing it themselves is to have it checked by a solicitor or by a legal expert from the Citizens' Advice Bureau.

Banks

Advice on wills and the administration of estates is carried out by the trustee companies of most of the major high street bbanks.

In particular, the services they offer are: to provide general guidance, to act as executor and to administer the estate. They will also introduce clients to a solicitor and keep a copy of the will – plus other important documents – in their safe, to avoid the risk of their being mislaid. Additionally, banks (as solicitors) can give tax planning and other financial guidance, including advice on inheritance tax. Some banks will draw up a will for you.

Solicitors

Solicitors offer to: draw up a will, act as executors and administer the estate. Like banks, they will also of course keep a copy of your will in safe keeping. If you do not know a solicitor, you can ask your bank or the Citizens Advice Bureau. Or you can write to the **Law Society**, 113 Chancery Lane, London WC2A 1PL. T:0171 242 1222.

Charges

These can vary enormously, depending on the size and complexity of the will. A basic will could be as little as £50 or the cost could run into many hundreds of pounds. Always ask for an estimate before proceeding. Remember too that professional fees carry 17.5 per cent VAT. Solicitors charge according to the time they spend on a job, so although the actual work may not take very long, if you spend hours discussing your will, or changing it every few months, the costs can escalate very considerably.

Legal aid

Legal aid is available to certain groups of people for making a will. These include, among one or two other categories: people aged over 70, people with a mental disorder and those who are blind, deaf or have no speech. Additionally, to qualify, they will need to satisfy the financial criteria. For further information enquire at your CAB.

Executors

You will need to appoint at least one executor to administer your will. An executor can be a beneficiary under the estate and can be a member of your family or a friend whom you trust to act impartially, always provided of course that he/she is willing to accept the responsibility. Or, and this is generally advisable for larger estates, you could appoint your solicitor or bank.

The fees will be additional. They are not paid at the time of making the will but instead come out of the estate. Pretty significant sums could be involved, so the advice on obtaining an estimate is, if anything, even more relevant. In certain instances, banks can be more expensive; in others, solicitors. The only way to discover is to get an estimate from each.

Banks publish a tariff of their charges. Solicitors render bills according to the time involved; so, although it is impossible for them to be precise, they should nevertheless be able to give a pretty accurate assessment – at least at the time of quoting. Both banks' and solicitors' fees may increase during the interval between their being appointed and fulfilling their duties as executor.

Other points

Wills should always be kept in a safe place – and their whereabouts known. The most sensible arrangement is for the solicitor to keep the original and for both you and the bank to have a copy.

A helpful initiative devised by the Law Society is a mini-form, known as a Personal Assets Log. This is for individuals drawing up a will to give to their executor or close relatives. It is, quite simply, a four-sided leaflet with space to record the essential information: name and address of solicitor; where the will and other important documents – for example, share certificates and insurance policies – are kept; the date of any codicils and so on. Logs should be obtainable from most solicitors.

Wills may need updating in the event of an important change of circumstances, for example: a divorce, remarriage or the birth of a grandchild. An existing will becomes invalid in the event of marriage or remarriage and should be revised. Any changes must be by codicil (for minor alterations) or by a new will, and must be properly witnessed.

Partners who wish to leave all their possessions to each other should consider including 'a survivorship clause' in their wills, as an insurance against the intestacy rules being applied were they both to be involved in the same fatal accident.

If you have views about your funeral, it is sensible to write a letter to your executors explaining your wishes and to lodge it with your will. If you have any pets, you may equally wish to leave a letter filed with your will explaining what arrangements you have made for their immediate/long term welfare. The charity PRO Dogs provides special cards for this purpose for owners to complete, obtainable from: **PRO Dogs**, National Head Office, Rocky Bank, 4 New Road, Ditton, Maidstone, Kent ME20 6AD. T:01732 848499.

If you would be willing to donate an organ which might help save someone else's life, you could indicate this in your will or alternatively obtain an organ donor card. These are available from most hospitals, chemists and Social Security offices as well as some charities.

Useful reading

Wills and Probate. Available from **Consumers' Association**, Castlemead, Gascoyne Way, Hertford X, SG14 1LH. £10.99.

Making Your Will. Free factsheet from **Age Concern England**, Astral House, 1268 London Road, London SW16 4ER (enclose sae).

'How Do I Make a Will?'. Free from the **Leonard Cheshire Foundation**, 26-29 Maunsel Street, London SW1P 2QN.

Will Information Pack. Free from **Help the Aged**, St James's Walk, Clerkenwell Green, London EC1R 0BE.

Money worries – and how to minimise them

Most people say that the first time they really think about death, in terms of what would happen to their nearest and dearest, is after the birth of their first baby. As children grow up, requirements change but key points that any family man or woman should consider – and review from time to time – include life insurance and mortgage protection relief.

Both husbands and wives should have **life insurance cover**. If either were to die, not only would their partner lose the benefit of their earnings, they would also lose the value of their services: home decorating, gardening, cooking and so forth.

Most banks and building societies urge homeowners to take out **mortgage protection schemes**. If you die, the loan is paid off automatically and the family home will not be repossessed.

Banks also offer **insurance to cover any personal or other loans**. This could be a vital safeguard to avoid leaving the family with debts.

Many people worry about **funeral costs**. These can vary, according to different parts of the country, from about £875 to £1,500 or even more depending on the choice of coffin and other arrangements. Although you may well hear of cheaper estimates, these are normally exclusive of disbursements which include minister's fees, cremation fees, medical certificate fees and other items.

As a way of helping, a number of insurance companies offer policies to cover funeral costs and while these could be sensible, a drawback is that you are budgeting today against an unknown cost in the future. Over the past five years, funeral costs have soared by about 30 per cent, so there would be no guarantee even with the best policies that the eventual pay-out would be sufficient to cover the expenses.

A rather different type of scheme, which overcomes the uncertainties and is growing in popularity, is the pre-paid funeral plan which is designed so you pay all the costs in advance, at present day prices. In other words, if you join today, the funeral is paid at today's price: whenever the service is actually required; and whatever the prices are at the time.

One such scheme is the Guaranteed Funeral Plan offered by **Chosen Heritage**, which is available through Age Concern. There are four options: the Basic plan, the Economy plan, the Popular plan and the Sovereign plan. Single payment prices (1995) are respectively £680, £895, £995, £2,620. Alternatively, payment may be spread over a number of monthly instalments, although this is more expensive. For further details, ask for a leaflet at your local Age Concern group or contact Tanvisha Longden, **Age Concern England**, Astral House, 1268 London Road, London SW16 4ER. T:0181 679 8000.

Additionally, **Golden Charter** (Freepost, London NW1 0YP, T:0800 833800) and **Dignity Ltd.** (Farringdon House, Wood Street, East Grinstead, West Sussex RH19 1EW, T:0800 269318) offer pre-arranged, pre-paid funeral plans, as do the Co-op and several regional insurance companies.

Alternatively you might like to investigate the Perfect Assurance pre-paid funeral plan – offered by the National Association of Funeral Directors – which is a 'bespoke' policy, as opposed to a package, so enabling you to choose all the details you want. For further information, contact: **National Association of Funeral Directors**, 618 Warwick Road, Solihull, West Midlands B91 1AA. T:0121 709 0019.

While most pre-paid funeral schemes are problem-free, as a recent **Office of Fair Trading** report warned, there can be pitfalls – including the risk of losing your money, if the company which sold you the plan should go out of business. Before making any advance payment you would be wise to investigate the following points: (1) whether your money will be paid into a trust administered by independent trustees (2) what fees are deducted from the investment (3) what exact expenses the plan covers and (4) if you cancel the plan, can you get all your money back – or only a part?

If you have a complaint either about a pre-payment scheme or funeral arrangements, the Ombudsman Scheme, which has power to award compensation of up to £50,000, might be able to help. The Ombudsman cannot assist unless the complainant has first tried to resolve the matter with the funeral company concerned. Also the company itself must be a member of the scheme. For further information, contact: **The Funeral Ombudsman**, 31 Southampton Row, London WC1B 5HJ. T:0171 430 1112.

Those in receipt of income support, family credit, housing benefit, council tax benefit or disability working allowance may qualify for a payment from the Social Fund to help with funeral costs. For details of eligibility and how you claim, see Leaflet D 49, *What To Do After a Death*, obtainable from any Social Security office. If the matter is urgent, make a point of asking for Form SF 200.

A very real crisis for some families is the need for immediate money while waiting for the estate to be settled. At least part of the problem can be overcome by couples having a **joint bank account**, with both partners having drawing rights without the signature of the other being required. Sole-name bank accounts and joint accounts requiring both signatures are frozen.

For the same reason, it may also be a good idea for any savings or investments to be held in the joint name of the couple. However, couples who have recently made any changes – or were planning to do so – as a result of independent taxation could be advised to discuss this point with a solicitor or qualified financial adviser.

Additionally, an essential practical point for all couples is that any financial and other **important documents should be discussed together** and understood by the wife as well as by the husband. Even today, an all too common saga is for widows to come across insurance policies and other papers, which they have never seen before and do not understand – often causing quite unnecessary anxiety. A further common-sense 'must' is for both partners to **know where important papers are kept**. Best idea is either to lock them, filed together, in a home safe; or to give them to the bank to look after.

If someone dies, **the bank manager should be notified as soon as possible**, so he can assist with the problems of unpaid bills and help work out a solution until the estate is settled. The same goes for the **suppliers of essential services**: gas, electricity, telephone and so on. Unless they know the situation, there is a risk of services being cut off if there is a delay in paying the bill. Add too any credit card companies, where if bills lie neglected, the additional interest could mount up alarmingly.

What to do when someone dies

There are formalities to be observed and arrangements to be made. The following two charts on pages 452-455, published by courtesy of Consumers' Association, whose book, *What to Do When Someone Dies*, provides a fund of practical information, illustrate what action is required. The first chart deals with the period immediately after death; the second, with the necessary arrangements for a funeral.

Useful reading
What to Do When Someone Dies. Available from **Consumers' Association**, Castlemead, Gascoyne Way, Hertford X, SG14 1LH. £9.99.
What To Do After a Death. Free booklet from your local Social Security office.
Arranging a Funeral, free factsheet from **Age Concern England**, Astral House, 1268 London Road, London SW16 4ER; or for those in Scotland, from **Age Concern Scotland**, 113 Rose Street, Edinburgh EH2 3DT (enclose large sae).

State benefits, tax and other money points

Some extra financial benefits are given to widows and, in more limited circumstances, to widowers. Several take the form of a cash payment. Others come in the form of a relief against tax.

Benefits paid in cash form
There are three important cash benefits to which widows may be entitled: widows' payment, widows' pension and widowed mother's allowance. To claim these, fill in Form BW 1, obtainable from any Social Security office. You will also be given a questionnaire (BD 8) by the Registrar. It is important that you complete this as it acts as a trigger to speed up payment of your benefits. All leaflets quoted are obtainable from any Social Security office.

Widows' payment. This has replaced what used to be known as the widows' allowance. It is a tax-free lump sum of £1,000, paid as soon as a woman is widowed provided that: (1) her husband had paid sufficient NI contributions (2) she is under 60; or (3) if she is over 60, her husband had not been entitled to retirement pension. Her claim will not be affected if she is already receiving a State pension, provided this is based on her own contributions. For more information, see leaflet NP 45 *A Guide to Widows' Benefits*.

Widowed mother's allowance. This is paid to mothers with at least one child for whom they receive child benefit. The value is £58.85 a week. The allowance is usually

CHART 1

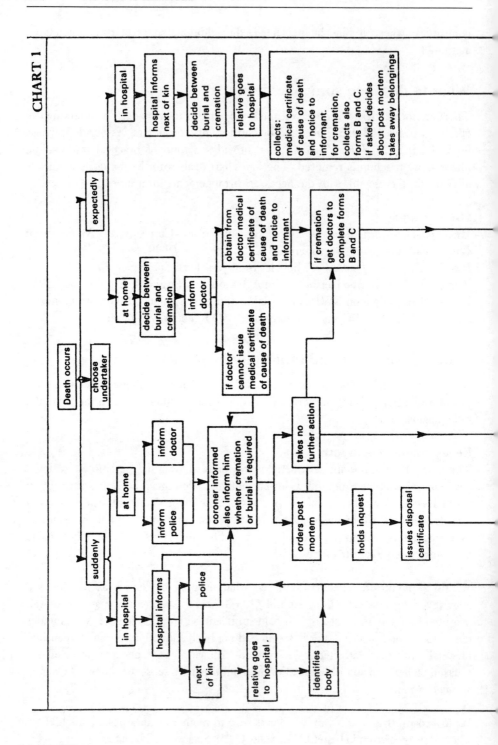

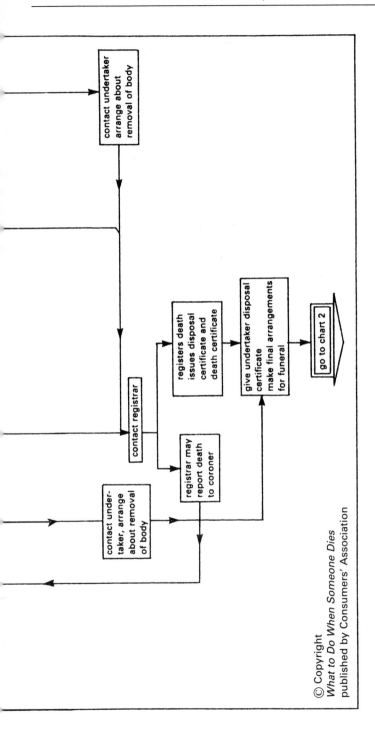

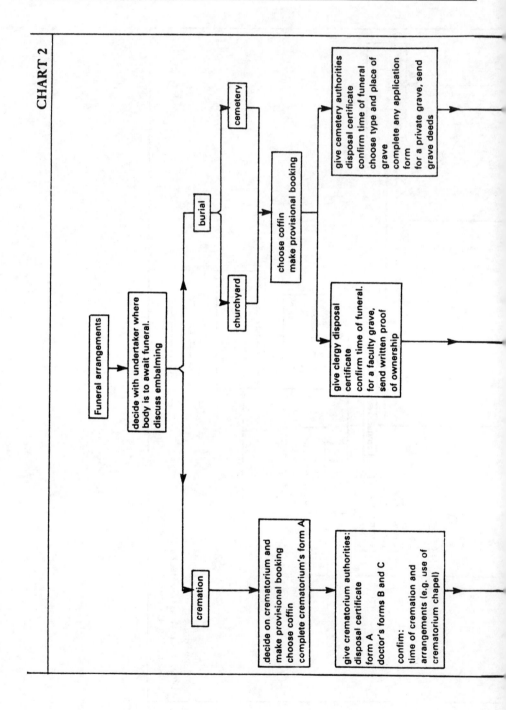

CHART 2

Funeral arrangements

decide with undertaker where body is to await funeral. discuss embalming

burial

churchyard

cemetery

choose coffin
make provisional booking

give cemetery authorities
disposal certificate
confirm time of funeral
choose type and place of grave
complete any application form
for a private grave, send grave deeds

give clergy disposal certificate
confirm time of funeral.
for a faculty grave,
send written proof
of ownership

cremation

decide on crematorium and
make provisional booking
choose coffin
complete crematorium's form A

give crematorium authorities:
disposal certificate
form A
doctor's forms B and C

confirm:
time of cremation and
arrangements (e.g. use of
crematorium chapel)

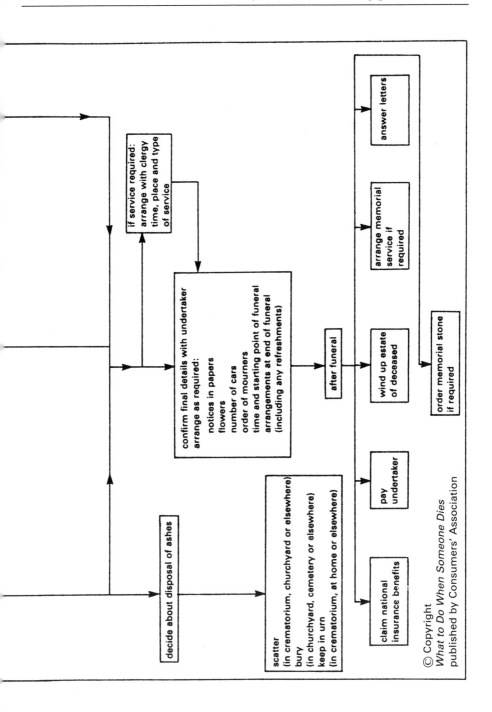

if service required: arrange with clergy time, place and type of service

confirm final details with undertaker arrange as required:
notices in papers
flowers
number of cars
order of mourners
time and starting point of funeral arrangements at end of funeral (including any refreshments)

decide about disposal of ashes

scatter (in crematorium, churchyard or elsewhere)
bury (in churchyard, cemetery or elsewhere)
keep in urn (in crematorium, at home or elsewhere)

after funeral

claim national insurance benefits

pay undertaker

wind up estate of deceased

arrange memorial service if required

answer letters

order memorial stone if required

paid automatically. If, for some reason, although eligible, you do not receive it, you should inform your local Social Security office. See leaflet NP 45.

Child dependency addition. This is a payment of £11.05 a week for each dependent child except for the eldest, for whom payment is only £9.85. The reason for the lower payment is because you receive more in child benefit for the eldest (or only) child. Information about child dependency addition is included in leaflet NP 45.

Widows' pension. There are various levels of widows' pension: the full rate which is described immediately below, and age-related widows' pension, which is described in the following paragraph.

Full-rate widows' pension is paid to widows who are between the ages of 55 and 59 inclusive when their husband dies; or when they cease to receive widowed mother's allowance. The weekly amount is £58.85, which is the same as the retirement pension received by a single person. Widows' pension is normally paid once you have sent off your completed form BW1; so if for any reason you do not receive the pension after about three weeks, you should enquire at your local Social Security office.

Age-related widows' pension. This is a pension for younger widows, who do not qualify for a full widows' pension. It is payable to a widow who is aged between 45 and 54 inclusive, when her husband dies; or when her widowed mother's allowance ceases to be paid. Rates depend on age and vary from £17.66 for 45-year-olds to £54.73 for those aged 54.

Retirement pension. Once a widow reaches age 60, she may choose whether to continue with her widows' pension or whether to receive retirement pension. After her 65th birthday, she no longer has a choice and will get retirement pension. If she is over 60 when her husband dies, she will usually receive a retirement pension rather than a widows' pension. If at the time of death the couple were already getting the State retirement pension, the widow will be entitled to her husband's share of their joint pension, if this is higher than her own.

An important point to remember is that a widow may be able to use her late husband's NI contributions to boost the amount she receives. See leaflets NP 46 *A Guide to Retirement Pensions*, FB 6 *Retiring? Your Pension and Other Benefits* and FB 32 *Benefits after Retirement*. **N.B.** A widower getting a retirement pension at less than the full rate may be able to use his late wife's NI contributions to get more pension.

Problems. As you will probably know, pension payments – including widows' pension – are dependent on sufficient NI contributions having been paid. Your Social Security office will inform you if you are not eligible. If this should turn out to be the case, you may still be entitled to receive income support, family credit, housing benefit, council tax benefit or a grant or loan from the Social Fund – so ask. If you are unsure of your position or have difficulties, ask at your Citizens' Advice Bureau who will at least be able to help you work out the sums and inform you of your rights.

Particular points to note

- Most widows' benefits are taxable. However, the £1,000 lump sum widow's payment is tax-free, as are war widows' pensions and the child dependency allowance.
- A reduced rate of benefit may be paid if there are any gaps in the husband's national insurance record.
- There is no widowers' pension. However, on retirement, a widower can substitute part of his late wife's contribution record for his own if this would be more beneficial.
- A widower with dependent children will receive child benefit; and normally also the £6.30 a week one-parent benefit for the first child.
- Men and women widowed after April 1979 will normally be able to inherit their spouse's additional pension rights, if he/she contributed to SERPS; or at least half their guaranteed minimum pension, if they were in a contracted-out scheme. Additionally, where applicable, all widows are entitled on retirement to half the graduated pension earned by their husband. Likewise, a widower can receive on retirement half the graduated retirement benefit based on his late wife's contributions.
- Widows who remarry, or live with a man as his wife, cease to receive widows' pension. They will, however, continue to receive a retirement pension if they remarry when they are aged 60 or over. A widow who has lived with a man as his wife and lost her entitlement to a widows' pension will, if the cohabitation ends, be entitled to claim it again. If she is over 60, the fact that she may be living with a man will not affect her entitlement to a retirement pension, based on her late husband's contribution record.

Tax and tax allowances

Widows and widowers receive the normal single person's tax allowance of £3,525 a year. If they have dependent children, they should also claim the additional personal allowance of £1,720 for single parents. Both widows and widowers are also entitled to any unused portion of the married couple's allowance in the year of their partner's death.

Widow's bereavement allowance. This is an extra allowance of £1,720, specially given to widows to assist them over the first difficult period. The only qualification is that a widow's late husband must have been entitled to the married couple's tax allowance at the time of his death. The allowance is given both in the tax year she became widowed and in the following tax year.

Important change. Since April 1995, tax relief on the additional personal allowance, married couple's allowance and widow's bereavement allowance has been restricted to 15 per cent. In other words, any taxpayer in receipt of one of these allowances will have their tax bill reduced by £258 (15 per cent of £1,720).

Useful Inland Revenue leaflets. These are available from any tax office.

IR 45: *Income Tax and CGT – What Happens When Someone Dies*
IR 90: *Tax Allowances and Reliefs*
IR 91: *A Guide for Widows and Widowers*
IHT 3: *An Introduction to Inheritance Tax.*

Advice. Many people have difficulty in working out exactly what they are entitled to – and how to claim it. The Citizens' Advice Bureau is always very helpful. Additionally, Cruse and the National Association of Widows (see below) can assist you.

Organisations that can help

Problems vary. For some, the hardest thing to bear is the loneliness of returning to an empty house. For others, money problems seem to dominate everything else. For many older women in particular, who have not got a job, widowhood creates a great gulf where for a while there is no real sense of purpose. Many widowed men and women go through a spell of feeling enraged against their partner for dying. Most are baffled and hurt by the seeming indifference of friends, who appear more embarrassed than sympathetic.

In time, all these feelings soften, problems diminish and individuals are able to recapture their joy for living with all its many pleasures. Talking to other people who know the difficulties from their own experience can be a tremendous help. The following organisations not only offer opportunities for companionship but also provide an advisory and support service.

Cruse – Bereavement Care, Cruse House, 126 Sheen Road, Richmond, Surrey TW9 1UR. T:0181 940 4818. Cruse offers free help to anyone who has been bereaved by providing both individual and group counselling through its 194 local branches. Practical advice can be given and there are also opportunities for social support. A list of publications and a newsletter are available. For a direct link to a counsellor, telephone Cruse Bereavement Line on 0181 332 7227 (Monday – Friday, 9.30 a.m. to 5 p.m.).

National Association of Bereavement Services, 20 Norton Folgate, London E1 6DB. T:0171 247 1080. Can put people who are bereaved or grieving for some other reason in contact with the most appropriate local service.

National Association of Widows, 54-57 Allison Street, Digbeth, Birmingham B5 5TH. T:0121 643 8348. The Association is a national voluntary organisation which offers a free and confidential advice and information service. Its many branches provide a supportive social network for widows throughout the country. Membership is £7.50 a year.

Many professional and other groups offer a range of services for widows and widowers associated with them. These include:

Civil Service Retirement Fellowship, 1b Deals Gateway, Blackheath Road, London SE10 8BW. T:0181 691 7411.

The War Widows Association of Great Britain, 17 The Earls Croft, Coventry CV3 5ES. T:01203 503298. From March 1996: 1 Coach Lane, Stanton-in-Peak, Derbyshire DE4 2NA. T:01629 636374.

Lesbian and Gay Bereavement Project, Vaughan M Williams Centre, Colindale Hospital, London NW9 5GH. T:0181 200 0511 (Monday to Thursday 10.30 a.m. to 4.30 p.m.); Helpline: 0181 455 8894 (7 p.m. to midnight every day). Offers telephone counselling and a drop-in centre for those affected by bereavement. The organisation is often able to find suitable clergy or secular officiants for funerals.

Many local Age Concern groups offer a counselling service. Trade unions are often particularly supportive, as are Rotary Clubs, all the armed forces organisations and most benevolent societies.

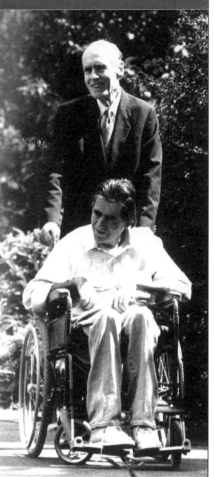

Index

add after a page number indicates that the organisation's address is included in that reference. References in italics indicate tables.

List of Advertisers

To: **Rosemary Brown**
Enterprise Dynamics Ltd.
9 Savoy Street
London WC2R 0BA

Tel: 0171 379 6515
Fax: 0171 379 3230

From:..
....
....
....
....

Suggestions:

....
....
....
....
....
....
....
....
....
....
....
....
....
....
....